Behavior Analysis in Education

Focus on Measurably Superior Instruction

Behavior Analysis in Education

Focus on Measurably
Superior Instruction

Edited by
Ralph Gardner, III
Diane M. Sainato
John O. Cooper
Timothy E. Heron
William L. Heward
John W. Eshleman
Teresa A. Grossi

THE OHIO STATE UNIVERSITY

Brooks/Cole Publishing Company
Pacific Grove, California

I(T)**P** ™
The trademark ITP is used under license.

Brooks/Cole Publishing Company
A Division of Wadsworth, Inc.

Printed in the United States of America
10 9 8 7 6 5 4 3 2 1

Library of Congress Cataloging-in-Publication Data
Behavior analysis in education : focus on measurably superior
  instruction / edited by Ralph Gardner, III . . . [et al.].
      p. cm.
    Papers presented at a conference sponsored by the Faculty in
  Applied Behavior Analysis, The Ohio University, Sept. 18-20, 1992.
      Includes bibliographical references and index.
      ISBN 0-534-22260-9
    1. Teachers--Rating of--Congresses. 2. Teaching--Evaluation-
-Congresses. 3. Behavioral assessment--Congresses. 4. Educational
tests and measurements--Congresses. 5. Early childhood education-
-Congresses. 6. Special education--Congresses. I. Gardner, Ralph,
1994
LB2836.B46 1994
371.1'44--dc20   93-46878
                                                                CIP

Sponsoring Editor: *Vicki Knight*
Editorial Assistant: *Lauri Banks Ataide*
Production Editor: *Penelope Sky*
Production Assistant: *Tessa A. McGlasson*
Manuscript Editor: *Robin L. Witkin*
Permissions Editor: *Carline Haga*
Interior Design: *Katherine Minerva*
Cover Design: *Gini Sardo*
Art Coordinator: *Lisa Torri*
Typesetting: *Joan Mueller Cochrane*
Printing and Binding: *Arcata Graphics/Fairfield*

To future behavior analysts

CONTRIBUTORS

Carmen Arreaga-Mayer
University of Kansas

Donald M. Baer
University of Kansas

Patricia M. Barbetta
Florida International University

Carl Binder
Precision Teaching and
Management Systems, Inc.

Don Bushell, Jr.
University of Kansas

Judith J. Carta
University of Kansas

Samuel M. Deitz
Georgia State University

Susan A. Fowler
University of Illinois

Howard Goldstein
University of Pittsburgh

Charles R. Greenwood
University of Kansas

R. Douglas Greer
Columbia University

Thomas G. Haring
University of California at
Santa Barbara

Gregory F. Harper
State University of New York
College at Fredonia

Betty Hart
University of Kansas

Andrew Hawkins
West Virginia University

Nancy Hepting
University of Pittsburgh

Timothy E. Heron
Ohio State University

William L. Heward
Ohio State University

Vikki F. Howard
Gonzaga University

Carolyn Hughes
Vanderbilt University

Daniel E. Hursh
West Virginia University

Mark A. Jackson
Western Michigan University

Kent R. Johnson
Morningside Academy

Louise Kaczmarek
University of Pittsburgh

Edward J. Kameenui
University of Oregon

Melinda Karnes
State University of New York
College at Fredonia

T. V. Joe Layng
Malcolm X College

Thomas C. Lovitt
University of Washington

Scott R. McConnell
University of Minnesota

T. F. McLaughlin
Gonzaga University

Larry Maheady
State University of New York
College at Fredonia

Barbara Mallette
State University of New York
College at Fredonia

Richard W. Malott
Western Michigan University

April D. Miller
The University of Southern
Mississippi

Samuel L. Odom
Vanderbilt University

H. S. Pennypacker
University of Florida

Roger Ray
Rollins College

Todd Risley
University of Kansas

Tom Sharpe
University of Nebraska–Lincoln

J. E. Stone
East Tennessee State University

Yolanda Tapia
University of Kansas

Vicci Tucci
Tucci Educational Services

Ron Van Houten
Mount Saint Vincent University

Dale Walker
University of Kansas

Paul Weisberg
University of Alabama

Betty F. Williams
Gonzaga University

PREFACE

This book was written to disseminate measurably superior instructional strategies to those interested in advancing sound, pedagogically effective, field-tested educational practices. All chapters were derived from papers presented at the September, 1992 conference titled *Behavior Analysis in Education: Focus on Measurably Superior Instruction,* sponsored by the Faculty in Applied Behavior Analysis, The Ohio State University. The chapters consist of original research, reviews, and/or position papers on higher education and professional development, research and measurement methodology, perspectives on the education of children and adults, and instructional applications. The authors share their assessment of past and present educational practice, as well as their vision for future reform. What is more important is that they communicate effectively to practitioners at all levels—universities, state departments of education, and local school districts—providing a technology to contribute to educational reform.

The book is divided into six parts. Part One contains 2 chapters that provide a futures view of behavior analysis in education. Part Two includes 4 chapters that focus on the theme of "promoting applied behaviors analysis." The 2 chapters in Part Three address early childhood intervention issues. Part Four, which contains 11 chapters, deals with measurably superior instructional practices for school-aged children. Part Five addresses the timely area of transition interventions and adult learners. Part Six integrates behavior analysis in education and public policy.

The completion of this project could not have occurred without the sustained commitment of the contributors. Numerous people worked to make the conference a success and this text a reality. We would like to acknowledge the efforts of our current and former colleagues: Judy Genshaft (now dean, College of Education, The State University of New York at Albany), James Wigtil, Thomas Stephens, Helen Sutherland, Donald Anderson (former dean of the College of Education, The Ohio State University),

and Nancy Zimpher, dean of the College of Education. We appreciate the efforts of Kelly Heckaman and Kimberly Weber, who compiled the author index. A special note of gratitude goes to the present students and past graduates of The Ohio State University Applied Behavior Analysis doctoral program, who served as authors and editors. Their individual and collective contributions to this project are greatly appreciated.

Ralph Gardner, III
Diane M. Sainato
John O. Cooper
Timothy E. Heron
William L. Heward
John W. Eshleman
Teresa A. Grossi

Royalties generated from the sale of this book will support future conferences or other activities for the advancement of behavior analysis in education.

CONTENTS

Part 1   1
Two Views of the Future of Behavior Analysis in Education

Chapter 1   3
Measurably Superior Instruction Means Close, Continual Contact with the Relevant Outcome Data. Revolutionary!
Don Bushell, Jr., Donald M. Baer

The Measurement Primer   4
Measuring Teaching   6
The Relevance of the Audience   7
References   9

Chapter 2   11
A Selectionist View of the Future of Behavior Analysis in Education
H. S. Pennypacker

Cultural Evolution   11
Institutional Contingencies   12
Variation and Selection in Education   15
The Future of Behavior Analysis in Education   16
References   18

Part 2   19
Promoting Applied Behavior Analysis

Chapter 3   21
Measurably Superior Instructional Methods: Do We Need Sales and Marketing?
Carl Binder

How We Have Failed   21
What Is Sales and Marketing?   22
The Public Versus the Private Sector   28
Deciding How to Proceed   29

Conclusions and Recommendations   30
References   30

Chapter 4   33
The Insignificant Impact of Behavior Analysis on Education: Notes from a Dean of Education
Samuel M. Deitz

Data and Dogma   34
Mice and Moose   36
Suggestions and Solutions   39
References   41

Chapter 5   43
"Mainstreaming" Applied Behavior Analysis Principles and Procedures into a Preservice Training Program for General Education Teachers
Larry Maheady, Gregory F. Harper, Barbara Mallette, Melinda Karnes

Educational Restructuring and Reform: An Opportunity to Respond for Behavior Analysts   43
RARE Program Philosophy and Major Components   45
RARE Program Organization and Instructional Procedures   47
Initial Outcomes from the RARE Program   52
Summary and Conclusions   55
References   56

Chapter 6   57
Developmentalism's Impediments to School Reform: Three Recommendations for Overcoming Them
J. E. Stone

Developmentalism as an Impediment to Reform   59
The Popular Acceptance of Developmentalism   63
The Developmentalist Ideal as a Benchmark   65
Recommendations   67
References   70

Part 3   73
Early Childhood Intervention

Chapter 7   75
Social Context, Social Validity, and Program Outcome in Early Intervention
Scott R. McConnell

A Brief Definition of Early Intervention   75
How Are Early Intervention and Applied Behavior Analysis Related?   76
Identifying the Goals of Early Intervention   77
Factors in Early Intervention   79
Community Involvement in the Evaluation of Early Intervention   82
References   83

Chapter 8   87
Contextualism and Applied Behavior Analysis: Implications for Early Childhood Education for Children with Disabilities
Samuel L. Odom, Thomas G. Haring

World Hypotheses   88
Behaviorism as a Mechanistic System   89
Behaviorism as a Contextualistic System   90
Contextualistic Behaviorism Within Early Intervention/ Early Childhood Special Education   93
Summary: Bringing the Context into Practice   97
References   98

Chapter 9   101
Communication Interventions: The Challenges of Across-the-Day Implementation
Howard Goldstein, Louise Kaczmarek, Nancy Hepting

Naturalistic Communication Interventions   101
Challenges to Implementation   106
Conclusions   111
References   111

Chapter 10   115
Helping Preschoolers from Low-Income Backgrounds Make Substantial Progress in Reading Through Direct Instruction
Paul Weisberg

Distar Reading   116
Teaching Early Reading   116
The Early Childhood Day Care Project   121
Evaluation   121
Concluding Remarks   127
References   128

Chapter 11   131
Children Prenatally Exposed to Alcohol and Cocaine: Behavioral Solutions
Vikki F. Howard, Betty F. Williams, T. F. McLaughlin

The Effects of Prenatal Substance Abuse   131
Early Intervention   135
Intervention with School-Aged Children   142
Conclusions   142
References   144

Part 4   147
School-Age Children

Chapter 12   149
Measurably Superior Instructional Practices in Measurably Inferior Times: Reflections on Twain and Pauli
Edward J. Kameenui

What's Right, Almost Right, and Not Even Wrong: Two Trends   149
Debating Words and Numbers   151
The Realities of Diversity   156
Summary   157
References   158

Chapter 13   161
The Measure of a Teacher
R. Douglas Greer

Identifying a Primary Measure of Teaching   161
The Validity of Learn Units   169
Conclusion   170
References   170

Chapter 14   173
The Morningside Model of Generative Instruction
Kent R. Johnson, T. V. Joe Layng

A History   173
The Morningside Model as Applied Science   177
Daily Operation of a Class Period or Course   186
A Summary and Conclusion   193
References   194

Chapter 15   199
Teaching Children with Learning Problems
Ron Van Houten

Setting the Stage for Learning   199
Overcoming Problems with Labeling and Memory   202
Teaching by Rules   205
Embedding Critical Material   208
Focusing on the Developing Rate   209
Teaching Adaptive Behavior   209
Summary   210
References   210

Chapter 16   213
The Opportunity to Respond and Academic Performance Revisited: A Behavioral Theory of Developmental Retardation and Its Prevention
Charles R. Greenwood, Betty Hart, Dale Walker, Todd Risley

Opportunity to Respond   214
Scope of the Problem   215
A Progression of Developmental Retardation   215
Review of Longitudinal Findings   216
Implications of the Problem and Its Cause   220
Discussion and Conclusion   221
References   222

Chapter 17   225
Ecobehavioral Assessment of Bilingual Special Education Settings: The Opportunity to Respond
Carmen Arreaga-Mayer, Judith J. Carta, Yolanda Tapia

Ecobehavioral Assessment: A Technology for Measuring Classroom Processes   226

ESCRIBE: The Ecobehavioral System for the Contextual Recording of Interactional Bilingual Environments   227
Pilot Study   229
Conclusions   236
Summary   237
References   238

Chapter 18   241
Toward Instructional Process Measurability: An Interbehavioral Field Systems Perspective
Andrew Hawkins, Tom Sharpe, Roger Ray

Conceptual Foundations   241
An Assessment Protocol   243
An Example of Interbehavioral Assessment   249
Implications and Applications   252
Conclusion   254
References   254

Chapter 19   257
Developing Competent Learners by Arranging Effective Learning Environments
Vicci Tucci, Daniel E. Hursh

Competent Learners   258
Repertoire Development   259
Learning Environments   260
The Competent Learner Model   261
Designing New Schools   262
References   264

Chapter 20   265
START Tutoring: Designing, Training, Implementing, Adapting, and Evaluating Tutoring Programs for School and Home Settings
April D. Miller, Patricia M. Barbetta, Timothy E. Heron

The Benefits of Using Students as Tutors   266
The START Tutoring Program   267
Conclusion   278
References   279

Chapter 21   283
Three "Low-Tech" Strategies for Increasing the Frequency of Active Student Response During Group Instruction
William L. Heward

The Learning Trial as the Basic Unit of Instruction   284
Active Student Response   286
Three Benefits of Increasing ASR During Instruction   290
The Visual Response System: High Technology for Increasing ASR During Group Instruction   293
Low-Tech ASR Teaching Strategies   294
Using High-ASR Teaching Strategies Across the Curriculum and Throughout the School Day   311
ASR Is Not a Silver Bullet   313
Much More Research Is Needed   314
Conclusion   315
References   316

Chapter 22   321
Applied Behavior Analysis: An Insider's Appraisal
Thomas C. Lovitt

A Few Significant Epochs   321
Message of the Education Crisis Issue   324
Applied Behavior Analysts' Responses to the Crisis in Education   325
Alternative Actions   326
What Do We ABAs Have to Disseminate?   328
What Problems Should We Address?   328
How Can Applied Behavior Analysts Influence Education?   328
Wrap Up   330
References   330

Part 5   333
Transition to Adulthood

Chapter 23   335
Teaching Generalized Skills to Persons with Disabilities
Carolyn Hughes

Traditional Instructional Models   335
Two Strategies for Promoting Generalization: Self-Instruction and Multiple-Example Teaching   336
A New Approach: The Generalized Skills Model   338

Systematic Replications of the Model   343
Future Areas of Research   343
Summary   346
References   346

Chapter 24   349
Helping High-Risk Black College Students
Mark A. Jackson, Richard W. Malott

The Problem of Attrition for Minority Students   349
The University's Perspective   350
Reasons for Attrition   351
Current Strategies Designed to Affect Attrition   354
An Alternative to the Traditional, Ineffective Retention Program: The Three-Contingency Model of Performance Management   358
References   362

Part 6   365
Behavior Analysis in Education and Public Policy

Chapter 25   367
Behavior Analysis in Education, and Public Policy: A Necessary Intersection
Susan A. Fowler

Considering Our Terminology: Does It Help or Hinder?   368
Building a Clear Vision of Our Goals for Education   368
Encouraging Appropriate Choices by Publishing Professional Standards   369
Promoting Consumer Input   369
Expanding Our Choices of Marketing and Dissemination Strategies   370
Building Coalitions with Other Constituency Groups   371
Promoting Public Advocacy   371
References   372

Name Index   373
Subject Index   381

PART 1

Two Views of the Future of Behavior Analysis in Education

Chapter 1
Measurably Superior Instruction Means Close,
Continual Contact with the Relevant Outcome
Data. Revolutionary!
    Don Bushell, Jr., Donald M. Baer

Chapter 2
A Selectionist View of the Future of Behavior
Analysis in Education
    Henry S. Pennypacker

CHAPTER 1

Measurably Superior Instruction Means Close, Continual Contact with the Relevant Outcome Data. Revolutionary!

Don Bushell, Jr.
Donald M. Baer

Measurably superior instruction will require four classes of knowledge. First, we must know what we mean by *superior instruction*. Second, we must know how to measure the degree to which instruction is superior. Third, we must know how to teach so that these measures improve. Fourth, we had better learn how to get our society to act on what we know—or the knowledge will remain academic.

We suggest that of these four kinds of knowledge, the second—how to measure the quality of instruction—is pivotal to the other three. Our thesis is that we already know a lot about teaching educational objectives. If "a lot" is not to be enough for measurably superior instruction, then we should learn more. However, "a lot" may well be more than enough. Perhaps the largest part of the problem is in getting what we already know to happen. If we can accomplish this, the results will clarify what we mean by superior instruction—and indeed, what anyone means by superior instruction. If we are not successful, it will not matter what we mean by superior instruction, and the topic will remain show business.

To begin, 30 years ago, Robert Mager (1962) taught us how to write instructional objectives that clarified what we wanted to teach. He did not teach

us what to want to teach. He only revolutionized educational techniques by showing us that some educational objectives can be written well enough to be measured and others cannot. By doing that, he rationalized two worlds of education, probably the only two of any importance. One is the world in which we choose everything we want to teach from the universe of measurable goals, and then find the teaching techniques to maximize those measures. In the other world, we choose only *how* we will teach, as if there were an a priori correct way; whatever we get by teaching that way then must be what we want or should want. It is especially easy to believe that, when what we want is not measurable—or at least not measured. Perhaps the second world is so consistently preferred over the first because the first is doubly embarrassing: It requires us to decide what we want to teach, and it is always embarrassing to discover that in some small part we don't know and in some small part we don't agree. And it exposes us to a series of surprises as we discover what techniques teach the goals better than others.

Therein lies the problem for this conference: We live in the first of these two worlds and our society lives in the second. Very likely, the great majority of us here choose all our objectives from the universe of measurable ones, and then develop teaching techniques that maximize those measures. But we first-worlders find ourselves a tiny minority. What our second-world society measures is mainly irrelevant, most often in the form of what it has been told to call an achievement test, and that near-irrelevancy is almost always measured too rarely and too late. Our society, being second world, judges its schools and its teachers by whether it likes the look of how they teach, not by whether how they teach maximizes their goals. Our society also blames the schools and the teachers when achievement-test scores decline. It does that by finding something that does not look so good after all, and demanding reform. For decades, those demands have taken the form of *A Nation at Risk*, or Silberman's *Crisis in the Classroom* (1970); that is, they have become media events. But, staunch in its second-worldliness, our society does not demand that reform be guided by whatever maximizes the achievement-test scores; instead, it demands a reform that looks good, as if what looks good *must* maximize achievement-test scores. It is typical of the second world to suppose that good process will yield good outcomes, rather than that good outcomes define good process. It is exceptionally difficult to ask them to remember and generalize "Handsome is as handsome does" and to admire whatever techniques teach what achievement tests measure.

The Measurement Primer

We first-worlders know how to measure. A large part of this skill is measuring how well our students learn every skill we teach as we teach it. For the second world, that is a puzzling, difficult, and expensive lesson. Perhaps we should offer them the measurement primer, as follows: If you don't know where you are, you're lost, and it doesn't matter that you know where you want to go. Many of us, even when we have well-defined objectives, are not always sure where we have been or where we are in relation to those objectives. We're lost.

Author Don Bushell has begun asking unwary acquaintances if last Thursday was a good day. A common response is "Not bad, why?" "How," he asks, "would you decide if Thursday was a good day or a bad day? Was Thursday better or worse than a week ago last Wednesday?" Interestingly, some of his friends suddenly discover that their glass needs refilling or remember an urgent errand. Fortunately, others humored him, and a lesson has unfolded.

For example, a clinician reflected a bit and then explained that Thursday had been a mixed day. Good, because several patients said they were improving—they felt better. Bad, because one patient was hospitalized after a drug overdose. It was a good day to the extent that it wasn't a bad day. And no, he couldn't remember a week ago last Wednesday well enough to compare.

A psychiatric-hospital aide explained that Thursday was a good day because he did not have to complete any injury reports, the entire staff showed up for work, and no one had to be placed in physical restraint. It was a good day because it wasn't a bad day. And no, he couldn't remember a week ago last Wednesday well enough to compare either.

A teacher decided that Thursday was a good day because there were no playground accidents, no disruptive intrusions by other teachers who needed to take children out for special lessons, no special requests from the main office or new forms from downtown, and a boy who often hit other students was absent. It was a good day because it wasn't a bad day. And no, she couldn't remember a week ago last Wednesday well enough to compare.

There is the lesson. You have noticed how persistently *good* is defined as the absence of *bad*, and how persistently memory is the only measure of how well people's professions went a week ago. Yet all of the informants consider themselves behaviorists. If pressed, they could construct exemplary statements of their objectives. But they had no easy way to measure where they were relative to those objectives or relative to where they were a week ago last Wednesday. Lacking some kind of outcome measurement, they relied on judgment born of professional experience, the essence of which apparently is that a good day is one that is not bad, and that it better have been recent.

Professional judgment is valuable, but it is different from measurement. Professional judgment is often correct, but its reliability at any given moment is unknown. It is superior to unprofessional judgment based on limited experience, but it is difficult to confirm. It is the product of the complex, unknowable, and irreproducible history of the professional interacting with clients or students who have their own complex, unknowable, and irreproducible histories. And their interaction occurs in settings that, despite similarities, can seem as individually distinctive to the people in them as the people themselves.

Using only professional judgment to decide where you are in relation to where you want to go is like navigating by dead reckoning. A few can use it often enough to survive, but most of us are uncertain about where we are relative to our objective until we arrive there—if we do—and we remain forever uncertain relative to where we were last week and last month. When we must navigate without measures, we are lost most of the time. No doubt that is why it is called *dead* reckoning.

By contrast, Skinner studied the behavior of organisms by entering every instance of the behavior into a permanent, cumulative record; he examined those records constantly. For the social sciences, that was a novel strategy. The method known as the experimental analysis of behavior, derived from that beginning, has been different from the methods of other social and behavioral sciences. Perhaps there is where the first world emerged as different from the second. Behavior analysts measure the behavior they are studying as it occurs, no matter how often or where. In part, the purpose of frequent and repeated measurement is to describe the natural history of the behavior. But more important, the purpose is to bring the *analyst's* behavior under the control of those data.

Skinner (1956) made that point in "A Case History in Scientific Method," noting that "the organism whose behavior is most extensively modified and most completely controlled in research of the sort I have described is the experimenter . . ." (p. 232). Skinner was explaining the effect of constantly observing the cumulative record written by the behavior. Sidman (1960) made a comparable observation when he urged the experimenter not to transform data much more than did the cumulative record. "It is a direct record of the subject's behavior; furthermore, it is an immediate

record, which permits the investigator to evaluate the moment-to-moment course of [an] experiment as it develops" (p. 399). By definition, behavior analysts measure the effects of their own behavior on the behavior of their subject, so they can analyze that behavior and earn their professional title.

In laboratories behavior analysts, even if they no longer respond to the pen line of a cumulative recorder, still make their decisions based on continual measures. So do applied researchers working in messier settings such as hospitals and schools. In applied research the interval between data points may be longer than in the lab and the measurement clumsier, but the function is the same: To produce data that tell us whether to persist in or change what we are doing—to keep us from being lost. If an applied program is behavior analytic, teams of people meet regularly to examine their graphs and make decisions based on what they see. Is it time to change procedures or should things continue as they are? Parsonson and Baer (1978, 1986) also described this distinguishing feature of applied behavior analysis:

> The behavior of the subject(s) controls the pace and procedures of the program through the data, which are continually available to the experimenter when graphed after each session. Judgments, decisions, and changes can be made as the program proceeds. [1986, p. 109]

Unfortunately, this definitive, crucial feature of behavior analysis has not made the transition from classroom research to classroom practice. So, although the operations of behavioral research programs are usually controlled by their data, the operations of classrooms seldom are. Why is this? Perhaps it is because researchers build measurement systems to withstand the scrutiny of editors and reviewers who emphasize reliability rather than economy or ease of use. Perhaps it is because research projects often budget for observers, and classrooms never do. Perhaps it is because researchers often talk to other researchers and seldom talk to teachers. We have produced a lot of classroom research that succeeds with great consistency, but we have yet to build a practical outcome-measurement system that classroom teachers will use in their day-to-day work. Like most practitioners, teachers rely on their professional judgment to guide them toward their objectives. The rare successful teacher, like the navigator without stars or instruments, responds to cues that are so subtle they cannot be recognized or described. Such teaching is admired for its artistry and prized for its rarity. It is too rare for a society to rely on.

Society needs measures that help all teachers become more effective—measures that inform day-to-day decisions. Good measures do not replace good judgment. The fact that physicians, engineers, dentists, pilots, and pharmacists all closely rely on continual measures does not mean they lack professional judgment. It is their continual use of *outcome* measures that shapes and develops their professional judgment. Professional decisions must be informed by both judgment and measures.

When such measures are proposed, they must be attractive to the teacher who has just explained rather abruptly, "I've got 26 kids. If you're talking about more measures, I haven't got time. Besides, I know the current abilities of every child. I don't need them." That teacher has set the specifications. To be practical, classroom measures must be useful, and seen as useful, cheap, and easy.

Measuring Teaching

These specifications can be met. Many years ago, in a Follow Through program that served Head Start graduates as they entered public school, author Bushell and his colleagues collaborated with teachers in classrooms all across the country. These more than 300 kindergarten through third-grade instructors were teaching reading, arithmetic, spelling, and handwriting to 8,000 students, and the researchers had to keep track of how the children were progressing on a weekly basis.

They created a measure by dividing the curriculum materials into sections or steps. Suppose, for example, that a first-grade arithmetic book has 300 pages. They set their objective at one-year's worth of material plus 20%. That's 360 pages in a 40-week school year. (There aren't really 40 weeks, however. Parent conferences, Thanksgiving, Halloween,

Valentine's Day, and other special events reduce a school year to 36 weeks.) So, 360 pages in 36 weeks is 10 pages a week. Every 10 pages was declared a new step. The teachers made sure that step placement stood for skill level by requiring at least 80% accuracy for advancement.

Each Friday afternoon, every teacher sent the researchers a class roster with five columns beside the column of names. The first column reported any absences during the week, and the other four reported each child's current step in reading, arithmetic, spelling, and handwriting. That information became four charts or graphs, with the steps listed on the vertical axis and 40 weeks along the horizontal. Each week the researchers entered the number of children who were reading on each step (e.g., two on step 8, three on step 10, one on step 11, five on step 12). The resulting set of charts painted a picture of what was going on in the classroom. One set of charts was kept in Kansas, and the teacher posted another set in the classroom. The charts showed when progress accelerated or decelerated, when a particular step was unusually difficult or easy, and when any student was leaping ahead or falling behind. Week by week, anyone could see how all the students were progressing toward their goals. In particular, the teacher could see the progress.

The teachers always knew where they were in relation to their objectives, and in relation to where they had been last week and last month. Their teaching had been brought into close, continual contact with its most relevant consequences. If you asked *those* teachers if it had been a good week, and how it compared to the previous week, they could answer exactly.

Taking less than 20 minutes a week to prepare— less time than the bulletin board—the resulting graphs became a source of meaningful instructional information—and of pride—for the teachers. The charts were posted in the classrooms where the principal, other teachers, and visiting parents could see them and compliment the teachers on their fine class. It may be that the most important function of these charts was their ability to recruit compliments for the teachers.

In the classroom, applause and compliments greeted the child who advanced to the next step. To compound the effect, the teachers made individual charts and sent them home every month so parents could see and delight in their child's progress. Each month the charts showed the student's current placement, where he or she had been each prior month, and the end-of-semester objective.

Presumably, at higher grade levels, the students themselves could keep comparable charts to record completed assignments. Whatever the level, the outcome recorded needs to be an event that can occur often, preferably daily. In this way, the charts can bestow what in other contexts may be labeled "a sense of progress."

Bushell's research on teaching is now conducted in day-care centers and Baer's is used in preschools and institutions, but the measurement questions are the same: How can we know what is happening and not happening; how can teaching behavior be kept in close, continual contact with its effects; how can teachers recruit contingent praise for their teaching; and how can students recruit contingent praise for what they learn?

The Relevance of the Audience

We began this argument with the premise that we already know a lot about measurement. We know that we need continual outcome measures whose function it is to control our research behaviors. As laboratory researchers we often assume that we are the correct and sufficient audience for our measures, but as applied researchers we know better. In application, outcome measures will function only when they are relevant to an audience that admires good performance—an audience that is beyond the researcher. We may not yet know a lot about recruiting such an audience, but we do know something. Hopkins (1968) enlisted the support of passersby in treating a boy with retardation who always looked unhappy. When the boy was out in the world, he wore a sign around his neck that read "If I smile, talk to me. If I look sad, ignore me." People obliged, and the boy was soon smiling at everyone he encountered. Subsequently, Stokes, Fowler, and Baer (1978) taught preschool children the simple social skills necessary to recruit

approval from their teachers, with highly salutary effects on their school performance. In Bushell's current day-care version, students who complete a curriculum step wear a paper tag around their neck. The tag usually says something like "I can count to 20 by 2s." Any adult who sees a child with a tag is likely to read the message. Some adults immediately congratulate the successful student, while others strengthen the skill by asking the child to demonstrate, "Let me hear you count to 20 by 2s."

This looks like reinforced practice and generalization programming: The newly mastered skill is rehearsed by new adults in new settings. Similar contingencies are likely to occur many times during the day and with particular enthusiasm when parents arrive at the end of the day. The events prompted by the tags are fun for the children and for their teachers. The children's progress—and the work of the teachers—is supported by an approving audience.

These are mere examples. Our general thesis is that close, continual contact with relevant outcome data is a fundamental, distinguishing feature of applied behavior analysis. *Close, continual contact with relevant outcome data* ought to be a fundamental feature of classroom teaching as well. It ought to become the most familiar acronym in the educational world: 3C/ROD, pronounced "three-cee-rod." But practitioners in general, and classroom teachers in particular, have not built these kinds of outcome measures, even though they could. Precision Teaching and Distar classrooms are occasional exceptions, but the rule is that the relevant outcome measures, which are direct measures of students' performances of what is taught as it is taught, are not a part of school practice. Why not?

Perhaps we have simply neglected to build the audience necessary to make outcome measures functional. Measures and audience must go together; an outcome measure that has no audience cannot function—it is not relevant. Consider a weight loss program that consists only of standing on the scale every day recording a number. The measure is appropriate, but for most of us the absence of an approving, encouraging audience leaves it irrelevant. We should expect the measurement behaviors to decline faster than the weight.

Neither measures nor audiences arise spontaneously. Both must be designed with care and developed with patience. Most important, the audience must be taught not only when to applaud, but when to remain silent. Some of the earliest applied studies taught preschool teachers to deliver their attention and approval to children only for improvements in their behavior. These teachers often found it unnatural not to attend to misbehavior, yet what worked best was attending exclusively to what was good and appropriate. Rather than say "Stop crying," the teachers had to reserve their attention for when the child was not crying; rather than say "Stop crawling," they had to attend only when the child was upright; rather than instruct "Don't be a wimp," they had to seem interested only when the child climbed the apparatus. The same general lesson has been taught hundreds of times since. Better, more skillful behavior is most consistently shaped by reinforcing improved approximations, not by criticizing or condemning.

That is one of the oldest and best disseminated lessons of our field. How often nonbehavioral practitioners have been advised to "catch them being good" rather than learn the mysteries of something called positive reinforcement! Even so, the technique is rarely practiced. When close, continual contact with relevant outcome data reveals a not-so-good performance, it may seem unnatural not to criticize. We must be taught how to find the few good things in the sea of the not-so-good. That can be exasperating, but it avoids the countercontrol or escape that criticism can generate. The implication of our argument is that someone who watches teachers teach should catch *them* being good—should praise their finding something good in each student's performance to praise—rather than criticize their frequent use of criticism. Who can do that for us?

Maybe 3C/ROD? Perhaps teachers in close, continual contact with outcome data that are made relevant by audience approval will discover, just as the researchers have, that criticism does not improve the outcome data nearly as well as praise reserved for good performances. Close, continual contact with the relevant outcome data makes experimenters of us all, even those untrained in research design. Indeed,

many forms of training in research design probably prevent teachers and practitioners from thinking they could ever do it in their daily practice.

Did we mistrain our Follow Through teachers? We taught them techniques; such as how to sequence materials, how to prompt, how to fade, how to attend differentially to improvements, how to catch students being good, how to praise and give tokens, how to use time-out. If we had started by teaching them 3C/ROD—how to collect and stay in close contact with outcome measures and how to display the data to parents and principals who could then praise improvements—they might have invented all those techniques themselves, and more. They might even have abandoned criticism.

Once again, we are in the midst of a new round of school reforms and criticism. Pessimism abounds. Goodlad has indicated that teacher education is not education. Cheney has just concluded that the tyrannical machines of education are beyond redemption. In a similar vein, Baer (1988) argued that schools as organizations follow certain descriptive laws. These laws predict that the public schools can grow worse more easily than better. Pennypacker (in Chapter 2 of this text), makes a closely related point in his behavior-analytic characterization of *Type S* organizations.

Still, some schools may be changing. The media warily report a voucher plan for poor children in Milwaukee, some events called school reforms in Kentucky, and the supposed decentralization of a certain amount of political control in the 547 Local School Councils of Chicago. And David Berliner (1992) used a great deal of available data to argue that American schools are not a gross failure, and that much of the current round of pessimism is a media event driven by disinformation. But these situations are not about teachers developing close, continual contact with relevant outcome data. Nothing like 3C/ROD appears in our media reports.

Occasional observers have noted that behavioral programs demonstrably and consistently make children smart. Then why haven't they been invited to do so? In part, perhaps because of the nature of politics and organizations. In another part, because when we present behavioral programs, teachers and other second-worlders simply do not like them. That fact should not set the occasion for us first-worlders to scorn the unenlightened in the second world. Instead, it must remind us of our own first principle: The subject is always right. If teachers do not like our lesson, we have not taught it correctly. In particular, we have not taught teachers how to recruit appreciative and responsive audiences for their continual outcome measures.

Neither have we appreciated the operating measures and audiences that influence teachers. It should be no surprise that these operating measures are of process rather than outcome. They describe daily attendance, the lunchroom count, the number of children in each teacher's room, and the number with special needs. Each of these measures is closely attended by the teacher partly because each has an attentive, responsive audience beyond the classroom. The school board and the administration understand that funding is based on daily attendance; the cooks understand daily lunch counts; central-office administrators understand the allocation of funds based on the number of children with special needs; and the teacher-pupil ratio is a basic datum in annual contract negotiations between the union and the school board. Outcome data, describing the effects of instruction, however, have no direct effect on either funding or contract negotiations. Outcome data have no audience and therefore, they are not relevant.

We first-worlders know how to measure how well our students learn what we teach as we teach it. We know how to design measures that provide close, continual contact with outcome data. We know how to be the kind of attentive, responsive audience that makes those data relevant. But we have not devised an adequate technology for turning our audience functions over to those others that make up a teacher's immediate community: students, principals, other teachers, and, most of all, parents and taxpayers. What kind of measures would particularly suit a principal and other administrators? How would they differ in content and timing from measures prepared for other teachers? What easy description of an outcome that is especially relevant to parents can engage their frequent and supportive attention? These are the people who need to witness and respond to the teachers' daily or weekly accomplishments. These are the audiences whose applause can make outcome data relevant. We have a fantasy that the end of a school day might someday be like the end of a basketball game. The teacher posts the score for the day, while the fans stand and applaud—it was a winning day. A good kind of winning—when we win, nobody loses. That fantasy may be close to reality if we can build a system that lets a teacher post the day's score where the principal can say "Nicely done," and later in the week a parent on the Local School Council can stop to say thank you.

We do not know exactly how to recruit the relevant audience. We are disadvantaged; we are university people and we usually have our audience recruited for us. A few of our colleagues are trying to sell applied behavior analysis, including behavior-analytic education and training, as if they were commercial products. The skills of recruiting the relevant audience will quickly be shaped in the repertoires of those who survive, because in large part that is how survival is defined. Thus we can watch for those who survive and prosper and study their recruitment repertoires; the necessary experiment is being done by them right now.

In summary, measurably superior instruction means close, continual contact with outcome data that are made relevant by attentive, responsive audiences. In the 30 years since Mager's important contribution, scores of technologies have come together to bring us nearer to the possibility of measurably superior instruction. If we can now devise ways to recruit and maintain audiences that, by their interest and attention, will define relevant outcome data, the completed package known as 3C/ROD could lead to measurably superior instruction in schools. That would indeed be revolutionary.

References

BAER, D. M. (1988). The future of behavior analysis in educational settings. In J. C. Witt, S. N. Elliott, & F. M. Gresham (Eds.), *Handbook of behavior therapy in education* (pp. 823–828). New York: Plenum.

BERLINER, D. C. (1992). *Educational reform in an era of disinformation.* Paper presented at a meeting of the American Association of Colleges for Teacher Education, San Antonio.

HOPKINS, B. L. (1968). Effects of candy and social reinforcement, instructions, and reinforcement schedule learning on the modification and maintenance of smiling. *Journal of Applied Behavior Analysis, 1,* 121–129.

MAGER, R. F. (1962). *Preparing instructional objectives.* Belmont, CA: Fearon.

NATIONAL Commission on Excellence in Education. (1984). *A nation at risk: The full account.* Cambridge, MA: USA Research.

PARSONSON, B. S., & Baer, D. M. (1978). The analysis and presentation of graphic data. In T. R. Kratochwill (Ed.), *Single-subject research: Strategies for evaluating change* (pp. 101–165). New York: Academic Press.

PARSONSON, B. S., & Baer, D. M. (1986). The graphic analysis of data. In A. Poling & R. W. Fuqua (Eds.), *Research methods in applied behavior analysis* (pp. 157–186). New York: Plenum.

SIDMAN, M. (1960). *Tactics of scientific research.* New York: Basic Books.

SILBERMAN, C. E. (1970). *Crisis in the classroom: The remaking of American education.* New York: Random House.

SKINNER, B. F. (1956). A case history in scientific method. *American Psychologist, 11,* 221–233.

STOKES, T. F., Fowler, S. A., & Baer, D. M. (1978). Training preschool children to recruit natural communities of reinforcement. *Journal of Applied Behavior Analysis, 11,* 285–303.

CHAPTER 2

A Selectionist View of the Future of Behavior Analysis in Education

H. S. Pennypacker

Public education in America has been under intense scrutiny. As one of the key institutions in a complex culture that is undergoing extensive change along many dimensions, education cannot escape the pressures that are shaping the future of our society. The evidence is available almost daily in the media, whether in the form of reports on education's role in the erosion of our international competitiveness or a feature story on a successful innovation. Most important, education is the subject of political debate as never before. Candidates are vying for votes on the basis of proposals for curriculum reform, national testing programs, and even financial restructuring.

Will any of this make any difference? Is our educational system likely to change and, if so, how? What role, if any, will behavior analysis play in the schools of the future? My purpose in this chapter is to address these questions from the perspective of a coherent world view that derives from the natural science of behavior. First, I present an overview of cultural evolution from a perspective that is compatible with behavior analysis, which shows that the current turmoil in education is predictable from our understanding of how cultural practices evolve. Second, I detail the impact of this evolutionary process on

education as we know it. In so doing, I highlight the contributions of behavior analysis to education and assess its future involvement.

Cultural Evolution

> Human behavior is the joint product of (i) the contingencies of survival responsible for the natural selection of the species and (ii) the contingencies of reinforcement responsible for the repertoires acquired by its members, including (iii) the special contingencies maintained by the social environment. [Ultimately, of course, it is all a matter of natural selection, since operant conditioning is an evolved process, of which cultural practices are special applications.] [Skinner, 1981, p. 502]

In this widely reproduced quotation, B. F. Skinner articulated the major unifying principle to emerge from his lifetime of research and writing. This is the principle of *selection by consequences*, which anchors a new paradigm within the life sciences known as *selectionism*. A basic tenet of this position is that all forms of life, from single cells to complex cultures, evolve as a result of selection with respect to function.

Thus, the morphological characteristics of a species are selected through differential reproduction by those individuals that have adapted and survived. The behavioral repertoires of individual organisms are determined by contingencies of reinforcement that select some forms of behavior over others as the organism interacts with the environment. Behavioral selection is thus both ontogenic and phylogenic. Susceptibility to these environmental contingencies of reinforcement, which select forms of behavior that mediate survival to the point of reproduction, will be transmitted genetically to subsequent generations.

The same selection principles operate on cultural practices. In this case, selection appears to occur with respect to the basic economic standard of *cost-benefit*, a composite defined by joint variation in the contingencies of production and reproduction (Harris, 1980). Thus, those cultural practices that enhance the group's productivity or reproductivity are retained while those that do not are selected out. Unlike phylogenic and ontogenic selection, however, cultural selection depends on the presence of verbal behavior, which, as we know, is the result of both phylogenic and ontogenic contingencies (Skinner, 1957).

Verbal behavior serves several functions in cultural evolution. First, it permits rapid induction and modification of behavioral repertoires by *rules*, that is, statements of contingencies that obviate the need for direct contact. "If you blow on the spark, it will become a flame" and "If you give me some of your food, I will protect you from the wolves" are apocryphal examples of rules with obvious cost-benefit to prehistoric cave dwellers.

Second, verbal behavior replaces (or at least supplements) genetics with respect to the transmission of successful cultural adaptations across generations. The existence of a spoken and preferably a written language permits history to be created. One generation can learn vicariously from the experiences of prior generations, providing that those experiences were chronicled and that succeeding generations include individuals who can interpret the chronicles.

Verbal behavior also permits codification of the rules of social conduct into a system of *laws*, or statements of the social contingencies that govern the behavior of members of a particular group. Archaeologists and anthropologists note that contemporaneous with this development is the emergence of government (Peltzman, 1980; Posner, 1980). Government extracts a portion of the collective pool of reinforcers in exchange for performing management and enforcement functions. With the advent of a medium of exchange, this process becomes formalized through mechanisms of taxation and subsequent redistribution of the results of production.

As long as the overall cost-benefit to the group remains positive, variations of this type are functional and may be differentially selected. In theory, if such a practice ceases to be cost-beneficial, it will disappear and be replaced by one that is. In reality, however, that may be a long and painful process. In the case of any particular culture or cultural practice, a positive outcome is by no means assured. An analysis of the contingencies operating within such cultural units will clarify the issue.

Institutional Contingencies

Individuals who assume, by whatever means, the role of manager within a cultural unit do not become exempt from the influence of contingencies of reinforcement. In fact, they are exposed to a different set of contingencies from those that prevail within the larger cultural unit. Power, prestige, social influence, and wealth are available, if they maintain their position. Thus, behavior that achieves these ends is selected, including forms of verbal behavior that transcend the functions discussed earlier. Specifically, explanations are invented for events that are otherwise unexplainable, and in the process, the inventor becomes endowed with special knowledge that justifies his or her position. The tribal witch doctor is the prototypical example of this ingenious adaptation.

In more complex cultures, this practice itself becomes institutionalized. A body of invented wisdom is established that serves the managers' immediate needs and indirectly the culture's needs. For example, during the Middle Ages, a system of laws of divine origin was sufficient to maintain civil order even as it maintained the preeminence of the clergy in all matters of secular and religious concern. This accounts for the fact that the clergy led the denunciations of Galileo and Darwin, whose offenses were to explain natural phenomena in ways that were inconsistent with the established body of invented wisdom (Johnston & Pennypacker, 1980; Pennypacker, 1992).

Of immediate importance is the fact that behavior within such an organization is shaped and maintained by contingencies that promote the organization's survival sometimes without regard for the impact on the surrounding culture. We call such organizations *Type S*(tatic). It is instructive to analyze the contingencies that operate within them.

Because survival is the standard against which selection operates, it is not surprising that variation in practice is discouraged. Behavior within such an organization is maintained primarily by a complex system of avoidance contingencies, defined independently of the external environment. Meeting deadlines avoids aversive consequences, "making waves" does not.

An organization that is chartered to solve a particular societal problem has, by definition, no interest in solving the problem if doing so would lead to its dissolution. Process and procedure are therefore emphasized over outcome; failure to make progress on the original problem justifies requests for additional resources and the growth of the organization. External proposals to solve the problem are met with fierce resistance; the proponents are attacked and the organization's resources are marshalled to the cause of its defense. When challenged by the external, supporting culture to provide evidence to justify its activities, the institution enlists learned exponents of the prevailing body of invented wisdom to document the sheer difficulty, if not the impossibility, of measuring progress in the area of concern. As a last resort, the institution will launch its own evaluation program with the help of consultants recruited from the ranks of the learned exponents.

The Antithesis of Type S Organizational Contingencies

The history of civilization makes clear that institution-serving contingencies are not the only determinants of cultural evolution. If they were, Western culture would have reached steady state about 1000 A.D. and Eastern culture would have frozen during the height of the Ming dynasty. In fact, no institution has evolved that can exert total control over all the natural contingencies impinging on the life of every member of the culture. This leaves room for variation in at least some practices and differential selection of those that are cost-beneficial.

Discovery of new knowledge is perhaps the most important, single cause of cultural variation. The highly complex form of verbal behavior we call science is the principal means by which new knowledge is generated. This behavior, like any other, is selected by its effects on the environment; technology and its benefits select and maintain scientific practice. To be sure, there are intermediate contingencies involving the scientist's verbal behavior and the maintaining audience of peers, but the ultimate selective forces are found in the culture at large and are essentially economic in nature (Harris, 1980; Pennypacker, 1992). Scientific enterprises that fail to produce anything of economic value eventually disappear.

The contingencies that support science and technology also permit the formation of organizations, but only to the extent that they are cost-beneficial for the larger enterprise. We call such organizations *Type F*(unctional). Such organizations are ad hoc in nature and tend to disappear when they are no longer needed. Because the survival of such organizations is so closely tied to economic utility, the contingencies that operate within them tend to be outcome oriented. Variation in practice is encouraged, and the status quo is constantly challenged. When an innovative practice of substantial cost-benefit emerges from within such an organization, the larger organization, and possibly the entire culture, changes accordingly. The personal computer revolution is a recent example.

Thus we see that the distinction between invented wisdom and discovered knowledge is fundamental to the evolution of two contrasting sets of organizational contingencies. These relations are summarized in Table 2.1.

A Refined Analysis of Cultural Evolution

Cultural history can be viewed as a series of dynamic interchanges between these two forms of organization. Static organizations form, grow, become

Table 2.1 Contingencies governing the selection of organizations.

Invented Wisdom	Discovered Knowledge
Selection is via consequences of social control.	Selection is via effects on the environment.
Power accrues to philosopher-kings, clergy, and guardians of invented wisdom.	Technology and its economic benefits select and maintain scientific practice.
↓	↓
Bureaucracy.	Ad hoc organization.
Negative reinforcement.	Maintained by mixed contingencies of positive and negative reinforcement.
Variability limited.	Variability encouraged.
Contingencies select for process, survival of the organization.	Contingencies select for cost-beneficial outcomes.
↓	↓
Type S Organizations	Type F Organizations

too large for the culture to support, and are displaced by functional forms that may then grow under their own contingencies and become static. How does the principle of selection by consequences extend our understanding of this process?

The selectionist paradigm unifies our understanding of change at the phylogenic, ontogenic, and cultural levels of analysis. We may borrow principles from the disciplines operating at any one of these levels and inductively apply them to any other level. For example, the principle of *reproductive fitness* states that the relative frequency of organisms that possess features critical to fertility increases the species probability of survival by natural selection (Andronis, 1992; Gould, 1989). Similarly, the principle of *operant conditioning* states that the higher the frequency of a particular response in an organism's repertoire, the more likely it is to contact reinforcement. This, in turn, further increases its relative frequency within the repertoire. From these principles, we may induce a corollary principle at the level of cultural selection: the higher the frequency of a cultural practice, the greater the likelihood of its retention by the culture.

But what accounts for these high frequencies, whether of fertility-related characteristics, operant response classes, or cultural practices? The answer, of course, is differential selection by consequences. In the case of the operant response class, frequency (probability?) of occurrence is a product of prior contingencies of reinforcement. When the contingencies change, response frequencies change as well. If the contingency change is too great, and the existing response frequency is too low, extinction occurs. Thus, the durability of a response in an organism's repertoire is a joint function of its frequency and the prevailing contingencies of reinforcement.

In the case of cultural practices, the durability, or probability of retention, of a cultural practice is a joint function of its current frequency and cost-benefit. This relationship can be symbolized as follows:

$$D = f(P) \, \emptyset \, cb(P)$$

where D is durability, P is cultural practice, f is frequency, cb is cost benefit, and $\emptyset$ is an operation of combination.

This relationship clearly shows that even if a cultural practice occurs at a high frequency, if its cost-benefit diminishes, so does its likelihood of survival. Similarly, if an innovative practice occurs at a low frequency but is highly cost-beneficial, its durability should increase. Eventually, it may overtake and replace the original practice, as when the automobile replaced the horse as the primary means of personal transportation.

The problem in applying this analysis to complex problems in our culture lies in determining the cost-benefit of a particular practice. In a democratic society like ours, practices (including education) that are the province of publicly supported institutions must include the burden borne by the taxpayers in the calculation of cost. The benefit side includes the livelihood of the individuals who populate the institution. Since these individuals are also voters, and since their frequency is both large and increasing, the political consequences for an elected official of acting to modify the practice may be untenable. The uproar over base closings in the wake of Department of Defense cutbacks illustrates this point.

On the other hand, there is growing evidence that the public is willing to modify those institutions that, in their view, have ceased to be cost-beneficial. The popular effort to limit the terms of elected officials, the outpouring of support for Ross Perot as a presidential candidate, and the recent periodic tax revolts suggest that certain governmental institutions and the services they provide are no longer publicly perceived as being worth what they cost. Unfortunately, as our earlier analysis points out, before a practice can disappear, an alternative with superior frequency and cost-benefit must be available. In the examples, clearly superior alternatives do not exist, although fiscal pressure has spawned numerous innovations. The increasing sensitivity of public policy to the role of consequences in behavior management has caused some localities to experiment with welfare reform, waste reduction, privatization of corrections, and even education (Pennypacker, 1992).

Variation and Selection in Education

Let us now consider the current upheaval in education in the light of this analysis of selection of cultural practices. The fact that there is an upheaval signifies that either the cost, the benefit, or both, of current practices is unsatisfactory. Though the debate often centers on issues of public versus private schools, voucher systems, parental choice, and national versus local standards, cost and benefit are the basic parameters of the problem. In fact, as Finn (1991) and others have documented, both elements are in severe need of adjustment.

Cost
Schmidt (1992) pointed out that since 1965, the United States has roughly doubled the level of per-pupil spending (after inflation) in the public schools. Although this places us ahead of Britain, France, Japan, and Germany in this index (*Wall Street Journal*, 1991), our educational outcomes do not compare favorably with these countries. Finn (1991, p. 37) estimated that less than half of the public educational dollar is spent on instruction, with the balance absorbed by inflated administrative costs. The situation is somewhat better in the private schools where

market forces place limits on marginal costs (Chubb & Moe, 1991).

Benefit
It is with respect to the outcomes of education, particularly public education, that the most intense concern is being voiced. The static picture in terms of standardized achievement-test scores, the high drop-out rates, and the alarming rate of illiteracy compared to other industrial nations has been with us for some time. In response, numbers of blue-ribbon commissions have been appointed to make recommendations, billions of dollars have been spent on educational research, and nothing has changed. It is as though a critical mass of concern could not be reached until some catalyzing event tipped the equilibrium.

That event, not surprisingly, was economic. The recent recession has dramatized the gradual decline in U.S. productivity and the corresponding decline in competitiveness. The documented failure of the educational system to produce sufficient numbers of trained workers has placed American industry at a competitive disadvantage in the international marketplace, and as a result, the American standard of living is declining. Suddenly, everyone is alarmed about the crisis in education. There is reason for cautious optimism concerning change in educational practices, if only because of the perceived relationship between the effectiveness of the educational system and economic well-being. There is also reason for pessimism, which derives from our earlier analysis of institutions within our culture.

A dramatic case history illustrates the scope of the obstacles facing those who would act to change our educational system. Watkins (1988) presented an analysis of the contingencies that govern the educational establishment as they emerged in the case of Project Follow Through, the most expensive educational experiment in U.S. history. Beginning in the 1970s, the federal government launched a program to evaluate several varieties of educational interventions that were designed to consolidate the gains attributable to Head Start. After several years, the programs were evaluated by an outside agency with respect to gains in basic skills, problem-solving skills, and self-concept.

Two programs, the Direct Instruction model from the University of Oregon and the Behavior Analysis model from the University of Kansas, were superior. Some of the other programs were actually harmful in comparison to the control effects of no intervention at all. These results were not only unexpected, they were contrary to some cherished tenets of invented wisdom embraced by the academic educational establishment. Consequently, the Department of Education averaged the outcomes across all programs, concluded that no change had occurred, and recommended that Congress increase funding for these least-effective or least-harmful programs. This is hardly an example of differential selection of practice based on demonstrated benefit!

The chief impediment to changing our educational practices is not lack of alternatives, but a system of institutional contingencies that cannot accommodate such change. Our analysis suggests that serious change will begin only when the economic consequences, and hence the political consequences, of past practices become sufficiently aversive. Then, those innovations that are blessed with sufficient frequency and positive cost-benefit will be selected. Will behavior analysis be among them?

The Future of Behavior Analysis in Education

Throughout its relatively brief history, behavior analysis has contributed significantly to education. From B. F. Skinner's early work with teaching machines and programmed instruction through the latest developments in Direct Instruction and Precision Teaching, behavior analysts have put forth a nearly continuous effort to improve some educational practice or other. These efforts have invariably led to superior performance on the part of learners, including grade school pupils (Skinner, 1968, 1984; Engelmann & Carnine, 1982), college students (Keller, 1968), special education populations (Haughton, 1972), factory workers (Gilbert & Gilbert, 1992), and illiterate adults (Johnson & Layng, 1992). The list is almost endless. Notwithstanding these accomplishments, and the critical need for improvement in the educational practices of our culture, the extent

to which any of these innovations has been adopted is disappointing (Carnine, 1992; Lindsley, 1992).

Reflecting on this state of affairs, Skinner wrote in 1984: "A culture that is not willing to accept scientific advances in the understanding of human behavior, together with the technology which emerges from these advances, will eventually be replaced by a culture that is" (p. 953). The question for us is, Why is the culture unwilling to accept these technologies? In terms of our present analysis, there are three possibilities: benefit, cost, and frequency. Let us consider these in order.

With respect to benefit, the data are clear. These technologies are superior if benefit is measured in terms of student achievement or, more technically, amount of student behavior change per unit of time or cost (Pennypacker & Binder, 1992). Watkins (1988) pointed out, however, that these are not the measures of benefit that interest the educational establishment.

Those who have experienced conflict with educational institutions as a result of implementing these technologies (Englemann, 1991; Pennypacker, Heckler, & Pennypacker, 1979) realize that these Type S institutions measure benefit by expansion of the top line, leading to growth of the institution. This has resulted in budgetary practices in which the fundamental unit is one body in place for one unit of time. Any practice that threatens to shorten the time required to provide the service is not viewed favorably. Given that a disparity exists between benefit for the student and benefit for the institution as a component of accounting, management has successfully defended the latter. The suggestion that accountability might better be fashioned in terms of behavior change (learning) per unit of time (money) receives even less consideration (Pennypacker & Binder, 1992).

With respect to the second factor—cost—little is known. Behavioral instruction technologies cost more, at least initially, because of one-time training costs. With respect to continued operation, however, such technologies as Precision Teaching and Direct Instruction can be added to the conventional public school for a few dollars per pupil per year. We need comparative data on *opportunity cost*: What do these technologies offer in terms of long-range savings by cutting the drop-out rates, the illiteracy rates, and the concomitant costs of corrections (Berlin & Sum, 1988)? As data bearing on these points become more available, they must become part of the public dialogue.

The third factor—frequency—is our biggest problem, but I am most optimistic about this factor. In spite of the systematic lack of reinforcement, even punishment, that the early innovators (Lindsley, 1992) experienced, our numbers seem to be increasing and our activities are becoming more diverse. Perhaps this is because we have begun to recognize the problems inherent in Type S institutions and have sought more hospitable environments in which to contribute to the culture. We have, in short, discovered that environments exist in which behavior change is valued and those who can engineer it are both valued and appropriately compensated. By providing appropriate reinforcers, these environments will increase our frequencies. We are being, and will continue to be, selected. Eventually, a critical mass will be reached and fundamental changes will emerge.

This is important because we will never make a major contribution to the massive problems of education unless we find a way to exert some leverage with respect to our pitifully small frequencies. If the powers that be were to decide tomorrow that public education should be immediately reformed in accordance with the prescriptions of behavior analysis, who would do it? The task would be enormous and we would be shorthanded. In the short run, however, we can make some basic contributions. Let me suggest a couple.

The hallmark of behavior analysis is its emphasis on direct measurement of behavior. Skinner's (1938) early emphasis on *frequency* as the proper unit was almost prescient in the light of subsequent discoveries of its fundamental role in selection by consequences. We now know that frequency is not just a good unit, it is also one of the dimensions of behavior that defines function. For a particular behavior to be functional, it must occur with appropriate form and at a frequency dictated by the reinforcing demands of the environment.

In the early 1970s, Eric Haughton (1972) began emphasizing tool skill frequencies in the development of more complex and durable academic behavior. His work was widely ignored until very recently when

Carl Binder (Binder, 1988; Binder & Watkins, 1990) and Kent Johnson (Johnson & Layng, 1992) began working with measures of *fluency*, defined as a joint measure of accuracy and frequency. Out of this work has come the realization that fluency is, or should be, the aim of any instructional intervention. Lacking fluency in tool skills, students flounder in their attempts to acquire more complex skills. With fluency, however, the complex skills sometimes emerge spontaneously (Johnson & Layng, 1992), as predicted by a selectionist analysis of survival in a changing environment. Thus, students with fluent computational math and reading skills can perform effectively on word problems with no formal instruction! Johnson and Layng have suggested the term *adduced contingencies* to account for this phenomenon.

What are the skills that an individual must exhibit at fluent levels to be functional in our society? What are the values of frequency and accuracy that define the fluency of these skills? Answers to these questions are presently unknown, but scores on the SAT or any other standardized achievement test will probably bear a small positive relation to these values. Put another way, if all individuals taking the SAT were fully functional in all the skills required for citizenship, there would be very little variance in the scores to explain. Instead of overhauling the system to improve SAT scores, why not teach fluencies?

Carl Binder and I (Pennypacker & Binder, 1992) recently took this a step further and suggested a system whereby students would be certified by independent examiners on achievement of fluency in each required skill. Such a system presupposes standards of fluency that behavior analysts are uniquely qualified to collect. How such fluency is acquired would be left to parents, schools, private venders, and others to determine. Skill certifications would be an outcome measure against which selection with respect to educational practices would finally become functional.

My final suggestion flows from all that has preceded. Many years ago, in a private moment with Eric Haughton, I asked him how he managed to remain so cheerful in the face of so little progress by behavior analysis in terms of acceptance by the educational establishment. Eric was an accomplished seaman and a mountain climber and his answer came from his experience in the mountains. I forget his exact words, but the metaphor is crystal clear even today. He said that when climbing a mountain, if all you ever do is look straight ahead at the summit off in the distance, you easily become tired and discouraged, and you may give up. If, however, when you stop to rest, you turn around and look at where you came from—at the town below, the clouds beneath you— and then look again at the summit, it will seem much closer. You may never reach it, but there will be renewed joy in the attempt.

We are on such a mountain. Some of us will never reach the summit. But I am confident of one thing: those fortunate ones who do should not be surprised if Eric is there to greet them.

References

ANDRONIS, P. T. (1992). *Selectionist connections between radical behaviorism and other fields such as ethology and biology.* In K. Johnson & T. Layng (Chairs), Workshop on selectionism and behavior analysis. Eighteenth annual meeting of the Association for Behavior Analysis, San Francisco, May 25–28.

BERLIN, J. A., & Sum, A. (1988). *Toward more perfect union: Basic skills, poor families, and our economic future.* New York: Ford Foundation.

BINDER, C. V. (1988). Precision teaching: Measuring and attaining academic excellence. *Youth Policy, 10,* 12–15.

BINDER, C. V., & Watkins, C. L. (1990). Precision Teaching and Direct Instruction: Measurably superior instructional technology in schools. *Performance Improvement Quarterly, 8,* 2–14.

CARNINE, D. (1992). Expanding the notion of teachers' rights: Access to tools that work. *Journal of Applied Behavior Analysis, 25,* 13–19.

CHUBB, J. E., & Moe, T. M. (1991). The public vs. private school debate. *Wall Street Journal,* July 26, p. A8.

ENGLEMANN, S. (1991). Why I sued California. *Direct Instruction News,* Winter, 1991.

ENGLEMANN, S., & Carnine, D. (1982). *Theory of instruction: principles and applications.* New York: Irvington Publishers.

FINN, C. E. (1991). *We must take charge: Our schools and our future.* New York: Free Press.

GILBERT, T. A., & Gilbert, M. B. (1992). Potential contributions of performance science to education. *Journal of Applied Behavior Analysis, 25,* 43–49.

GOULD, S. J. (1989). *Wonderful life.* New York: Norton.

HARRIS, M. (1980). *Cultural materialism: The struggle for a science of culture.* New York: Random House.

HAUGHTON, E. C. (1972). Aims: Growing and sharing. In J. B. Jordan & L. S. Robbins (Eds.), *Let's try doing something else kind of thing.* Arlington, VA: Council on Exceptional Children.

JOHNSON, K. R., & Layng, T. V. J. (1992). Breaking the structuralist barrier: Literacy and numeracy with fluency. *American Psychologist, 47*(11), 1475–1490.

JOHNSTON, J. M., & Pennypacker, H. S. (1980). *Strategies and tactics of human behavioral research.* Hillsdale, NJ: Lawrence Erlbaum Associates.

KELLER, F. S. (1968). Good-bye, teacher. *Journal of Applied Behavior Analysis, 1,* 79–89.

LINDSLEY, O. R. (1992). Why aren't effective teaching tools widely adopted? *Journal of Applied Behavior Analysis, 25,* 21–26.

PELTZMAN, S. (1980). The growth of government. *Journal of Law and Economics, 23,* 209-287. Reprinted in G. Stigler (Ed.), *Chicago Studies in Political Economy.* Chicago: University of Chicago Press, 1988.

PENNYPACKER, H. S. (1992). Is behavior analysis undergoing selection by consequences? *American Psychologist, 47*(11), 1491–1498.

PENNYPACKER, H. S., & Binder, C. V. (1992). Triage for American education. *Administrative Radiology Journal, 11*(1), 19–25.

PENNYPACKER, H. S., Heckler, J. B., & Pennypacker, S. F. (1979). A university-wide system of personalized instruction: The Personalized Learning Center. In A. C. Catania & T. A. Brigham (Eds.), *Handbook of applied behavior analysis: Social and instructional processes* (pp. 584–602). New York: Irvington Publishers.

POSNER, R. A. (1980). A theory of primitive society, with special reference to law. *Journal of Law and Economics, 23*(1), 1–53. Reprinted in G. Stigler (Ed.), *Chicago Studies in Political Economy.* Chicago: University of Chicago Press.

SCHMIDT, Jr., B. C. (1992). Educational innovation for profit. *Wall Street Journal,* June 5, p. A10.

SKINNER, B. F. (1938). *The behavior of organisms.* New York: Appleton-Century-Crofts.

SKINNER, B. F. (1957). *Verbal behavior.* New York: Appleton-Century-Crofts.

SKINNER, B. F. (1968). *The technology of teaching.* New York: Appleton-Century-Crofts.

SKINNER, B. F. (1981). Selection by consequences. *Science, 213,* 501–504.

SKINNER, B. F. (1984). The shame of American education. *American Psychologist, 39,* 9947–9954.

SUMNER, W. G. [1906] (1959). *Folkways.* New York: Ginn & Co. Reprinted by Dover Publications.

WALL Street Journal. Staff. (1991). The schools' burdens (editorial). *Wall Street Journal,* May 10, p. A10.

WATKINS, C. L. (1988). Project Follow Through: A story of the identification and neglect of effective instruction. *Youth Policy, 10*(7), 7–11.

PART 2

Promoting Applied Behavior Anlaysis

Chapter 3
Measurably Superior Instructional Methods:
Do We Need Sales and Marketing?
  Carl Binder

Chapter 4
The Insignificant Impact of Behavior Analysis
on Education: Notes from a Dean of Education
  Samuel M. Deitz

Chapter 5
"Mainstreaming" Applied Behavior Analysis Principles
and Procedures into a Preservice
Training Program for General Education Teachers
  Larry Maheady, Gregory F. Harper,
  Barbara Mallette, Melinda Karnes

Chapter 6
Developmentalism's Impediments to School Reform:
Three Recommendations for Overcoming Them
  John E. Stone

CHAPTER 3

Measurably Superior Instructional Methods: Do We Need Sales and Marketing?

Carl Binder

This chapter expands on previous discussions of the importance of taking a sales and marketing approach to the dissemination and promotion of effective instructional technology (Binder & Watkins, 1989; Binder, 1990, 1991a, 1991b). Behavioral educators who have developed measurably effective instructional methods and materials must do a better job of targeting markets and customers, identifying their needs, developing and packaging specific solutions for those needs, describing these offerings with language that will influence customers' buying decisions, and inducing customers to adopt or literally purchase the solution. Stated with a more commercial intent, we need to learn how to package and promote what we do to sell it in sufficient quantity and generate sufficient revenues to guarantee continued, independent funding of our research and development. This is the most pressing challenge for instructional technologists today if we seek to make significant, lasting contributions.

How We Have Failed

Many academics and human services practitioners seem to view sales and marketing as beneath them. Yet many express surprise or indignation when measurably superior instructional methods are not more widely adopted. As scientists motivated by empirical data, or as practitioners encouraged by observable results, we often lack sympathy for those who are not likewise motivated. For example, in moving from educational research and teacher preparation into private-sector corporate consulting and training development, I assumed that measured results would "sell" effective instructional methodologies. This naive assumption turned out to be incorrect. Although data work to support adoption or buying decisions made by those in need of objective justification, such decisions seem largely influenced by other factors, including the emotional connotations of the words used to describe products, services, and their benefits (Miller & Heiman, 1987). Objective data seem to be relevant only when they relate directly to a problem or need of which the customer is clearly aware. Customers must be able to identify results that they perceive to be desirable, and there seems to be a substantial emotional component in this anticipation. The behavior of our prospective customers—educators and administrators, for the most part—suggests that we have often failed to successfully identify reinforcers for their behaviors, effectively enable them to anticipate those reinforcers, or bring them under the stable control of the positive consequences of adopting our methods.

Malott (1992) made the point that "behavior analysis can save the world by focusing on the added, effective, performance management contingency. We can best contribute by designing and implementing contingencies with outcomes that are sizable and probable" (p. 19). Our difficulty has not been with the effectiveness of our solutions. Indeed, we have been able to produce remarkably powerful solutions to pressing educational problems (e.g., Watkins, 1988; Binder & Watkins, 1990; Johnson & Layng, 1992). Rather, in large part we have failed to attractively package, market, and sell our products. This has been true both for those working within schools and human services agencies and for consultants or academics attempting to influence education on a large scale from the outside. We might benefit, therefore, from adopting methods used in private enterprise to market and sell products and services.

What Is Sales and Marketing?

The marketing and sales approach is largely a matter of verbal behavior that is designed to prompt and reinforce successive approximations to a "buying decision." Marketing and sales has at least four discernible functions: (1) market researchers identify and survey potential markets for products or services, (2) product development and product marketing professionals create products and services that meet the target customers' perceived needs or wants. (3) marketing communications people craft vision statements, product literature, and advertising copy to increase the likelihood of positive buying decisions, and (4) sales professionals use questioning strategies to prompt customers to discuss their perceived problems, their needs, and the value of solutions to those problems. Once customers have expressed their needs and the potential payoff for addressing those needs, salespeople can introduce solutions and explain how they address those needs, as a step toward "closing the sale."

Every step in the process is designed to introduce or strengthen the establishing operations or to shape customers' verbal behavior toward buying decisions. Although this chapter is not intended to provide an exhaustive or technically precise behavioral description of this process, others could contribute significantly to our understanding by carrying out such an analysis. Instead, I will simply introduce and discuss some of the basic principles and procedures of sales and marketing and suggest how they might apply to our efforts to promote effective instructional methods.

Market Research: The Problem of Identifying Markets

The first step in an effective sales and marketing process involves research, with varying degrees of formality, aimed at identifying prospective markets or customer groups and their needs. Market research consists of procedures for checking in advance the correctness of marketing, sales, and product decisions (Breen & Blankenship, 1982). These decisions can be related to all aspects of the product development, marketing, and sales process. As a starting place, however, we need to discover who might be willing and able to buy what we have to offer.

As academics and practitioners, we are not ignorant of market research, although we probably have not conceived of our activities as such. Indeed, the processes of grantsmanship and academic publication frequently involve searching for granting agencies interested in funding research or applied programs, or investigating journals to determine which are likely to publish what we write and how we should position what we write so that it will be accepted. In these processes we conduct a narrow version of market research by scanning potential markets to target customers and identify their needs.

On the other hand, our grant-seeking and publication efforts differ from private-sector market research in several critical aspects. In seeking grants, for example, we are often communicating with our peers—academics, practitioners, or bureaucrats—whose jargon and perspectives we share. Consequently, we may not need to conduct extensive research to determine the best language for describing their problems or needs. We may not have to reduce our communication efforts to plain English, expressed in terms that an otherwise unfamiliar audience might understand. To the contrary, in many cases the more academic jargon or "bureaucratese" we use the better, since using such language with these audiences might convey credibility. In market research, as it is described here, one goal is to identify and adopt the vocabulary of the customer—language that might be quite different from our own.

Although there is certainly an element of selling involved in grantsmanship and publication, the motivation of our customers in these situations may be significantly different than in the commercial environment. In many cases, we need only seek the agencies or journals whose published standards correspond with what we are already doing, rather than adapt our work in any significant way to the needs of the market. In some cases, granting agencies and journal editors have the equivalent of quotas to fulfill and accept the best of whatever proposals or manuscripts they receive. Participation in this process may therefore be far different than inducing an otherwise uninterested prospective customer to buy something.

To more widely promote and sell our educational technologies, we must identify those customers who control decisions to adopt or buy our products or services; capture the language they use to describe their problems, needs, and wants; and use that language to communicate the benefits of our products and services. We must identify those customers who have serious problems or needs that we can address with unique or compelling cost-effectiveness or emotional impact and in sufficient numbers to generate a significant return on our investment, both financial and in overall impact or visibility.

An important difference between the process of identifying potential customers and of securing grants is that the grant-getting process does not always promote development of products and services that will outlast the grant. Grants can significantly contribute to our survival only if they are viewed as "seed capital" to develop products and services that will be successful in the marketplace. Otherwise, as has occurred so often in research and program development, grants are analogous to "feeding the deer"—once the artificial source of sustenance ends, the deer starve to death because the free food has discouraged adapta-

tion to the natural contingencies. From a selectionist perspective (Johnson & Layng, 1992), grants often select programs that cannot stand on their own. The benefit of conducting market research as a precursor to exposing ourselves to the contingencies of the marketplace is that it increases the likelihood of survival by identifying the needs we must satisfy in order to be sustained by natural, economic contingencies. That is, market research helps us define the parameters of products and services we must develop, package, and offer to increase the likelihood of adoption and support in the free market environment.

Methods for conducting market research vary. They may include relatively informal analyses as well as formal controlled studies and significant statistical and demographic research (Breen & Blankenship, 1982). Simply listing the types of prospective users and buyers of our technologies and creating preliminary descriptions of their potential problems and needs is a way to begin considering which products and services to develop for whom. Scanning the media for information about potential markets and needs and recording the language used to describe them may also be a good preliminary step. Once having defined the characteristics of potential buyers, using readily available sources of demographic and statistical data to estimate market size is another common exploratory method. Working with marketing professionals to apply more sophisticated methods, whether as paid consultants or as academic colleagues, may offer behavioral educators an entry into more sophisticated phases of the market research process. It may also lead to new types of research for behavioral educators, such as studies aimed at empirically determining optimal conditions and target markets for dissemination of behavioral technology.

Some market research methods are similar to those used by instructional designers in the process of needs assessment (Zemke & Kramlinger, 1982). For example, using surveys and questionnaires with samples of a prospective customer base to determine the types and magnitudes of their problems and needs, and the language they use to describe them, is a relatively easy way of beginning to formulate products and services likely to be successful in particular markets. Using focus groups—structured group discussions—with various customer types is another important tool for identifying markets, customer needs, and effective marketing language. Telephone interviews can produce a large amount of data about specific questions and topics at relatively low cost, given phone lists of appropriate interviewees. An important emphasis for all of these methods is to identify significant markets with pressing needs that can be addressed in powerful ways. In the process, a narrowly defined "niche" market may often provide a more secure or predictable customer base than a larger market, which is less predictable because of its broader parameters.

Examples of potential markets for our services might include the growing number of parents willing to invest in after-school programs for their children; adults needing to pass certification or licensing exams in specific fields; adult literacy; home study markets for children whose parents purchase materials at check-out counters in common retail outlets; computer training; many areas of corporate and industrial training; public schools willing to contract with outside providers in specific curriculum areas; people willing to pay for health maintenance programs; foreign language training in specific market segments; and various types of recreational instruction such as chess, bridge, and golf, where the skills might be taught more efficiently.

For each potential market, we need to define a customer profile; obtain estimates of size and indications of ability and willingness to spend; identify perceived problems, needs, or wants; and gather information about actual or potential competition. (By the way, markets with existing successful providers are often ripe for additional competitors and may sometimes offer greater potential than new, untested markets.)

Product Development: The Problem of Defining a Product

Effective sales and marketing relies on having a product. Once we have conducted market research to identify a significant market with specific problems or needs, the purpose of the product development phase is to create and package a product or service that is designed precisely to address those needs and be attractive to target customers. Just as it is often a mistake to assume that a broadly defined market will be more lucrative than a narrowly and more precisely defined market segment, developing a generic product or service may be perceived as "for no one" because it is for everyone. Prospective customers must be able to easily identify the product or service as a solution to their particular problems, in both its description and packaging. In the process of product development, we would be wise to conduct research about whether our prospective customers can readily identify our offering as specifically intended for them.

The more tangible our solution is to specific needs, the easier it will be to describe, demonstrate, and sell. A major difficulty for instructional technologists, and for behavioral educators in particular, is that we often attempt to sell methods or an approach rather than a well-defined product or service. Because we are frequently involved in academic pursuits, and have ourselves been sold on the concepts and principles of behavior analysis, we often promote our general methodology on the merits of its logic and overall measures of success. Combined with our frequent use of jargon and abstract terminology, this approach places us at a significant disadvantage.

An interesting trend toward "packages" of behavioral interventions began in the 1970s with such products as Foxx and Azrin's (1974) popular toilet-training book for parents. This was an example of applying general principles and procedures to a specific problem for a particular audience and using language that was easy for that audience to accept and understand. Some criticism arose in the field of applied behavior analysis when academic publications reported the results of "packaged" combinations of interventions without analyzing the effects of each component (Birnbrauer, 1979). This controversy, however, might have been clarified by distinguishing between marketing packages created to disseminate technology and the science of behavior analysis, which should strive to determine the effects of each variable and its interactions.

In recent years there have been many examples of educational packages being marketed by nonbehaviorists directly to the public. Ads in airline magazines, for example, portray language learning self-study programs that are clearly and attractively aimed at busy professionals. *Hooked on Phonics* (1987), a popular audiotape and workbook reading-instruction package marketed on television, and the videotape study skills program *Where There's a Will There's an . . . A* (Olney, 1989) are examples of mass-marketed educational packages aimed at specific segments of parents and students. Those who need these programs can easily identify them as potential solutions to their problems.

Some behaviorists have also been successful in creating and marketing specific products. Behavioral educator Michael Maloney of Ontario, Canada, for example, has successfully marketed educational software called *Math Tutor* (1985) for teachers, parents, and children. (In fact, this series of programs has received awards for excellence from both *Curriculum Digest* and *Parents Choice* magazines.) Trying to sell behavioral education, or even such specific methodologies as Precision Teaching or Direct Instruction, may be far more difficult than selling "The Morningside Program" for children and adults with learning problems (Johnson & Layng, 1992) or *Teach Your Child to Read in 100 Easy Lessons* (Engelmann, Haddox, & Bruner, 1983). These types of packaged, targeted products are far more likely to be commercially successful, thus serving as effective vehicles for disseminating our technologies, than the generic methods on which they are based.

There may even be evidence that the more specifically we define and package our products, moving away from general methodologies toward particular solutions, the more effective they will be. An example, from the now-famous Project Follow Through study (Watkins, 1988), is that the Direct Instruction model, which included both a methodology and very specific curriculum materials and procedures, was more effective at teaching basic skills to young children than the Behavior Analysis model, which relied on a generally "behavioral" methodology of contingency management but did not include curriculum materials that were developed and refined for effectiveness specifically with the target population. The Morningside model, which integrates principles from Precision Teaching, Direct Instruction, and other behavioral methodologies, appears to be more effec-

tive in teaching literacy, numeracy, and study skills than any of its component methodologies in isolation (Johnson & Layng, 1992).

Marketing Communication: The Problem of Description

Having identified customers and needs and developed and packaged a solution, the next step is to communicate with prospective customers about the product and how it addresses their needs or desires. Marketing communication involves identifying and using audience-specific language, describing products and services as need-solutions that appeal to target customers, and crafting language that carries appropriate emotional connotations for its target audience and conveys the relevant facts.

As scientists, we have learned to communicate in ways that are ineffective when used with those outside our profession. In particular, academic encouragement of passive sentences and technical jargon has created barriers between us and the general literate public. Using behavioral terminology to communicate with prospective customers is similar to using engineering jargon to sell cars (Binder, 1991b)—it simply doesn't work very well. Yet, we are so attached to our language because of its technical power and precision that we tend to resist plain English. We often seek to convert others to our philosophy and therefore to our way of speaking. Although this goal might be a worthy one in the context of academic or philosophical discourse, it may not support wide dissemination of our methods.

As the originator of the phrase *measurably superior instructional methods* (Binder, 1990, 1991a)— the tag line for the 1992 Ohio State University Conference on Behavior Analysis in Education—I can speak from experience about the need to obtain feedback from the market about our use of language. In an effort to substitute plain descriptive language for such terms as Precision Teaching, Direct Instruction, and Behavioral Education, I created the phrase *measurably superior instructional methods* because it emphasizes our measured results. However, recent feedback from nonbehaviorists and relatively naive readers has convinced me that the air of haughty superiority connoted by this phrase probably outweighs any descriptive improvement it represents. Our persistence in using the term *behavioral* is an example of our failure to take the audience into account. For whatever reason, this term raises mechanistic, even inhumane, images for many people. We may wish it were otherwise, but we will probably not be very successful in promoting our products and services if we insist on tagging them with language that does not appeal in the marketplace.

A good illustration of using plain English to describe our methods to a general audience is *Don't Shoot the Dog!* (Pryor, 1985), a paperback written by an accomplished animal trainer applying behavioral principles to common human situations. Even seeking to translate the language of our methods for prospective buyers, at least until after they are thoroughly satisfied customers, may be a mistake. We need to exercise extreme care in this area, especially because of the more attractive language used by our "competitors" in psychology and education who begin with a natural marketing communications advantage.

As Malott (1992) observed, "Cognitivism is a lay view in intellectual's clothing. With its expectancies, values, beliefs, and self-efficacies, cognitivism lends legitimacy to the misconceptions of the person on the street" (p. 19). Unfortunately, the language of cognitive developmentalists expresses what behavior analysts believe to be inaccurate descriptions of learning and behavior in terms that are attractive to the general public (Stone, 1991). In recent years, for example, the term *cognitive science* has acquired a high and seldom questioned degree of legitimacy in popular publications and discourse. Its models of commonly accepted processes and mental events based on the language of computer systems seem to add scientific credibility to an already popular vocabulary of mentalistic explanations. In many popular discussions of related topics, cognitive science is assumed to have superseded the old behavioristic notions of the 1950s and 1960s.

Thus, we start out with a handicap—the language we ordinarily use to describe our methods. It does not communicate, except to a small number of specialists. Moreover, it carries mechanistic or "robotic" connotations that seem to offend the average person. Because

we are technologists, like technologists in other fields we tend to emphasize technical language in discussing the features of our products and services rather than present the benefits and unique strengths of what we offer in plain English that describes how they address our customers' perceived needs. The fact that we often promote our general methodologies rather than specific products and services adds to the problem, because in addition to being full of jargon, our descriptions are abstract, even when they describe outcomes or benefits.

An approach that is more aligned with effective marketing communication suggests that we must adopt language that (1) is specific and concrete rather than abstract, (2) is familiar, emotionally attractive to our customers, and easily identifiable as "for" them, and (3) describes solutions to their problems or needs and the feelings associated with those solutions, rather than focusing on the features of our methods and materials.

A look through current popular news publications, in their almost daily reporting of efforts to improve American education, should help us identify words and phrases for describing commonly perceived problems and needs for education and training. A useful step in attempting to describe our products and services might involve focus groups for recording language used by typical customers to describe their problems and needs, the types of solutions they would like to see, and what those solutions would offer them (both objectively and emotionally). We might follow up with individual interviews or questionnaires to confirm and refine their language choices for describing needs and problems, products and services, and solutions and payoffs. In such questionnaires, for example, we might ask prospective customers, "What would you more likely buy, X or Y?" where the alternatives are different descriptions of the same thing.

An interesting precedent in behavioral research on the effects of language was a Burns's (1984) dissertation with Roland Tharp at the University of Hawaii. In this study, behavior modification procedures were described in two ways: standard behavioral terminology and humanistic language. Burns reported that the subjects viewed the behavioral description more negatively than the more humanistic description. This study lends credence to the argument that while it is important to preserve the technical precision of our own terminology as part of behavioral science and engineering, we should not make the error of using such language to market our wares.

Sales: The Problem of Inducing a Purchase

Sales is a process of prompting and shaping prospective customers toward a purchase; that is, the verbal and nonverbal behavior involved in choosing to exchange value (or personal support) for products or services. Although there are many models of the sales process, perhaps the most data-based approach is called SPIN® selling, derived by a researcher who observed and counted the behaviors of effective salespeople (Rackham, 1988). Rackham observed that the most effective salespeople asked certain types of questions with relatively high frequencies when speaking with prospective customers. These questions (summarized by the SPIN acronym) were *s*itua-tion questions, probing for descriptions of current conditions; *p*roblem questions, prompting discussion of current or anticipated difficulties; *i*mplication ques-tions, aimed at inducing the customer to expand on the range and magnitude of difficulties associated with each problem; and *n*eed-payoff questions, prompting explicit statements of needs and descriptions of the expected value to the customer of addressing those needs. This sequence supports a highly effective methodology for prompting and reinforcing the verbal behavior likely to lead to a purchase (assuming that the customer is in a position to buy the particular product or service).

In contrast to such a needs-oriented sales process, many salespeople simply "pitch" the features of their products, attempting to convince prospective cus-tomers of their benefits. Technologists, in particular, often engage in such "feature dumping" rather than asking questions that will lead to customers' identify-ing their perceived problems and needs and the value of solutions. Behavioral technologists frequently fail in this regard, attempting to promote the elegance and power of our methods rather than probing customers to discover their needs before presenting our solu-tions. Viewed in this context, our common practice of citing objective data to support the effectiveness of our methods is likely to be successful only if it follows a sequence in which the prospective customer has explicitly stated problems or needs and the data represent evidence for our compelling solutions to those needs.

Other elements of successful sales are generally subsumed under "sales strategy," a topic Rackham (1989) also covered in detail. For example, when attempting to promote our products or services in competition with others, we may need to adopt strategies for shaping the customer's priorities and buying criteria, shifting the customer's focus from the perceived weaknesses of our products to their per-ceived strengths. Analyzing customer behavior during the process of purchasing a product or service (the "buying cycle") can help us select strategies at each point that effectively prompt and shape behavior toward the final purchase. After the purchase, under-standing how buyers behave during the stages of adoption and implementation can lead to prompting, reinforcement, and problem solving that will ensure continued support and repeated purchase of our products and services.

Another important component of sales behavior involves elementary acts of interpersonal communication. One sales-training program, for example, teaches people to discriminate the affect of the prospective customer at each point in a sales discussion and then respond with a "matching" affect, while prompting and shap-ing them toward a "positive attitude" that is likely to support a buying decision (*Par Sales Training*, 1983). This program can serve as a useful antidote to the all-too-common approach among behavioral educators and researchers of responding with indignation and self-righteousness to anything other than enthusiastic accep-tance by the prospective customers (as though they were stupid for not coming to the "correct" conclusion). In our own frustration, arising from histories of frequent extinction and punishment, we often forget that "the organism is always right." If Skinner's understanding that organisms behave lawfully applies any-where, it certainly must be true of the customers we would like to adopt our products and services. In the midst of the sales process, we must remember to adjust our own behavior accordingly, shaping and reinforcing our customers' responses toward the buying decision.

Qualifying the Customer

A recommended prerequisite step is known as "qualifying the customer." Before pursuing prospective customers, sales professionals set criteria that are intended to screen out those who are unlikely to purchase. Typical qualification criteria include whether prospects can afford a purchase and the absence or presence of various obstructions or positive influences on their ability to control the purchase or on the likelihood of their making purchasing decisions. Depending on the products or services being sold, and often on specifics related to customer types or market segments, qualification criteria may vary a great deal from one sales situation to another. We should also consider what factors might define our prospects' probability of purchase before expending time and energy trying to influence their behavior. Given limited sales resources, we need to "choose our battles"—allocate our efforts where they can be most effective.

The Public Versus the Private Sector

In marketing and selling educational products and services, a primary qualifying criterion might involve the distinction between the public school system and the private sector. For example: What are the conditions under which we are more likely to have an impact on the effectiveness of education? Can we ever hope to significantly impact the public education system from the inside?

The probability of changing public education is addressed by Benno Schmidt, recently president of Yale University and now president of the private-sector Edison Project, an enterprise intended to create hundreds of private for-profit schools that will compete with public schools during the next decade on effectiveness and price. Business Week ("Saving Our Schools," 1992), quoted Schmidt as saying, "I asked myself: What is the chance that public education would make the investment in innovation and have the freedom to experiment and set itself the kind of competitive conditions in which innovations can flourish? There is no chance" (p. 72). Watkins (1988) conducted a contingency analysis of the American public education system and came to much the same conclusion.

Although many of us continue to propose significant technical and structural changes for public education (e.g., Pennypacker & Binder, 1992), there is little reason to believe that the system will allow us to develop and apply optimally effective instructional methods and programs on a large scale any time soon. On the other hand, small-scale private-sector educational enterprises developed and implemented by behavioral educators have been able to achieve significant impacts on students' learning and performance, while selling their programs to markets eager for improved educational practices. One of our best current examples is Dr. Kent Johnson's Morningside Program, which began in Seattle as a private school and demonstrated the capacity to dramatically accelerate the learning rates of adults and children with learning problems. Since 1991, the Morningside program has taken hold at Malcolm X Community College in inner-city Chicago, and community support has swelled because of the dramatic effects on students in summer and regular programs (Johnson & Layng, 1992).

How, then, should we approach the educational market? One strategy is to understand what is possible in each market segment, public and private, and to decide in groups or as individuals on specific goals for each. In public schools, for example, we might focus on specific curriculum areas, geographical sectors, or other target markets where we (1) are most likely to be allowed to teach as effectively as possible, (2) can produce results that have especially powerful economic or political impact and visibility, and (3) are likely to receive public credit that will lead to additional opportunities. Although it is not clear what these markets might be, given the history of nonfunding and punishment for effective educational programs (not merely "behavioral" ones) in this country (Matthews, 1988; Binder, 1991b), many of our colleagues may still choose to focus their energies in this direction for personal or political reasons.

As a compromise, we might develop programs or materials outside the public system that can then be sold into it. "Private practice" educators in some states have developed specific programs (e.g., foreign language) which they deliver on contract to public schools (Lochhead, 1991). They are held accountable contractually for results but have comparative freedom within their programs to develop and deliver the methods and materials that they see fit. Some corporations provide management and instructional services for entire public schools under contract (Holmes, 1990). These emerging markets may offer significant opportunities for enterprising behavioral educators, allowing them comparatively greater freedom to implement effective programs in public school environments.

Finally, self-contained private schools, after-school programs, and publishing enterprises can serve as laboratories for developing and marketing optimal instructional systems and packages, staff performance management systems, organizational structures, and efficient development and publishing operations. So far, our private-sector colleagues have focused mainly on packaging and promoting instructional methods and programs as *services* (e.g., Morningside Academy in Seattle; The Learning Centres in Ontario, Canada; Ben Bronz Academy in West Hartford, CT; Haughton Learning Center in Napa, CA), although a few examples of publishing efforts with *products* also exist (e.g., Engelmann-Becker Corporation's DISTAR programs). The results of some programs have been staggering and have attracted significant public attention (Binder & Watkins, 1989, 1990; Binder, 1991b, 1992; Johnson & Layng, 1992). In the future, behaviorists might combine instructional and performance-management technologies to produce superschools and then conduct systematic sales and marketing efforts to sell these programs to the general public. Major private enterprise programs such as Sylvan Learning Centers (one of several national franchise after-school programs), Kumon (a Japanese import after-school program that uses timed practice sheets), and the Edison Project (an effort of Whittle Communications Corp. to open 2,000 schools around the nation) serve as precedents for a free-market approach that behavior analysts might profitably choose to emulate while incorporating our superior instructional technology.

Deciding How to Proceed

The individual decision to "go private" or remain in the public sector combines personal, professional, and business considerations. At a personal level, starting

any business is a risk, especially if it takes us away from the security of a regular public school job. On the other hand, many startup businesses have begun as part-time enterprises until they become large enough for full-time involvement. Private enterprise requires a range of skills, high energy, and persistence, and many educators may feel that they lack one or more of these prerequisites. Nonetheless, there are few better environments for shaping skills and effort than the economic contingencies of the free market. And many educators are already working far beyond the call of duty in their public education jobs.

Professionally and as a field, we must examine the trade-offs between public- and private-sector efforts. Starting a learning center, school, or program materials company can challenge professional skills and knowledge in extraordinary ways, while accelerating professional development and helping shape how offerings are presented to potential customers. A successful undertaking will allow us to apply all the best techniques and approaches we know with few limitations, unlike most public-sector environments. (If truly successful, in the sense of establishing a stable customer base, it will also insulate us from the instability of public budgets and the threat of layoffs.) Nonetheless, some argue that for political, moral, and cultural reasons we should not abandon the public system altogether, since most students will continue to receive their education in that environment. Our decision becomes a choice between a challenging private-sector environment that may support accelerated development of the effectiveness and marketability of our methods and a challenging public education environment in which we may be more frequently frustrated and risk burn-out but still maintain the hope of slow change from within. We can probably predict that most of our colleagues will remain in the public environment, but that some of our most powerful changes and innovations will come from private-sector efforts.

Many of those who have already chosen to "go private," including this author, have come to the conclusion that our only real hope is to be able to demonstrate extraordinary effectiveness in the private sector, while learning to market and sell what we do. We hope that combining dramatic effectiveness of our private-sector programs and published products with efforts to communicate and sell directly to parents, business people, and the general public will eventually lead to a significant impact on the educational system, because of pressure from our satisfied customers demanding comparable effectiveness in public schools. Whether this strategy is ultimately successful, exposure to the contingencies of the marketplace will shape and refine the technology itself.

Conclusions and Recommendations

This chapter provides an overview of some key principles and procedures taken from private-sector sales and marketing. It emphasizes the importance of assuming a needs-driven orientation to product development, packaging, and communication with customers. Some specific suggestions that behavioral educators can begin to apply, in the public system and the private sector, are also included:

- Work to understand your potential customers, perceived problems and needs, using formal and informal surveys, interviews, and group discussions.
- Design concrete solutions for very specific target groups, being sure to package and describe these solutions in ways that appeal to your intended audience so they can clearly see the objective and emotional payoffs.
- Capture the language of the intended adopters or customers in interviews, group discussions, surveys, and popular literature reviews—especially the language they use to describe their problems and needs and the characteristics they seek in solutions. Use that language when discussing your products and services and how they will address needs and problems.
- Use questions for prompting prospective adopters or customers to discuss their problems, the implications of these problems, and the value of solving their problems or addressing their needs. Shape their verbal behavior toward telling you what they need in terms that you can use to describe what you offer as solutions.
- Pick your battles, focusing on those you can win with significant impact, and be clear about the trade-offs between job security, cultural impact, opportunity to advance the technology, and long-term personal and professional goals.

This chapter, and my previous publications, have encouraged behavioral educators to learn more about sales and marketing principles. No matter how effective our methods and programs might be, they will have little impact on our culture if they are not adopted. After decades of successful research and development, the current challenge for behavioral educators may be effective sales, marketing, and implementation on a wide scale. From a selectionist perspective, our effectiveness in this area may well determine whether our methods will be adopted by the culture at large in the future or whether behavioral educators will become instead extinct. Whether we can "sell" what we offer may make a difference with respect to the survival and success of our species as a whole.

References for this chapter include a number of books and training programs that provide further information and guidelines for selling and marketing— guidelines that might be applied to promoting effective instruction. I sincerely hope my colleagues will study some of these documents and programs, perhaps adding the precision of behavior analysis to their content, and consider their implications for effective dissemination and implementation of behavioral technology.

References

BINDER, C. (1990). Efforts to promote measurably superior instructional methods in schools. *Performance and Instruction, 29*(9), 32–34.

BINDER, C. (1991a). The 9th International Precision Teaching conference: Highlights and future directions. *Future Choices, 2*(3), 39–49.

BINDER, C. (1991b). Marketing measurably effective instructional methods. *Journal of Behavioral Education, 1*(3), 317–328.

BINDER, C. (1992). Morningside Academy: A private sector laboratory for effective instruction. *Future Choices, 3*(2), 61–66.

BINDER, C., & Watkins, C. L. (1989). Promoting effective instructional methods: Solutions to America's educational crisis. *Future Choices, 1*(3), 33–39.

BINDER, C., & Watkins, C. L. (1990). Precision Teaching and Direct Instruction: Measurably superior instructional technology in schools. *Performance Improvement Quarterly, 3*(4), 74–95.

BIRNBRAUER, J. S. (1979). Applied behavior analysis, service and the acquisition of knowledge. *Behavior Analyst, 2*(1), 15–21.

BREEN, G., & Blankenship, A. B. (1982). *Do-it-yourself marketing research.* 2nd ed. New York: McGraw-Hill.

BURNS, C. (1984). Does a behavioral presentation reduce acceptance of classroom management techniques? Ph.D. diss., University of Hawaii, Honolulu.

ENGELMANN, S., Haddox, P., & Bruner, E. (1983). *Teach your child to read in 100 easy lessons.* New York: Simon & Schuster.

FOXX, R., & Azrin, N. (1974). *Toilet training in less than a day.* Champaign, IL: Research Press.

HOLMES, S. A. (1990). In Florida, a private company will operate a public school. *New York Times,* December 6, pp. A2, A15.

HOOKED on phonics. (1987). Orange, CA: Gateway Educational Products, LTD.

JOHNSON, K. R., & Layng, T. V. J. (1992). Breaking the structuralist barrier: Literacy and numeracy with fluency. *American Psychologist, 47*(11), 1475–1490.

LOCHHEAD, C. (1991). A lesson from private practitioners. *Insight,* December 24, pp. 34–36.

MALOTT, R. W. (1992). Notes from a radical behaviorist: Commitment vs. adherence and cognitivism vs. behaviorism. *ABA Newsletter, 15*(3), 19–20.

MATH Tutor. (1985). New York: Scholastic, Inc.

MATTHEWS, J. (1988). *Escalante: The best teacher in America.* New York: Holt.

MILLER, R. B., & Heiman, S. E. (1987). *Conceptual selling.* Walnut Creek, CA: Miller-Heiman.

OLNEY, C. W. (1989). *Where there's a will there's an . . . A.* Paoli, PA: Chesterbrook Educational Publishers.

PAR Sales Training. (1983). Atlanta: Par Training Corporation.

PENNYPACKER, H. S., & Binder, C. (1992). Triage for American education. *Administrative Radiology,* Jan., 19-25.

PRYOR, K. (1985). *Don't Shoot the Dog!* New York: Bantam Books.

RACKHAM, N. (1988) *SPIN Selling.* New York: McGraw-Hill.

RACKHAM, N. (1989). *Major Account Sales Strategy.* New York: McGraw-Hill.

SAVING our schools. (1992, Sept. 14). *Business Week,* 70–78.

STONE, J. E. (1991). Developmentalism: A standing impediment to the design of the "New American School." *Network News and Views, 10*(12), 1–3.

WATKINS, C. L. (1988). Project Follow Through: A story of the identification and neglect of effective instruction. *Youth Policy, 10*(7), 7–11.

ZEMKE, R., & Kramlinger, T. (1982). *Figuring things out: A trainer's guide to needs and task analysis.* Reading, MA: Addison-Wesley.

CHAPTER 4

The Insignificant Impact of Behavior Analysis on Education: Notes from a Dean of Education

Samuel M. Deitz

It is disconcerting, though not uncommon, to invent a better mousetrap and find that no one is very interested. This seems to be the case with the application of behavior-analytic principles to educational practice. For over 35 years, behavior analysts have presented effective solutions to some of the most pressing problems of American education. Unfortunately for behavior analysts and educational consumers, almost no one is listening.

However, this may be a new time in American education. There is a strong renewed awareness by politicians, business leaders, and professional educators that the education offered through our nation's schools is inadequate. National and state policies are being reformulated; politicians are presenting solutions ranging from creating goals for American schools (America 2000) through drafting laws about teacher preparation and certification to lotteries and other plans for increased educational funding. Business leaders recommend adopting successful business practices in schools and forming partnerships and school "adoptions." Professional educators are discussing the importance of preschool experience for all children, school restructuring, and major changes in teacher preparation.

A relatively small group calls for fundamental changes in the classroom practices of teachers and other school personnel; they are advocating better teaching. This group is primarily, but not exclusively, made up of behavior analysts who with increasing frustration discuss their better mousetraps and wonder why the public is not beating a path to their door. A recent issue of the *Journal of Applied Behavior Analysis* (1992) was devoted to "the educational crisis." Many prominent behavior analysts discussed a wide variety of problems and solutions to the ineffectiveness of American schools. Topics included what techniques behavior analysis has available for education, why these advances have not been accepted, and what behavior analysts need to do to ensure that these advances become a part of schooling in America.

These are important issues if behavior analysis is to help solve the problems of education. I am going to discuss these issues from a different context than most behavior analysts. For the past three years, I have been the dean of a large college of education. I have listened to what my colleagues think about ineffective education (every professional educator, no matter how traditional, believes that the practices they teach their students are superior to what actually occurs in most schools). I have attended professional meetings of mainstream educators and read articles by both traditional educators and nonbehavioral, nontraditional educational authors. These experiences have given me a different view on the relations between mainstream education and behavior analysis.

This altered viewpoint does not change one important issue concerning behavior analysis and education. More data are not needed to show that behavior analysis has had an insignificant impact on education (see Sulzer-Azaroff, 1986). We can go into almost any school in this country and find little or no evidence of behavior analysis. We can examine the curriculum of almost every teacher education preparation program and find little or no evidence of behavior analysis (with the exception of special education). We can read almost any mainstream educational journal and find little or no evidence of behavior analysis. Even the report of the APA Task Force on Psychology in Education essentially ignores the contribution of behavior analysis ("For the Record," 1992). From my experiences as a dean of education, I believe that there are clear and compelling issues that explain, if not justify, this state of affairs. Presenting and analyzing these issues and some potential solutions is the purpose of this chapter.

Data and Dogma

One tenet of the behavioral position is the reliance on data-based decision making. Behavior analysts posit that schools should base their decisions about what occurs on solid data. There are two problems with this position. First, behavior analysts must recognize that data-based decisions are almost exclusively the activity of scientists (and even scientists do not always agree on what constitutes good data). It is not common in our country to rely on data when making decisions in politics (school board members are usually elected officials) or even in most businesses. In fact, politicians often ignore data when creating legislative solutions and businesses rely more on advertising than on data on quality in selling their products. Research is rarely used for most decisions in most

contexts. Even in the face of this overwhelming evidence, behavior analysts continue to expect research data to convince school officials to turn to behavior analysis for reasonable alternatives to education problems. I will not argue that this *should not* be the case, only that it is *not now* the case.

Second, behavior analysts often go beyond their own data in making claims about behavioral solutions for schools (I made this point in 1978 and unfortunately it still appears to be accurate; see Deitz, 1978). Behavior analysts have an enviable though spotty record for supporting claims that behavioral solutions can improve education in the United States. When it comes to improving education, behavior analysts, like many mainstream educators, ignore a careful analysis of available data and claim to have answers to the problems of public education when that simply is not yet the case. Examining the behavior-analytic literature shows that there are considerable data for effectiveness in some limited areas, but almost no data exist in many other areas.

To claim that behavioral procedures are effective for *schooling*, analysts must be able to show that whole schools and school systems have been changed by behavioral methods. They must show that their methods can be effective with the 46 million children in U.S. schools (*American Education at a Glance*, 1992). There must be evidence with children whose abilities range from disabled to gifted and whose ages range from preschool through high school. Finally, there must be evidence of change affecting the whole school, not just classrooms or individual students within classrooms.

This is not to say that there is little or no evidence of the effectiveness of behavioral procedures. Behavioral journals have published numerous demonstrations of excellent behavioral solutions. Significant progress has been made in some areas, most notably in special education and the education of young children in basic skills. Recently, Engelmann and his colleagues expanded direct instruction curricular materials to other curricular areas with older elementary children. Personalized Systems of Instruction, or PSI (Keller, 1968), have been shown to be effective in limited cases with older children in public schools and extensively with college-age students in a broad array of subject matters. While published data are difficult to find, reports have been positive on the effectiveness of Precision Teaching (Lindsley, 1992a). Greer (1992) makes a case for a still broader base of effectiveness than has existed in the past, although mostly in private elementary schools. Greenwood, Terry, Arreaga-Mayer, and Finney (1992) presented important classroom-based data on peer tutoring.

But evidence is still lacking in many other areas. There are no data that support behavioral effectiveness in a variety of types of schools from inner city to suburban to rural and in the wide array of subjects taught to large groups of children with wide ranges of ability—foreign language, calculus, physics, chemistry, history, art, English as a second language, music, geography, and so forth.

Much of the data demonstrating the effectiveness of behavioral procedures have been collected with children with disabilities. Special education in this country, at least in the areas of severe and profound retardation, is dominated by behavior analysis. It is ironic, however, that this has worked to the disadvantage of behavior analysts. Demonstrating effectiveness with children who are difficult to teach should have encouraged mainstream educators to look at behavioral procedures as potentially effective for all students (if it works for the most difficult problems, it should work even better for the less difficult problems). If anything, the opposite occurred. As Axelrod (1992) explained, these data were seen as products of conditions that were dramatically different than those in regular classrooms—fewer students with more resources. These procedures were not seen as feasible for regular classrooms. "Normal" and especially "gifted" children would need a very different type of educational practice. To overcome this bias will require more data on behavioral procedures in regular classrooms with regular children doing regular classwork (see Axelrod, 1992).

Fantuzzo and Atkins (1992) understood that more research in the regular classroom was necessary before certain claims could be made. They suggested that behavior analysts need to "develop more adaptive and effective strategies that teachers and school personnel *can* and *will* actually use" (p. 37). They ex-

plained that behavior analysts have not looked at "factors involved in entering complex school systems" (p. 38). Fantuzzo and Atkins advocated a long-term commitment to classrooms and showed that there is no longer a need for "experimenter-centered demonstrations" (p. 41). Behavior analysts need to enter school systems and work with the broad range of students and subject matters and document that they can be effective in those settings. They need to execute research that goes beyond demonstrations with some students in some subject matters; they need to document solutions for all the students in all the subject matter areas in American schools.

Fantuzzo and Atkins's (1992) advice is important if behavior analysts are to increase their influence in education. Many educational issues deal with complex school systems, and are not even considered by behavior analysts. For example, U. S. school systems are notorious for hiring teachers to teach out of their field of preparation. While 83% of the elementary teachers in our country are trained in elementary education, only 69% of the social studies or special education teachers, 62% of all science teachers, and 54% of math teachers are certified in their areas of teaching.

Also, there is growing evidence that those trained in the art of education are better teachers than those who only receive subject matter preparation. Behavior analysts should agree that training in the practice of teaching will improve teaching. Behavior analysts must demonstrate that the teachers they would produce can be more effective than the teachers from excellent colleges of education who are then employed to teach in their area of specialization. This should not be a difficult task if behavioral methods are clearly superior. Since so few behavior analysts work in colleges of education, it may be difficult to arrange the proper conditions to conduct such a study (for an important exception in the field of special education, see Marchand-Martella & Lignugaris/Kraft, 1992).

My argument is not that convincing data are totally lacking or that they would be impossible to obtain. Many behavioral innovations can be of great assistance in improving American education; some could even provide revolutionary relief. But to claim that behavioral procedures have been proven effective and that with them, behavior analysts are now ready to revolutionize education is to practice deception. While advocating that all educational proposals should be evaluated, Carnine (1992) stated that mainstream educators often make decisions based on "dogma and current fads" (p. 13) rather than on a scientific basis. When behavior analysts go beyond data in making claims about changing American education, they can be accused of the same practice.

Mice and Moose

Inventing a better mousetrap is of little use if one is hunting moose. Behavior analysts have presented a mousetrap consisting of essential information for improving teaching practices. However, in the broad context of U.S. education, many concerns extend beyond effective teaching. Behavior analysts rarely discuss these concerns, but they are essential to mainstream educators and the politicians who control schooling. There are also misunderstandings among behavior analysts about the goals and practices of mainstream education. These issues help explain the lack of influence that behavior analysis has on education; while some educators admire what behavior analysis can accomplish in instruction, they claim that it presents only a small part of the solution for problems in American education.

There are critical problems in schools today that extend beyond those soluble by more effective instructional practices. Homeless children move from school to school throughout the year as their parents move from shelter to shelter. Too many children have no decent meals from the free lunch in school on Friday until free breakfast in school on Monday. Almost 40% of U.S. children live below the poverty level. Prostitution is a growing problem in elementary schools. Our children are murdering each other and are having children at alarmingly increasing rates. Our society and our schools are becoming resegregated. These issues are a moral outrage, and they point out that improving schools in the 1990s requires more than improved instruction. It requires a revolutionary examination of social issues that stretch far beyond the classroom but affect schooling. With very few exceptions, neither mainstream educators nor behavior analysts are addressing these issues with much success.

However, mainstream educational thought at least discusses some of these issues as well as other important topics, most of which are of little apparent interest to behavior analysts. For example, the theme of an issue of the *Journal of Teacher Education* (1992) was "cultural diversity." Articles appeared on programs for teaching culturally diverse children, teacher stereotyping, and restructuring schools for multicultural education. Cultural diversity is critical in a country in which over half of our schoolchildren by the year 2010 will be nonwhite and almost one-quarter will not speak English as their native language. The themes for 1993 in the *Journal of Teacher Education* include teacher assessment, the impact of accreditation on teacher education, school and college restructuring, and teacher education in relation to the national goals of education. All these topics are important to mainstream education, but no topic has received more recent attention than school restructuring; that is, the attempt to reconstruct the organization and structure of schools and the roles of teachers within those schools. Mainstream educators are also interested in tracking, teacher testing, self-esteem, and gender issues. Behavior analysts, however, do not appear to be examining any of these areas.

An irony for some of us who spent considerable time working with classroom discipline in the 1970s (Deitz & Hummel, 1978) is that another concern of mainstream educators is safety, especially but not exclusively in our nation's urban areas. School administrators are interested in ensuring that major felonies are not committed within schools, but they also need help for the more common problems associated with misbehavior in classrooms. Until 1972, when Winett and Winkler warned behavior analysts not to spend so much time examining issues that taught children only to "be still, be quiet and be docile," behavior analysts were national leaders in this area. Rather than extending the research to discipline procedures that create effective learning conditions in normal classroom settings, especially in middle and high schools, behavior analysis almost disappeared as a behavioral contribution to mainstream education, except in special education. Now it is needed more than ever and behavior analysts are not responding with effective solutions.

There are other issues that relate to effective schooling. The length of the school year is important when one considers that U.S. students rank low on tests in relation to students in many other countries. Japan requires 243 days in school, Korea requires 220 days, Canada 196, but the United States only requires 180 days. Behavior analysts need to examine whether "simply" extending the schoolyear is enough. For example, Japan initiated a "reversal" for the 1992 schoolyear by eliminating classes on one Saturday a month. Also, although the educational systems in other countries are considered more effective than ours, none have been shown to be paragons of behavioral education. Behavior analysts should consider cross-cultural research, which may discover that these countries employ solutions that are more compatible with behavior analysis than those in the United States.

Mainstream educators are interested in issues related to the goals of education. Recently, the goals specified through the America 2000 initiative have received considerable attention. These goals state that *all* children from *all* backgrounds should begin school ready to learn and then progress through world-class standards in subject matter areas to lifelong learning and accomplishment. Behavior analysts have not presented data showing how their procedures effectively address these goals. In fact, in some ways the advice of some behavior analysts runs counter to these goals. Lindsley (1992b), for example, proposed an athletic analogy for education. The problem was not in claiming that "it is amazing that educators and the public accept the need for disciplined regular daily practice in the performing arts and in athletics, yet reject it in academics" (p. 23). The lack of such practice in education today may be one important cause of academic problems (a "commonsense" issue that has surprisingly little documentation). However, Lindsley continued his analogy advocating competition, stating that "competition is welcomed in athletics and is seen to strengthen the participants" (p. 23). But athletics competition is not designed to ensure that all children become excellent athletes, rather it weeds out the weak athletes so that only the best remain to play on competitive teams. "Weeding out" weak students is hardly compatible with a goal of *all* students meeting world-class standards.

Another issue relates to differences in emphasis between student-centered and teacher-centered

education. Behavior analysts discuss education as teacher centered; that is, the teacher directs what goes on and ensures that students learn. Mainstream educators discuss student-centered education; that is, the teacher is less directive and works with student interest toward what may be different outcomes. A student-centered approach need not be counterproductive, nor is it necessarily parallel to the unproductive, practices of a patient-centered medicine as Carnine (1992) implied. It does not mean that the student chooses all he or she does, or what will be learned, or how a teacher should teach; student-centered does not mean student-directed. Rather, in the traditions of Dewey through Foxfire, (1) work should flow from student concern; (2) the teacher is a collaborator or team leader; (3) students are active; (4) there is much use of peer teaching, small-group work, and teamwork; (5) connections are stressed between the classroom, work, and communities; (6) the use of imagination and reflection are stressed; and (7) there is honest, ongoing evaluation ("The Principles of Foxfire," 1992). Most of these principles are compatible with behavioral education. Behavioral systems always require active student participation and evaluation; PSI stresses peer tutoring (Keller, 1968). As these student-centered concepts become compatible with cultural expectations for schooling and more acceptable to the community at large, discussing behavioral procedures within their structure could help behavioral concepts become more acceptable as well.

One advantage of a student-centered approach is an emphasis on groups and teams. Behavior analysts have ignored student-centered group processes, cooperative learning, and teams, while stressing individual accomplishment. Although the skills and abilities of all students should reach high levels, one of the most important skills needed today in businesses and other places of employment is the ability to work in teams and to lead teams. Working alone in an office and traditional views of the boss are remnants of the past; behavior analysts could gain more influence in education if they were to construct systems that incorporated these concepts and furthered these skills.

Discussing student-centered education may also help behavioral educators solve the dilemma of imposed and natural contingencies. As Sulzer-Azaroff (1992) stated:

> Natural or functional reinforcers, the stimulus events produced by the instrumental (learning) responses, are integral to the behavior, follow it everywhere, and support its continued maintenance. They require no time from educators, nor can society, educators, parents, or students take issue with their use on philosophical or ethical grounds. Indeed, natural reinforcement is best and the way to go, provided (a) that the learning objective *does* produce a natural reinforcer and (b) that the natural reinforcer *is more powerful* than any competing punishers inherent in the task or reinforcers for competing responses. [p. 81]

She goes on to examine those issues demonstrating that natural reinforcers are not always obtainable. It is possible, however, that using the principles of a student-centered approach that stresses student interest and ties school activity to outside concerns may make the identification and use of natural reinforcement more likely.

A student-centered approach could also require behavior analysts to move beyond stressing "the right answer" as the product of education. While no mainstream educator would argue that getting the right answer is unimportant, they would claim that it is insufficient. Children need to know why an answer is correct and they need to know and be able to accomplish the process used to arrive at that answer. Behavior analysts do appear to stress "just" learning facts, while others stress learning skills and thinking. Behavior analysts need to devise research that documents that children who learn facts through behavioral procedures also learn why those facts are true, how to arrive at those facts, and how the facts fit into broader fields. Direct Instruction is the only behavioral approach to teaching that clearly identifies the need to study the structure of subject matter (concepts) in order to define effective instruction for that subject matter (Engelmann & Carnine, 1982). Their approach, while not well accepted in many schools, ensures that students do more than just get the right answer.

One reason behavior analysts do not discuss these topics is that the language of behavior analysis differs markedly from the language of most American cultures. Debate has arisen about how functional the language of behavior analysis is for communication with those who are not behavior analysts, even with scientists who are not behavioral scientists. Hineline (1980) argued that the language of behavior analysis is its calculus and needs its precision. Others (Deitz, 1986; Deitz & Arrington, 1983, 1984) have argued that when behavioral language uses borrowed technical terms (extinction) or ordinary terms in extraordinary ways (behavior), the major result is confusion, at least in communication with members of mainstream culture and often even among members of the behavioral community. Axelrod (1992) understood that behavior analysts use language that differs markedly from the language of the typical culture and that these differences strengthen the image (deserved or not) that behavioral approaches are "coercive and controlling" (p. 31). To affect mainstream education, behavior analysts need to address this issue directly. They need to decide whether the function served by scientific purity in the language of behavior analysis is more important than the function served by communication. This is not a simple decision. Different languages may need to be devised for different purposes and translation may need to become common behavioral practice. Solving those issues can ensure that language no longer interferes with the acceptance of behavior analysts by mainstream educators.

By stressing effective instruction, behavior analysts have invented a better mousetrap. However, emphasizing improved teaching came without analyzing broader issues (behavior analysts have not even thoroughly examined what is necessary to prepare teachers to present these better methods). This is not to say that the interests of mainstream educators are more important than those of behavior analysts. But these differences can ensure that mainstream educators do not attend to the issues of behavior analysts. If behavior analysts began showing how their procedures help schools solve the problems clarified by mainstream educators, their acceptance could increase and the mousetrap could become effective for catching moose.

Suggestions and Solutions

Mainstream education needs effective solutions to the problems of education in the United States. If the solutions offered by behavior analysts are to be considered, there is much they need to do. Above all, they need to move into more schools to collect more data on more students of all ages and with many ability levels who are working on the whole range of subject matters. Behavior analysts need to commit to schools and school systems for long-term restructuring, not just for demonstrations of effectiveness. They can continue to operate private schools that are open to all types of children and document their effectiveness, but they must also work extensively in public schools. In all schools, they must move beyond an emphasis on special students or young children.

More data are essential. To affect mainstream education, however, other issues need equal attention. Behavior analysts need to investigate issues that are important to mainstream educators but are not part of behavioral education. They need to examine cultural diversity, tracking, assessment, self-esteem, and cross-cultural analyses; they need to return to the area of classroom discipline and consider the issues presented by a student-centered approach to education.

It is essential that behavior analysts become directly involved in teacher preparation. This will require moving from psychology to education and obtaining proper credentials. Behavior analysts in special education need to extend their expertise into regular classrooms. Schools and colleges of education rarely hire psychologists, even educational psychologists, with little or no formal training in schooling. Also, most positions in teacher education are in subject matter areas and behavior analysts must move into these areas.

This involvement will also prepare behavior analysts to work for school systems. Today, a considerable amount of teacher preparation takes place through staff development workshops and classes arranged by the local school systems. Outside experts are often hired to conduct these classes, but larger systems hire permanent staffs to arrange and teach their staff development offerings. In any case, school systems most often hire professional educators, not psychologists.

If behavior analysts are to gain influence in the preparation of teachers and administrators either through colleges and universities or through staff development, they must go beyond behavioral training and begin to study in the few colleges of education that offer proper credentials and behavioral training. They must earn degrees in areas within education (see Axelrod, 1992), if they are to affect mainstream education.

Behavior analysts also need to begin presenting their concepts and data to nonbehavioral audiences. While the special issue of the *Journal of Applied Behavior Analysis* (*JABA*) was a valuable contribution, like many presentations at behavioral conventions and publications in behavioral journals, its impact will be limited if the audience is made up of those who are already convinced (preaching to the converted reinforces the preacher but does not reach the audience in need of conversion). Not many traditional educators read *JABA*. Many behavior analysts will argue that mainstream journals will not publish behavioral concepts or data. I think that is an empirical question and one that needs repeated testing.

It is also a solution that may require some creativity and linguistic skill. Behavioral articles may be rejected for two reasons. First, the concepts presented may be of little interest to mainstream educators. As stated earlier, behavior analysts devote little attention to many issues that concern mainstream educators. But, where there is relevance, behavioral data need to be couched in the interests of the audience. Showing how these data relate to important concepts in mainstream education can be an effective way of making them more acceptable. Of course, behavior analysts will have to closely examine articles presented in mainstream educational journals to learn more about these issues. Second, the presentation of the data may be unacceptable. Some mainstream educational journals are hesitant to accept articles based only on single-subject analyses. This is a more difficult problem but as behavior analysts move into broader areas with larger "samples" that issue may be solvable by combining single-subject and traditional statistical analyses. Publishing in mainstream educational journals will also require the linguistic skill to write behaviorally sound articles that do not totally confuse the audience.

Reading mainstream journals without prejudice can expose other interesting issues. Some interests are compatible with behavioral thought. For example, many "cognitive solutions" are similar to those presented by behavior analysts, although they are described in very different terms. When Anderson (1989) discussed "scaffolding" and "fading" (pp. 105–107) from a "cognitive-mediational perspective" (p. 103), she was discussing stimulus control. While the interpretation of why her procedures are effective differs dramatically according to her conceptual orientation, her solutions rest on what is done with the student before and after a student acts. Requiring readers to accept a particular theory is quite restrictive. More often, behavior analysts disagree more with the explanation of the data than with the data themselves. This point is true for mainstream researchers as well. Behavior analysts must not let their strong theoretical beliefs interfere with being open to all suggestions, since they expect others to be open to behavioral interpretations. As Sidman (1960) stated, "Good data are always separable, with respect to their scientific importance, from the purposes for which they were obtained" (p. 3).

Reading and studying other points of view will show that the concept of contingency is not uniformly ignored outside the world of behavior analysis. For example, in a recent issue of a nonbehavioral journal, Moellenberg (1992) discussed the importance of contingency in the decline of communism:

> When the contingency between behavior and consequence is eroded, performance declines. Communism failed to differentiate rewards between excellent and shoddy performance, which would have been sufficient in itself to cause the dramatic failures that characterized the collective farms and factories of the Soviet system. [p. 348]

More relevant to behavior analysis is the suggestion that the most current thinking in cognitive psychology may be moving back to an appreciation of contingency as a necessary component to understanding complete episodes of action (Donahoe & Palmer, 1989).

Finally, behavior analysts need to use what they know about the contingencies that affect behavior to overcome their insignificant impact on education.

Axelrod (1992) reminded behavior analysts of Sulzer-Azaroff's contribution (1986) when he stated, "If the educational community does not embrace behavioral strategies, the appropriate antecedent and consequent conditions are not in place" (p. 33). It is time for behavior analysts to turn toward public relations, partnerships, and politics to increase their effect on the mainstream educational community. Public relations must go beyond marketing (Binder, 1991). It must be a concerted effort on many fronts to demonstrate that behavioral procedures are not only effective but that they can be generally acceptable to the community and to educators. First, this will require a campaign to emphasize that data-based decisions are essential. Second, behavior analysts must convince educators that behavioral procedures "fit" with the generally accepted views of what teachers should do. In other words, the general opinion that behavioral procedures are coercive, punitive, or restrictive must be overcome; normal behavioral language will probably need to be altered. One important direction is to emphasize teacher empowerment (Fantuzzo & Atkins, 1992) within restructured schools.

The behavioral discussions should emphasize what is positive and avoid the critical comments that are too common in behavioral writing. Comments in some of the articles in the special issue of the *Journal of Applied Behavior Analysis* (1992) are surprisingly insulting to mainstream educators (Why would I listen to you when you keep telling me how wrong/stupid I am?). Some of the solutions also create resistance. Carnine (1992), for example, called for a "national advisory board with representatives from mature professions, such as medicine, engineering, and law" (p. 17) to recreate certification standards. How should mainstream educators react to the implication that they are part of an "immature" profession or that it takes individuals with no experience or education in a field to determine the standards for that field? The tone of some comments and solutions can surely create enemies.

Behavior analysts need to find businesses that emphasize data-based decisions and try to form partnerships with them. These partnerships can take two forms. First, behavior analysts could form partnerships with existing education-related businesses to improve the effectiveness of their products. Better software, more effective schools, and improved educational materials could be the result. Second, schools and school systems are moving toward relationships with businesses in their communities. Entering the system with a readily accepted business partner will help behavior analysts gain acceptance.

Finally, behavior analysts need to enter the political realms of mainstream education. This will require more than obtaining credentials and positions in colleges of education. Behavior analysts will need to join and participate in professional educational organizations, teachers' organizations and unions, and parent organizations, both nationally and locally. And to be effective, they will need to learn the language of education and translate the language of behavior analysis so that better communication is possible. It will require working in school system bureaucracies and the establishment in Washington. It is a long-term process but one through which impressive influence can be gained.

Behavior analysts possess a theory, data, and a technology with great promise for education. With some changes, they can significantly increase their effectiveness. These changes will include new approaches, some reconceptualizations of old approaches, and new training strategies leading to new professional possibilities. In other words, behavior analysts will have to admit that an excellent mousetrap is insufficient. That is a considerable task for a group that has already presented much that is effective and excellent. But these changes are necessary if behavior analysis is to gain the significant influence in mainstream education it so richly deserves.

References

AMERICAN education at a glance. (1992). Washington, DC: National Center for Educational Statistics, Office of Educational Research and Improvement, U.S. Department of Education.

ANDERSON, L. M. (1989). Classroom instruction. In M. C. Reynolds (Ed.), *Knowledge base for the beginning teacher* (pp. 101–115). New York: Pergamon Press.

AXELROD, S. (1992). Disseminating an effective educational technology. *Journal of Applied Behavior Analysis, 25*, 31–35.

BINDER, C. (1991). Marketing measurably effective instructional methods. *Journal of Behavioral Education, 1*(3), 317–328.

CARNINE, D. (1992). Expanding the notion of teachers' rights: Access to tools that work. *Journal of Applied Behavior Analysis, 25, 13–19.*

DEITZ, S. M. (1978). Current status of applied behavior analysis: Science versus technology. *American Psychologist, 33*, 805–814.

DEITZ, S. M. (1986). Understanding cognitive language: The mental idioms in children's talk. *Behavior Analyst, 9,* 161–166.

DEITZ, S. M., & Arrington, R. L. (1983). Factors confusing language use in the analysis of behavior. *Behaviorism, 11*, 117–132.

DEITZ, S. M., & Arrington, R. L.. (1984). Wittgenstein's language games and the call to cognition. *Behaviorism, 12,* 1–14.

DEITZ, S. M., & Hummel, J. H. (1978). *Discipline in the schools: A guide to reducing misbehavior.* Englewood Cliffs, NJ: Educational Technology Publications.

DONAHOE, J. W., & Palmer, D. C. (1989). The interpretation of complex human behavior: Some reactions to *Parallel distributed processing,* edited by J. L. McClelland, D. E. Rumelhart, and the PDP Research Group. *Journal of the Experimental Analysis of Behavior, 51*, 399–416.

ENGELMANN, S., & Carnine, D. (1982). *Theory of instruction: Principles and applications.* New York: Irvington Publishers.

FANTUZZO, J., & Atkins, M. (1992). Applied behavior analysis for educators: Teacher centered and classroom based. *Journal of Applied Behavior Analysis, 25,* 37–42.

FOR the record. (1992). *Division 25 Recorder,* 27.

GREENWOOD, C. R., Terry, B., Arreaga-Mayer, C., & Finney, R. (1992). The classwide peer tutoring program: Implementation factors moderating students' achievement. *Journal of Applied Behavior Analysis, 25*, 101–116.

GREER, R. D. (1992). L'enfant terrible meets the educational crisis. *Journal of Applied Behavior Analysis, 25,* 65–69.

HELLER, F. S. (1968). "Good-bye, teacher . . ." *Journal of Applied Behavior Analysis, 1*(1), 79–89.

HINELINE, P. N. (1980). The language of behavior analysis: Its community, its functions, and its limitations. *Behaviorism, 8,* 67–86.

JOURNAL of Applied Behavior Analysis. (1992). 25.

JOURNAL of Teacher Education. (1992, March–April). *43*(2).

LINDSLEY, O. R. (1992a). Precision Teaching: Discoveries and effects. *Journal of Applied Behavior Analysis, 25,* 51–57.

LINDSLEY, O. R. (1992b). Why aren't effective teaching tools widely adopted? *Journal of Applied Behavior Analysis, 25,* 21–26.

MARCHAND-MARTELLA, N. E., & Lignugaris/Kraft, B. (1992). Preservice teacher performance in a direct instruction practicum using student teachers and university personnel as supervisors. *ADI News, 11,* 2–8.

MOELLENBERG, W. P. (1992). Restoring the foundations of freedom. *Educational Forum, 56*(7), 347–360.

SIDMAN, M. (1960). *Tactics of scientific research.* New York: Basic Books.

SULZER-AZAROFF, B. (1986). Behavior analysis and education: Growing achievements and crying needs. *Division 25 Recorder, 21,* 55–65.

SULZER-AZAROFF, B. (1992). Is back to nature always best? *Journal of Applied Behavior Analysis, 25,* 81–82.

THE principles of Foxfire. (1992). *Atlanta Constitution,* February 3, p. A6.

WINETT, R. A., & Winkler, R. C. (1972). Current behavior modification in the classroom: Be still, be quiet, be docile. *Journal of Applied Behavior Analysis, 5,* 499–504.

CHAPTER 5

"Mainstreaming" Applied Behavior Analysis Principles and Procedures into a Preservice Training Program for General Education Teachers

Larry Maheady
Gregory F. Harper
Barbara Mallette
Melinda Karnes

How familiar are preservice general education trainees with the basic principles and procedures of applied behavior analysis? Can most general educators entering the public schools distinguish between punishment and negative reinforcement contingencies, reward versus bribery conditions, or describe the differential effects that result from varied reinforcement schedules? More important, can general education trainees implement sound behavior analysis programs or use direct instructional teaching practices within their own classrooms when they complete their preservice training programs? Even the most optimistic behavior analysts among us would be inclined to respond negatively to such questions, and with good reason. A casual review of program requirements in "traditional" preservice training programs for elementary and secondary teachers, and an analysis of current research on teacher preparation practices in general, reveals a very limited role for applied behavior analysis (e.g., Cuban, 1988; Hall, 1991; Kohler & Strain, 1992). This is, indeed, unfortunate because applied behavior analysis has much to offer future classroom teachers (e.g., Axelrod, 1991; Hall, 1991; Kohler & Strain, 1992).

The purpose of this chapter is to describe a different preservice training program for general education trainees.

The Reflective and Responsive Educator (RARE) program, a newly developed model at the State University of New York College at Fredonia, integrates basic behavior analysis principles and procedures into the educational coursework and practicum experiences of future teachers. In this chapter we describe the primary components of the RARE program and discuss the process by which the model was developed within the context of a traditional teacher-training program. We then describe some common instructional methods and teaching arrangements that have been used to develop more behaviorally responsive classroom teachers. Finally, we present some initial data regarding the efficacy, perceived efficiency, and social acceptability of our primary preparation methods. Since the RARE program is still being implemented and evaluated, a completely defined model has not yet been developed.

Educational Restructuring and Reform: An Opportunity to Respond for Behavior Analysts

In a recent article, Kohler and Strain (1992) suggested that applied behavior analysis has essentially been ignored by those involved in the general restructuring of America's public schools. For whatever reasons, educational reformers have not embraced the many potential contributions that behavior analysts can make to improve the quantity and quality of the instruction provided in our schools (Axelrod, 1991; Binder, 1991; Engelmann, 1991; Hall, 1991). Rather than being offended by this apparent oversight, however, Kohler and Strain (1992) argued that it should serve as a stimulus to do more about getting behavior analysis principles and practices assimilated into traditional educational practice. At Fredonia, we have made a modest effort to do so.

Spurred on by New York State Department of Education mandates to restructure existing preservice training programs for elementary and secondary education trainees, we attempted "to seize the day." We used the state mandate as an opportunity to infuse behavior analysis principles and procedures throughout the four-year program for future classroom teachers. More specifically, we (1) integrated behavioral content into basic curriculum requirements for all preservice trainees; (2) altered existing service delivery arrangements to include more direct teaching opportunities with increased levels of systematic feedback; and (3) adopted an outcome-based decision-making model for evaluating and adapting current teaching practices. Making such substantial structural changes in a traditional teacher preparation program was not an easy task, but in the process we have learned much about program change and "selling" our methods to a nonbehavioral constituency.

Breaking Tradition

The preparation of elementary and secondary education trainees has been a primary mission of the State University College at Fredonia (SUC-Fredonia) since its earliest beginnings as a normal school. Throughout the years, SUC-Fredonia has prepared substantial numbers of teachers in western New York and has developed and maintained good working relationships with surrounding school districts. Significant changes in the demographic makeup of the general student population and increased calls for more integrated instructional programming in the public schools, however, have resulted in many more

hard-to-teach children being placed in general education classrooms (Gartner & Lipsky, 1987; Hodgkinson, 1985; Lilly, 1986; Maheady & Algozzine, 1991; Will, 1986). Traditionally, such youngsters—the poor, the culturally and linguistically diverse, the exceptional—have not fared well in the public schools. They have been much more likely to experience academic and behavioral failure. They have been retained in grade level more often than their peers, dropped out from school at excessively high rates, and been placed into special and remedial education programs at rates disproportional to their numerical representation in school (Ysseldyke, Algozzine, & Thurlow, 1992). These same students, however, *have* been well served by instructors who apply behavior analysis and Direct Instruction teaching procedures (Carnine & Kinder, 1985; Gersten & Dimino, 1991; Maheady, Harper, & Mallette, 1991). The initial intent of our restructuring efforts, therefore, was to ensure that our future teachers could implement validated instructional practices with the types of students who would be entering their classrooms in years to come.

Using our collective knowledge base on applied behavior analysis, we attempted to restructure SUC-Fredonia's traditional teacher preparation program. To do so, we got directly involved in the change process; that is, we volunteered for important curriculum committees. Maheady was named the chairperson of the two most influential committees. Throughout the two years of meetings, we attended and responded differentially to others' input. We acknowledged and reinforced program proposals that were consistent with our general program philosophy and intended structural changes, while withholding attention from disparate proposals. Interestingly, we found that through the use of a common, nonbehavioral language we were able to reach agreement on a set of basic beliefs, goals, and program outcomes. For example, the committees readily agreed that students in our undergraduate teacher preparation program must acquire "demonstrably effective teaching strategies." We, however, insisted that only those strategies supported by research evidence be included, thus effectively eliminating popular but unsupported practices like "life space interviewing." The committees also agreed on the desirability of "responsive teaching," but we convinced them that this could only be accomplished through curriculum-based assessment and a decision-making model based on empirical student data. In general, by making commonly accepted goals operational, we were able to retain scientific rigor without sacrificing consensus.

After gaining faculty support for our program proposals, we kept the change process going by "modeling" proposed modifications in our own courses. These modeling efforts served at least two functions. First, they demonstrated our commitment to the restructured program. By teaching new field-based courses, we influenced the instructional content and avoided placing additional instructional responsibilities on other faculty members. This appeared to make them much more receptive to the proposed changes. Second, by piloting our new field-based coursework, we were able to refine our training methods, develop good working relationships with critical school personnel, and develop a replicable model for helping others implement their field-based courses.

Finally, we collected outcome data from our initial field-based courses to demonstrate the efficacy of our training efforts. We then used these data to evoke and maintain support for our new program from critical consumers (i.e., students, classroom teachers, and district and college administrators) and to seek external funding for our efforts. As a result, approximately three-quarters of the new program was in effect by Fall 1992, with the remaining components to be implemented over the next three semesters. In subsequent sections, we describe the general philosophy underlying the RARE model, outline the primary components of the program, and discuss some common instructional arrangements that have been used to facilitate participants' acquisition, retention, and use of important behavioral principles and procedures.

RARE Program Philosophy and Major Components

The RARE model's general philosophy is deceptively simple yet highly consistent with the basic tenets of applied behavior analysis. We believe that all children can learn, and that they can learn best when

they are taught by classroom teachers who are both reflective and responsive. To be reflective, a teacher must understand that an individual learns most about teaching when he or she looks back on and analyzes what has happened during instructional episodes (Schon, 1987). This professional reflection should include a self-analysis of the efficacy of selected teaching strategies and an objective assessment of the pupils' responsiveness to such methods. In essence, teachers must become the pupils of their students (Skinner, 1972). Reflection alone, however, is not enough. In addition, teachers must *respond* effectively to the information they glean from their reflection and analysis. In other words, they must make "informed" decisions regarding their instructional practice. Informed decision making is demonstrated when classroom teachers (1) continue to use or develop instructional strategies that accelerate successful student responding, and (2) discard or adapt teaching procedures that produce insufficient improvements in the pupils' performance. Since no one instructional practice will work with all students, all the time, and in all different instructional domains, the RARE program emphasizes ongoing evaluation and adjustment of instruction in response to pupil performance as the *preferred* method for teaching children and youth.

A second principle underlying the RARE program philosophy is that children and adults learn best by doing. A considerable database from the ecobehavioral literature suggests that many hard-to-teach children fail simply because they receive insufficient opportunities to learn (Greenwood, Delquadri, & Hall, 1984). A similar scenario can be projected for preservice educators; many may fail to learn how to teach effectively because they have received too few teaching opportunities. Reitz and Kerr (1991) articulated this concern by noting that "teacher trainees spend hour after hour sitting in college classrooms learning about education and how students learn, but little time actually engaged in the process of teaching others" (p. 362). The traditional preparation program at SUC-Fredonia (and many other schools as well) did not offer formal teaching opportunities for preservice educators until the final year of their professional preparation (i.e., methods and student teaching). Quite often, this was too little, too late. A top priority for RARE, therefore, was to provide preservice educators with more direct teaching opportunities. Moreover, these instructional opportunities were to occur earlier and throughout their preparation program. Finally, they were to be highly structured, carefully sequenced, and conducted with as many high-risk learners as possible.

The five primary components of the RARE program are (1) four years of highly structured field-based experiences, (2) systematic training in specific validated intervention strategies, (3) direct training in peer collaboration skills, (4) an objective evaluation system to assess effectiveness, efficiency, and social acceptability of training procedures, and (5) a conceptual framework that emphasizes reflective decision making and lifelong learning

The first component is a set of four required teaching experiences. Typically, these experiences begin in the freshman year and consist of teaching assistant–type activities (e.g., assist with the implementation of teacher-specified instructional and noninstructional tasks). In the sophomore year, preservice general educators assume greater instructional responsibility by serving as reading tutors for children and youth with identified learning and behavioral disabilities. In their junior year, RARE participants teach *small groups* of high-risk learners through the use of cooperative learning and other peer-mediated instructional methods (e.g., Classwide Peer Tutoring). During their senior year, participants assume instructional responsibility for entire classrooms of students. In this instance, they are placed into classes that contain at least two high-risk learners and teachers who have been nominated by their peers as being unusually effective with such youngsters. This senior-level experience is a full year in length and requires participants to demonstrate competence on a predetermined set of instructional objectives. Careful inspection of the RARE training sequence reveals an attempt to "shape" preservice trainees' instructional competence. RARE trainees *gradually* assume greater teaching responsibilities as they proceed through the program. They move from providing noninstructional services, to teaching individual pupils with specific learning needs, to instructing small heterogeneous learning groups, to ultimately serving an entire class of youngsters.

This gradual shifting of instructional responsibility should facilitate RARE participants' acquisition and mastery of specific teaching competencies, make them more comfortable in working with children, and ensure that no one proceeds to more demanding instructional arrangements until they have demonstrated competence in less rigorous teaching situations.

The second major component of the RARE program is direct training in the use and evaluation of specific, validated teaching practices. The rationale underlying the inclusion of this component is as follows. First, not all instructional interventions are equally effective. Some instructional methods, in fact, have empirical evidence to suggest that they are more effective than other teaching approaches (e.g., Classwide Peer Tutoring, Direct Instruction, Classwide Student Tutoring Teams, Question-Answer-Relationships). RARE participants are taught that they must be "wise consumers" of instructional products. They should select those methods that have the highest probability of being successful, particularly with high-risk learners. In this regard, applied behavior analysis has provided our students with numerous teaching options. We also provide intensive preparation on specific teaching practices because we want our students to do some instructional things very well. In many traditional teacher-training programs, preservice trainees are exposed to an eclectic array of teaching methods but are rarely required to demonstrate competence in any particular approach. Often the result is that trainees know a little about a lot of different teaching approaches, but they lack the overall knowledge and skills to implement any of these approaches effectively in the classroom (Reitz & Kerr, 1991).

The third component involves systematic training in collaborative decision making. Throughout their four-year preparation program, RARE trainees are given direct opportunities to work collaboratively with their peers. Through the use of cohort learning groups that remain intact across semesters, partner pairings for practice and field-based activities, small-group cooperative-learning sessions, and specific peer-coaching assignments, we teach our preservice trainees to work together effectively. The rationale for teaching collaborative work skills stems primarily from changes that are taking place in the public schools. For example, current nationwide restructuring efforts emphasize concepts such as collaborative problem solving, teacher empowerment, site-based management, and shared responsibility for high-risk learners. The assumption underlying this so-called professional reform model (Elmore, 1991; Sykes, 1991) is that schools have failed to educate students effectively primarily because of poor working conditions for classroom teachers. Inservice teachers often work alone, receive little feedback regarding their instruction, have few opportunities to learn from one another, and are generally treated in a less-than-professional manner. Typical reform proposals have included increasing time allocations for teacher collaboration, establishing buildingwide support and decision-making teams, and providing greater access to new knowledge and alternative instructional techniques through ongoing staff development programs. While we do not believe that better working conditions alone will ameliorate the extensive problems that schools are facing, there is value in increasing classroom teachers' opportunities to collaborate and solve their own classroom-based problems. Moreover, our experiences with peer-mediated teaching procedures have taught us that numerous instructional benefits (e.g., a greater number of problem solutions, improved communication skills, and enhanced interpersonal relationships) often accrue when individuals are allowed to work together.

The final two components of the RARE program are an objective evaluation system for assessing program outcomes, and a conceptual framework that prepares trainees as "reflective decision makers" and "lifelong learners." The rationale for selecting objective program evaluation criteria needs no detailed explanation in a chapter written for applied behavior analysts. However, the inclusion of reflective decision making and lifelong learning may require some discussion. These concepts are very popular among current educational reformers, particularly those who ascribe to a cognitive and social constructivist philosophy (e.g. Schon, 1987; Patriarca & Lamb, 1990; Zeichner & Liston, 1987). We see great utility in these outcomes. For example, reflective decision makers examine their own teaching practice in relation to student performance. In those instances where insufficient progress is being made, reflective practitioners adjust their teaching practices. This concept is certainly consistent with procedures espoused by applied behavior analysts. Similarly, the notion of a lifelong learner as one who will never "know it all" is highly compatible with behaviorists' understanding that we cannot control all sources of variance in real-life settings.

RARE Program Organization and Instructional Procedures

All RARE participants complete a minimum of 120 credit hours. Approximately 40 credit hours are devoted to coursework to meet General College Program (GCP) requirements for all undergraduate students, and another 30 credit hours are taken in a student-selected liberal arts concentration. The remaining 50 credit hours are taken to meet Education Department requirements for graduation and certification. This 50-credit-hour requirement for RARE participants is shown in Table 5.1.

On initial analysis of education program requirements, we decided that the most logical and feasible place to infuse behavior analysis content was in the "new" field-based coursework. Therefore, the following discussion focuses primarily on what happens within each field-based course. Applied behavior analysis, however, is discussed in other required (e.g., Educational and Developmental Psychology) and elective (e.g., Classroom Management) courses.

Preservice educators first encounter applied behavior analysis concepts and procedures during their freshman year. All education majors enroll in the field-based course Introduction to Contemporary Education. Traditionally, this course had been an elective for education majors and was based on lectures. In the RARE model, however, this course is the freshman field experience. It follows an instructional pattern that includes six weeks of lecture-based instruction followed by ten weeks of "in-school" activities. Students enroll in cohorts of 30, and in turn, these cohorts are assigned to partner pairs for their ten-week field experience. Partner pairs are assigned to elementary classrooms that contain at least two high-risk learners and a teacher who has been nominated by peers as effective in dealing with such pupils. The college instructor, in conjunction with the classroom teacher and the partner pairs, then completes a Teaching/Learning Contract (see Table 5.2) that outlines the course expectations for all involved parties.

The Teaching/Learning Contract lists a variety of noninstructional and instructional functions that partner pairs can serve. The classroom teacher identifies at least three specific duties that *each* participant should perform on a regular basis. These duties are then written directly on the contract and all parties receive a copy of the agreement. In one classroom, for example, freshman participants spend a significant portion of their time "catching pupils being good" during independent seatwork. They give raffle tickets and social praise to all students who are on task and completing assignments. This gives participants an opportunity to practice the contingent application of positive consequences. In another classroom, RARE students edit and conference with pupils about recent writing assignments. The classroom teacher rates freshman participants on each of their assigned duties,

using a 7-point Likert-type scale; for example, 1 = unsatisfactory performance, 4 = adequate performance, and 7 = outstanding performance. These ratings are given on a biweekly basis and provide ongoing feedback. In turn, the formative evaluation data are used to make decisions regarding each participant's ongoing rate of progress. Ultimately, our goal is to create local norms regarding below-average, average, and above-average performance, and then to develop, implement, and evaluate a variety of intervention strategies to improve deficient participant performance. In addition, the use of Teaching/Learning Contracts allows us to quantify many aspects of the freshman field experience, such as the type and range of instructional and noninstructional services provided.

At the sophomore level, RARE participants get their second exposure to applied behavior analysis concepts and methods. Preservice educators again enroll in a required field-based course, Introduction to the Exceptional Child, in cohorts of 30 or 60. The course follows an instructional pattern of six weeks of lecture-based instruction followed by ten weeks of field experience. RARE participants, in this instance,

Table 5.1 Education requirements for RARE participants

Year	Course		Number of credits
Freshman	ED 105	Introduction to Contemporary Education (field-based)	3
Sophomore	ED 225	Developmental Psychology	3
	ED 250	Introduction to the Exceptional Child (field-based)	3
	ED 230	The Electronic Classroom	3
	ED 215	Historical and Philosophical Foundations of Education	1
Junior	ED 349	Educational Psychology	3
	ED 305	Multicultural Education (field-based)	3
	ED 315	Sociological Foundations of Education	1
Senior	ED 410	Instructional Methods in the Disciplines (field-based)	14
	ED 420	Student Teaching (field-based)	15
	ED 415	Legal Foundations of Education	1

Table 5.2 Sample Teaching/Learning Contract for freshman field experience

I. Purpose of This Contract

The purpose of the Learning Contract is twofold: to provide RARE participants with a specific set of instructional experiences for children and youth with disabilities, and to provide cooperating teachers with the individualized types of assistance that they will need in meeting the needs of their mainstreamed students. Listed below are a variety of possible instructional and noninstructional duties that RARE participants may perform. Please decide *collaboratively* which of these educational experiences would be most beneficial to you (cooperating teacher), to your mainstreamed learners, and to your RARE participants. Place a checkmark next to each duty you would like your college helpers to perform. Select at least *three* specific duties for *each* participant. These duties can be the same or different for each participant. Next, list these specific duties right on this form. After this information has been reviewed with your RARE participants, you and your helpers should sign the form and each keep a copy. Periodically, you will be asked to rate (i.e., from 1 to 7) your participants' performance of their assigned duties.

II. Possible Participant Duties

Instructional Duties	*Noninstructional Duties*
___ Listen to child read.	___ Collate tests or other materials.
___ Read to children.	___ Run off dittos.
___ Discuss reading and writing activities.	___ Pass out and collect materials.
___ Edit and conference with pupils on writing tasks.	___ Pass out awards.
___ "Catch pupils being good" (praise and recognize pupils).	___ Collect paperwork (e.g., permission slips, notes from home, etc.).
___ Assist with arts and crafts activities.	___ Collect homework and record who turned in assignments.
___ Correct homework and in-class assignments.	___ Write schedule/activities on board.
___ Work with pupils in content area assignments.	___ Organize displays/learning centers.
___ Teach small-group lesson or whole-class lesson.	___ Collect materials on teacher-selected topic.
___ Observe small- or large-group lessons.	___ Assist in transition, lunch, or recess.

Please list any other instructional or noninstructional duties that you would like your participants to perform on a regular basis in your classroom. _____

_____

_____

III. List Three Specific Duties

1._____   2._____   3._____

IV. Collaborative Agreement

We, the undersigned, agree to participate in the types of activities that have been mutually agreed on. We acknowledge that fulfillment of this learning contract will partially meet the requirements for ED 105.

_____   _____
Cooperating Teacher   Date

_____   _____
RARE Participant   Date

_____   _____
RARE Participant   Date

are given a direct opportunity to teach special-needs learners in the area of reading. Preservice educators are trained, in pairs, to implement a highly structured reading tutoring program with children who have been identified by the public schools as disabled or at-risk for special education placement. Major components of the sophomore-level reading tutoring program are outlined as follows:

1. **Direct instruction in reading comprehension**
   A. In-class teacher-led instruction.
   B. Partner pairing for in-class practice activities.
   C. Fidelity checks on use of specific reading tutoring strategies (e.g., collecting and graphing CBA data).
2. **Reading and teacher-led review of tutoring manual**
   A. A 12-page manual that describes:
      1. Proper etiquette in schools.
      2. General tutoring procedures (i.e., dates and times of tutoring sessions, overview of methods, etc.).
      3. Specific tutoring procedures (i.e., recommended activities for prereading, oral reading, story grammar, and listening comprehension phases of tutoring sessions).
      4. Procedural fidelity checklist for conducting individual tutoring sessions.
      5. Detailed directions for conducting, scoring, and graphing daily reading rate measures.
3. **Package" of recommended teaching practices**
   A. A 20-page packet of material that reviews the major facets of reading instruction (i.e., decoding, word meaning, story grammar, reading and listening comprehension strategies).
   B. Each class participant is required to teach one topic to members of their small groups.
4. **Assignment as tutoring partners**
   A. Two college sophomores work with one special-needs learner.
   B. Tutor partners reverse roles and share instructional responsibilities.
   C. Receive specific guidelines for conducting peer-coaching sessions.

5. **Weekly meetings with instructor and small groups**
   A. RARE participants are assigned to small heterogeneous groups and meet on a weekly basis for the final ten weeks of the semester.
   B. Small groups serve both an instructional and a support function.
   C. Small groups meet with instructor every week to discuss how things are going in tutoring sessions.
6. **Direct observation of individual tutoring sessions**
   A. RARE participants are observed on an almost daily basis while they work with special-needs learners.
   B. Random fidelity checks are taken and used to provide feedback to tutors.

Twice each week for one hour, partner pairs work in an after-school tutoring program. Tutoring partners alternate teaching and observing roles and meet collaboratively to evaluate pupil progress. To help monitor progress, RARE participants are systematically taught to collect and graph curriculum-based assessment (CBA) data on their tutees' oral reading fluency rates. Partner pairs also follow scripted peer-coaching procedures for conducting their feedback sessions.

In addition, each week RARE trainees return to campus to participate in small learning groups of five or six members. These groups serve both an instructional and a supportive function. Each team member is given a packet of information on one facet of reading instruction, such as word meaning, story grammar, or reading comprehension strategies. He or she is required to read the material, discuss it with members of other teams who have the same topic, and then teach it to his or her teammates the following week. During these teaching sessions, the team leaders model specific instructional strategies, which the other team members must then use in brief, *role-play* activities. Afterward, the leaders provide positive, corrective feedback to each team member. Teammates, in turn, complete a peer evaluation inventory, which consists of a 5-item questionnaire in which team members anonymously assign grades to the presenter for specific aspects of the presentation. The inventory is worth 10% of the presenting student's total grade. At the end of the semester, course participants are given an objective exam that tests their knowledge of all facets of reading instruction. In addition, RARE trainees must display their newly acquired teaching strategies during field-based assignments. These evaluation activities build in a measure of individual accountability to the cooperative learning arrangement and place course participants under an interdependent group contingency (Rhode, Jenson, & Reavis, 1992; Slavin, 1990). The small-group cooperative learning arrangement also seems to serve a social function. Team members enjoy hearing how other RARE participants are doing in the field. They share instructional concerns, discuss individual successes and failures, and frequently exhort one another to try something different. Small-group sessions have also been a valuable source of information for course instructors, who can move among the groups, listen to their discussions, observe their presentations, and see how well they are able to work together.

RARE trainees teach small heterogeneous learning groups during their junior-level field experience. The field experience accompanies enrollment in a Multicultural Education course. The general purposes of this particular course are to (1) introduce RARE trainees to the nature and needs of children and youth from diverse cultural and linguistic backgrounds, (2) provide preservice educators with an opportunity to teach such children in small-group learning arrangements, and (3) give trainees the opportunity to implement validated cooperative learning and peer-mediated teaching procedures. As in the two previous field-based courses, a variety of instructional arrangements are used to promote trainees' acquisition of specific course objectives. During the initial six weeks of campus-based instruction, RARE trainees are exposed to a variety of peer-teaching formats, such as Numbered Heads Together, Classwide Peer Tutoring, and Think-Pair-Share. They are then assigned to small heterogeneous teams and required to collaboratively develop, implement, and evaluate a series of peer-teaching activities with small groups of elementary or secondary students. The primary service delivery vehicles for the junior-level field experience are after-school Cultural Enrichment Clubs. These clubs are being developed through

partnerships with local school districts. Cultural Enrichment Club membership includes students of all academic abilities and diverse ethnic and cultural backgrounds (e.g., African American, Native American, and Hispanic). Clubs meet twice each week for approximately two hours. RARE trainees are required to develop instructional activities that promote awareness and respect for all cultures and that can be used with small learning groups. These instructional activities must use children's literature books, written by individuals from that particular culture, as the medium to help students learn about diverse cultural beliefs and practices. For example, *Casa Means Home* (Campion, 1970) is a fictional story that introduces a variety of important concepts about growing up in the Puerto Rican culture. RARE trainees might read this book (as a group) and plan collaboratively a set of peer-mediated instructional activities that will help their small learning groups acquire and retain the information. Trainees are given direct training in the use of specific cooperative-learning and peer-teaching procedures and must demonstrate competence in the use of these methods on campus before using them "in the field." Course instructors use fidelity checklists to monitor the trainees' accuracy in implementing specific peer-teaching procedures and provide positive and corrective feedback throughout the term. During the semester, RARE participants may use three or four different children's literature books, each representative of a different cultural group, and implement a similar number of peer-teaching procedures. Peer-teaching arrangements were selected primarily because there are ample data to suggest that they are quite effective with children from diverse cultural and linguistic backgrounds and they expand preservice educators' instructional repertoires (Tiedt & Tiedt, 1990). Moreover, these types of instructional procedures require RARE trainees to assume greater instructional responsibilities in that they must plan for and instruct more than one learner .

The capstone experience in the RARE program occurs during the trainees' senior year. At this time, they are expected to assume instructional responsibility for entire classes of children and youth, including those who are at-risk for academic or behavioral failure. In the past, students enrolled for one semester of professional methods courses that included an eight-week field placement, followed by a semester of student teaching that involved two separate field placements. One of the major problems with this arrangement for professional methods faculty was that they rarely saw their students after the initial methods courses, because much of the field supervision at the senior level is conducted by adjunct faculty members. Moreover, the traditional arrangement of separate methods courses by academic discipline, such as science methods or social studies methods) was inconsistent with existing curricular reform movements toward thematic or integrated instructional units within the public schools. The new senior experience is an integrated "professional year" in which methods courses are organized around common instructional themes and students return to campus and their original instructors halfway through their whole-class teaching experiences. The professional year consists of six weeks on campus, ten weeks in the field, six weeks on campus, and ten weeks in the field. Moreover, the faculty use a performance-based evaluation approach as their preferred assessment method. Finally, returning to campus provides trainees with a unique opportunity to refine their whole-class teaching skills and to assess, from an experiential perspective, their own instructional needs. This, in turn, permits the faculty to be more responsive to their trainees' questions and concerns.

The public schools have done much to inform our professional-year curriculum. By establishing partnerships with local school systems and designating certain schools as teaching centers, we have been able to gain valuable input on preferred practices from those in the field. Interestingly, many of their preferred practices are also consistent with an applied behavior-analytic or direct-instruction philosophy (although we have never heard them referred to as such). Our ongoing consultation and increased visibility in the schools has also strengthened our previously good relationships with the public schools and become a valuable source of instructional expertise that had been untapped.

In summary, applied behavior analysis principles and procedures have been infused throughout our four-year field-based teacher preparation program. Faculty members model validated instructional prac-

tices in on-campus segments of specific courses. Preservice trainees are then given an opportunity to practice these procedures with peers through analogue arrangements and must demonstrate applied competence (via fidelity checklists) before working with children. While working with children in each field-based course, trainees gain additional fluency in the use of specified teaching techniques and meet regularly with course instructors and peers to evaluate and discuss their progress. Finally, RARE participants are observed directly throughout their field-based experiences and evaluated specifically on predetermined sets of performance-based criteria. In the next section, we discuss some initial outcomes that have been associated with the RARE program.

Initial Outcomes from the RARE Program

To date, we have collected evaluation data from significant individuals working within the public schools (i.e., classroom teachers and building principals) on our preservice trainees and on the children they serve. More specifically, we have collected fidelity of implementation data on the trainees' use of specific reading comprehension strategies, academic outcome data (i.e., oral reading rates) on schoolchildren, and social validity data from children, preservice trainees, and significant school personnel. To facilitate (and limit) our discussion of specific program outcomes, we will only present data from *one* course, Introduction to the Exceptional Child, that was offered during *one* instructional semester, Spring Term, 1992.

As noted earlier, this course is the sophomore-level field experience in which RARE trainees work two-on-one with a special-needs learner in an after-school reading tutoring program. The target schools come from a racially and ethnically diverse school district of low- to middle-socioeconomic status (SES). During the semester, 110 preservice trainees provided a total of 1,088 hours of direct reading instruction to 68 special-needs learners (some RARE trainees worked one-on-one because the schools had more tutees than we had tutors). A "typical" tutor pair used an average of six children's literature books with their respective tutee and spent approximately 8 hours listening to them read orally from these texts. In addition, tutor pairs used an average of five specific reading comprehension strategies during the semester and generated approximately 320 comprehension questions to assess their pupils' listening and reading comprehension skills.

Procedural reliability data were collected on a sample of 36 trainees during their tutoring sessions. In general, we assessed the accuracy with which trainees implemented specific components of the tutoring package, such as prereading, oral reading, and comprehension tasks. The components were assessed as either present or absent and a composite percentage of the components present was derived. On average, RARE trainees implemented 89% of the reading tutoring components (range = 0.67–1.00). In addition, we also calculated the percentage of trainees who accurately used each of the specific tutoring components. These data are depicted in Table 5.3. As seen in Table 5.3, the majority of RARE trainees implemented most tutoring components. The tutoring components implemented by the most participants were oral reading, listening and reading comprehension, and prereading activities. The components implemented by the fewest RARE trainees were daily reading rate and comprehension modeling strategies. Clearly, a more fine-grained analysis of specific implementation practices is needed before we can make more definitive statements about our trainees' instructional competence.

RARE trainees were also required to collect and graph curriculum-based assessment data on their tutees' oral reading fluency rates at the end of each tutoring session. Representative data from four tutor pairs can be seen in Figure 5.1. Once again, we found that tutor pairs were able to adequately collect and graph their CBA data (at least those who regularly used daily reading rates). A total of 36 RARE trainees collected usable reading rate data on their tutees. Examination of these data revealed an average increase of approximately 20% in the pupils' oral reading rates over the ten-week tutoring period (range: 2%–54%). Using children's literature books as the source of our CBA data, however, created a number of measurement problems that we are presently working to rectify. Moreover, although we have been able to demonstrate trainee competence in the collection of

CBA data, we have not yet assessed their competence in using these data to make "informed" instructional decisions.

Finally, we have collected social validity data from our preservice trainees, their tutees, and significant building personnel. Each group was given a consumer satisfaction survey to complete anonymously. All surveys asked participants to evaluate the importance of the program's instructional goals, the acceptability of existing teaching procedures, and the general level of satisfaction with program outcomes. Participants rated each item on a 3-point Likert-type scale and the resulting data were averaged across all three target groups. Only the major findings will be summarized here (i.e., actual data can be obtained by contacting the first author). For the most part, RARE participants recognized the need for earlier hands-on experiences in reading and for direct work with spe-

Table 5.3 Percentage of tutors using specific tutoring components (N = 36)

Tutoring Components	Composite Percentage	Range[a]
1. Use informal discussion/activity to "break the ice."	0.94	--
2. Conduct informal questioning on previously read material.	0.96	--
3. Conduct a systematic review of previous content.	0.80	--
4. Introduce new vocabulary from upcoming reading passages.	0.93	0.78–0.96
5. Ask tutee comprehension questions from upcoming passages before oral reading.	0.90	--
6. Explain or model specific comprehension strategies before reading.	0.68	--
7. Ask tutee to read aloud important sight words from upcoming passages.	0.96	0.92–1.00
8. Ask tutee to read aloud from text.	0.98	0.94–1.00
9. Ask tutee to retell details of story.	0.84	--
10. Instruct tutees to continue reading.	0.98	--
11. Collect daily reading rate data.	0.78	--
12. Read orally and ask tutee comprehension questions.	0.96	--
	0.89	--

[a]Some procedural components contain two or three subcomponents; therefore, the range represents the lower (lowest) and higher (highest) percentage of participants who used those particular subcomponents.

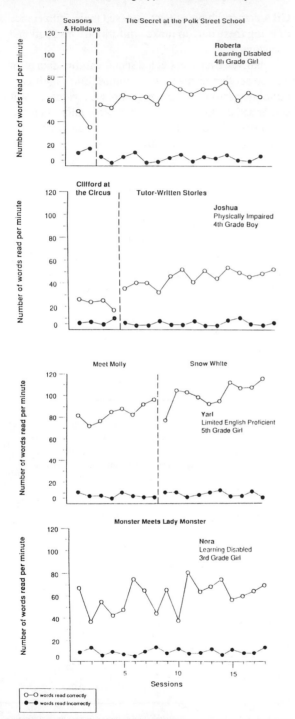

Figure 5.1. Sample Daily Reading Rate Data Collected and Prepared by RARE Participants.

cial-needs learners. Moreover, they enjoyed going to the schools, working in pairs, and doing most tutoring activities. The most-preferred activities included listening comprehension tasks, keeping a tutoring journal, and meeting on a weekly basis with small groups; the least-preferred included collecting CBA data and doing oral reading activities. Overall, trainees were quite satisfied with the outcomes of their tutoring project. Almost 90% reported that they were very satisfied with their performance during the semester and a comparable number felt that their tutees were equally satisfied. Interestingly, when asked if they would take the course over with or without the field-based component, 109 out of 110 selected the field-based alternative.

Classroom teachers and building principals provided similar positive reactions in their consumer satisfaction surveys. Once more, they cited the need for earlier field experiences, specifically in reading and with special-needs learners. They were also unanimous in their support for on-site placement of preservice trainees and for the use of tutoring partners. Classroom teachers also rated most tutoring activities as acceptable, although some instructors were concerned about the collection of daily reading rate data. The school is presently divided between whole-language and skills-based approaches to reading instruction, thus their concerns seem to reflect deeper philosophical differences regarding preferred teaching practices. All district personnel, however, were very satisfied with program outcomes. If given a choice to continue or terminate the program, 100% wanted the program to continue. Finally, all building personnel reported that their children made sufficient academic progress during the tutoring program and that they enjoyed participating in the after-school experience.

The primary recipients of the tutoring program—special-needs learners—were also assessed with regard to their satisfaction with the tutoring program. For the most part, they too reported that it was important for them to improve their reading performance and that working with college students was a good way to do so. Ninety-six percent of the children liked having college students come to their school and a comparable number enjoyed working with two tutors.

With regard to specific tutoring components, they liked the prereading and listening comprehension activities the most and the oral reading tasks the least. Interestingly, 81% reported liking CBA activities "very much," while only 7% said that they did not like these activities at all. These data differ somewhat from the responses of both preservice and inservice teachers. Finally, 96% of all students felt that they had improved in reading and wanted to be in the program the following year.

Summary and Conclusions

Applied behavior analysis does, indeed, have much to offer general education. Besides providing a variety of effective instructional interventions, behavior analysis can offer an objective measurement and evaluation system that will permit educators to be more responsive to their learners' needs, whether at the public school or higher education level. In Kohler and Strain's words, applied behavior analysis can offer a "methodological blueprint for developing and evaluating *any* attempts to improve America's schools" (1992, p. 31). Behavioral technology can also be applied to significant staff development and innovation dissemination problems presently facing educational reformers (e.g., Elmore, 1991; Rowan, 1991). It is highly unlikely, however, that applied behavior analysis will be of any value to future classroom teachers or children, unless the knowledge base is integrated effectively into preservice teacher-training programs (Hall, 1991). In this chapter, we described an initial attempt to mainstream behavior analysis principles and procedures into a preservice training program for general education students. To date, we have successfully implemented about three-fourths of the RARE model and have obtained administrative and faculty support to infuse the remaining components as well. Our attempts to integrate behavioral content into a traditional preservice training program have taught us much about institutional change and our own teaching practice.

On the positive side, we have learned that it is possible to integrate much of the behavior analysis content into the "mainstream" of preservice teacher preparation practice, although it is easier to do so if one refrains from the excessive use of "behavioral" language. Moreover, our students like the explicit nature of our new instructional arrangements and are generally turned on by the "behavioral message." Highly structured field-based experiences provide an appropriate vehicle for giving preservice educators an opportunity to practice their newly acquired instructional skills, and peer collaboration appears to be a feasible means for providing students with more frequent individual feedback. Overall, preservice educators have taken their instructional responsibilities seriously (i.e., attendance rates were above 95% for field experiences), and they have learned to work well together when planning, implementing, or evaluating specific teaching episodes. Finally, much good can come from the formation of "true" partnerships with local school systems. We have found that schools contain many good instructional models for our students, that district personnel are often valuable sources of input regarding program development, and that school officials are quite responsive when treated as peers. In effect, we have learned that our role as behavioral messengers is often more important than the behavioral message itself.

On the down side, institutional change is a long and often painstaking process. While most, if not all, program components will ultimately be in place, such changes have not come without their costs. Some faculty members remain skeptical about the model itself, others are carrying much of the additional workload, and a few have elected not to participate in program implementation. This is unfortunate because our initial intent was to develop a program that would be acceptable to everyone and implemented by all. In reality, this may simply be an inappropriate expectation or goal for our restructuring efforts. We have also learned that there are many "bugs" to work out in the routine implementation of a field-based program. In particular, making accommodations for transfer students and those who declare an education major late in their academic program has become a recurrent problem. Another important lesson is that many of our nonbehavioral constituents are turned off by the use of technical terms and some of our more intrusive data collection procedures (e.g., multiple observers within a classroom setting). Presently, we are exploring evaluation methods that are less intrusive, and we plan to expand the role of peers in the data collection process.

With regard to future programmatic endeavors, we intend to refine and extend the RARE model into both the early childhood and secondary education programs. Clearly, the field-based placements, partner pairings, and small-group arrangements can be replicated in other course offerings. Additionally, we must conduct more in-depth analyses and evaluations of the RARE program. Thus far, our training and evaluation efforts have lacked the same empirical rigor that characterized our applied studies. We must develop more systematic training procedures, use more refined observation measures, and design more controlled studies that will link our training efforts to more objective pupil outcomes. Finally, we must develop or locate some institutionwide mechanisms to prompt and reward continued involvement in program development and the effective preparation of classroom teachers. The bottom line is that many people are working harder than they ever have before. Unless we can evoke systemwide support for these increased efforts, it is highly unlikely that we can maintain the existing practice for years to come.

References

AXELROD, S. (1991). The problem: American education. The solution: Use behavior analytic technology. *Journal of Behavioral Education, 1,* 275–282.

BINDER, C. V. (1991). Marketing measurably effective instructional methods. *Journal of Behavioral Education, 1,* 317–328.

CAMPION, N. (1970). *Casa means home.* New York: Holt Publishing.

CARNINE, D., & Kinder, B. D. (1985). Teaching low performing students to apply generative and schema strategies to narrative and expository material. *Remedial and Special Education, 6* (1), 20–30.

CUBAN, L. (1988). Why do some reforms persist? *Educational Administration Quarterly, 24,* 329–336.

ELMORE, R. F. (1991). Introduction: On changing the structure of public schools. In R. F. Elmore (Ed), *Restructuring schools: The next generation of educational reform* (pp. 1–28). San Francisco: Jossey-Bass.

ENGELMANN, S. (1991). Change schools through revolution, not evolution. *Journal of Behavioral Education, 1,* 295–304.

GARTNER, A., & Lipsky, D. K. (1987). Beyond special education: Toward a quality system for all students. *Harvard Educational Review, 57,* 367–395.

GERSTEN, R., & Dimino, J. (1991). Reading instruction for at risk students—Implications of current research. *Direct Instruction News,* Winter, 9–20.

GREENWOOD, C. R., Delquadri, J. C., & Hall, R. V. (1984). Opportunity to respond and student academic performance. In W. L. Heward, T. E. Heron, D. S. Hill, & J. Trap-Porter (Eds.), *Focus on behavior analysis in education* (pp. 58–88). Columbus, OH: Charles E. Merrill.

HALL, R. V. (1991). Behavior analysis and education: An unfulfilled dream. *Journal of Behavioral Education, 1,* 305–316.

HODGKINSON, H. L. (1985). *All one system.* New York: Institute for Educational Leadership.

KOHLER, F. W., & Strain, P. S. (1992). Applied behavior analysis and the movement to restructure schools: Compatibilities and opportunities for collaboration. *Journal of Behavioral Education, 2,* 367–390.

LILLY, M. S. (1986). The relationship between general and special education: A new face on an old issue. *Counterpoint,* March, p. 10.

MAHEADY, L., & Algozzine, B. (1991). The Regular Education Initiative: Can we proceed in an orderly and scientific manner? *Teacher Education and Special Education, 14* (1), 66–73.

MAHEADY, L., Harper, G. F., & Mallette, B. (1991). Peer-mediated instruction: An illustrative review with potential applications for learning disabled students. *Reading, Writing, and Learning Disabilities International, 7,* 75–103.

PATRIARCA, L., & Lamb, M. A. (1990). Preparing secondary special education teachers to be collaborative decision-makers and reflective practitioners: A promising practicum model. *Teacher Education and Special Education, 13,* 228–232.

REITZ, A. L., & Kerr, M. M. (1991). Training effective teachers for tomorrow's students: Issues and recommendations. *Education and Treatment of Children, 14,* 361–370.

RHODE, G., Jenson, W. R., & Reavis, H. K. (1992). *The tough kid book.* Longmont, CO: SOPRIS West.

ROWAN, B. (1991). Applying conceptions of teaching to organizational reform. In R. F. Elmore (Ed.), *Restructuring schools: The next generation of school reform* (pp. 209–250). San Francisco: Jossey-Bass.

SCHON, D. A. (1987). *Educating the reflective practitioner: Toward a design for teaching and learning in the professions.* San Francisco: Jossey-Bass.

SKINNER, B. F. (1972). The shame of American education. *American Psychologist, 27,* 947–954.

SLAVIN, R. E. (1990). *Cooperative learning: Theory, research, and practice.* Englewood Cliffs, NJ: Prentice Hall.

SYKES, G. (1991). Fostering teacher professionalism in schools. In R. F. Elmore (Ed.), *Restructuring schools: The next generation of educational reform* (pp. 59–96). San Francisco: Jossey-Bass.

TIEDT, P. L., & Tiedt, I. M. (1990). *Multicultural teaching* (3rd ed.). Boston: Allyn & Bacon.

WILL, M. C. (1986). Educating children with learning problems: A shared responsibility. *Exceptional Children, 52,* 411–415.

YSSELDYKE, J. E., Algozzine, B., & Thurlow, M. L. (1992). *Critical issues in special education* (2nd ed.). Boston: Houghton Mifflin.

ZEICHNER, K. M., & Liston, D. (1987). Teaching student teachers to reflect. *Harvard Educational Review, 57,* 23–48.

CHAPTER 6

Developmentalism's Impediments to School Reform: Three Recommendations for Overcoming Them

J. E. Stone

Behavior analysts and various educational researchers have developed experimentally vindicated educational practices; yet, in spite of a crying need for educational reform, schools have failed to adopt them (Ellson, 1986; Walberg, 1990, 1992; Watkins, 1988). Instead, a search for radically new schools has been inaugurated (New American Schools Development Corporation, 1991). A broadly construed doctrine of developmentalism has been implicated as a major impediment to effective educational practice of any stripe (Stone, 1991). Found in a variety of educational and psychological theories, developmentalism is a theoretical perspective that emphasizes (1) the sufficiency of a natural inclination to learning, (2) the limits posed by biological and environmental constraints on learning, and (3) the desirability of instruction tailored to learner attributes and proclivities.

A belief in the value of teaching informed by developmental principles has been a central theme in educational psychology for well over 100 years.

By understanding the nature of children and adolescents as behaving organisms, [William] James was convinced teaching could be improved. He saw the importance of tailoring educational material to fit the learner's true condition, not the condition that the teacher assumed the learner should be in [Sprinthall & Sprinthall, 1987, p. 13].

From James to Dewey to Piaget to present-day proponents of whole-language instruction, the idea of spontaneous, stimulating, and successful learning experiences catalyzed by teaching tailored to the learner's developmentally determined attributes has seduced theorists, educators, and the public. Today, it threatens to prevent adoption of desperately needed changes in American schooling.

Dewey's fear that schooling could be subverted by a wrongful understanding of child-centered teaching was realized in the excesses of "progressive education" (Dewey, 1902). Regrettably, many of these (now) intuitively appealing concepts and practices are again conventional wisdom within the educational establishment; and they appear to be especially well represented within schools of education (Kramer, 1991). Whereas progressive education was based on Dewey's pragmatic philosophy and practical-minded observations of children, today's developmentalism is based primarily on theories such as those advanced by Piaget, Erikson, Kohlberg, and Maslow. The premises may not be Dewey's, but the conclusions are largely the same (Reschly & Sabers,

1974). For a recent illustration of developmentalism's pervasive influence, see *Excellence in Teacher Education: Helping Teachers Develop Learner-Centered Schools* (Darling-Hammond, Griffin, & Wise, 1992), published by the National Education Association's Professional Library Series. Darling-Hammond is a well-known educational policy analyst, formerly with Rand Corporation, and Wise is the executive director of the National Council for Accreditation of Teacher Education. Indeed their proposals for teachers are as constricted as those that would be recommended for physicians if herbalists were in charge of the medical schools.

I argue that behavior analysts should work to promote school reform by:

1. Drawing attention to developmentalism's counterproductive implications,
2. Collaborating with educational reformers who seek to ensure, not merely expect, student performance at the classroom level, and
3. Supporting public calls for student commitment to schoolwork and to the nation's future.

My suggestions are not intended primarily as a means of advancing the use of behavior analysis. Rather they are proposed as an avenue whereby behavior analysts might collaborate with other *reform-minded* persons in the public interest. I would hope, however, that such collaborations would bring the advantages of competently applied behavior principles to the attention of educational reformers, many of whom are unfamiliar with or misinformed about behavioral concepts.

There are a growing number of reformers and other interested parties whose backgrounds are not in education and the helping professions. Many of them have not been indoctrinated with the precepts of developmentalism. They recognize the failure of the educational establishment to significantly improve learning outcomes, and they seek pragmatic and cost-effective solutions to education's problems. I refer here to the numerous corporate participants in educational reform, educational traditionalists, the New American Schools Development Corporation's (NASDC) design teams such as the Modern Red School-house (Bennett, 1992), and Whittle Corporation's The Edison Project (1992). These are partners with whom

behavior analysts should seek to collaborate. Unlike typical members of the elementary, secondary, and teacher education establishments, their first priority is academic results.

Behavior analysis is likely to appeal to pragmatists because it offers a manageable and relatively cost-effective means of overcoming student deficiencies. It enables fulfillment of the traditional promise of education; namely, education as a tool of personal betterment and social reform. In contrast, much present-day educational thinking holds that schooling cannot succeed without prerequisite societal change. Behavior analysis is unique in this respect. Its effectiveness has been demonstrated both experimentally and clinically with an array of deficiencies, disabilities, handicaps, and disorders. Typically, these limitations are as daunting as those that many educators consider insurmountable. In truth, the typical learner limitations stemming from deficient or adverse socioeconomic conditions are mild versions of those limitations routinely overcome by special educators using behavior analysis.

Educators who limit their interventions to those deemed developmentally appropriate are like physicians who forgo medications and surgery. They may do no harm, but neither do they confront any real educational challenges. By contrast, behavior analysts assert that students (and parents) have a "right to effective education" (Barrett et al., 1991).

Although behavior analysts must maintain their intellectual and scientific integrity, they can contribute more regularly to educational reform by cooperating with others who seek to ensure student performance (i.e., pragmatic nondevelopmentalists). Not only are such opportunities increasing as a function of growing public insistence on change, but educational reformers are recognizing that behavioral methods produce *results*. A literature of "productive" teaching practices identifies behavioral approaches as among the most potent, but not the only effective approaches to instruction (Ellson, 1986; Walberg, 1990, 1992).

Pragmatists such as lawmakers in the states of Kentucky and Tennessee appear to be influenced by these findings. Because their interest is in educational impact, not doctrinal purity, they seem to favor eclectic models of educational practice, ones that are not inherently uncongenial to behavior analysis. For example, pursuant to its 1984 Comprehensive Educational Reform Act, the state of Tennessee adopted a plan called the Tennessee Instruction Model. It was very similar to Madeline Hunter's Mastery Teaching Program and included elements of Popham's (1981) thinking about behavioral measurement and criterion-referenced educational objectives ("Not Everyone," 1991). Another example is the Modern Red Schoolhouse proposal recently funded by NASDC. It employs "a demanding individualized curriculum," "mastery learning," and other elements that seem entirely compatible with a behavioral approach to instruction (Bennett, 1992).

The incentives for schools to focus on academic gain instead of educational process are changing as well. Kentucky's Educational Reform Act (1990) required schools to produce objectively measurable results or suffer prescribed consequences. Tennessee's recently enacted Education Improvement Act (1992) mandated a value-added system of school and teacher accountability for student performance gains. Significantly, a state income tax proposed to boost school funding was rejected in the same year. NASDC and the America 2000 program both encourage schools to seek a world-class level of student attainment. Such aims and accountability measures will cause schools to seek teaching practices that not only work, but work in a more efficient manner.

Developmentalism as an Impediment to Reform

Developmentalism accounts for the emergence of human characteristics as a product of maturation interacting with environmental factors over time. As a conceptual tool for behavioral scientists, it is useful, benign, and accepted by virtually all scientific perspectives of human development. As a guide to educational practice, however, it is fraught with implications that are contrary to that which is demonstrably effective (Binder & Watkins, 1989; Stone, 1991).

Learning of the kind that educators want invariably requires study and practice, and study and practice require an adequate degree of student motivation.

Unfortunately, and for reasons pertaining to their beliefs about human nature, developmentalists hold that students cannot and should not be "extrinsically"—that is artificially or externally—motivated. Thus they recommend that teachers merely provide attractive opportunities for learning rather than attempt to induce any particular degree of student effort. They believe that the most desirable form of learning occurs as life circumstances and maturation converge to produce a spontaneous motivation for achievement. "Because learning is developmental, it follows that one learns better when one is ready to learn . . ." (Clark & Starr, 1991, p. 37). The teacher education classic, *Psychological Foundations of Education* (Bigge & Hunt, 1962) stated the concept simply: "A young person is ready to learn something when he has achieved sufficient physiological maturation and experiential background so that he not only can learn but wants to" (p. 377). The teacher's role is to be sensitive to the student and to provide (developmentally) appropriate instruction as readiness emerges.

In contrast, teachers throughout the Far East (and American teachers of an earlier era) do not assume that teachers should merely afford attractive opportunities for the student. Instead, they believe that students are responsible for making a determined effort to learn regardless of their disposition or ability; and they succeed with many students developmentalists would consider unready for instruction (Stevenson & Stigler, 1992). Contrary to developmentally informed practice, teachers in the Far East do not presume that lack of performance implies lack of ability to perform. Reliance on developmentalism impedes educational reform in several ways:

1. Developmentalism has not worked, especially with at-risk students, yet developmentally informed educational concepts, such as "discovery learning," continue to be widely employed in attempts to improve schools. For example, almost all of NASDC's design teams (1992) are shaped by developmentalist principles and practices. Many sound as if their authors were steeped in Dewey's and Piaget's ideas about hands-on learning experiences. Developmentalist practices based on the principles of progressive education (i.e., the child-centered curriculum) were discredited in the 1950s after 40 years of classroom

trials (Ravitch, 1983).   John Dewey (1963), the originator of progressive education, disavowed the practices of child-centered educators in 1938. More recent versions of developmentalism—open education, responsive education, the Bank Street model—and other developmentally informed programs in the 1960s and 1970s fared poorly in the quasi-experimental trials conducted by the Follow Through project (Proper & St. Pierre, 1980).

To date, perhaps developmentalism's most critical and telling failure is outlined in a report commissioned by the United Kingdom's Secretary of State and coauthored by the Chief Inspector of Her Majesty's Inspectorate and the Chief Executive of the British Government's National Curriculum Council (Alexander, Rose, & Woodhead, 1992). Titled *Curriculum Organization and Classroom Practice in Primary Schools, the widely noted report concludes: "Over the last few decades the progress of primary pupils has been hampered by the influence of highly questionable dogmas* [italics added] which have led to excessively complex classroom practices and devalued the place of subjects in the curriculum" (p. 1). These highly questionable dogmas are none other than the Piagetian developmentalism that enjoyed great popularity in the United Kingdom during the late 1960s and was subsequently imported into the United States (Reschly & Sabers, 1974). Developmentally informed teaching may be appropriate for students whose maturity and life circumstances ensure that they are well prepared and motivated for schooling; but even for those individuals, it may expect too little.

2. Developmentalism hinders the use of educational practices that might otherwise be effective, because it implies that attempts to teach the unready or unmotivated student may do grave harm and it ignores the deficiencies resulting from insufficient instruction (Stone, 1991). For example, the National Association for the Education of Young Children (NAEYC) "Position Statement on Developmentally Appropriate Practice in the Primary Grades" declares:

> Compelling evidence exists asserting that over-emphasis on mastery of narrowly defined reading and arithmetic skills and excessive drill and practice of skills that have been mastered

threaten children's dispositions to use the skills they have acquired. [Bredekamp, 1988, p. 68]

Similar cautions are found throughout a Professional Library publication of the National Education Association titled *Motivation and Teaching: A Practical Guide* (Wlodkowski, 1986). Offering an eclectic mix of developmentally informed practices and ad hoc advice, the publication effectively rules out the use of either requirements or incentives:

> We often do this ["make" students learn] under the rationale that, "learning to read and write is more important than *waiting for students to learn*." [italics added] But is it?. . .
>
> "Making" a student learn appears to have severe long-range effects. [p. 15]
>
> . . . .
>
> We need to look more at the process and performance of our students and less at the more narrow and self-defeating emphasis of product or acquisition. [p. 16]

. . . .

There is significant concern that through a total reinforcement approach to learning, students will be turned into "reinforcement junkies" who must always have something extra in order to learn. There is also the very real danger that extrinsic reward systems may interfere with and decrease intrinsic motivational properties within the learning behavior itself. [p. 154]

In essence, developmentalism discourages the use of any educational methods that call for inducing student performance. Virtually all teaching strategists reject strongly aversive incentives such as threat, intimidation, and duress. Milder forms of pressure such as teacher approval and disapproval are also discouraged but not outrightly rejected. Developmentalists permit certain other forms of pressure—for example, asking students to commit to making an effort—as concessions to educational accountability and practical necessity (Wlodkowski, 1986). They similarly discourage the use of positive reinforcement because "intrinsic motivation" may be undermined (Dickinson, 1989).

Developmentalists cite the rate of suicide among Japanese youth as evidence of the dire effects of teacher insistence on academic performance. In truth, suicide rates among American youth are higher (U.S. Department of Education, 1987). Furthermore, it is no more known whether pressure to succeed in school is responsible for Japanese suicide rates than it is certain that drug abuse, alcohol abuse, and teen pregnancy are caused by the use of developmentally informed practices in American schools. Yet developmentalists rely on such evidence to suggest that the Japanese emphasis on the need for effortful study has a "dark side" (Arthur, 1990).

Whether or not Japanese educational methods are responsible for the mental health problems seen among their youth, none of the "productive" educational strategies cited by Walberg (1990) and Ellson (1986) suggest the use of inducements that are even suspected of precipitating suicide. As to the hazards of positive reinforcement, the use of artificial and extrinsic rewards with already motivated students, can reduce subsequent motivation. However, competent application of behavioral principles has always discouraged the unnecessary use of artificial and contrived contingencies. For example, contrary to Wlodkowski's apparent understanding, positive reinforcement does not involve "always" giving students "something extra." Rather, best-practice uses of positive reinforcement are scientifically informed applications of the rule "work before pleasure." Artificial and contrived contingencies are recommended only when natural contingencies cannot be enhanced and so-called intrinsic motivation is insufficient.

Developmentalist concerns about inducing student performance range from the exaggerated to the unfounded. Clearly they are misplaced with respect to the competent application of behavior principles. Contrary to that which is suggested by the developmentalist view, behavior principles are routinely employed by school psychologists and special educators. They are used because they are demonstrably effective, and they have never been known to induce any disorder when used competently.

Behavioral science, cognitive science, and trial-and-error offer valuable recommendations about how to teach, but none of these practices is likely to be adopted by educators who are preoccupied with being developmentally correct. In theory, developmentalists avoid interfering with optimal developmental processes. In practice, their inaction fails to offset the deleterious effects of naturally occurring conditions such as ineffective parents or delinquent peers—conditions John Eshleman calls the "default contingencies" (personal communication, 26 February 1993). Deprived of any effective way to induce student performance, developmentally oriented teachers are encouraged to direct their efforts not toward objectively determined academic outcomes, but toward subjective aspects of the student's experience as a learner; namely, the learning "process" (Bredekamp, 1988; Wlodkowski, 1986). Conceptually, they believe that if the teacher is actively seeking to facilitate learning, everything that can safely be done for the student is being done.

An excellent illustration of developmentalist opposition to inducing student performance can be found in an emerging conflict between the NAEYC's guidelines for developmentally appropriate practice (DAP) and the psychoeducational interventions employed in the field of early childhood special education (Carta, Schwartz, Atwater, & McConnell, 1991). The desirability of early intervention into the lives of children with disabilities is the raison d'etre for early childhood special education's existence as a professional specialty, and the conflict between its guiding philosophy and the NAEYC's DAP concept is striking.

Proponents of DAP in early intervention programs (Johnson & Johnson, 1992) have been remarkably frank about developmentally appropriate practice and its implications for educational practice. They characterize the concept as emerging less as a product of scientific and educational considerations and more as an outcome of an "overriding concern . . . to build a consensus and to advance the field of ECE [early childhood education] as a whole and to enhance the status of the profession" (p. 441). Consistent with developmentalist principles, they argued that schools and society should be less concerned with the educational and developmental progress of these children and more tolerant of their deficiencies. Clearly, in the developmentalist view, educational outcomes are secondary to concerns about the educational process.

3. The most counterproductive feature of developmentalism may be that it invites student immaturity and complacency instead of independent effort and dedication to socially valued forms of achievement. Developmentalists encourage schools to spare neither effort nor resources in fitting instruction to students while expecting little from them in return. Student inattention and apathy are met with herculean efforts to stimulate interest and enthusiasm. Deficient outcomes are countered by reducing expectations to the level of whatever the student seems willing to do. Even the practice of affording students accurate feedback about accomplishments is deemed questionable because of its purported detrimental effect on intrinsic motivation and self-esteem. The students' recurrent failure to attain even minimal achievements is accepted as lamentable but unavoidable and treated accordingly. In short, developmentalism requires only the teacher to work, not the student (Tomlinson & Cross, 1991). It is inherently an inefficient and expensive approach to instruction.

In contrast to the pattern permitted by developmentalist principles, the classic working relationship between teacher and student has been one of teacher assistance conditioned on student commitment to study. It is an arrangement in which students must do their part. They are not permitted to waste expensive time, resources, and opportunities. Critics of American public schooling correctly observe that American schools cost far more and produce far less than their foreign counterparts and that substantial increases in funding have produced meager results. Given the nature of developmentalist practices, such a state of affairs is not surprising.

Developmentalist views are not unique in their emphasis on teacher action. Environmentalist concepts such as behavior analysis presume teachers to be responsible for learning outcomes but with the clear understanding that student action is also and invariably required. Unlike developmentalists, behavior analysts regard the degree of student effort and level of performance as a function of contingency arrangements that, at least in principle, are alterable by the teacher. Using those arrangements, they attempt to induce improved student performance to the extent permitted by maturation. In contrast, developmentalists consider student effort and performance to be governed by autonomous developmental characteristics. They encourage teachers to accommodate expectations to whatever the student seems inclined to put forth and to otherwise await whatever enhancements might be produced by naturally occurring environmental conditions interacting with biologic maturation.

Behavior analysts recognize that student time and effort devoted to study and practice is indispensable to school success. It is this understanding that makes behavioral prescriptions for educational reform uniquely compatible with the views of pragmatists and of most Americans. Other educational reforms propose enhancements of the educational process or changes in prerequisite conditions, such as plans to stimulate interest, enhance creativity, improve self-esteem, build cognitive skills, relieve social and economic conditions, and so on. Behavioral proposals, however, seek to directly induce study and performance and recognize such student activity as the linchpin of improved schooling.

In addition to failing to induce study and learning, the widespread use of developmentalist practices may be creating or at least contributing to a larger cultural and social complacency about student achievement. Inadequate school performance seems to have gained a substantial degree of social acceptance, and the attainment of broadly valued levels of achievement may be eroding as a culturally recognized objective (Adler et al., 1992; DeLoughry, 1992; Lederman, 1992; Stevenson & Stigler, 1992). Instead of responding to continuing student deficiencies with alarm, teachers, parents, and the public are coming to think of academic standards as a kind of arbitrary requirement imposed at the behest of academic traditionalists and elitists (Allis, Bonfante, & Booth, 1991; Brock, 1987). Instead of reporting student accomplishments relative to recognized standards, teachers now seem to feel justified in using more flexible and forgiving standards, a practice quietly accepted by school administrative bureaucracies (Welsh, 1992). With performance judged by standards of this kind, it is not surprising that surveys of parents and students reveal a far more positive perception of school and student performance than that held by professors and employers (Harris Education Research Center, 1992).

Developmentalism's deemphasis of student effort may be contributing to other widely held attitudes. There is growing evidence that America is producing generations of citizens whose response to life's adversities is as hapless individuals victimized by insensitive economic, social, and political circumstances (Birnbaum, 1991). They believe that their lack of success implies deficiencies in the conditions that surround them rather than any deficiency in their attempts to help themselves. While the relationship of these attitudinal characteristics to school experiences is unknown, such attitudes bear a remarkable resemblance to the dependent and immature responses that might be expected from students who have experienced developmentally oriented schools. Rather than receiving encouragement to exert themselves in the face of learning challenges, students taught by developmentalist methods are expected to perform only when there is assistance, encouragement, and enthusiasm for the task at hand. Accomplishments are expected to come easily without sacrifice or boredom; and if they fail, students are taught not to be overly concerned. It may be that these students are being given an object lesson that seriously undermines the time-honored American belief in personal effort as a means to accomplishment. It would be difficult to contrive conditions less conducive to self-reliance or a work ethic.

Clearly, such an attitude was reflected in a recent survey of employers by the National Association of Manufacturers ("Survey," 1991). The survey results showed that many young people were attitudinally unprepared for responsibility in the workplace. Apparently they do not understand the reciprocity of pay for performance; that is, performance that meets competitive or organizational standards. The reason may be that they only know effort and attainment as judged by the minimal expectations set by their teachers and themselves.

The Popular Acceptance of Developmentalism

The appeal of developmentalism is buttressed by social, political, and economic factors. Public schools have tried to maintain a culturally neutral position in curricular matters, thus they are comfortable with developmentalism's deemphasis of specified performance outcomes (Ravitch, 1983). Teachers have found the concept of developmental readiness a very convenient excuse for teaching ineffectiveness; in other words, academic failure is maturational failure (Tomlinson & Cross, 1991). Parents and students have found comfort in having academic failure explained by developmental shortcomings rather than inattention to school work (Wang, Reynolds, & Walberg, 1987). The testing/diagnosis/child-labeling industry to which failing students are referred has a vested interest in the idea that student performance deficiencies are caused by developmental inadequacies, deficiencies in aptitude, and other factors beyond the control of schools, teachers, and parents. As a licensed educational psychologist and school psychologist, I see legions of psychologists, physicians, social workers, and counselors who make a living by blaming student failure on suitably remote causes. Significantly, those who implicate more familiar factors (e.g., lack of serious attention to homework) often find their advice is less often sought and even less often enthusiastically received (Vargas, Spangler, Stone, & Wishon, 1990).

Beyond its value to vested interests, developmentally informed teaching appeals to certain well-respected American values. It promises to make learning more spontaneous, enjoyable, and successful, and it requires less student exertion in the bargain. It also promises to be efficient if one does not consider the time and effort lost in groping for signs of student readiness:

> Individuals are ready to learn something when they have matured enough to learn it efficiently; when they have acquired the skills, knowledge, and strengths prerequisite to learning it; and when they are sufficiently motivated. When students have reached such a state of readiness, the teacher's job is relatively easy; when they have not, the teacher's job is more difficult and sometimes absolutely impossible. [Clark & Starr, 1991, p. 37]

Theoretically, spontaneous, or intrinsically motivated, learning would lessen the need for teachers to be taskmasters (Wlodkowski, 1986). Presumably, intrinsically motivated students are inclined to study independently, thus they would require less teacher time and achieve better outcomes. Assuming that developmentally emergent motivation is sufficient to propel student performance, expanded use of developmentally informed teaching would seem to offer an ideal means of educational reform; that is, reform that produces better results with less time, money, and effort.

The great popularity of developmentalism's previous incarnation—progressive education—was due in considerable part to its contrast with the demanding, unpleasant "lockstep" recitation methods that dominated 19th-century schools. Progressive education promised pleasant, higher-quality learning—learning that would reach higher levels of "social, cultural and intellectual meaning" (Ravitch, 1983, p. 47). The prospect of classrooms filled with independent, enthusiastic learners instead of passive, resistant conscripts appealed to both teachers and parents, especially those who had themselves endured "the rule of the hickory stick." Today, the idea that a developmentally informed teaching could engender similar benefits and do so in the face of apparent social, economic, and educational decline is quite appealing.

Progressive education's concept of natural spontaneous learning made sense from a personal intuitive standpoint. Are not children naturally inclined toward curiosity and discovery, and has not everyone experienced enjoyable and enthusiastic learning when they are really interested? If the nature of the child could be better understood and if conditions conducive to natural interest could be better approximated in classrooms, could schooling be vastly improved? Few questioned whether it would be possible for teachers to consistently inspire the required student interest (i.e., the interest of most students, in most subjects, most of the time), and fewer still questioned whether interest in learning alone would be sufficient to sustain the performance of students immersed in a world of other attractions. Thus a set of commonsense observations and suppositions survived unchallenged as the popularly understood bases for the "project method," the "child-centered school," "life adjustment education," and other mainstays of progressive

education. To doubt their efficacy was to doubt the essential goodness of human nature (Tenenbaum, 1951).

Developmentalist views of teaching and learning are no less premised on a faith in the wholesome powers of human nature, and here again the premises have gone more or less unchallenged. Bigge and Hunt (1962) identified developmentalism's philosophic origins in Rousseau's romantic naturalism and Hegel's concept of growth as unfoldment. It is a faith not without basis in theory or credible evidence. Without question, the ability to acquire adaptive behavior from the naturally occurring environment has been "selected for" in the human species, and such "natural learning" is a very significant factor in the increased competence children exhibit as they "grow up." However, whether schools that provide mass public education can rely on natural abilities alone (i.e., phylogenetically determined abilities enhanced by naturally occurring ontogenetic histories) is another issue.

Public schools must not only educate, they must do so at a rate commensurate with social, cultural, and economic requirements, and they must succeed with many children whose naturally occurring ontogenetic histories are known to be deficient or detrimental. Given that extensive efforts to alter the causative social and economic conditions have proven insufficient, greater reliance on artificial methods of overcoming their adverse effects will be required for the foreseeable future. Consistent with this observation, industrial and technological societies worldwide are increasingly reliant on formal education and seem to select this institutional arrangement. Societies with greater degrees of formal education seem to be providing greater health and prosperity for their members.

Even if developmentally informed instruction will work under optimal societal conditions, there remain significant practical and economic problems. The chief difficulty is that there is no certain means of matching experiences with emergent abilities and inclinations or scheduling their availability. The only time teachers can be sure of adequate readiness is when they actually observe learning taking place (Bigge & Hunt, 1962). Thus affording the right opportunities at the right time can present an imposing logistical problem. From the learner's standpoint, even spontaneously motivated learning requires time and effort, which usually implies less time and energy for other, perhaps more attractive or more important, activities. From the standpoint of teachers, schools, and society, when and how often an individual experiences the necessary confluence of conditions and where these episodes of readiness will fall with respect to the availability of teachers, schools, and other resources is problematic. Also there is the practical question of economic support for the learner while society awaits the emergence of a natural thirst for scholastic achievement. In fact, many individuals become highly motivated only when they encounter the demands of college or a job; but at that point in their lives, schools, teachers, parental support, and freedom from economic responsibilities are not as likely to be available. Others rarely, if ever, seem to experience "teachable moments."

The Developmentalist Ideal as a Benchmark

Widespread acceptance of developmentalist concepts has established an uncommon, precarious experience as the benchmark against which teachers judge the quality of proposed teaching methods. Developmentalists acknowledge that learning can be artificially induced by methods that involve teacher insistence, student commitment, and anguish about outcomes. "Good" teaching (i.e., developmentally informed teaching), however, produces learning in ways that are stimulating yet minimally obtrusive, challenging yet requiring only comfortable levels of exertion. In essence, good teaching teaches the way romanticists from Rousseau to James and Dewey to the present have imagined that everyday experience teaches (Bigge & Hunt, 1962).

Teachers implicitly subscribe to the developmentalist ideal when they avoid empirically validated teaching methods in favor of continual attempts to optimize the match of instruction with student attributes. Good teaching, they believe, involves creativity, innovation, and experimentation in response to differences and changes in student readiness. The fact of student differences precludes an optimal match by any one method, and the danger of intervention requires all innovations to be minimally obtrusive.

Because developmental attributes are unobservable and learning outcomes are not immediately evident, teachers arrange activities that are, first and foremost, attractive to and well received by students. If students are unreceptive to an innovation, the developmentally sensitive teacher experiments with another approach or alters the expectation for student response. In theory they optimize learning, in practice they optimize student satisfaction. Persisting with an activity that is not well received is not only deemed ineffective, it threatens student curiosity, creativity, and self-esteem. In essence, teachers informed by developmental theory fail to employ "what works" because they are preoccupied with finding something that better fits the developmentalist ideal.

In spite of failure to meet cultural and economic requirements for learning, developmentally informed teachers continue to believe that learning is best produced by instruction working in harmony with nature. They believe that developmentally appropriate teaching cannot be expected to produce results on any kind of externally imposed schedule, so they see their sporadic successes as vindication and their failures as inevitable and they never seriously question their strategy. Theirs is an especially unfortunate criterion for validation of practice because, in truth, almost any method of teaching might be expected to work occasionally.

Given the developmentalist ideal, alternative methods of instruction, even ones that have well-demonstrated effectiveness (Walberg, 1990, 1992), are often questioned and rejected. Consistently effective instruction inevitably requires students to devote necessary levels of time and effort to study and other academic tasks regardless of naturally occurring propensities or competing attractions (Tomlinson & Cross, 1991). All effective methods explicitly or implicitly require student efforts to be made within the time frames loosely dictated by schedules and by the availability of resources, and not simply when the individual is ready. All effective methods are in one manner or another intrusive in that they require student action to somehow be reliably produced by teaching.

Developmentalists hold that accomplishments produced by intrusive methods are mere performances rather than meaningful learning (Clark & Starr, 1991). Implicitly, they challenge proponents of nondevelopmentalist views to prove otherwise. What goes unquestioned in their critique is whether learning produced by developmentally appropriate instruction is anything other than mere performance. In truth, this question is unanswerable because no psychological or educational perspective can experimentally demonstrate a link between observed performance and the underlying mental attributes and events that developmentalists believe characterize "true" learning. The only evidence of academic learning that can be observed by any present-day investigation is "mere performance."

Not incidentally, developmentalism and its philosophic predecessors have enjoyed enduring popularity, in part because the developmental hypothesis cannot be falsified. Rather, the failure of developmentally appropriate practice to engender expected results is always subject to an escape clause: The expected performance did not occur because of unobservable deficiencies in development or life circumstances. It is precisely because teachers are never certain whether deficient performance is due to inadequate readiness, poor instruction, or simply a poor match between the two that they are encouraged to sympathetically accept or excuse student failure and to lower expectations instead.

Developmentalists are not in favor of any teaching practices that call for induction of change in classroom performance. In particular, they have subjected behavior-analytic practices to virtual damnation. Behavior analysts have tried to defend their views by arguing that they can produce *better* educational outcomes using methods that are far more humane and effective than those teachers actually use. Of course, these arguments fall on deaf ears because behavioral approaches conflict at too many points with the developmentalist ideal. Behavioral approaches can produce educational outcomes in a demonstrably consistent way, but they cannot do so without inducement of consistent student effort. Neither can they succeed without well-informed teachers who are able to structure educational experiences, arrange contingencies, and monitor student performance. Thus they require

an unaccustomed form of teacher effort. Although developmentalists acknowledge behavioral methods such as positive reinforcement as more humane than the "lockstep" recitation fought by Dewey, even positive reinforcement requires certain "establishing operations" (i.e., preconditions) and denial of student desires (developmentalists would say "needs") until performance criteria are met. The greatest differences, however, are that behavioral approaches seek to induce student performance; they are considered invasive of the student's naturally occurring environment, and they are believed to harm intrinsic motivation (Dickinson, 1989).

Even in the matter of educational objectives, behavioral views differ from developmental ones. Behavior analysis contemplates the attainment of socially valued levels of scholastic performance. Developmentalism, in contrast, expects idiosyncratic outcomes such as those sought by multiculturalists. In fact, idiosyncratic outcomes can be considered socially valued when they are thought of as the product of multicultural experiences—a consideration that may play a role in multiculturalism's surging popularity within the educational establishment. Yet there may be another reason for multicultural education's evident growth: multicultural outcomes tend to confound the expectations for quality implicit in most educational accountability schemes.

Given this formidable array of differences, it is not surprising that behavioral approaches have not found their way into the mainstream of educational methods even when disguised by nonbehavioral names and concepts. Behavioral methods not only differ from the developmental ideal, they suggest a different set of educational priorities.

Shorn of its equivocal concessions to pressures for educational accountability, developmentalist doctrine can be seen as strikingly at odds with publicly supported educational aims. If the educational outcomes produced by developmentalist methods seem out of touch with the expectations of the American public, developmentalists say that public opinion must change:

• The expectation that American students can attain the academic performance levels exhibited by students in other countries is unrealistic, unfair, and contrary to developmental science's understanding of learning. Foreign schools are selective and draw on more culturally homogeneous populations.

- Uniformly high achievement in American schools will require extensive prerequisite change in the social and economic conditions that impact developmental readiness. In the meantime, marginal improvements can be made by better equipping schools to facilitate individual differences and needs. Lowering pupil-teacher ratios is the primary means to this end.

- As American society becomes more culturally, racially, and ethnically diverse, the need to individualize will only become greater. Under these circumstances, the expectation that schools and teachers be held accountable for specific educational outcomes, much less outcomes of uniform academic quality (i.e., world-class outcomes), is entirely inappropriate.

Most school reforms have not been well accepted by teachers, because neither the proposed reforms nor their expected outcomes are compatible with the developmentalist ideal. In truth, no truly satisfactory reforms will be found so long as teachers implicitly compare field-tested reform proposals to the myth envisioned by developmentalists—a myth recognized by B. F. Skinner (1973) in his analysis of Rousseau's *Emile*. Until the developmentalist ideal is recognized for what it is, implementing workable reforms in the real world of publicly funded mass education will continue to be an exercise in exasperation for everyone involved.

Recommendations

In the interest of turning the educational establishment from its infatuation with developmentalism, I suggest the following steps be taken by behavior analysts individually and by behaviorally oriented organizations such as the Association for Behavior Analysis.

1. *Apprise the parties who are concerned with educational reform of developmentalism's counterproductive implications: (a) its record of failure and its similarity to the failed doctrine of progressive education, (b) its emphasis on assumed student limitations, (c) its over-emphasis of the dangers of intervention, and (d) its*

tendency to foster student and teacher complacency about achievement.

Enhanced public awareness of these impediments may pay great dividends. There is a very large audience concerned with the nation's educational deficiencies. They have no clear fix on the cause, and they are running out of money to throw at the problem. Attention to developmentalism can make it clear that a central problem in implementing effective educational reform is the educational establishment's predictable comfort with a new version of "progressive education."

Developmentalism is a doctrine that questions both the need and the desirability of requiring young people to work hard at their studies. Parents, teachers, and the taxpaying public need to know that a primary reason schools in other countries are more successful and less costly is that students are expected to do their part in learning. Developmentalist concerns about academic performance requirements having an adverse impact on the personal development, mental health, and other facets of student well-being are scientifically unwarranted generalizations drawn from limited and equivocal findings. Certainly there is no credible evidence that the behavioral interventions employed and recommended by school psychologists and special educators are in any way harmful, much less causative of mental health problems.

A sound case can be made that the limitations on human potential posed by immaturity, lack of aptitude, disabilities, and handicaps have been vastly exaggerated. In many cases, they serve as nothing more than excuses for educational and parental ineffectiveness. Those who focus on such limitations overlook countless cases of children who overcame limitations with the help of dedicated parents and teachers. Special education teachers have been especially effective in demonstrating what can be done even in the most challenging cases. Clearly the greater danger to American children today is failure to achieve their potential as a result of interventions that are far too timid.

In particular, the corporate and philanthropic community should be alerted, because many such groups often seem to be unwitting advocates of the very developmentalist concepts that undermine their goals.

For example, an organization as notable for its advocacy of reform as the Business Roundtable rightly calls for comprehensive preschool programs. Yet the statement detailing this objective explicitly stipulates that such programs be "developmentally appropriate." The same term is found in the America 2000 objectives for school readiness (U.S. Department of Education, 1991). In the absence of competent educational practice, the stipulation of developmental appropriateness may legitimately insulate some children from adverse social pressures, but it does so at the expense of failing to enhance the potential had by others whose talents would flourish with greater stimulation.

The phrase *developmentally appropriate instruction* reflects the recommendations of the National Association for the Education of Young Children, an organization strongly committed to developmentalist teaching practices for children aged 5 through 8. The NAEYC has issued position papers that explicitly reflect the developmentalist thinking of David Elkind (1981), the well-known Piagetian scholar (*The Hurried Child*) and former NAEYC president. Not incidentally, their position papers and curriculum guides clearly oppose requirements, expectations, and inducements of any kind. For example, the following practices are termed "developmentally inappropriate":

> Teachers attempt to motivate children through the use of external rewards and punishments. The teacher's role is to correct errors and make sure the child knows the right answer in all subject areas. Teachers reward children for correct answers with stickers or privileges, praise them in front of the group, and hold them up as examples. [p. 76]

. . . .

> Teachers try to motivate children by giving numerical (85%) or letter grades, stickers, gold stars on charts, candy, or privileges such as extra minutes of recess. [Bredekamp, 1988, p. 77]

The same concern applies to developmentalist recommendations coming from state departments of education and other regulatory agencies. For example, in spite of extensive evidence that student self-esteem is a product, not a cause, of school achievement (Scheirer & Kraut, 1979), the Tennessee State Department of Education continues to promote programs that attempt to boost school achievement by enhancing student self-esteem. In other words, both the achievement and the self-esteem of Tennessee's students would be better served by focusing on learning and not on the developmentally salient matter of self-esteem.

2. *Recognize that just as managers, coaches, and others who are untrained in any particular methodology can get young people to learn, educators employing a variety of concepts may teach successfully. Behavior analysts should collaborate with all educators who seek to induce improved student academic performance. Such methods might be termed* educationally appropriate *rather than* developmentally appropriate.

In a synthesis of over 8,000 studies, Walberg (1992) identified nine factors that produce potent, consistent, and widely generalizable learning effects. Of the factors that were directly alterable at the classroom level, "Skinnerian reinforcement and acknowledgment of correct performance" produced the largest overall effect. In a similar article published in *Phi Delta Kappan*, Walberg (1990) asserted that ". . . the effects of cues, engagement, reinforcement and corrective feedback on student learning are enormous. The research demonstrating these effects has been unusually rigorous and well controlled" (p. 471). In a review also published in the same journal, Douglas Ellson (1986) cited 75 "research studies—largely ignored by school and university establishments—that report great differences in one or more quantitative indices of teaching productivity. . . ." (p. 111). Among those mentioned prominently and favorably were programmed learning, programmed teaching (e.g., Direct Instruction), performance-based instruction, and Personalized System of Instruction—methods all derived from applied behavior analysis.

Clearly, there are researchers and educational practitioners who are concerned with directly stimulating changes in student performance and are not philosophically hostile toward behavioral methods. Significantly, they too lament the fact that schools know about effective methods but do not use them (Walberg, 1992). Behavior analysts need to join with them in calling for the use of teaching methods and curricula that are in keeping with academically valued educational objectives, not the assumed developmental characteristics of students. The term *educationally appropriate* might be used to distinguish teaching that matches methods and curriculum to the student with the aim of inducing, not merely permitting, achievement.

A willingness to collaborate with nondevelopmentalist colleagues in research and school reform proposals, to convene with them in professional associations (such as the National Association of School Psychologists), and to join them in addressing developmentalism would benefit all concerned. The credibility and exposure of the collaborating parties would be enhanced, and the public interest would be served. Behavior analysts today are sufficiently well established to maintain their independent identity, and the rapprochement of behavioral scientists in the national interest could publicly underline the urgency of rethinking educational reform.

3. *All behavioral scientists and helping professionals who are concerned with educational reform need to give far more public attention to the potential that students have to benefit themselves and the nation by "being the best they can be." At the same time, less attention should be accorded the view that students are helpless victims of poor teaching, poor schools, and an uncaring society.*

Behavior analysts obviously hold a deterministic view of human behavior, yet they recognize better than virtually any of the players in educational reform that nothing can be accomplished without the students' active participation. Educators tend to interpret Skinner's concept of environmental determinism in terms of a simplistic stimulus-response model. Instead it is a selectionist view in which environment selects for and against behaviors that are products of phylogenetic and ontogenetic history (Johnson & Layng, 1992; Vargas, 1991). The behavioral concept of determinism is in no way opposed to the recognition of socially occasioned and spontaneously emergent verbal and written expressions as potent influences on behavior (i.e., it envisions "self-determined" behavior). Skinner argued for the necessity of abandoning the concepts of freedom and dignity, but he was addressing the need to promote public understanding of social and cultural contingencies as shapers of behavior. Ever the empiricist, however, he would agree that cultural enshrinement of freedom, dignity, personal responsibility, and a work ethic may be vital to national survival in an economically competitive world.

In our enthusiasm to build teacher repertoires, behavior analysts tend to overlook the point that schooling can succeed without good or energetic teaching, but it cannot overcome a lack of time and effort devoted to study. A public call for students to work hard at their studies would be a culturally acceptable and cost-effective way of prompting more and better learning. Perhaps as important, such a call would crystallize the recognition that the only reforms that can work are those that ensure change in the time and effort students devote to study and practice.

Concerned parents, teachers, and members of the general public would find the message direct and comprehensible. With an explicit public consensus, teachers would be empowered to respond more effectively to insufficient student effort. Their mission would be greatly clarified. Developmentalist concerns would be thought of more as hurdles to be overcome by hard work rather than as insurmountable deficiencies. Supportive public policies and their relevant contingencies would have a far greater likelihood of public acceptance. For example, under such conditions, a policy of conditioning youth driving privileges and work permits on scholastic standing could be employed extensively. Not incidentally, behavioral and other approaches known to produce results would be publicly distinguished as part of the solution rather than as part of the problem.

As an important incidental benefit, those who work with students would be accorded the recognition they deserve. The parent and teacher efforts that ensure student performance also depend on socially controlled incentives. Those who call for greater parental involvement sometimes forget that inducing student effort can be challenging. Even a scientifically informed practice such as positive reinforcement requires establishing operations, performance monitoring, and steadfast contingency arrangements.

A significant impact is possible. American youth may be self-indulgent and intellectually unengaged, but they are competitive and patriotic. Watching and participating in sports has taught them well. The nation's reaction to Desert Storm indicates the kind of public response that could be aroused if the present loss of jobs and living standards were more explicitly and emphatically linked to the present and future international economic competition.

In any case, we cannot continue to talk as if the educational system and society are exclusively to blame for the lack of student attainment and expect students to heed the message that they need to work much harder. Local, state, and national leaders as well as responsible elements of the private sector need to appeal directly and emphatically to the youth of America. The plain and honest message is that we are about to lose the battle for America's future, almost without a fight. If our fortunes are to be reversed, American youth are going to have to give their best effort. The truth is that their country cannot make it without them.

From a public leadership standpoint, I believe that such a message would be well received by young people especially if it were addressed directly to them. I believe they would be honored and empowered by being recognized for their vital role. John F. Kennedy said; "Ask not what your country can do for you, ask what you can do for your country," and the youth of America responded. A call for young people to work hard in school could have a similar effect. Certainly, it is consistent with President Clinton's call for "sacrifice" in the public interest. Such a message would neither preempt honor as does the student-as-victim-in-need-of-help approach, nor would it preclude honor as does a blame-and-shame, student-as-irresponsible-and-in-need-of-redemption approach.

Critics might argue that those who call for student effort want to "blame the victim" (Tomlinson & Cross, 1991). However, the popular alternative of blaming everyone *but* the victim is fallacious and counterproductive. At the very least, students who fail to make their best effort are guilty of "contributory negligence." In any case, I doubt that such a pessimistic assessment of our young people and their ability to help their country would be very well received by the youth themselves. Surely the public assertion that young Americans are not helpless and that their country needs them is a powerful and constructive message. Rather I would expect that public opinion

might turn away from growing fatalism about schools to a belief that much can be accomplished without more bureaucracy and taxes.

In truth, schools are not going to improve until most students make a significantly greater effort to study, and the nation cannot wait until all the factors that might limit such an effort are removed from their lives. The sooner the educational establishment faces this fact, the sooner the schools will be on the road to recovery. Quality learning inevitably requires student time, effort, and commitment. These contributions to the learning process are rarely without sacrifice or cost. In other words, with learning as with so many things in life, it can be said: *No pain, no gain*.

Many teachers and parents understand this fact of life, but they are reluctant to buck the tide of developmentalism. They need to be assured that young people around the world are called on to make sacrifices as a matter of family and civic duty. They need to be assured that young people are capable of responding, and that they will be better for their efforts. Equally as important, students need public recognition and credit for their efforts if they are to devote time to schoolwork rather than more attractive pursuits. Behavior analysts and other members of the professional and academic community would do a great service by publicizing America's need for students to begin helping their country now.

References

ADLER, J., Wingert, P., Wright, L., Houston, P., Manley, H., & Cohen, A. D. (1992). Hey, I'm terrific. *Newsweek*, February 17, pp. 46–51.

ALEXANDER, R., Rose, J., & Woodhead, C. (1992). *Curricular organization and classroom practice in primary schools, a discussion paper*. London (SW1P 3BT) Department of Education and Science.

ALLIS, S., Bonfante, J., & Booth, C. (1991). Whose America? *Time*, July 8, pp. 12–17.

ARTHUR, L. (1990). *Do or die: Educational pressure and teenage suicide in Japan*. Paper presented at the annual meeting of the American Reading Forum. ERIC Document Reproduction Service No. ED 332–906.

BARRETT, B., Beck, R., Binder, C., Cook, D., Engelmann, S., Greer, R., Kyrklund, S., Johnson, K., Maloney, M., McCorkle, N., Vargas, J., & Watkins, C. (1991). The right to effective education. *Behavior Analyst, 14*(1), 79–82.

BENNETT, W. J. (1992). *The modern red schoolhouse. A project of the Hudson Institute and the New American Schools Development Corporation.* Indianapolis: Hudson Institute.

BIGGE, M. L., & Hunt, M. P. (1962). *Psychological foundations of education: An introduction to human development and learning.* New York: Harper & Row.

BINDER, C., & Watkins, C. L. (1989). Promoting effective instructional methods: Solutions to America's educational crisis. *Future Choices, 1*(3) 33–39.

BIRNBAUM, J. (1991). Crybabies: Eternal victims. *Time,* August 12, pp. 16–18.

BREDEKAMP, S. (1988). NAEYC position statement on developmentally appropriate practice in the primary grades, serving 5 through 8 year-olds. *Young Children,* January, pp. 64–84.

BROCK, D. (1987). A philosopher hurls down a stinging moral gauntlet. *Insight,* May 11, pp. 10–12.

CARTA, J. J., Schwartz, I. S., Atwater, J. B., & McConnell, S. R. (1991). Developmentally appropriate practice: Appraising its usefulness for young children with disabilities. *Topics in Early Childhood Special Education, 11*(1), 1–20.

CLARK, L. H., & Starr, I. S. (1991). *Secondary and middle school teaching methods.* 6th ed. New York: Macmillan.

DARLING-Hammond, L., Griffin, G., & Wise, A. (1992). *Excellence in teacher education: Helping teachers develop learner-centered schools.* Washington, DC: National Education Association.

DELOUGHRY, T. (1992). Top U.S. higher-education official wants colleges to raise sights. *Chronicle of Higher Education,* p. A28.

DEWEY, J. (1902). *The child and the curriculum.* Chicago: University of Chicago Press.

DEWEY, J. (1963). *Experience and education.* New York: Collier Books.

DICKINSON, A. (1989). The detrimental effects of extrinsic reinforcement on "intrinsic motivation." *Behavior Analyst, 12*(1), 1–15.

THE Edison Project. (1992). Knoxville, TN: Whittle Communications.

EDUCATION and cultural exchange opportunities. (1986). Washington, DC: U.S. Department of State, Bureau of Cultural Affairs.

EDUCATION Improvement Act of 1992, TN Code Ann. Titles 8 and 49 (1992).

ELKIND, D. (1981). *The hurried child.* Reading, MA: Addison-Wesley.

ELLSON, D. (1986). Improving productivity in teaching. *Phi Delta Kappan, 67*(2), 111–124.

HARRIS Education Research Center (1992). *An assessment of American education.* New York: Committee for Economic Development.

HEYNEMANN, S. P. (1990). Education in the world market. *American School Board Journal, 177*(3), 28–30.

JOHNSON, J. E., & Johnson, K. M. (1992). Clarifying the developmental perspective in response to Carta, Schwartz, Atwater and McConnell. *Topics in Early Childhood Special Education, 12*(4), 439–457.

JOHNSON, K. R., & Layng, T. V. J. (1992). Breaking the structuralist barrier: Literacy and numeracy with fluency. *American Psychologist, 47*(11), 1475–1490.

KENTUCKY Education Reform Act of 1990, KRS }} 156.010 (1990).

KRAMER, R. (1991). *The ed school follies, the miseducation of America's teachers.* New York: Free Press.

LEDERMAN, D. (1992). Arthur Ashe, defender of black athletes, urges colleges to help them meet more-stringent academic standards. *Chronicle of Higher Education,* February 12, pp. A37, A40.

NATIONAL Association for the Education of Young Children. (1991). *Guidelines for appropriate curriculum content and assessment, position statement of NAEYC and NACFS/SDE.* Washington, DC: NAEYC.

NEW American Schools Development Corporation. (1991). *Designs for a new generation of American schools, request for proposals.* Washington, DC: NASDC.

NEW American Schools Development Corporation. (1992). *NASDC facts.* Washington, DC: NASDC.

NOT everyone plays Madeline Hunter's game. (1991). *TEA News, 23*(3), 14.

POPHAM, W. J. (1981). *Modern Educational Measurement.* Englewood Cliffs, NJ: Prentice-Hall.

PROPER, E. C., & St. Pierre, R. G. (1980). *A search for potential new follow through approaches: Executive summary.* Cambridge, MA: Abt Associates.

RAVITCH, D. (1983) *The troubled crusade: American education 1945–1980.* New York: Harper-Collins.

RESCHLY, D., & Sabers, D. (1974). Open education: Have we been here before? *Phi Delta Kappan, 55*(10), 675–677.

SAYLOR, J. G., & Alexander, W. M. (1966). *Curriculum planning for modern schools.* New York: Holt, Rinehart & Winston.

SCHEIRER, M. A., & Kraut, R. E. (1979). Increasing educational achievement via self-concept change. *Review of Educational Research, 49*(1), 131–150.

SKINNER, B. F. (1973). The free and happy student. *Phi Delta Kappan, 55*(1), 13–16.

SPRINTHALL, N. A., & Sprinthall, R. C. (1987). *Educational psychology: A developmental approach.* 4th ed. New York: Random House.

STEVENSON, H. W., & Stigler, J. W. (1992). *The learning gap.* New York: Summit Books.

STONE, J. E. (1991). Developmentalism: A standing impediment to the design of the "New American School." *Network News & Views, 10*(12), 1–3.

SURVEY: Fewer skilled workers. (1991). *Johnson City Press,* December 10, p. 14.

TENENBAUM, S. (1951). *William Heard Kilpatrick: Trail blazer in education.* New York: Harper & Bros.

TOMLINSON, T. M., & Cross, C. T. (1991). Student effort: The key to higher standards. *Educational Leadership, 49*(1) 69–73.

U.S. Department of Education. (1987). *Japanese education today.* Washington, DC: U.S. Government Printing Office.

U.S. Department of Education. (1991). *America 2000, an education strategy.* Rev. ed. Washington, DC: U.S. Department of Education.

VARGAS, E. A. (1991). Behaviorology: Its paradigm. In I. Waris (Ed.), *Human behavior in today's world* (pp. 139–147). New York: Praeger.

VARGAS, E., Spangler, R., Stone, J., & Wishon, P. (1990). *Behaviorists in non-behavioral places: Practicing a discipline without a profession*. Submitted for publication.

WALBERG, H. J. (1990). Productive teaching and instruction: Assessing the knowledge base. *Phi Delta Kappan, 71*(6), 470–478.

WALBERG, H. J. (1992). The knowledge base for educational productivity. *International Journal of Educational Reform, 1*(1), 1–10.

WANG, M. C., Reynolds, M. C., & Walberg, H. J. (1987). *Handbook of special education*. New York: Pergamon.

WATKINS, C. L. (1988). Project Follow Through: A story of the identification and neglect of effective instruction. *Youth Policy, 10*(7), 7–11.

WELSH, P. (1992). It takes two to tango. *American Educator, 16*(1), 18–23, 46.

WLODKOWSKI, R. J. (1986). *Motivation and teaching: A practical guide*. Washington, DC: National Education Association.

PART 3

Early Childhood Intervention

Chapter 7
Social Context, Social Validity, and
Program Outcome in Early Intervention
    Scott R. McConnell

Chapter 8
Contextualism and Applied Behavior Analysis:
Implications for Early Childhood Education for
Children with Disabilities
    Samuel L. Odom, Thomas G. Haring

Chapter 9
Communicative Interventions: The Challenges
of Across-the-Day Implementation
    Howard Goldstein, Louise Kaczmarek,
    Nancy Hepting

Chapter 10
Helping Preschoolers from Low-Income
Backgrounds Make Substantial Progress in
Reading Through Direct Instruction
    Paul Weisberg

Chapter 11
Children Prenatally Exposed to Alcohol and
Cocaine: Behavioral Solutions
    Vikki F. Howard, Betty F. Williams,
    Timothy F. McLaughlin

CHAPTER 7

Social Context, Social Validity, and Program Outcome in Early Intervention

Scott R. McConnell

Many issues confront those of us who are interested in applied behavior analysis, the tenets of radical behaviorism, and their application to the practical problems of early intervention. Interestingly, the development of these two somewhat distinct human service disciplines—applied behavior analysis and early intervention—have followed parallel and complementary paths. Over the last 30 years, applied behavior analysis has evolved from a small, relatively focused set of procedures demonstrating the direct application of principles that were developed under the auspices of experimental behavioral analyses (often of nonhuman subjects) to a rich, varied discipline encompassing many different aspects of human behavior. During this same period, the early intervention field has grown from initial demonstrations of the importance of early stimulation on the development of language and cognitive skills (Hunt, 1961) to the development of programs for children who have developmental and other disabilities (Odom & Karnes, 1988) and who are growing up in poverty (Farran, 1990). Today, early intervention is a comprehensive set of service delivery systems designed and implemented to increase the likelihood that all children—particularly those at risk due to poverty, disability, or culture—acquire basic skills or competencies during their preschool years.

This chapter addresses current developments in the area of overlap between applied behavior analysis and early intervention. In particular, some of the challenges that are confronting us as early interventionists are discussed, along with the ways in which behavior analytic approaches may help address these challenges.

A Brief Definition of Early Intervention

In the United States today, early intervention can be defined as a loosely structured confederation of publicly and privately funded home- and classroom-based efforts that provide (1) compensatory or preventive services for children who are assumed to be at risk for learning and behavior problems later in life, particularly during the elementary school years, and (2) remedial services for problems or deficits already encountered. Typically, early intervention services are provided to children who have developmental or other disabilities and who are at risk for disabilities due to poverty, homelessness, native language, parenting or caregiving experiences, or other known and unknown factors.

Two federally mandated programs account for many of the children enrolled in programs meeting

75

this definition. Head Start was created in the 1960s to promote school success by providing early educational and related services to children from low-income homes. Next, the Individuals with Disabilities Education Act required that preschool children with disabilities receive special education and related services, contingent on diagnosis of developmental delay or disability (somewhat like the diagnostic criteria used for many older students in special education). A host of other early intervention programs also exist, from local efforts supported by nonprofit organizations to statewide efforts for particular groups of children.

How Are Early Intervention and Applied Behavior Analysis Related?

There has been a substantial overlap in the development of applied behavior analysis and early intervention. From the perspective of applied behavior analysis, some of the earliest demonstrations of successful application of social attention as a reinforcer for human behavior were conducted with preschool children (Allen et al., 1964). Additionally, much of the early work in several "basic" behavioral interventions—such as incidental teaching (Hart & Risley, 1975), correspondence training (Rogers-Warren & Baer, 1976), social interaction skill training (Strain & Timm, 1974), peer-mediated behavior change (Strain, 1981), and overall behavior management—began with research conducted in early intervention programs. In this way, early intervention has contributed directly to the development and evolution of applied behavior analysis.

So too has applied behavior analysis contributed to the development of early intervention programs. Perhaps not too surprisingly, many of these basic behavioral interventions also serve as fundamental procedures in early intervention programs. Behavior-analytic procedures also contributed substantially to the development of other fundamental aspects of early intervention, including environmental or classroom organization (Goetz, 1982; LeLaurin & Risley, 1972), instructional interaction (Wolery & Brookfield-Norman, 1988), social integration (Odom, McConnell, & McEvoy, 1992), and language intervention (Warren & Kaiser, 1988). Indeed, from one vantage point,

there is a great deal of "good" and "important" applied behavior-analytic work going on in early intervention, and some of the leading researchers, policy makers, and program developers are from the applied behavior-analytic perspective.

However, applied behavior analysis in early intervention seems to be at a crossroads; events of the past few years, and the next few, are likely to have a large impact on the ongoing interaction between these two disciplines. On the one hand, this is a period of expansion in early intervention, and with this expansion comes the real possibility of increased impact of applied behavior analysis. In the past few years, the federal government has enacted legislation that extends the special education mandate to all children with disabilities from their third birthday and provides additional incentives to serve these children from birth (Public Law 99-457). Additionally, the federal government has greatly increased the amount of money available for Head Start. Many states and local governments are not only implementing these federal mandates but are also considering (and in some cases adopting) expanded educational and related services for children considered at risk for learning and behavior problems. Taken together, the numbers of children receiving early intervention services, and perhaps the array of service options provided to these children and their families, will become a major educational enterprise in the coming years. With this expansion, and with the central position of applied behavior analysis and applied behavior analysts in the early intervention field, one could expect increased involvement (and perhaps expanded impact) for our field in the design, evaluation, and provision of services for young children.

On the other hand, however, many early interventionists (particularly, those with less of a "behavioral" perspective) are questioning the purposes and procedures of early intervention (especially behavioral procedures) and exerting substantial social control to support some practices and limit others. This movement is perhaps best characterized by the operationalization of "developmentally appropriate practice" or DAP, a set of guidelines for what preschoolers should do and how preschool programs should help them do it.

These guidelines were originally articulated by the National Association for the Education of Young Children, or NAEYC (Bredekamp, 1987), as a distillation of theoretical and empirical research on child development. Their purpose is to help early intervention program staff members and consumers (1) select or monitor the development of age-appropriate competencies in various developmental domains (e.g., social, cognitive, communication), and (2) plan and implement programs that support the development of these competencies and build on intervention strategies tailored to the identified, idiosyncratic characteristics of children of different ages or developmental levels.

Whether intended or not, NAEYC's guidelines occurred simultaneously with increased attention in the early intervention community to the targets of our intervention programs and to the ways in which we program for the acquisition of these targets. Some researchers (e.g., Elkind, 1981) have argued that we should deemphasize the acquisition of behavior-specific "skills" for young children and instead emphasize the development of more general competencies and approaches to learning. A corollary of this position has been an active diminishment in the importance of the identification, evaluation, and teaching of "preacademic" skills such as number recognition, writing, and early reading. Elkind (1981) and others have suggested that intervention for these skills too early in a child's life leads to incomplete learning, produces unnecessary stress, and fails to produce better long-term outcomes.

Building on these positions, other researchers have argued that early intervention programs must not be "structured" by teachers but must encourage and support children's active engagement with materials and self-directed learning. Attributing this position to the work of Jean Piaget, proponents of this child-centered view suggest that participants in early intervention programs will naturally seek out information and stimulation that best matches their current developmental level and that the processes of assimilation and accommodation, and therefore learning, will be maximized (Mahoney, Robinson, & Powell, 1992).

Finally, some analysts would suggest that children's performance under such child-directed activities represents the most appropriate rate of development, and

that any deliberate effort to intervene in this process is not only doomed to failure but may create problems by setting unrealistically high expectations for some children, particularly those with disabilities. This view suggests that intervention programs, like those we might describe as behavior analytic, work against the natural developmental progressions of young children with learning and behavior problems.

Current discussions of the purpose, design, implementation, and evaluation of early intervention programs frequently voice these perspectives, or their derivatives (appropriate and otherwise). The questions that are raised from these perspectives often sound familiar to behavior analysts, covering each point of what we think of as social validity (cf., Schwartz & Baer, 1991). These are as follows: (1) What targets or goals should we hold for children in early intervention programs? (2) What are the most appropriate methods for reaching these targets or goals? (3) Once an intervention program has been implemented, is the treatment effect obtained meaningful?

Unfortunately, it has been my experience (and that of some of my colleagues) that the questions of some early interventionists are often not phrased so openly. Instead, concerns are raised over behavior-specific intervention targets, over efforts to explicitly arrange environments to produce these targeted changes, and over the judged lack of importance of the effects obtained, even when other professionals or the child's parents may judge them to be worthwhile. Given the frequency (and intensity) with which these concerns are voiced, and the status of the individuals voicing them with respect to funding and policy making, applied behavior analysts in early intervention had better understand what the goals should be for early intervention and what controls the acceptability of the interventions to meet these goals. In addition, we must identify those factors that contribute to judgments of meaningful outcomes for children enrolled in these programs.

Identifying the Goals of Early Intervention

On what basis can we turn discussion of the goals of our intervention efforts toward a more open analysis of these questions of social validity in early intervention? Direct discussions of more vaguely defined terms, such as *developmentally appropriate practice* or *child-centered intervention*, are tangential to the core issues, relying more on an individual's theoretical or conceptual model than on direct analysis. While these discussions are certainly academically engaging, one cannot be certain they contribute to the development of meaningful activities in early intervention. Instead, the field may be better served by a more fundamental analysis of our mandate and mission, both in early intervention in particular and in human services in general.

Previously, early intervention was defined as a "loosely structured confederation of . . . [programs that] provide compensatory or preventive services for children." According to this definition, early intervention (like other educational enterprises) is substantially directed by a set of federal and state laws that mandate and regulate services.

Across enacting legislation and procedural regulations, one can extract an implicit goal for early intervention programs in this county. Simply put, early intervention must provide early identification and provision of services to reduce or eliminate the effects of disabilities or to prevent the development of other problems, so that the need for subsequent special services is reduced (Public Law 99-457).

Additionally, laws and regulations set some general constraints on the provision of early intervention services. For instance, federal laws mandating and regulating the provision of early childhood special education services (i.e., early intervention for children with developmental disabilities) require that programs for children 3 to 5 years of age are individualized, are provided in the least-restrictive environment, and include substantial input from each child's parents in the design and operation of intervention services. For younger children, these same laws require that services are not directed to the child's needs per se, but rather are family centered, with intervention designed to increase the family's capacity to promote the child's development.

Without question, some empirical support exists for each of these mandated features: We know that, under some conditions, early intervention programs do "reduce or eliminate the need for subsequent special education services" (Odom & Karnes, 1988) and that, under the right conditions, individualized programs and programs provided in normalized settings promote increased gains for young children (e.g., Carta, Schwartz, Atwater, & Connell, 1989; Guralnick, 1988). Similarly, we have early evidence that programs can be designed to substantially involve parents and families and that effective services can be directed at these larger social units rather than at individual children (Bailey et al., 1986).

However, the empirical support for these, and numerous other, defining features of early intervention is only a small part of the reason that practitioners provide services as they do. Instead, many features of early intervention are "desired" by policy makers, practitioners, or consumers and thus represent socially defined parameters for the ways in which early intervention ought to be provided (Odom & McClean, 1992).

This analysis is not problematic for applied behavior analysis; it sounds like a description of social validity variables that might be considered in anyone's work. There is a long history of applied behavior analysts in early intervention who devoted substantial effort to the development and evaluation of intervention procedures and to systems that create the effective implementation of these desired features. For instance, individualized programming (e.g., Bricker & Cripe, 1992; Neisworth & Bagnato, 1988) matches well with behavioral assessment, idiographic intervention, and evaluation activities that are core to applied behavior analysis. Similarly, a growing number of behavior-analytic studies demonstrate the ways in which classroom design and intervention can promote interaction in normalized, or least-restrictive, environments (McEvoy, Twardosz, & Bishop, 1990; Odom, Chandler, Ostrosky, Reaney, & McConnell, 1992; Osnes, DaVerne, & Stokes, 1992).

Yet, behavior analysts cannot profitably and efficiently work, and the field of early intervention cannot progress, when the socially desired characteristics of early intervention are poorly articulated and understood, under constant revision, or controlled by factors other than those related to program outcomes for children. It is becoming increasingly clear that applied behavior analysts in early intervention must understand the social context for these desired features of early intervention, the ways in which the social context influences, both formally and informally, the application of behavior-analytic and other procedures in early intervention, and ways in which we can influence this social context.

This is not a call for an increased conceptual and philosophical discussion of vague and potentially unimportant variables. Instead, there may be value in applying a behavior-analytic perspective to the ways we *do* early intervention and to the identification of variables that control *our behavior* as behavior analysts. As behavior analysts, we may be reinforced by the identification of controlling variables and the articulation of functional relationships between cultural factors, social behaviors, and early intervention. As practitioners in early intervention, we may also be reinforced by influencing or controlling some of those variables that, in turn, control the provision of early intervention. In either case, we will be better informed of the factors that shape and maintain the enterprise of early intervention and more able to improve the effectiveness or efficiency of that effort.

A behavior analysis of behavior analysis, even in the focused area of early intervention, is clearly beyond the scope of this chapter. Instead, the remainder of this chapter is devoted to (1) a review of some of the "behaviors" of early intervention and the factors that may control them, and (2) an overview of some of the ways we might proceed to better understand, and control, the provision of early intervention services. To do this, we must first consider, in a general way, causal relationships that shape the design and provision of early intervention, and the factors influencing these causal relationships.

Factors in Early Intervention

Program Outcome

Let us begin this discussion at the most basic level of applied behavior analysis: the interaction between behavior change agents and the participants (or "subjects") in the behavior change activities. Like behavior analysts in other applied arenas, early

interventionists at this level of analysis are interested in identifying functional relationships between ecobehavioral variables and the behaviors of individual child participants. At the level of program outcomes (or the effects of program participation on the behavior of enrolled students), changes in the behavior of the children are due to the instrumental action, programmed or not, of behavior analysts. This is the core of applied behavior-analytic early intervention: the careful selection and specification of dependent and independent variables, arrangement of the environment to control for the delivery of independent variables, and objective evaluation of changes in the rates of the dependent variable as a function of delivery or nondelivery of that independent variable (Baer, Wolf, & Risley, 1968).

At this level, much of the work in early intervention will sound familiar to other applied behavior analysts. For instance, early interventionists have demonstrated increased rates of transitions from one classroom activity to another when using either "transition buddies" or simple reward activities (Sainato, Strain, Lefebvre, & Rapp, 1987), decreased aggression and aggressive theme play when restricting such activities to small spaces (Sherburne, Utley, McConnell, & Gannon, 1988), or acquisition of labeling and matching skills when using various prompts and time delays (Wolery & Gast, 1984).

To some extent, however, recent work has also started to expand how we might define "behavior analyst" (or at least behavior change agent) at this level of analysis. For instance, Strain, Shores, and Timm, (1977), Odom et al., (1992), Goldstein and Ferrell, (1987), and others have developed, demonstrated, and refined various procedures by which peers monitor classmates' behavior and provide antecedents or consequences that produce reliable changes in the behaviors. Similarly, in a growing number of examples, teachers are trained to implement standardized interventions so that (1) intervention procedures are reliably implemented and (2) significant changes are produced in their students' behavior (e.g., Carta et al., 1989; McConnell et al., 1990; Odom & McConnell, 1991). A significant feature of these interventions is that, while procedures are based on principles of applied behavior analysis, the behavior of the teacher or other primary intervention agent is controlled more by a manual or treatment plan than by day-to-day measures of child behavior (Odom, 1988).

Thus, whether conducted by "certified" behavior analysts or by individuals with whom these behavior analysts work, early intervention programs have used applied behavior analysis to produce significant and enduring change in the behavior of young children. Yet, in spite of this longstanding success, only recently have we directed concerted attention to the ways in which we select the targets for these intervention efforts. Although analyses and critiques of target behavior selection have been around for many years (Hawkins, 1975; Winnett & Winkler, 1972), and although we have long discussed and measured social validity (e.g., Wolf, 1978), there has been a sudden increase in attention in the past few years, both in applied behavior analysis (Schwartz & Baer, 1991) and in early intervention (Bredekamp, 1987). In short, many applied behavior analysts work under the assumption that individual program goals, as well as evaluations of success, rest in the hands of the consumers of our intervention efforts.

Social Validity

At the risk of oversimplifying a complex relationship, consumers' preferences or verbal reports control the selection of goals and the evaluation of appropriateness for intervention programs implemented by applied behavior analysts. Although this relationship often might be more reciprocal (for example, the development of an Individualized Educational Plan), we assume, for the sake of discussion, that consumers (particularly the parents of young children with disabilities) hold major responsibility for determining the social validity of any early intervention program.

Schwartz and Baer (1991), in the lead article of a recent section of the *Journal of Applied Behavior Analysis* devoted to this topic, described social validity as a measure of the acceptability or viability of a particular intervention effort. They suggested that the collection and use of social validity data might occur in two parts: the collection of opinions from an "accurate and representative sample" of consumers, and the use of that information to "sustain satisfactory

practices or effect changes in the program to enhance its viability" (Schwartz & Baer, 1991, p. 190). From this perspective, social validity, as measured by consumer opinion or preference, clearly has a key role in shaping applied behavior-analytic efforts.

At this point, however, an important question emerges: Who *are* the consumers of early intervention programs? In the simplest sense, children enrolled in a program (along with their parents and other family members) are the most *direct* consumers. Indeed, through the development and review of Individualized Educational Plans, their preferences are sampled and used to shape intervention activities in many programs.

However, as Schwartz and Baer (1991) suggested, there may be other consumer groups whose preferences or evaluations affect the viability of, and thus might shape, early intervention efforts. In addition to the direct consumers, then, the opinions of indirect consumers, members of the immediate community, and members of the extended community might also be sampled.

Indirect consumers, or those who fund programs or are directly affected by the behavior change of child participants, are perhaps easy to identify. They might include school board members or administrators, project officers at funding agencies, the future teachers of child participants, or others who interact with these children outside the immediate treatment setting. Individuals in this group might offer evaluations on the *extent* of behavior change, the *maintenance and generalization* of that effect, or the extent to which the program achieved its original goals or worked in a *cost-effective* way. In early intervention, we routinely sample the evaluations of individuals in this group and are developing a better understanding of how to integrate these evaluations into our program development efforts.

We have less experience, however, in assessing or using the evaluations of members of the immediate or extended community. Whereas members of the immediate community interact regularly with consumers of an intervention, members of the extended community (including classmates, neighbors, and taxpayers) are less likely to do so. Nonetheless, members of both groups stand to gain short- and long-term benefits from intervention efforts. We will return to this point toward the end of this chapter.

Once the consumers of an early intervention effort are identified, perhaps another question occurs: Who decided *they* were experts, or that their opinions should guide our educational efforts? As behavior analysts, we might describe "consumer evaluations" as the verbal behavior of classes of individuals. Given this description, we might then analyze controlling variables for the verbal evaluations of different program elements by different individuals or groups of consumers. In short, analysts may try to determine what the setting events, discriminative stimuli, and reinforcers are for program evaluations of social validity by consumers.

Social Context

Features of the social context and cultural practices of a given community will influence or control the evaluations of social validity for individual consumers. Rather than suggesting some vague relationship among "values," "attitudes," and "behavior," social context and its relationship to consumer evaluations and program outcomes can be analyzed.

An emerging body of work supports this analysis. Building on the work of Stephen Pepper's *contextualism* (1942) and Marvin Harris's *cultural materialism* (1979), several behavior analysts have offered suggestions for analyses of larger social units that are consistent with, and support, the individual-specific behavior analysis (e.g., Biglan, Glasgow, & Singer, 1990; Glenn, 1988; Malagodi, 1986).

Sigrid Glenn (1988) defined a cultural practice as "a subset of interlocking contingencies of reinforcement in which the behavior and behavioral products of each participant function as environmental events with which the behavior of other individuals interacts" (p. 167). The challenge is to identify not only these interlocking contingencies of reinforcement, but *also* the metacontingencies that control their various relationships.

What cultural practices and metacontingencies control the verbal behavior of consumers and community members regarding early intervention program outcomes, and the procedures and costs associated with these outcomes? What is the role of science, and the potentially selective dissemination of theoretical and empirical analyses, in the evolution and maintenance of these cultural practices? What controls and counter-controls operate on the evolution, maintenance, and revision of cultural practices related to early intervention? A review of the literature on early intervention suggests that we are only beginning to conduct analyses that address these types of questions, but these analyses might prove essential to the ongoing development of applied behavior analysis in early intervention.

The Relationship Among Program Outcomes, Social Validity, and Social Context

To this point, we have examined simple, unidirectional relationships among program outcomes, social validity, and social context. In reality, the relationships are probably not that simple. Figure 7.1 suggests the more likely *reciprocal* and *interactive*

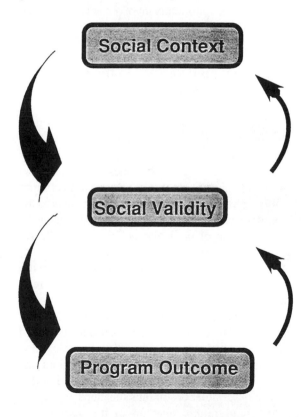

Figure 7.1. Schematic representation of multivariate effects of social context, social validity, and intervention procedures for producing outcomes in early intervention.

relationship among these factors. This figure depicts the order of relationships "from the top down," reflecting an assumption that social context controls social validity, which in turn controls the selection of goals for program outcome. These relationships may also occur "from the bottom up"; that is, program outcomes (particularly successful ones) may shape and maintain consumer evaluations of desired outcomes, which in turn produce changes in cultural practices like legal mandates, funding, and social support. Or, these factors may be related "from the top down" *and* "from the bottom up," or they may not be related at all.

An assumption of reciprocity and interaction among these variables may provide guidance for the selection of some future activities of applied behavior analysts in early intervention. One such activity may be to elicit more community involvement in the design and evaluation of early intervention activities.

Community Involvement in the Evaluation of Early Intervention

The relationships depicted in Figure 7.1 suggest that, under some conditions, communities of individuals might "learn"; that is, cultural practices, consumer evaluations, and program outcomes might change in a systematic and developmental way as a function of the differential *success* of specific actions, such as the adoption of particular procedures or programs or the implementation of particular policies. This "learning" would require a standard or measure of "success," and a systematic way of informing the community of the outcomes of different actions relative to this standard.

As Schwartz and Baer (1991) suggested, the "standards of success" might be selected or developed through a participatory democratic process. However, these standards are still verbal behaviors and thus are subject to change due to variations in other controlling variables or stimulus situations (e.g., changes in demographic makeup of the community, economic status, or development in other scientific disciplines [such as health care]). Perhaps the greatest challenge is to develop ways to systematically inform the community of the success of different actions. Consumer education may be one vehicle (Schwartz, 1991), but it alone may not be sufficient.

Early interventionists have a more complex example that might provide some measure of guidance. Over the past few years, the state of Oregon developed a new way of allocating publicly funded health care resources to members of its community. While the plan has not yet been implemented and some of its details have proven controversial, its structures and operation are of interest.

In simple terms, a committee of Oregon citizens evaluated the importance or worth of a large number of medical procedures on the basis of their cost, efficacy (including contribution to the "quality of life" of intervention recipients), and incidence in the population. Using these data and a calculation of available funds, the state rank-ordered medical procedures and then drew a line that indicated, based on incidence and cost, what interventions could be afforded. Procedures *above* the line would be available to all eligible persons, while procedures *below* the line would not be funded with public dollars.

The rank ordering of procedures and the drawing of the line reflect, in some senses, measures of social validity with the ranks demoting the importance of the intervention and the line reflecting the available resources. Like other social validity measures, these are arbitrary and can change as consumer evaluations change.

If a system like this were implemented, it might provide information to a community regarding the effects of earlier important decisions. Questions might include: Do individuals receive the health care they "need"? Do nomothetic models of disease, treatment, and outcome work in all individual cases? Does the allocation of more money, or the reordering of medical procedures, produce more desirable outcomes? And can some community practices change to promote health and avoid cost?

Through an iterative process of rank ordering, allocation, and evaluation, the citizens of a community using this approach might develop a system that directs individual practitioners and influences cultural practice. In this way, a community might "learn" what its health care system can be. And this learning would reflect the reciprocal influences among individual interventions, consumers' evaluations of the effects of these interventions, and cultural practices regarding the value of these interventions, both for contributing to the quality of life of all community members and for determining the allocation of scarce resources within and across intervention domains.

As behavior analysts and early interventionists, we must direct more effort to identifying variables that control the consumer evaluations and cultural practices that in turn control *our* behavior as practitioners. What does our community of direct and indirect consumers know about early intervention, and how do they judge the goals, procedures, and costs associated with these programs? Perhaps more important, what information (and what conditions) will contribute to systematic review and evolution of these community standards for early intervention? Can we gather evidence that this type of widescale participation in the design and evaluation of our intervention efforts makes these efforts "better"?

To achieve any of these goals, or to ask any of these questions, we must first develop a system that solicits the involvement of a broader community, that increases the rate of "trials" in which that community directs and evaluates early intervention efforts, and, therefore, contributes more directly to the evolution of cultural practices and consumer evaluations that promote program outcomes for young children. Perhaps in this way we will expand the attention and concern directed to the behavioral development of these children and to the intervention efforts designed to contribute to this developmental process.

Acknowledgment

I want to acknowledge the preliminary discussions of topics presented in this paper with Ann Johnson and Mary McEvoy, and to thank members of the Early Childhood Research Programs at the Institute on Community Integration, as well as Diane Sainato and Teresa Grossi for their comments on an early version of this paper. Preparation of this paper was supported by grants H024B00068 (Ecobehavioral Programming for Individual Children), H024R10004 (Early Childhood Research Institute on Substance Abuse), and H023C10092 (Prenatal Cocaine Exposure and Social Development of Young Children) from the U.S. Department of Education. Correspondence should be directed to Scott McConnell, Institute on Community Integration, 102 Pattee Hall, University of Minnesota, Minneapolis, MN 55455.

References

ALLEN, K. E., Hart, B., Buell, J. S., Harris, F. R., & Wolf, M. M. (1964). Effects of social reinforcement on isolate behavior of a nursery school child. *Child Development, 35*, 511–518.

BAER, D., Wolf, M. M., & Risley, T. R. (1968). Some current dimensions of applied behavior analysis. *Journal of Applied Behavior Analysis, 1,* 91–97.

BAILEY, D. B., Simeonsson, R. J., Winton, P. J., Huntington, G. S., Comfort, M., Isbell, P., ODonnell, K. J., & Helm, J. M. (1986). Family-focused intervention: A functional model for planning, implementing, and evaluating individualized family services in early intervention. *Journal of the Division for Early Childhood, 10*, 156–171.

BIGLAN, A., Glasgow, R. E., & Singer, G. (1990). The need for a science of larger social units: A contextual approach. *Behavior Therapy, 21*, 195–215.

BREDEKAMP, S. (Ed.) (1987). *Developmentally appropriate practice in early childhood programs serving children from birth through age 8.* Washington, DC: National Association for the Education of Young Children.

BRICKER, D. M., & Cripe, J. (1992). *Activity-based intervention.* Baltimore: Brookes.

CARTA, J., Schwartz, I., Atwater, J., & Connell, M. (1989). Teaching classroom survival skills to students with learning problems. Paper presented at the annual meeting of the Division of Early Childhood, Council for Exceptional Children, October, Minneapolis.

ELKIND, D. (1981). *The hurried child: Growing up too fast too soon.* Reading, MA: Addison-Wesley.

FARRAN, D. C. (1990). Effects of early intervention with disadvantaged and disabled children: A decade review. In S. J. Meisels & J. P. Shonkoff (Eds.), *Handbook of early intervention* (pp. 501–539). Cambridge: Cambridge University Press.

GLENN, S. S. (1988). Contingencies and metacontingencies: Toward a synthesis of behavior analysis and cultural materialism. *The Behavior Analyst, 11*, 161–180.

GOETZ, E. M. (1982). Behavior principles and techniques. In K. E. Allen & E. M. Goetz (Eds.), *Early childhood education: Special problems, special solutions* (pp. 72–103). Rockville, MD: Aspen.

GOLDSTEIN, H., & Ferrell, D. R. (1987). Augmenting communicative interaction between handicapped and non-handicapped preschool children. *Journal of Speech and Hearing Disorders, 52,* 200–211.

GURALNICK, M. J. (1988). Efficacy research in early childhood intervention programs. In S. L. Odom & M. B. Karnes (Eds.), *Early intervention for infants and children with handicaps* (pp. 75–88). Baltimore: Brookes.

HARRIS, M. (1979). *Cultural materialism: The struggle for a science of culture.* New York: Simon & Shuster.

HART, B., & Risley, T. (1975). Incidental teaching of language in the preschool. *Journal of Applied Behavior Analysis, 8,* 411–420.

HAWKINS, R. P. (1975). Who decided *that* was a problem? Two stages of responsibility for applied behavior analysts. In W. S. Wood (Ed.), *Issues in evaluating behavior modification* (pp. 195–214). Champaign, IL: Research Press.

HUNT, J. M. (1961). *Intelligence and experience.* New York: Ronald Press.

LELAURIN, K., & Risley, T. R. (1972). The organization of day-care environments: "Zone" versus "man-to-man" staff assignments. *Journal of Applied Behavior Analysis, 5,* 225–232.

MAHONEY, G., Robinson, C., & Powell, A. (1992). Focusing on parent-child interaction: A bridge to developmentally appropriate practice. *Topics in Early Childhood Special Education, 12,* 105–120.

MALAGODI, E. F. (1986). On radicalizing behaviorism: A call for cultural analysis. *Behavior Analyst, 9,* 1–18.

MCCONNELL, S. R., Peterson, C., Fox, J., & Odom, S. L. (1990). Effects of child-specific intervention on social interaction rates for young children with handicaps: Selection of treatment components. Unpublished manuscript, May, Vanderbilt-Minnesota Social Interaction Project, University of Minnesota.

MCEVOY, M. A., Twardosz, S., & Bishop, N. (1990). Affection activities: procedures for encouraging young children with disabilities to play with their peers. *Education and Treatment of Children, 13,* 159–167.

NEISWORTH, J. T., & Bagnato, S. J. (1988). Assessment in early childhood special education: A typology of dependent measures. In S. L. Odom & M. B. Karnes (Eds.), *Early intervention for infants and children with handicaps* (pp. 23–49). Baltimore: Brookes.

ODOM, S. L. (1988). Research in early childhood special education. In S. L. Odom & M. B. Karnes (Eds.), *Early intervention for infants and children with handicaps (pp. 1–21). Baltimore: Brookes.*

ODOM, S. L., Chandler, L. K., Ostrosky, M., McConnell, S. R., & Reaney, S. (1992). Fading teacher support in peer-initiation interventions for young children with disabilities. *Journal of Applied Behavior Analysis, 25,* 307–318.

ODOM, S. L., & Karnes, M. B. (1988). *Early intervention for infants and children with handicaps.* Baltimore: Brookes.

ODOM, S. L., & McClean, M. (1992). Best practices in early intervention for infants and young children with disabilities.

Arlington, VA: Division of Early Childhood, Council for Exceptional Children.

ODOM, S. L., & McConnell, S. R. (1991). Comparison of interventions for promoting peer social competence of young children with disabilities. Paper presented at the biennial meeting of the Society for Research in Child Development, April, Seattle.

ODOM, S. L., McConnell, S. R., & McEvoy, M. M. (1992). *Social competence of young children with disabilities: Nature, development, and intervention.* Baltimore: Brookes.

OSNES, P., DaVerne, K. C., & Stokes, T. (1992). Social integration effects for young, at-risk children and their typically developing peers. Paper presented at the 18th annual convention of the Association for Behavior Analysis, May, San Francisco.

PEPPER, S. (1942). *World hypotheses.* Berkeley: University of California Press.

ROGERS-Warren, A., & Baer, D. M. (1976). Correspondence between saying and doing: Teaching children to share and praise. *Journal of Applied Behavior Analysis, 9,* 335–354.

SAINATO, D. M., Strain, P. S., Lefebvre, D., & Rapp, N. (1987). Facilitating transition times with handicapped preschool children: A comparison between peer-mediated and antecedent prompt procedures. *Journal of Applied Behavior Analysis, 20,* 285–292.

SCHWARTZ, I. (1991). The study of consumer behavior and social validity: An essential partnership for applied behavior analysis. *Journal of Applied Behavior Analysis, 24,* 241–243.

SCHWARTZ, I., & Baer, D. M. (1991). Social validity assessments: Is current practice state of the art? *Journal of Applied Behavior Analysis, 24,* 189–204.

SHERBURNE, S., Utley, B. L., McConnell, S. R., & Gannon, J. (1988). Decreasing violent/aggressive theme play among preschool children with behavior disorders: A comparison of two freeplay management strategies. *Exceptional Children, 55,* 166–172.

STRAIN, P. S. (1981). *The utilization of classroom peers as behavior change agents.* New York: Academic.

STRAIN, P. S., & Timm, M. A. (1974). An experimental analysis of social interaction between a behaviorally disordered preschool child and her classroom peers. *Journal of Applied Behavior Analysis, 7,* 583–590.

STRAIN, P. S., Shores, R. E., & Timm, M. A. (1977). Effects of social initiations on the behavior of a withdrawn child. *Journal of Applied Behavior Analysis, 10,* 289–298.

WARREN, S. F., & Kaiser, A. P. (1988). Research in early language intervention. In S. L. Odom & M. B. Karnes (Eds.), *Early Intervention for infants and children with handicaps: An empirical base.* Baltimore: Brookes.

WINNETT, R. A, & Winkler, R. C. (1972). Current behavior modification in the classroom: Be still, be quiet, be docile. *Journal of Applied Behavior Analysis, 5,* 499–504.

WOLERY, M., & Brookfield-Norman, J. (1988). (Pre)Academic instruction for handicapped preschool children. In S. L. Odom & M. B. Karnes (Eds.), *Early intervention for infants and children with handicaps: An empirical base* (pp. 89–128). Baltimore: Brookes.

WOLERY, M., & Gast, D. L. (1984). Effective and efficient procedures for the transfer of stimulus control. *Topics in Early Childhood Special Education, 4(3)*, 52–77.

WOLF, M. M. (1978). Social validity: The case for subjective measurement, or how applied behavior analysis is finding its heart. *Journal of Applied Behavior Analysis, 11*, 315–329.

Contextualism and Applied Behavior Analysis: Implications for Early Childhood Education for Children with Disabilities

Samuel L. Odom
Thomas G. Haring

Young children with disabilities regularly participate in the American educational system. The movement to provide early intervention/early childhood special education (EI/ECSE) services to these children began with the individual initiatives of parents and local school districts in the late 1960s, was encouraged by Public Law 94-142 in the mid-1970s, increased in momentum in the 1980s, and became mandated by law (for preschool children) in the 1990s through Public Law 99-457 (reauthorized by Public Law 102-119). As services expanded, educators have examined with much interest practices that would best meet the children's needs. Strain and colleagues (1992) proposed that behaviorism has much to offer program developers and professionals who work with young children with disabilities and their families: (1) it provides a theory of developmental retardation that focuses on variables that are observable and perhaps treatable; (2) it contains a flexible research methodology that is useful for children with a variety of characteristics; (3) its assessment methodologies emphasize factors that maintain or influence children's behavior; and (4) its intervention procedures emphasize quality of implementation, effectiveness, and social validity.

Within behavior analysis, there has been much discussion of the philosophical bases that guide theory and practice (Haring & Kennedy, in press; Marr, 1993; Morris, 1992a). Traditionally, applied behavior analysis (in particular) has been seen as a mechanistic system that focuses on the elements of behavior. However, some researchers and clinicians have questioned whether mechanism is the most useful or accurate philosophical framework for behavior analysis (Biglan, 1992; Morris, 1988) and have proposed that contextualism is a more useful philosophical perspective (Hayes, Hayes, & Reese, 1988; Morris, 1988).

The purpose of this chapter is to describe a contextualistic view of behavior analysis and examine the implications of this view for educational practice in early childhood special education. First, we review Pepper's (1942) four world views. Next, we specifically contrast the application of mechanistic and contextualistic views of behavior analysis and suggest some possible advantages of the latter view. Also, we identify instructional or intervention procedures within early childhood special education that reflect contextualism in general and contextualistic behaviorism specifically. Last, we discuss the implications of contextualistic behaviorism for future trends in EI/ECSE practices.

World Hypotheses

In his seminal work published in 1942, Pepper sought to study "hypotheses about the world as objects in the world" (p. 1). In his view, individuals organized their understanding of the world in both commonsensical and "disciplined" ways (i.e., through formal hypotheses, theories, and empirical confirmation). However, even disciplined thought depends on commonsensical metaphors or analogies that serve as the basis for understanding events in the world and organizing information. Pepper called these "root metaphors." Individuals uncovered or understood the structure of these root metaphors by developing concepts (which he called "categories") from experiences or data that they collect.

Pepper proposed that essentially four root metaphors were commonly used in philosophy and science and were the basis for the formation of the four basic "world hypotheses." Each world hypothesis, along with its root metaphor, contained associated categories (which we will not describe in detail) as well as the truth criterion by which an individual verified that events in the world reflected or fit with the particular world view. The four world views, root metaphors, goals, truth criteria, and examples from psychology and education are presented in Table 8.1 and are described in the following paragraphs.

Formism

The root metaphor for formism is similarity, and the goal of many philosophies and scientific endeavors is to discover the reoccurrence of forms in nature. The truth criterion within formism is correspondence between forms of objects that are alike or similar. Formism is reflected by the philosophies of Plato, Aristotle, the scholastics, and the neorealists

Table 8.1 World hypothesis and their elements

World Hypotheses	Root Metaphor	Goal	Truth Criterion	Examples in Psychology and Education
Mechanism (Democritus, Descartes, Locke)	Machine	To discover the parts and the relations among the parts	*Correspondence* between verbal construction and new facts implied by the construction	Some forms of behaviorism, some information processing and computer models of intelligence
Formism (Plato, Aristotle)	Similarity	To discover the reoccurrence of recognizable forms, as a whole	*Correspondence* between verbal constructions and facts	Ethological examination of animal behavior; cross-section and longitudinal research that describes children's development (Gesell's work)
Organism (Hegel)	Dynamic, evolving organic system	To discover the steps involved in the organic process and the principle features in the organic structure achieved	*Coherence* of facts that lead to a conclusion	System's theories of Bronfenbrenner; Piaget's work; constructivist orientation in Early Childhood Education
Contextualism (James)	Ongoing act in context or historical event (as it *unfolds*)	To understand an event as part of a contextual whole. Parts are discernable, but only have meaning as they relate to the other parts	*Successful working*: analyses are true only to the extent that they accomplish their particular goal	Some forms of behaviorism; pragmatic approach to language acquisition; activity-based intervention

(Pepper, 1942). Examples of work within psychology and education are ethological investigations of behavior patterns in animals and humans (Blurton-Jones, 1972) and the descriptive cross-sectional or longitudinal research on child development such as the work of Gesell and his colleagues (Gesell, 1925). Haring and Kennedy (in press) also noted that the analytic work associated with general case training (Horner & McDonald, 1982) and direct instruction (Engelmann & Carnine, 1982) represent a formistic world view within behavior analysis.

Mechanism

The root metaphor for mechanism is the machine, and the goal of mechanism is to discover the parts of a phenomenon and the relationship among those parts. The truth criterion for mechanism lies in verbal constructions that reflect the world or a phenomenon (especially as they reflect the way aspects of a mechanism interrelate) and facts from the world that support such a verbal construction. Mechanism is embedded in the philosophies of Democritus, Lucretius, Galileo, Descartes, Hobbes, Locke, Berkeley, and Hume. The early behaviorism of John Watson and Thorndike, information processing theory (Lachman, Lachman, & Butterfield, 1979), Bandura's (1977) social learning theory, and computer models of human cognition (Winograd, 1987) all reflect a mechanistic world hypothesis. Pepper noted that both formism and mechanism were analytic world hypotheses in that they attempt to understand a phenomenon by pulling it apart and examining the similarities or relationships among its aspects.

Organism

The root metaphor for organism is the process inherent in a dynamic organismic system. The goal of organism is to discover the process(es) inherent in an evolving organismic system as well as the structure of the system. The truth criterion is the coherence or integration of facts that lead to a conclusion about a phenomenon. Organism is reflected in the philosophies of Schelling, Hegel, Green, and Bradley (Pepper, 1942). Bronfenbrenner's (1986) ecological systems theory, Piaget's (1952) theory of cognitive development, and the general constructivist orientation in early childhood education (DeVries & Kohlberg, 1987) are all current reflections of organism.

Contextualism

The root metaphor for contextualism is the historical event as it unfolds (i.e., the ongoing act in context). The goal of contextualism is to understand an event as part of a contextual whole. The parts of an act or event have meaning only as they relate to other aspects of the context. The truth criterion for contextualism is successful working; an understanding is true only to the extent that it accomplishes a particular goal. Contextualism is reflected in the philosophies and psychology of William James, Pierce, Bergson, and Dewey. Current reflections of contextualism include pragmatic analyses of communication skills and intervention, some conceptualizations of behaviorism (as we will see), naturalistic language-training approaches (Hart, 1985), and activity-based intervention approaches (Bricker & Cripe, 1992). Pepper noted that both organism and contextualism were synthetic world hypotheses in that they attempted to understand the phenomenon as a whole rather than by separating aspects from the system or the context.

Behaviorism as a Mechanistic System

Behaviorism has been described as a mechanistic system. The behavior of organisms may be analyzed in terms of their component parts by examining individual parts in relationship to the other parts. These relationships can be stated in terms of laws that determine or predict the mechanism's future actions. Laws or principles reflect that the actions of a mechanism (i.e., an organism, event, phenomenon) are represented by its individual parts and their relationship. Pepper (1942) used the examples of the lever and fulcrum and the dynamo to illustrate mechanistic relationships. Relatively static parts (in the former) and dynamic parts (in the latter) may be viewed in isolation and in action to understand the relationship among the parts.

Within behaviorism, the three-term contingency that Skinner (1938) contributed to the analysis of behavior has been interpreted as a mechanistic relationship of environmental events and human behavior. Within a mechanistic perspective, the relationships among the discriminative stimulus (S^D), the response (R_o), and the reinforcing stimulus (S^{r+}) are of critical interest, yet each can be examined in isolation (see Figure 8.1). From the mechanistic perspective, each term can be seen as a separate part with the emphasis in the analysis on understanding the relationships among the parts. From the contextualistic perspective, the interest is on the entire action in context, with the separate terms representing the textures that constitute the action in context. For example, basic experimental researchers have conducted a great deal of research on the principles of reinforcement. In such research, the investigations are carried out to determine how the frequency or timing of reinforcement (one element of the three-term contingency) relates to the frequency of a response (another element). The notion is that reinforcement, as an entity, can be separated into an element that can be varied and the effect can be seen on the covariation in another separate element, the response. From the applied literature, the use of reinforcement menus to determine specific reinforcers for individuals (in the absence of a response or setting) is an example of a mechanistic application of behavior-analytic techniques.

Radical behaviorism may also be represented as a selectionistic perspective. Behaviors are "selected" by their consequences for the individual (see Pennypacker, Chapter 2 in this text). The selectionist perspective represents an analysis of two terms of the three-term contingency with the emphasis continuing to be placed on separate elements (terms) of the contingency (i.e., the response and the consequence).

It is quite possible that depicting theoretical operant behaviorism as a mechanistic system represents a "strawman" position against which a contextualistic perspective might be built (Marr, 1993). In fact, Hayes and Hayes (1992) noted that Skinner described behaviorism in both mechanistic and contextualistic terms. However, the application of behavioral principles in special education (as in much of applied behavior analysis) has been primarily mechanistic in nature. Haring and Kennedy (in press) noted that many applications of task analysis are examples of a mechanistic perspective. Individual behaviors are analyzed into component parts, with each part potentially serving as an objective or behavioral unit that would be the focus of instruction. Within early childhood special education, the past practice of identifying specific behaviors from criterion-referenced assessments and teaching them in formal instructional formats without linking them to natural discriminative stimuli and consequences may reflect a mechanistic application of behavioral principles. This perspective is not unique to special education; Brown, Collins, and Duguid (1989) proposed that much academic instruction in elementary and high schools takes place in a similar (although less individualized) format.

Behaviorism as a Contextualistic System

Hayes, Hayes, and Reese (1988) and Morris (1988, 1992a, 1992b) proposed that behaviorism, at least operant behaviorism, is an inherently contextualistic system. Within contextualism, the components of a phenomenon can be separated into elements. One element is the *quality* of an act, or the total (unanalyzed) nature of the act. The second is the *texture*, or the parts that make up the quality. However, the quality cannot be completely understood in terms of its individual textures (i.e., the sum is greater than the total of the parts). To illustrate this point, Pepper used an example originally noted by William James. Lemonade is made of lemon juice, sugar, and water. The quality of lemonade (experienced by tasting, smelling, and drinking it) is different from each of its individual textures. However, within contextualism there is a sliding frame of reference, in which an observer can shift his or her analysis from

Mechanistic Perspective	S^d	--	R_o	--	S^{r+}
	Peer Present Toy Present		Request		Receiving Toy

Requesting Toy

Contextualistic Perspective	S^d	R_o	S^{r+}
	Peer Present Toy Present	Request	Receiving Toy

Figure 8.1. Two versions of the three-term contingency.

the act or object in context to its textures; the texture then becomes the quality (focus of the analysis), which is in turn made up of other textures. In the lemonade example, the analysis could be shifted to sugar, which then becomes the quality and the color, gradual makeup, and taste become the textures. In turn, the lemonade might be a texture of a larger "act in context," such as relaxing on a hot summer day. In such a situation, the textures might also include a shady tree, a soft place to slt, a cool breeze, and a blue sky.

A contextual perspective on behaviorism could also use Skinner's three-term contingency as a basis for understanding behavior. However, in this conceptualization, the quality of an act is represented by the conjoined nature of the three terms; the S^D, R_o, and S^{R+} would be the textures (Morris, 1988). In essence, an individual's behavior (R_o) can only be understood within the context of the stimuli that set the occasion for the behavior to occur and the environmental stimuli that increase or support the probability that the behavior will occur again. For example, if requesting a material from a peer is a behavior of interest (the R_o), the S^Ds for such a behavior could be the presence of a peer, a sufficient supply of materials that the peer could share, and a history of sharing by the peer or positive interactions with the peer. Similarly, the S^{R+} could be receiving the material from the peer, the peer pointing to where the material could be obtained, or the peer telling the teacher that the child needs a material. The topography of the requesting response alone provides an incomplete picture of the act in context. The characteristics of the S^Ds and the S^{R+}s do not provide meaning for the action. The three elements essentially define one another, and if any are missing, the understanding of requesting is incomplete.

An aspect of contextualism that is compatible with behaviorism is the truth criterion employed—successful working. The adequacy of a contextualistic perspective is judged by the degree to which the goals of the explanation are achieved. In behavior analysis, the goals are prediction and control of behavior. Behaviorists measure the successful working of their hypotheses about children's behavior by examining the functional relationships that exist between environmental variables and the individuals' responses.

The public nature of contextualism also reflects a theme inherent within behaviorism. To quote Pepper:

> One of the strong arguing points for contextualism is that all categories are derived from the immediacy of any given present event, and that the public world about us is directly derived from these and does not need to be inferred. . . . The contextualist insists that a study of any private event carries of itself into a public world. [1942, p. 265]

Certainly, the emphasis on public rather than private events in behaviorism would be compatible with this description of contextualism.

Advantages of a Contextualistic Perspective in Behaviorism

The primary advantage of following a contextualistic perspective in applied behavior analysis is that it requires the investigator to focus on the behavior in context rather than on the behavior as an element separable from its antecedent stimuli and reinforcers. In behavior analysis, at least as applied in the field of early childhood special education over the past 20 years, a greater emphasis has been placed on identifying a specific behavior and potential reinforcers for the behavior. Until recently, less emphasis had been placed on stimuli that set the context for the behavior to occur. Within the experimental analysis of behavior, there has been a history of research on antecedent stimuli that provide the initial context for behavior. This may be seen in Skinner's (1931) third variables, Kantor's (1933) setting factors, the "setting events" of Bijou and Baer (1978) and Wahler and Fox (1981), Gewirtz's (1972) contextual determinants, and Michael's (1982) establishing operations.

An example of such a shift to a greater analysis of contextual antecedents may be seen in Sidman's (1986) discussion of conditional discriminative stimuli. As we noted, the three-term contingency might serve as the basis of our examination of behavior. However, there may be conditions within the broader context that affect whether an event may serve as a discriminative stimulus. Sidman proposed that a fourth or fifth term could be added to the contingency to illustrate the conditional nature of the immediate S^d event. Using our example of the child's requesting behavior, a friendly peer with a sufficient number of blocks to share is in a play area next to a child. Blocks are one of the child's preferred activities. In this context, on Monday and Tuesday, the child requests the blocks from the peer. On Wednesday and Thursday, the teacher places a set of colorful cars and trucks next to the play area, but at some distance from the other peers. On these days, the child does not request materials from the peer, even though the same environmental stimuli are present (rather, she plays with the cars and trucks). On Friday, the cars and trucks are not present and the child again requests blocks from the peer. In this example, the peer with the blocks was a conditional S^D, with the presence of the cars and trucks serving as an event that influenced its effectiveness. The events that were effective S^ds in one context were not effective in a second context.

If we were to follow a contextualistic approach to applied behavior analysis, what might we do differently than the mechanistic behavior-analytic approaches? Contextualistic behavior analysis moves the unit of analysis from the response to all three terms of the three-term contingency. So immediately, it eliminates the possibility of discussing or planning behavioral interventions without examining the events that set the context for and reinforce the behavior. Perhaps more important, it may open the possibility for creating larger units of analysis. Thompson and Lubinski (1986) have argued that behavior analysis has not adequately handled well the existence of larger units of behavior. Similarly, Biglan and colleagues (Biglan, Glasgow, & Singer, 1990; Biglan & Hayes, 1991) have proposed that for behavior analysis to continue to become a viable basis for clinical treatment, the field must look toward larger units of behavior in our practices. Biglan, Glagow, and Singer (1990) pushed this theme further in suggesting that cultural materialism as a philosophy (Harris, 1979) and as applied to behavior analysis by Glenn (1988) could serve as an important basis for treatment.

The undisciplined movement to larger (more than three terms) units of analysis could potentially be confusing and counterproductive. Taking Sidman's analysis to its logical extreme, a sixth conditional term could be found for the fifth term in the contingency, a seventh for the sixth, and so on. The question becomes How large a unit is sufficient? The truth criterion within contextualism, and behavior analysis, provides the basis on which a researcher or teacher can determine the size of the contextual-behavioral unit. From the contextualist perspective, when an explanation of an action does not meet the investigator's or intervenor's goals (i.e., successful working does not occur), then the unit of analysis is either too large or inaccurate. Similarly, in behavior analysis, when a functional relationship is not established between the variables, then the explanation of their relationship is inadequate. A pragmatic empiricism guides the contextualistic behavior-analytic approach.

So, the first, primary, and ultimate criterion for judging the usefulness of a contextual world hypothesis for behavior analysis is its own truth criterion; if it allows the investigator or teacher to predict and control behavior to a greater extent than other perspectives, it is justified. *If, and only if, this basic truth criterion is met*, then at least two other advantages may accrue to the field of behavior analysis and specifically the field of early childhood special education.

A contextualist world view may provide a point of common perspective with individuals from other theoretical orientations or disciplines. For example, Hayes and Hayes (1992) described how a contextualistic behaviorism, applied through stimulus equivalence work, may allow researchers to speculate about cognition. Their work on rule-governed behavior represents a step in such a direction. From outside behavior analysis, Brown, Collins, and Duguid (1989) and the Cognition and Technology Group at Vanderbilt (1990) based their academic instructional programs on "situated cognition." Learning and using academic skills in context, with the range of cues needed for direct application, is the key feature of this approach. Sternberg (1985) based his investigations and theories of human intelligence on practical problem solving in real-world situations. Lerner (1991) proposed a developmental contextual perspective for understanding the basic processes of child development, and similarly, Fogel et al. (1992) proposed following a "radical contextualism" in understanding the development of emotional expression in young children. Although different theoretical perspectives on child development or teaching can exist within contextualism, a shared perspective (at the metatheoretical level) could provide a point of reference for dialogue that is now nonexistent. Some may feel that such a dialogue may be unimportant or unnecessary. Yet, the majority of psychology and education professionals believe that behaviorism was an early and appropriate victim of the cognitive revolution in the 1960s (e.g., Bruner, 1990). At best, behaviorism may be viewed as a benign and somewhat irrelevant subdomain, at worst as a harmful and inappropriate application to education (especially for young children). If behaviorism is to contribute significantly to future education, a common frame of reference will need to be established with professionals who may have different theoretical perspectives. Such a point of reference may allow behaviorists to convey that behaviorism is still an active, vital theoretical perspective.

A contextualistic perspective may also make behavioral interventions more palatable and acceptable for practitioners. Early childhood education is driven by a constructivistic theoretical orientation (Bredekamp, 1987; Bredekamp & Rosegrant, 1992; DeVries & Kohlberg, 1987). The current view of behavioral teaching strategies for young children is of structured, teacher-directed programs in which children sit in seats all day, work on academic worksheets, and receive edible reinforcers for their correct responding (i.e., a misapplied, mechanistic perspective). A contextualistic behavior analysis, which embedded teaching and interventions within an ongoing routine that includes both child- and teacher-initiated activities, is much closer to the model that operates in early childhood education.

These two advantages are very real but are secondary in nature. They exist only if the primary truth criterion of behavior analysis is met: that of greater prediction and control of behavior.

Contextualistic Behaviorism Within Early Intervention/Early Childhood Special Education

Contextualism is an emerging perspective within behavior analysis, and as such its direct application within early childhood special education has been limited. That is, EI/ECSE professionals have not directly identified their intervention approaches as having a theoretical base in contextualistic behaviorism, but many EI/ECSE practices are compatible with and even reflections of this perspective. In this section, we discuss dimensions of EI/ECSE that fit within the contextualist behavioristic perspective.

The Child as the Setting Event for Intervention

EI/ECSE, like behavior analysis, is idiographic in nature; the individual child is the focus of interventions or teaching strategies. These strategies reflect the individual's special needs, both in terms of the skills to be acquired (to be discussed later) and the characteristics or abilities that the child brings to the learning activity. As such, factors or variables related to the child may serve as the context or setting events for the types of instruction that the teacher plans. A contextualistic behaviorism would not propose that the teacher use hypothetical constructs to infer the child's readiness for a learning activity, but rather base her or his judgment on overt cues or actions.

For example, in early intervention programs for infants with disabilities, one goal is to promote positive parent/infant interactions. To do this, parents are sometimes taught to read and understand the behavior cues their infants provide. These cues reflect the infant's readiness to be engaged in interaction and essentially the probability that the child will respond to the parent in a positive way. One such cue is the infant's state of arousal. Infants vary in their states of arousal from deep sleep at the low end, to active alert in the middle, to highly aroused at the high end. Parents and professionals can readily detect these states by using such scales as the Carolina Record of Individual Behavior (Simeonsson, 1979) (see Table 8.2) or the Brazelton Neonatal Behavioral Assessment (Brazelton, 1984) and by conducting an informal observation. If a parent makes an appropriate initiation to the infant when he or she is at either end of the arousal continuum, it is unlikely that the child will respond in a positive manner. If the child is in an active alert state, there is a higher probability that the child will respond. The child's state of arousal is an intrachild variable reflected by overt actions that set the context for the interaction. In many ways, it is similar to the conditional S^d that Sidman (1986) noted.

Table 8.2 The Carolina Record of Individual Behavior

State 1   Deep sleep, eyes closed, regular respiration, no movements.

State 2   Intermediate sleep, eyes closed, few minor facial, body and/or mouth movements, respiration is "periodic," alternating periods of shallow and deep breathing.

State 3   Active sleep, eyes closed, irregular respiration, some gross motor activity (stirring, writhing, grimacing, mouthing, or other facial expression).

State 4   Drowsiness, eyes open and closed intermittently, fluttering eyelids, eyes have glassy appearance, frequent relaxation followed by sudden jerks.

State 5   Quiet awake, relatively inactive, eyes open and appear bright and shiny, respiration regular.

State 6   Active awake, eyes open, diffuse motor activity of limbs or whole body, vocalizations of a content nature.

State 7   Fussy awake, eyes open, irregular respirations, diffuse motor activity, vocalizations of fussy, cranky variety.

State 8   Mild agitation, eyes open, diffuse motor activity, moderate crying, tears may or may not be present.

State 9   Marked uncontrollable agitation, screaming, eyes open or closed, tears may or may not be present.

Source: Carolina Record of Individual Behavior by R. J. Simeonsson, 1979. Unpublished assessment instrument. Chapel Hill, NC: Frank Porter Graham Child Development Center, University of North Carolina. Reprinted by permission. *Note:* This scale displays the range of states of arousal for individuals. Such states may serve as conditional discriminative stimuli for responding by infants and young children.

Teachers frequently use such information about children to make decisions about their actions and learning activities. For example, they position children with motor impairments to allow them greater voluntary movement and engagement in learning activities, pace their interactions differently when they know a child is on a certain type of seizure medication that slows response time, or provide a prompt or teaching suggestion when the child is actively engaged and attending to a certain activity that he or she may have selected. All teachers reflect the child's characteristics as part of the context that influences behaviors central to the learning activity.

Prediction and Control of Behavior as a Shared Goal

The goal of contextualistic behaviorism is prediction and control of behavior (Biglan & Hayes, 1991; Morris, 1992). EI/ECSE holds the same goals, although they are stated somewhat differently. Predic-

tion reflects a teacher's ability to predict the effect that classroom activities or intervention plans may have on children and families. Control, which is not meant in the authoritarian sense, reflects the actual effects of such interventions; that is, the intervention actually accomplished the intended effect.

The issue of control is important and controversial in early childhood education and EI/ECSE. Behavioristic special education programs are often seen; they are teacher directed and place control at the "teacher-prompting and children responding" level (Odom, Skellenger, & Ostrosky, 1993). However, control does not necessarily mean the use of direct and immediate teacher behavior that controls individual child behaviors. Many early childhood education and EI/ECSE programs follow a child-centered curriculum in which children are given freedom to initiate their participation in activities. A contextualistic behavioral perspective would advocate for such a teaching approach, which embeds teaching and learning directly in the "act in context." In such settings, teachers still exert control by planning and providing activities that will foster the children's active engagement in learning activities. If their activities do not enhance (or control) active engagement, then they will change the activity to provide a greater enhancement (or control) of the child's participation in the environment. Thus, prediction and control of behavior could be seen as shared goals of contextualistic behaviorism and EI/ECSE.

Selection of Learning Objectives

Professionals in EI/ECSE place a great emphasis on identifying a child's "functional" skills (Neisworth, 1993). The term *functional* means that the skills have relevance for the child's life; that is, they will be useful in the current or future context. Such skills should be identified by using several sources of information: (1) the child's current functioning level determined by formal or informal assessment of skills; (2) the skills that the child needs to be independent in the home as reflected by the family's information, priorities, and concerns; (3) the skills the child needs in the immediate environment, as reflected by an ecological analysis; and (4) the skills the child needs in the next or future environments. By sampling the behavioral requirements (for independence and success) of each of these environmental contexts as well as the developmental and behavioral context of the child's current skills, teachers, parents, and other professionals may determine skills (acts in context) that could serve as the basis for the intervention programs. Such a skill selection process would be compatible with a contextualistic behavioral orientation.

Embedding Learning Within the Context

Recently in EI/ECSE, professionals have attempted to identify practices or procedures that reflect the state of the art (DeStefano et al., 1991; Hanson & Lynch, 1989; McDonnell & Hardman, 1988). In the largest effort to-date, a nationwide sample of professionals and parents participated in identifying practices in 14 different aspects of EI/ECSE (DEC Recommended Practices Task Force, 1993). A theme that ran across intervention areas was that learning experiences should be embedded in the children's natural routines or environments, rather than being taught solely in didactic instructional settings (McLean & Odom, in press). At some point, the learning experience must affect the act in context. Two specific intervention approaches are provided as examples of teaching in context.

Activity-based intervention is a frequently used strategy in EI/ECSE. As defined by Bricker & Cripe (1992), it is a child-directed, transactional approach in which the environmental context sets the occasion for the child's use of or practice on a specific skill (or set of skills) in regular classroom or home routines. The teacher embeds training in these routines. She or he does this by first identifying the child's functional skills and then analyzing the classroom or home environment to determine when these skills might naturally be used. In this analysis, he or she determines the logically occurring antecedents (S^ds) and consequences (S^{r+}) and plans for occasions during the identified routine for the child to participate in learning events. To promote generalization and maintenance, the teacher varies the times, activities, and adults involved in the child's use of the skill. Activity-based intervention, and an earlier similar strategy called "individualized curriculum sequencing" (Mulligan et al., 1980), is

applicable to the range of functional skills commonly identified as instructional targets for infants and young children with special needs.

A set of similar interventions, couched under the terms *naturalistic language training* (Hart, 1985) and *milieu training* (Warren, 1992), also reflect the contextualistic behavioral theme in EI/ECSE. In these teaching approaches, the teacher's role is to first arrange the environment to set the context for the child to engage in the targeted functional skill (the act in context). For example, the functional skill might be the child requesting assistance from a teacher. During an art activity, the teacher may give the child a glue jar whose lid is slightly too tight for the child to open. Following a milieu-training approach, if the child does not make a verbal request after trying to open the jar, the teacher might provide a mand ("Juanita, What do you need?") or a model ("Juanita, say 'Help, please.'"). If the child has a history of following a teacher prompt in such contexts, the teacher could delay providing the verbal prompt for a short time, allow the child to make the request on his or her own, and then provide the model or mand if necessary. If the child makes the verbal request spontaneously, the teacher may elaborate on or prompt the child to make a slightly more sophisticated request (e.g., a request that labels the action "open the glue"). The strategies of mand (first example), model (second example), delayed prompting (third example), and incidental teaching (fourth example) all are part of milieu training (Kaiser, Yoder, & Keetz, in press). These strategies have been applied primarily to language training, but they could be adapted to promote other functional skills. Like activity-based intervention (ABI), the milieu-training approaches are compatible with a contextualistic behavioral approach to EI/ECSE.

Transition Planning and Analysis of Environments

Both by law (Public Law 102-119, as specified for infant and toddler programs) and professional consensus (Bruder & Chandler, 1993), planning and supporting the transition of children and families across agencies is an important part of EI/ECSE. Implicit in this requirement is the assumption that different classroom settings may have different requirements for children; that is, the contexts may differ substantially.

As part of the preparation for transition, the teacher may collect information on the skills that will be necessary in the next context and choose those skills as objectives for the child's current program. At times, the teacher may need to change the environmental context to more closely resemble the next setting or have the same types of requirements that may occur in the next setting. For example, if in kindergarten, all children have to carry their lunch tray in the lunchroom, then teaching the children to carry their tray and requiring it as a part of the lunch routine could be strategies that a preschool teacher might employ.

Another way that teachers might support a successful transition is through communication across professionals. Such communication could help the receiving teacher (the teacher next year) understand the developmental or behavioral characteristics of the child entering her or his class as well as contextual variables within this next classroom that might be helpful in supporting this transition. Understanding the relationship of the contextual features of the different environment and the child's functional skills are key to a successful transition from the home to a classroom setting or across classrooms.

The Family-Centered and Culturally Appropriate Nature of Early Intervention

Although most discussions of family involvement and participation in EI/ESCE flow from a systems perspective (Bailey et al., 1986; Dunst & Trivette, 1988), the family-centered practices are also compatible with a contextualistic behavioral orientation. Similarly, practices within families reflect their larger culture as well as the idiosyncratic microculture that is really the essence of being a family. Issues in EI/ECSE related to families and culture are similar in that they reflect the values or, as Sigrid Glenn (1988) suggested, the metacontingencies that operate in each context.

Cultural materialism, a perspective within anthropology and sociology, can provide a conceptual base for examining the larger contextual variables of families and cultures (Biglan et al., 1990). Society, as reflected through cultural and family practice, can be understood through two basic functions that must be achieved: individuals must have food and other essentials for physical survival and they must reproduce.

For our purposes, reproduction would be characterized as both giving birth to children and raising them to be productive members of society. Family and cultural practices can be understood in terms of the (meta)contingencies between such practices and the two basic outcomes (Glenn, 1988; Harris, 1979). Of course, when these functions are met satisfactorily, other functions might emerge (e.g., leisure, religion, science, sports).

EI/ECSE family-centered practices reflect the basic assumptions of cultural materialism. First, families have basic needs and priorities that may take precedence over intervention programs designed for their children. These needs dictate actions that occur within family contexts. When a family does not have sufficient food, clothing, or shelter, parents cannot be expected to contribute great energy to an EI/ECSE program that focuses on their children's development. Professionals, especially when working at the infant and toddler level, attempt to determine the family's needs and priorities. If basic survival needs are not present, service coordinators try to locate community services to meet those needs (Vincent & Beckett, 1993).

Second, the reproduction function influences family practice in ways that support the development of children within the family. With regard to EI/ECSE, the family members would become invested in early intervention plans that could be conducted at home or that occur at a center-based program (given that the survival functions are sufficiently met). Although the option is always given for families not to participate, the implicit assumption is that most families will want to be involved at some level.

Cultural appropriateness.   From a cultural materialism and contextual behaviorism perspective, cultural practices reflect the metacontingencies that exist among the multiple functions noted earlier. Practices (responses and contingencies) differ across cultures; so to understand acts in context (or the skills that should be selected for children in programs), one has to understand the practices occurring within the culture. Designing and implementing culturally appropriate interventions has become central to the practice of EI/ECSE (Odom & McLean, 1993). Such planning requires that professionals have a "cultural competence" that involves an awareness of their own culture, knowledge about the cultural norms of the family and child with whom they are working, and skills to communicate directly or through an interpreter in the language that the family uses (Lynch, 1992). Such cultural competence should allow EI/ECSE professionals to seat the skills that are important for individual children directly in the cultural context of their families and communities.

Summary: Bringing the Context into Practice

A contextualistic behavioral approach to EI/ECSE could be presented as in Figure 8.2. In this figure, the three-term contingency is still used, with the understanding that the first term could be extended into longer analyses of conditional and unconditional discriminative stimuli if necessary. Within this analysis, contextual factors are listed under the S^D, but they actually are not separable from the other terms in this contingency. These contextual factors include cultural variables, family variables, child variables, and current environments; all of which might be related to a single discriminative stimulus or class of stimuli.

The S^D, within the complex of variables, would set the occasion for or signal the occurrence of the functional response(s) that are the focus of an intervention plan for a child. Again, the form and function of the response is determined by, and therefore not separable from, the contextual factors that influenced the S^D. In fact, its embeddedness or relationship to the contextual factors is what makes it a functional response (i.e., appropriate for the cultural, family, or classroom environmental circumstances). The consequences that occur after the response may either be positive (immediately or in the future) or result in removal of negative events or experiences. Again, the positive and negative quality is functionally determined by the effects on the behavior but practically determined by the contextual variables (i.e., child factors, family factors).

In this chapter, we reviewed contextualism as a world hypothesis and proposed it as an organizing conceptual framework for behavior analysis. We then described how practices within EI/ECSE reflect or are at least compatible with a contextualistic behavioral approach. As the field moves toward a normalized, family-centered form of service provision operating within a culturally pluralistic society, such an approach could provide beneficial use as a conceptual foundation for EI/ECSE. However, its ultimate utility will always need to be measured against the truth criterion within contextualism: successful working. If the contextualistic behavioral perspective helps professionals successfully meet the goals for families and children with disabilities, then its values would be reflected by this success. In the end, it is a pragmatic and empirical issue.

$$S^D \qquad R_o \qquad S^{r+}$$

Contextual Variables
Immediate environment
Intrachild variables
Family variables
Cultural variables

Figure 8.2. The range of contextual variables that may influence the "action in context" for children with disabilities.

Acknowledgment

Many of the ideas contained in this chapter emerged from a reading group on Contextualism and Behavior Analysis at the University of California at Santa Barbara, which occurred while the first author was there as a postdoctoral fellow. In addition to the two authors, members of that group included Marta Valdez-Menchaca, Robert Koegel, Lynn Koegel, Craig Kennedy, Mike Gerber, and a number of doctoral students. Support for the first authors was provided by a Leadership Training Grant from the U.S. Office of Special Education, for which Mel Semmel serves as director. Support for the final preparation of this manuscript was provided by Project No. HO24B10108-93, funded by the Office of Special Education.

As this chapter went through the publication process, Tom Haring died. Tom was a leader in the fields of Applied Behavior Analysis and Special Education. Although relatively young, his work had already contributed substantially to both fields and had directly affected the lives of individuals with disabilities. The lives of those who knew him are a lesser place without Tom. This chapter is dedicated to Tom, his wife and collaborator, Cathy Breen, and his three daughters.

References

BAILEY, D. B., Simeonsson, R. J., Winton, P. J., Huntington, G. S., Comfort, J., Isbell, P., O'Donnell, K. J., & Helm, J. (1986). Family-focused intervention: A functional model for planning, implementing, and evaluating individualized family services in early intervention. *Journal of the Division for Early Childhood, 10,* 156–172.

BANDURA, A. (1977). *Social learning theory.* Englewood Cliffs, NJ: Prentice-Hall.

BIGLAN, A. (1992). *A functional contextualist: Framework for community intervention.* Paper presented at the Conference on Varieties of Contextualism, January, Reno.

BIGLAN, A., & Hayes, S. C. (1991). *Should the behavioral sciences become more pragmatic? The case for functional contextualism in research on human behavior.* Oregon Research Institute. Manuscript submitted for publication.

BIGLAN, A., Glasgow, R. E., & Singer, G. (1990). The need for a science of larger social units: A contextual approach. *Behavior Therapy, 21,* 195–215.

BIJOU, S. W., & Baer, D. M. (1978). *Behavior analysis of child development.* Englewood Cliffs, NJ: Prentice-Hall.

BLURTON-Jones, N. G. (1972). *Ethological studies of child behavior.* Cambridge: Cambridge University Press.

BRAZELTON, T. B. (1984). *Neonatal Behavioral Assessment Scale.* Philadelphia: Lippincott.

BREDEKAMP, S. (Ed.). (1987). *Developmentally appropriate practice in early childhood programs serving children from birth through age 8.* Washington, DC: National Association for the Education of Young Children.

BREDEKAMP, S., & Rosegrant, T. (Eds.). (1992). *Reaching potentials: Appropriate curriculum and assessment for young children,* Vol. 1. Washington, DC: National Association for the Education of Young Children.

BRICKER, D., & Cripe, J. J. (1992). *An activity-based approach to early intervention.* Baltimore: Brookes.

BRONFENBRENNER, U. (1986). Ecology of the family as context for human development research perspectives. *Developmental Psychology, 22,* 723–742.

BROWN, J. S., Collins, A., & Duguid, P. (1989). Situated cognition and the culture of learning. *Educational Researcher, 18*(1), 32–41.

BRUDER, M. B., & Chandler, L. (1993). Recommended practices in promoting transitions across programs. In DEC Recommended Practices Task Force (Eds.), *DEC Recommended Practices: Indicators of quality in programs for infants and young children with special needs and their families* (pp. 96–106). Reston, VA: Council for Exceptional Children.

BRUNER, J. (1990). *Acts of meaning.* Cambridge, MA: Harvard University Press.

COGNITION and Technology Group at Vanderbilt. (1990). Anchored instruction and its relationship to situated cognition. *Educational Researcher, 19*(5), 2–10.

DEC Recommended Practices Task Force. (1993). *DEC Recommended Practices: Indicators of quality in programs for infants and young children with special needs and their families.* Reston, VA: Council for Exceptional Children.

DESTEFANO, D. M., Howe, A. G., Horn, E. M., & Smith, B. A. (1991). *Best practices: Evaluating early childhood special education programs.* Tucson: Communication Skill Builders.

DEVRIES, R., & Kohlberg, L. (1987). *Constructivist early education: Overview and comparison with other programs.* Washington, DC: National Association for the Education of Young Children.

DUNST, C. J., & Trivette, C. M. (1988). A family systems model of early intervention with handicapped and developmentally at-risk children. In D. Powell (Ed.), *Parent education as early childhood intervention: Emerging directions in theory, research, and practice* (pp. 131–180). New York: Ablex.

ENGELMANN, S., & Carnine, D. (1982). *Theory of instruction: Principles and applications.* New York: Irvington Publishers.

FOGEL, A., Nwokah, E., Dedo, J. Y., Messinger, D., Dickson, K. L., Matusov, E., & Holt, S. A. (1992). The social process theory of emotion: A radical contextualist perspective. *Social Development, 1,* 147–150.

GESELL, A. (1925). *The mental growth of the preschool child.* New York: Macmillan.

GEWIRTZ, J. L. (1972). Some contextual determinants of stimulus potency. In R. D. Parke (Ed.), *Recent trends in social learning theory* (pp. 7–33). New York: Academic Press.

GLENN, S. S. (1988). Toward a synthesis of behavior analysis and cultural materialism. *The Behavior Analyst, 11,* 161–180.

HANSON, M. J., & Lynch, E. W. (1989). *Early intervention: Implementing child and family services for infants and toddlers who are at risk or disabled.* Austin: PRO-ED.

HARING, T. G., & Kennedy, C. H. (in press). Philosophic foundations of behavior analysis in developmental disabilities. In K. Haring, D. Lovett, & N. Haring (Eds.), *Integrated lifestyle services for persons with disabilities: A theoretical and empirical perspective.* New York: Springer Verlag.

HARRIS, M. (1979). *Cultural materialism.* New York: Random House.

HART, B. (1985). Naturalistic language training techniques. In S. Warren & A. Rogers-Warren (Eds.), *Teaching functional language* (pp. 63–88). Baltimore: University Park Press.

HAYES, S. C., & Hayes, L. J. (1992). Some clinical implications of contextualistic behaviorism: The example of cognition. *Behavior Therapy, 23,* 225–249.

HAYES, S. C., Hayes, L. J., & Reese, H. W. (1988). Finding the philosophical core: A review of Stephen C. Pepper's *World hypotheses: A study in evidence. Journal of the Experimental Analysis of Behavior, 50,* 97–111.

HORNER, R. H., & McDonald, R. S. (1982). A comparison of single instance and general case instruction in teaching a generalized vocational skill. *Journal of the Association for Persons with Severe Handicaps, 7*, 7–20.

KAISER, A. P., Yoder, P., & Keetz, A. (in press). The efficacy of milieu language intervention. In S. Warren & J. Reichle (Eds.), *Causes and effects of communication and language intervention*. Baltimore: Brookes.

KANTOR, J. J. (1933). In defense of stimulus-response psychology. *Psychological Review, 40*, 324–336.

LACHMAN, R., Lachman, J. L., & Butterfield, E. C. (1979). *Cognitive psychology and information processing*. Hillsdale, NJ: Lawrence Erlbaum Associates.

LERNER, R. M. (1991). Changing organism-context relations as the basic process of development: A developmental contextual perspective. *Developmental Psychology, 27*, 27–32.

LYNCH, E. W. (1992). Developing cross-cultural competence. In E. Lynch & M. Hanson (Eds.), *Developing cross-cultural competence* (pp. 35–59). Baltimore: Brookes.

MCDONNELL, A., & Hardman, M. (1988). A synthesis of "best practice" for early childhood services. *Journal of the Division for Early Childhood, 12*, 328–341.

MCLEAN, M. E., & Odom, S. L. (in press). Practices for young children with and without disabilities: A comparison of DEC and NAEYC identified practices. *Topics in Early Childhood Special Education*.

MARR, M. J. (1993). Contextualistic mechanism or mechanistic contextualism?: The straw machine as tar baby. *The Behavior Analyst, 16*, 59–65.

MICHAEL, J. (1982). Distinguishing between the discriminative and motivational functions of stimuli. *Journal of the Experimental Analysis of Behavior, 37*, 149–155.

MORRIS, E. K. (1988). Contextualism: The world view of behavior analysis. *Journal of Experimental Child Psychology, 46*, 289–329.

MORRIS, E. K. (1992a). The aim, progress, and evolution of behavior analysis. *Behavior Analyst, 15*, 3–29.

MORRIS, E. K. (1992b). *What it would be like to be a mechanist*. Paper presented at the symposium, Mechanism and Contextualism Contrasted at the annual convention of the Association for Behavior Analysis, San Francisco.

MULLIGAN, M., Guess, D., Holvoet, J., & Brown, F. (1980). The Individualized Curriculum Sequencing Model (I): Implications from research on massed, distributed, or spaced trial training. *Journal of the Association for the Severely Handicapped, 5*, 325–337.

NEISWORTH, J. T. (1993). Recommended practices in assessment of infants and young children. In DEC Recommended Practices Task Force (Eds.), *DEC recommended practices: Indicators of quality in programs for infants and young children with special needs and their families* (pp. 11–18). Reston, VA: Council for Exceptional Children.

ODOM, S. L., & McLean, M. E. (1993). Establishing recommended practices for program for infants and young children with special needs and their families. In DEC Recommended Practices Task Force (Ed.), *DEC recommended practices: Indicators of quality in programs for infants and young children with special needs and their families* (pp. 1–10). Reston, VA: Council for Exceptional Children.

ODOM, S. L., Skellenger, A., & Ostrosky, M. (1993). Ecobehavioral analysis of engagement and child initiation for children with and without disabilities. Paper presented at the Biennial Conference of the Society for Research in Child Development, New Orleans.

PEPPER, S. C. (1942). *World hypotheses: A study in evidence*. Berkeley: University of California Press.

PIAGET, J. (1952). *The origins of intelligence in children*. New York: International Universities Press.

SIDMAN, M. (1986). Functional analysis of emergent verbal classes. In T. Thompson & M. Zeiler (Eds.), *Analysis and integration of behavioral units* (pp. 213–245). Hillsdale, NJ: Lawrence Erlbaum Associates.

SIMEONSSON, R. J. (1979). *Carolina Record of Individual Behavior*. Unpublished assessment instrument. Chapel Hill: Frank Porter Graham Child Development Center, University of North Carolina.

SKINNER, B. F. (1931). The concept of reflex in the description of behavior. *Journal of General Psychology, 5*, 427–458.

SKINNER, B. F. (1938). *Behavior of organisms*. New York: Appleton-Century-Croft.

STERNBERG, R. J. (1985). *Beyond I.Q.: Toward a triarchic theory of intelligence*. Cambridge, MA: Cambridge University Press.

STRAIN, P. S., McConnell, S. R., Carta, J. J., Fowler, S. A., Neisworth, J. T., & Wolery, M. (1992). Behaviorism in early intervention. *Topics in Early Childhood Special Education, 12*, 121–141.

THOMPSON, T., & Lubinski, D. (1986). Units of analysis and kinetic structure of behavioral repertoires. *Journal of the Experimental Analysis of Behavior, 46*, 219–242.

VINCENT, L., & Beckett, J. A. (1993). Recommended practices in family participation. In DEC Recommended Practices Task Force (Eds.), *DEC recommended practices: Indicators of quality in programs for infants and young children with special needs and their families* (pp. 19–29). Reston, VA: Council for Exceptional Children.

WAHLER, R. G., & Fox, J. J. (1981). Setting events in applied behavior analysis: Toward a conceptual and methodological expansion. *Journal of Applied Behavior Analysis, 14*, 327–338.

WARREN, S. F. (1992). Enhancing communication and language development with milieu teaching procedures. In E. Cipani (Ed.), *A guide to developing language competence in preschool children with severe and moderate handicaps* (pp. 68–93). Springfield, IL: Charles C. Thomas.

WINOGRAD, T. (1987). *Understanding computers and cognition: A new foundation for design*. Reading, MA: Addison-Wesley.

CHAPTER 9

Communication Interventions: The Challenges of Across-the-Day Implementation

Howard Goldstein
Louise Kaczmarek
Nancy Hepting

Helping young children learn communication skills is no longer considered the exclusive purview of speech-language pathologists. Collaborative and transdisciplinary education efforts are initiated with increasing prevalence, especially in classrooms serving preschoolers with communication impairments. Integrating communication interventions into classroom environments has been widely advocated (Cole & Dale, 1986; Hart, 1985; Miller, 1989; Nietupski, Scheutz, & Ockwood, 1980; Wilcox, Kouri, & Caswell, 1991). Consequently, investigators have explored ways of using effective instructional procedures to teach communication skills across the day. In our own research efforts, teachers, teaching assistants, and even peers have served as communication intervention agents throughout the preschool day.

In classroom-based communication intervention, consultants (typically, speech-language pathologists) seek to change the interaction styles of intervention agents in the classroom who in turn affect the children's communication and language learning. This task is challenging in self-contained or reverse mainstreamed programs for children with disabilities, but it is likely to be even more challenging in traditional preschool programs that include children with

disabilities. In comparison to special education programs, most programs for typical preschoolers have larger class sizes, lower staff-child ratios, less time dedicated to inservice training, and little training on teaching children with disabilities.

To understand the challenges inherent in implementing communication interventions across the school day, we need to review the full range of intervention strategies that can be used in the classroom. First, we present an overview of interventions that were designed for, or can be adapted to, use in children's everyday or "natural" environments. Then we discuss suggestions for meeting the many challenges of implementing intervention on an across-the-day basis.

Naturalistic Communication Interventions

The term *naturalistic interventions* refers to interventions implemented in real or simulated activities that are typical of the home, school, or community environments in which a child normally functions. Naturalistic interventions vary in the extent to which they depart from the didactic teaching strategies historically implemented in "pull-out" models of treatment for communication disorders. Typically, naturalistic interventions are characterized by their use of dispersed learning trials, attempts to base teaching on the child's attentional lead within the context of normal conversational interchanges, and orientation toward teaching the form and content of language in the context of normal use (Warren & Bambara, 1989). Didactic intervention approaches, on the other hand, have been conducted using substitute stimuli (e.g., pictures, puppets) or simulation settings that are amenable to teaching specific skills using mass trials. Naturalistic approaches were developed as an alternative to didactic language intervention, because children often experienced difficulties in generalizing new skills to everyday contexts where they were needed. To avoid generalization problems, naturalistic communication interventions are programmed within the context of normal routines and activities. Interventions that are implemented across the day within usual routines and activities might be considered the most natural; the more an intervention alters what usually occurs in the natural environment, the less natural the intervention. For example, playing a specially designed game is less natural than integrating procedures into a mealtime or bedtime context. Setting the occasion for functional language use in this way could be quite effective. The use of naturalistic contexts does not ensure that intervention programming is effective. Effectiveness more likely relates to instructional techniques; that is, ensuring that the child learns to respond to relevant stimuli and that the behaviors that are taught evoke positive consequences from other adults and children in everyday contexts (e.g., LeBlanc & Ruggles, 1982).

Most naturalistic interventions focus on restructuring the interaction patterns between the child and the adults in the environment. Methods of restructuring these patterns differ in whether or with what specificity intervention agents set language objectives, control environmental stimuli, and modify the language used in interactions (Fey, 1986). With adult-directed approaches, the intervention agents explicitly control these variables. Adult-directed approaches tend to focus on *structuring the antecedents* to provide optimal opportunities for the child to communicate (e.g., the adult wishes the child to say "cookie," so he

holds up a cookie and asks, "What do you want?"). Child-oriented approaches are characterized by the child's control of what and when something is communicated. Child-oriented approaches tend to focus primarily on *structuring adult responses* to a child's communication (e.g., when the child picks up a cookie and says "coo-ee," the adult repeats "Yes, cookie").

Review of Naturalistic Communication Intervention Packages

The many naturalistic communication intervention packages that have been developed differ in the combinations of techniques they include. These techniques are directed to multiple aspects of adult-child interaction (e.g., directing or responding to the child's focus of attention; providing the child a model of appropriate language); the procedures for sequencing the use of techniques depend on the child's behavior (e.g., requesting a child to repeat a model after he or she fails to respond correctly to a question; repeating what a child has said with the addition of one new word). Characteristics of a number of communication intervention packages and their effects are reviewed in the following paragraphs.

Interactive model of intervention. Interactive approaches are often considered child oriented because they strive to emulate interaction patterns that are typical of mothers with children whose language is developing normally. The individuals present in children's natural environments are taught to use multiple techniques for promoting interaction, modeling language, and following the child's lead (Tannock & Girolametto, 1992). Language modeling techniques include: self-talk and parallel talk (i.e., describing what you or the child is doing, seeing, feeling, or hearing), repetitions, expansions (i.e., repeating a child's utterance with the addition of a new syntactic or semantic element(s)), extensions (i.e, providing additional information), and recasts (i.e., presenting the same semantic material by using different syntactical forms). Specific language objectives typically are not targeted with this general stimulation approach. No didactic language teaching procedures are used, and the intervention techniques are intended to be used across the day regardless of setting or specific activities (Tannock & Girolametto, 1992).

Most research on the interactive model has focused on mother-child interactions. To date, research on these approaches with children with language impairments has shown that mothers' interaction styles change when they incorporate the techniques. Improvements have been demonstrated in adult-child interactions on a variety of dimensions such as exhibiting more balanced exchanges and fewer adult turns (Girolametto, 1988; Mahoney & Powell, 1988), following the child's lead more often (Girolametto, 1988; Mahoney & Powell, 1988), and giving fewer commands (Mahoney & Powell, 1988; Weistuch & Lewis, 1985; Weistuch, Lewis, & Sullivan, 1991). Some mothers, however, adopted only one or two of the techniques, as Tannock and Girolametto (1992) pointed out in their review of interactive approaches. They also suggested that the intensive training typical of these approaches may not be necessary to produce the expected effects. Furthermore, acquisition of these new adult behaviors has typically been measured in contrived play sessions conducted outside the mother and child's natural environment and everyday routines. Thus, it is difficult to determine the extent to which the procedures were actually carried out across the day in home environments. Measures of child outcomes have been limited to general measures such as the mean utterance length (MUL). Tannock and Girolametto (1992) suggested that evidence of changes in mother-child interaction is common, but that evidence of children learning new language forms is lacking in these studies.

Interactive approaches have been carried out in classroom environments in studies that have compared this approach to other communication intervention approaches (Cole & Dale, 1986; Friedman & Friedman, 1980; Weller, 1979; Wilcox, Kouri, & Caswell, 1991). Cole and Dale (1986) found an interactive approach that used environmental arrangement strategies and concentrated on snacktime and free play activities within the classroom to be as effective as didactic instruction. Wilcox and colleagues (1991) compared individual therapy and a classroom-based interactive model and found the interactive model to be equally effective. They gathered mother-child language samples in the home and reported somewhat better generalization to home environments by the

children treated with the interactive model. Overall, classroom implementation of interactive approaches has shown improved performance on standardized language tests, but treatment comparisons have not yielded conclusive comparative results favoring these approaches.

Hybrid intervention approaches. Hybrid approaches (Fey, 1986) combine the use of some of the interactive techniques with adult-directed strategies. Specific language objectives are typically identified for individual children. Some hybrid approaches, such as milieu language teaching (Hart & Risley, 1968; Warren & Kaiser, 1986) and vertical restructuring (Schwartz et al., 1985), require a child to respond verbally. Others, such as focused stimulation (Leonard, 1981) and responsive interaction (Yoder & Davies, 1990) do not require verbal responding. Most investigations of these approaches have implemented intervention techniques in special areas set aside within the classroom or during one or two selected classroom activities. Intervention agents have primarily been researchers or trained classroom personnel rather than parents. Milieu language teaching and responsive intervention are widely used and have been evaluated in our own research (Goldstein, Mousetis, Hepting, & McDonnell, 1993; Yoder et al., 1993).

Milieu language teaching, an approach derived from incidental teaching (Hart & Risley, 1968), focuses on establishing functional communication by using such techniques as time-delay (Halle, Baer, & Spradlin, 1981; Halle, Marshall, & Spradlin, 1979), mands for verbalization (Warren, McQuarter, & Rogers-Warren, 1984), prompted imitation, and expansion. These techniques are structured into a system of most to least prompts for introducing new language behaviors. When the child initiates interest in an event or object and the intervention agent uses this opportunity to teach language through use of the specific techniques, the procedure is called "incidental teaching." The implementation of milieu language teaching requires intervention agents to learn a set of sequenced procedures requiring no more than two replications of each of three basic techniques. In a recent review of the literature, Kaiser, Yoder, and Keetz (1992) concluded that milieu teaching has consistently produced improvements in the use of target behaviors within treatment settings. The generalized effects on performance outside the treatment settings, however, have not been supported sufficiently. Further research is needed to study the effects of milieu teaching when implemented across the day.

Responsive interaction (Yoder & Davies, 1990) is a hybrid adapted from the INREAL model (Weiss, 1981), a classroom-based, interactive, across-the-day communication intervention approach. Like other more adult-directed interventions, responsive interaction differs from the interactive approaches in that specific language objectives are targeted. This approach was implemented in a group design study that compared it to across-the-day milieu language teaching (Yoder et al., 1993). Both approaches resulted in significant improvements in general language performance measures. Aptitude-by-treatment interactions indicated that responsive interaction was relatively more effective with children with more advanced language (e.g., higher MLUs) and milieu teaching was more effective with children with less developed communication skills. Results from another treatment comparison study were similar; milieu teaching was found to have somewhat better effects for lower functioning children, whereas a didactic approach had somewhat better effects for higher functioning children (Yoder, Kaiser, & Alpert, 1991). However, the two treatments did not differ significantly overall in their effects on general language performance measures.

Goldstein and his colleagues (1993) developed a hybrid *responsive interaction plus milieu language teaching* model was to teach elaborated requests and comments. They evaluated the relative effects of teaching preschool children communication skills in small-group intervention outside the classroom versus classroom intervention implemented by teachers and teacher assistants. Specifically, they investigated whether acquisition and generalization of targeted language goals differed when addressed twice weekly during a small-group instructional format as compared to daily in the classroom using a hybrid of milieu and responsive interaction instructional formats. An alternating treatments comparison revealed that both interventions were effective in teaching children with

different developmental levels to produce new language skills in the training settings and in a generalization setting with an adult not associated with either approach. The teachers and aides were taught to implement seven intervention techniques. Although the teachers' facility at using the different techniques varied, their overall rate of communication intervention across the day was high and the effects were impressive.

There is little evidence in the research literature to indicate that certain communication intervention packages are more effective than others. However, when multiple-component intervention packages have been fully implemented, they resulted in desired changes in adult-child interaction patterns and improvements in language use or language learning. The lack of differential effects may be a result of a long-standing problem in studying language development; that is, the paucity of sensitive and reliable measures. Alternatively, the various intervention packages may be effective because, regardless of specific techniques, each intervention alters the presence and frequency of important variables of which children's language use is a function. With each package, children are presented an abundance of appropriate models of language, salient antecedent stimuli in motivating contexts, lots of opportunities for language use supplemented by various prompting and fading strategies, and functional reinforcers for language use.

Table 9.1 summarizes the techniques identified in evaluations of naturalistic approaches to communication intervention. We have classified 11 techniques based on the emphasis each places on the manipulation of antecedent stimuli or the broader environmental contexts to evoke children's language behavior or the delivery of consequent events to influence children's communication. The interventions, which are numbered along the horizontal axis, have been ordered roughly from those that are more adult directed to those that are more child oriented based on the teaching techniques employed. Each study evaluated an intervention package consisting of a unique set of techniques. More than one intervention may be described in single studies when treatment comparisons were conducted. An examination of in-

Table 9.1 Summary of the teaching techniques used in studies of communication interventions

Study Number*	Didactic Approaches				Hybrid Intervention Approaches																				Interactive Approaches							
	1	2	3	4	5	6	7	8	9	10	11	12	13	14	15	16	17	18	19	20	21	22	23	24	25	26	27	28	29	30	31	32
Manipulations of Antecedents																																
Prompting imitation	x	x	x		x	x	x	x	x	x	x	x	x	x	x	x	x	x	x	x	x	x				x	x	x				
Manding verbalization	x	x	x		x	x	x	x	x	x	x	x	x	x	x	x	x	x	x	x	x	x	x	x	x	x	x	x	x	x	x	x
Waiting for initiation or response											x	x	x	x				x	x	x	x		x	x			x	x				
Requesting clarification or elaboration								x	x	x											x							x				
Modeling			x									x			x	x	x	x	x		x	x	x		x	x	x		x	x	x	x
Descriptive talking																						x			x		x		x	x	x	x
Repeating, expanding, etc.	x		x		x	x	x		x	x				x	x	x			x		x	x	x	x	x	x		x	x	x	x	x
Arranging the environment			x		x	x	x	x	x	x	x		x	x	x	x		x	x	x	x	x	x		x		x		x	x	x	x
Manipulations of Consequences																																
Praising	x	x	x	x	x	x	x	x	x		x	x		x				x	x	x		x									x	
Using minimal encouragers									x												x	x		x			x	x				
Delivering desired consequence		x	x		x	x	x	x	x	x	x	x	x	x	x	x	x	x	x	x	x	x	x	x			x	x				

*Studies (Note that the *a*'s and *b*'s refer to studies that compare treatments.):

1. Yoder et al., 1991b
2. Cole & Dale, 1986a
3. McGee et al., 1985b
4. Neef et al., 1984a
5. Hunt et al., 1986
6. MacDonald et al., 1974
7. Neef et al., 1984b
8. Rogers-Warren & Warren, 1980
9. Warren et al., 1984
10. McGee et al., 1985a
11. Halle et al., 1981
12. Cavallaro & Bambara, 1982a
13. Gobbi et al., 1986
14. Oliver & Halle, 1982
15. Angelo & Goldstein, 1990
16. Haring et al., 1987
17. Yoder et al., 1991a
18. Charlop et al., 1985
19. Hart & Risley, 1974
20. Hart & Risley, 1975
21. Warren & Bambara, 1989
22. Warren & Gazdag, 1990
23. Hart & Risley, 1968
24. Schwartz et al., 1985
25. Weistuch & Lewis, 1985
26. McLean & Vincent, 1984
27. Cavallaro & Bambara, 1982b
28. Giralometto, 1988
29. Mahoney & Powell, 1988
30. Weiss, 1981
31. Cole & Dale, 1986b
32. Wilcox et al., 1991

tervention studies reveals a good deal of overlap between the teaching techniques used in interactive and hybrid intervention approaches.

Each of the studies reviewed documented language gains in most of the children or groups of children who received treatment. Treatment packages that include more treatment components do not necessarily yield superior outcomes. The lack of clear differential effects in treatment comparison studies argues against advocating the use of particular packages of teaching techniques. Although there have been some indications that certain treatment approaches may be better suited to more or less sophisticated language learners, results are not consistent and confirmatory studies have yet to be conducted (Connell, 1987; Cole & Dale, 1986; Cole, Dale, & Mills, 1991; Friedman & Friedman, 1980; Yoder, Kaiser, & Alpert, 1991). Including too many teaching techniques when designing across-the-day communication interventions may not be wise. High-quality implementation may be especially difficult to establish in classroom contexts if treatment packages are too complex. Careful consideration should be given to the many challenges to designing effective naturalistic communication interventions.

Challenges to Implementation

An emphasis on across-the-day implementation represents a radical departure from the traditional pull-out model of communication intervention. One of the biggest challenges for practitioners is the change in roles of the personnel involved. Speech-language pathologists, who traditionally have taken children out of their classrooms for therapy, must now release at least a portion of their role to teachers (Nietupski, Scheutz, & Ockwood, 1980). The role of the speech-language pathologist shifts from conducting direct therapy to training teachers and facilitating the delivery of communication interventions within the classroom environment. To ensure fidelity of treatment and monitor the progress of the intervention within the classroom, speech-language pathologists need to be able to demonstrate for, team teach with, coach, observe, and provide feedback to classroom personnel. The roles of teachers and other classroom

staff also shift. They must accept responsibility for delivering at least a portion of the communication instruction to certain children. In addition to collaborating with speech-language pathologists on the design of classroom communication interventions, teachers, who generally do not possess the same level of expertise on communication development as speech-language pathologists, must be trained to implement communication interventions within the classroom, must feel comfortable being observed, and must accept feedback on their implementation.

The fidelity of implementation of across-the-day interventions is critical to maximizing treatment effects. Both the accuracy and frequency of implementation of the teaching techniques across the day are vital to success. Through our efforts to establish across-the-day communication intervention programs, four issues related to the fidelity of treatment have been identified for further discussion: activities preliminary to training, inservice training of teachers, strategies for establishing high-quality implementation, and strategies for promoting maintenance and generalization of implementation.

Activities Preliminary to Training

In our research efforts over the past six years, we have worked with teachers and teacher assistants in both integrated and segregated preschool programs to implement naturalistic language interventions (i.e., milieu, responsive interaction, and a hybrid of the two approaches) in an across-the-day format. It is not surprising that some teachers are intimidated by a set of new expectations. The key to minimizing such anxiety and resulting resistance remains illusive. A combination of factors needs to be considered. Rapport must be built before training begins. While establishing reliability and conducting child assessments, we have done just that. By devoting time to help teachers in the classroom and by talking about the children before and after school, we have established a reputation for helpfulness, dependability, trustworthiness, and caring about students and teachers. Thus, a consistent and strong presence during startup has been advantageous in developing relationships with classroom staff that set the stage for a collaborative intervention effort.

Our first step in implementing naturalistic communication interventions has been to convince teachers that the interventions will be useful and fairly easy to implement. Not surprisingly, many teachers have expressed a reasonable amount of initial skepticism on both counts: "Sure, this intervention has good results in research studies, but what makes you think it will work and that I can do this, given the extraordinary demands of the kids in my classroom and my diverse job responsibilities." Perhaps such concerns can be mitigated by adding some extra steps in the training process. In particular, focusing more attention on *assessing attitudes and practices* could be very helpful.

Social validation assessments are an initial, formative step in the training process (Fawcett, 1991). In the past, we have administered consumer satisfaction questionnaires at the end of our studies. For example, when we asked teachers about different intervention strategies, their overall ratings indicated that (1) the procedures are minimally to moderately difficult to learn; (2) some change is manifested in classroom curriculum, classroom management, or interaction styles; (3) moderate to high enjoyment is associated with implementing the strategies; and (4) perceived effectiveness is rated as moderate to high. However, some relevant distinctions were made. For milieu teaching, time delay and incidental teaching procedures were judged as being more difficult to implement than model and mand-model procedures. Responsive-interaction intervention, sustained attention, and following the child's lead were judged as more difficult to implement than the descriptive talking and the repeat/expand procedures. Following the child's lead was judged as somewhat more effective than the other responsive-interaction procedures. Sustained attention was perceived as less effective and less enjoyable to implement. Perceptions of acceptability of specific procedures and their likely effectiveness also can be assessed *prior* to training.

The following example illustrates a social validity assessment conducted before training. We asked 18 early childhood specialists representing a number of disciplines to watch videotapes and to make judgments about the teacher-child interactions they observed. Half of the judges showed strong preferences;

3 preferred more structured interactions and teacher-directed techniques, whereas 6 preferred less structured interactions and child-directed techniques. These preferences might influence decisions in choosing to focus on milieu language teaching versus responsive interaction. At the end of the session, we also asked these judges to rate the likelihood that various aspects of these teacher-child interactions would facilitate language learning. Mean ratings for those judgments are presented in Table 9.2. Interestingly, these ratings did not reflect disparate judgments of the perceived effectiveness of adult-directed versus child-oriented procedures like those shown for the videotape ratings.

One goal of social validation is to assess the perceived acceptability of different treatment procedures before training (Schwartz & Baer, 1991). Our experiences thus far have led us to the following revision of our social validation assessments. Teachers are asked to make informed decisions about the acceptability of seven strategies that could be used in a hybrid model of across-the-day language intervention. Allowing teachers to make informed decisions about unfamiliar intervention strategies is a bit tricky. To improve upon our past method, we propose providing a brief description of each strategy and its basic objective and then presenting a brief videotape to illustrate the implementation of the strategy with several examples. Acceptability could be rated for each strategy in succession using a Likert-type scale.

Table 9.2 Mean ratings of the likelihood of facilitating language learning

Interaction	Mean Rating
Focusing on specific language objectives for each child.	4.5
Giving children ample opportunity to direct conversation.	3.9
Using corrective feedback.	4.4
Following the child's topic or interest.	4.3
Not asking many questions.	2.7
Getting children to repeat specific utterances.	3.6
Limiting teacher talking so that child can talk more.	3.6
Responding to child utterances by repeating or adding to it.	4.6
Requiring children to request needed materials.	4.1
Not requiring children to say specific words or sentences.	2.4

Note: 1 = very unlikely; 5 = very likely.

This pretraining assessment could be used to individualize the selection of training goals. We assume that teachers will be more enthusiastic about learning and implementing strategies they have rated as acceptable. The teacher's role in the selection process is meant to encourage a sense of ownership and commitment to the strategies being learned. Strategies rated as less acceptable might be excluded from training, but taught later, with greater sensitivity to teachers' attitudes or opinions. This form of social validity assessment assesses attitudes after giving teachers adequate information to make judgments about their interest in learning intervention techniques. Such an assessment presupposes that the consultant(s) or trainers will then use that information when designing inservice training programs.

A second type of social validity assessment relates to teachers' attitudes about what communicative behaviors are important in educational contexts. In particular, we are interested in the opportunities for language use that teachers provide. Our observations indicate that teachers provide ample opportunities for children to answer questions and follow instructions. It is important to determine whether these are the communicative functions most valued by teachers. If they think other communicative functions are important, do they give the children plenty of opportunities to use their language to express these other functions? Figure 9.1 provides an example of how we might assess teachers' perceptions of the importance of and opportunities for different communicative functions. Observational data could be taken in addition to or perhaps instead of the perception-of-opportunities survey.

Before asking teachers to change the way they interact with children in their classrooms, it is useful to gain insight into individual differences in their attitudes and practices. The information garnered from the type of questionnaire presented in Figure 9.1, as well as observational data, could be used to demonstrate to teachers that the intervention strategies that they will be learning match what they (as well as

---

Communication Functions

Competent communicators express a variety of communication functions. Some of the functions that preschoolers might express include:

Requesting (e.g., requests for information, action, objects, acknowledgment)
Responding (e.g., responding to questions and requests, clarifying, protesting)
Commenting (e.g., describing events, properties of objects, feelings)
Conversational amenities (e.g., attention getters, politeness terms, greetings)
Social supplements (e.g., jokes, teasing, warnings)

Indicate your rating of the *importance* for students in your class to express each of these general functions, using the following scale:

1=essential, 2=very important, 3=moderately important, 4=minimally important, 5=not important

Requesting	1	2	3	4	5
Responding	1	2	3	4	5
Commenting	1	2	3	4	5
Conversational amenities	1	2	3	4	5
Social supplements	1	2	3	4	5

Now estimate how many *opportunities per day* currently exist in your classroom for children to display these communication functions:

Requesting	< 5	5–10	10–20	20–40	> 40
Responding	< 5	5–10	10–20	20–40	> 40
Commenting	< 5	5–10	10–20	20–40	> 40
Conversational amenities		< 5	5–10	10–20	20–40	> 40
Social supplements	< 5	5–10	10–20	20–40	> 40

Figure 9.1. Questionnaire to assess communication functions in preschool classrooms.

parents and others) view as important. For example, teachers who think instructional procedures for teaching *requesting* are too structured and too difficult to carry out might initially be better candidates for learning procedures for teaching *commenting*. It seems likely that teachers will execute an intervention that they have selected with greater fidelity and higher rates of implementation than other interventions.

Inservice Training

Numerous investigators have questioned whether isolated inservice training workshops are effective in changing professional practices (Burke, McLaughlin, & Valdiviesco, 1988; Evans, 1981; Odom, 1987). Some of the features believed to enhance the effects of inservice training include: (1) tailoring the training to individual and program needs (Evans, 1981; Klein & Sheehan, 1987; Lieberman & Miller, 1979; Rogers, Lewis, & Reis, 1987); (2) active support and involvement of program administrators (Evans, 1981; Klein & Sheehan, 1987); (3) linking inservice training workshops with on-site technical assistance (Emrick & Peterson, 1977; Janney & Meyer, 1990); and (4) evaluating the effects of training by using multiple measures, including preobservations and postobservations of targeted skill usage in context and changes in the children's performance (Rogers, Lewis, & Reis, 1987; Weissman-Frisch, Crowell, & Inman, 1980).

Part of tailoring an initial workshop about communication intervention to individual and program needs involves conveying realistic expectations. Three key points illustrate our expectations for teachers involved in across-the-day communication intervention. First, communication between adults and target children involves reciprocal influences. Raising one's consciousness of how interactions potentially influence language learning may profoundly impact behavior. Second, although "teaching episodes" with target children may differ from typical conversational interactions, the intervention techniques are largely comprised of communication skills already in the repertoires of competent communicators. Those behaviors are repackaged, however, to be used in a more systematic manner. In fact, later in training we use flow charts to illustrate how these behaviors are chained. Thus, training entails bringing teachers' communication skills under new

stimulus control to optimize learning opportunities for target children. Third, some facilitative strategies run counter to communicators' natural tendencies. Perhaps the most difficult subcomponent of these behavior chains is getting teachers and speech-language pathologists to attend to communication partners and wait for a child's response or especially an initiation. Our culture does not tolerate silence in conversational contexts. Yet this delay technique (or waiting silently and expectantly) may be crucial in providing opportunities for communication turns for children with disabilities (Halle, Marshall, & Spradlin, 1979, 1981; Weiss, 1981).

After elaborating on key expectations, we introduce general guidelines for creating opportunities for teaching interactions. Teachers are asked to consider environmental arrangement strategies that can increase the number of opportunities for functional language use (Halle, 1988). Next, the training of specific intervention techniques involves the fairly standard steps of modeling and directing guided practice during a workshop.

Subsequent technical assistance within the classroom involves additional guided practice with children, shifting to more varied and realistic implementation contexts, and monitoring and providing feedback for independent practice. Technical assistance can be delivered through different forms of consultation, ranging from the expert model in which the consultant directs the consultee to the collaborative model in which consultant and consultee together develop target objectives, implementation strategies, and evaluation plans (Babcock & Pryzwansky, 1983). The collaborative model, which most teachers (Babcock & Pryzwansky, 1983; File, 1992; Pryzwansky & White, 1983), appears to be the most compatible with implementing across-the-day communication intervention. Collaborative consultation skills are not innate forms of interaction; both consultants and consultees require training to become proficient (Idol & West, 1987; West & Cannon, 1988; West & Idol, 1990).

Strategies for Establishing High-Quality Implementation in the Classroom

Three additional strategies that take place after the initial training have enhanced the effects of training.

First, initially concentrating implementation of the intervention on particular activities during the day has helped develop realistic expectations for "across-the-day" interventions. Second, involving teachers in training other teachers has helped solidify learning. Third, requiring teachers to self-monitor their implementation helps avoid underutilization of the procedure.

We have begun the implementation of across-the-day language intervention by initially concentrating on selected activities and several children and then gradually expanding implementation to more activities and increasing numbers of children. As a result, teachers have not found implementation to be overwhelming, because they have been able to refine their implementation of the procedures in fewer contexts before expanding their application across the entire day.

When implementation of language intervention results in marked improvements in children's communication repertoires, word tends to spread quickly within a program. For example, teachers in one program asked us to provide inservice training to staff members of classrooms that were not involved in a language study. Rather than providing the inservice workshop ourselves, we enlisted these teachers to deliver the workshop. We helped them prepare, including the development of handouts and video segments, and rehearse. Teaching colleagues the procedures bolstered learning and validated the procedures in the eyes of the novice teachers in other classrooms. Because they were a part of the program's culture, the inservice presenters knew and understood the types of techniques, examples, and strategies that would work well in presenting the information and practicing the various procedures with their colleagues.

Finally, asking teachers to self-monitor their implementation has helped avoid underutilization of procedures with "missed" children (Goldstein et al., 1993). Tear-off tabs (like those found on bulletin-board advertisements with tear-off phone numbers) were taped to children's backs. Each child's objective was written on the paper, and each time a teacher engaged a child in a language-teaching episode, the teacher would tear off one of the tabs. The use of the tabs reminded the teachers of each child's target objective, ensured a minimum level of implementation, and communicated at a glance to the teachers the status of each child's teaching episodes during the day. Our participant questionnaire results revealed that most teachers liked the tabs.

Strategies for Promoting Maintenance and Generalization of Implementation

We contend that long-term implementation is a long-term problem. Intervention strategies that bring about meaningful improvements in children's communication and social skills are likely to be maintained through natural contingencies of reinforcement. An apparent lack of maintenance or diminished effectiveness is more likely a problem of generalization rather than of maintenance.

Long-term implementation requires teachers to generalize the procedures across different target behaviors and children. One problem that we have experienced is the repeated application of the procedures without much modification once a child has achieved the objective. A lack of timely readjustments has two implications. First, some children who have started to make marked progress in their communication repertoires may begin to show slower progress if new objectives are not identified and targeted for intervention. Thus, procedures need to be put in place to monitor progress and to select new target objectives.

Second, the novelty of the specific application seems to "wear off" with some children who do not maintain performance of their targeted language objective. Some children may show interest in the situation that previously set the stage for the objective but "refuse" to display their objective, whereas others may show varying degrees of disinterest, from a marked change in preferences for toys to clear avoidance when the environmental arrangement is initiated. Thus, teachers must adapt their strategies to maintain a child's interest in communicating.

Kaczmarek (1990) pointed out the important role that listener preparatory behaviors (e.g., selecting an appropriate listener, establishing proximity, and obtaining attention before delivering a message) play in establishing spontaneous use of communication skills. Kaczmarek and her colleagues (1992) combined training of listener preparatory behaviors with milieu language teaching to facilitate spontaneous language. Their strategy for instituting enough systematic variation to promote generalization of children's target objectives, maintain their interest, and vary the therapy set is conceptualized as a matrix generalization model. Generalization probes were constructed based on a 6-by-4 matrix. Table 9.3 shows the vertical dimension of the matrix, consisting of four levels of gradually decreasing demands for listener preparatory behaviors followed by two, more advanced milieu teaching procedures (i.e., time delay and mand). Displaying a target behavior under conditions representing greater demands for listener preparatory behaviors represents a higher level of spontaneous language than displaying them in situations in which such demands are not as great.

The horizontal dimension of the matrix consisted of four combinations of setting and communication partner variables, proceeding from characteristics that were most like training to those that were least like it. In Level A, the trainer implemented the probe in the training environment. In the other levels, the probes were implemented by a nontrainer in the training setting (Level B), a trainer in the nontraining setting (Level C), and a nontrainer in the nontraining setting (Level D). This generalization matrix offers teachers and speech-language pathologists a plan for assessing and promoting spontaneity while continuing to en-hance a child's interest by varying the conditions that set the occasion for the target objective.

Conclusions

Convincing teachers that they should target communication skills and demonstrating that they can accurately implement instructional techniques may not be sufficient. Additional challenges need to be addressed, such as how best to individualize instruction and how to shape implementation so it becomes increasingly integrated into the school day and endures over time. The quality of implementation, the robustness of results, and the extent of acceptance of across-the-day language intervention are highly interrelated. These issues are likely to have considerable impact on the extent to which children with disabilities learn functional communication skills and generalize them for use in naturalistic contexts across the day.

References

ANGELO, D. H., & Goldstein, H. (1990). Effects of a pragmatic teaching strategy for requesting information by communication board users. *Journal of Speech and Hearing Disorders, 55,* 231–243.

BABCOCK, N. L., & Pryzwansky, W. B. (1983). Models of consultation: Preferences of educational professionals at five stages of service. *Journal of School Psychology, 21,* 359–366.

BURKE, P., McLaughlin, M., & Valdiviesco, C. (1988). Preparing professionals to educate handicapped infants and young children: Some policy considerations. *Topics in Early Childhood Special Education, 8*(1), 73–80.

CAVALLARO, C. C., & Bambara, L. M. (1982). Two strategies for teaching language during free play. *Journal of the Association for Persons with Severe Handicaps, 7,* 80–92.

CHARLOP, M. H., Schreibman, L., & Thibodeau, M. G. (1985). Increasing spontaneous verbal responding in autistic children using a time delay procedure. *Journal of Applied Behavior Analysis, 18,* 155–166.

COLE, K., & Dale, P. (1986). Direct language instruction and interactive language instruction with language-delayed preschool children: A comparison study. *Journal of Speech and Hearing Research, 29,* 206–217.

COLE, K., Dale, P., & Mills, P. (1991). Individual differences in language-delayed children's responses to direct and interactive preschool instruction. *Topics in Early Childhood Special Education, 11,* 99–124.

Table 9.3 Generalization probe procedures: Vertical dimension

Level 4	Face child, 10–15 feet away, attention directed elsewhere. Object held in field of vision.
Level 3	Same as level 4, but *look at* child.
Level 2	Approach, face same direction without looking at child. Object in field of vision.
Level 1	Eye contact, joint attention. Object visible but not prominent.
Time Delay	Object directly in front of child. Alternate eye contact from child to object.
Mand	Provide verbal mand for target response.

CONNELL, P. J. (1987). An effect of modeling and imitation teaching procedures on children with and without specific language impairment. *Journal of Speech and Hearing Disorders, 30,* 105–113.

EMRICK, J., & Peterson, S. (1977). *Evaluation of the national diffusion network.* Menlo Park, CA: Stanford Research Center.

EVANS, J. (1981). Inservice training for the 1980's. *Journal of the Division for Early Childhood, 2,* 67–73.

FAWCETT, S. (1991). Social validation: A note on methodology. *Journal of Applied Behavior Analysis, 24,* 235–239.

FEY, M. E. (1986). *Language intervention with young children.* San Diego: College-Hill Press.

FILE, N. (1992). The consultation process: Implications for early intervention. *Occasional Paper Series, 1,* 1–24.

FRIEDMAN, P., & Friedman, K. (1980). Accounting for individual differences when comparing the effectiveness of remedial language teaching methods. *Applied Psycholinguistics, 1,* 151–170.

GIROLAMETTO, L. (1988). Improving the social-conversational skills of developmentally delayed children: An intervention study. *Journal of Speech and Hearing Disorders, 53,* 156–167.

GOBBI, L., Cipani, E., Hudson, C., & Lapenta-Neudeck, R. (1986). Developing spontaneous requesting among children with severe mental retardation. *Mental Retardation, 24,* 357–363.

GOLDSTEIN, H., Mousetis, L., Hepting, N., & McDonnell, B. (1993). Classroom versus small group instruction: Acquisition and generalization of language goals by preschoolers with developmental disabilities. University of Pittsburgh.

HALLE, J. (1988). Adopting the natural environment as the context of training. In S. N. Calculator & J. L. Bedrosian (Eds.), *Communication assessment and intervention for adults with mental retardation* (pp. 155–185). Boston: College-Hill Press.

HALLE, J. W., Baer, D. M., & Spradlin, J. E. (1981). Teachers' generalized use of delay as a stimulus control procedure to increase language use in handicapped children. *Journal of Applied Behavior Analysis, 14,* 389–409.

HALLE, J. W., Marshall, A. M., & Spradlin, J. E. (1979). Time delay: A technique to increase language use and facilitate generalization in retarded children. *Journal of Applied Behavior Analysis, 12,* 431–439.

HARING, T. G., Neetz, J. A., Lovinger, L., Peck, C., & Semmel, M. I. (1987). Effects of four modified incidental teaching procedures to create opportunities for communication. *Journal of the Association for Persons with Severe Handicaps, 12,* 218–226.

HART, B. (1985). Naturalistic language training techniques. In S. Warren & A. Rogers-Warren (Eds.), *Teaching functional language* (pp. 63–88). Baltimore: University Park Press.

HART, B. M., & Risley, T. R. (1968). Establishing use of descriptive adjectives in the spontaneous speech of disadvantaged preschool children. *Journal of Applied Behavior Analysis, 1,* 109–120.

HART, B. M., & Risley, T. R. (1974). Using preschool materials to modify the language of disadvantaged children. *Journal of Applied Behavior Analysis, 7,* 243–256.

HART, B. M., & Risley, T. R. (1975). Incidental teaching of language in the preschool. *Journal of Applied Behavior Analysis, 8,* 411–420.

HUNT, P., Goetz, L., Alwell, M., & Sailor, W. (1986). Using an interrupted behavior chain strategy to teach generalized communication responses. *Journal of the Association for Persons with Severe Handicaps, 11,* 196–204.

IDOL, L., & West, J. F. (1987). Consultation in special education (Part II): Training and practice. *Journal of Learning Disabilities, 20,* 474–494.

JANNEY, R., & Meyer, L. (1990). A consultation model to support integrated educational services for students with severe disabilities and challenging behaviors. *Journal of the Association for Persons with Severe Handicaps, 15,* 186–199.

KAISER, A. P., Yoder, P. J., & Keetz, A. (1992). Evaluating milieu teaching. In S. F. Warren & J. Reichle (Eds.), *Causes and effects in communication and language intervention* (pp. 9–47). Baltimore: Brookes.

KACZMAREK, L. (1990). Teaching spontaneous language to individuals with severe handicaps: A matrix model. *Journal of the Association for Persons with Severe Handicaps, 15,* 160–169.

KACZMAREK, L., Hepting, N., & Dzubak, M. (1992). The application of a matrix model to the examination of milieu language generalization. University of Pittsburgh.

KLEIN, N., & Sheehan, R. (1987). Staff development: A key issue in meeting the needs of young handicapped children in day care settings. *Topics in Early Childhood Special Education, 7*(1), 13–27.

LEBLANC, J. M., & Ruggles, T. R. (1982). Instructional strategies for individual and group teaching. *Analysis and Intervention in Developmental Disabilities, 2,* 129–137.

LEONARD, L. B. (1981). Facilitating linguistic skills in children with specific language impairment. *Applied Psycholinguistics, 2,* 89–118.

LIEBERMAN, A., & Miller, L. (1979). *Staff development: New demands, new realities, new perspectives.* New York: Teachers College Press.

MACDONALD, J. D., Blott, J. P., Gordon, K., Spiegel, B., & Hartmann, M. (1974). An experimental parent-assisted treatment program for preschool language-delayed children. *Journal of Speech and Hearing Disorders, 39,* 395–415.

MCGEE, G. G., Krantz, P. J., & McClannahan, L. E. (1985). The facilitative effects of incidental teaching on preposition use by autistic children. *Journal of Applied Behavior Analysis, 18,* 17–31.

MCLEAN, M., & Vincent, L. (1984). The use of expansions as a language intervention technique in the natural environment. *Journal of the Division for Early Childhood, 9,* 57–66.

MAHONEY, G., & Powell, A. (1988). Modifying parent-child interaction: Enhancing the development of handicapped children. *Journal of Special Education, 22*(1), 82–96.

MILLER, L. (1989). Classroom-based language intervention. *Language, Speech, and Hearing Services in Schools, 20,* 153–169.

NEEF, N. A., Walters, J., & Egel, A. L. (1984). Establishing generative yes/no responses in developmentally disabled children. *Journal of Applied Behavior Analysis, 17,* 453–460.

NIETUPSKI, J., Scheutz, G., & Ockwood, L. (1980). The delivery of communication therapy services to severely handicapped students: A plan for change. *Journal of the Association for Persons with Severe Handicaps. 5,* 13–23.

ODOM, S. (1987). The role of theory in the preparation of professionals in early childhood special education. *Topics in Early Childhood Special Education, 7*(3), 1–11.

OLIVER, C., & Halle, J. W. (1982). Language training in the everyday environment: Teaching functional sign use to a retarded child. *Journal of the Association for Persons with Severe Handicaps, 8,* 50–62.

PRYZWANSKY, W. D., & White, G. W. (1983). The influence of consultee characteristics on preferences for consultation approaches. *Professional Psychology: Research and Practice, 14,* 457–461.

ROGERS, S., Lewis, H., & Reis, K. (1987). An effective procedure for training early special education teams to implement a model program. *Journal of the Division for Early Childhood, 11,* 180–188.

ROGERS-Warren, A. K., & Warren, S. F. (1980). Mands for verbalization: Facilitating the generalization of newly trained language in children. *Behavior Modification, 4,* 230–245.

SCHWARTZ, I. S., & Baer, D. M. (1991). Social validity assessments: Is current practice state of the art? *Journal of Applied Behavior Analysis, 24,* 189–204.

SCHWARTZ, R. G., Chapman, K., Terrell, B., Prelock, P., & Rowan, L. (1985). Facilitating word combination in language-impaired children through discourse structure. *Journal of Speech and Hearing Disorders, 50,* 31–39.

TANNOCK, R., & Girolametto, L. (1992). Reassessing parent-focused language intervention programs. In S. F. Warren & J. Reichle (Eds.), *Causes and effects in communication and language intervention* (pp. 49–76). Baltimore: Brookes.

WARREN, S. F., & Bambara, L. M. (1989). An experimental analysis of milieu language intervention: Teaching the action-object form. *Journal of Speech and Hearing Disorders, 54,* 448–461.

WARREN, S. F., & Gazdag, G. (1990). Facilitating early language development with milieu intervention procedures. *Journal of Early Intervention, 14,* 62–86.

WARREN, S. F., & Kaiser, A. R. (1986). Incidental language teaching: A critical review. *Journal of Speech and Hearing Disorders, 51,* 291–299.

WARREN, S. F., McQuarter, R. J., & Rogers-Warren, A. K. (1984). The effects of mands and models on the speech of unresponsive language-delayed preschool children. *Journal of Speech and Hearing Disorders, 49,* 43–52.

WEISS, R. S. (1981). INREAL intervention for language handicapped and bilingual children. *Journal of the Division for Early Childhood, 4,* 40–51.

WEISSMAN-Frisch, N., Crowell, F., & Inman, D. (1980). In-servicing vocational trainers: A multiple perspective evaluation approach. *Journal of the Association for Persons with Severe Handicaps, 5,* 158–173.

WEISTUCH, L., & Lewis, M. (1985). The language interaction intervention project. *Analysis and Intervention in Developmental Disabilities, 5,* 97–106.

WEISTUCH, L., Lewis, M., & Sullivan, M. W. (1991). Project profile: Use of a language interaction intervention in the preschools. *Journal of Early Intervention, 15,* 278–287.

WELLER, C. (1979). Training approaches on syntactic skills of language-deviant children. *Journal of Learning Disabilities, 12,* 46–55.

WEST, J. F., & Cannon, G. S. (1988). Essential collaborative consultation competencies for regular and special education. *Journal of Learning Disabilities, 21,* 56–63.

WEST, J. F., & Idol, L. (1990). Collaborative consultation in the education of mildly handicapped and at-risk students. *Remedial and Special Education, 11*(1), 22–31.

WILCOX, M. J., Kouri, T. A., & Caswell, S. B. (1991). Early language intervention: A comparison of classroom and individual treatment. *American Journal of Speech-Language Pathology, 1,* 49–62.

YODER, P., Goldstein, H., Kaiser, A., Alpert, C., Mousetis, L., & Kaczmarek, L. (1993). A comparison of milieu and responsive-interaction language teaching in preschool classrooms: Towards matching children with language teaching methods. Vanderbilt University, Nashville.

YODER, P., Kaiser, A., & Alpert, C. (1991). An exploratory study of the interaction between language teaching methods and child characteristics. *Journal of Speech and Hearing Research, 34,* 155–167.

YODER, P. J., & Davies, B. (1990). Do parental questions and topic continuations elicit developmentally delayed children's replies? A sequential analysis. *Journal of Speech and Hearing Research, 33,* 563–573.

CHAPTER 10

Helping Preschoolers from Low-Income Backgrounds Make Substantial Progress in Reading Through Direct Instruction

Paul Welsberg

If given the green light to launch preschool programs for at-risk 4-year-olds at your public schools, would you want to begin by teaching the children to read? Consider this important ramification. Having the ability to read can help expand the child's range of language concepts and fund of world information. Normally, the primary source of this early knowledge comes from listening to and conversing with others. This process "naturally" generates a listening vocabulary. Reading accelerates vocabulary and world knowledge acquisition and encourages an appreciation of the subtleties of language. However, such sophisticated by-products must follow the establishment of strong reading skills.

Now consider the at-risk child. The disadvantaged, school-aged child is caught in an educational dilemma. Not able to understand what is read because of a poorly developed listening vocabulary and not able to expand his or her reading vocabulary because of inadequate reading skills, the child is instructionally at a standstill. Providing early, intensive language instruction should help overcome some deficiencies in listening vocabulary. Complementing language instruction would be the early introduction of reading so that the young child not only knows how

to read but reads in order to learn concepts and information in a society that places increasing emphasis on achieving literacy (Resnick & Resnick, 1977).

The literature on early intervention does not dwell on the description and potential benefits of preschool reading programs (Consortium for Longitudinal Studies, 1983; Karweit, 1989). Instead, it reports changes in general cognitive processes, with improvements in IQ as the major means of gauging program success (Locurto, 1991). If mentioned, reading is treated as a specific set of behaviors that is expected to emerge as a by-product of improvements in several general abilities and a favorable attitude toward school (Weisberg, 1992). However, because so many disadvantaged youngsters graduating from preschool intervention projects still encounter reading difficulties in the primary grades (Gray, Ramsey, & Klaus, 1982; Haskins, 1989), the claim that preschool curricula produce emerging literacy behaviors is suspect.

The building of a powerful reading repertoire in the preschool years will require extensive teaching, probably spanning at least two years before first grade. Is there evidence that preschoolers from low-income backgrounds can master sophisticated reading repertoires prior to first grade? Are there any reading approaches that can satisfy this challenge?

Some early childhood interventionists agree with Stone's (1979) advice that Head Start preschoolers should not "learn to read and write ahead of the (elementary) school schedule" (p. 166). Some may continue to agree with Morphett and Washburne's (1931) early assertions that reading should be delayed until the child's mental age reaches 6 1/2 years. Still others will say that early reading is acceptable if self-taught in natural settings, and they will point to the retrospective reports of parents of early readers (Durkin, 1966). Finally, there is Mason's (1984) suggestion, and to some extent Adams' (1990) as well, that those children who have not obtained reading concepts dealing with phonemic awareness through incidental and informal sources should receive organized instruction in these concepts before first grade or they will probably flounder in school. Because children who are behind at the beginning of first grade often turn out to be poor readers, catching them up in first grade may be a myth.

I believe that much more can be done for economically disadvantaged preschoolers if we are willing to adopt a synthetic phonics program, originally known as *Distar Reading* (Engelmann & Bruner, 1969), and use it systematically and intensively. The nature of this approach and the outcomes generated by it are the focus of this chapter.

Distar Reading

Preskills

Distar Reading, now called "Reading Mastery," is not a reading program intended for older, primary-grade children that has been simplified or extended downward for preschoolers. The first two levels, Reading I and Reading II (Engelmann & Bruner, 1969), were initially implemented with preschool and kindergarten children with a fair degree of success (Engelmann, 1970). Only later, in the Follow Through Project, were the same and more advanced levels successfully employed with older primary-grade children (Becker, 1992).

Many primary-grade programs are not readily adaptable for younger children, because they presume

entry knowledge and skill attainments that young children, especially those who are at risk, do not have. The rate of presentation of new concepts and multistep operations is usually too accelerated for most instructionally naive preschoolers and the opportunity for practice and review is usually insufficient. Thus, teaching reading to the children who need it most must be delayed. But, consider this alternative: using a reading program found successful for at-risk preschool children for primary-grade children. Such a program should work at both age levels, although children who learn the content at a faster-than-average rate can start the same program at an advanced level and move through it more quickly.

Space restrictions prevent a detailed description of the prerequisite skills for Reading I. These skills, all teachable to preschoolers, include identifying sounds, segmenting the sounds in words, blending them together, and carrying out the sounding-out process in a left-to-right order. The essentials for teaching, integrating, and sequencing these skills can be found in Carnine, Silbert, and Kameenui (1990).

Number and Rate of New Words Targeted

Figure 10.1 shows the cumulative number of new words introduced in Reading I and II in terms of blocks of 20 lessons. Clearly, a preschooler given two program years will likely read over 1,400 words and possibly decode a sizable number of never-taught words, all before first grade.

Teaching Early Reading

Self-Taught Readers

We all have probably encountered preschoolers who show an unusual interest in being read to and in actively identifying and entertaining themselves with words seen almost everywhere—on TV commercials, on food packages, on street signs, and in the countless books they own. Because of their additional fascination with printing and spelling words, Durkin (1966) fittingly described them as "paper and pencil kids." Torrey (1979) argued that the efforts of these children are voluntary because they begin to read within informal home settings, where reading is not compulsory and not bound by a standard instructional procedure. They are considered self-taught because they start to read before beginning first grade.

The incidence of early readers is never more than 4%, despite differences in the measurement of reading proficiency and in sampling selection characteristics (Durkin, 1966; King & Friesen, 1972; Morrison, Harris, & Auerbach, 1971). The vast majority score high on IQ tests (Durkin, 1966; Torrey, 1979), although that aspect is not necessarily a precursor of early reading because children with average or slightly below-average IQs also end up as early readers (Durkin, 1966).

Surveys of early readers frequently reveal a higher proportion coming from middle- or upper-class families where the mother's educational attainments were higher than the control families (King & Friesen, 1972; Torrey, 1979). A notable exception to the association between SES level and incidence of early readers comes from Durkin (1966). In her California survey of 5,100 children, there was an overrepresentation of families from lower socioeconomic-status (SES) levels; one-third were classified as "lower-middle" and one-half as "upper-lower." The paradox is resolved when one considers whether mothers knew or subscribed to the prevailing view that children should learn to read in school, not before. Upper-middle-class mothers held this attitude, and many said they refused to help when their child asked questions about words. On the other hand, fewer working-class parents of early readers knew or subscribed to the conventional wisdom. With her New York City survey, conducted when it was less fashionable to discourage home instruction, Durkin (1966) found more early readers from families of higher SES levels.

Several investigators (Durkin, 1966; Goetz, 1979; Mason, 1980) have proposed or implemented early-reading programs modeled after the development of early readers. Although the program outcomes are modest, some of the assumptions and procedures for teaching beginning reading, especially to young children not so inclined to take a natural interest in print, can be questioned. The primary goal of these efforts was to introduce popular words, usually nouns represented by pictures. Since these programs stopped short of teaching function words that are not easily illustrated (prepositions, auxiliary verbs, articles), learning to read sentences of any complexity became problematic. Early readers do not show an immediate tendency to induce the sounds for letters (Durkin, 1970). It takes about one or two years before a few children develop that ability (Mason, 1980), and the skill is often lacking in entering first-graders (Durkin, 1970; Weisberg, 1989). Advocates of models that assume slow development of letter-sound knowledge are not likely to adopt reading programs that emphasize the initial teaching of this skill.

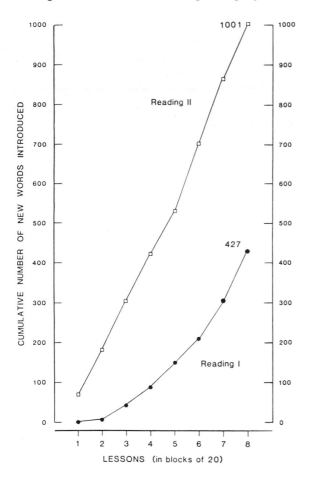

Figure 10.1. Cumulative number of words taught in Distar Reading I and II. SOURCE: "Direct Instruction in the Preschool," by P. Weisberg, 1988, *Education and Treatment of Children, 11(4), 349–363. Copyright 1988 by PRO-ED, Inc. Reprinted by permission.*

Early-reading approaches further presume that early readers seem to learn in natural ways, and thus the teaching of reading should be guided by naturalistic interventions. Such an emphasis overlooks many opportunities in which effective reading strategies can begin with the teaching of skills in very unnatural ways. For example, when Distar-taught children initially decode words, they say the sounds in the word slowly without pausing between the sounds. Thus, the word *mad* is sounded as *mmmaaad* and then said quickly as *mad*! Weisberg and Savard (in press) noted that this routine hardly every occurs spontaneously and reliably in young children; it must be explicitly modeled and frequently practiced before they learn to do it almost automatically.

Through Preschool Instruction

This section presents five preschool reading projects (Table 10.1) in which (1) reading instruction was relatively long-lasting, usually spanning a six- to

nine-month preschool year; and (2) at the end of the preschool and kindergarten years, measures of the child's ability to read (e.g., word recognition, word meaning, and/or sentence or paragraph comprehension) were obtained. I did not consider studies that limited measurement to reading readiness scores or to the presumed components or prerequisites of reading (e.g., letter naming or phonemic awareness).

After one year of reading training, the majority of children could read 30 tested words in Durkin's (1970) project and some number less than that in Fowler's (1971). (Fowler also administered the first-grade level of the Gates Primary Reading Test and discovered that 91% of the children identified no more than 3 words.) What are we to make of the sum of these results? We could say that the outcomes are too meager and we should not waste time teaching reading to preschool children. We could say that the outcomes are modest and the children would have some advantage if read-

Table 10.1 Summary of early reading studies

Source	Subjects	Reading Approach	Word Recognition Performance
Durkin (1970)	36 (upper-lower & lower-middle class) IQs = 114[a]	Language arts	30 words: 1st year 124 words: 2nd year
Fowler (1971)	69 (middle & upper-middle class) IQs = 122	Analysis and synthesis of words/sentences	< 30 words: 1st year
Bereiter & Engelmann (1966; 1968)	13 (poverty-level) IQs = 93	Linguistic approach	WRAT GE Scores[b] *M* GE = 1.0: 1st year *M* GE = 1.5: 2nd year
Engelmann (1970)	12 (poverty-level from above continued for 2nd year) IQs = 95	Prepublication Distar scripts	M GE = 2.6: 2nd year
	18 (middle-class) IQs not reported	Prepublication Distar scripts	M GE = 2.4: 1st year
	7 (middle-class from above continued for 2nd year)	Prepublication Distar scripts	M GE = 3.4: 2nd year
Anderson (1971); Knudson (1970)	42 (from Salt Lake County; SES not given) IQs = 105	Distar	M GE = 1.8: 1st year M GE = 2.6: 2nd year

Notes: [a]All studies used the Stanford-Binet test to determine IQ for entering preschoolers except Anderson, who used the Peabody Picture Vocabulary Test. [b]WRAT = Wide-Range Achievement Test; Reading Subtest given; GE = grade-equivalent scores.

ing is continued. Durkin's (1970) readers who were given a second year of reading quadrupled their rate, ending up reading about 124 tested words. However, there is a third possibility. Perhaps, Durkin's and Fowler's early reading approaches greatly underestimated the amount of reading achievement possible with preschoolers and, different approaches could have established a substantial, productive reading repertoire, even with children from poverty-level backgrounds.

Direct Instruction

Bereiter and Engelmann (1966) did not report the number of words presented in Bloomfield and Barnhart's (1961) linguistic approach. Reflecting on all academic outcomes, Bereiter and Engelmann (1968) freely admitted that after finishing two program years, "it was in reading (as opposed to arithmetic and spelling) that the (economically disadvantaged) children exhibited the most frequent and frustrating failures to 'get it' and 'hold on to it'" (p. 32). Apparently, "missing it" was an inability to induce letter sounds from whole words as a result of the analytic-phonic methods they initially used. So, without being able to recall "letter sounds," the children were at a loss when blending the sounds in words. The result was probably an absence of a consistent word-attack strategy both for reading the words taught and for figuring out nontaught words.

Undaunted by these and other problems, Engelmann designed a different approach that became known as *Distar Reading*. Englemann used the prepublication formats of Distar to teach economically disadvantaged and middle-class children, and Anderson (1971) used the published version (Engelmann & Bruner, 1969). Previously, Engelmann (1970) had addressed teaching at-risk students more (of the critical skills) in less time and attaining mastery-level performance. Still, no mention is made, either by Engelmann (1970) or by Anderson (1971), of the number of Distar lessons that would render an approximation of the number of words taught (Figure 10.1). Also, criterion-referenced outcomes regarding the accuracy of reading throughout the Distar program are not provided. Instead, psychometric information in the form of grade equivalents (GE) on the *Wide-Range Achievement Test* (WRAT) was used to gauge reading performance. The WRAT is a frequently used instrument for pre-first-grade children (Gersten

et al., 1984; Weisberg, 1973), because raw score conversions to GE scores are permissible for children as young as 4 and traditional psychometric indices, like GE scores and percentiles, are possible starting at age 5.

A GE of 1.0 can be obtained without being able to read any of the 75 WRAT words. All that is needed is a total raw score of 22 from the first three reading subtests (Jastak & Jastak, 1978): (1) labeling any two letters in the participant's name for 2 points, (2) recognizing and matching letters for 10 points, and (3) letter naming for 13 points. A GE of 1.0 thus reflects a sampling of "reading" behaviors expected of the average child entering first grade. That is, an ability to recognize and identify most alphabet letters but an inability to read words. Pre-first-grade disadvantaged children who obtain GEs of 1.0 exhibit this profile (Weisberg, 1984).

Assuming a raw score of 22, the number of words needed to get the GE scores in Table 10.1 can be determined. For Bereiter and Engelmann's (1968) one-year and two-year program groups, the GEs of 1.0 and 1.5 signify, respectively, only 0 and 2 WRAT words. Because several WRAT words fit the linguistic word-family groups taught (e.g., *cat, red, his, him,* and *lip*), Bereiter and Engelmann (1968) concluded that the only explanation for low word-identification scores was that the children were simply poor readers.

By implementing the pre-Distar formats, Engelmann (1970) elevated both the WRAT GE scores and the number of WRAT words read correctly. The GE scores of 2.6, 2.4, and 3.4 in Table 10.1 convert to word-identification scores, respectively, of 16, 13, and 27 WRAT words. The GE scores of 1.8 and 2.6 for Anderson's (1971) project convert to 5 and 16 WRAT words. The WRAT words overlap somewhat with those taught directly in Reading I and II, but for children to do an outstanding job in WRAT reading they must decode words that haven't been taught. They must grapple with novel words like *size, weather, lame, stuck, stalk, cliff, glutton,* and *threshold*. It was truly a spectacular problem-solving feat to see preschoolers in my program read these and similarly difficult words; this feat is accomplishable with two years of Distar Reading (Weisberg, 1984). These accomplishments are consistent with the generalized decoding strategies that Distar Reading has furnished to primary-grade children (Gersten et al., 1984).

Comprehension

There are questions about measures of comprehension. Durkin's (1970) initial teaching of popular words in the form of high-interest, picture-prompted nouns, without much teaching of not easily illustrated and perhaps low-interest function words, makes it unlikely that the children read sentences of any substance. Eventually, some grammatical forms were introduced and sentences were provided, but no information on the composition, length, or understanding was given. With the linguistic approach, Bereiter and Engelmann (1966) provided their children with phrases and sentences. Given their difficulties at identifying words, it is doubtful that any sentence comprehension existed at all.

Fowler (1971) evaluated reading comprehension through criterion-referenced tests, using brief stories that were thematically related to and that contained the same vocabulary words as the stories in the study's seven primers. The number of primers completed varied among the children. Correct comprehension answers ranged from 67% (primer 2) to 88% (primer 4), and the overall mean across the seven primers was 80%. However, a majority of the children mastered less than 30 words. Thus, the nature of the comprehension questions was fairly simple. Illustrations accompanied the stories and both the questioning and answering were done orally. Most likely, all questions required direct, literal answers.

Engelmann (1970) did not provide any measure of reading comprehension. The WRAT does not evaluate reading comprehension. Since Distar-taught children do well on WRAT decoding, the often-heard myth that Distar Reading only teaches word calling and not comprehension can be perpetuated. That is hardly the case. Soon after some words can be read in isolation, they appear as two- and three-word phrases on worksheets, which the children take home. The Take-Home stories increase in length, and midway through Reading I, storybooks are provided. The stories are about zany cartoonlike characters, including animals, that have human qualities. They appeal to children from diverse backgrounds because the adventures or everyday problems are culture free.

The story line of Reading I stories is simple and straightforward. Comprehension is assessed both orally when children immediately answer direct, literal ques-

tions, and when they write answers to story questions that appear in the Take-Home. Correct answers are selected from a multiple-choice set or written in a blank space. The stories do not contain the extensive vocabulary and syntactical structure needed for successful end-of-first-grade reading. The comprehension exercises, however, do encourage beginning readers to reflect upon what they read and to communicate this understanding to others in oral and written form.

The stories in the Reading II storybook get progressively longer and become syntactically and semantically more complex. The first five Reading II stories average 13 sentences and 100 words compared to 45 sentences and 361 words for the last five stories. Whereas Reading I and half of Reading II teach children the process of how to read, the last half of Reading II emphasizes reading as a tool for learning. The Reading II storybooks and Take-Homes provide exercises that entail following printed instructions, understanding written directions in order to search for details in pictures, reading rules in order to make logical deductions and apply them both to illustrations and to printed information, and reading for sheer enjoyment.

Completing Reading II should prepare a child to start second-grade reading and to do a creditable job on a reading achievement test normed for the end of first grade. Such an outcome was expected of children from Anderson's (1971) preschool project who supposedly had two program years of Distar Reading (Table 10.1). These pre-first-graders were given the Gates and MacGinitie (1965) Primary Test of Reading. Unfortunately, they did poorly on comprehension measures: Vocabulary (14th percentile) and Story Reading (12th percentile) (see Knudson, 1970). It is possible that the children simply did not complete a sufficient number of Reading II lessons and therefore didn't do a stellar job on reading comprehension.

Extension of Early-Reading Studies

The small amount of literature on long-term teaching of preschool reading suggests a relationship between the length of teaching and the extent of reading progress. This relationship was examined at a campus-based facility, known as the Early Childhood Day Care Center (ECDCC). The preschoolers attended it for one or two years and were evaluated annually on criterion-referenced and norm-referenced instruments. Measurements included word identification abilities and the neglected measures of reading comprehension. The central question was whether before beginning first grade, poverty-level youngsters could acquire and maintain accelerated forms of reading abilities never before documented in the literature.

The Early Childhood Day Care Project

The Children and Their Families

The Early Education Day Care Project (ECDCC) had a Title XX contract with the state to provide full-day, year-round services to 3- to 6-year-old children. The local welfare office determined parent eligibility and assigned children to the ECDCC and to other Title XX day-care contractors on the basis of which facility was next in line to receive a child.

Family income was below or close to poverty levels: 52% needed day care in order to work; 34% received public assistance through the Aid to Families with Dependent Children (AFDC) program; and 14% were court-appointed foster parents of children who suffered family abuse or abandonment. Family demographics (see Weisberg, 1984) indicated that those children needing day care and those eligible for AFDC came from low SES backgrounds that were similar to the backgrounds reported in other intervention projects (Engelmann, 1970; Gray, Ramsey, & Klaus, 1982).

Group Breakdown

For present purposes, the children are grouped according to the last reading lesson completed. Not all children received reading instruction. During the period 1976 to 1985, of 156 preschoolers 21% (33) attended for less than three months and either got no reading instruction or a minimal amount; that is, less than 20 lessons. Nine percent (14) remained longer but could not be retained in a reading group because of their sporadic attendance or nonmastery of the prerequisite reading skills.

The remaining 109 children were placed in one of three groups. The Limited Reading Group ($N = 12$) completed 20 to 70 of the 160 Reading I lessons, leaving the children with an incomplete strategy for decoding words. The One-Year Group ($N = 43$) completed at least two-thirds of Reading I but not more

than 35 of the 160 lessons of Reading II. Practically speaking, these children received one year of reading instruction. The Two-Year Group ($N = 44$) finished at least 75 Reading II lessons and 73% came within 30 lessons of completing Reading II. Ten children did not fall within these designations and their data are not included in the length of training effects.

The Two- and One-Year Groups did not differ on gender (55% girls versus 58% boys) or on entry Slossen IQ (89.4 versus 89.1). On entry to the ECDCC, no child was able to read, print words, spell, or do arithmetic computations.

Starting in 1983, the ECDCC increased its enrollment from 24 to 35 and accepted children from economically advantaged families on a fee-paying basis. Although these children also received reading and other academic instruction, only the outcomes for the 99 disadvantaged children will be reported.

Direct Instruction Implementation Practices

For the initial year, Distar Reading and Language were taught only to 5-year-olds. Following successful progress, these programs plus Distar Arithmetic (Engelmann & Carnine, 1976) were phased in and taught to prekindergarten, 4-year-olds as well. Groups of five to eight children met with a teacher daily. The beginning lessons were short, lasting 10 to 15 minutes. As the children mastered the content-area skills, the lessons gradually lengthened to 30 to 45 minutes, with another 15 minutes given to spelling and special classroom activities (reading library books, drawing, and composing short stories).

Evaluation

Continuous Progress Tests

Children in Reading I were checked after every 10 to 20 lessons on tasks that measured identifying sounds, decoding of words, reading sentences, and answering comprehension items. The group size for these evaluations varied from 20 to 30 children. Correct identification of familiar and recently taught sounds was almost perfect across all evaluation sessions; this means that the children had probably mastered all 44 letter sounds taught in Reading I. Their decoding of a sample of previously taught words was consistently high, averaging 93% correct and implying an ability to read most of the 427 words taught. (Weisberg & Savard [1993] found similarly high levels of sound identification and, with appropriate sounding out of words, equally high word-identification abilities with Reading I instruction.) Their decoding of nontaught words, composed of previously taught sounds, averaged 80%, thus indicating the application of a general-case decoding strategy. Evaluation of comprehension began after lesson 120 and consisted of reading a three-sentence story and answering oral questions, circling the correct answer from among three choices, and matching sentences to pictures. Correct answers on these tasks averaged between 90% and 95%.

WRAT Outcomes

Standard scores on WRAT Reading were markedly affected by length of training; $F(2,96) = 54.09$, $p < .0001$, with the three intergroup comparisons significant, all $ps < .0001$. The Two-Year Group is one standard deviation (SD) unit higher than the One-Year Group, which in turn is more than two SD units higher than the Limited Reading Group. The Limited Reading Group was at the 22nd percentile, which is the perfor-

mance benchmark of poverty-level children on standardized tests (Gertsen et al., 1984). The One-Year Group was at the 90th percentile and obtained a mean GE score of 1.8, which is compatible with Anderson's (1971) one-year group but lower than the middle-class children in Engelmann's (1970) one-year group (Table 10.1). The Two-Year Group was at the 99.2 percentile and obtained a GE score of 3.3, which exceeds all previously reported two-year groups on the WRAT and is close to Engelmann's (1970) seven middle-class children who were given two years of Distar Reading (Table 10.1).

A WRAT GE score of 3.3 does not necessarily mean that a child can read books at the third-grade level. It means that the child's reading proficiency is much above that of same-age peers who, in this case, are the 6-year-olds starting first grade. The grade level at which these children are capable of reading will be addressed next.

Reading Achievement on First-Grade Standardized Tests

The reading abilities of beginning first-graders on standardized tests are given in Figure 10.2. For every evaluation period (the spring before first grade), the

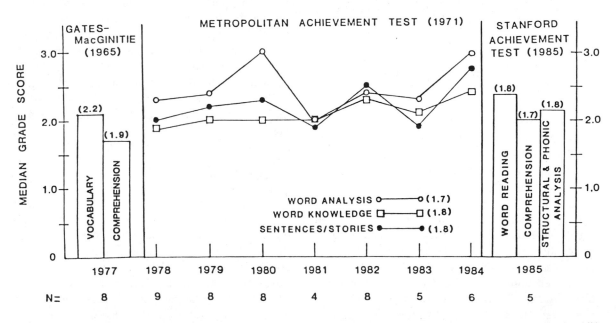

Figure 10.2. Reading abilities of pre–first-graders on standardized tests.   SOURCE: "Direct Instruction in the Preschool," by P. Weisberg, 1988, *Education and Treatment of Children, 11(4)*, 349–363. *Copyright 1988 by PRO-ED, Inc. Reprinted by permission.*

Table 10.2 MAT subtest and total reading scores of beginning first grade and beginning kindergarten children

Type of Measure	Starting First Grade		Starting Kindergarten
	Two Years ($N = 37$)	One Year ($N = 11$)	One Year ($N = 17$)
Word Knowledge			
Median GE	2.4	1.5	1.4
Median percentile	80th	26th	18th
Word Analysis			
Median GE	2.7	1.7	1.4
Median percentile	92nd	46th	24th
Reading Sentences and Stories			
Median GE	2.5	1.4	1.4
Median percentile	89th	20th	20th
Total Reading			
Median GE	2.4	1.5	1.4
Median percentile	88th	20th	20th

Note: GE = grade equivalent score

median GE scores of ECDCC children approximate or are often much higher than the normative values. For example, on the 1985 Stanford Achievement Test, the grade scores for the end of the first grade that correspond to the 50th percentile are 1.8 (word reading), 1.7 (comprehension), and 1.8 (structural and phonic analysis). The median grade scores for the ECDCC pre-first graders on each subtest are at 2.0 or higher.

The beginning first-graders reported in Figure 10.2 had unequal amounts of reading training. A breakdown of their Metropolitan Achievement Test (MAT) performance according to two years of reading versus one year is provided in Table 10.2. The MAT performance of some beginning kindergarten children with one year of reading is also reported. The between-group differences for each MAT subtest and for Total Reading are significant, all $Fs(2,62) > 47.04$, all $ps < .0001$. The absolute differences in subtest and total scores for the first–grade starting group with two years of reading ranges from 0.9 to 1.3 GE points higher than the other two one-year taught groups; these differences are what one would expect from an extra year of reading.

Both groups of children who received instruction for one year, whether starting kindergarten or first grade, had a hard time with the Word Knowledge subtest, which requires selecting one of four words that best identifies an aspect of a given illustration. They were also less able with more difficult reading comprehension items, as manifested by the Reading Sentences and Reading Stories sections. Reading Sentences requires the selection of one of three sentences that best describes an illustration. Reading Stories requires the selection of one of three words or phrases that best answers a comprehension item based on a short story.

One factor working against the children is that they did not have the full complement of decoding skills to tackle many words. They have not yet learned to use the silent-*e* rule; they are unfamiliar with many letter-sound combinations (*ea, ou, al*); and they have not yet been phased out of the helpful Reading I orthography. Another restraint is that these two MAT subtests are timed, and since the Reading I program stresses reading for accuracy, many items are left incomplete. What they do complete, however, is more often correct than not.

Not only are the one-year children penalized for taking their time to decode words, many of which are irregular, they have trouble with the meaning of many MAT words—namely *special, favorite, starry night*—and they may not know certain idioms, such as "to catch a bus" or "water meets land." Although able to cope with straightforward comprehension items, they were less able to deal with unfamiliar syntactical styles and inferential-based comprehension items that presume much outside information and verbal sophistication.

What can be done for the one-year readers who are fine on their continuous progress performance and on WRAT Reading but suffer on the comprehension section of an end-of-first-grade achievement test? Put them in Reading II and give them another year of reading before first grade. The two-year children were in the same predicament before they received another year of reading. During that second year, their promising decoding skills were expanded to include a broader set of words and they were taught to read with increased fluency and expression both within and outside of class. The increasing development in

Reading II of a host of comprehension skills, aided by the use of Distar Language II, which features more complex syntax, semantic relationships, and an enlarged vocabulary, inevitably helped them read for information and understand more subtle meanings.

Children in the Two-Year Group are competent to read second-grade texts. These and other competencies gained from Distar Language and Distar Arithmetic should inculcate a high degree of school confidence. Children in the One-Year Group are more fragile. If placed in a kindergarten class where their emerging reading repertoires lie dormant or in a first-grade class where the reading approach discourages consistent decoding and comprehension strategies, the initial promise these children have in reading is likely to diminish.

The MAT Word Analysis subtest calls for the ability to match a dictated word (say *song*), with one of four highly similar printed words (*sing*, *sang*, *song*, and *sung*). Using items of this kind and finding that children with mental ages below 7 were unsuccessful at this task, Dolch and Bloomster (1937) concluded that phonics training should be delayed until average IQ children are 7 years old. The kind of phonics training they had in mind was analytic phonics, where children are to induce sounds from known whole words. However, in Distar Reading, learners are taught how to combine sounds to form words. Called synthetic or explicit phonics, it is the approach Chall (1983) found that works best, especially with children from at-risk backgrounds. The 6-year-olds who are starting first grade with two years of reading are at the 92nd percentile on Word Analysis; those with a year of reading are holding their own at the 46th percentile (Table 10.2). Clearly, these positive findings raise serious questions about the sweeping generalizations concerning the age to start teaching reading in general and the specific age for phonics training. An examination of the reading approaches on which such magical ages are based would be a worthy endeavor.

Comparison with Other Preschool Programs

The ECDCC children, who were tested in the spring of 1980 and found to be similar in intellectual and academic performance to ECDCC children from other program years (Weisberg, 1984), were compared to children from low-economic backgrounds enrolled in several local intervention projects. The comparison groups contained children who attended two local Head Start programs and a child development program operated by the Department of Home Economics. These projects, in operation for at least eight years, essentially followed a Structured-Cognitive Model (Weisberg, 1992), in which the primary aim was to develop general cognitive processes or abilities. Many presumed prereading activities were provided, including recognizing and naming alphabet letters, listening to stories, and completing perceptual-motor tasks. Words were taught using a whole-word, meaning-emphasis approach, usually in the context of labeling objects in a theme-based unit. (For more details, see Weisberg, 1984).

The ECDCC group did not differ from the comparison groups on the WRAT Reading, nonreading subskills. These skills include labeling letters in the child's name, recognizing letters, and naming letters. These rudimentary or mediocre skills contain operations that most children can do before first grade or that will be taught within the first several weeks. In WRAT Spelling, rudimentary skills include writing one's name and copying shapes; in WRAT Arithmetic, they include identifying numerals and counting objects.

The ECDCC children did differ from the comparison children in terms of the more difficult WRAT skills, which only a few children can do before first grade and often are not mastered until well into first or second grade. Certainly, being able to read is a substantial skill and it is this skill that distinguished ECDCC children from comparison children. ECDCC children of beginning kindergarten and first-grade beginning age read 9 and 28 WRAT words, respectively; however, 97% of the comparable children from the comparison groups could not read a single WRAT word. Other WRAT substantial skills that also favored the ECDCC children, both statistically and by large absolute score differences, were writing dictated spelling words and solving oral and written arithmetic problems.

Children can still look good on WRAT Reading if they are competent in the rudimentary academic skills. The average comparison-group child who was ready to start kindergarten scored at the 42nd percentile. While not outstanding, these values are still about two-thirds of a SD unit higher than the 20th percentile level reported for low-income children (Gersten et al., 1984). Proficiency in the rudimentary skills should not be considered a trivial accomplishment, since in a large-scale Head Start project many of the preschoolers in several intervention projects failed to establish even the first three subskills of the WRAT (Weisberg, 1973). In that project, the substantive WRAT subskills of reading, spelling, and solving arithmetic computations could not be administered because they proved to be "clearly too difficult for Head Start children" (Weisberg, 1973, p. 33).

It is heartening to know that given two years of Distar Reading before first grade, children from poverty-level backgrounds can acquire sophisticated reading competencies. This advancement becomes even more significant when children with similar demographics have not achieved these levels even after two years of preschool intervention and a year of first grade (Gray et al., 1982) and when minority first-graders are stymied by traditional reading approaches (Slavin, 1991).

Some Consequences of Early Reading

More important than their accomplishments on standardized tests was what the literacy competencies of the children who had been taught for two years furnished them in everyday circumstances. They eagerly and independently read library books and children's classics to others and to themselves both at school and at home, where their parents also found them browsing through magazines and books, including the Bible. When it came time to sing Christmas carols and other songs, they rehearsed by reading the scores. Instead of depending on teachers for information, they found it themselves through reading. For example, hours after they had described the morning weather (by searching the sky and other surroundings and gauging the temperature from a thermometer), these children read and answered questions about these earlier reports to promote their memory of it. They also compared that day's weather report to what they had described on a previous day and then matched it to what they read in the local newspaper.

Many had become the "paper and pencil" children reminiscent of Durkin's (1966) early-reading project. They asked questions about words, copied them from reading material, and engaged in self-invented spelling play. As testimony to their sophistication with sounds, many children spelled some unfamiliar words as they were dictated during the WRAT Spelling test in this manner: *edvis* (advise), *reaznabl* (reasonable), *nacher* (nature), *sixsex* (success), *amaghery* (imaginary), *ocyuple* (occupy). The children freely expressed their thoughts on chalkboards, on paper, and in many humorous, adventurous, and personal stories (Weisberg, 1984). These stories were often accompanied by freehand drawings, which visiting teachers judged as thoughtful and provoking. Sims, Weisberg, and Sulentic (1983) found that these representative drawings reflected greater clarity of detail than those of preschoolers from child-development programs that stressed art activities.

The Distar Language program enabled these children to describe and subsequently read about a multitude of relationships among objects and events, including the expression of similarities and differences, of past, present, and future actions, of if-then and other rule-governed statements, and of verbal analogies premised on higher-order classification and knowledge about object parts, location, materials, and use. The program furnished them with a fund of useful world knowledge about seasons, occupations, and natural phenomena that was embellished through reading. It also provided interactive stories linked to the concepts that had been taught and introduced them to poetry.

In accord with the whole-language approach, reading instruction at the ECDCC came to be interrelated with other forms of communication, such as listening, speaking, and writing. The big difference is that the process of reading was demystified by giving early, systematic instruction in phonics and word-attack strategies as Adams (1990) and Chall (1983) advocated. Before using Distar Reading, my wife (an experienced elementary school teacher) and I tried many of the now-popular whole-language immersion procedures. Unfortunately, reading ability did not emerge to any serious levels and all of the preschoolers were left without an effective decoding strategy. They were troubled by similar-looking words and by freely substituted words, especially if the word in text differed from the name of a referent implied in an illustration; and in general, they ended up guessing at words (Weisberg, 1984). The teaching of accurate, fluent reading does not mean that other facets of communication come to a standstill. While the reading strategy was under way, the teachers continually read stories of fictional intrigue and humor to the children, intending to excite them and draw them to literature, helped them express themselves orally, and taught them to print and spell. If anything, as reading and comprehension improved, the other components of the language arts program appeared easier for the teachers to present and for the pre-schoolers to understand.

Primary Grade Follow-Up

Table 10.3 shows the first and second grade reading achievement outcomes of the ECDCC and comparison groups on the California or Stanford Achievement Tests given by the local school district. The length of instruction in preschool reading continued to have a major impact, although the advantage was larger in first grade than in second. Relative to the comparison groups, a significantly higher percentage of one- and

two-year ECDCC children were above grade level and more competent in reading. Although their second-grade performance levels dropped some, the differences between groups were still pronounced. That the two-year ECDCC children were at the 56th percentile, with 57% above the second-grade level is remarkable, given a baseline on reading tests that hovers around the 20th to 27th percentile for disadvantaged children.

A sizable length of program effect appeared for the Direct Instruction Model in the Follow Through project (Becker, 1992). At the end of third grade (when intervention ceased), kindergarten-starting children were more than 0.7 grade points higher in reading than children starting first grade, and these starting-age differences were maintained into ninth grade. Not surprisingly, the reading outcomes at ninth grade were not as strong as at third grade. An attempt to realize even greater benefits with the Direct Instruction Model by implementing Distar Reading earlier with beginning 4-year-olds did not materialize because of implementation difficulties (Weisberg, 1984).

Clearly, intensive, well-implemented intervention efforts using effective programs can go a long way in overcoming reading failures. It is equally clear that a

Table 10.3 First- and second-grade outcomes by Distar (ECDCC) and comparison children

Variable	None or Limited	ECDCC Reading Training One-Year	Two-Year	Child Development & Head Start
First Grade				
Number of children	13	19	41	40
Percentage above 50th percentile	15.4	84.2	92.7	21.0
GE Status	5 mos below	2 mos above	8 mos above	4 mos below
Median percentile	20th	64th	87th	30th
Second Grade				
Number of children	8	22	35	38
Percentage above 50th percentile	0.0	45.4	57.1	15.0
GE status	8 mos below	1 mos below	2 mos above	6 mos below
Median percentile	18th	44th	56th	27th

prekindergarten-kindergarten effort, by itself, is not the entire answer for long-term effectiveness any more than a kindergarten-third grade effort is. A program that merges serious preschool intervention with the continued impact that Direct Instruction can have in the elementary grades and throughout the school years needs to be implemented.

Concluding Remarks

I originally considered teaching reading to preschoolers in order to bring their achievement to levels far beyond that predicted by their demography. Madden and colleagues (1991) suggested that an intervention project needs to start early when learning deficits are relatively small and the learner has few deleterious competing habits. They argued for a less costly, proactive approach to help children who are at risk for school failure. Let me urge that the intervention start in preschool and that the same kind of systematic, strategic instruction begun with Direct Instruction be continued throughout the school years.

How will early childhood decision makers react to the teaching approach and the outcomes observed in the sophisticated readers who had two years of the program? Some will acknowledge the findings but will choose to develop or continue preschool reading by approaches that lead to weak, fragmented outcomes. Still others will act on gimmicky, trendy solutions, and when reading proficiency is not realized, they will cite a lack of readiness as the cause for failure rather than an incorrect theory of decision making.

Lobbying groups such as the National Association for the Education of Young Children (1987) discourages academically oriented instruction for preschool age children. The half-day preschool reading projects of the 1960s and 1970s, which attempted to prepare the at-risk child for future school success, filled the day largely with cognitive and academic activities. At the ECDCC, structured academic activities consumed less than 2 1/2 hours of its 8 1/2-hour preschool day. The remainder was filled with traditional recreational and play-related activities (make-believe, block building, puzzles, arts and crafts, and music) plus normal day-care routines. However, if the

ECDCC day were to be shortened, our academic program would prevail because, after witnessing its importance for their children's future, the teachers and parents would insist on its continuation.

The NAEYC opposes having young children engage in workbook activities that furnish drill-in-readiness activities. This concern is well justified. The frequent hodgepodge of activities, often containing unclear directions and loaded with dead-end irrelevant reading-readiness skills, should not be tolerated in any school setting, preschool or otherwise. It is easy to turn children off to learning. This holds true whether the task is academic or nonacademic. Design tasks as a series of difficult discriminations, limit the opportunity for practice and review, present lessons in a drony, slow-paced fashion without eye contact and acknowledged progress, and children will fail. Academic learning, like other routines, need not be as sterile, joyless, and irrelevant as the NAEYC portrays it.

From 1970 to 1975 before Distar Reading, the ECDCC tried to teach high-level academics to preschoolers through traditional teaching and curriculum strategies. Our intense concern and efforts were humbling experiences for our successes were only marginal. We persevered, learned about the critical changes that were needed, and are satisfied that we at last served our youngsters well. The unresolved puzzle for me is the lack of interest or commitment by early childhood program decision makers to learn the important features of good instructional design. There are many words published about commitment, but little evidence that empirically validated methods are being embraced. There are children in our society who desperately need competencies for success. How sad that what is known to work in preschool settings is, for the most part, largely ignored.

Acknowledgment

Roberta S. Weisberg has been a source of encouragement and an invaluable contributor to the Early Childhood Day Care Center Project from its inception. Her comments in connection with this chapter are greatly appreciated.

References

ADAMS, M. J. (1990). *Beginning to read: Thinking and learning about print.* Cambridge, MA: MIT Press.

ANDERSON, B. E. (1971). An evaluative study: Teaching three and four-year olds in a structured education program in Granite school district. Unpublished master's thesis, University of Utah, Salt Lake City.

BECKER, W. C. (1992). Direct instruction: A twenty-year review. In R. P. West & L. A. Hamerlynck (Eds.), *Designs for excellence in education* (pp. 71–112). Longmont, CA: Sopris West.

BEREITER, C., & Engelmann, S. (1966). *Teaching disadvantaged children in the preschool.* Englewood Cliffs, NJ: Prentice-Hall.

BEREITER, C., & Engelmann, S. (1968). An academically oriented preschool for disadvantaged children: Results from the initial experimental group. In D. W. Brison & J. Hill (Eds.), *Psychology and early childhood education* (pp. 17–36). Ontario: Institute for Studies in Education.

BLOOMFIELD, L., & Barnhart, C. (1961). *Let's read: A linguistic approach.* Detroit: Wayne State University Press.

CARNINE, D. W., Silbert, J., & Kameenui, E. J. (1990). *Direct instruction reading.* 2nd ed. Columbus, OH: Charles E. Merrill.

CHALL, J. S. (1983). Learning to read: The great debate. Updated ed. New York: McGraw-Hill.

CONSORTIUM for Longitudinal Studies (1983). *As the twig is bent.* Hillsdale, NJ: Erlbaum.

DOLCH, E., & Bloomster, M. (1937). Phonic readiness. *Elementary School Journal, 38,* 201–205.

DURKIN, D. (1966). *Children who read early.* New York: Teachers College Press, Columbia University.

DURKIN, D. (1970). A language arts program for pre-first grade children: Two-year report. *Reading Research Quarterly, 5,* 534–565.

ENGELMANN, S. (1970). The effectiveness of direct instruction on IQ performance and achievement in reading and arithmetic. In J. Hellmuth (Ed.), *Disadvantaged child,* Vol. 3 (pp. 339–361). New York: Brunner/Mazel.

ENGELMANN, S., & Bruner, E. (1969). *Distar Reading: Levels I and II.* Chicago, Science Research Associates.

ENGELMANN, S., & Carnine, D. (1976). *Distar Arithmetic: Levels I & II.* Chicago: Science Research Associates.

FOWLER, W. A. (1971). A developmental learning strategy for early reading in a laboratory nursery. *Interchange, 2,* 106–125.

GATES, A. I., & MacGinitie, W. H. (1965). *Gates-MacGinitie reading tests (Primary A).* New York: Teacher's College Press.

GERSTEN, R. M., Becker, W. C., Heiry, T. J., & White, W. A. T. (1984). Entry IQ and yearly academic growth of children in Direct Instruction programs: A longitudinal study of low SES children. *Educational Evaluation and Policy Analysis, 6,* 109–121.

GOETZ, E. M. (1979). Early reading: A developmental approach. *Young Children, 34,* 4–13.

GRAY, S., Ramsey, B., & Klaus, R. (1982). *From 3 to 20: The early training project.* Baltimore: University Park Press.

HASKINS, R. (1989). Beyond metaphor: The efficacy of early childhood education. *American Psychologist, 44,* 274–282.

JASTAK, J. F., & Jastak, S. (1978). *Wide-Range Achievement Test.* 2nd ed. Wilmington, DE: Jastak Associates.

KARWEIT, N. (1989). Effective preschool programs for students at-risk. In R. Slavin, N. L. Karweit, & N. A. Madden (Eds.), *Effective programs for students at-risk* (pp. 23–51). Boston: Allyn & Bacon.

KING, E. M., & Friesen, D. T. (1972). Children who read in kindergarten. *Alberta Journal of Educational Research, 18,* 147–161.

KNUDSON, G. P. (1970). *An evaluation of two preschool programs.* Unpublished master's thesis, University of Utah, Salt Lake City.

LOCURTO, C. (1991). Beyond IQ in preschool programs? *Intelligence, 15,* 295–312.

MADDEN, N. A., Slavin, R. E., Karweit, N. L., Dolan, L. T., & Wasik, B. A. (1991). Success for all. *Phi Delta Kappan, 72,* 593–599.

MASON, J. M. (1980). When do children begin to read: An exploration of four year-old children's letter and word reading competencies. *Reading Research Quarterly, 15,* 203–227.

MASON, J. M. (1984). Early reading from a developmental perspective. In P. D. Pearson, R. Bass, M. L. Kamil, & D. Mosenthal (Eds.), *Handbook of reading research* (pp. 505–543). New York: Longman.

MORPHETT, M., & Washburne, C. (1931). When should children begin to read? *Elementary School Journal, 31,* 496–503.

MORRISON, C., Harris, A. M., & Auerbach, I. T. (1971). The reading performance of disadvantaged early and non-early readers from grades 1 through 3. *Journal of Educational Research, 65,* 23–26.

NATIONAL Association for the Education of Young Children. (1987). *Developmentally appropriate practice.* Washington, DC: NAEYC.

RESNICK, D. P., & Resnick, L. (1977). The nature of literacy: An historical exploration. *Harvard Educational Review, 47,* 370–385.

SIMS, E. V. J., Weisberg, P., & Sulentic, C. (1983). Direct instruction improves drawing skills with preschoolers. *Direct Instruction News,* Spring, pp. 4–5.

SLAVIN, R. E. (1991). Chapter 1: A vision for the next quarter century. *Phi Delta Kappan, 72,* 586–592.

STONE, J. G. (1979). General philosophy: Preschool education within Head Start. In E. Zigler & J. Vallentine (Eds.), *Project Head Start: A legacy of the war on poverty* (pp. 163–174). New York: Free Press.

TORREY, J. W. (1979). Reading that comes naturally: The early reader. In T. G. Waller & G. E. Mackinnon (Eds.), *Reading research: Advances in theory and practice* (pp. 117–144). New York: Academic Press.

WEISBERG, H. I. (1973). *Short-term cognitive effects of Head Start programs: A report on the third year of planned variation—1971–72.* Cambridge, MA: Huron Institute.

WEISBERG, P. (1984). *Accelerating reading and comprehension in poverty-level preschoolers using a synthetic phonic program.* Tuscaloosa, AL: Center for Learning and Development Disorders. (ERIC Document Reproduction Service No. ED 250 076)

WEISBERG, P. (1989). What Head Start and preschool children know about academic concepts and operations before they start the primary grades. Unpublished manuscript, University of Alabama, Department of Psychology, Tuscaloosa.

WEISBERG, P. (1992). Education and enrichment approaches. In C. E. Walker & M. C. Roberts, *Handbook of clinical child psychology,* 2nd ed. (pp. 919–932). New York: Wiley.

WEISBERG, P., & Savard, C. (1993). Teaching preschoolers to read: Don't stop between the sounds when segmenting words. *Education and Treatment of Children, 16*, 1–18.

CHAPTER 11

Children Prenatally Exposed to Alcohol and Cocaine: Behavioral Solutions

Vikki F. Howard
Betty F. Williams
T. F. McLaughlin

Substance abuse by pregnant women tends to affect prenatally exposed children across a continuum of dimensions. At one end of the continuum, fetal alcohol syndrome (FAS) presents the most dramatic and severe impact and is also the most extensively researched and documented. Cocaine use appears to cause subtle effects for which the long-term impact has yet to be determined. Marijuana, heroin, methamphetamines, tobacco, and caffeine also have documented deleterious effects of greater and lesser degrees along the continuum. Of these pharmacological teratogens, the most frequently used secondary drugs are marijuana and alcohol (Hingson et al., 1982). Confounding the issues related to prenatal substance abuse is the prevalence of polydrug abuse. Most cocaine abusers, for example, also abuse other drugs, making the effects of cocaine alone difficult to determine. The presence of such polydrug use seems to worsen birth outcomes for exposed infants (Kaye, Elkind, Goldberg, & Tytun, 1989) in regard to birth weight, gestational age, and length of hospital stay. In addition, the form of ingestion may differentially affect the mother and fetus. For example, infants of crack cocaine abusers displayed poorer outcomes than those exposed to other forms of cocaine in regard to birth weight and adverse neurologic signs. Although many drugs are known to have teratogenic effects when used during pregnancy, this chapter focuses primarily on alcohol, crack/cocaine, and polydrug use. Several factors were weighed in this decision. First, alcohol and cocaine have both high frequency use and broad-based damage to the fetus. Second, the developmental and behavioral characteristics observed in these infants and young children appear to overlap substantially, which renders the analysis relevant for both. Finally, fetal alcohol syndrome, prenatal cocaine exposure, and polydrug use are widely considered the most troubling and preventable disabilities of the late 20th century.

The Effects of Prenatal Substance Abuse

Fetal Alcohol Syndrome

A diagnosis of FAS is warranted when a child has a cluster of disorders within three diagnostic areas: central nervous system dysfunction, craniofacial malformations, and prenatal and postnatal growth disorders (Griesbach & Polloway, 1990). The diagnosis is made when at least two or more craniofacial defects are present in a child, and the growth rate is below the 10th percentile for height and weight (Griesbach & Polloway, 1990). Children who meet some but not all criteria for a clear diagnosis and who have a history of prenatal alcohol exposure may be labeled fetal alcohol effects (FAE) or alcohol-related birth defects (ARBD) (Warren & Bast, 1988). For the purposes of this discussion, the term *FAS* will be used to refer to children with FAS, FAE, and ARBD, while acknowledging that the most serious of the three is clearly FAS.

Fetal alcohol syndrome is the leading known cause of mental retardation with prevalence figures surpassing Down's syndrome, cerebral palsy, and spina bifida (Luke, 1990; Streissguth, 1986; Streissguth et al., 1991). Though worldwide prevalence figures place the rate of FAS at about 1.9 per 1,000 live births in the general population (Warren & Bast, 1988), birth rates among chronically alcoholic women average about 25 per 1,000 (Burd & Martsolf, 1989). Researchers have concluded that the fetus is most vulnerable to alcohol teratogenic effects during the first trimester, but they have not determined a threshold for safe ingestion of alcohol during pregnancy. Yet, even with the well-publicized risk of alcohol's harmfulness, every year between 6,000 and 11,000 children are born with major or minor physical birth defects caused by prenatal alcohol exposure (Burd & Martsolf, 1989).

The short- and long-term prognosis for children with FAS is poor. For example, Jones and Smith (1973) found that 17% of children born to alcoholic mothers died during the first week of life. Of those who survived, 32% had abnormal facial features and 55% had borderline to moderate mental retardation (Overholser, 1990). More specifically, Streissguth and colleagues (1991) found that these children have a 44% chance of having full FAS and a 66% chance for partial effects. When an older sibling has already been identified with FAS, the probability that the younger sibling will also have the syndrome increases; specifically, births among younger siblings averaged 77% FAS per 1,000 births (Abel, 1988; Warren & Bast, 1988).

An unstable family environment may compound the problems of these children. For example, they go through an average of five different homes within their lifetimes. Only 9% are raised with both biological parents; another 3% with the biological mother alone.

Contributing to this instability is the mothers' chronic alcohol dependency. In fact, Streissguth and colleagues (1991) reported that by adolescence, 69% of the biological mothers were known to be dead and 33% of the children were never raised by their biological mothers. Native American children, a disproportionate number of whom have FAS, are in foster care at a rate five times higher than the national rate (Griesbach & Polloway, 1990).

Children Prenatally Exposed to Cocaine

Like alcohol, prenatal exposure to cocaine appears to have deleterious effects on later development; however, there are significant differences in our understanding of cocaine exposure. First, interest in cocaine-affected infants is a more recent phenomenon and the incidence of abuse is probably less than that of alcohol. Second, because cocaine use is illegal, it is difficult to obtain accurate reports of use. Finally, the saliency of characteristics, though similar in kind, seems to be less apparent than for children with FAS. So, while children may be described in a similar fashion, there appear to be distinct qualitative differences.

The use of cocaine by pregnant women has rapidly increased in recent years (Chasnoff et al., 1986). In 1990 Kusserow estimated that 100,000 babies were born to cocaine-using women each year. Hospitals conducting urine tests on newborns found that 10% to 15% proved positive for cocaine (Miller, 1989) and ranged as high as 45.8% in San Francisco (Osterloh & Lee, 1989). In fact, the Perinatal Center for Chemical Dependence in Chicago found that the primary drug used by 58% of pregnant drug abusers was cocaine (Chasnoff, 1989a).

In spite of the alarm sounded by the popular media, a majority of infants exposed to cocaine demonstrate no physical abnormalities or immediate effects (Griffith, 1990). It is possible that subtler, less physical symptoms of neurological impairment will be present as long-term effects (Barford, 1989). Those infants *who are symptomatic* demonstrate the characteristics described in Table 11.1.

Factors Covarying with Exposure to Alcohol and Cocaine

The long-term characteristics observed in children prenatally exposed to substance abuse may be due to causes beyond the direct drug exposure. Numerous

Table 11.1 Characteristics of children prenatally exposed to alcohol and cocaine

Characteristics	Fetal Alcohol Syndrome	Cocaine
Growth retardation, low birth weight or failure to thrive	Burd & Martsolf, 1989; Clarren & Smith, 1978; Luke, 1990; Majewski & Goecke, 1982	Chasnoff, 1989b; Fulrother, Phillips, & Durand, 1989
Neonatal neurological indexes: tremulousness, abnormal muscle tone, hyperextension, abnormal reflexes, anxiety seizure	Griesbach & Polloway, 1990; Elliot & Johnson, 1983	Chasnoff, 1986/1987; Schneider & Chasnoff, 1987
Sleep disturbances	Rossett, 1980	Ward et al., 1986
Delays in cognitive development	Overholser, 1990	--
Abnormal EEG or ultrasonograph	--	Dixon & Bejar, 1989
Hyperirritability (inability to habituate to environmental stimuli)	Griesbach & Polloway, 1990; Streissguth, 1986	van Baar, Fleury, & Ultee, 1989
Facial anomalies: thin upper lip; flattened bridge; short, upturned nose; underdeveloped groove between upper lip and nose; hydroplasia epicanthal fold; narrow eye slit; low-set unparallel ears; narrow receding forehead; microcanthea	Luke, 1990; Overholser, 1990; Phillipson, 1988; Rossett, 1980	
Physical anomalies: cardiac, renal, skeletal defects	Luke, 1990; Majewski & Goecke, 1982; Phillipson, 1988	Hoyme et al., 1990
Motor dysfunctions	Barr et al., 1990	Schneider & Chasnoff, 1987
Reduced immune response	Burd & Martsolf, 1989; Griesbach & Polloway, 1990; Majewski & Goecke, 1982	
Premature labor	Griesbach & Polloway, 1990	MacGregor et al., 1987
Attentional deficits and hyperactivity	Streissguth et al., 1991; Warren & Bast, 1988	Chasnoff, 1989c
Language delays	Becker, Warr-Leeper, & Leeper, 1990; Carney & Chermak, 1991; Warren & Bast, 1988	--
Behavioral problems: impulse control, excess aggression, rule breaking, conduct problems— lying, cheating, stealing	D'Entremont, 1990; Streissguth et al., 1991	
Social skills deficits: social intrusiveness, poor peer relations	D'Entremont, 1990; Streissguth et al., 1991	Van Dyke & Fox, 1990
Learning disabilities: judgment, comprehension, abstraction	Streissguth & LaDue, 1985, 1987	Van Dyke & Fox, 1990
Poor academic achievement	Streissguth, Aase, Clarren, Randels, LaDue, & Smith, 1991	Van Dyke & Fox, 1990
Affective: insecure attachments		Ainsworth et al., 1978; Howard, Beckwith, & Kropenske, 1989
Respiratory difficulty	Jones & Smith, 1973	Chasnoff et al., 1989

competing explanations exist for observed dysfunctional behavior, language, and development. These explanations need to be noted, since assignment of blame to substance abuse alone might lead to a largely misplaced preoccupation and ignore social issues of broader impact (Dixon, 1990; Weston et al., 1989). The following alternative hypotheses should be considered as competing with the effects of exposure to substance abuse on the behavior of young children (Williams & Howard, in press):

1. *Prenatal care.* Women using drugs were more likely to have lower than average weight-to-height ratios, sexually transmitted disease, and poorer prenatal histories. Prenatal care is a significant factor related to postnatal health and developmental risk.

2. *Premature birth.* Prematurity is also linked to other variables that occur in tandem with drug use, such as maternal malnutrition and cigarette smoking.

3. *The natural home environment.* Approximately one-half to three-quarters of those children identified at birth as being prenatally exposed to drugs returned home with their mother or a relative. Because of the lack of treatment options for women who are addicted to drugs (Dodd, 1990; Lubinski, 1990; Miller, 1989), a large percentage of women remain users or return to drug use. A task force in New York City found that from 1985 to 1988 there was a 72% increase in child abuse as a result of drug abuse, primarily crack (Briggs et al., 1990).

4. *Poverty.* Outcomes for children associated with poverty alone include malnourishment, attention deficit disorder, significant developmental lags, increased crime and violent behavior, and a constellation of other preventable behaviors.

5. *Racial inequities.* Even though drug use pervades all segments of society, low-income and minority groups are overrepresented (Dixon, 1990). Minority students comprise a high-risk group that tends to have a considerable disadvantage in the education system. This is unfortunate since minority status is confounded by socioeconomic class, and poverty alone may be the critical factor limiting educational attainment (Vacha & McLaughlin, in press).

6. *Social welfare.* Finally, and perhaps most significantly, the failure of our social welfare system to deal with an abundance of infants who are found at birth to have been prenatally exposed to drugs is a compounding factor in determinants of later child development. In many states child protective programs have been overwhelmed by the number and difficulty of drug-related pediatric cases. These factors contribute to changes in data related to foster care, such as younger average age of entry, substantially longer average stay in foster care, decreasing availability of foster families, and lack of adequate training for foster care parents. One result is that children are often shifted from foster home to foster home, after brief stays with a single family (Briggs et al., 1990; Dodd, 1990; Weston et al., 1989). All of these factors have the potential to contribute to the types of behaviors that have been noted anecdotally in "drug babies."

Behavioral Intervention

Considerable attention has been paid lately to the characteristics and needs of children who have FAS/FAE or prenatal exposure to cocaine/crack or other drugs (Burgess & Streissguth, 1992; Griffith, 1992). There are an ever-increasing number of children with such a history, and since these children display problems that are complex and often severe, there are no simple solutions. Management strategies used in cognitive and social skills training for other children have had little impact on this population. It is plausible, however, that strategies developed to intervene with children exhibiting similar behaviors will also be effective for the constellation of behaviors observed in children with FAS or other substance abuse histories. Behavior analysis has contributed the most consistently effective interventions for children with social and academic problems, although several factors have limited the extent to which this technology has been linked to FAS and cocaine-exposed behaviors. The adoption of behavior interventions has been limited for the following reasons: (1) behavioral strategies provide neither simple nor short-term solutions; (2) a lack of understanding or adoption of behavior analysis has obscured its potential to the mainstream; and (3) until now, the need for widespread adoption of behavior analysis has not been as critical, since children with such challenging needs represented a relatively small percentage of students in public schools.

The following analyses identify probable behavior-analytic intervention solutions for the most troubling characteristics of children exposed to substance abuse. These strategies are illustrative of the range of behavioral solutions that should be investigated. To a very large degree, the recommended solutions need rigorous research. Hence, this chapter provides the basis for initial efforts to functionally link the knowledge base of behavior analysis to the behavioral remediation of children who were prenatally exposed to drugs.

Early Intervention

Functional Analysis of Behaviors

Because the operational conditions for acquiring or maintaining difficult behaviors are seemingly subtle in this population, intensive measurement using functional analysis is needed. O'Neill and colleagues (1989) described the multiple outcomes of functional analysis, which were to (1) operationally define the target behaviors, (2) identify conditions under which behavior is likely to occur, and (3) define functions that the behaviors serve for the individual (reinforcers). Each of these outcomes would contribute significantly to the understanding and eventual intervention of problem behaviors associated with prenatal exposure to drugs.

A prerequisite to functional analysis is the elimination of known physiological conditions—such as metabolic, organic, and physical state conditions—as contributors to the problem behavior. Infants who were prenatally exposed to alcohol tend to be hypersensitive to environmental stimuli, so much so that episodes of excessive crying are common. This crying, however, may be functional rather than pathological, as these infants are often victim to the physiological conditions that frequently accompany FAS and polydrug exposure such as otitis media, upper respiratory infection, and gastrointestinal disturbances. Thorough medical evaluations should be conducted before beginning more intensive behavioral investigations.

Systematic Desensitization, Shaping, and Fading

Griffith (1992) attributed much of the aberrant behavior observed in polydrug-exposed children to a reduced threshold for overstimulation. A procedure of systematic desensitization using stimulus-shaping and fading technology would accomplish the dual goals of preventing overstimulation while promoting adaptation (Budzynski & Stoyva, 1969). Since infants with FAS and other prenatal substance exposure syndromes tend to be overly sensitive to auditory, tactile, and visual stimulation, they may be more easily disrupted from sleeping than other children. Following a consistent pattern for putting a child to sleep, a caregiver should attempt to reduce extraneous stimulation. Swaddling a child tightly in a flexed position (arm and leg joints bent), the caregiver should follow gradual, discrete steps for placing a child in bed. Taking one deliberate step at a time (swaddle, rock, move to bed, lay in bed, turn light off), a caregiver would complete the process by placing the child in a side-lying position. Lights, music, children at play, and other potential disturbances should initially be kept to a minimum to avoid waking the child. To initially minimize disturbances during sleep, white noise might be used and gradually faded to systematically develop habituation (adaptation) to natural conditions. Because parents may be negatively reinforced when tactics such as white noise are successful, they may be reluctant to attempt fading. However, fading is a critical element of behavior management, since failure to do so may prevent or delay adaptation.

Children who have been prenatally exposed to drugs sometimes exhibit unusual patterns of awakening, whereby they bypass normal stages of awareness and move directly into high-pitched crying. These children miss critical periods for verbal or social interactions during which reciprocal conditioned reinforcement takes place. Again, to avoid such episodes, desensitization using the gradual introduction of stimuli to assist the child in awakening might be an effective tactic (see Figure 11.1). Using one stimulus change at a time, an adult would turn the child over, lift the child, rock the child gently, softly coo, and then slowly introduce degrees of light. If the child cries, the caregiver would move back to a previous step by reducing sound and visual stimuli, but attempt to reintroduce stimulation quickly to prevent reinforcing avoidance or escape behavior.

As described earlier, caregivers and clinicians have frequently noted aberrant sleep patterns that persist through childhood in infants affected by prenatal exposure to drugs. For example, Griesbach and Polloway (1990) noted that children with FAS tended to sleep less and slept in a more restless state than other children. As a neonate, disturbances in sleep patterns could be related to various physiological problems such as persistent drug effects, mild neurological disruptions, or metabolic difficulties. However, long-term sleep problems probably result from an early interaction between physiology and environment (Benoit, Zeanah, Boucher, & Minde, 1992). Benoit and colleagues (1992) found that infants and young children who had erratic sleep patterns tended to be poorly attached to their mothers. That is, their mothers did not become conditioned reinforcers to their children, and the children themselves were not reinforcing to caregivers. This would be a logical outcome for children who are difficult to comfort, hypersensitive to environmental stimuli, and experience multiple placements (Williams & Howard, in press). Early caregiver responses to infants' sleep/wake behaviors may actually lead to long-term problems that become highly resistant to change (see Figure 11.1). For example, adults commonly respond immediately to infants who wake and cry during the

night. This attention includes holding, cooing, feeding, rocking, and other attempts at comfort until the child either falls asleep or is sufficiently calmed to return to bed (Figure 11.1). For a typically developing child who cries, immediate and consistent attention is considered appropriate, if not desirable. However, because infants with FAS and those exposed to other substances tend to be more difficult to comfort, the frequency and length of attention may be extensive. The infant may quickly learn that he or she can not only get, but keep an adult's attention by waking, crying, and staying awake. The beginning of long-term childhood sleep disturbances may be maintained in this way. Such a hypothesis requires carefully controlled research to determine if a functional relation-ship does occur.

To eliminate patterns of night waking, caregivers can implement a systematic plan for shaping increasingly longer periods of independence (Berman, Nino-Murcia, & Roehrs, 1990). Extinction is one strategy that has been effective. However, because crying children tend to make parents uncomfortable, they might be more willing to consistently implement more positive systems. One behavioral strategy gradually increases the length of time between the child awakening and the adult responding (Figure 11.2). The caregiver initially gives brief, managerial attention to the child and places him or her back in bed. The next time the infant wakes, the caregiver waits 15 to 30 seconds before attending to the child. Gradually, the interval between the child awakening and receiving adult attention is lengthened. In this manner, the

Hypersensitivity

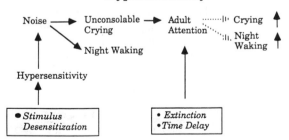

Figure 11.1. Hypersensitive children respond to noise by waking suddenly and crying unconsolably. Adult attention is probably punished by continued crying. To change this, the child should be awakened with the gradual introduction of stimuli, adding one dimension at a time; first touch, then voice, then lights, while maintaining quiet responding. Withdrawing adult attention (extinction) or time delay may interrupt the chain to reduce night waking.

Frustration

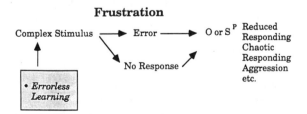

Figure 11.2. When complex tasks are presented, children who have been prenatally exposed to drugs may make errors or fail to respond, which results in frustration and reduces "trying" or persistence. Using errorless learning techniques with sufficient prompting to ensure success avoids frustration and its punishment.

caregiver reduces the strength of adult reinforcement for night awakening.

Children with attentional deficits, who are unable to remain at a task for a *reasonable* length of time given their developmental age, seem to be unable to discriminate between irrelevant and critical environmental stimulation (Barkley, 1990). Hence, they perceive visual, tactile, auditory, and gustatory sensations with greater intensity than for those who are able to adjust to multiple sensations more adaptively. Even in early infancy, it is critical to gradually increase a child's tolerance for multiple stimuli. For example, caregivers might hold a child for a while, then begin talking quietly, then rock, then play with toys, and so on until the child is able to deal with many sensations. Shaping a child's tolerance to increasingly complex environments will enable him or her to be more successful in natural school and adult situations. Again, negative reinforcement is likely to prevent parents from attempting systematic introduction of multiple sensations. In fact, avoidance of complex environments by adults might in fact lead to persistent hypersensitivity in the infant.

Children with prenatal drug histories often experience difficulty in making transitions or adjusting to changing conditions or situations (Figure 11.3). For example, an infant may refuse to use a bottle when it is filled with anything other than formula, even though he or she is willing to drink other fluids from a cup. A recommended intervention might include a fading procedure (Bijou & Baer, 1967). To use the formula example, a caregiver would gradually add milk to the formula, while reducing the amount of formula, so that eventually the child is left with only milk. Since our lives involve constant change, it is important that caregivers help children experience successful transitions early and with as little trauma as possible. The principles of shaping and fading strategies can be used to help children adapt to alterations in environment.

Task Analysis and Errorless Learning

Observations indicate that children with FAS/FAE have generally delayed cognitive skills and, along with other children with prenatal substance histories, have low tolerance for frustration (Griffith, 1992). To address both these concerns, two promising techniques for efficient instruction are task analysis (Sulzer-Azaroff & Mayer, 1991) and errorless learning strategies (Billingsley & Romer, 1983).

To avoid frustration in learning new skills, two principles of instruction should be followed. First, for a child to learn from an activity, it must be within a child's skill range (including skills slightly beyond mastery level). Tasks that are too difficult will result in failure and frustration. A task analysis helps caregivers break down a task and pinpoint the appropriate placement within the task sequence where the child will be successful. Just being successful, however, is not sufficient; children should be gradually assisted to develop more complex skill repertoires. Errorless learning, a second tactic illustrated in Figure 11.2, can be used to move a child from the point of mastery within a task analysis to more complex levels without unnecessary failure (frustration). Errorless learning tactics, which have broad research bases for individuals with mental retardation, include time delay, shaping and fading, graduated guidance, system of least prompts, and most-to-least prompts (Ault et al., 1989).

Differential Reinforcement

Much of the disruptive social behavior observed in children with prenatal substance histories might be

Demand Motivated Avoidance

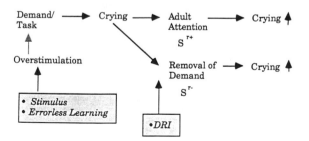

Figure 11.3. The infant may perceive a demand or task as overstimulation to which he or she responds by crying. This in turn obtains adult attention or the removal of the demand and thus results in increased crying. This situation may be avoided by presenting only tasks at which the child may be successful or by providing positive consequences for behavior that is incompatible with crying.

described as escape-motivated behavior. For example, fussy, easily irritated, and difficult-to-calm infants quickly learn that they can avoid or escape uncomfortable situations by crying. Though crying is a natural way for infants to learn control over their environment, babies who cry often and for long periods may receive excessive attention, which is highly contingent on crying. This very attention may strengthen the crying itself. Children who learn that a demand can be avoided or retracted when they cry engage in escape-motivated behavior for that purpose (Figure 11.3). Furthermore, caregivers may become so sensitive to the antecedent stimuli associated with impending fussiness that they will be negatively reinforced for eliminating all potential demands that might lead to crying.

To reduce crying, caregivers might allow children to cry, sometimes for long periods, attending only when there is a break in the infant's crying. This strategy, known as Differential Reinforcement of Incompatible behavior (DRI) (Sulzer-Azaroff & Mayer, 1991), has been used effectively for children with disabilities and for typical children. After ensuring that an infant is not hurt, sick, or wet, the adult removes his or her attention until the child calms. Once a child stops crying, the adult immediately provides attention, ensuring that the interaction is positive while not being so intrusive that the child cannot adjust to the level of stimulation.

The term *demand-motivated aberrant behavior* also refers to having "taught" children to act out (e.g., cry, throw things, self-abuse) in order to avoid a situation that places demands on them. As mentioned earlier, adults are frequently immediately reinforced for removing demands because the removal often results in a reduction of the child's inappropriate behavior. Rather than risk inciting further unpleasantness, caregivers avoid reintroducing the demand. Children learn that they can avoid even weak demands by acting out. Children with prenatal substance histories have been reported to exhibit extreme forms of aberrant behavior, which might largely be attributed to escape or avoidance behavior.

Schedules

Mace and colleagues (1988) described a strategy for eliciting high levels of compliance with previously noncompliant individuals. A method of task variation is used, whereby high-frequency task demands are interspersed among low-frequency task demands. As a result, individuals experienced high levels of success and developed generalized compliance. Sailor and Guess (1983) contended that the use of concurrent schedules of task presentation would result in higher levels of success. Each of these strategies is likely to be useful in minimizing levels of frustration, distractedness, and noncompliance (Figure 11.4). Finally, the systematic manipulation of reinforcement schedules to achieve high levels of attention to task, compliance, and efficient learning will contribute to efficient and effective intervention.

Verbal Behavior

Reciprocal conditioning. When caregiver attention to an infant's primitive needs (hunger or discomfort) is paired with primary reinforcers, the caregiver and the attention become conditioned social reinforcers (Bijou & Baer, 1967). Similarly, when adult attention to an infant's needs is consequated with positive feedback from the infant, the adult is reinforced for his or her attention (Figure 11.5a). The reciprocity of this relationship is sometimes referred to as bonding or attachment (Chess & Thomas, 1984). A significant disruption in the conditioning of adults or infants during the initial months of life may result in a failure

Distractedness

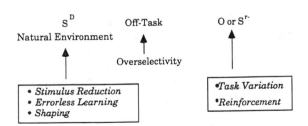

Figure 11.4. The natural environment may be highly distracting for the child who has been exposed to drugs. Structuring the environment through stimulus reduction, errorless learning, and shaping may prevent some overstimulation. Using task variation and structured reinforcers will increase the likelihood of attentive responding.

Mutual Conditioned Reinforcement
(Attachment/Bonding)

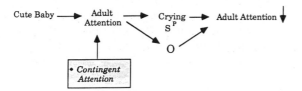

Figure 11.5a. A cute baby typically elicits adult attention, but the infant exposed to drugs tends to respond to this attention with crying or little positive affect, which tends to punish the attending adults. It is critical that contingent adult attention continue in order to provide opportunities for socialization and language development.

to bond (see Figure 11.5b). Several factors related to the ecology of a child exposed to multiple drugs may result in such disruptions. Bonding between infants and caregivers is generally considered a critical stage in socioemotional development, but it is a phenomenon that is not well understood. For example, the exact period of development for critical neonatal-to-infant attachment is not known, nor is it known if the absence of bonding during this period results in behavior that is resistant to later attachment and in serious emotional problems (Chess & Thomas, 1984).

One factor that may be a contributing factor to the caregivers' failure to become conditioned reinforcers

is that children who were prenatally exposed to drugs are placed in multiple foster care settings. Research indicates that children are entering the foster care system at younger ages and staying in the system for longer periods. Some children are difficult to care for and do not respond to attention. These children who come from environments where caregivers are unable to provide consistent nurturing are probable candidates for disrupted development of attachment (reciprocal conditioned reinforcers). Also, adults may actually become conditioned punishers to neonates in neurological distress. Those infants who are overstimulated by touch, sound, or even the sight of their mother's face find these stimuli aversive. The consistent pairing of adults with aversive overstimulation may condition the parent as an aversive stimulus, and other humans in general as generalized punishers (Figure 11.6). This might help explain the observed lack of affection shown by children with FAS and other polydrug exposure. Hence two levels of intervention are to teach adults to provide consistent nurturance within stimulation tolerance levels, and to provide nurturance in spite of unpleasant infant behaviors.

Nurturing is defined as a supportive relationship based on warmth, security, and mutual trust (Bijou & Baer, 1967; Siegel-Causey & Guess, 1989). Siegel-Causey and Guess (1989) identified several contin-

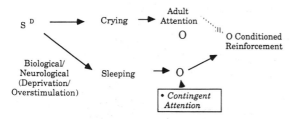

Figure 11.5b. The infant exposed to drugs may respond to stimulation in two ways: by crying or by "shutting down" in deep sleep. This reduces adult attention, and therefore adults in general fail to become conditioned reinforcers. If adult attention is given despite crying or "shut down," these infant actions may not become negatively reinforced by the avoidance of stimulation.

Conditioned Punishment

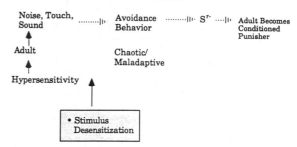

Figure 11.6. Another explanation of the child's lack of socialization is the punishment paradigm. For some children who were exposed to drugs, adult stimulation is aversive due to the child's hypersensitivity and the pairing of these aversive stimuli with adults makes adults conditioned punishers. If adults are careful to gradually introduce increasing stimuli, the punishment factor may be removed.

gent adult behaviors that caregivers might use to foster affectionate bonding. Establishing reciprocal eye gaze, by following the child's line of vision until eye contact is established, is considered critical. Animated facial expressions and the display of joy capture the child's attention and create a positive atmosphere. Furthermore, when caregivers adjust their language to a child's, a style known as "motherese," there is a feeling of warmth and security. Specifically, Siegel-Causey and Guess (1989) recommended the following four strategies to enhance nurturance: (1) provide regular, natural opportunities for comfort, support and affection; (2) establish a positive physical and social setting for interactions; (3) attend and respond to social and physical needs that are expressed through child-initiated behavior; and (4) focus on the child's world and the things that are of interest to the child. Providing warmth and affection to infants should not be noncontingent or unpredictable. Rather, positive interactions are most likely to develop when caregivers systematically nurture children when they engage in acceptable behavior.

Building verbal repertoires. Cognition, language, and social skills are all integrally related developmental domains. Hence, factors that affect one of these areas also affect the others either directly or indirectly. Children with FAS have deficits in all three areas. Children prenatally exposed to cocaine/crack are said to have problems in social and language skills. A lack of interpersonal communication skills will disrupt an individual's ability to develop reciprocal relations with others (McCormick & Schiefelbusch, 1990). Building these skills begins early in life, when children *first* recognize that they can have an impact on their environment. A child's first evidence of language is crying—crying because they are wet, crying because they are hungry, crying because they are uncomfortable. Neonates quickly learn that this crying communicates certain needs to adults, since adults typically contingently negatively reinforce crying to reduce states of discomfort. Gradually, adults learn to recognize other means of communication, and by reinforcing such attempts, infants learn alternate means of establishing verbal control over

their environment (Skinner, 1957). Children exposed to substance abuse, however, who cry often and sometimes for very long periods, may not discriminate between differential adult attention. Moreover, disruptions in an adult's sensitivity to an infant's communication attempts, or failures to respond in communication-enhancing ways, result in deficits in language and social skills. Language deficits can also occur when adults try to do too much for a child without expecting language, or when adults are unfamiliar with subtle forms of communication in children who are not very social (Figure 11.7).

Use of Positive Reinforcement

Although in general there are sound arguments to avoid the use of aversives in the form of negative reinforcement and punishment (Sidman, 1989), these arguments may be more urgent for children with prenatal substance histories. It is probable that many children who fall into these categories have acquired histories of being managed through negative reinforcement and punishment. Research indicates that children who have been affected by prenatal exposure to cocaine and alcohol are environmentally at risk. Factors such as poverty, single-parent families, lack of adult social support networks, persistent adult substance abuse, and multiple placements in foster families are all associated with clinical if not subclini-

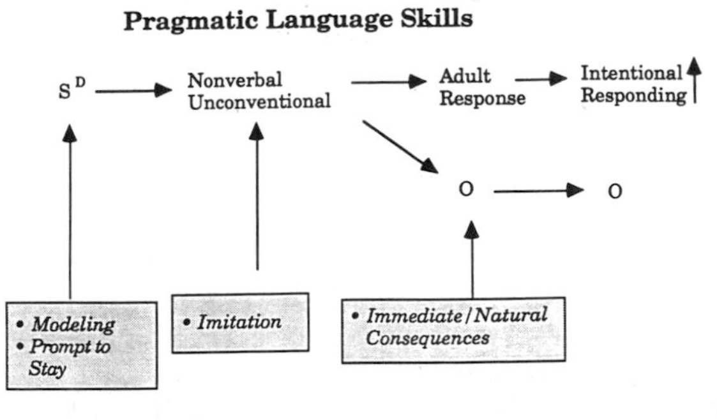

Figure 11.7. Effective language instruction involves sustained attention to the interaction. This may be enhanced by modeling and prompting, by imitating the child's own communications, and by interpreting initially nonconventional communication as intent and providing immediate and natural reinforcers.

cal child abuse and neglect. Add to this equation, children who are unusually difficult to manage, and one understands why a high incidence of child abuse occurs with this population.

The predicted consequences of coercion (negative reinforcement and punishment) are aggression, escape and avoidance, drop-out and countercontrol (Sidman, 1989). The chronic aberrant behavior and social skills deficits observed in children with prenatal cocaine or alcohol histories, fit the coercion paradigm (Figure 11.8) described by Sidman (1989) and may be largely attributed to histories of coercion. Therefore, it is likely that further use of aversives to manage behavior will only strengthen these maladaptive behaviors. For children with characteristics of substance exposure, powerful behavioral tactics that involve environmental engineering and positive reinforcement are likely to have a much healthier and more sustained effect. Specific strategies are discussed later in this chapter.

Weak Rule-Governed Behavior

An individual whose behavior is said to be controlled by weak rules generally appears to behave in the absence of consequences (Barkley, 1990). That is, the consequences are so subtle or weak, that they may not even be clear to the behavers themselves (Figure 11.9). Some practitioners have explained such behavior as intrinsically motivated. In fact, it is controlled by weak

consequences, which have become functional due to a history of pairing weak rules with consequences.

Barkley (1990) theorized that children with attention deficit hyperactivity disorder (ADHD) are insensitive to consequences (reinforcers and punishers), particularly mild and social consequences. He further hypothesized that the cause of this insensitivity is *differential neurological functioning*. Often children with prenatal cocaine or alcohol histories also lack such weak rule-governed behavior and seem to be controlled by more immediate consequences. Several factors may contribute to a reliance on contingency controlled behavior: (1) disruptive lifestyle may prohibit consistent rule-governed behavior training and (2) early behavioral problems (i.e., crying, hypersensitivity) that result in adult attention may build resistance to tolerance for delay of gratification of personal needs.

Investigation of the theory of weak rule-governed control has significant implications. Malott (1980) identified four prerequisites before a person can engage in weak rule-governed behavior. These strategies include (1) an ability to state the rule; (2) an ability to break down a task into minirules; (3) an ability to verbalize self-praise; and (4) an ability to evaluate rule compliance. It may well be that establishing rule-governed behavior will increase the child's ability to recruit and be controlled by reinforcers within the natural environment. Improved compliance is also likely to decrease the

Social Skills

S^D ──────▶ Aggression ──────▶ S^P ──▶ Aggression, Escape, Countercontrol, etc.
Overstimulation   Chaotic Behavior

▲
|
┌─────────────────────┐
│ • *Errorless Learning* │
│ • *Stimulus Reduction* │   ┌──────────┐
└─────────────────────┘   │ •*DRI* │
                                 └──────────┘

Figure 11.8. Overstimulation may produce aggressive or chaotic behavior, which punishes the child for social interaction. This same aggressive or chaotic behavior may also offend others and reduce their interaction; which negatively reinforces the child's use of the behavior as an escape function. Reducing initial stimulation or prompting for greater success may avoid a child's aggressive response. Likewise, providing reinforcement for behavior incompatible with aggression may reduce the negative aspects of the situation.

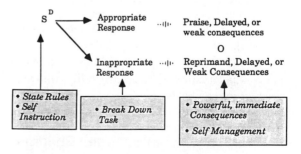

Figure 11.9. Tasks that result in weak or delayed consequences result in poor compliance. Such behaviors may be strengthened by programming self-instruction as an initial discriminative stimulus or by providing strong immediate consequences or even self-consequation.

frequency of negative parent-child interactions (Barkley, 1990).

Generalization

Adults who work with children who were prenatally exposed to cocaine describe behaviors that can be broadly categorized as failure to make stimulus and response generalizations. Burgess and Streissguth (1992) indicated that students with FAS/FAE lacked the ability to generalize to new settings, were unable to predict consequences, and failed to make good judgments. As another example, observers reported that a child would play with a toy as an adult had demonstrated but did not show an inclination to explore or solve problems, perhaps experiencing delays in the development of processes of stimulus equivalence (Stromer, 1991) and recombinative generalization (Goldstein, 1983; Striefel, Wetherby, & Karlan, 1978). These examples indicate that these children may need specific training to teach subtle stimulus and response generalization. Behavior analysts have developed a sophisticated technology of generalization that might be applied to this population. Specifically, Haring (1988) and Horner, Dunlap, and Koegel (1988) have provided sophisticated technologies of generalization. Though both technologies were presented as solutions for children with severe disabilities, their potential application should not be limited to that population. Haring (1988) described a set of decision-making rules to enhance the generalization of social, functional, and language skills. Horner, Dunlap, and Koegel (1988) described a six-step process for "teaching generalization with precision": (1) defining the instructional universe, (2) defining the range of relevant stimulus and response variation, (3) selecting, (4) sequencing (5) teaching examples and nonexamples, and (6) testing with nontrained probe examples.

Intervention with School-Aged Children

Some of the most disturbing characteristics of children with FAS are those related to their inability to follow rules and recognize consequences for their actions (especially delayed consequences), and their tendency to engage in aggressive behavior. These behaviors make children especially vulnerable to punitive control by adults as they get older, since positive intervention systems that are systematically introduced may have weaker immediate results. Conduct disorders of this nature are likely to become more pervasive and resistant to treatment the longer intervention is delayed. Control of attention deficits, self-management, and acquisition of basic skills become critical as these children age. Although a complete review of these strategies is beyond the scope of this chapter, we have provided in Table 11.2 examples of interventions that might be effective in solving problems observed in children with prenatal exposure to alcohol or cocaine. Thoughtful research studies, designed to validate these conjectures and proposals for new or alternative solutions, should follow.

Conclusions

It is probable that the seemingly intractable behavior observed in children who have been described by the popular media as "drug babies" is subject to the same principles of behavior as all other persons. Hence, we have not presented new behavioral strategies for addressing the complex problems often observed in children who have been prenatally exposed to cocaine or alcohol. Rather, we have tried to establish a research and training agenda for behavior analysts (see Table 11.2). There is a need to investigate functional relationships between early infant behavior associated with neurological disruptions and later behavior problems. Behavior analysts might also contribute to a set of practices that will be useful in teaching these children skills in social adaptation, linguistic competence, and academic and functional adaptation. It seems clear to us that the solutions for this population are often complex and may require sophisticated behavioral engineering. Given the growing number of children who fall into this group, it is unreasonable to think that the present cadre of well-trained behavior analysts will be sufficient to meet the demand. Moreover, caregivers (parents, grandparents, and foster caregivers) need to possess skills that will enable them to cope. This will require the development of a more user-friendly behavioral technology.

Table 11.2 Intervention Strategies

Problem Behavior	Intervention Strategy	Author/Date	Subject	Target Behavior
Attention to task	Task variation	Charlop, Kurtz, & Milstein, 1992	Five children with autism	Acquisition of following direction
	Behavioral momentum	Mace et al., 1988	Adults with mental retardation	Compliance with "do" and "don't" commands
	Self-monitoring	Hertz & McLaughlin, 1990	Two students with mild disabilities	On-task behavior
Tolerance for frustration	Errorless learning	Ault et al., 1989	Students with moderate and severe disabilities	Review of comparative studies
Escape-motivated behavior	Behavioral momentum	Mace & Belfiore, 1990	Women with severe retardation	Stereotypic behavior
	Differential reinforcement of incompatible behavior	Iwata et al., 1990	Seven children with mental retardation	Self-injurious behavior
Language delays	Incidental teaching	McGee, Krantz, & McClannahan, 1985	Three language-delayed children with autism	Expressive use of prepositions
	Language scripts	Goldstein & Cisar, 1992	Six typical and three children with disabilities	Social communicative interaction
	Conversational recruitment	Yoder, Davies, & Bishop, 1992	Nineteen preschoolers with developmental delays and their parents	Frequency, length, and content of linguistic utterances
Attention Deficit Hyperactivity Disorder	Medication therapy and behavior therapy	Abramowitz et al., 1992	Three boys ages 10 and 11 with ADHD	On-task behavior
	Token economy	Freidling & S. O'Leary, 1976	Eight 7- and 8-year-olds with hyperactivity	On-task behavior and academic performance in reading and math
Conduct disorders: Noncompliance	Behavioral contracting	Allen et al., 1993	Three elementary school boys	On-task behavior
	Self-recording	McLaughlin, 1984	Twelve elementary students with behavior disorders	On-task behaviors and assignment completion
Complex academic behaviors	Direct instruction	Gurney et al., 1990	Seven high school students with learning disabilities	Comprehension of literature passages
	Stimulus equivalence	Stromer & Mackay, 1992	Three students with mental retardation	Spelling
Generalized social interaction skills	Modeling, behavioral rehearsal, prompting, and praise	Barton & Ascione, 1979	Thirty-two preschool children	Physical and verbal sharing
	General case training	Horner & McDonald, 1982		Generalized vocational skills
	Direct teacher prompting of confederates and rewarding confederates	Odom et al., 1985	Three preschoolers with disabilities	Sharing, requesting, assistance, affection, and compliments

References

ABEL, E. L. (1988). Fetal alcohol syndrome in families. *Neurotoxicol Teratology, 10,* 1–2.

ABRAMOWITZ, A. J., Eckstrand, D., O'Leary, S. G., & Dulcan, M. K. (1992). ADHD children's responses to stimulant medication in two intensities of a behavioral intervention program. *Behavior Modification, 16,* 193–203.

AINSWORTH, M., Blethar, M., Waters, E., & Wall, S. (1978). *Patterns of attachment.* New Jersey: Lawrence Erlbaum.

ALLEN, L. J., Howard, V. F., Sweeney, W. J., & McLaughlin, T. F. (1993). Use of contingency contracting to increase on-task behavior with primary students. *Psychological Reports, 72,* 905–906.

AULT, M. J., Wolery, M., Doyle, P. M., & Gast, D. L. (1989). Review of comparative studies in the instruction of students with moderate and severe handicaps. *Exceptional Children, 55,* 346–356.

BARFORD, D. (1989). Substance abuse in pregnancy. *Inland Empire Perinatal Center Newsletter, 2,* 5.

BARKLEY, R. A. (1990). *Attention deficit hyperactivity disorder: A handbook for diagnosis and treatment.* New York: Guilford.

BARR, H. M., Darby, B. L., Streissguth, A. P., & Sampson, P. D. (1990). Prenatal exposure to alcohol, caffeine, tobacco, and aspirin: Effects on fine and gross motor performance in 4-year-old children. *Developmental Psychology, 26,* 339–348.

BARTON, E. J., & Ascione, F. R. (1979). Sharing preschool children: Facilitation, stimulus generalization, response generalization, and maintenance. *Journal of Applied Behavior Analysis, 12,* 417–430.

BECKER, M., Warr-Leeper, G. A., & Leeper, H. A. (1990). Fetal alcohol syndrome: A description of oral motor, articulatory, short-term memory, grammatical, and semantic abilities. *Journal of Communication Disorders, 23,* 97–124.

BENOIT, D., Zeanah, C. H., Boucher, C., & Minde, K. K. (1992). Sleep disorders in early childhood: Association with insecure maternal attainment. *Journal of the American Academy of Child and Adolescent Psychiatry, 31,* 86–93.

BERMAN, T. E., Nino-Murcia, G., & Roehrs, T. (1990). Sleep disorders: Take them seriously. *Patient Care,* June, 85–112.

BIJOU, S. W., & Baer, D. M. (1967). *Child development: Readings in experimental analysis.* New York: Appleton-Century-Crofts.

BILLINGSLEY, F. F., & Romer, L. T. (1983). Response prompting and transfer of stimulus control: Methods, research, and a conceptual framework. *Journal of the Association for the Severely Handicapped, 8*(2), 3–12.

BRIGGS, E. D., Johnson, K. R., Seelman, K., Bratton, B., Brown, S. S., & Graham, L. (1990). H. H. S. releases report on crack babies. *Focus,* Spring, 1,8.

BUDZYNSKI, T. H., & Stoyva, J. M. (1969). An instrument for producing deep muscle relaxation by means of analog information feedback. *Journal of Applied Behavior Analysis, 2,* 231–237.

BURD, L., & Martsolf, J. T. (1989). Fetal alcohol syndrome: Diagnosis and syndromeal variability. *Physiology & Behavior, 46,* 39–43.

BURGESS, D. M., & Streissguth, A. P. (1992). Fetal alcohol syndrome and fetal alcohol effects: Principles for educators. *Phi Delta Kappan, 74,* 24–29.

CARNEY, L. J., & Chermak, G. D. (1991). Performance of American Indian children with fetal alcohol syndrome on the test of language development. *Journal of Communication Disorders, 24,* 123–134.

CHARLOP, M. H., Kurtz, P. F., & Milstein, J. P. (1992). Too much reinforcement, too little behavior: Assessing task interpersonal procedures in conjunction with different reinforcement schedules with autistic children. *Journal of Applied Behavior Analysis, 25,* 795–808.

CHASNOFF, I. J. (1986/1987). Cocaine and pregnancy. *Childbirth Educator,* Winter, 37–38, 42.

CHASNOFF, I. J. (1989a). *National epidemiology of perinatal drug use.* Paper presented at a conference on Drugs, Alcohol, Pregnancy and Parenting: An Intervention Model, July, Spokane.

CHASNOFF, I. J. (1989b). Cocaine, pregnancy, and the neonate. *Women & Health, 15*(3), 23–35.

CHASNOFF, I. J. (1989c). *The nation's educational system should prepare.* Paper presented at a Conference of the National Association for Perinatal Addiction Research and Education, September, Miami.

CHASNOFF, I. J., Burns, K. A., Burns, W. J., & Schnoll, S. H. (1986). Prenatal drug exposure: Effects on neonatal and infant growth and development. *Neurobehavioral Toxicology and Teratology, 8,* 357–362.

CHASNOFF, I. J., Hunt, C. E., Kletter, R., & Kaplan, D. (1989). Prenatal cocaine exposure is associated with respiratory pattern abnormalities. *American Journal of Diseases of Children, 143,* 583–587.

CHESS, S., & Thomas, A. (1984). *Origins of behavior disorders.* New York: Brunner/Mazel.

CLARREN, S. K., & Smith, D. W. (1978). The fetal alcohol syndrome. *New England Journal of Medicine, 298,* 1063–1066.

D'ENTREMONT, D. M. (1990). *Intervention strategies for school age children.* (Report No. CG023529). University of Southern Maine. (ERIC Document Reproduction Service No. ED 334514).

DIXON, S. D. (1990). *Infants of substance abusing mothers: Demographics and medical profile.* A paper presented at Babies and Cocaine, New Challenges for Educators, September, San Francisco.

DIXON, S. D., & Bejar, R. (1989). Echoencephalographic findings in neonates associated with maternal cocaine and methamphetamine use: Incidence and clinical correlates. *Journal of Pediatrics, 115,* 770–778.

DODD, C. J. (1990). *Falling through the crack: The impact of drug-exposed children on the child welfare system.* Testimony presented to the United States Senate Subcommittee on Children, Family, Drugs, and Alcoholism, March.

ELLIOT, D. J., & Johnson, N. (1983). Fetal alcohol syndrome: Implications and counseling considerations. *Personnel and Guidance Journal, 62,* 67–69.

FREIDLING, C., & O'Leary, S. G. (1976). Effects of self-instructional training on second- and third-grade hyperactive children: A failure to replicate. *Journal of Applied Behavior Analysis, 12,* 211–219.

FULROTHER, R., Phillips, B., & Durand, D. J. (1989). Perinatal outcome of infants exposed to cocaine and or heroin in utero. *American Journal of Diseases of Children, 143,* 905–910.

GOLDSTEIN, H. (1983). Recombinative generalization: Relationships between environmental conditions and linguistic repertoires of language learners. *Analysis and Intervention in Developmental Disabilities, 3,* 279–293.

GOLDSTEIN, H., & Cisar, C. L. (1992). Promoting interaction during sociodramatic play: Teaching scripts to typical pre schoolers and classmates with disabilities. *Journal of Applied Behavior Analysis, 25,* 265–280.

GRIESBACH, L. S., & Polloway, E. A. (1990). *Fetal alcohol syndrome: Research review and implications.* (Report No. EC232650). Lynchburg, VA: Lynchburg College. (ERIC Document Reproduction Service No. ED 326035)

GRIFFITH, D. R. (1990). The effects of perinatal drug exposure on child development: Implications for early intervention and education. A paper presented at Babies and Cocaine, New Challenges for Educators, September, San Francisco.

GRIFFITH, D. R. (1992). Prenatal exposure to cocaine and other drugs: Developmental and educational prognoses. *Phi Delta Kappan, 74,* 30–34.

GURNEY, D., Gersten, R., Dimino, J., & Carnine, D. (1990). Story grammar: Effective literature instruction for high school students with learning disabilities. *Journal of Learning Disabilities, 23,* 335–342.

HARING, N. G. (Ed.) (1988). *Generalization for students with severe handicaps: Strategies and solutions.* Seattle: University of Washington Press.

HERTZ, V., & McLaughlin, T. F. (1990). Self-recording effects for on-task behavior of mildly handicapped adolescents. *Child and Family Behavior Therapy, 12*(3), 1–10.

HINGSON, R., Alpert, J. J., Day, N., Dooling, E., Kayne, H., Morelock, S., Oppenheimer, E., & Zuckerman, B. (1982). Effects of maternal drinking and marijuana use on fetal growth and development. *Pediatrics, 70,* 539–546.

HORNER, R. H., & McDonald, R. S. (1982). Comparison of single instance and general case instruction in teaching a generalized vocational skill. *Journal of the Association for Persons with Severe Handicaps, 8,* 7–20.

HORNER, R. H., Dunlap, G., & Koegel, R. L. (1988). *Generalization and maintenance: Life-style changes in applied settings.* Baltimore: Brookes.

HOWARD, J., Beckwith, L., & Kropenske, V. (1989). The development of young children of substance abusing parents: Insights from seven years of intervention and research. *Zero to Three, 9*(5), 8–12.

HOYME, H. E., Jones, K. L., Dixon, S. D., Jewett, T., Hanson, J. W., Robinson, L. K., Msall, M. E., & Allanson, J. E. (1990). Prenatal cocaine exposure and fetal vascular disruption. *Pediatrics, 85,* 743–747.

IWATA, B. A., Pace, G., Kalsher, M. J., Cowdery, G. E., & Cataldo, M. F. (1990). Experimental analysis and extinction of self-in-

jurious behavior. *Journal of Applied Behavior Analysis, 23,* 11–28.

JONES, K. L., & Smith, D. W. (1973). Recognition of the alcohol syndrome in early infancy. *Lancet, 2,* 999–1001.

KAYE, K., Elkind, L., Goldberg, D., & Tytun, A. (1989). Birth outcomes for infants of drug abusing mothers. *New York State Journal of Medicine,* 256–261.

KUSSEROW, R. P. (1990). *Crack babies.* A Report of the Office of Inspector General, Department of Health and Human Services, February, Washington, DC.

LUBINSKI, C. (1990). Addressing the impact [of cocaine] on women, children and families. Paper presented at Babies and Cocaine: New Challenges for Educators Conference, August, Washington, DC.

LUKE, B. (1990). The metabolic basis of the fetal alcohol syndrome. *International Journal of Fertility, 35*(6), 33–337.

MCCORMICK, L., & Schiefelbusch, R. L. (1990). *Early language intervention.* Columbus, OH: Merrill.

MACE, F. C., & Belfiore, P. (1990). Behavioral momentum in the treatment of escape-motivated stereotypy. *Journal of Applied Behavior Analysis, 23,* 507–514.

MACE, F. C., Hock, M. L., Lalli, J. S., West, B. J., Belifiore, P., Pinter, E., & Brown, D. K. (1988). Behavioral momentum in the treatment of noncompliance. *Journal of Applied Behavior Analysis, 21,* 123–141.

MCGEE, G. G., Krantz, P. J., & McClannahan, L. E. (1985). The facilitative effects of incidental teaching on preposition use by autistic children. *Journal of Applied Behavior Analysis, 18,* 17–32.

MACGREGOR, S. N., Keith, L. G., Chasnoff, I. J., Rosner, M. A., Chisum, G. M., Shaw, P., & Minogue, J. P. (1987). Cocaine use during pregnancy: Adverse prenatal outcome. *American Journal of Obstetrics and Gynecology, 157,* 686–690.

MCLAUGHLIN, T. F. (1984). A comparison of self-recording and self-recording plus consequences for on-task and assignment completion. *Contemporary Educational Psychology, 9,* 185–192.

MAJEWSKI, F., & Goecke, T. (1982). Alcohol embryopathology. In E. Abel (Ed.), *Fetal alcohol syndrome,* Vol. II: *Human studies.* Boca Raton, FL: CRC Press.

MALOTT, R. W. (1980). A radical behavioral analysis of behavior modification. *Notes from a Radical Behaviorist, 2*(6), 1–2.

MILLER, G. (1989). Addicted infants and their mothers. *Zero to Three, 9*(5), 20–22.

ODOM, S. L., Hoyson, M., Jamieson, B., & Strain, P. (1985). Increasing handicapped preschoolers' peer social interactions: Cross setting and component analysis. *Journal of Applied Behavior Analysis, 18,* 3–16.

O'NEILL, R. E., Horner, R., H., Albin, R. W., Storey, K., & Sprague, J. R. (1990). *Functional analysis of problem behavior.* Sycamore, IL: Sycamore Publishing Company.

OSTERLOH, J. D., & Lee, B. L. (1989). Urine drug screening in mothers and newborns. *American Journal of Diseases of Children, 143,* 791–793.

OVERHOLSER, J. C. (1990). Fetal alcohol syndrome: A review of the disorder. *Journal of Contemporary Psychotherapy, 20*(3), 163–176.

PHILLIPSON, R. (1988). The fetal alcohol syndrome—recent international statistics. *Australia and New Zealand Journal of Developmental Disabilities, 14* (3&4), 211–217.

ROSSETT, H. L. (1980). A clinical perspective on fetal alcohol syndrome. *Alcohólism, 4,* 119–122.

SAILOR, W., & Guess, D. (1983). *Severely handicapped students: An instructional design.* Boston: Houghton Mifflin.

SCHNEIDER, J. W., & Chasnoff, I. J. (1987). Cocaine abuse during pregnancy: Its effects on infant motor development—A clinical perspective. *Topics in Acute Care and Trauma Rehabilitation, 2,* 59–69.

SIDMAN, M. (1989). *Coercion and its fallout.* Boston: Author's Cooperative.

SIEGEL-Causey, E., & Guess, D. (1989). *Enhancing nonsymbolic communication interactions among learners with severe disabilities.* Baltimore: Brookes.

SKINNER, B. F. (1957). *Verbal behavior.* New York: Appleton-Century-Crofts.

STREISSGUTH, A. P. (1986). The behavioral teratology of alcohol: Performance, behavioral, and intellectual deficits in prenatally exposed children. In J. R. West (Ed.), *Alcohol and brain development* (pp. 3–8). New York: Oxford University Press.

STREISSGUTH, A. P., Aase, J. M., Clarren, S. K, Randels, S. P., LaDue, R. A., & Smith, D. F. (1991). Fetal alcohol syndrome in adolescents and adults. *Journal of American Medical Association, 265,* 1961–1967.

STREISSGUTH, A. P., & LaDue, R. A. (1987). Fetal alcohol syndrome and fetal alcohol effects: Teratogenic causes of mental retardation and developmental disabilities. In S. R. Schroeder (Ed.), *Toxic substances and mental retardation* (pp. 1–32). Washington, DC: American Association on Mental Deficiency.

STRIEFEL, S., Wetherby, B., & Karlan, G. R. (1976). Establishing generative verb-noun instruction follwing behavior in retarded children. *Journal of Experimental Child Psychology, 22,* 247–260.

STROMER, R. (1991). Stimulus equivalence: Implications for teaching. In W. Ishaq (Ed.), *Human behavior in today's world* (pp. 109-122). New York: Praeger.

STROMER, R., & Mackay, H. A. (1992). Delayed constructed response identity marching improves the spelling performance of students with mental retardation. *Journal of Behavioral Education, 2,* 139–158.

SULZER-Azaroff, B., & Mayer, G. R. (1991). *Behavior analysis for lasting change.* New York: Holt, Rinehart, & Winston.

VACHA, E. F., & McLaughlin, T. F. (in press). The social structural, family, school and personal characteristics of at-risk students: Policy recommendations for school personnel. *Journal of Education.*

VAN BAAR, A. L., Fleury, P., & Ultee, C. A. (1989). Behaviour in first year after drug dependency pregnancy. *Archives of Disease in Childhood, 64,* 241–245.

VAN DYKE, D. C., & Fox, A. A. (1990). Fetal drug exposure and its possible implications for learning in the preschool and school-age population. *Journal of Learning Disabilities, 23,* 160–163.

WARD, S. L., Schuetz, S., Kirshna, V., Bean, X., Winger, T. W., Wachsman, L., & Keens, T. G. (1986). Abnormal sleeping ventilatory patterns in infants of substance abusing mothers. *American Journal of Diseases in Children, 140,* 1015–1020.

WARREN, K. R., & Bast, R. J. (1988). Alcohol-related birth defects: An update. *Public Health Reports, 103*(6), 638–642.

WESTON, D. R., Ivins, B., Zuckerman, M. D., Jones, C., & Lopez, R. (1989). Drug exposed babies: Research and clinical issues. *Zero to Three,* 9(5), 1–7.

WILLIAMS, B. F., & Howard, V. F. (in press). Children exposed to cocaine: Characteristics and implications for research and intervention. *Journal of Early Intervention.*

YODER, P. J., Davies, B., & Bishop, K. (1992). Getting children with developmental delays to talk to adults. In S. F. Warren & J. Reichle (Eds.), *Causes and effects in communication and language intervention*: Vol. 1 (pp. 255–276). Baltimore: Brookes.

PART 4

School-Age Children

Chapter 12
Measurably Superior Instructional Practices
in Measurably Inferior Times: Reflections on
Twain and Pauli
Edward J. Kameenui

Chapter 13
The Measure of a Teacher
R. Douglas Greer

Chapter 14
The Morningside Model of Generative Instruction
Kent R. Johnson, T. V. Joe Layng

Chapter 15
Teaching Children with Learning Problems
Ron Van Houten

Chapter 16
The Opportunity to Respond and Academic
Performance Revisited: A Behavioral Theory of
Developmental Retardation and Its Prevention
Charles R. Greenwood, Betty Hart, Dale Walker,
Todd Risley

Chapter 17
Ecobehavioral Assessment of Bilingual Special
Education Settings: The Opportunity to Respond
Carmen Arreaga-Mayer, Judith J. Carta,
Yolanda Tapia

Chapter 18
Toward Instructional Process Measurability:
An Interbehavioral Field Systems Perspective
Andrew Hawkins, Tom Sharpe, Roger Ray

Chapter 19
Developing Competent Learners by Arranging
Effective Learning Environments
Vicci Tucci, Daniel E. Hursh

Chapter 20
START Tutoring: Designing, Training,
Implementing, Adapting, and Evaluating Tutoring
Programs for School and Home Settings
April D. Miller, Patricia M. Barbetta,
Timothy E. Heron

Chapter 21
Three "Low-Tech" Strategies for Increasing the
Frequency of Active Student Response During
Group Instruction
William L. Heward

Chapter 22
Applied Behavior Analysis: An Insider's Appraisal
Thomas C. Lovitt

Measurably Superior Instructional Practices in Measurably Inferior Times: Reflections on Twain and Pauli

Edward J. Kameenui

In this chapter, I anchor my thoughts to the clever words of two prominent writers, Mark Twain and Wolfgang Pauli, who are well known outside the fields of education, psychology, and social science. Literary folklore has it that Mark Twain once made the following observation: "The difference between the almost right word and the right word is really a large matter—'tis the difference between the lightning-bug and the lightning." Science folklore has it that when he was asked to comment on a highly speculative proposal in physics, Wolfgang Pauli, the noted physicist, responded, "It's not even wrong" (Flanagan, 1988, p. 226; Kameenui, 1993). So between the words of Mark Twain and Wolfgang Pauli, we can construct a semantic framework for thinking about what is *right*, what is *almost right*, which for all practical purposes is wrong (according to Twain), and what is so far off-base, it's *not even wrong*.

Discerning what is right, what is almost right, and what's not even wrong is a troublesome task these days for educators, educational researchers, teachers, teacher educators, administrators, educational publishers, and the education community in general. This task is made particularly troublesome by two current trends—one sociological and the other pedagogical,

perhaps even epistemological. Not surprisingly, these trends inevitably interact. As is the case with most interactions, be they statistical or human, it is difficult to "unpack" this interaction of epistemology and sociology in ways that allow for clarity and confidence in identifying the causes of the interaction, the sources of error, and the simple main effects.

What's Right, Almost Right, and Not Even Wrong: Two Trends

The first trend that makes it difficult for educators to discern what is right, almost right, or not even wrong rests in part in responding to the unique and diverse needs of learners in the classroom. The realities of this diversity were made stark in a recent article by Hodgkinson (1991) "Reform Versus Reality." According to Hodgkinson:

- Since 1987, one-fourth of all preschool children in the U.S. have been in poverty.
- On any given night, between 50,000 and 200,000 children have no home. (In 1988, 40% of shelter users were families with children.)

- The "Norman Rockwell" family—a working father, a housewife mother, and two children of school age—constitutes only 6% of U.S. households.
- In 1987 child protection agencies received 2.2 million reports of child abuse or neglect—triple the number received in 1976.
- One-fourth of pregnant mothers receive no physical care of any sort during the crucial first trimester of pregnancy. About 20% of handicapped children would not be impaired had their mothers had one physical exam during the first trimester, which could have detected potential problems.
- About one-third of preschool children are destined for school failure because of poverty, neglect, sickness, handicapping conditions, and lack of adult protection and nurturance. [p. 10]

These facts, according to Hodgkinson (1991), are indicative of education's "leaky roof," a metaphor he used "for the spectacular changes that have occurred in the nature of the children who come to school" (p. 10).

Hodgkinson's (1991) demographic analysis is also reinforced by an unceasing wave of stories in the popular press. For example:

> The child poverty rate rose by more than 11% during the 1980s, reaching 17.9% in 1989. Black children were the most likely to fall into this group. In 1989, a black child had a 39.8% chance of living in poverty, a Native American child a 38.8% chance and a Hispanic child a 32.2% chance. The figure for Asian children was 17.1% and for white children 12.5%. [*Time*, 1992, p. 15]

Similarly, an advertisement for the Children's Defense Fund reads:

> Approximately 2.5 million American children were reported abused or neglected last year . . . Fourteen nations boast smarter 13-years-olds than the United States. [*SV Entertainment*, 1992, p. 13]

Hodgkinson (1991) concludes his analysis by offering a poignant soliloquy on the current slings and arrows of education's outrageous fortunes:

> There is no point in trying to teach hungry or sick children. From this we can deduce one of the most important points in our attempts to deal

with education: *educators can't fix the roof all by themselves.*   It will require the efforts of many people and organizations—health and social welfare agencies, parents, business and political leaders—to even begin to repair this leaky roof. There is no time to waste in fixing blame; we need to act to fix the roof. And unless we start, the house will continue to deteriorate, and all Americans will pay the price. [p. 10]

The sociological facts reported by Hodgkinson describe conditions that are so far off-base, so far from being right, that they are, in the words of Wolfgang Pauli, not even wrong. In short, they reflect the measurably inferior economic times in which we live. Given these times, one would think it imperative to heed Hodgkinson's call to fix the leaky roof. In the face of these difficult economic times, the importance of effective practices or "measurably superior instructional practices" are especially pronounced. Unfortunately, what makes Hodgkinson's data particularly chilling are not the facts themselves, but the dynamics of the educational discourse currently taking place under education's leaky roof.

The current debates about literacy and beginning reading (Adams, 1990, 1991; Bower, 1992; Chaney, 1991; Kameenui, 1988), whole language and direct instruction (Chall, 1992; Goodman, 1992; Liberman & Liberman, 1990; Mather, 1992; Yatvin, 1991), constructivism and positivism, skill-based and meaning-based learning, the "transmission" paradigm and the problem-solving paradigm in mathematics, all make it difficult to discern what is right, almost right, and not even wrong in pedagogy and classroom practice.

While scholarly debates about theory, pedagogy, and practice are important in the marketplace of ideas, in the current context of education's leaky roof, they appear indifferent to students with diverse learning and curricular needs. In some cases, the debates reflect tensions that have simply gone awry. For example, the debate about how best to teach beginning reading was reignited by Marilyn Jager Adams's (1990) book, *Beginning to Read: Thinking and Learning About Print.* To the uninitiated, the debate about beginning reading instruction and the role of phonics is not just another debate; it is a bitter family feud and like most family fights, it is passionate, heated, and painful. Adams's (1991) opening statement in a special issue of *The Reading Teacher* devoted exclusively to a critique of her book revealed the troubling tenor of this debate.

> I freely admit that I did not welcome this assignment. The debate over beginning reading instruction had long since admitted polemic and propaganda alongside well-founded research and responsible argumentation. People told me that I would lose old friends and make new enemies. People told me that I would be shot. [pp. 371–372]

"People told me that I would be shot." When asked about this statement, Marilyn assured me it was not delivered in jest. The gravity of that statement is absolutely chilling—that an academic scholar could actually be killed for examining the scientific evidence and bringing it to bear on a rather simple question: Is it better to sound out a word (*sssaaaat*) or simply read it whole (*sat*)? Words. What's particularly sobering about Adams's revelation is the thought that an academic debate could melt down to a level in which, as Dostoevski put it, a thought "will not enter words" (Vygotsky, 1962).

This is not right, in fact, it's not even wrong.

Debating Words and Numbers

The interaction between the realities of diversity as described by Hodgkinson (1991) and the current debates about "superior instructional practices" is a messy one. But the urgency of fixing the leaky roof requires at the very minimum, a reasonable understanding of some of the tensions associated with identifying and measuring superior instructional practices.

In the next section, I examine two general areas of the current discourse on educational reform: The first area of difficulty, in fact, has to do with words, and it is evident in the current debate on how best to teach beginning readers how to read. This debate is age-old—perhaps more than 100 years old—and according to Stanovich reaches back to the "beginning of pedagogy" (Bower, 1992, p. 138). It seems the older that debate gets, the more passionate and tenacious the voices become.

The second area of difficulty in discerning what is right, almost right, or not even wrong has to do not with words, but numbers. It centers on the curriculum and teaching standards promoted by the National Council for Teachers of Mathematics (NCTM), standards about which there has *not* been much serious debate; that in itself should be sufficient cause for concern. After years of passionate debate, has the field of mathematics education finally reached a consensus on how best to teach math? It's unlikely.

Beginning to Read

Adams's book, *Beginning to Read* (1990), is the result of a congressional mandate for an evaluation of phonics instruction. She was commissioned by the Center for the Study of Reading at the University of Illinois to carry out the evaluation as part of the 1986 Human Services Reauthorization Act.

What does Adams say about beginning to read? I'll let her speak for herself, words are not a problem for her, they flow effortlessly and with an eloquence that belies their historical and pedagogical weight:

1. The question of how much phonics is optimal is of genuine practical importance. Teaching phonics is a task that requires disciplined, sequenced coverage of individual elements and their interrelations, as well as continuous evaluation of students' levels of mastery. By its nature it entails lots of detail to attend to and to do. It is easy to imagine the busy teacher who shortshrifts the effort, whether by teaching too little about everything or everything about too little. But it is equally easy to imagine the teacher who becomes all too immersed in the system, treating it as an end in itself, neglecting its purpose or taking that appreciation for granted. [p. 51]
2. The alphabetic principle is subtle. Its understanding may be the single most important step toward acquiring the code. [p. 63]
3. Deep down in the machinery of our brains and long before we get to school, each of us has established a thorough familiarity with the phonemes of our language . . . But despite our working knowledge of phonemes, we are not naturally set up to be consciously aware of them. [pp. 65–66]
4. In the end, the great value of research on prereaders may lie in the clues it gives us toward determining

what the less prepared prereaders need most to learn. For these children, we have not a classroom moment to waste. [p. 90]

5. Skillful reader's processing of text seems far too fast and efficient to be based on letterwise processing of its print. Similarly each of these hypotheses has been transported to the educational domain with the same well-intentioned motivation: If we could release children from letterwise processing of text, we could expedite their graduation into efficient, skillful readers. Yet the single immutable and non-optional fact about skillful reading is that it involves relatively complete processing of the individual letters of print. On reflection, we realize that none of these hypotheses is entirely wrong. The problem is that none of them is sufficiently right. [p. 105]

6. Phonological awareness, letter recognition facility, familiarity with spelling patterns, spelling-sound relations, and individual words must be developed in concert with real reading and real writing and with deliberate reflection on the forms, functions, and meanings of texts. [p. 422]

In the final two pages of her text, Adams (1990) asked, ". . . Why is there so much outward dispute?" She answered:

My best guess is that by virtue of human nature, people tend to conceive of some instructional activities as "key" and others as "support." But the process of reading cannot be divided into key and support activities. All of its component knowledge and skills must work together within a single integrated and interdependent system. And it is in that way that they must be acquired as well: It is not just eclecticism that makes a program of reading instruction effective; it is the way in which its pieces are fitted together to complement and support one another, always with full consideration of the needs and progress of the young readers with whom it will be used. [p. 423]

These appear to be pretty reasoned words, so what's the problem? In part, the problem has to do with the words that Adams chooses. As Twain noted, the difference between the right word and the almost

right word is indeed a large matter. For example, in the "Afterword" to Adams's text, Dorothy Strickland and Bernice Cullinan stated: "Terms such as 'prereaders,' 'reading readiness,' or 'prerequisite skills' do not reflect the latest thinking on literacy development . . . The term emergent literacy, coined by Marie Clay in her 1966 dissertation 'Emergent Reading Behavior,' is a more apt descriptor of children in the process of becoming literate" (1990, p. 426).

The conception of young children as "emergent" readers is deliberate and central. Strickland and Cullinan noted, "The difference in terminology reflects a critical difference in our perspective. The process of becoming literate is developmental, and we use the term 'emergent readers' to characterize the developmental nature of learning to read" (1990, p. 427). However, they went on to state, "We sincerely hope that this book draws disparate groups in our profession together instead of providing further ammunition to continue the futile discussions of phonics or no phonics. We believe that the proponents of whole language can accommodate the essence of this book if phonics instruction is recognized as a part of an integrated approach to teaching" (p. 432).

Others have not been as generous as Strickland and Cullinan (1990) in assessing Adams's analysis of the research on beginning reading. Instead of accepting her words, other critics have studied her motive and intent. As Chaney (1991) stated, "On a daily basis I encounter increasing numbers of teachers who are seeking ways to make literacy acquisition purposeful and meaningful for their students . . . Given these teachers' efforts to change, Adams's book seems conspiratorial. Congressional mandate notwithstanding, I hope I have misinterpreted her intent" (pp. 374–375).

The prominence of an educational issue is in part reflected in the amount and kind of press it captures and Adams's book has attracted the attention of the frivolous and the serious. The *Chicago Tribune* featured a column with the headline, "Book beats drum for phonics—but will schools hear?" (Beck, 1990). Even *Science News: The Weekly Newsmagazine of Science,* devoted an article to this debate entitled, "Reading the Code, Reading the Whole" in its February 29, 1992, issue. In addition, the March 1991 issue of *Psychological Science* ran a feature review of

Adams's book that included commentaries by Charles Perfetti, Keith Stanovich, and Frank Vellutino. Finally, in the February 1992 issue of *Phi Delta Kappan,* Frank Smith published an article entitled, "Learning to Read: The Never-Ending Debate."

All of these articles are required reading to appreciate the heat and substance of the debate on beginning reading. However, two other works are also compelling in their analyses of what's right, what's almost right, and what's not even wrong: Cunningham's (1991) annual review of research address to the National Reading Conference, and an article by Liberman and Liberman (1990) of Haskins Laboratories.

Cunningham reviewed what we know about "how good readers read words." In her review she identified "specific facts . . . pertinent to the question of what kind of phonics instruction we should have" (1991, p. 12). These facts include the following:

1. Readers look at virtually all of the words and almost all the letters in those words.
2. Readers usually recode printed words into sound.
3. Readers recognize most words immediately and automatically without using context.
4. Readers accurately and quickly pronounce infrequent, phonetically regular words.
5. Readers use spelling patterns and analogy to decode words. [Cunningham, 1991, pp. 12–15]

Cunningham's review of what we know about "how children learn to read words" included the following:

1. Children from literate homes have over 1,000 hours of informal reading and writing encounters before coming to school.
2. Phonemic awareness is critical to success in beginning reading.
3. Children who can decode well learn sight words better.
4. Lots of successful reading is essential for readers to develop automaticity and rapid decoding. [Cunningham, 1991, pp. 16–19]

Cunningham's review appears to be in concert with Adams's findings on beginning to read. Their convergence of findings appear to suggest what's right for the teaching of beginning reading.

In another view of what is right or almost right in beginning reading, I turn to Alvin and Isabel Liberman's (1990) recent paper, "Whole Language vs. Code Emphasis: Underlying Assumptions and Their Implications for Reading Instruction." The Libermans do not mince words, because words are their business and for them, thoughts enter words with unusual ease:

> To find the important differences between Whole Language and Code Emphasis, one must put aside the easy truisms and look more deeply into the assumptions the two views make about the nature of language. . . . What we see there . . . is that the basic assumptions of Whole Language are wrong, and that they lead to recommendations about reading instruction that we consider grievously misguided. [p. 54]

Whole Language appears to pivot on the singular principle that speaking is naturally easy to learn and therefore, reading should be equally easy; that as Liberman and Liberman stated, ". . . learning to read is, or can be, as natural a part of language development as learning to speak" (p. 55). The Libermans asked, "Is reading, like speaking, really all that natural . . .?" (p. 54). Their answer sounds much like Wolfgang Pauli's response to that speculative proposal in physics, "It's not even wrong." The Libermans stated:

> Just because learning to speak and learning to read can both be viewed as forms of language development—in the vacuous sense that both reflect the effect of experience on language behavior—it simply does not follow, as Whole Language would have it, that they are equivalent forms of development, or that they can be instructed by experience in the same natural, unconscious way. [1990, pp. 55–56]

Another assumption that Whole Language makes about the reading process is that reading, as Goodman (1976) argued, is a "psychological guessing game." That is, a reader need not read every word but "merely sample the print, apprehending some words and skipping others" (Liberman & Liberman, 1990, p. 62). The assumption is that the reader will gain the meaning by relying on the message's context and his or her own background knowledge. As the parent-teacher guide for Goodman's *What's Whole in Whole Language* makes clear, the reason for this strategy is that "readers are seeking meaning, not sounds or words" (p. 38; cited in Liberman & Liberman, 1990, p. 67). The guide also stated that "trial and error risk-taking on the part of the learner is an absolute requirement" (p. 67). Errors are not only encouraged but "celebrated" (p. 47). In their article, the Libermans quoted an issue of *The Whole Language Newsletter* that says, "Good Things to Do include skip it, use prior information . . . read ahead, re-read, or put in another word that makes sense" (1990, p. 69).

What's peculiar and puzzling about Goodman's form of Whole Language is that it seems to betray the very language it views as whole. Language is made of words and sounds. In fact, as Voltaire first noted, language is often difficult to put into words (Baumann & Kameenui, 1991). But in Goodman's language, words don't really count. In fact, *contrary* to Twain, the difference between the right word and almost the right word is not a large matter at all. In Goodman's Whole Language, any word will do—skip it, read ahead, reread, put in another word—after all, readers seek meaning, not words. As the Libermans asked, how does one reach meaning "without grasping the words"? (p. 67).

As an undergraduate major in English literature, I was taught to attend to words, the words were all, and the right words in the right place made the difference between James Joyce, Robert Penn Warren, Emily Dickinson, Franz Kafka, Euripides, or Shakespeare. To skip a word or ignore a comma when reading Shakespeare's *Hamlet,* for example, is to miss the meaning the bard intended:

> Not a whit, we defy augury.
> There is special providence in the fall of a sparrow.
> If it be now, tis not to come;
> If it be not to come, it will be now;
> If it be not now, yet it will come.
> The readiness is all. [Barnet & Hubler, 1963, p. 167]

One of the interesting contradictions about Whole Language is that the words of emergent literacy and Whole Language are themselves quite poetic and captivating. Who could argue with the "sense of influx" (Vygotsky, 1962, p. 147) stirred up by the wholeness and naturalness of a child's emerging language and literacy? When I think back 15 years to the class I

took from Roach Van Allen at the University of Arizona, I remember the words he spoke about the Language Experience Approach. He likened the teaching of reading to an Eskimo carving a figure in a piece of ivory. According to Van Allen, the Eskimo doesn't really carve a figure. Instead, he merely releases a figure already embedded in the ivory. Those words captured my imagination then and I'm glad I didn't skip them or substitute my own.

NCTM Standards

The changing landscape in reading and writing (known in some circles as critical literacy) parallels the changes in the third R that used to be 'rithmetic (i.e., adding, subtracting, multiplying, and dividing). But arithmetic too has given way to thinking strategies (Cobb & Merkel, 1989), understanding (National Council of Teachers of Mathematics, Working Groups of the Commission on Standards for School Mathematics, 1989), and problem solving (Cobb, Yackel, & Wood, 1989). In 1989, the National Council of Teachers of Mathematics (NCTM) published a document entitled *Curriculum and Evaluation Standards for School Mathematics (Standards)*. NCTM states three reasons for adopting and publishing the *Standards*: (1) ". . . to ensure that the public is protected from shoddy products", (2) ". . . as a means for expressing expectations about goals", and (3) ". . . to lead a group toward some new desired goals." (p. 2)

Two of the three reasons given for establishing the *Standards* relate to mathematics education goals. The goals stated in the *Standards* for all students are that (1) they learn to value mathematics, (2) they become confident in their ability to do mathematics, (3) they become mathematical problem solvers, (4) they learn to communicate mathematically, and (5) they learn to reason mathematically.

The goals are certainly reasonable: Who could quarrel with building confidence in mathematics, becoming a mathematical problem solver, or reasoning and communicating mathematically? However, one of the main problems is the implication the *Standards* hold for low performers and students with disabilities, or as NCTM refers to them, students with "different needs and interests." Their unique curricular needs are duly acknowledged by the *Standards*:

We believe that *all* students can benefit from an opportunity to study the core curriculum specified in the *Standards*. This can be accomplished by expanding and enriching the curriculum to meet the needs of each individual student, including the gifted and those of lesser capabilities and interests. We challenge teachers and other educators to develop and experiment with course outlines and grouping patterns to present the mathematics in the *Standards* in a meaningful, productive way. [NCTM, 1989, p. 253]

Educators are not recommending a watered-down or second-rate mathematics content for at-risk students. Rather, the goal is to devise curriculum and instruction so that these students understand the kind of mathematics that includes higher-order thinking, problem solving, and reasoning.

Insisting that all students can benefit from an "opportunity to study the core curriculum" is easy. However, "expanding and enriching the curriculum" to meet the needs of those with "lesser capabilities and interests," as called for by the NCTM standards, is not easy. The kind of educational tools and actual classroom instruction implied are currently not in place, at least not for students who are at-risk or have disabilities.

The challenges to meet these standards are enormous, if not paralyzing. For instance, how do teachers in the Los Angeles Unified School District enrich and expand the curriculum to respond to the 82 different languages that are spoken in that district alone? How should we expand the curriculum for students identified as learning disabled and at risk, whose language and reading deficits contribute indirectly to their difficulties in solving verbal mathematics problems? How do we expand and enrich the curriculum for students whose knowledge base is already in serious jeopardy? What knowledge do we expand and enrich?

Not surprisingly, the burden of expanding and enriching the core curriculum will ultimately fall to classroom teachers. Curriculum development activities in mathematics are not easy for teachers, as Good and Grouws (1979) pointed out more than a decade ago. In addition, the presence of low-achieving students in the classroom raises questions about the teachers' ability to accommodate these students' learning and curricular needs. For example, in a recent study of factors that influence change in individual teacher practice, Smylie (1988) noted, "The lower the achievement level of students in the class, the less likely teachers seem to believe that they can affect student learning despite the level of confidence they may have in their knowledge and skills related to teaching" (p. 23).

If you recall, the NCTM *Standards* for students with different needs and interests issued the following challenge:

We challenge teachers and other educators to develop and experiment with course outlines and grouping patterns to present the mathematics in the *Standards* in a meaningful, productive way. [1989, p. 253]

I accept that challenge, but I don't think the answer is in "expanding" the curriculum by developing and experimenting with "course outlines" and "grouping patterns." Instead, I think a two-part strategy, at the minimum, is required. The first part of the answer is given by Stanovich (1986), who argued that instructional questions surrounding students who are in serious educational jeopardy require very specific answers: "The cycle of escalating achievement deficits must be broken in a more specific way to short-circuit the cascade of negative spinoffs. This suggests that the remedy for the problem must be more of a 'surgical strike' (to use a military analogy)" (1986, p. 393). In short, the kind of instruction and curriculum required for successful kids will simply not do for those who are less successful in school.

The second part of the answer can be found in the educational tools employed in schools. Most of the teaching that takes place in school is organized around certain tools—textbooks, activity guides, computer programs, films, and so on. These tools are used in a range of settings—lectures, cooperative learning, independent projects, and so on. For the most part, the tools are designed for general education students from middle-class backgrounds, yet they are used in practically every school. The tools designed for middle-class students are not developed and designed for students with different needs and interests.

To improve the quality of educational tools, we must begin by addressing the following questions:

1. What are the learning characteristics of students with learning problems?
2. How do their learning characteristics align with the attributes of educational tools (e.g., curriculum programs, electronic media, software) used in the general education classroom?
3. What are the key principles for designing, expanding, and enriching the curriculum for these students?

When the characteristics of students with learning problems are considered, then the criteria for evaluating mathematics programs take on the tedious details required by Stanovich's (1986) call for surgical strikes:

1. What provisions are made to ensure that students have the relevant prior knowledge to perform the target task?
2. Is the rate of introducing new information reasonable?
3. Is there logical coherence in the presentation of strategies?
4. Is there adequate transition in the form of teacher support or scaffolded instruction between the initial teaching stages and the stages where students work independently?
5. Is adequate review of newly taught material provided to ensure that students will remember what they've learned?
6. Are topics taught for exposure or are they covered thoroughly? In the areas of mathematics and reading, the question is not "whether to reform," but "where to begin" the surgical strikes.

The Realities of Diversity

In light of the debates about beginning reading and the teaching of mathematics within the context of the new NCTM *Standards*, how do we begin to respond to Hodgkinson's assertion that "There is no time to waste in fixing blame; we need to act to fix the roof"? As noted earlier, the details of this response are of particular significance to students who reside in the basement of the house with the leaky roof—children identified

as poor readers, reading disabled, at risk, low performers, mildly disabled, language delayed, and culturally disadvantaged—and who have diverse learning and curricular needs. Like pedagogy, literacy, and other peculiar constructs of education, the face of diversity is equally complex, and at this point defies a definition comprised of only the right words (Garcia, Pearson, & Jimenez, 1990).

Despite the differences that these children bring to school, what is profoundly and unequivocally the same is that they are behind in their academic development, particularly in reading and language development. Moreover, they constantly face the "tyranny of time" in trying to catch up with their peers, who continue to advance in their critical literacy development (Kameenui, 1993). For student who are behind, simply keeping pace with their peers amounts to losing more and more ground. This predicament has been referred to as "Matthew effects," a concept resurrected and insightfully applied to reading by Stanovich (1986), in which the literacy-rich get richer, and the literacy-poor get poorer in reading opportunities, vocabulary development, written language, general knowledge, and so on.

The pedagogical clock for students who are behind in reading, literacy development, vocabulary, mathematics, and so forth continues to tick mercilessly, and the opportunities for these students to advance or catch up diminish over time. The realities that poor readers remain poor readers (Griffith & Olson, 1992; Juel, 1988), that insufficient opportunities to read seriously deter reading progress (Adams, 1990; Allington, 1980, 1983, 1984; O'Sullivan et al., 1990), and that particular instructional arrangements (e.g., whole-class instruction) fail to promote adequate reading growth (Byrne, Freebody, & Gates, 1992; Durkin, 1990) set the stage for educators to reconsider the needs of students who face pedagogy's ticking clock. As Kameenui (1993) pointed out, the experiences required for these students can be derived and constructed from at least seven general pedagogical principles. While these principles do not prescribe a single method and by no means represent an exhaustive list, they do offer a conceptual framework for informing our decisions about how to develop the early learning experiences of these students:

1. *Instructional time is a precious commodity; do not lose it.* If a reading strategy, concept, or problem-solving analysis can be taught two different ways and one is more efficient, use the more efficient.

2. *Intervene and remediate early, strategically, and frequently.* The magnitude of growth in the early years for students who are behind is influenced substantially by what we teach and how we teach. As Stanovich (1986) argued, "educational interventions that represent a *more of the same* approach will probably not be successful . . . the remedy for the problem must be more of a *surgical strike*" (p. 393).

3. *Teach less more thoroughly.* The conventional wisdom in working with students who have diverse learning and curricular needs is to teach more in less time (Kameenui & Simmons, 1990; Kameenui, 1990). While the logic of this advice seems reasonable (i.e., children who are behind in conceptual knowledge and skills must be taught more in a shorter period in order to catch up), the actual practice simply ignores the constraints of teaching. Instead, by selecting and teaching only those objectives that are essential, more can be learned more thoroughly in the limited time available.

4. *Communicate strategies in a clear and explicit manner, especially during initial phases of instruction.* For many students with learning problems, new concepts and strategies should be explained in clear, concise, and comprehensible language. Explicit instruction is still most effective for teaching concepts, principles, and strategies to at-risk students.

5. *Guide student learning through a strategic sequence of teacher-directed and student-centered activities.* Teacher-directed instruction is necessary if students are to catch up and advance with their able-reading peers.

6. *Examine the effectiveness of the instruction and educational tools by formatively evaluating student progress.* To adapt instruction to meet the needs of learners, teachers must formatively evaluate the effectiveness of their instructional approaches and materials. As a guideline, current research suggests that measuring student performance twice per week provides an adequate basis for instructional decision making (Deno & Fuchs, 1987).

7. *Develop instructional strategies around "big ideas."* To respond to the NCTM *Standards* to meet the learning and curricular needs of students with learning problems requires, not "expanding" the curriculum, as called for by the *Standards*, but shrinking the curriculum to teach less and use generalizable "big ideas" as concepts or strategies (e.g., Calfee, 1991; Calfee, Chambliss, & Beretz, 1991; Carnine & Kameenui, 1992) to strategically teach less more thoroughly. Strategically selecting what critical strategies to teach, teaching less more thoroughly, and anchoring what's taught to big, conceptual ideas and principles is the best way to enrich the curriculum. Building strategies around "big ideas" that are most central to understanding that domain facilitates a broad understanding (Porter, 1989; Prawat, 1989).

Summary

To enrich and expand the curriculum to meet the demands of learners with different needs and interests will require a different kind of educational reform than currently offered by Whole Language and the NCTM. Specifically, a review of the research by Adams (1990), Cunningham (1991), Liberman and Liberman (1990), Stahl and Miller (1989), and many others do not support the Whole Language mandate. In rejecting Marilyn Adams's (1990) research and analysis, Goodman stated, "Innovative (whole-language) practice is leaping ahead of research" (cited in Bower, 1992, p. 140). Indeed it is.

There is also evidence that the innovative practices recommended by NCTM *Standards* are themselves leaping ahead of the research. Near the beginning of the *Standards*, the authors stated that they were protecting the American public from shoddy practices, just as the Food and Drug Administration does. However, in the same document the authors called for "the establishment of some pilot school mathematics programs based on these standards to demonstrate that all students—including women and under-served minorities—can reach a satisfactory level of mathematics achievement" (NCTM, 1989, p. 253). So much for protection against shoddy practices.

The current debates in reading and mathematics are not really about how best to teach reading and how to teach children to understand numbers and complex mathematical operations. Instead, the debates represent age-old tensions that reflect epistemological, philosophical, and even ontological differences about the nature of learning and children. Moreover, the debates reflect again how different communities of researchers frame questions and select the tools to use to answer those questions. In short, it has to do with what passes as research in education today, and ultimately, what we decide is false and fashionable (Kameenui, 1991). The exchanges are represented by the current debates between the quantitative/qualitative approaches to inquiry. The heart of that debate beats with equal force in the debates between those who view human behavior from a holistic/phenomenological perspective, and those who view it from a behavioral and positivistic vantage point.

One could argue that this paradigmatic instability is destructive, because it invites and perhaps encourages false and fashionable practices that ultimately hurt children. The paradigm wars suggest that the standards for deciding when educational practice is right, almost right, or not even wrong are ambiguous. This situation in educational discourse is in contrast to other scientific disciplines. For example, in particle physics, a theory is said to suffer from anomalies if it violates certain laws of conservation of electric charge and conservation of energy-momentum. These conservation laws are firmly entrenched as fundamental rules of physics. If they are violated, the theory is regarded as incoherent and is automatically dismissed (Regis, 1987, p. 268).

We need to settle the paradigm wars before we can decide what to accept as reasonable practice. That is not likely to happen anytime soon. The universe of neutrinos and dark matter as the famous physicist Stephen Hawking knows it, may be governed by well-defined laws, but the laws of human nature are a different matter altogether.

These laws notwithstanding, we must change the way we do business and, more important, how we think about our business. If schooling is to be meaningful for all learners, then educators must have access to effective tools analogous to those that empower other professions (Carnine, 1992, p. 8). The tools of professions other than education are usually tested extensively—prescription drugs, pajamas, electronic imaging machines, toys, playground equipment, automobiles, and so forth (Carnine, 1992, p. 2). In contrast, the educational tools themselves (e.g., textbooks, computer programs) are rarely systematically field-tested. Untested and ineffective tools discriminate most harshly and insidiously against low performers—those who are already victims of education's leaky roof. Measurably superior instructional practices are currently available, and their use in these measurably inferior times (Hodgkinson, 1991) is not only right, but imperative. Superior instructional practices offer the greatest hope for eschewing practice that is "almost right" or "not even wrong."

References

ADAMS, M. J. (1990). *Beginning to read: Thinking and learning about print.* Cambridge, MA: MIT Press.

ADAMS, M. J. (1991). Beginning to read: A critique by literacy professionals. *Reading Teacher, 44*(6), 371–372.

ALLINGTON, R. L. (1980). Poor readers don't get to read much in reading groups. *Language Arts, 57,* 872–876.

ALLINGTON, R. L. (1983). The reading instruction provided readers of differing reading abilities. *Elementary School Journal, 83,* 548–559.

ALLINGTON, R. L. (1984). Content coverage and contextual reading in reading groups. *Journal of Reading Behavior, 16,* 85–96.

BARNET, S., & Hubler, E. (Eds.). (1963). *Signet Classic Shakespeare. Hamlet.* New York: New American Library.

BAUMANN, J. F., & Kameenui, E. J. (1991). Vocabulary instruction: Ode to Voltaire. In J. Flood, J. Jensen, D. Lapp, & J. R. Squire (Eds.), *Handbook of research on teaching the English language arts* (pp. 604–632). New York: Macmillan.

BECK (1990). Book beats drum for phonics—but will schools hear? *Chicago Tribune,* April 23, Section 1, p. 15.

BOWER, B. (1992). Reading the code, reading the whole: Researchers wrangle over the nature and teaching of reading. *Science News, 141*(9), 138–141.

BYRNE, B., Freebody, P., & Gates, A. (1992). Longitudinal data on the relations of word-reading strategies to comprehension, reading time, and phonemic awareness. *Reading Research Quarterly, 27*(2), 141–151.

CALFEE, R. (1991). What schools can do to improve literacy instruction. In B. Means, C. Chelemer, & M. S. Knapp (Eds.), *Teaching advanced skills to at-risk students* (pp. 176–203). San Francisco: Jossey-Bass.

CALFEE, R. C., Chambliss, M. J., & Beretz, M. M. (1991). Organizing for comprehension and composition. In W. Ellis

(Ed.), *All language and the creating of literacy* (pp. 79–93). Baltimore: Orton Dyslexia Society, Inc.

CARNINE, D. W. (1992). *Reforming educational leaders: The role of science.* Eugene: University of Oregon, National Center to Improve the Tools of Educators.

CARNINE, D., & Kameenui, E. J. (1992). *Higher order thinking: Designing curriculum for mainstreamed students.* Austin: Pro-Ed.

CHALL, J. (1992). Whole language and direct instruction models: Implications for teaching reading in the schools. Paper presented at the meeting of the International Reading Association, May, Orlando.

CHANEY, J. H. (1991). Beginning to read: A critique by literacy professionals. *Reading Teacher, 44*(6), 374–375.

COBB, P., & Merkel, G. (1989). Thinking strategies: Teaching arithmetic through problem solving. In P. Trafton (Ed.), *1989 Yearbook of the National Council of Teachers of Mathematics* (pp. 70–81). Reston, VA: NCTM.

COBB, P., Yackel, E., & Wood, T. (1989). Young children's emotional acts while engaged in mathematical problem solving. In D. B. McLeod & V. M. Adams (Eds.), *Affect and mathematical problem solving: A new perspective* (pp. 117–148). New York: Springer-Verlag.

CUNNINGHAM, P. (1991). What kind of phonics instruction will we have? Paper presented at National Reading Conference, Palm Springs.

DENO, S., & Fuchs, L. (1987). Developing curriculum-based measurement systems for data-based special education problem solving. *Focus on Exceptional Children, 19*(8), 1–16.

DURKIN, D. (1990). Matching classroom instruction with reading abilities: An unmet need. *Remedial and Special Education, 11*(3), 23–28.

FLANAGAN, D. (1988). *Flanagan's version: A spectator's guide to science on the eve of the 21st century.* New York: Vintage.

GARCIA, G. E., Pearson, P. D., & Jimenez, R. T. (1990). *The at risk dilemma: A synthesis of reading research.* Champaign: University of Illinois, Reading Research and Education Center.

GOOD, T. L., & Grouws, D. A. (1979). The Missouri mathematics effectiveness project. *Journal of Educational Psychology, 71,* 355–362.

GOODMAN, K. (1992). Whole language and direct instruction models: Implications for teaching reading in the schools. Paper presented at the meeting of the International Reading Association, May, Orlando.

GOODMAN, K. S. (1976). Reading: A psycholinguistic guessing game. In H. Singer & R. B. Ruddell (Eds.), *Theoretical Models and the Process of Reading.* Newark, DE: International Reading Association.

GRIFFITH, P. L., & Olson, M. W. (1992). Phonemic awareness helps beginning readers break the code. *Reading Teacher, 45*(7), 516–523.

HODGKINSON, H. (1991). Reform versus reality. *Phi Delta Kappan, 73,* 9–16.

JUEL, C. (1988). Learning to read and write: A longitudinal study of fifty-four children from first through fourth grade. Paper presented at the annual meeting of the American Educational Research Association, April, New Orleans.

KAMEENUI, E. J. (1988). Direct instruction and the Great Twitch: Why DI or di is not the issue. In J. R. Readence and S. Baldwin (Eds.),

Dialogues in literacy research: Thirty-seventh yearbook of the National Reading Conference (pp. 39–45). Chicago: NRC.

KAMEENUI, E. J. (1990). The language of the REI —Why it's hard to put into words: A response to Durkin and Miller. *Remedial and Special Education, 11*(3), 57–59.

KAMEENUI, E. J. (1991). Guarding against the false and fashionable. In J. Baumann & D. Johnson (Eds.), *Publishing professional and instructional materials and language arts* (pp. 17–28). Newark, DE: International Reading Association.

KAMEENUI, E. J. (1993). Diverse learners and the tyranny of time: Don't fix blame; fix the leaky roof. *Reading Teacher, 46*(5), 376–383.

KAMEENUI, E. J., & Simmons, D.C. (1990). *Designing instructional strategies: The prevention of academic learning problems.* Columbus, OH: Merrill Publishing Company.

LIBERMAN, A., & Liberman, I. (1990). Whole language vs. code emphasis: Underlying assumptions and their implications for reading instruction. *Annals of Dyslexia, 40,* 52–76.

MATHER, N. (1992). Whole language reading instruction for students with learning disabilities: Caught in the cross fire. *Learning Disabilities Research & Practice, 7,* 87–95.

NATIONAL Council of Teachers of Mathematics (1989). *Curriculum and evaluation standards for school mathematics.* Reston, VA: NCTM.

O'SULLIVAN, P. J., Ysseldyke, J. E., Christenson, S. L., & Thurlow, M. L. (1990). Mildly handicapped elementary students' opportunity to learn during reading instruction in mainstream and special education settings. *Reading Research Quarterly, 25*(2), 131–146.

PORTER, A. C. (1989). A curriculum out of balance: The case of elementary school mathematics. *Educational Researcher, 18*(5), 9–15.

PRAWAT, R. S. (1989). Promoting access to knowledge, strategy, and disposition in students: A research synthesis. *Review of Education Research, 59,* 1–41.

REGIS, E. (1987). *Who got Einstein's office? Eccentricity and genius at the Institute for Advanced Study.* Boston: Addison-Wesley.

SMYLIE, M. A. (1988). The enhancement function of staff development: Organizational and psychological antecedents to individual teacher change. *American Educational Research Journal, 25,* 1–30.

STAHL, S. A., & Miller, P. D. (1989). Whole language and language experience approach for beginning reading: A quantitative research synthesis. *Review of Education Research, 59,* 87–116.

STANOVICH, K. E. (1986). Matthew effects in reading: Some consequences of individual differences in the acquisition of literacy. *Reading Research Quarterly, 21,* 360–407.

STRICKLAND, D., & Cullinan, B. (1990). Afterword. In M. J. Adams, *Beginning to read: Thinking and learning about print.* Cambridge, MA: MIT Press.

SV Entertainment. (1992). July, p. 13.

TIME. (1992). Growing up poor in US. July 20, p. 15.

YATVIN, J. (1991). *Developing a whole language program for a whole school.* Richmond: Virginia State Reading Association.

VYGOTSKY, L. S. (1962). *Thought and language.* Cambridge, MA: MIT Press.

CHAPTER 13

The Measure of a Teacher

R. Douglas Greer

The identification and use of a primary measure of teaching is essential to the maturation of a science of pedagogy. The basic unit should represent a natural fracture of teaching in the same fashion that the operant became the basic unit of the science of behavior (Skinner, 1953). Such a measure would lead to (1) better research, (2) better teacher training, (3) more accurate measures of teacher and school effectiveness, and (4) ways to determine the cost and benefits of education.

Identifying a Primary Measure of Teaching

Why is such a measure so important? Throughout the last three decades, teacher research has moved away from assessments of intervening variables (e.g., teacher personality measures) and toward more observable entities (e.g., classroom organization). That is, notions like teacher warmth or coldness, directness or indirectness, degrees of authoritarianism, and enthusiasm were more characteristic of much of the research of the 1960s (Stephens, 1967). By the end of the 1970s, teacher effectiveness had to do with keeping students "engaged" or "on task"—actual teacher

operations. Engaged became engaged academic time, and a teacher's ability to maximize engaged academic time and to allocate more time to academic tasks was generally recognized as important (Stallings, 1980). Engaged academic time seemed to be related even to what some were identifying as more effective schools (Edmonds, 1979).

In the early 1980s, research by behavior analysts at the Juniper Garden Children's Project had demonstrated relationships between the opportunity to respond and student learning (Greenwood, Delquadri, & Hall, 1984). This was clearly a significant step beyond engaged time and time on task. Students who received more opportunities to respond gave more responses and more correct responses. The students may have even appeared more on task, as a by-product of receiving more opportunities to respond. Ayllon and Roberts (1974) had shown the importance of reinforcing academic responding relative to being on task. While on-task or engaged time was in some cases a corollary or by-product of academic responding, some data suggested that simply producing on task did not lead to more learning (Wolpow, 1976). This led Winett and Winkler (1972) to proclaim that behavior modifiers (that day's term for applied behavior analysts) were mostly interested in "sit-down-and-be-quiet responses" from students. This criticism of behavior-analytic work in education was voiced by individuals both inside and outside the field (Brophy, 1983; Deitz, 1978). The work on "opportunity to respond" moved us substantially beyond engaged time and time on task; as a substantial contribution to our field, it was included in the collection of published papers from the first Ohio State University Conference on Behavior Analysis in Education (Greenwood, Delquadri, & Hall, 1984).

In the 1960s, behavior analysts responded to teachers' calls for help. The research showed teachers how to use praise and how to ignore to manage their class (Madsen, Becker, & Thomas, 1968). Clearly, teacher behaviors that resulted in cooperative students who were not unruly were a necessary step toward improved academic responding. Thus, teachers who praised certain behaviors consistently and ignored others had students who could be engaged in more academic responding. Teachers who made reinforcement errors or who disapproved more than they approved were ineffective at teaching students to respond as targeted, whereas those who praised contingently and frequently, while ignoring inappropriate (e.g., incorrect) responding, got more good behavior.

The Direct Instruction group fused behavioral teaching operations to carefully sequenced curricula in reading and mathematics (Becker, 1992). Flawless or accurate teacher operations (e.g., correct reinforcement and presentations) were scripted into the presentation of the curriculum. Teachers who were taught Direct Instruction procedures produced more student responding and consequated that responding more frequently and accurately. Apparently, what we knew about teacher behavior from applied behavior analysis worked for academic responding equally as well as it did for producing more good classroom behavior and less bad behavior. In fact, since the 1960s, the Personalized System of Instruction (PSI) and Precision Teaching groups have worked on academic responding.

During the 1970s, another program of research found that not only were these teacher behaviors important for gaining student attention and producing more correct academic responding, but stimuli that were previously nonpreferred became preferred when teachers properly used teaching tactics derived from behavior-analytic research (Greer, 1981; Greer et al., 1973). Use of disapproval resulted in the students' avoiding what was taught in separate free-time settings, while approval resulted in the opposite effect. This seemed an important advance, because not only is it important to teach students to read, do math, or learn new music, but it is also important to increase the reinforcement value of what is taught if the associated stimuli are to have generalized stimulus control outside of the instructional setting.

In the 1980s, a research program that built on earlier findings led to the study of a systemwide application of behavior analysis to entire schools. This comprehensive application of behavior analysis to schooling (CABAS) drew on teacher training and observation procedures that we called the Teacher Performance Rate/Accuracy measure (TPRA).[1] This procedure allowed us to measure rates of teacher behavior that the literature had found effective (e.g., accurate teacher performance and inaccurate performance), while measuring student correct and incorrect responses. The results of several years and several studies showed that accurate teacher performance (higher TPRA scores) functioned to produce more correct responses by students and inaccurate teacher performance (lower and even negative TPRA scores) produced more incorrect responses by students (Greer, McCorkle, & Williams, 1989; Ingham & Greer, 1992). Moreover, teachers' TPRA performance with individual students could be used to predict their accuracy with all of their students collectively throughout the day (Ingham & Greer, 1992). Finally, the more TPRA observations the supervisors conducted, the more accurate the teachers were, and this led to more and correct responding from students (Babbitt, 1986; Greer, McCorkle, & Williams, 1989).

---

[1]The Teacher Performance Rate/Accuracy measure allows the collection of data on the teacher's accurate and inaccurate reinforcement or correction of student responses and the student's correct and incorrect response to scripted or programmed instruction. The data for each are summarized by rate of response. Student data result in rate per minute correct and incorrect. Teacher data result in rate per minute correct and incorrect or the algebraic product of correct subtracted from incorrect and converted to rate. The procedure is described in detail in Ingham and Greer (1992) and Greer (in press).

In addition to research data, a large body of data was produced in two schools during the 1980s (Greer, in press). For several years teachers in the CABAS schools collected daily data on all the academic responding of all of their students. In the CABAS schools teachers are observed multiple times weekly using the TPRA procedure. Trained behavior analyst supervisors make the observations and check the measures of teacher and student behavior for interobserver agreement; thus, the data are reliable. The data for over 11 years in one school showed high, positive correlations between accurate (high TPRA scores) teacher performance and correct student responding as well as achievement of criterion-referenced objectives consistent with the data published in Greer, McCorkle, and Williams (1989). Functional or "causal" relations between high TPRA scores and student achievement were found in several studies (Albers & Greer, 1991; Ingham & Greer, 1992) and as part of a package in other studies (Babbitt, 1986; Lamm & Greer, 1991; Selinske, Greer, & Lodhi, 1991).

The Direct Instruction group and the research in programmed instruction had taught us about the importance of scripting curricula (Becker, 1992). Thus, CABAS schools scripted or used published scripted curricula for all instruction given to students. Each instructional presentation or trial was scripted along with an opportunity to respond and the consequence (reinforcement operation or correction operation). The TPRA observations were designed for student trials that were three-term contingency units. Thus, since we measured all our students' responses to all instruction, and since we scripted the antecedent and consequence, all of our data on students were then teacher-presented three-term contingency trials (Greer, 1992). The data obtained on all instruction for over seven years in six different schools showed that the numbers of three-term contingency trials presented by teachers predicted the number of correct responses and the attainment of correct objectives by students. When those three-term contingency trials were accurately presented at high rates, even more learning occurred (Greer, 1992).

When teacher consequation was provided for opportunities to respond, students learned from two to seven times more than they did in baseline when teacher consequences were infrequent (Albers & Greer, 1991). That is, when we increased the accuracy and rate of teachers' presentations and consequations to students' responding, the number of correct responses increased and incorrect responses decreased (Albers & Greer, 1991; Ingham & Greer, 1991). This effect was found not only with individual teachers and classrooms, but with entire schools, across as many as three years (Lamm & Greer, 1991; Selinske, Greer, & Lodhi, 1991).

Both the students and teachers appeared to be learning when three-term contingency instructional units were the focus of observation and training. The teachers learned from their effects on their students just as the students learned. These teacher communications were interlocking operants that had the potential to teach the teacher as much as the student. Because of the confusion engendered by the term *trial*, we renamed these units *learn units*. Heward (see Chapter 21) describes a similar concept, which he terms a "learning trial."

Learn units incorporate antecedents-behaviors-consequences for teachers and students that interlock with each other. An effective teacher presents or manages the presentation of instructional antecedents to the student under the control of the student's current and prior performance. The student is induced to respond; the response in turn results in the immediate or delayed consequence by the teacher controlled by the student's response. The teacher either performs a correction operation or a reinforcement operation followed by recording the accuracy of the student's performance, still another control over the teacher's behavior. The skilled teacher learns from the student's behavior what he or she should do for the next learn unit or series of learn units. A series of types of student responding (e.g., correct or incorrect) evokes certain teacher operations. Table 13.1 provides examples of simple learn units.

Teacher Contingencies and Learn Units
When teacher behavior is accurate, the student is presented an unambiguous antecedent and attends to the relevant attributes of the stimulus at the time (teacher antecedent and target antecedent or only the

target antecedent). The teacher then provides an appropriate interval for the student to respond, sometimes preceded by constant or progressive response delays or prompts. The student's response or lack of response occasions the teacher to deliver a correction if the response was incorrect or a reinforcement operation if the response was in a correct range. The well-trained teacher then records the response and observes the cumulative progress of the student vis-à-vis criterion-referenced objectives, which in turn serves as a consequence. All of the teacher responses are deemed correct or incorrect based on the responding of the student and the scripted program. In the course of the scripted learn unit, a teacher who is under the accurate control of the student's three-term contingen-

cy is involved in at least 2 three-term contingencies, as shown in Table 13.1.

When the student's unit is incidental or a captured operant, his or her behavior evokes a consequation by the teacher, and the consequence is the data record. Thus, in the scripted presentation two or more three-term units occur for the teacher, whereas in the incidental or free-operant event a minimum of a single three-term contingency results for the teacher.

Teachers consistently present complete and accurate learn units only after they have been trained to do so. Learn units that have all of the necessary components apparently do not occur naturally in the repertoire of an untrained teacher. Teachers do not correctly consequate academic responding any more than they reinforce following classroom rules unless they are trained to do so. The databases for this assertion are from several sources.

1. In a two-year multiexperiment study, baseline teacher performance showed that teacher errors matched or exceeded correct teacher presentations (Ingham & Greer, 1992). Following the regular use of TPRA observation by a supervisor, errors were eliminated and the correct rate was increased to a significant level.

2. In two other experiments (Lamm & Greer, 1992; Selinske, Greer, & Lodhi, 1991), the teacher error rate was as high or higher than teacher correct performance before training. In fact, in the Lamm and Greer (1992) study, there were *no* teacher consequences and very few clear antecedents during the baseline phases.

3. Observations of 25 teachers in a school for students with developmental disabilities showed that the teachers, most of whom had 10 or more years' experience, emitted high numbers of teacher errors. Moreover, they completed few learn units. Their data were comparable to the baseline data in Ingham and Greer (1992).

The teacher data cited thus far were collected in classrooms for students who performed at what I call *pre-independent reader status* (Greer, in press). That is, most or all learn units had to be presented directly by teachers. When students achieve *independent reader and writer* status, the potential numbers of possible learn units increases geometrically since

Table 13.1 Two examples of interlocking operants between teacher and student

Type of Learn Unit	Event	Operant Components
Programmed, scripted, or planned	"What is two times two?"	Student antecedent and teacher behavior (attention of student was the prior teacher antecedent)
	"Four."	Student behavior and teacher consequence and antecedent
	Reinforcement operation performed.	Teacher behavior and consequence for student
	Response recorded.	Teacher consequence
Incidental or captured	"Coat, please." (presence of coat, deprivation of coat, presence of a listener to deliver coat result in antecedent and motivation)	Student antecedent and behavior and teacher antecedent
	Coat presented.	Student consequence and teacher listener behavior
	Coat taken or put on.	Teacher consequence and also antecedent for recording correct response

learn units may be presented indirectly via print stimuli (e.g., texts, workbooks, computer programs). The following databases illustrate teacher accuracy in classrooms with pupils who have independent reader and writer status.

4. In a math class for seventh-graders, Albers and Greer (1991) found that the baseline rates of teacher presentations without consequences (incomplete learn units or two-term contingency trials) were equal to or exceeded presentations that included all components of the learn unit. Thus, while the rates of students responding in *independent reader and writer* classrooms increased dramatically over *pre-independent classrooms*, the ratio of accurate learn units to inaccurate teacher presentations was similar to the data discussed earlier. The teacher omitted consequences until he or she was prompted in the classroom to make complete learn-unit presentations.

Our data show that once the teacher increases the rate of learn-unit presentations, student correct rates increase dramatically and incorrect rates remain low. This finding is consistent across several studies where increases in teacher accuracy (more correctly done learn units) have shown either functional effects on student responding (see Albers & Greer, 1991; Ingham & Greer, 1992) or a strong positive correlational relationship (Greer, McCorkle, & Williams, 1989).

5. I recently completed observations of five teachers teaching the core subjects in a small high school for students with a range of independent reader and writer repertoires. This is a public high school in a middle to high socioeconomic area. In other words, this is a well-funded program where teachers are long-term employees. The student-teacher ratio is 10 to 1 and the purpose of all the instruction at that time was practice for the Regents or state examination. It is reasonable to say that these observations represented high rates of learn units for these teachers. The data show that the average student received an opportunity to respond every 8 minutes and to complete a learn unit every 15 minutes. These are very low rates of learn units and response opportunities. Table 13.2 summarizes teacher performance and student response opportunities to incomplete and complete learn units.

In short, samples of teaching in programs for students with developmental disabilities and pre–independent reader status as well as in programs for the secondary grades (independent readers and writers) with students who have no developmental disabilities show that these teachers made frequent errors. The result was that few complete learn units occurred for students. Response opportunities were not what they should be and learn units were even more infrequent.

The most frequent teacher error was the omission of corrections or reinforcements. This suggests that the student response, written or vocal and gestural, stops teacher behavior. Whereas when the teacher is trained, student behavior evokes further teacher behavior, including consequence operations and data recording.

The behavior analysts from the Juniper Gardens Children's Project have demonstrated the importance of increased responding by students (Greenwood, Delquadri, & Hall, 1984). Teachers who have continuous presentations and continuous student responding have classrooms in which students achieve more. To this, we suggest that the complete and accurate

Table 13.2 Learn units for high school teachers and students: Rates per minute and latencies

Teacher Performance

1. Written and vocal mean rates of presentations, all teachers and all students	=	5.37 per minute (mean per teacher for all students in the classsroom)
2. Rate of written and vocal presentations that were complete and accurate learn units	=	2.35 per minute
3. Inaccurate or incomplete learn units	=	3.02 per minute
4. Teacher performance rate/accuracy score	=	0.69

Received by Students for Entire School Day (Allocated Time)

1. Mean latency in minutes between responding (average for students)	=	8.79
2. Mean latency in minutes between correct responses (average for students)	=	11.19
3. Mean latency in minutes between incorrect responses (average for students)	=	33.15

learn unit is a next step for both teaching and measurement purposes.

The Albers and Greer (1991) study and the Ingham and Greer (1992) study suggested the additive effect of the consequence. Moreover, several other studies indirectly suggested a similar conclusion (Babbitt, 1986; Lamm & Greer, 1991; Selinske, Greer, & Lodhi, 1991; Greer, McCorkle, & Williams, 1989). Recently, one of our doctoral students did a pilot study comparing low opportunity and high opportunity to respond with low learn units and high learn units (Diamond, 1992). This pilot study was done with high school students in a basic math class. The data showed that learn-unit presentations resulted in higher rates of correct and lower rates of incorrect than did presentations and response opportunities without consequences. High rates of learn-unit presentations were superior to low rates and low rates of learn units were superior to the high or low opportunity-to-respond rates. These findings, however, need further scrutiny.

In still another series of experiments done by another doctoral student (Kelly & Greer, 1992), students with assaultive or self-injurious behaviors decreased or stopped the problem behaviors contingent on significant increases in the teachers' learn-unit presentations. This occurred with no behavior decrease or punishment operations in effect and without the use of psychotropic medication. These data suggest that teachers who have classrooms in which students receive high rates of individually appropriate learn units are less likely to have behavior management problems. Rather than using DRO (differential reinforcement of other behavior) tactics that effectively decrease maladaptive responding but do not necessarily increase student learning, the use of high rates of learn units not only decreases the bad behavior but carries out the function of schools—to teach the mandated curriculum. In effect, the student responding to instruction was differentially reinforced.

Learn units are critical measures of teaching. First, the number of learn units received by students is a measure of teacher productivity. Second, measures of teachers' accuracy in delivering learn units are critical to increasing the quality or effectiveness of teaching because when that accuracy is improved, student learning increases. Measures of teacher accuracy prescribe what needs to be done to improve teacher effectiveness.

Learn units *must*, however, be considered together with the measurement of criterion-referenced instructional objectives. Since the CABAS and other scripted or programmed curricula prescribe the learning objectives and their criteria, the achievement of objectives can be measured simultaneously with learn units. If learn-unit correct responses remain high without regular dips, then we typically find that the teacher is not moving the student on to new objectives or new curricular programs. Of course, if learn-unit responses are low and the objectives are infrequent, more attention and expertise vis-à-vis learn-unit presentations is needed, or the objectives need to be broken down, or a combination of both.

Learn Units and Stages of Instruction

There are several functional stages of instruction based on the students' verbal behavior repertoires (Greer, in press). These repertoires and stages govern the type and frequency of learn units presented and the related student responses. Learn units and rates must be considered in light of the types of instruction. The instructional response types include whether the objective of the curriculum is to produce multiple-choice, point-to, or construct functions. Each incorporates different antecedents. Curricula also include traditional structural categories (e.g., social studies, mathematics, English composition). Thus, learn units and objectives are categorized by functional and subject matter components of curricula. The type of instruction and related responding affects learn-unit rates.

In addition, the composition of each classroom determines baseline learn-unit rates and the achievement of objectives. That is, rates for students who are at prespeaker, prereader, or prewriter stages differ for students who are independent readers and writers (Greer, in press). Learn-unit rates and teacher rate/accuracy data are used for within-teacher and instruction analyses, not for between-teacher comparisons.

The analysis of learn unit and objectives is used continuously in CABAS schools by all teachers and supervisors to improve the students,' the teachers,' and the supervisors' learning. Evaluation of the student is done via archival records or portfolios of achievement and deficits (we use behavioral inventories of repertoires). The same holds true for the teacher and supervisor in these schools, both of whom have inservice curricula consisting of individualized criterion-referenced objectives. The learn-unit productivity and accuracy serves as instructional or curricular-based assessment on a continuous basis and the achievement of objectives is preserved in student, teacher, and supervisor archival records. For a description of the role of the learn unit in inservice training for teachers, see Greer, McCorkle, and Williams (1989).

Cost-Benefit Analysis

The lack of a universal and absolute unit to measure teaching and student learning has contributed to our inability to measure the cost and benefits of education. By using the learn unit as the measure of teaching and learning, we have been able to determine the costs of instruction in terms of its products, correct responding, and achievement of objectives. By dividing the numbers of learn units presented, correct responses, and objectives achieved, respectively, by school time, we have been able to determine actual instructional costs (McCorkle, 1992). The results of these calculations for the Fred S. Keller Preschool are shown in Table 13.3.

To compare the relative costs of a behavioral program versus a nonbehavioral program, I drew on observations made in a school with students comparable to those at the Margaret Chapman school (pre-independent readers and prelistener stages). Using the data I obtained by observation, I prorated the tuition rates for the comparative school to give an estimated comparison for the same week of the school year (see Table 13.4). These data are presented for heuristic rather than archival purposes. More stringent studies are needed in order to determine the actual comparative costs.

The costs for the control school are based on extensions of my observation, not on records of all learn units taught, since the school, like most schools, has no such records. However, it is safe to say that the estimates of the number of learn units taught are probably low and the costs are probably underestimated.

In the high school for students with independent reader and writer status (see Table 13.2), the costs (using a conservative $5,000 per annum estimate) are $2.95 per learn unit and $2.32 per correct response. No data were available for the objectives, but given the long latency (33 minutes) between incorrect responses, the cost per objective is likely very high since these data suggest that the students are not acquiring new learning objectives.

The ability to measure learn units, objectives, and related costs prepares the way for future estimates of cost benefits. Schools that provide these measures prepare the way for determining the relationship be-

Table 13.3 Mean latencies between learn units and costs per learn unit and objectives over a five-year period at the Fred S. Keller preschool[a].

| Year | Number of Students in the School | Student-Received Unit | | Correct Student Responses | | Reliable Criterion-Referenced Objectives | |
		Minutes Between	Costs Per Unit	Minutes Between	Costs Per Response	Number	Costs Per Objective
1986–1987	32	2.30	$.60	3.42	$.88	899	$155.55
1987–1988	52	1.89	$.64	2.47	$.90	4,598	$ 88.87
1988–1989	62	2.98[b]	$.69	4.16[c]	$.96	3,648	$153.62
1989–1990	71	1.45	$.70	1.94	$.93	11,873[d]	$ 62.18
1990–1991	73	1.16	$.65	1.48	$.84	15,634	$ 55.58

Notes: [a]These costs are not adjusted for inflation; thus, the actual costs are lower when a constant dollar is used.
[b]Increased costs are due to the initial costs of an additional site.
[c]New, untrained staff replace teachers who were promoted to supervisory responsibilities.
[d]Generalization objectives for communicative verbal behavior are included in total objectives for the first time.

Table 13.4 Mean latencies between learn units and objectives and costs for the Margaret Chapman School (a comprehensive behavioral school for students with severe developmental disabilities) and a control school with comparable students[a]

| | Student-Received Unit | | | Correct Student Responses | | Reliable Criterion-Referenced Objectives | |
	Minutes Between	Costs Per Unit	Number of Students	Minutes Between	Costs Per Response	Number	Costs
Control School[b]	30.00	$16.80	72	45.00	$25.22	No reliable figures available	
The Margaret Chapman School[c]	1.89	$ 0.40	65	2.68	$ 0.54		$136.00

Notes: [a]These observations were conducted by a single observer—the author. Thus, interobserver agreement is based on calibrated accuracy to videotape standards. The agreement with three standard videotapes ranged from 96% to 100% and the mean was 98%.
[b]These are estimated figures projected from Teacher Performance Rate/Accuracy Observations done of all of the teachers. Typically, however, the mean latency between learn units is much lower during teacher observations than for periods when teachers are not observed.
[c]These are the actual costs for the fiscal year 1990–1991.

tween what is learned and taught in schools and their effects on the working world. That is, as we learn more about which objectives and their costs are related to successful workplace repertoires, we can make more informed decisions about the costs and benefits of learn units and curricula vis-à-vis the workplace market. We can also do similar analyses of school learning and leisure or lifestyles.

Our current evidence suggests that schools that are driven by a science of pedagogy and continuous assessment can produce more learning and more instruction than comparable schools. Thus, comprehensive behavioral schools are probably very cost-effective comparatively. Of course, this means that the teachers in these schools simply are more effective also by both learning and financial criteria.

Feasibility

The fact that teachers and supervisors in the CABAS schools have been measuring all of the learn units received in several schools for up to 11 years demonstrates that it is feasible to do so. Additional research is needed to develop ways to increase learn-unit measurement in a variety of schools. The fact that CABAS schools have conducted these measurements for no more or less cost than schools that do not do it demonstrates that it is economically feasible. In fact, by using our measurement of the effects of schooling,

schools that measure learn units are dramatically more cost-effective than those schools that we have observed that do not measure learn units or use the science of pedagogy comprehensively.

Types of Learn Units

The learn unit is an "antecedent-behavior-consequence" presentation for a student and involves one or more three-term contingencies for the teacher. Some are learner controlled as when a student moves through automated instruction with a programmed textbook or personal computer program, or does one-minute timings with flashcards. Others are massed as in teacher-presented or textural learn units, whereas still others are dispersed. In the latter case, a learn unit for one student or subject matter is alternated with another student or subject. Still other learn units are captured or incidental. In this case, learn units for targeted objectives are captured in natural settings or settings are created to simulate natural ones. Frequently, the latter type are generalization training opportunities that are turned into learn units. Our teachers are quite good at capturing and recording learn units while they are doing scripted or programmed learn units. It is likely, however, that captured learn units are not always recorded.

Captured learn units can incorporate the necessary motivational conditions to improve the effect of the learn-unit presentation and the curriculum. At the same time, we can perform planned establishing operations that provide all of the benefits of captured learn units but with the advantage of increasing the numbers of learn units (Greer et al., 1991; McCorkle & Greer, in progress).

The Validity of Learn Units

Learn units and criterion-referenced data are valid to the degree that what has been mastered leads to or is directly related to subsequent learning and usefulness in the world at large (e.g., habilitation). Hawkins (1986) described the criteria for habilitation as the development of behaviors that maximize long-term reinforcement opportunities and minimize punishment occasions. It is also important for those repertoires that are reinforced to be useful ones for society as well as the individual. Instructional objectives need to lead to or result in student expertise. That is, that which is learned should be habilitative for the individual and utilitarian for society. The habilitative outcomes of education can be tested via behavior analyses once learn units and criterion-referenced objectives are available for students.

What about short-term tests of validity? One traditional source has been the standardized achievement test. However, it is important to keep the proper perspective on such tests. First, they are designed to predict what has been taught in classes through sample measures. But, what if what was taught has been mastered, but the test item or test items are based on an unsubstantiated belief about cognition? For example, the student has learned how to describe and categorize conceptual subject matter and even use that subject matter usefully, but he or she has not been taught an exemplar identification repertoire (multiple-choice responding). The test item presumed correspondence between two repertoires (i.e., describe and use versus exemplar identification); that is, the item presumes a cognitive intervening variable has been "tapped" by the test item regardless of the fact that two independent responses were involved (Chase, Johnson, & Sulzer-Azaroff, 1985). A curriculum-based assessment is more accurate provided the teacher is appropriately trained.

Thus, for standardized tests to be useful for determining the validity of learn units and criterion-referenced objectives, certain criteria must be applied to the use of these tests. These include (1) the response and antecedent conditions measured in the test must be the same as those taught, (2) the student must have responded incorrectly to the item before instruction, (3) learn units and objectives related to the item must have been reliably measured and criteria achieved (in short, items not taught in class should be omitted); and (4) items that test for inference ability (an unsubstantiated intervening variable) should be excluded. If these criteria are applied, standardized tests may prove useful as one assessment of entire schools, but they still are not the ultimate test. With or without standardized test items, the validity of the learn units and criterion-referenced objectives can be determined by inspecting the objectives vis-à-vis their long-term effects and the associated data and reliability of the teachers as accurate transducers of student behavior.

After leaving school, and even in a good graduate course, multiple-choice repertoires are never used (Chase, Johnson, & Sulzer-Azaroff, 1985). Other than answering questions on quiz shows, the world-at-large has little, if any, use for multiple-choice responding. Yet multiple-choice responding permeates schooling. Perhaps the critics of multiple-choice tests and instruction have been correct all along. Graduates need to precisely characterize phenomena consistent with our best disciplines. This clearly is the repertoire needed by individuals who provide the world with the expertise for solving problems. Or, do we teach learn units for multiple-choice responding in order for students to perform well on standardized tests, even though they will have an inadequate writing or speaking repertoire? We can definitively answer these questions about the validity of curriculum using learn-unit measurement and controlled experimentation, but we will never answer them without a standard unit of learning and teaching like the learn unit. So, the answer to the question "How valid is the learn unit?" is "How valid is the instruction?" The answer can, as far as I can see, be ascertained only with measures like the learn unit.

The Learn Unit and Teacher Training

The use of the learn unit provides the tools and the conceptual framework for teaching teachers a true expertise in pedagogy. The nucleus learn unit draws on the full range of the science of behavior vis-à-vis pedagogy. Teachers in CABAS schools learn to analyze student responses in terms of the antecedent and consequent stimuli, the instructional history as a history of learn units, setting events and stimuli, and their manipulation as establishing operations in terms of their effects on the student's learn-unit performance. Typically, inadequate teaching operations are traceable to three sources: the teacher's presentation of the learn unit, deficits in the student's instructional history, or setting events and stimuli that affect the postcedent operations to the student response (Greer, 1992).

The use of the learn unit and criterion-referenced objectives can focus research in pedagogy directly on instructional interventions that can be replicated. There is no need to blame the problem on an unsubstantiated psychological construct. Teachers can be taught strategies for analyzing learn units, the student's instructional history, and the setting events and setting stimuli that affect the nucleus learn unit. The acceptance of a standardized absolute unit of teaching and learning would have an effect on research in pedagogy comparable to the effect that the acceptance and use of the operant did for the generic science of behavior!

Conclusion

The measure of a teacher is one that incorporates student and teacher behavior and the rate and accuracy of the behaviors of both. It is a measure that is related to criterion-referenced objectives and can be summarized in archival inventories of deficits and achievement. The teacher accuracy with the learn unit predicts student achievement—the more learn units presented, the more student learning. Fewer teacher errors result in even more learning. The unit can be related to all types of curricular responding and all levels of curriculum from students with no listener repertoires (e.g., no instructional control) to students who function as writers and as their own readers (i.e., sophisticated self-editing repertoires).

The measure is not used for between-teacher comparisons, but for within-teacher and within–subject matter comparisons. Baselines are determined for each student, each teacher, and each classroom. These measures are used to teach and assist teachers just as they are used by teachers to assist students. In the CABAS schools each teacher sets his or her teacher accuracy and learn-unit objectives on an incremental basis together with the supervisor or principal.

The measure can be used to determine the costs and benefits of instruction based on in-classroom learning and instruction rather than on projective test measures that are of questionable relevance to classroom instruction. The measure allows for the rigorous test of the long- and short-term benefits of instruction.

Finally, the learn unit provides the most critical measure for a teacher—a means to determine how to ensure student learning. The use of strategic analyses of the enlarged concept of the learn unit (e.g., instructional history and setting events) provides the way to train, monitor, and motivate the behaviors that are the core of a science of pedagogy. They are teaching operations for all children that derive from and contribute to measurably superior strategies.

References

ALBERS, A., & Greer, R. D. (1991). Is the three-term contingency trial a predictor of effective instruction? *Journal of Behavioral Education, 1* (3), 337–354.

AYLLON, T., & Roberts, M. D. (1974). Eliminating discipline by strengthening academic performance. *Journal of Applied Behavior Analysis, 7,* 71–76.

BABBITT, R. L. (1986). Computerized data management and the time distribution and rate of tasks performed by supervisors in a data-based educational organization. (Doctoral dissertation, Columbia University, 1986). *Dissertation Abstracts International, 47,* 3737a.

BECKER, W. (1992). Direct instruction: A twenty-year review. In R. West & L. Hammerlynck, *Designs for educational excellence: The legacy of B. F. Skinner* (pp. 71–112). Longmont, CO: SoprisWest.

BROPHY, J. E. (1983). If only it were true: A response to Greer. *Educational Researcher, 12,* 10–13.

CHASE, P. M., Johnson, K. R., & Sulzer-Azaroff, B. (1985). Verbal relations within instruction: Are there subclasses of interverbal? *Journal of the Experimental Analysis of Behavior, 43,* 301–313.

DEITZ, S. (1978). Current status of applied behavior analysis: Science vs. technology. *American Psychologist, 33,* 805–814.

DIAMOND, D. (1992). Beyond time on task: Comparing opportunities to respond and learn units to determine an accurate means of measuring educational gains. Unpublished paper, Teachers College, Columbia University.

EDMONDS, R. (1979). Effective schools for the urban poor. *Educational Leadership, 37,* 15–21.

GREENWOOD, C. R., Delquadri, J., & Hall, R. V. (1984). Opportunity to respond and student academic performance. In W. Heward, T. Heron, D. Hill, & J. Trap-Porter (Eds.), *Behavior analysis in education* (pp. 58–88). Columbus, OH: Charles E. Merrill.

GREER, R. D. (1981). An operant approach to motivation and affect: Ten years of research in music learning. In *Documentary report of the Ann Arbor symposium: Application of psychology to the teaching and learning of music.* Washington, DC: Music Educators National Conference.

GREER, R. D. (1992). *L'enfant terrible* meets the educational crisis. *Journal of Applied Behavior Analysis, 23,* 65–69.

GREER, R. D. (in press). *Teaching operations for all children.* Boston: Allyn & Bacon.

GREER, R. D., Dorow, L. G., Wachhaus, G., & White, E. R. (1973). Adult approval and students' music selection behavior. *Journal of Research in Music Education, 21,* 345–354.

GREER, R. D., Dorow, L. G., Williams, G., McCorkle, N., & Asnes, R. (1991). Peer-mediated procedures to induce swallowing and food acceptance in young children. *Journal of Applied Behavior Analysis, 24,* 783–790.

GREER, R. D., McCorkle, N., & Williams, G. (1989). A sustained analysis of the behaviors of schooling. *Behavioral Residential Treatment, 4,* 113–141.

HAWKINS, R. P. (1986). Selection of target behaviors. In R. O. Nelson & S. C. Hayes (Eds.), *Conceptual foundations of behavioral assessment* (pp. 331–385). New York: Guilford Press.

INGHAM, M., & Greer, R. D. (1992). Functional relationships between supervisors' observations of teachers in observed and generalized settings. *Journal of Applied Behavior Analysis, 25,* 153–164.

KELLY, T. M., & Greer, R. D. (1992). Functional relationships between learn units and maladaptive behavior. Paper presented at the International Conference of the Association for Behavior Analysis, May, San Francisco.

LAMM, N., & Greer, R. D. (1991). A systematic replication of CABAS. *Journal of Behavioral Education, 1*(4), 427–444.

MCCORKLE, N. (1992). Are CABAS schools cost effective? Paper presented at the international convention of the Association for Behavior Analysis, San Francisco.

MCCORKLE, N., & Greer, R. D. (in progress). Multiple experiments on peer-mediated establishing operations. Unpublished data.

MADSEN, C. H., Becker, W. C., & Thomas, D. R. (1968). Rules, praise, and ignoring: Elements of elementary classroom control. *Journal of Applied Behavior Analysis, 1,* 139–150.

SELINSKE, J., Greer, R. D., & Lodhi, S. (1991). A functional analysis of the comprehensive application of behavior analysis to schooling. *Journal of Applied Behavior Analysis, 24,* 220–249.

SKINNER, B. F. (1953). *Science and human behavior.* New York: Macmillan.

STALLINGS, J. (1980). Allocated academic learning time revisited, or beyond time on task. *Educational Researcher, 9,* 11–16.

STEPHENS, J. M. (1967). *The process of schooling.* New York: Holt, Rinehart & Winston.

WINETT, R., & Winkler, R. (1972). Current behavior modification in the classroom: Be still, be quiet, be docile. *Journal of Applied Behavior Analysis, 5,* 499–504.

WOLPOW, R. I. (1976). The independent effects of contingent social and academic on the on-task behavior and performance of profoundly retarded adults. *Journal of Music Therapy, 14,* 29–38.

CHAPTER 14

The Morningside Model of Generative Instruction

Kent R. Johnson
T. V. Joe Layng

We first introduced the formal characteristics of the Morningside Model of Generative Instruction in a special issue of the *American Psychologist* honoring B. F. Skinner (Johnson & Layng, 1992). Although the model, its conceptual history, and its foundations in selection science were discussed, space precluded elaboration of several key points. This chapter is a further specification of the Morningside Model of Generative Instruction. We first address the organizational history of Morningside Academy and its Chicago offspring at Malcolm X College. Next, we explain how the Morningside Model is an example of applied science, including further elucidation of generative instruction, instructional design features, retention–endurance–application–performance–stability REAPS), and the importance of standard celeration charting. Finally, we provide a thumbnail sketch of 14 daily operational procedures of a classroom employing the Morningside Model.

A History

Morningside Academy: The Seattle Children's School

To develop the model of teaching presented here, Kent Johnson established a private, nonprofit (501 (c) 3)

corporation—the Morningside Learning Center—13 years ago in Seattle, Washington. Initially, Morningside offered a broad array of academic and training services, letting the Seattle community determine its focus (Pennypacker, 1992; Skinner, 1971, 1981). These services included providing psychoeducational and vocational assessment, training human service personnel, teaching time management and study skills to college learners, and improving the academic skills of children and adults. Students, their families, or various social service agencies paid for the services. Within nine months, the parents of tutored children surfaced as the most frequent and stable users of Morningside's services. Since many of their children needed more intensive academic services than could be offered during weekly tutoring, Morningside Learning Center became Morningside School, a summer program for children with learning and attention problems. That fall, at the request of the parents of the summer-school children, Morningside became a full-fledged, year-round school, accredited by the state of Washington.

Morningside Academy, a name its students eventually petitioned the director to use, is a basic skills catchup school; learners participate between one and three years before they are ready to be successful students elsewhere. The program teaches them the fundamental component skills necessary to learn successfully in a content class like history or biology. Learners who could achieve an "A" in such classes probably would not need to attend Morningside Academy.

The Current Morningside Academy Curriculum

The curriculum is a comprehensive sequence in the basics: reading, decoding, and comprehension; mathematics concepts, calculation and problem solving; language arts, including handwriting, composing, grammar, spelling, and mechanics; computer basics, including keyboarding, document organization, and word processing; time management, materials organization, and learning to learn; and critical thinking, reasoning, and argumentation.

The instructional materials represent a combination of Engelmann's Direct Instruction programs in reading (Engelmann & Bruner, 1988a, 1988b; Engelmann, Carnine, & Johnson, 1978; Engelmann & Hanner, 1988a; 1988b; Engelmann et al., 1988a; 1988b), writing (Engelmann & Davis, 1991; Engelmann, Arbogast, & Davis, 1991; Engelmann & Silbert, 1983, 1985, 1991, 1993; Engelmann & Grossen, 1993), and mathematics (Engelmann & Carnine, 1992a, 1992b, 1992c, 1993a, 1993b), Morningside's fluency supplements to Engelmann programs (e.g., Johnson & Kevo, 1993), Archer and Gleason's (1989) Direct Instruction programs in organizational and study skills and our own programs in mathematics (Johnson, 1993a, b, c, d, e, f, g, h, i; Johnson & Streck, 1993a, 1993b) and thinking skills (Layng, Jackson, & Robbins, in preparation). We plan to formally design and package all of our current instructional programs and fluency supplements.

Although many of its school functions, such as organized physical education during the lunch hour, monthly field trips, and parent potlucks, help create the atmosphere of a typical school, Morningside Academy is essentially a learning laboratory for designing instructional programs and classroom procedures, with a laserlike focus on the essential skills for school success and a 13-year research base (Binder, 1991a).

The Morningside Academy Guarantees

At Morningside Academy, students typically gain between two and three grades in each academic skill per year, as measured by national standardized achievement tests (Johnson & Layng, 1992; Snyder, 1992). Table 14.1 presents Morningside students' gains over the past 11 years.

Due to its successes, Morningside Academy now offers parents two money-back guarantees. The first is for children who are two or more years behind in school. Many children in this group have been officially classified as "learning disabled" by public school personnel. These learners, who have rarely gained more than half a year in any one academic year, will gain at least two grade levels per school year or their parents will receive a tuition refund in proportion to the shortfall. The second guarantee is for any other learners who are not much behind in grade-level achievement but who stand apart from their peers because they do not coordinate visual and motor skills effectively, as is most apparent in their handwriting. These students are also highly distractible, hyperactive, disorganized, and have poor study and independent learning skills. Many children in this group have been officially classified by their pediatricians or other medical personnel as "attention deficit disordered" (ADD). Morningside Academy guarantees that these learners will increase their time-on-task endurance from their typical 1 to 3 minute spans to 20 minutes or more—an attention span longer than that

Table 1 Morningside Academy Children's Mean Standardized Achievement Test Grade-Level Gains

Year	Reading Mean	Language Arts Mean	Math Mean
1981–1982	2.4	1.6	2.1
1982–1983	2.3	1.9	1.9
1983–1984	2.4	1.9	2.0
1984–1985	2.5	2.7	2.2
1985–1986	2.0	3.0	2.5
1986–1987	2.3	2.3	1.9
1987–1988	2.3	3.5	2.2
1988–1989	2.5	3.0	2.7
1989–1990[a]	2.8	3.3	2.4
1990–1991[a]	2.2	3.8	3.9
1991–1992[a]	2.6	3.9	3.1

Note: [a]Metropolitan Achievement Test (MAT 6). All others: California Achievement Test. SOURCE: From "Breaking the Structuralist Barrier: Literacy and Numeracy with Fluency, by K. R. Johnson and T. V. J. Layng, 1992, *American Psychologist, 47*, 1475–1490. Copyright 1992 by the American Psychological Association. Reprinted by permission.

of the average college learner (Reese & Johnson, 1975). Morningside Academy also guarantees that students with visual or motor coordination deficiencies will learn word processing skills to communicate in writing. Furthermore, Morningside guarantees to bring these learners above the 65th percentile of their peer group nationally before they transition to another school. In the seven years since the assurances have formally been in place, Morningside has never had to refund tuition for failure to meet its money-back guarantees (Binder, 1988; Johnson & Layng, 1992).

Morningside Academy and the So-Called Learning and Attention Disorders

Morningside Academy began with no particular focus on learning disabilities or attention deficit disorders, populations with which it is now closely associated. Its strengths connected with a sector of the population that needed them in a microcultural evolution. Morningside Academy is now considered among the top agencies in the Northwest specializing in "learning and attention disorders," even though none of its faculty, including its director, has had any training in neuropsychology, a predominant field in the "treatment" of these "disorders." Behavior analysis has evolved a technology powerful enough to override certain hypothesized organic barriers to successful school functioning. By so doing, it created the irony of environmental effectiveness in an area most often approached from a physiological perspective.

The Seattle Literacy Project

In 1987 Morningside Academy began its adult literacy program, providing remedial basic skills education to minority youth and adults who did not have high school diplomas and were seriously deficient in reading, mathematics, and writing skills. Some participants took the Morningside Academy program concurrently with job-training skills programs, others as preparation for specific occupational-skills training courses. The project was funded by the Job Training and Partnership Act (1985), a revival of the Comprehensive Employment Training Act (CETA) program sponsored by Lyndon Johnson and the Great Society, and proposed by the unlikely duo of Ted Kennedy and Dan Quayle. Funding for the project was contingent on Morningside's proposal that no payment would be requested for any learner who progressed less than two grade levels.

Morningside's initial literacy project serviced 52 African American men and Asian American women. Forty-eight of these learners acquired skills at or above the national eighth-grade literacy standard and progressed more than two grade levels to do so (Johnson & Layng, 1992; Snyder, 1992). This was remarkable given the unstable lives of many of the participants, from homelessness to drug and other criminal activity. Learners advanced at an average rate of 1.8 grades per month (20 hours of instruction and practice)—a figure that contrasts sharply with the U.S. government standard of one grade-level progress per 100 hours of instruction (Binder & Watkins, 1989; Johnson, 1990, 1991; Johnson & Layng, 1992; Snyder, 1992). Part of the reason for the speedy progress was perhaps related to the economic contingencies: the faster learners advanced, the sooner Morningside Academy was paid.

Figure 14.1 illustrates the progress of four representative learners (KR, WB, DM, and JK) in the adult literacy project. The dot-dashed lines in each graph represent the individual's predicted gains, which were calculated by dividing the entering grade-level performances by the number of years spent in school. The dashed lines drawn on the diagonal of each graph represent the standard progress expected of the learner in school: one year of progress for one year of schooling. The solid lines represent the individual's gains in the Morningside program. In each case the participants' actual progress far exceeds both the standard and predicted progress.

Morningside Academy's literacy program attracted many visitors, including representatives from the U.S. Department of Labor, U.S. Department of Energy, the Washington State Employment Security Department, various Washington county youth employment and training programs, local television and radio personalities, and hundreds of parents, teachers, and professionals in medical and social service. (Curiously, no one from the U.S. Department of Education has ever visited.)

The Chicago Precollege Institute of Malcolm X College

In January 1991 T. V. Joe Layng became director of the Academic Support Center at Malcolm X Col-

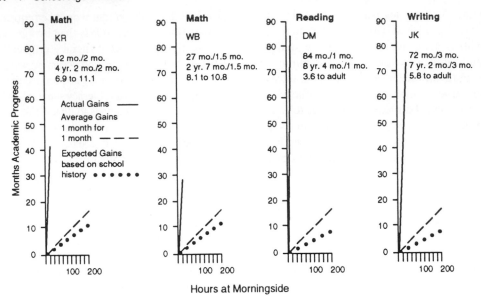

Figure 14.1. The progress of four adults. SOURCE: From "Breaking the Structuralist Barrier: Literacy and Numeracy with Fluency," by K. R. Johnson and T. V. J. Layng, 1992, *American Psychologist, 47*, 1475–1490. Copyright 1992 by the American Psychological Association. Reprinted by permission.

lege in Chicago. As we had previously collaborated on other projects (including formalizing the various elements that define the Morningside Model), and with the success of the Morningside Academy adult education JTPA project, we designed and implemented a pilot project.

Thus began the formal dissemination of the Morningside Model. We launched a training program for tutors in the Academic Support Center, who expressed interest in working in a summer program for people who were behind in mathematics skills. The program was to be called "Academic Storm: The Mother of All Summer Programs." Academic Storm was the pilot project and foundation for the new Precollege Institute, to begin in the fall of 1991, for learners with high school diplomas who attempted to register at Malcolm X College but had reading skills below the sixth-grade level. The main purposes of the institute would be to accelerate the building of precollege skills in one to two semesters, preventing learners from dropping out before they achieve college-level status, and to guarantee the success of learners in college courses (Johnson & Layng, 1992; Johnson, Layng, & Jackson, 1993; Snyder, 1992).

During five weeks in January, April, May, June, and July, Kent Johnson trained the tutors to teach a sequence of over 250 objectives in mathematics, from simple addition through solving ratios and equations with one unknown, a span of about six grade levels. The tutors also learned about the generic components of effective instruction and practice. Between training visits, the tutors practiced their new teaching technologies with each other at Malcolm X College.

Beginning July 1st, learners and teachers participated in the Academic Storm *Morningside Mathematics* (Johnson & Streck, 1993a) program Mondays through Thursdays, from 9 A.M. to 12 P.M., for six weeks. Every Friday we gathered the tutors and the fall supervisor-in-training to share charts, discuss successes, brainstorm problems, and ask the detailed questions about the model that arise only after direct contact with the system's contingencies. Learners with entry math skills at the fifth-grade level who participated in the full Morningside technology gained over six years in math computation and over two years in math concepts and problem solving. After only 20 hours in timed reading rate practice, learners gained an average of 1.1 years in reading (Johnson & Layng, 1992; Snyder, 1992).

Malcolm X College's Precollege Institute (PCI) program now includes instruction in reading, mathematics, writing, and thinking skills for those who test below the sixth-grade level. Early follow-up data indicate that in addition to dramatic grade-level gains (Layng & Johnson, in press), following as little as eight weeks in the program, learners who finish their first semester in the college credit curriculum are exceeding the stated PCI goal of a 2.5/4.0 GPA and achieving some of the highest within and semester-to-semester retention rates in the college. All of these gains with children and adults in Seattle and Chicago occurred without any homework (to complete or to evaluate)!

The Morningside Model as Applied Science

The Morningside Model of Generative Instruction is an outgrowth of *applied science* because it attempts to incorporate built-in, databased self-correcting procedures (Bronowski, 1965). It is instructional design, based on scientific findings—as electrical engineering is to physics. Every step a learner takes, every procedure a teacher uses produces data that they use to direct them to their next activity. The Morningside Model is designed so that both the instructional technology and the students' learning continually improve as more and more learners and teachers participate in its implementation. *Self-correcting mechanisms* are crucial to the evolution of a model. Such programs "have a life of their own," helping perpetuate their own survival. They contain inherent features that both investigate the program's effectiveness and evolve improvements along the way.

As in all design, there is an artistic component—unspecified contingency-shaped designer repertoires—that is not easily subject to obvious self-correction. This component is determined by the complex histories of the designers. It makes each implementation a unique instance of the model. Each implementation maintains its stability and integrity, however, by adhering to the basic instructional design, related scientific findings, and the use of rate of change in learner performance to provide continuous self-correcting feedback.

The Role of Frequency Data

Experimental psychology had a strong influence on the measurement features of the Morningside Model. Some of the learning literature in experimental psychology, particularly the experimental analysis of behavior, uses *frequency* measurement, whether of responses or time between responses. Much has been written about the sensitivity of frequency measurement and the continuous orderly data it produces (Ferster, 1953; Skinner, 1953; Ferster & Culbertson, 1982; Ferster & Skinner, 1957). But perhaps the most important feature of frequency is that it can accurately predict future action (Ferster, 1953; Ferster & Culbertson, 1982). In everyday talk, terms such as *habit, disposition, tendency*, and *personality* attempt to predict what someone will do based on the frequency with which they have behaved that way in the past. For example, a person who "has a habit" of whistling tunes does so regularly and will probably do so in the future. Someone who "has a high disposition" or "tendency" to speak out about politics will do so when the occasion arises. Someone who "has an addictive personality" engages in behaviors that may be detrimental at high frequencies, such as drugging or gambling. Indeed, some (see Binder, Chapter 3 in this text) suggest that frequency may be considered a separate dimension of behavior along with the commonly accepted dimensions of duration, intensity, and form (topography).

From the outset, Morningside Model programs measured frequencies of accurate performance, and built performance to high frequencies, a technology Carl Binder called "fluency building" (Binder, 1977–1983, 1988, 1991b). Fluent performance is useful, permanent, and easily applied to new learning, features to which we return later in this chapter. Perhaps more important, Morningside Model programs use changes in frequency—*acceleration* of accurate learner performance—to develop permanent and useful learner success. This focus on acceleration meets the needs of children who have always progressed "slowly," as well as the concerns of parents who see the implications of having a child falling further and further behind (decelerating). A focus on acceleration also alleviates the frustration of teachers faced with increasing differences in learner performance levels and progress within the same classroom, resulting in increasing teacher work and decreasing reinforcement for that work (i.e., burnout from ratio strain).

Fortunately, a simple graphical chart—Ogden Lindsley's *Standard Celeration Chart*—is available to record learning accelerations (and decelerations). This chart is the fundamental teaching tool for a self-identified community of teachers with a distinct set of methods called Precision Teaching (Lindsley, 1972, 1990, 1991). The Standard Celeration Chart provides the foundation for setting fluency aims and for making students' learning accelerations the basis for curricular changes—everything from decisions about seating arrangements, to effective staffing, the use of commercially available material, and the design

of materials and teaching methods. The Standard Celeration Chart appears in Figure 14.2.

Defining Academic Behavior I: Cumulative Programming of Intellectual Skills

The animal learning literature in experimental psychology influenced not only Morningside Academy's measurement practices, but also focused the model on acquisition, retention, endurance, and transfer of learning (Kling & Riggs, 1971). The verbal learning and cognitive processes literature provided further direction for teaching acquisition, retention, endurance, and transfer or application. Current applications of the model focus on *intellectual skills*, those concepts, principles, and strategies that go beyond rote learning and verbal repertoires (Gagne, 1970). The distinction between verbal repertoires and intellectual skills is the difference between knowing

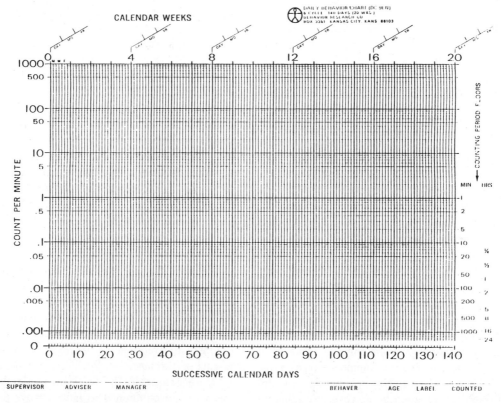

Figure 14.2. Daily Standard Celeration Chart. SOURCE: Reprinted by permission of and available from Behavior Research Company, Box 3351, Kansas City, KS 66103.

about and knowing *how* (Gagne, 1970; Tiemann & Markle, 1990). We can know about Pythagoras and geometry, as demonstrated by what we say about him in a historical account (verbal repertoire); and we can also know how to find the length of the hypotenuse of a right triangle by applying the formula $c^2 = a^2 + b^2$ (intellectual skill). We can know about reinforcement by saying its definition. We can show reinforcement know how, by identifying it when we see instances of it in the real world and by applying reinforcement procedures when we deem them necessary.

Conceptual behavior, identifying instances of things and events, is the foundation for intellectual skills. Concept formation research with humans and other animals (Clark, 1971; Gagne & Brown, 1961; Johnson & Stratton, 1966; Tiemann & Markle, 1990) tells about how to teach conceptual behavior with a cluster of tasks that includes a range of positive and negative instances (*examples* and *nonexamples*). During *discrimination training* with a range of examples and nonexamples of a concept, experimenters reinforce learners' identification of examples as examples and nonexamples as nonexamples. Identification of nonexamples as examples is either ignored (i.e., extinction) or corrected. Using these *differential reinforcement* and correction procedures, learner performance comes under the fine-grained control of the stimulus features that embody the concept. Once each concept is mastered, the resulting conceptual behavior can be related to others in a variety of ways to form more complex relations or principles (Tiemann & Markle, 1990). In the Morningside Model's programs, learners know about their fine-grained intellectual skills as well, by learning to answer questions such as "Is this an example? How do you know? Is this one? Why not?" (Markle, 1991).

An example from Morningside's study skills curriculum emphasizes intellectual skill building, beginning with conceptual behavior (Layng, Jackson, & Robbins, in preparation). Learners are taught to generate a special type of question as they study texts and notes. The questions they generate promote the continual hypothesis-testing behavior shown by experts within a given discipline. These "focusing" questions are special because they focus on material learners have not read but are about to read. Specifi-

cally, a focusing question must contain the following characteristics or attributes: (1) it must make a response request, (2) it must be about what one is preparing to read (not what one has already read), and (3) it must be a complete sentence.

If any one of these features is missing, the question or statement would not qualify as a focusing question. For example, a section heading or topic sentence of a paragraph might begin: "Almost everyone wants economic growth." Examples of a good focusing question might be "Why does almost everyone want economic growth?" or "Distinguish between those who want economic growth and those who do not." Notice that although only one example is stated as a question, both make a response request, both ask about the text about to be read, and both are complete sentences. Nonexamples include, "People typically want more of everything" (no response request); "What do most people want?" (asks about material already read); and "Why economic growth" (incomplete sentence).

The teaching sequence begins by providing students with scripted instruction featuring the rules for identifying focusing questions, and exercises using examples and nonexamples of the concept. So-called generalization is taught, not left to chance. Examples are drawn from a wide variety of subject matters, types of things questioned (e.g., topic sentences, headings, captions, and charts), and complexity of text until students can identify new examples not previously encountered in instruction. Nonexample work concludes when students reject all new statements or questions that do not include all three of the critical features of the concept. As a result, the students learn to discriminate focusing questions from nonfocusing questions. This sequence provides them with *automatic reinforcement* (Skinner, 1957) from a discriminative repertoire with which they are able to judge whether the questions they later produce are focusing questions. That is, the learners are able to correct themselves or at least know when they need assistance.

Building on this discriminative repertoire, students are introduced to the more complex skill of writing a focusing question by simply showing them how to add a question word and an action word (verb) to the material being questioned and then check to see that it is a grammatically correct complete sentence. They then practice writing focusing questions for a wide range of written material drawn from a variety of topics. Next, students apply their ability to write focusing questions to entire passages of text with and without headings. Once question writing is established, similar procedures are used to teach the students to generate brief answers to their questions, to read to answer their questions, and finally to compare their answers to the answers provided by the text—hypothesis testing.

Defining Academic Behavior II: Cumulative Programming of Concurrent Intellectual Skills

Like student like teacher. The skills that we teach teachers to implement with their learners require the same intellectual skill-building technologies that we use with the learners themselves. The faculty at Morningside learn concepts embodying positive approaches to decelerating behavior, such as Goldiamond's (1974) constructional approach, differential reinforcement of other behavior (DRO), differential reinforcement of alternative behavior (Alt-R), differential reinforcement of low rates of behavior (DRL), and differential reinforcement of diminishing rates of behavior (DRD) (Sulzer-Azaroff & Mayer, 1991). Each procedure is taught as conceptual behavior through discrimination training with examples and nonexamples. As each successive concept is mastered and added to the cumulative mix of scenarios, the faculty are required to discriminate each one from all of the others.

Less formal applications of cumulative programming of concurrent intellectual skills occur when teachers require learners to integrate (i.e., discriminate among) the skills they are learning from typical textbooks. For example, most mathematics texts treat topics in isolation. Learners may solve addition story problems in one section and subtraction problems in the next section. However, learners rarely practice solving both types together. Teachers may apply cumulative programming principles by writing practice worksheets that successively and continuously add each new math topic to the preceding topics. Teachers have applied cumulative programming to other subject matters, such as grammar, social science, and natural science.

Component/Composite Analysis

At about the same time that Kent Johnson founded Morningside Academy, T. V. Joe Layng was collaborating independently at the Behavior Analysis Research Laboratory of the University of Chicago, with Paul Andronis and Israel Goldiamond, its director, on basic animal research on the conditions responsible for combining previously trained simple nonsocial behaviors, such as pecking a disk and walking back-and-forth between other disks, into complex untrained social patterns (aggression in this case), such as increasing the number of times another bird had to peck its disk for food (Andronis, Goldiamond, & Layng, 1983). This and other basic research both at Chicago and elsewhere (Epstein, 1985, 1991) led to formalizing some of the key practices at work in the model from the outset and later provided research protocols we are using to formally investigate the human intellectual skills that lie at the heart of the model.

Both Morningside Academy's methods and the Chicago laboratory investigations were preceded by yet other contributing observations by both Johnson and Layng and their colleagues in the mid-1970s. These included Johnson's work with Carl Binder and Beatrice Barrett teaching developmentally disabled adults the activities of daily living skills, such as showering, brushing teeth, and washing hands. Their work used Eric and Elizabeth Haughton's observation of the importance of establishing very basic component motor skills before training more complex composite skills. The Haughtons called their basic motor skills list the big 6 + 6, which included reach, point, touch, grasp, place, release, push, pull, twist, squeeze, tap, and shake. Layng's work in inpatient psychiatry with Paul Andronis led to the observation that so-called pathological composite behavior could often be traced to everyday component behaviors that had been established earlier in other contexts (see Layng & Andronis, 1984). A patient's "symptom choice," such as pulling up clotheslines while screaming that they were blasphemous representations of the cross, could often be understood as a reinforced composite of previously learned religious and other component social patterns that resulted in loved ones rallying to the patient's assistance in the past.

This relation between basic behavioral components and more complex composites of these components may be the single most-important reason the Morningside Model has had the successes reported to date. Component/composite analysis is the foundation of the Morningside Model.

By combining (1) component/composite analysis of behavior with (2) cumulative instruction that includes a range of positive and negative instances of the component skills and (3) procedures that increase the frequency of the component behaviors, a powerful technology of instruction emerges—one that addresses performance acquisition, retention, and application. When practitioners apply this technology, new and complex repertoires emerge as a function of simply presenting a context for their combination, such as an activity, game, or simulation; component behaviors taught in the instructional sequence combine into new, untaught complex behavior as a result of the requirements imposed by the game, activity, or simulation. The application of fluent skills to new contexts and combinations without the need for instruction is the result, and therefore the meaning, of *generative instruction* (Alessi, 1987; Epstein, 1991).

Three Examples of Morningside Instructional Design

Let us take a brief look at the teaching of three complex academic skills—factoring equations in algebra, sentence writing, and debating—to illustrate component/composite analysis, cumulative teaching with positive and negative instances, and building the component skills thus acquired to higher frequencies. The composite behavior, factoring an equation like $4x^2 - 10xy + 4y^2$, stumps many beginning algebra learners. Much has been written about teaching such mathematical problem solving, including some direct, programmed instruction produced by people of a behavioral bent (Eraut, 1970). Nearly all of this literature supposes that teaching the complex skill requires a complex algorithm and fairly elaborate methods. Cognitive science research in education, the whole language movement, and even the elaborate programmed instruction procedures that incorporate fading and chaining procedures based on task analysis, attempt to teach skills at the level of their observed complexity.

In contrast, the Morningside Model builds the component skills involved in factoring equations from the bottom up. Number writing, addition facts (i.e., numbers with sums to 18; Johnson, 1993a), subtraction facts (differences between numbers through 18 minus 9; Johnson, 1993a), multiplication facts (through 9 times 9; Johnson, 1993b), isolating and solving for X in a simple linear equation (Johnson, 1993e), squaring and factoring squared numbers (Johnson & Streck, 1993), and certain organization and sequencing skills are first firmly established and then practiced until they occur at high frequencies. With high-frequency (fluent) component skills, learners learn how to factor within minutes by simply learning which operations go in which position within which set of parentheses to produce the answer: $(4x-2y)(x-2y)$. This complex skill is not learned by complex teaching procedures, but by a quick, three-step method: (1) show and tell the operation, (2) provide mnemonics to remember the sequence (i.e., FOIL—first numbers, outside numbers plus inside numbers, last numbers give the equation), and (3) discrimination training/testing with examples and nonexamples (e.g., "Is this equation factored correctly? Why not? Is it factored correctly now? How do you know?" and so on; Johnson, 1993b).

English textbook authors usually spend several pages teaching learners how to write and correctly punctuate appositives like that illustrated in the middle of the following sentence:

John F. Kennedy, president of the United States in the early 1960s, was assassinated in 1963.

However, at Morningside Academy, when we brought the component skills—relative pronouns (e.g., who, which), nonrestrictive relative clauses (e.g., who was president of the United States in the early 1960s), and the linking "to be" verb (e.g., am, was)—to fluency first, instruction in appositives for our middle school students was errorless after two-rule sentences:

Appositives are like nonrestrictive relative clauses using *which* or *who* and a linking verb. However, in an appositive, the relative pronoun and linking verb are left out.

With only three examples, all five learners so instructed immediately began fluency building in appositives. No learner ever made an error.

How about debating? Morningside begins with argumentation rules from one of Engelmann's Direct Instruction programs, like "Just because two things happen at the same time doesn't mean one causes the other" (Engelmann, Hanner, & Haddox, 1980). One rule is taught at a time. Learners apply the rules to short passages that follow or violate the rules:

> The rooster crows on my farm every morning before the sun rises. I think I better bring him with me on my trip to New York City. They don't have roosters there, so the sun may rise later than usual, if at all.

Argumentation rules are cumulatively programmed. Learners eventually catch the violations of *many* rules simultaneously in *lengthy* prose passages through discrimination training procedures (e.g., "What argument rule does the passage violate? How do you know? Is a rule broken in this passage? How about this one? Which one?" and so on).

Learners also build these skills almost to their reading rates. For example, a learner who can read 100 words per minute should be able to detect faulty logic in passages at his reading rate divided by 1.2, to account for covert reasoning skills (a little "thinking time"). Thus, 100 divided by 1.2 = 80 words of faulty logic detection per minute. Such automaticity guarantees retention of the skill and thereby its immediate availability for combination with related debating skills to form a new and complex composite skill. When skills are not at our fingertips they may be temporarily forgotten, or may occur only after a long delay, as when we get into bed and remember how we could have countered a colleague's argument earlier that morning.

The debating instructional program gradually shifts from written passages to vocal statements requiring listening skills. Finally, the rules of debating protocol are learned by discrimination training with examples and nonexamples and cumulative programming. Learners serve as debate referees who catch violations of debating rules at higher and higher frequencies in live simulations, before they practice them on their own.

As in the algebra factoring problem, the complex repertoire, seen in the act of actual debating, is a function of simpler component skills. In our approach, as skills get more complex they actually get easier to learn, because they are combinations of simpler high-frequency repertoires. Because the more complex repertoires are easier to learn, they are also easier to teach. The tendency is to add more interventions, more directions, more teaching to complex situations. But our experience has taught us that this is not necessary. Morningside teachers do not follow elaborate algorithms or programmed sequences to teach debating. In its later stages, teaching debating is about guiding or coaching—like inserting brief tips and quips to steer an ongoing, complex, generative repertoire when it goes off-course. Intensive, teacher-directed instruction occurs in the *early* stages, when component skills are learned.

Contingency Adduction

Component skills, initially shaped under separate circumstances, may be recruited in a substantially different context into a new composite skill. Andronis and Layng call this sudden combination of component elements *contingency adduction* (Andronis, 1983; Andronis, Goldiamond, & Layng, 1983; Layng & Andronis, 1984; Johnson & Layng, 1992). The examples of factoring equations, sentence writing, and debating illustrate contingency adduction. The Morningside Model of Generative Instruction is *itself* an instance of adduction from teaching repertoires that embodied applied experimental science, frequency measurement, a focus on multiple learning processes, and cumulative programming of sequences of component skills, derived from component/composite analyses, and established through discrimination training. All of these examples of contingency adduction illustrate the rearranging of existing repertoires (after Ferster, 1965) through rules, prompts, and activities.

When teachers use the Morningside Model, they need to be on the lookout for an increase in *unintended* contingency adduction. Learner repertoires may combine in ways other than those planned. The school environment may intersect with and adduce repertoires *without* any rules or instruction! An example of unintended contingency adduction occurred in our adult literacy program at Malcolm X College (Johnson & Layng, 1992; Snyder, 1992).

At one point in *Morningside Mathematics* (Johnson & Streck, 1993), learners are introduced to word problems involving fractions. This is a terribly difficult juncture for most learners, as many of us who never really mastered the fractions word problem skill can attest. Universal, defective conventional instructional practices prevailed in our thinking that surely no adduction would occur at this juncture. Indeed, as we reported earlier (Johnson & Layng, 1992), on a course pretest of problem solving with fractions, four learners' performance ranged from 3 to 7 problems correct out of 14. Significant component skills that were weak or nonexistent at the time of the pretest, however, were now occurring at high frequencies. These repertoires included the elements of problem solving with whole numbers and fractional computation. Now, with no instruction or even a mention of problem solving with fractions, learner performance ranged from 13 to 14 correct out of 14. Assessing for contingency adduction saved teachers and learners many hours of instruction! The learners simply completed fluency-building exercises to assure the retention of this adduced repertoire.

This is why every lesson in the *Morningside Mathematics* program (Johnson & Streck, 1993) contains a short adduction exercise, consisting of each of the component and composite skills to be taught in the lesson, to be sure that the learner really needs the instruction before it occurs. Since different learners bring different histories to the classroom, different numbers of them skip the instructional portion of each lesson, and either practice the skills taught in the lesson to high frequencies, or move to the next lesson if already automatic. As the program proceeds, more and more skipping occurs as an ongoing, complex, generative repertoire snowballs. We call these contingency-adduced repertoires *curriculum leaps* (Johnson & Layng, 1992).

Retention–Endurance–Application–Performance–Stability, and Fluency

The Morningside Model of Generative Instruction is an adduction of many findings in experimental psychology over the last five decades. Increased learner contingency adduction was one unintended

result. Another was the discovery of criterion frequency dimensions that predict that behavior will be retained after significant periods of no practice, will endure over extended periods, will be easily applied in more complex situations, and will be stable in the face of distractions. The discovery of retention–endurance–application–performance–stability (Haughton, 1980, 1981) led Precision Teachers—most notably, Eric and Elizabeth Haughton, Bea Barrett, and Carl Binder—to coin and use the term *fluency* to describe behavior that meets REAPS. Thus began a distinction between accurate and fluent performance. Accuracy, unlike fluency, rarely predicts whether performance will be retained, endure, transfer to more complex situations, combine with other repertoires under the same contingencies, and remain stable during distracting conditions. For example, learners may be taught to spell words that follow the rule: double the final consonant before adding an ending that begins with a vowel. The typical teacher complaint is that many learners, even those who spell the words with 100% accuracy on the Friday spelling test, misspell them when writing their compositions. This occurs because the new skill is accurate but not fluent and can therefore be disrupted when it must occur along with other skills or in new situations.

The discovery of REAPS led many Precision Teachers to abandon goal setting and competency defining by norm-based frequency criteria. Three norm-based criteria have been used most often. One derives the average performance in a school or work setting, such as the rate of math facts per minute of all fifth-graders at a certain school or district. A second method derives the average from people judged to be "truly competent," such as all kids scoring above the 90th percentile on the California Achievement Test in Math Computation at a certain school or district. A third method derives the average rate of math facts per minute of people who choose a certain career, such as all tellers at all branches of U.S. Bank. REAPS significantly altered the selection of criterion rates by focusing on rates of math facts that ensure retention, endurance, transfer, and stability.

Seven Tenets of the Morningside Model
These two discoveries—contingency adduction and REAPS—were unintended adductions that crys-

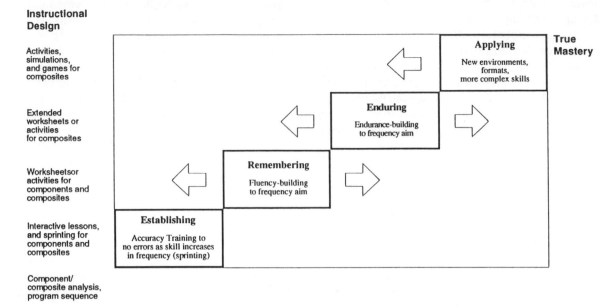

Change the procedures for a step, go up and down the steps, based upon learner performance.

Figure 14.3. The Morningside Model of Generative Instruction. SOURCE: From "Breaking the Structuralist Barrier: Literacy and Numeracy with Fluency," by K. R. Johnson and T. V. J. Layng, 1992, *American Psychologist, 47,* 1475–1490. Copyright 1992 by the American Psychological Association. Reprinted by permission.

tallized the seven tenets of the Morningside Model of Generative Instruction, illustrated in Figure 14.3.

1. Identify the component elements of instructional objectives.
2. Measure their frequency until true mastery, defined by REAPS, reached (Binder, 1988).
3. Establish a component behavior through highly interactive, contingent exchanges between learner and teacher, until behavior stays accurate at gradually increasing frequencies.
4. Build the component skills to fluency aims to ensure remembering.
5. Build the endurance of component skills that are repeated in succession en masse in the real world.
6. Include application activities that allow multiple component skills to combine in ways that define the higher-level complex activities of an expert in a field.
7. Alter the procedures for implementing the Morningside Model according to the data collected.

These are seven tenets, not procedures. A range of possible procedures can be used to achieve each step. The arrows next to the boxes in Figure 14.3 also indicate that procedures for meeting the goal of each step could be implemented in overlapping fashion. For example, some learners could begin building fluency while still establishing their skills; others need to wait to build fluency until establishment is complete. Individual-learner performance data should dictate which procedures to use to meet the goals of a step, when work on a new step should begin, and when return to a previous step for more work is warranted.

The simple-to-complex sequence of tasks learners encounter in the Morningside Model contrasts sharply with currently popular cognitive science and whole language approaches. These methods attempt to use complex activities to teach component elements. For example, debating is used to teach argumentation, and conducting a scientific experiment is used to teach observation skills. Indeed, cognitive science approaches may not bother with the component elements at all (e.g., Engelmann, 1992; Resnick, 1988)! Learning by activities, as illustrated by whole language and other cognitive science approaches to teaching, stand the Morningside Model on its head!

Self-Correction and the Three-Term Contingency

Tenet 7, the dynamic mechanism, is what makes the Morningside Model applied science. The self-correcting mechanism operates at the level of the *three-term contingency*: the *presentation* of a moment of instruction, the learner's *performance* at that moment of instruction, and the immediate *consequences* of the learner's performance: confirmation and praise, or corrections, depending on the adequacy of the learner's performance (Sherman & Ruskin, 1978). *The self-correcting mechanism is defined by reverberations through the three-term contingency.* Any given presentation of information, materials, tasks, or problems, including course procedures, may or may not be appropriate to the learner's current knowledge and skills—learner performance helps teachers adjust the presentation until the learner is successful. Likewise, learner performance determines the nature of consequences: praise or corrections. The consequences also help adjust the next moment of instruction, and so on, through cycles of presentation–performance–consequence reverberations that make the system viable for each learner.

More frequent opportunities for learner performance increase the interactivity of the teacher and the learner, reverberations through the three-term contingency, and thus self-correction (see Heward, Chapter 21 in this text). Optimal interactivity, defined by reverberation frequency, depends on the complexity of the task presentation, learner performance, and performance consequence. Optimal interactivity also depends on the efficiency of learning—reverberations produced by unnecessary tasks and learner responses that occur too frequently don't alter the presentation–performance–consequence cycle and thus delay mastery of skills. The most efficient use of the model occurs when teachers and learners take the largest instructional step that produces successful performance.

Selectionist Versus Essentialist Applied Science

By operating under the assumption that complex performance can be understood as a product of simpler elements, the Morningside Model is an example of a *selection science,* like evolutionary biology and paleontology. Selection sciences seek to find the more molecular processes that are sufficient to produce molar order (Donahoe, 1986, 1991; Palmer & Donahoe, 1992). Such sciences are in stark contrast to those Palmer and Donahoe (1992) called *essentialist* in character. Essentialist sciences, often typified by cognitive science, view complexity as an expression of inherent processes operating at the level of observed events. Every observation has its proposed mechanism to explain it. For example, some cognitive theories explain the activity of remembering by ascribing to it a structure (memory) that is composed of highly organized semantic networks (Palmer & Donahoe, 1992). A selectionist science, often typified by behavior analysis, explains remembering as just that—an activity that describes particular occasion-behavior relations that were initially reinforced and now occur at a later time (Palmer, 1991).

Essentialist-designed instruction attempts to teach complex skills at the same level of complexity that is observed in an expert or highly skilled performer. Indeed, instruction that is essentialist in nature often eschews any attention paid to simple components or their sequence (Resnick, 1988). Cognitive science approaches to instructional design (e.g., Stahl & Miller, 1989; Stepich, 1991), and the educational movements on which they are loosely based (e.g., whole language), exemplify this approach.

By contrast, instruction designed according to principles of selection science focuses on the simple elements that comprise complex behavior (Layng, 1988, 1989, 1991). When the elements occur at high frequencies, activities, games, and simulations can be arranged to promote the adduction of complex repertoires. The Morningside Model exemplifies this approach. *It assumes that learning and teaching get easier, not harder.* It is only the accumulation of weak component skills that makes learning harder and harder. As we noted in an earlier paper (Johnson & Layng, 1992), of the nearly 10 million learners who make it to high school mathematics courses each year, only 800 go on to earn doctorates in math (Mullis et al., 1991). Cumulative ignorance may be a primary cause of the fallout. For most of us, studying calculus is like climbing a mountain with a bag of bricks on our back, each brick representing a weak component skill. When instruction is designed from the bottom up, people may be able to learn calculus at a cocktail party on a napkin!

A selectionist approach also calls into serious question most tutoring practices and remedial approaches to learning. Learners who are tutored almost invariably have deficient component repertoires, yet are kept afloat in their studies by tutors who focus on the complex repertoires needed for next week's chemistry or history test and neglect the very component skills that would make adduction of the complex skills likely. The problem is that learners move through the educational system based on their age and on the credits they have accumulated, not on their competencies. The time available to study for next week's chemistry test makes it unlikely that either the tutor or the learner will focus on learning any deficient component skills needed for the test.

An insidious problem results from the educational establishment's developmentalism (see Stone, Chapter 6 in this text). Learners react emotionally to the suggestion that they are not appropriately placed in a particular academic sequence based on their age or the time they have spent in school. Eric and Elizabeth Haughton met much resistance from McGill University students to their approach to helping learners who were doing poorly in calculus. Students wanted help in differential equations, not number-writing skills, math facts, adding, and the like. However, with no tutoring in calculus and instead focusing on simple component elements that were deficient, learners substantially improved their calculus grades. *The problem presented is not always the problem to solve!*

Daily Operation of a Class Period or Course

Physical Space

Figure 14.4 shows a typical arrangement of a Morningside classroom. At station 1, learners work with a teacher in small groups to establish new component skills. There is a desk or at least bookshelves at station 1 for the teacher to keep materials for immediate use. At station 5, learners build fluency individually, in pairs, or in triads, and may work with a fluency coach, who may be the teacher, a teacher's aide, or an ad-

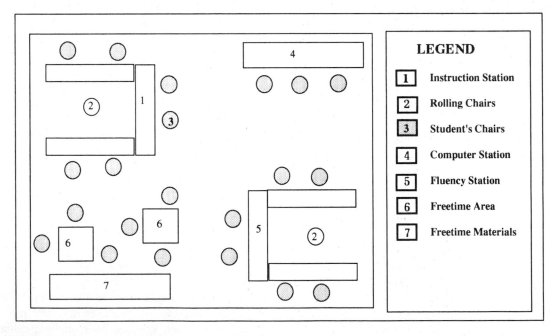

Figure 14.4. Recommended floor plan.

vanced learner. Somewhere in the classroom, each learner has a personal shelf or cubby space to store materials. In larger settings, learners may have personal desks at which to study or an area for self-study. In applications with children and youth, there is an area, 6–7, for leisure activities. The area contains activities for reinforcement, such as construction toys, computer games, cards, books, puzzles, and board games. Children earn points throughout the class or school day that can be exchanged throughout the class or day for minutes in the leisure-time activities area.

Personnel and Their Roles

In addition to designing instruction and teaching new skills, instructors usually serve as supervisors of the system, making sure materials are readily available, recordkeeping is organized and up-to-date, and daily operation is smooth, especially in making databased adjustments for learners. Supervisors also monitor their staff in vivo and provide written and oral feedback on their performance.

In addition to the instructor, learners are assisted by *coaches* before working by themselves and with each other to build their skills to fluency. In programs for children and youth, coaches can be the teacher, teacher aides, parents, or other paraprofessionals skilled in the subject matter. Coaches can also be learners in higher grades or otherwise advanced in the subject matter, in a kind of cross-age tutoring (see Miller, Barbetta, & Heron, Chapter 20 in this book). Ultimately, coaches need to come from the ranks of the learners in the program.

In programs for college and adult learning, coaches can be the teachers themselves or tutors hired by a university, college, or learning center. As with children and youth, coaches can be advanced students working for credits; eventually learners in the course can dominate coaching.

Much has been written about *peer coaching*, particularly at the college level (Johnson & Ruskin, 1977; Sherman, Ruskin, & Semb, 1982). Strain (1981) edited a comprehensive book on the use of children and youth peers as classroom behavior-change agents. Unfortunately, almost nothing has been written about the minutiae of coaching to increase skill frequency to fluency aims. The procedures involved in training

peer coaching are beyond the scope of this paper. The job description is clear, however. Coaches increase the opportunity for practice, measurement, and feedback and contribute significantly to the self-correcting reverberations of the system. They help maximize learner and teacher productivity by increasing the number of performances that can be monitored, praised, and corrected. Coaches can also be the incidental locus for learning organizational, observational, and learning-to-learn skills. Coaches are also the source of interpersonal social reinforcers in the system, and are often the best source for adjusting the system for the learner's benefit. Coaches can be formally trained to provide all these services.

The best peer coaches have skills that overlap with the learners' current skills to a far greater degree than an expert such as the instructor (Skinner, 1957; Johnson, 1977; Johnson & Ruskin, 1977). *Overlapping repertoires* produce more fine-grained, frequent changes, and learning proceeds at a more rapid pace. Athletes show such judicious selection of coaches when they select their practice partners from those who play just a little better than they do. Many of the staff in the adult learning program at Malcolm X College built their component teaching skills in shifts to positions of more responsibility in the system. One person recently moved in steps from coach to supervisor, another from adult literacy student to coach.

Daily Operational Procedures

The following is a thumbnail sketch of 14 daily operational procedures employed in a typical Morningside Model classroom. The suggested time frames assume that 60 minutes are available each day.

I. **Lesson plan.** Divide up the daily course or skill area class period into three parts. All three parts can occur simultaneously, but for different learners at different times. Each of these three daily segments can be divided into several specific tracks, each focusing on a different skill. Every day the teacher must map the course the learner is to follow the next day, based on careful analysis of the learner's performance that day. We strongly recommend daily classes over classes that meet only one or two days per week. The more

infrequently a course or skill is studied, the less efficient the learner's daily map may be, due to variations
in dysfluent skills from one class period to the next,
and the slower the learner's progress will be.

2. Precision placement. Pretesting learners frequently keeps the instructor current on what skills they need
to learn. Learners bring entering repertoires to a
course or class, and new repertoires may be adduced
during a course of study. A beginning course or
program pretest will give information about entering
repertoires. Individual lesson pretests will tell more
details about entering behavior, plus any new repertoires that have been adduced since the course began.
*No learners should participate in an instructional
episode if they already have the skills to be taught.*
The composition of instructional groups should change
from day to day, according to pretesting results. Careful
pretesting can greatly improve the efficiency of learning and teaching, and may play a large role in the
grade-level gains that we have reported thus far.

3. Public progress records. Entering and adduced
behavior can be marked on a public wall chart that lists
the learners on the vertical axis and the lessons to be
mastered on the horizontal axis. Teachers can refer to
the chart to call only those learners to the instructional
table who need to learn the skills taught in the lesson.
As learners establish and build fluency on the skills in
the lessons, additional marks can be made on the chart.
At Malcolm X College, learners, with their instructors
or coaches, make a small circle in the cell of a lesson
when they have participated in instruction. They
make the circle larger after they have successfully
built some frequency with coach support and then
completely color in the cell when they reach the
fluency aim. The progress chart is also used as the
occasion for daily meetings between the instructor and
coaches. Public progress records also help maintain
the pace (Johnson & Ruskin, 1977) and quality (Van
Houten, 1980) of performance.

4. Tool skill fluency. Each course or skill has a number of fundamental component elements or *tool skills*.
For example, an analysis of addition and subtraction
of whole numbers reveals nine tool skills that are
fundamental to the majority of their concepts and
operations, including number writing and reading,
math facts, and math language skills with symbols and
terms (Johnson & Streck, 1993). Reading has prerequisite pointing, decoding, and scanning skills. Writing has critical transcriptive and dictation tool skills,
with both pen and paper and computer keyboards.
Studying has critical organizational and cooperative
learning tool skills.

Learners should be given ample time to practice
three to four tool skills daily. Typically, five to ten
minutes is sufficient practice to make a noticeable
improvement in one tool skill compared to the previous day.

5. Establishing new skills. In the Morningside Model,
instructors provide highly interactive lessons to establish new skills and knowledge. Lessons are taught to
small groups of no more than 12, and only to those
who need them. Instructors examine the public wall
chart for a particular lesson and call only the learners
who have blank cells. The other learners practice the
objectives until they are fluent and work on other
fluency assignments.

At least three instructional procedures contain the
ingredients necessary for establishing new skills efficiently. The first is Engelmann's *Direct Instruction (DI)*
(e.g., Engelmann & Carnine, 1982; Kinder & Carnine,
1991). The second is *Programmed Instruction (PI)*
(e.g., Markle, 1991; Gilbert, 1962; Evans, Homme, &
Glaser, 1962). The third is Keller and Sherman's
Personalized System of Instruction (*PSI*) (Keller,
1968; Sherman & Ruskin, 1978; Sherman, Ruskin, &
Semb, 1982). We will describe our applications of
each of these instructional strategies in turn.

In Direct Instruction at Morningside, a small group
of learners gather with a teacher at a horseshoe-shaped
table for 20 to 30 minutes. During that time, the
teacher stands in front of the group, either in front of
a blackboard or next to an overhead projector. Next
to the teacher on a music stand is a scripted instructional presentation, which he or she refers to when
necessary. The script provides the exact lines
the teacher will use for instruction. The lines are
relatively brief, allowing learners to chorally respond
to the teacher on signal approximately 10 times a

minute, an excellent frequency for beginning skill establishment.

Rapid recognition of progress and correction of errors occurs throughout the instructional episode, maximizing the self-correcting mechanism of the system at this important step: *establishing*. Instructors teach two to three DI groups in a given subject per day.

The learners' choral responding in interaction with the instructor during DI lessons is very rhythmic and enthusiastic, like singing and dancing in the classroom. Children, youth, and adults alike enjoy and learn. Various parents and community leaders in Chicago's African American community have likened it to the "call and response" African oral tradition that is evident in some church services even today! Heward, Courson, and Narayan (1989) provided an excellent introduction to choral responding.

Direct Instruction teaching procedures comprise a complex system that requires training in its own right. Kinder and Carnine (1991) provided an excellent introduction to gaining competence in Direct Instruction. Janie DeNapoli and Paul McKinny (1992), of J/P Associates, have created excellent DI training videotapes.

Direct Instruction procedures are highly teacher directed. The live, oral manner of presentation is a very efficient approach to teaching basic skills like reading, arithmetic, and writing. As learners increase their competency in these basic skills, instruction can become less teacher dependent while maintaining a highly interactive character. Programmed Instruction, or textbook/study guide concoctions typical of PSI courses, are examples.

In Programmed Instruction the teacher's scripted lines are text to which learners respond in writing at their own paces (Markle, 1969, 1991; Skinner, 1954, 1968). The text may be in a book, computer program, or audiovisual format. Each response the learner makes is followed by an answer to which learners compare their answers. Sometimes the program will direct the learner to specific remedial sequences if an error was made.

In PSI courses teachers write a study guide to accompany standard text (Keller, 1968; Sherman & Ruskin, 1978; Sherman, Ruskin, & Semb, 1982). The study guide contains tasks for the learners to complete as they study the text. Usually these tasks are not as bite-sized as the tasks presented in programmed instruction sequences—there may be only 2 or 3 tasks presented per textbook page. The study guide also contains clarifications, corrections, and additions to text, and is most successfully presented in a personalized framework, as if a tutor or study partner were present when the learner is studying the text. In most PSI courses learners do not receive confirmation of their responses to the teacher's tasks; they must take the initiative to clarify any problems they have with course personnel before testing. This relatively sophisticated format for learning puts PSI procedures at the other end of the continuum of establishing procedures: Direct Instruction–Programmed Instruction–Personalized System of Instruction.

6. Sprinting. Immediately following Direct, Programmed, and/or Personalized Instruction, learners put the finishing touches on establishing new skills by engaging in *sprinting* exercises for five to ten minutes with a coach (Johnson & Layng, 1992). The coach may be the instructor who continues this work with the learners, or another person who steps in. A number of learners may test out of Direct, Programmed, or Personalized Instruction, and go directly to sprinting.

During sprinting, learners gradually increase the frequency of the new component skills that they have learned, and the coach ensures that these skills don't break down as frequency is increased from 10 to 20 or more per minute. Coaches introduce activities such as, "How many can you complete in twenty seconds? Let's see. Then we'll see if you can get more done in the next round," or "Let's see how long it takes you to complete three of these. Say 'done' when you're done. I'll tell you the time it took you. You write that time down. We'll see if you can beat that time in the next round." As learners practice, they record their frequencies and/or durations. Coaches rotate among learners as they put some rate behind their skills, noting and changing elements of their practice that slow them down, and further firming their accuracy if errors begin to occur as their rates increase. Coaches let the learners who are doubling their frequencies leave the group to fluency-build with one another; they continue to coach only those learners who need further guided practice.

Establishing involves not only making component skills firm (accurate at 10 or so per minute), but also *setting them in celeration motion*, to new frequencies that predict retention, endurance, and application. Thus, establishing is a combination of Direct Instruction and Precision Teaching, with their foci on accuracy and charted daily frequencies of performance (Kinder & Carnine, 1991; Binder & Watkins, 1990; Lindsley, 1972, 1990). Establishing charts the course of initial lower frequencies of performance and helps guarantee that steep celerations will occur with further practice.

7. Fluency building with peer coaches. Once learners have doubled or tripled their rates in short spurts without making errors, they engage in timed practice with each other to build their frequencies until they meet *fluency aims*. Fluency aims are those frequency ranges that predict retention, endurance, and application. For example, the fluency aim for math facts is 80 to 100 per minute; for oral reading 200 to 250 words per minute; for solving math word problems 12 to 15 per minute, for writing paragraphs 20 to 25 words per minute. Miller and Heward (1992) provided a detailed description of timed practice procedures (see also Miller, Barbetta, & Heron, Chapter 20 in this text). Visitors to a Morningside classroom liken sprinting and *fluency building* to an academic gymnasium, complete with warm-ups, sprints, longer endurance training, monitoring, coaching, stretching, and resting.

For 15 to 20 minutes each day, each pair of learners fluency-builds the skills learned in the day's instruction, along with other recently learned skills that need more practice to be fluent. They also keep track of their progress on recording sheets. Peer-coaching procedures allow learners to become independent of teachers by the end of the course. Under these procedures, star learners emerge as fluency coaches (and instructors!). Peer coaching requires training, a description of which is beyond the scope of this paper.

Fluency building is a combination of Precision Teaching (PT), with its focus on daily timings and charting, and the Personalized System of Instruction, with its reliance on the peer as a proctor to guide individual learning. As such, it is about instruction and practice intertwined, but differently than the way they are intertwined during establishment. There, the accuracy of accelerating performance is at issue; here, the issue is celeration itself and how to increase it.

Instructional materials. Sprinting and fluency building require multiple timers with features that allow the timing of duration and the length of a specific period. The timers must electronically signal the latter, with a beep or ring, to prevent the learner from having to continually check the timer while completing the exercise. (So stop watches and sandglasses are out.)

Teachers must also make a great many copies of practice exercises, because each learner will complete multiple timings, over several days, to reach a fluency aim. An alternative is to cover a practice sheet with Mylar. By using a hard-tipped marking pen, each timed practice can be easily erased with a moist sponge.

Design. As in establishing skills, many instructional design considerations should be followed to construct practice sheets and set fluency aims for them. Further description of sound instructional materials design is beyond the scope of this paper. To keep the focus on REAPS and to avoid using norm-referenced fluency standards, we offer the following beginning points.

To design a practice sheet and set a fluency aim for it, an instructor sums the basic reading and writing tool skills that the learners will be required to use while completing the tasks to be practiced and divides this number by 1.2 to allow for a little thinking time. Consider our earlier example of building fluency with argumentation rules, in which learners identify faulty reasoning in text passages. One design option is to write 50-word passages that contain 0–2 broken rules. Learners can identify the broken rules by writing the number of the rule that the argument breaks next to the sentence that violates it. The tool-skill aim for writing numbers is 160–180 per minute. The tool skill aim for reading text is 200–250 words per minute. In a 2-minute timing, learners could read 4–5 passages and write their numbers. To allow a little think time, the teacher could set the aim at 3–4 passages per minute.

Sometimes learners are not fluent in their basic tool skills. It is extremely important for teachers to make tool-skill fluency building a priority for these learners. The rate of learning more complex skills may be impossible without fluent tool skills. Complex skill learning may also accelerate with fluent tool skills (Gagne & Foster, 1949; Haughton, 1972; Johnson & Layng, 1992).

While learners with deficient tool skills are building tool-skill rates, teachers can set fluency aims by dividing their current rates by 1.2. For example, if a learner reads at 150 words per minute, the aim for the argumentation rule task would be 2–3 passages per minute. This procedure is chancy, however; learners' argumentation skills might not automatically increase with their tool-skill increases. If they do not, the learners will not have reached fluency and the skill may be forgotten. Periodic checks during tool-skill building will reveal whether additional practice with argumentation rules is necessary.

Several versions of a fluency practice sheet should be designed to avoid memorization. The learner responses should also be as efficient and task related as possible. We could ask learners to write out the broken argumentation rule each time faulty logic in the passage occurs, but practice in writing the rule is not the point of the exercise, catching faulty logic is (Markle, 1991)! A minimum of page turning or cross-page referencing will guarantee that the materials themselves don't impede building of the skill. The practicing should also be learner paced, not teacher paced, for the same reasons (Binder, 1977–1983; Precision Teaching Project, 1984; White & Haring, 1980).

Using classtime wisely. Figure 14.5 shows the relative proportion of time learners engage in various activities specified by the Morningside Model of Generative Instruction. Fluency building is by far the predominant activity, involving 70% or more of the learner's time, depending on what the data show. Conventional classroom time is proportioned in reverse, with about 70% spent establishing skills, 20% practicing, and 10% testing. When the authors provide training in the Morningside Model to schools, districts, and colleges, many teachers' first reaction to

the "happy learner" is disbelief: "How can you spend so much time practicing? I barely cover the year's curriculum (or the course's objectives) with much more time devoted to establishing. How can you produce two to three year gains this way?" The answer lies in the inefficiency of instruction that is top-heavy in establishment. Unless learners become fluent in the skills established, they lose them. There is also far less likelihood of curriculum leaps. Learners in classrooms that are top-heavy in establishing recycle through learning and forgetting and relearning during "review" sessions. The learn–forget–review–forget cycle is far more time-consuming than Morningside's learn-it-once-and-for-all approach.

8. Standard celeration charting. In Morningside programs, learners use standard celeration charts to monitor fluency building. Learners plot the daily frequency of each skill. They also draw miminum celeration lines on their charts to show daily progress that doubles in frequency each week. They first examine their charts for yesterday's performance frequency and record it on a practice record form. Next, they set the day's progress aim by determining what frequency would keep them on or above their mini-

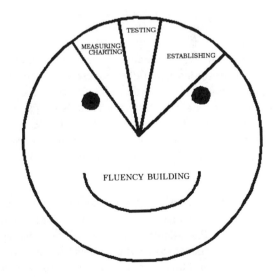

Figure 14.5. The happy learner (SOURCE: adapted from a transparency by Eric and Elizabeth Haughton, 1978).

mum celeration line, and record this information. Next, learners practice until they meet the day's progress aim. Once this occurs, the instructor or fluency coach is called to give a final timing, which verifies the achievement. The learner then plots the final timing on the chart.

Learning how to use the standard celeration chart is easy. The interested reader may consult several sources for good training (e.g., Precision Teaching Project, 1984; Pennypacker, Koenig, & Lindsley, 1972). In one article, 5-year-old Stephanie Bates tells her friends how to chart while her father takes notes (Bates & Bates, 1971)!

9. Decision-making and fluency-building interventions. In most cases, timed practice itself is the intervention needed to build fluency. Sometimes, however, learners will experience *performance locks* (Elizabeth Haughton, personal communication, August 1978). Try as they may, they don't achieve x 2 (read "times 2") weekly progress through repeated timings. This is more often the experience of learners with learning and attention problems. There are a multitude of procedures to help learners build fluency when their performance is locked, but these are beyond the scope of this chapter. The interested reader should consult a variety of resources to gain these competencies; most notably, Haughton (1980) and Binder's (1977–1983) *Data-Sharing Newsletter.*

At Morningside, fluency-building interventions occur whenever learners fail to double their acceleration each week. Some of these interventions require the instructor's skills, others a coach's skills, and still others can be implemented by the learners themselves. An important goal of any Morningside program is to teach all learners to make their own interventions.

10. Clearing a backlog. It may take several days or even a week or more to reach the fluency aim of a given skill. Periodically, learners will accumulate more skills established in instructional lessons that need fluency building than there is time in the day or class period to practice, leaving no time to attend new establishing lessons. This is okay. At Morningside

Academy and Malcolm X College, learners may skip a day or two of new instruction until they reach fluency on the skills established in previous days. The number of skills that constitutes a backlog and hence an instruction-skip day will vary according to the amount of time devoted to daily practice. As a general rule of thumb, each skill requires about 10 to 15 minutes of daily practice. If 45 minutes of daily practice is allotted, learners would skip instruction if they needed to practice more than four skills that day.

11. Endurance building. Some skills need to be repeated at high frequencies for longer periods than others. For example, column addition and subtraction lasts 15 minutes or more when balancing a monthly checkbook statement. Reading a chapter in a textbook may last 45 minutes or more. Editing a paper may take two hours or more. Writing or typing may occur for a whole workday! We set *endurance aims* by multiplying the fluency aim by the number of additional minutes required for endurance. For example, our silent-reading fluency aim is 500 words per minute; our 15-minute silent-reading endurance aim is 500 x 15 = 7,500 words in 15 minutes.

Although reaching a fluency aim often predicts the skill will endure for longer periods, this is not always the case. Sometimes reaching a higher fluency aim produces endurance; other times learners need to practice the skill over the anticipated time period. (See Johnson & Layng, 1992, for a more in-depth discussion.) Judicious examination of the curriculum, particularly at composite skill junctures, is necessary to identify skills slated for *endurance building*. These skills should be written in their appropriate places in the sequence on the public progress charts so that the work won't be overlooked.

Sometimes learners will show endurance problems even while building fluency. For example, some children and adults diagnosed with so-called attention deficit disorder slack off in performance frequency during a one-minute timing. Teachers can ascertain suspected endurance problems during fluency building by keeping track of frequencies during successive ten-second intervals of the minute. If frequency diminishes, learners need to gradually build their rates over successively longer intervals up to one minute. Binder, Haughton, and Van Eyk (1990) have described excellent procedures for accomplishing this.

12. Applying. Once several component skills are fluent, instructors can schedule planned activities to promote the complex and creative behaviors characteristic of experts in a field. There are at least three kinds of activities to promote such contingency adduction. The first kind promotes a relatively simple transfer of training from one context to another, as when learners apply cumulative decoding skills learned in controlled basal readers to reading newspapers and magazines. A second kind of activity promotes chaining of separately taught repertoires, as when learners consult a dictionary or thesaurus for an adjective to describe a feeling as they write a composition about the winter holiday season.

A third kind of activity promotes a recombination of components, an intertwining of behavior, as when learners debate, solve a math problem, write a research paper, create a stock exchange simulation in their classroom, or publish a classroom newspaper. Planning these latter adduction activities involves assembly of skills from multiple domains, as component skills from seemingly disparate subject areas can be brought into play. For example, creating a stock exchange involves component skills learned from mathematics, language arts (e.g., persuasive writing), organizational skills, and reference skills. With such extended sequences of instruction, learners may take six months of instruction before they are ready to design a classroom newspaper or a personal budget; they may take two or more years of a course of study before it will be fruitful to arrange a debate, or the design of a school yearbook or scientific experiment.

Games and simulations can also be scheduled to bring together component repertoires. Thiagarajan and Stolovitch (Stolovitch & Thiagarajan, 1980; Thiagarajan, 1990; Thiagarajan & Stolovitch, 1978) have written extensively on this motivating approach to applying component skills.

13. Unintended contingency adduction: Monitoring for curriculum leaps. As mentioned earlier, curriculum leaps will occur at junctures other than during planned

activities, games, and simulations. Component skills will combine at odd times, in complex and unusual ways, additively or multiplicatively, to the higher complex skills exhibited by experts. Curriculum leaping will accelerate as learners progress through a course of study. Careful pretesting before each lesson will ensure that a learner doesn't miss a chance to skip instruction and accelerate progress.

14. Integrity between criteria and progress. Morningside instructors make the contingencies between reaching criterion and progress through the program explicit at each step, every minute of the day. Each reverberation through a three-term contingency, at each learning step—establishing, fluency building, endurance building, and applying—tells instructors to either go forward or to provide the extra instruction or practice necessary for learners to achieve success. Skinner (1968) estimated that 42,000 contingencies probably occurred during a 50-minute observation of his daughter's elementary school math lesson! Adjusting the learner's contact with the Morningside system on the basis of even a small fraction of the three-term contingency reverberations will make a big difference.

A Summary and Conclusion

Table 14.2 summarizes 14 daily operational steps to a successful implementation of the Morningside Model of Generative Instruction. Several places in the overview contained in this paper need to be magnified with greater attention to detail. Direct Instruction training, Standard Celeration Chart training, fluency-building procedures training, peer-coaching training, and instructional materials design training may all be necessary.

Besides the usual classroom materials, teachers will need timers for practice; one-third the number of learners in the program will be sufficient. Standard celeration charts are required, as well as a wall chart for marking progress through the program. If copying is at a premium, the teacher will also need sponges, Mylar, and marking pens. Since learners will perhaps be more self-directed than teachers have been used to,

Table 14.2 Summary of daily procedures in the Morningside Model of Generative Instruction

1. Arrange each class period to allow for new instruction, tool skill fluency building, and sprinting/fluency building of skills recently established.
2. Pretest learners at the beginning of the course and before each lesson. Place students in instruction precisely matched to their current performance levels.
3. Keep public progress records to direct daily learner activities and reinforce progress.
4. Build prerequisite tool skills to high frequencies, to facilitate the mastery of curriculum objectives.
5. Use Direct Instruction to establish new skills with learners who don't have fluent reading, writing, and studying skills; use programmed instruction, or texts with study guides in a PSI format with experienced learners.
6. Coach the gradual beginning of skill acceleration with sprinting exercises.
7. Use peer coaching and testing to build skills to fluency aims, those levels of performance that guarantee retention, endurance, and application following significant periods of no practice.
8. Monitor fluency building on standard celeration charts.
9. Use acceleration criteria: change fluency-building procedures whenever skills are not doubling their rates per week.
10. Include catchup days of all practice and no instruction whenever a learner gets backlogged.
11. Build skill endurance on certain skills and sets of component skills.
12. Arrange application activities for contingency adduction.
13. Skip instruction when students make curriculum leaps.
14. Guarantee that the contingencies for reaching criterion are met before learners move forward in the program—every minute of the day.

the teachers should make sure that the learners don't have to ask for materials.

Instructors have a threefold job during class sessions: alternating between teaching from scripts, troubleshooting with learners who need special fluency-building procedures, during sprinting or peer fluency building, and reinforcing learner-coach and learner-learner interactions. For a year the teacher will be busier teaching than ever before. Eventually, however, the system will perpetuate itself and the teacher will find that very little daily preparation is needed. If the teacher has never taught with others, there will be a need to adjust to the cooperative nature of the Morningside Model. Instructors have three levels of meetings with their coaches: daily meetings, using the wall chart as a point of departure; weekly

work sessions, with the wall chart and standard celeration charts governing their interactions; and monthly training sessions to teach new skills.

Anything can be taught with the Morningside Model. Its use, however, may be circumscribed by three factors: (1) local policies and procedures that place constraints on curriculum, teaching methods, or the availability and use of paraprofessionals and advanced learners; (2) courses in which goals cannot be specified; and (3) courses designed to select, rank, or sort learners (Sherman & Ruskin, 1978).

We have argued that certain generative effects—occurring as they do without direct intervention and often described as intuitive leaps, insight, problem solving, sudden realization, and expert knowledge—are a product of the contingency adduction of interacting alternative contingency sets that have in the past occurred independently at high frequencies. Although we have accumulating evidence to support our argument, the research effort and its application is in its infancy. Many questions still need to be answered, and more still have to be asked. The model we present here is designed to promote this research effort, increase its efficiency, and make it available to everyone.

References

ALESSI, G. (1987). Generative strategies and teaching for generalization. *Analysis of Verbal Behavior, 5,* 15–27.

ANDRONIS, P. T. (1983). Symbolic aggression by pigeons: Contingency coadduction. Unpublished doctoral dissertation. The University of Chicago, Department of Psychiatry and Behavior Analysis, Chicago.

ANDRONIS, P. T., Goldiamond, I., & Layng, T. V. J. (1983). "Symbolic aggression" by pigeons: Contingency coadduction. Paper presented at the meeting of the Association for Behavior Analysis, May, Milwaukee.

ARCHER, A., & Gleason, M. (1989). *Skills for school success, Books 3-7.* North Billerica, MA: Curriculum Associates.

BATES, S., & Bates, D. F. (1971). ". . . and a child shall lead them": Stephanie's chart story. *Teaching Exceptional Children, 3,* 111–113.

BINDER, C. V. (1977–1983). *Data Sharing Newsletter.* Nonantum, MA: Precision Teaching & Management Systems.

BINDER, C. V. (1988). Precision teaching: Measuring and attaining academic excellence. *Youth Policy, 10,* 12–15.

BINDER, C. V. (1991a). Morningside Academy: A private sector laboratory for effective instruction. *Future Choices, 3,* 62–63.

BINDER, C. V. (1991b). The ninth international precision teaching conference: Highlights and future directions. *Future Choices, 2,* 39–50.

BINDER, C. V., & Watkins, C. L. (1989). Promoting effective instructional methods: Solutions to America's educational crisis. *Future Choices, 1,* 33–39.

BINDER, C. V., & Watkins, C. L. (1990). Precision teaching and direct instruction: Measurably superior instructional technology in schools. *Performance Improvement Quarterly, 3,* 2–14.

BINDER, C. V., Haughton, E., & Van Eyk, D. (1990). Increasing endurance by building fluency: Precision teaching attention span. *Teaching Exceptional Children, 22,* 24–27.

BRONOWSKI, J. (1965). *Science and human values.* New York: Harper & Row.

CALIFORNIA Achievement Tests. (1985). Monterey, CA: CTB/McGraw-Hill.

CARNINE, D. (1992). The missing link in improving schools—reforming educational leaders. *Association for Direct Instruction News, 11,* 25–35.

CLARK, D. C. (1971). Teaching concepts in the classroom: A set of teaching prescriptions derived from experimental research. *Journal of Educational Psychology, 62,* 253–278.

DENAPOLI, J., & McKinny, P. (1992). Becoming an engineer of instruction: Advanced correction and firming procedures for Reading Mastery and Corrective Reading. A videotaped inservice program. Baldwinsville, NY: J/P Associates.

DONAHOE, J. W. (1986). How shall we understand complexity? In P. N. Chase & L. J. Parrott (Eds.), *Psychological aspects of language: The West Virginia lectures* (pp. 36–43). Springfield, IL: Charles C. Thomas.

DONAHOE, J. W. (1991). Selectionist approach to verbal behavior: Potential contributions of neuropsychology and computer simulation. In L. J. Hayes & P. N. Chase (Eds.), *Dialogues on verbal behavior* (pp. 119–145). Reno, NV: Context Press.

ENGELMANN, S. (1991). Why I sued California. *Direct Instruction News, 10*(2), 4–8.

ENGELMANN, S. (1992). *War against the schools' academic child abuse.* Portland, OR: Halcyon House.

ENGELMANN, S., & Bruner, E. (1988a). *Reading mastery I.* Chicago: Science Research Associates.

ENGELMANN, S., & Bruner, E. (1988b). *Reading mastery II.* Chicago: Science Research Associates.

ENGELMANN, S., & Carnine, D. (1982). *Theory of instruction: Principles and applications.* New York: Irvington Publishers.

ENGELMANN, S., & Carnine, D. (1992a). *Connecting math concepts A.* Chicago: Science Research Associates.

ENGELMANN, S., & Carnine, D. (1992b). *Connecting math concepts B.* Chicago: Science Research Associates.

ENGELMANN, S., & Carnine, D. (1992c). *Connecting math concepts C.* Chicago: Science Research Associates.

ENGELMANN, S., & Carnine, D. (1993a). *Connecting math concepts D.* Chicago: Science Research Associates.

ENGELMANN, S., & Carnine, D. (1993b). *Connecting math concepts E.* Chicago: Science Research Associates.

ENGELMANN, S., & Davis, K. L. S. (1991). *Reasoning and writing A.* Chicago: Science Research Associates.

ENGELMANN, S., & Grossen, B. (1993). *Reasoning and writing E.* Chicago: Science Research Associates.

ENGELMANN, S., & Hanner, S. (1988a). *Reading mastery III.* Chicago: Science Research Associates.

ENGELMANN, S., & Hanner, S. (1988b). *Reading mastery IV.* Chicago: Science Research Associates.

ENGELMANN, S., & Silbert, J. (1983). *Expressive writing I.* Chicago: Science Research Associates.

ENGELMANN, S., & Silbert, J. (1985). *Expressive writing II.* Chicago: Science Research Associates.

ENGELMANN, S., & Silbert, J. (1991). *Reasoning and writing C.* Chicago: Science Research Associates.

ENGELMANN, S., & Silbert, J. (1993). *Reasoning and writing D.* Chicago: Science Research Associates.

ENGELMANN, S., Arbogast, A. B., & Davis, K. L. S. (1991). *Reasoning and writing B.* Chicago: Science Research Associates.

ENGELMANN, S., Carnine, D., & Johnson, G. (1978). *Word attack basics.* Chicago: Science Research Associates.

ENGELMANN, S., Hanner, S., & Haddox, P. (1980). *Concept applications.* Chicago: Science Research Associates.

ENGELMANN, S., Osborn, J., Osborn, S., & Zoref, L. (1988a). *Reading mastery V.* Chicago: Science Research Associates.

ENGELMANN, S., Osborn, J., Osborn, S., & Zoref, L. (1988b). *Reading mastery VI.* Chicago: Science Research Associates.

EPSTEIN, R. (1985). The spontaneous interconnection of three repertoires. *Psychological Record, 35,* 131–143.

EPSTEIN, R. (1991). Skinner, creativity, and the problem of spontaneous behavior. *Psychological Science, 2,* 362–370.

ERAUT, M. (1970). *Fundamentals of elementary algebra.* New York: McGraw-Hill.

EVANS, J. L., Homme, L. E., & Glaser, R. (1962). The RULEG system for the construction of programmed verbal learning sequences. *Journal of Educational Research, 55,* 513–518.

FERSTER, C. B. (1953). The use of the free operant in the analysis of behavior. *Psychological Bulletin, 50,* 263–274.

FERSTER, C. B. (1965). Verbal behavior as magic. Paper presented at the 50th Anniversary Conference of the Graduate School of Education, the University of Pennsylvania, May. In C. B. Ferster, S. A. Culbertson, & M. C. P. Boren. (1975). *Behavior principles.* 2nd ed. (pp. 563–568). Englewood Cliffs, NJ: Prentice-Hall.

FERSTER, C. B., & Culbertson, S. A. (1982). *Behavior principles.* 3rd ed. Englewood Cliffs, NJ: Prentice-Hall.

FERSTER, C. B., & Skinner, B. F. (1957). *Schedules of reinforcement.* Englewood Cliffs, NJ: Prentice-Hall.

GAGNE, R. M. (1970). *The conditions of learning.* 2nd ed. New York: Holt, Rinehart & Winston.

GAGNE, R. M., & Brown, L. T. (1961). Some factors in the programming of conceptual learning. *Journal of Experimental Psychology, 62,* 313–321.

GAGNE, R. M., & Foster, H. (1949). Transfer to a motor skill from practice on a pictured representation. *Journal of Experimental Psychology, 39,* 342–355.

GILBERT, T. F. (1962). Mathetics: The technology of education. *Journal of Mathetics, 1,* 7–73.

GOLDIAMOND, I. (1974). Toward a constructional approach to social problems: Ethical and constitutional issues raised by applied behavior analysis. *Behaviorism, 2,* 1–84.

HAUGHTON, E. C. (1972). Aims: Growing and sharing. In J. B. Jordan & L. S. Robbins (Eds.), *Let's try doing something else kind of thing* (pp. 20–39). Arlington, VA: Council on Exceptional Children.

HAUGHTON, E. C. (1980). Practicing practices: Learning by activity. *Journal of Precision Teaching, 1,* 3–20.

HAUGHTON, E. C. (1981). REAPS. *Data Sharing Newsletter,* March. Nonantum, MA: Precision Teaching & Management Systems.

HEWARD, W. L., Courson, F. H., & Narayan, J. S. (1989). Using choral responding to increase active student response. *Teaching Exceptional Children,* Spring, 72–75.

JOB Training and Partnership Act, Pub. Law No. 97-300 (1985).

JOHNSON, D. M., & Stratton, R. P. (1966). Evaluation of five methods of teaching concepts. *Journal of Educational Psychology, 57,* 48–53.

JOHNSON, K. R. (1977). Proctor training for natural control. *Journal of Personalized Instruction, 2,* 230–237.

JOHNSON, K. R. (1990). Literacy training: JTPA adults and youth at risk. Presented at the Ninth International Precision Teaching Conference, November, Boston.

JOHNSON, K. R. (1991). About Morningside Academy. *Future Choices, 3,* 64–66.

JOHNSON, K. R. (1993a). *Morningside mathematics fluency.* Vols 1–3, Addition and subtraction math facts. 2nd ed., Seattle: Morningside Academy.

JOHNSON, K. R. (1993b). *Morningside mathematics fluency.* Vols 4–6, Multiplication and division math facts. 2nd ed. Seattle: Morningside Academy.

JOHNSON, K. R. (1993c). *Morningside mathematics fluency.* Vols 7 & 8, Reading and writing whole numbers and decimals. 2nd ed. Seattle: Morningside Academy.

JOHNSON, K. R. (1993d). *Morningside mathematics fluency.* Vol. 9, Place value, rounding, greater than less than. 2nd ed. Seattle: Morningside Academy.

JOHNSON, K. R. (1993e). *Morningside mathematics fluency.* Vol. 10, Addition and subtraction equations. Seattle: Morningside Academy.

JOHNSON, K. R. (1993f). *Morningside mathematics fluency.* Vol. 11, Addition and subtraction problem-solving. Seattle: Morningside Academy.

JOHNSON, K. R. (1993g). *Morningside mathematics fluency.* Vol. 12, Addition and subtraction computation of whole numbers 2nd ed. Seattle: Morningside Academy.

JOHNSON, K. R. (1993h). *Morningside mathematics fluency.* Vol. 13, Multiplication and division computation of whole numbers. 2nd ed. Seattle: Morningside Academy.

JOHNSON, K. R. (1993i). *Morningside mathematics fluency.* Vol. 14, Multiplication and division tool skills. Seattle: Morningside Academy.

JOHNSON, K. R., & Kevo, H. (1993). *Morningside phonics fluency.* Seattle: Morningside Academy.

JOHNSON, K. R., & Layng, T. V. J. (1992). Breaking the structuralist barrier: Literacy and numeracy with fluency. *American Psychologist, 47,* 1475–1490.

JOHNSON, K. R., & Ruskin, R. S. (1977). *Behavioral instruction.* Washington, DC: American Psychological Association.

JOHNSON, K. R., & Streck, J. (1993a). *Morningside mathematics.* Seattle: Morningside Academy.

JOHNSON, K. R., & Streck, J. (1993b). *Addition and subtraction equations: Equations and problem solving.* Seattle: Morningside Academy.

KELLER, F. S. (1968). "Goodbye, teacher . . ." *Journal of Applied Behavior Analysis, 1,* 79–89.

KINDER, D., & Carnine, D. (1991). Direct instruction: What it is and what it is becoming. *Journal of Behavioral Education, 1,* 193–214.

KLING, J. W., & Riggs, L. A. (1971). *Woodworth & Schlosberg's experimental psychology.* 3rd ed. New York: Holt, Rinehart & Winston.

LAYNG, T. V. J. (1988). Problem solving: The role of metaphorical extension. Paper presented at symposium, Problem Solving: The State of the Science. Association for Behavior Analysis convention, May, Philadelphia.

LAYNG, T. V. J. (1989). Problem solving: Elements made absent. Paper presented at symposium, Problem Solving: The State of the Science II. Association for Behavior Analysis, convention, May, Milwaukee.

LAYNG, T. V. J. (1991). A selectionist's approach to verbal behavior: Sources of variation. In L. J. Hayes & P. N. Chase (Eds.), *Dialogues on verbal behavior* (pp. 146–150). Reno, NV: Context Press.

LAYNG, T. V. J., & Andronis, P. T. (1984). Toward a functional analysis of delusional speech and hallucinatory behavior. *Behavior Analyst, 7,* 139–156.

LAYNG, T. V. J., Jackson, P. J., & Robbins J. K. (in preparation). Fluent thinking skills: A generative approach. Chicago: Malcolm X College.

LAYNG, T. V. J., Johnson, K. R., & Jackson, P. J. (1993). Literacy, numeracy and the Morningside Model of Generative Instruction: The role of staff training in rapid learner progress. Research report. Chicago: Malcolm X College.

LINDSLEY, O. R. (1972). From Skinner to precision teaching: The child knows best. In J. B. Jordan & L. S. Robbins (Eds.), *Let's try doing something else kind of thing* (pp. 1–11). Reston, VA: Council for Exceptional Teaching.

LINDSLEY, O. R. (1990). Precision teaching: By teachers for children. *Teaching Exceptional Children, 22,* 10–15.

LINDSLEY, O. R. (1991). Precision teaching's unique legacy from B. F. Skinner. *Journal of Behavioral Education, 1,* 253–266.

MARKLE, S. M. (1969). *Good frames and bad: A grammar of frame writing.* 2nd ed. New York: Wiley & Sons.

MARKLE, S. M. (1991). *Designs for instructional designers.* Champaign, IL.: Stipes Publishing Company.

MILLER, A. D., & Heward, W. L. (1992). Do your students really know their math facts? Using daily time trials to build fluency. *Interventions in School and Clinic,* November, 98–104.

MULLIS, I., Dorsey, J., Owen, E., & Phillips, G. (1991). *The state of mathematics achievement: Executive summary.* Washington, DC: National Center for Education Statistics, U.S. Department of Education.

PALMER, D. C. (1991). A behavioral interpretation of memory. In L. J. Hayes & P. N. Chase (Eds.), *Dialogues on verbal behavior* (pp. 261–279). Reno, NV: Context Press.

PALMER, D. C., & Donahoe, J. W. (1992). Essentialism and selectionism in cognitive science and behavior analysis. *American Psychologist, 47,* 1344–1358.

PENNYPACKER, H. S. (1992). Is behavior analysis undergoing selection by consequences? *American Psychologist, 47,* 1491–1498.

PENNYPACKER, H. S., Koenig, C. H., & Lindsley, O. R. (1972). *Handbook of the standard behavior chart.* Lawrence, KS: The Behavior Research Company.

PRECISION Teaching Project. (1984). *Precision Teaching Project Training Manual.* 8th ed. Longmont, CO: Sopris West.

PRESCOTT, G., Balow, I., Hogan, T., & Farr, R. (1986). *Metropolitan Achievement Tests MAT6.* San Antonio: Psychological Corporation.

REESE, E. P., & Johnson, K. R. (1975). *Defining, Observing and Recording Behavior: Instructor's Manual.* Department of Psychology, South Hadley, MA: Mount Holyoke College.

RESNICK, L. (1988). Teaching mathematics as an ill-structured discipline. In R. I. Charles & E. A. Silver (Eds.), *The teaching and assessing of mathematical problem-solving.* Hillsdale, NJ: Lawrence Erlbaum and National Council of Teachers of Mathematics.

SHERMAN, J. G., & Ruskin, R. S. (1978). *The instructional design library.* Vol. 13, The personalized system of instruction. Englewood Cliffs, NJ: Educational Technology Publications.

SHERMAN, J. G., Ruskin, R. S., & Semb, G. B. (1982). *The personalized system of instruction: 48 seminal papers.* Lawrence, KS: TRI Publications.

SKINNER, B. F. (1953). Some contributions of the experimental analysis of behavior to psychology as a whole. *American Psychologist, 8,* 69–78.

SKINNER, B. F. (1954). The science of learning and the art of teaching. *Harvard Educational Review, 24,* 86–97.

SKINNER, B. F. (1957). *Verbal behavior.* Englewood Cliffs, NJ: Prentice-Hall.

SKINNER, B. F. (1968). *The technology of teaching.* Englewood Cliffs, NJ: Prentice-Hall.

SKINNER, B. F. (1971). *Beyond freedom and dignity.* New York: Knopf.

SKINNER, B. F. (1981). Selection by consequences. *Science, 213,* 501–504.

SNYDER, G. (1992). Morningside Academy: A learning guarantee. *Performance Management Magazine, 10,* 29–35.

STAHL, S., & Miller, P. (1989). Whole language and language experience approach for beginning reading: A quantitative research synthesis. *Review of Educational Research, 59,* 87–116.

STEPICH, D. (1991). From novice to expert: Implications for instructional design. *Performance & Instruction, 30,* 13–17.

STOLOVITCH, H., & Thiagarajan, S. (1980). *Frame games.* Englewood Cliffs, NJ: Educational Technology Publications.

STRAIN, P. S. (Ed.). (1981). *The utilization of classroom peers as behavior change agents.* New York: Plenum Press.

SULZER-AZAROFF, B., & Mayer, G. R. (1991). *Behavior analysis for lasting change.* Fort Worth: Holt, Rinehart & Winston.

THIAGARAJAN, S. (1990). *Games by Thiagi.* Bloomington, IN: Workshops by Thiagi.

THIAGARAJAN, S., & Stolovitch, H. (1978). *Instructional simulation games.* Englewood Cliffs, NJ: Educational Technology Publications.

TIEMANN, P. W., & Markle, S. M. (1990). *Analyzing instructional content: A guide to instruction and evaluation.* Champaign, IL: Stipes Publishing Company.

VAN HOUTEN, R. (1980). *Learning through feedback: A systematic approach for improving academic performance.* New York: Human Sciences Press.

WATKINS, C. L. (1988). Project Follow-Through: A story of the identification and neglect of effective instruction. *Youth Policy, 10,* 7–11.

WHITE, O. R., & Haring, N. G. (1980). *Exceptional teaching.* 2nd ed. Columbus, OH: Charles E. Merrill, Inc.

CHAPTER 15

Teaching Children with Learning Problems

Ron Van Houten

It has been estimated that between 3% and 28% of school-aged children have learning disabilities (Bryant & McLoughlin, 1972). The wide variation between these estimates results from the use of different criteria to define the occurrence of learning disabilities. However, whatever the criteria employed for identifying children as exhibiting learning problems, many children are affected. Children with learning disabilities often require considerable extra resources. Even when these resources are available, many children continue to have difficulty in school. Behavior analysis provides a useful approach for assisting these children to succeed in school.

Children who have problems learning specific material can receive assistance in the regular classroom in numerous ways, such as through teacher's aides or peer tutoring. Specialist teachers working in a resource room or self-contained classroom can also provide assistance. Finally, applying the analytic principles and information obtained through research can increase the effectiveness of the persons delivering the services.

Setting the Stage for Learning

Individuals with learning problems experience difficulty and failure more frequently. If someone fails a task often enough, he or she will find the task aversive and will try to escape it. Because children with learning disabilities find a large portion of schoolwork difficult and often experience failure, they can be expected to engage in a good deal of escape behavior such as refusing to work and engaging the teacher in protracted discussions of non-academic issues. Therefore, it is essential that the teaching setting be designed to maximize opportunities for reinforcement and to minimize aversive features.

Flashcard Instruction

Flashcards are often valuable in teaching children with learning problems. Several variables have been shown to influence the effectiveness of flashcard instruction (Van Houten & Rolider, 1989). To be effective, teachers should be able to see the children's faces in order to monitor their attention to the task. Teachers should also be close enough for their social consequences to be effective. One way to minimize escape behavior is by using an effective seating arrangement. It has been demonstrated that children with learning problems learn more rapidly in a knee-to-knee seating arrangement without a desk or any other barrier between the teacher and the child. In this seating arrangement, the teacher and the student sit facing each other, with the teacher's knees outside the student's knees. Similar results can also be obtained by working at a round table, with the student and teacher facing each other at a 90-degree angle.

Another variable that can influence the effectiveness of flashcard instruction is the type of correction procedure employed. Van Houten and Rolider (1989) compared presenting missed items again after one interspersed item with presenting items in sequential blocks. They found that missed items were learned more rapidly when they were presented after one interspersed item.

Motivation

Nothing succeeds like success. Therefore, the best way to motivate children with learning problems is to design the curriculum so they can succeed. However, children also need to see their success. One way to enable them to do so is to provide quantitative graphic feedback (Van Houten, 1980). By using innovative data-based instructional techniques, students can easily master material they did not think they were capable of learning. The use of effective techniques, will make learning more reinforcing and thereby reduce the need to escape.

Many methods used to motivate students can also be used to reduce the escape behavior frequently exhibited by children with learning disabilities. Escape behavior can be minimized by providing the best instructional techniques available and by focusing initial instruction on tasks and techniques that provide a heavy density of success. Another way to minimize escape is to provide frequent praise for success and, in particular, to provide descriptive praise when students stick with the task despite encountering difficulty. Tell the students they are tenacious, and explain the meaning of the word.

Although an all-positive approach to teaching has been promoted by a number of educators, the data show that reprimands have more effect on the behavior of hyperactive children than praise (Abramowitz et al., 1992; Pfiffner, Rosen, & O'Leary, 1985; Rosen et al., 1984). Sometimes teachers do not reprimand when teaching, because they fear it will have a negative impact on learning. The data in Figure 15.1 show that children with learning problems acquired a task more rapidly when they received correction plus a simple reprimand (saying no) than when they received correction alone (Van Houten & Rolider, 1989).

Because inappropriate behavior can quickly get out-of-hand, the teacher must correct the behavior early in the chain. The moment the inappropriate behavior begins to occur, the teacher should interrupt it by establishing eye contact and making a brief firm, but not loud, statement of disapproval, followed by an immediate request to engage in the appropriate behavior (Van Houten & Doleys, 1983).

The timing of teacher reactions is another factor that can influence its efficacy. The most important skill needed to use reprimands effectively is to identify the behaviors associated with the onset of an episode. For example, the teacher should deliver disapproval after the first couple of words when it is apparent that the student is saying something that is clearly inappropriate, such as challenging the teacher's authority. Similarly, if a child clenches her fists before engaging in tantrum behavior, disapproval should follow fist clenching. Teachers can also give directions as reminders about how the student should behave before beginning activities that have been associated with escape behavior in the past.

When faced with noncompliance, it is also important to give firm directions. Many factors have been shown to be related to the level of compliance with requests. First, children are more likely to follow requests when the teacher demands eye contact before making the request (Hamlet, Axelrod, & Kuerschner, 1984). Second, the teacher can set the occasion for following a request that has been associated with noncompliance by first providing several other instructions that have a high probability of compliance (Mace et al., 1988). Third, a firm tone of voice influences compliance with requests. In general, people

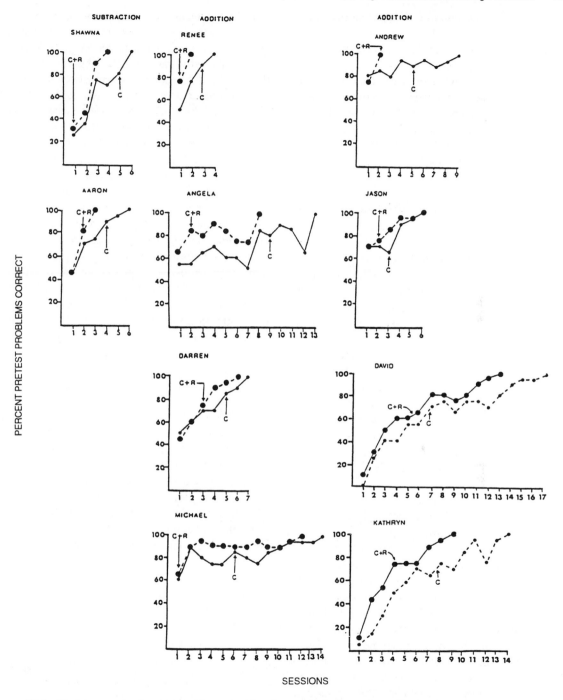

Figure 15.1. The percentage of pretest problems completed correctly during each session for the problem set taught with the simple correction procedure (C) and for the problem set taught with the correction plus reprimand (C + R) procedure.   SOURCE: *From "An Analysis of Several Variables Influencing Flashcard Instruction," by R. Van Houten & A. Rolider, 1989,* Journal of Applied Behavior Analysis, 22, *111–118. Copyright 1989 by* Journal for Applied Behavior Analysis. *Reprinted by permission.*

are less likely to respond to a request that involves a questioning inflection (an increase in pitch on the last word) than one that employs a more assertive inflection (a decrease in pitch on the last word or a steady low pitch). Fourth, whenever, the child emits the requested response, the teacher must provide immediate social reinforcement. For approval to be effective, the teacher must deliver it in a way the child finds reinforcing. Teachers can best discover these features through experience with each child.

Overcoming Problems with Labeling and Memory

Many young children have difficulty learning to label numbers, letters, and letter sounds. Memorizing number facts is a related problem, since it also involves matching a problem to a number. To make such discriminations, a child must learn to match written symbols, such as a letter or number, with a verbal response or another symbol. Although most young children learn to discriminate and label letters and numbers with little difficulty, some have problems learning to discriminate between mirror images while others have difficulty learning to label anything at all. Those children who have difficulty learning to label abstract stimuli such as numbers or letters benefit from specific behavioral teaching strategies.

Mediational Techniques

An alternative approach to teaching labeling involves the use of mediated transfer procedures. For example, if a child can label several colors correctly, the label for a particular color could be chained to the label for a particular number; for example, "Red three." If the numeral in question is then printed in the color associated with its verbal label, the child should be able to label the letter through a verbally mediated chain. If the child is also taught to match the numeral with its color, it should be possible to remove the prompt abruptly without disturbing the discrimination because the relevant stimuli would be linked via stimulus equivalence. For example, the number two could be written in red ink. The student would be shown the colored number at the start of the first teaching session

and told that it was "Red two." If he did not call it "red two" on any trial, he would be corrected: "No, this is red two. What number?" This correction procedure would also be followed on trials when the subject said the number (i.e., "two"). After the child correctly labeled the number for five consecutive sessions, the color would be dropped and the black number introduced. This procedure is represented schematically in Figure 15.2.

My colleague and I (Van Houten and Rolider, 1990) employed this procedure to teach number labels to three boys who had been identified by the school psychologists as having a learning disability. Initially, we taught these children with the method of flashcard instruction we found to be most effective (Van Houten and Rolider, 1989). The data in Figure 15.3 show that none of the boys made progress in learning the labels until the color-mediation procedure was introduced.

Other mediational procedures include size; characteristics of the line such as fat, thin, wavy, and spiked; or a pictogram that looks like the letter or number. Several examples are presented in Figure 15.4.

These techniques can be employed to teach number and letter labeling. I would not recommend using these techniques to teach letter names but instead would use them to teach the letter sounds. I have obtained good results teaching children the short vowel sounds needed to progress in direct instruction reading material. Because children with learning disabilities often have difficulty learning from unstructured reading programs that focus on learning sight words, I recommend using *Teach Your Child to Read in 100 Easy Lessons* (Engelmann, Haddox, & Bruner, 1983). Once the child can read the ten sounds introduced in the first 20 lessons, she is ready to start the book.

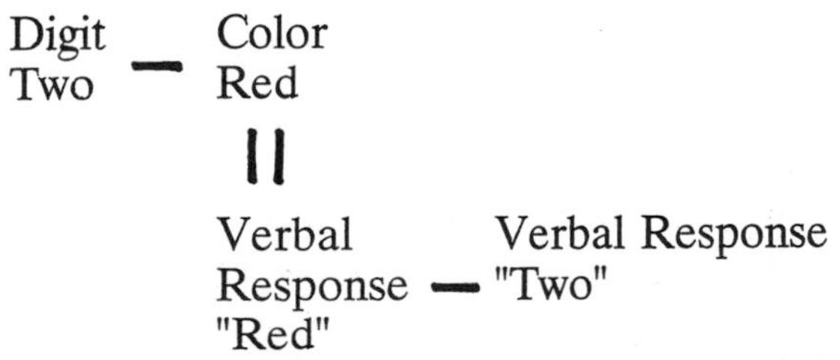

Digit — Color
Two — Red

‖

Verbal — Verbal Response
Response — "Two"
"Red"

Figure 15.2. A schematic representation of the color-mediation procedure.

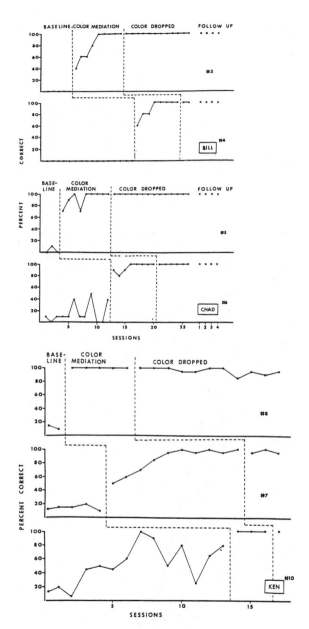

Figure 15.3. The percentage of correct labeling trials for three children during baseline and color-mediation conditions. SOURCE: *From "The Use of Color Mediation Techniques to Teach Number Identification and Single Digit Multiplication Problems to Children with Learning Problems," by R. Van Houten, & A. Rolider, 1990,* Education and Treatment of Children, 13, *216–225. Copyright 1990 by Education and Treatment of Children. Reprinted by permission.*

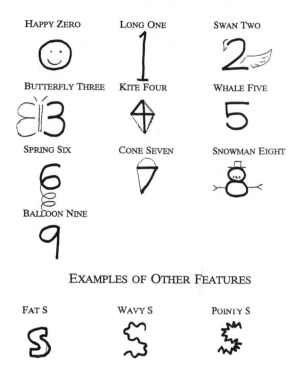

Figure 15.4. Examples of various other characteristics and features that can be used to mediate labeling responses.

The color-mediation approach can also be employed to teach children difficult number facts. Each number fact to be taught is printed in a different color on a flashcard. The answer to each problem is printed in its associated color on a separate card. The procedure involves three steps. First, the child is taught to look at the answer cards and say the color and the answer. For example, if the problem was 8 times 8, the student might say "Green sixty-four." This procedure is continued until the probe trial— "What answer is green?"—indicates that the child can respond with the answer when given the color. Second, the child is given practice with the colored number facts. Before presenting the problems the first time, the student is prompted to answer with the color and the number together; for example, "Green sixty-four." Third, without the cards the student is asked what color each of the multiplication problems are; for example, "What color is eight times eight?" After four days at 100% accuracy on this step, the student receives pretraining on the answer cards (step 1), and two blocks of trials with the colored flashcards (step 2), followed by four blocks of trials with the problems written in black. After two more sessions, the two blocks of trials using the colored flashcards are dropped and all six blocks of trials are presented using the flash-cards with black print. During all sessions when students are presented with black flashcards, they are instructed to answer by naming the color as well as the number. Finally, all color prompts are dropped.

We (Van Houten & Rolider, 1990) taught children multiplication facts using this procedure. The data presented in Figure 15.5 show that the children rapidly acquired the multiplication facts after the color-media-tion procedure was introduced and that the color-mediation procedure was dropped after the seventh and eighth sessions, respectively.

Memory Aids

The average person's memory span for auditory material is approximately seven items (Miller, 1956). Some children with learning disabilities have consid-erably short auditory memory spans. One would ex-pect auditory memory span to be important in the establishment of long verbal chains involved in spell-ing. Children should learn to spell short words more rapidly than long words. Students should also be better able to recall how to spell long words if the words are grouped in familiar units such as syllables, thus breaking a long verbal chain into several shorter

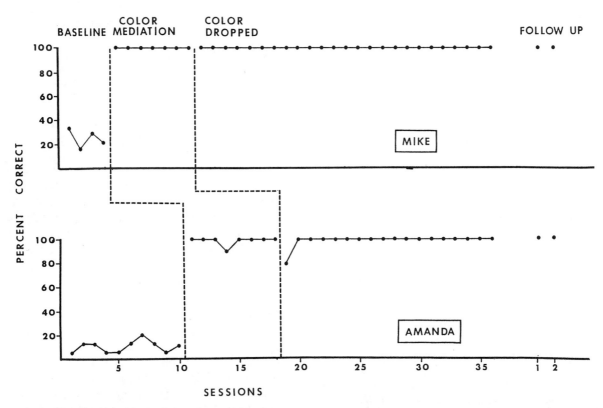

Figure 15.5. The percentage of number facts correct during each session. SOURCE: *From "The Use of Color Mediation Techniques to Teach Number Identification and Single Digit Multiplication Problems to Children with Learning Problems," by R. Van Houten, & A. Rolider, 1990,* Education and Treatment of Children, 13, *216–225. Copyright 1990 by Education and Treatment of Children. Reprinted by permission.*

chains. Finally, letters that frequently appear in the same order such as common prefixes, suffixes, and letter combinations should be learned as units.

My colleague and I (Van Houten & Van Houten, 1991) compared breaking words into syllables with teaching them intact. Five children who experienced problems learning to spell (two of them learning disabled) participated in this study. We taught the children using an oral recitation method. Each word was written on a 3-by-5-inch (7.65 cm x 12.70 cm) index card in a horizontal presentation format. The teacher and student sat facing each other in a knee-to-knee seating arrangement. The teacher held up a flashcard with the word facing the student and said the word. The student was instructed to say the word and orally spell it three times in succession. The experimenter then turned the card away from the student and asked her to spell it. If the word was spelled correctly, the teacher provided verbal praise and presented the next word, if not, he said no and repeated the procedure. After each word was taught, the teacher asked the student to spell the words taught that session; then using the same procedure, he retaught any word that was misspelled. After the student spelled all five words in the set, the teacher reviewed the words until the student correctly spelled each of the five words consecutively. If no errors were made, this criterion could be reached in 16 presentations. The words were all 8 to 12 letters long.

During the broken-word procedure, each word was printed as a series of letter groups separated by spaces of one letter width (e.g., *pro vin cial*). We determined the word division by written syllable, except in cases where individual syllables contained 5 or more letters. These syllables were further divided at the natural articulatory breaks when spelling (e.g., *nei gh bor ly* instead of *neigh bor ly*); this exception occurred in only 8% of the words used. We asked the students to spell the words orally, pausing briefly at each space.

The results of this study are presented in Figure 15.6. The introduction of the broken-word procedure led to a marked reduction in the number of presentations required to reach criterion, and the amount of time needed to teach the words. Performance was nearly errorless during the broken-word condition. We used an alternating treatments design in an earlier study. However, we found that children would generalize the broken-word strategy to the unbroken words after one or two sessions. Children would also break the word at a convenient point on their own. We have also seen students generalize other behavioral procedures, such as self-scoring and timing, to new tasks.

This approach could be employed to teach children to spell the words most frequently used when writing stories. Thomas (1979) developed a list of the 3,000 words most frequently used by Canadian adults and students in grades 2 through 8. The words are arranged on the list by decreasing probability of use. The first 100 words make up 59% of the total word count in student stories, whereas the entire list of 3,000 words accounts for 95% of the total word count. The method employed in this study could be used with a peer-tutoring approach to teach children the first 100 words. Other data indicate that some young children with learning problems benefit from breaking down words that only have five letters.

These results also support the value of Dixon's (1977) morphographic approach to teaching spelling, because the overlap of morphemes between words reduces the amount of "new" material making up long complex words. However, even direct instruction spelling programs require students to learn a set of root spelling words. Our instructional method (Van Houten & Van Houten, 1991) could prove useful for teaching these core words.

Teaching by Rules

Two hallmarks of the direct instruction approach are the explicit teaching of rules and strategies and the correction of rule misapplication by prompting the use of the rule (Gersten, Carnine, & White, 1984). Studies have also shown that simply requiring students to repeat a rule does not guarantee that the student will actually apply the rule (Carnine, Kameenui, & Maggs, 1982; Ross & Carnine, 1982). The need for guided practice suggests that, in order to be effective, rules must become incorporated as discriminative stimuli in behavioral changes.

Basic number facts are usually taught either by rote or by counting sets of objects. Baroody (1985) sug-

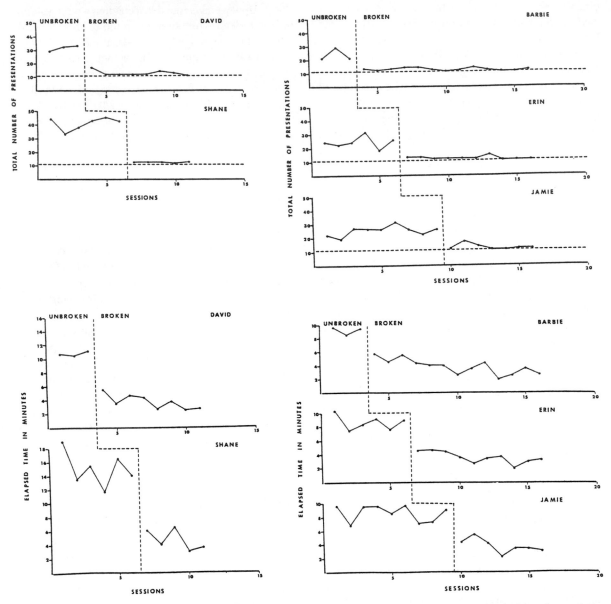

Figure 15.6. The total number of presentations required to teach the spelling words and the elapsed time in minutes during the unbroken and broken teaching conditions.   SOURCE: *From "The Effects of Breaking New Spelling Words into Small Segments on the Spelling Performance of Students with Learning Disabilities," by R. Van Houten, & J. Van Houten, 1991.* Journal of Behavioral Education, 1, *399–411. Copyright 1991 by the Journal of Behavioral Education. Reprinted by permission.*

gested that children use rules to learn number facts and that children who have a learning disability in math may not be able to learn these rules without explicit teaching. Baroody (1989) also provided evidence that children use rules to add 0 and 1 to a number.

The use of rules can reduce the number of facts a child needs to learn. For example, if children have learned addition facts, they can be taught subtraction facts involving a subtrahend of 7, 8, or 9 in the following way. First, they are told, "There is an easy trick to use when subtracting nine from a number in the teens. You simply add one to the digit above the nine." The student is then asked to state the rule: "What do you do when you subtract nine from a teen number?" If the student does not answer correctly, the correct response is prompted—"Add one to the digit above the nine"—and the teacher repeats the question. This procedure is repeated until the student can answer correctly.

On the first session, the student should be prompted to use the rule with each problem. On all subsequent sessions, a rule correction procedure should be employed. Whenever the student responds incorrectly, the experimenter asks the student to state the rule.

If the child cannot remember the rule, the teacher should prompt it. Then the teacher should go over the whole application of the rule: "Fifteen take away nine is six because the digit above the nine is five, and one plus five equals six."

I (in press) employed this rule procedure to teach students subtraction facts that involved subtrahends of 7, 8, and 9. In the first experiment, children from a self-contained classroom for children with learning disabilities served as participants. The results of this experiment, presented in Figure 15.7, show that all of the children learned the subtraction facts more rapidly when they were taught by a rule-teaching and correction strategy than when taught by a rote-teaching

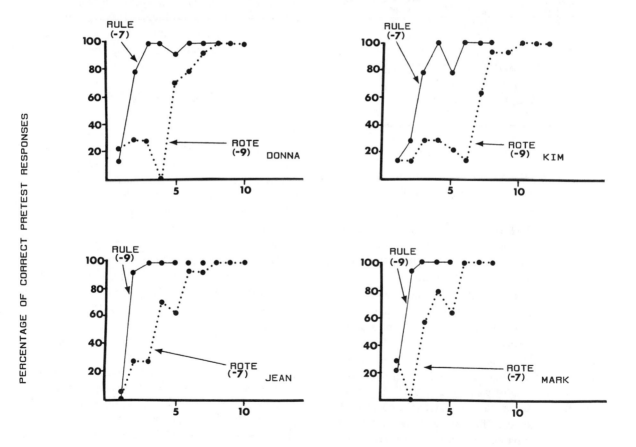

Figure 15.7. The percentage of pretest problems completed correctly during each session for the problem set taught using rules and the problem set taught using rote procedures.

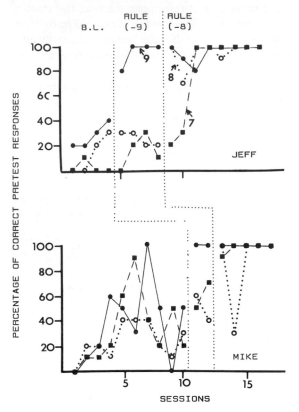

Figure 15.8. The percentage of pretest problems worked correctly by each student for the three problem sites.

approach. The results of another experiment, presented in Figure 15.8, show that children generalized the use of the rule to the third problem after being taught to use the rule for the first two problems. As in the spelling study, students will generalize effective strategies to new situations. Because children, including those with learning disabilities, are adaptive and can often apply strategies to new situations, they should be taught as many strategies as possible to help them compensate for any limitations.

Rules can also be used to teach the 0, 1, 2, 5, and 9 multiplication facts and to help children overcome problems with algorithms used for solving addition, subtraction, multiplication, division, and fraction problems.

Whitman and Johnston (1983) demonstrated that requiring students to state the rules involved in working subtraction problems with regrouping produced a marked increase in the percentage of problems worked correctly. Dunlap and Dunlap (1989) also increased students' accuracy in solving subtraction problems by having them fill out a procedures checklist following the completion of each problem.

It is important to employ parity when using rules that involve the student asking questions. For example, the following rule could be used to prompt students to regroup when solving subtraction problems. If the student answers the question "Is the bottom number larger than the top?" in the affirmative, then the answer to the question "Do I regroup?" is also yes. If the answer to the first question is no, then the answer to the second question is also no. A teacher can adapt this strategy to any problem that a student is having difficulty with, provided he or she can identify the rule that the student is using to solve the problem. This type of rule application is also employed to solve word problems in direct instruction mathematics programs.

Embedding Critical Material

Another technique that can improve the performance of children with learning disabilities is embedding critical information in the problem. One reason for the color-mediation procedure's effectiveness is that the mediating prompt is embedded in the symbol. In other words, the prompt is presented within the stimulus rather than outside the stimulus or in an extra-stimulus manner (Schreibman, 1975).

There are other ways to use embedded prompts to facilitate learning. For example, children can be taught to add sums up to 10 using an embedded prompt procedure. The first line of Figure 15.9 shows how set size can be embedded in the digits 2 through 5. Children can be taught to add two digits rapidly by saying the larger of the two numbers and then adding the dots onto the smaller number as the students touch the dots with their pencils. However, they must first be able to count on from a spoken number. For example, if the teacher says "Four," the students should be able to say "Five, six, seven, eight, nine, ten." If they have not mastered this skill, the teacher should teach it in isolation before introducing the dots. The teacher should also introduce the rule "Say the

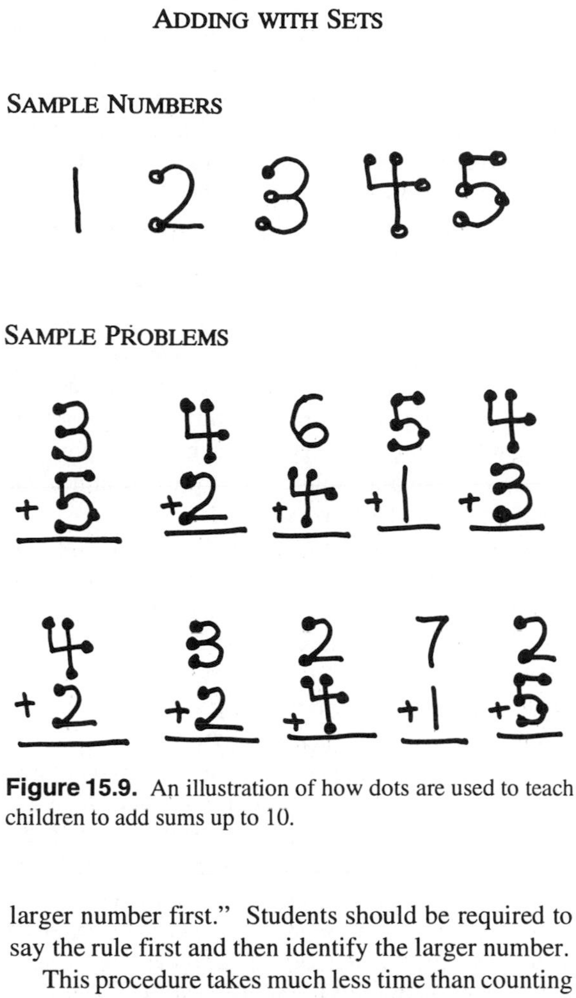

ADDING WITH SETS

SAMPLE NUMBERS

SAMPLE PROBLEMS

Figure 15.9. An illustration of how dots are used to teach children to add sums up to 10.

larger number first." Students should be required to say the rule first and then identify the larger number.

This procedure takes much less time than counting manipulative materials, and children continue to count the sets when the dots are abruptly removed by placing their pencil points where the dots used to be. Many children also begin to see that 3 plus 2 equals 5 because they see the five dots when they look at the problem. This new perception is more likely to occur when external counters are used or when the sets appear next to the digits.

Focusing on the Developing Rate

Children with learning disabilities are often moved on to new material before they have effectively mastered previous material. The use of a precision teaching approach helps ensure that the student has reached an adequate standard of competency on the material (Lindsley, 1990). It is often helpful to have children reread material until they can read it more fluently. A similar approach should be adopted with math and spelling fundamentals. Sometimes beginning with very short timing intervals (six or ten seconds) and gradually increasing the timing interval as the rate increases helps students avoid frustration.

Teaching Adaptive Behavior

Teaching a Child to Focus Attention

One way to teach a child to focus attention is to shape longer and longer periods of work on a task. First, the teacher gives the child a brief independent task, instructing him that he must finish without pausing for more than two seconds. The teacher explains that if he makes a mistake or pauses for more than two seconds he will have to begin the task again. Once the child is successful at sticking with a short task, the teacher can gradually increase the amount of work to be done. It is essential that the teacher make the student start again from scratch each time he makes an error or pauses for more than the set criterion. When the student is successful, the teacher provides praise, and when the student is unsuccessful, the teacher delivers a reprimand and asks the child to begin again.

To not frustrate the student when shaping attention to task, only those tasks that are at the mastery level should be used. The student must be able to complete the task in an errorless manner. If the child has no difficulty working simple addition problems with sums up to 10, it would be good to start with this task. Once the student can work independently at a reasonable rate for a long period, the teacher can fade out of the situation by gradually moving farther away from the student. At this point, it is important to determine how long it takes the child to complete the task. In the final phase, the teacher can instruct the student to start the task and then leave the room. The teacher should check on the student every minute. If the student has made a mistake or worked too slowly, as determined by the initial timed samples, the teacher should reprimand him and have him repeat the entire task. Gradually, the frequency of checks can be reduced until the student is completing the entire task on his own.

Once the student has mastered the first task independently, a second task should be introduced. The second task must be sufficiently different from the first to promote generalization to other tasks. If the first task is a math task, the second task could be a printing task or a reading task.

Teaching a Child to Accept Correction

Sometimes children with learning problems have difficulty accepting correction from teachers. These children can be taught to accept correction by setting up a structured teaching situation where frequent correction can be delivered for errors. The student should be told that the purpose of the exercise is to teach her to better handle correction. Before beginning, the teacher should speak with the student and motivate her to learn a more mature way to handle correction. This can often be accomplished by explaining how an inappropriate reaction to being corrected can lead to negative consequences in the future as well as in the present. Ask what would happen if she responded that way to a boss, a spouse, a police officer, or a friend. Immediately before providing correction, the teacher should prepare the student by telling her that he is about to provide correction. The teacher should also prompt the student how to respond. With some students, it may be necessary to role play how to respond to correction before expecting her to respond on her own. Once the student can handle correction when she is immediately prepared for it, the teacher should introduce a short delay between the prompt and providing correction. Gradually, the interval between the prompt and giving correction can be increased until the student is able to handle correction without prompts.

Summary

Children with learning disabilities often have a long history of failure and disappointment. To set the stage for successful learning, it is important to provide these students with an opportunity to succeed by using effective instructional procedures and offering one-on-one instruction. One of the most effective ways to motivate these children is to allow them to achieve success through the use of effective instructional techniques. It is also important to provide good feedback so these children can see their success. Many children with learning disabilities have learned ways to escape teaching situations. Teachers working with these children should know how to react to escape behavior.

Students with learning problems benefit less than their classmates when teachers use traditional instructional techniques. One way to overcome some problems is to use mediational procedures, especially when the student has difficulty with symbol learning or memorization. Memory aids such as breaking long material into smaller units can also prove useful when traditional methods fail.

Another helpful technique for teaching material that would otherwise require memorization is the use of rules and strategies. Direct instruction materials are often ideal for children with learning disabilities because they employ rules and strategies. However, direct instruction procedures may need to be adapted to meet the needs of a particular student.

Embedding prompts in the material to be taught is also helpful. Embedded prompts are more likely to become associated with the stimulus that is to ultimately acquire control over the student's academic responding. Students must also learn material to a mastery level. The emphasis on rate advocated by precision teaching researchers can prove very beneficial to children with learning disabilities.

Behavioral techniques can also be used to teach these children adaptive behavior such as focusing attention and accepting correction. An individualized approach is often required to solve these problems, and mediational chains such as notes and reminders can also be helpful.

References

ABRAMOWITZ, A. J., Eckstrand, D., O'Leary, S. G., & Dulcan, M. K. (1992). ADHD children's responses to stimulant medication and two intensities of a behavioral intervention. *Behavior Modification, 16*, 193–203.

BAROODY, A. J. (1985). Mastery of basic number combinations: Internalization of relationships or facts? *Journal for Research in Mathematics Education, 16,* 83–98.

BAROODY, A. J. (1989). Kindergartner's mental addition with single-digit combinations. *Journal for Research in Mathematics Education, 20,* 159–173.

BRYANT, N. D. (1972). Subject variables: Definition, incidence, characteristics, and correlates. In N. D. Bryant & C. E. Kass (Eds.). *Leadership Training Institute in Learning Disabilities* (vol. 1). Washington, DC: Bureau of Education for the Handicapped.

CARNINE, D. W., Kameenui, E. J., & Maggs, A. (1982). Components of analytic assistance: Statement saying, concept training, and strategy training. *Journal of Educational Research, 75,* 374–377.

DIXON, R. (1977). *Morphographic spelling.* Eugene, OR: E-B Press.

DUNLAP, L. K., & Dunlap, G. (1989). A self-monitoring package for teaching subtraction with regrouping to students with learning disabilities. *Journal of Applied Behavior Analysis, 22,* 309–314.

ENGELMANN, S., Haddox, P., & Bruner, E. (1983). *Teach your child to read in 100 easy lessons.* New York: Simon & Schuster.

GERSTEN, R., Carnine, D., & White, W.A.T. (1984). The pursuit of clarity: Direct instruction and applied behavior analysis. In W. L. Heward, T. E. Heron, D. S. Hill, & J. Trap-Porter (Eds.), *Focus on behavior analysis in education.* Columbus: Charles C. Merrill.

HAMLET, C. C., Axelrod, S., & Kuerschner, S. (1984). Eye contact as an antecedent to compliant behavior. *Journal of Applied Behavior Analysis, 17,* 381–387.

LINDSLEY, O. R. (1990). Precision teaching: By teachers for children. *Teaching Exceptional Children, 22,* 10–15.

MACE, C., Hock, M. L., Lalli, J. S., West, B. J., Belfiore, P., Pinter, E., & Brown, D. K. (1988). Behavioral momentum in the treatment of noncompliance. *Journal of Applied Behavior Analysis, 21,* 123–141.

MILLER, G. A. (1956). The magical number seven, plus or minus two: Some limits on our capacity for processing information. *Psychological Review, 63,* 81–97.

PFIFFNER, L. J., Rosen, L. A., & O'Leary, S. G. (1985). The efficacy of an all-positive approach to classroom management. *Journal of Applied Behavior Analysis, 18,* 257–261.

ROSEN, L. A., O'Leary, S. G., Joyce, S. A., Conway, G., & Pfiffner, L. J. (1984). The importance of prudent negative consequences for maintaining the appropriate behavior of hyperactive students. *Journal of Abnormal Child Psychology, 12,* 581–604.

ROSS, D., & Carnine, D. W. (1982). Analytic assistance: Effects of example selection, subjects' age and syntactic complexity. *Journal of Educational Research, 75,* 294–298.

SCHREIBMAN, L. (1975). Effects of within-stimulus and extra-stimulus prompting on discrimination learning in autistic children. *Journal of Applied Behavior Analysis, 8,* 137–138.

THOMAS, V. (1979). *Teaching spelling.* 2nd ed. Toronto: Gage Publishing.

VAN HOUTEN, R. (1993). Rote vs. rules: A comparison of two teaching and correction strategies for teaching basic subtraction facts. *Education and Treatment of Children, 16,* 147–159.

VAN HOUTEN, R. (1980). *Learning through feedback.* New York: Human Sciences Press.

VAN HOUTEN, R., & Doleys, D. M. (1983). Are social reprimands effective. In S. Axelrod & J. Apsche (Eds.), *The effects of punishment on human behavior.* New York: Academic Press.

VAN HOUTEN, R., & Rolider, A. (1989). An analysis of several variables influencing flashcard instruction. *Journal of Applied Behavior Analysis, 22,* 111–118.

VAN HOUTEN, R., & Rolider, A. (1990). The use of color mediation techniques to teach number identification and single digit multiplication problems to children with learning problems. *Education and Treatment of Children, 13,* 216–225.

VAN HOUTEN, R., & Van Houten, J. (1991). The effects of breaking new spelling words into small segments on the spelling performance of students with learning disabilities. *Journal of Behavioral Education, 1,* 399–411.

WHITMAN, T., & Johnston, M. B. (1983). Teaching addition and subtraction with regrouping to educable mentally retarded children: A group self-instructional training program. *Behavior Therapy, 14,* 127–143.

CHAPTER 16

The Opportunity to Respond and Academic Performance Revisited: A Behavioral Theory of Developmental Retardation and Its Prevention

Charles R. Greenwood
Betty Hart
Dale Walker
Todd Risley

At the 1982 conference on Behavior Analysis in Education held at Ohio State University, our group at the Juniper Gardens Children's Project reviewed the results of a program of interrelated descriptive and experimental studies. Based on these studies, we argued that the frequently observed delays in the academic competence of inner-city, low-SES (socioeconomic status) students was a function of their academic instruction and their teachers' use of instructional strategies that failed to optimally engage the students' academic behavior for sufficient periods each day (Greenwood, Delquadri, & Hall, 1984). The instruction used with these students was not discriminative for reinforcement (that is, teachers provided low rates of approval relative to higher rates of disapproval), the instructional stimuli did not control relevant academic responding (e.g., high levels of spelling inaccuracy and low oral reading rates were observed following instruction), and the stimuli that were effective controllers of academic responding were used infrequently (e.g., less than the scheduled amount of time for reading or spelling instruction was actually provided along with few specific opportunities to respond to academic trials).

The cumulative effect of this instruction was lower rates of daily academic behavior in the classroom and lower rates of academic growth and achievement. As evidence, a group of inner-city fourth-grade students who were lower in measured IQ and standardized achievement were also engaged less in active academic behaviors (12 minutes less per day), than a similarly aged group of suburban students. We defined academic engagement in terms of a composite of seven active responses—writing, academic game play, reading aloud, silent reading, academic talk,

This research was supported by grant No. 03144 from the National Institute of Child Health and Human Development to the University of Kansas. Additional support was obtained through the Kansas Mental Retardation Research Center. The ideas expressed in this chapter are exclusively those of the authors and not the agency. We would like to thank the project staff during the past 10 years: Carmen Arreaga-Mayer, Judith J. Carta, Granger Dinwiddie, Marleen Elliott, Rebecca Finney, Verona Hughes, Frank Kohler, Betsy Leonard, David Rotholz, Barbara Terry, and Debra Kamps. We acknowledge the help of our office staff: Carmen Root, Betty Smith, Alva Beasley, Bernadine Roberts, and Mary Todd. Thanks also to observer team directors Dan Schulte and Debra Montagna and to the observer team, to the school staff, including research director Don Moritz, and to the principals, teachers, parents, and students of the Kansas City, Kansas district USD #500.

Reprints of this chapter can be obtained from Dr. Charles R. Greenwood at the Juniper Gardens Children's Project, 1614 Washington Boulevard, Kansas City, Kansas 66102.

answering questions, and asking questions—that had been demonstrated to be correlates of academic achievement as measured by standardized tests (Greenwood et al., 1981). When compounded over an entire schoolyear, the total difference in engaged time was the equivalent of 1.6 additional school months per year. Beyond the usual explanations of the significantly lower levels of measured achievement and IQ of these students in the literature at this time—such as undereducated parents, neighborhood, race, and other socioeconomic factors—we suggested that this daily difference in classroom engagement was one causal factor, one that was alterable through changes in instruction (Greenwood, Delquadri, & Hall, 1984).

In our related intervention work with teachers, we described strategies for solving this stimulus control problem in terms of *increasing the opportunity to respond*. This term logically conveyed the need to promote higher rates of academic behavior for all students for longer periods by ensuring that instruction occasioned active academic responding in the classroom.

Opportunity to Respond

The opportunity to respond is a metaphorical description of the three- and four-term contingency transactions that make up caregiving, parenting, and instruction. It refers specifically to Skinner's (1953, 1968) definition of teaching: "The arrangement of contingencies of reinforcement . . . [from which the effects are] the expedition of learning, the hastening of the appearance of behavior which would otherwise be acquired slowly or . . . the appearance of behavior which might otherwise never occur" (1953, pp. 64–65). Thus, classroom instruction may be arranged to set the occasion for important behaviors in one of two ways: "In the first place, stimuli which have already become discriminative are manipulated in order to change probabilities [of behaviors] . . . In the second place, we may set up a discrimination in order to make sure that a future stimulus will have a given effect when it appears" (pp. 109–110).

The opportunity-to-respond construct describes this functional analysis of teaching and classroom academic behavior in terms that teachers can easily understand in the context of efforts to improve instruction.

> Opportunity to respond can be defined as the interaction between (a) teacher formulated instruction . . . (the materials presented, prompts, questions asked, signals to respond, etc.), and (b) its success in establishing the academic responding desired or implied by materials, the subject matter goals of instruction. [Greenwood, Delquadri, & Hall, 1984, p. 64]

When used to improve teaching, opportunity to respond assumes an analysis of the environmental arrangement as described by Skinner, including the antecedent events that have a strong establishing or occasioning relationship to students' academic responding; for example, the scheduling of instruction time during which academic subject matter is taught, supporting objects and materials and classroom organization as they are all applied in the effort to guide and select student responding. Opportunity to respond also implies the use of parenting and teaching tactics within interactions that involve presenting, questioning, correcting, and consequating behaviors that ensure that students have made the response and received reinforcement for doing so. It also implies a focus on active rather than passive student responding with respect to content goals (e.g., topics or subject matter to be learned).

The opportunity-to-respond construct was initially based on informal classroom observations followed by studies that employed direct observational assessment and curriculum-based and standardized measures of achievement. Emerging from and consistent with the strategy of increasing the opportunity to respond to improve achievement have been a number of instructional procedures including group-oriented contingencies, classwide peer tutoring, and cooperative learning groups. Efforts to record and analyze teachers' three-term interactions (Greer, McCorkle, & Williams, 1989; Narayan, Heward, & Gardner, 1990; Selinske, Greer, & Lodhi, 1991) have also emerged as a basis for improving instructional intervention.

In the intervening ten years, this original work with fourth-graders has been extended to the lifelong analysis of academic development, including a ten-year study of the effects of classwide peer tutoring, and to the problems of teaching special populations (Greenwood, Carta, & Atwater, 1991; Kamps et al., 1989). Work with special populations has included procedures to improve the instruction of children with autism and developmental disabilities (e.g., Kamps et al., 1991a, 1991b) instruction of children in preschool special education (Carta et al., 1990) or children at risk for special education placement (Cooper & Speece, 1990), and the functional assessment of instruction to ESL (English as a second language) students (Arreaga-Mayer & Tapia, 1991). From this work, a behavioral theory of academic development and instruction has emerged.

Scope of the Problem

We face the problem of well-known, persistent, diverging developmental trajectories in basic skills; that is, the gap between low- and high-SES students. This gap is not just a static difference in the skills of the school, however; with increasing age, it becomes a gap in academic competence, standard of living, and quality of life that is transmitted from one generation to the next. The lifelong effects of poor instruction for the learner and society are transferable to the larger society in terms of a lower collective pool of basic academic skills. Although several empirically based, comprehensive models of schooling have developed in recent years, they have not addressed instruction sufficiently to contribute to a measurable improvement in practice or outcome (e.g., Reynolds, 1991). What is the behavioral-environmental explanation for the transmission of lower academic skills from one generation to the next, and why is it so intractable in the face of efforts to prevent and ameliorate it?

We know from research that the gap between children from low-SES versus high-SES families emerges very early in terms of home language learning, mental age, and academic readiness skills (Hart & Risley, 1992; Walker et al., 1991), followed developmentally by an expanding gap in basic academic skills, early academic failure, school dropout, and parenthood—it is an intergenerational cycle (Greenwood et al., 1992). What we know about this form of developmental retardation

in poor children at the Juniper Gardens Children's Project has been learned through 15 years of research designed to alter it (Hall et al., 1989; Greenwood et al., 1992). This work sought to determine the long-term effects of systematic interventions in the school (Greenwood, 1991a, 1991b; Greenwood et al., in press) and the precursors of academic development in the home (Hart & Risley, 1992; Walker, Carta, Greenwood, Hart, & Taylor, 1991).

In this work, we used observational assessment protocols to determine the quality of language that parents expressed to their children in the home and the types of academic subject matter taught in school. The behaviors of the child or student—those reflecting active engagement and participation in the activities presented by the home and school environments—were also operationalized, validated, and assessed in the same prospective design. What follows is a synthesis of what has been learned.

A Progression of Developmental Retardation

Research has led to a hypothetical intergenerational progression of developmental retardation as illustrated in Figure 16.1. The key concept reflected in this progression is how a cumulative experiential deficit (defined as hours of engagement with relevant topics/subject matter) is transmitted to low-SES children over the preadult life span. This progression describes one particular path for developmental retardation in terms of low academic achievement and early school failure. The lines in the progression include: (1) Limiting parenting practices that produce low rates of vocabulary growth in early childhood (Hart & Risley, 1992), (2) instructional practices in middle childhood and adolescence that produce low rates of academic engagement during the schoolyears (Greenwood, Delquadri, & Hall, 1989), (3) lower rates of academic achievement and early school failure, (4) early school dropout, and finally (5) parenthood and continuance of the progression into the next generation.

As of this writing, all of the links in this progression are supported by collected data except for those between school dropout and parenthood (Greenwood, Delquadri, & Hall, 1989; Greenwood et al., in press;

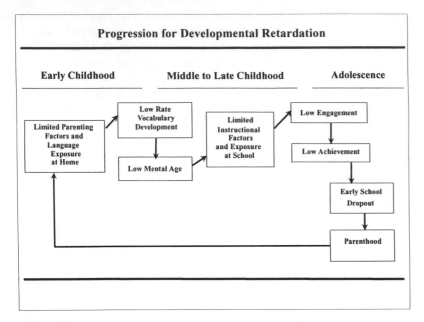

Figure 16.1. Progression of developmental retardation.

Hart & Risley, 1989, 1992; Walker et al., 1991). The school dropout–parenthood link, while theoretically consistent with the literature, is still untested and remains for future research. Although this progression represents one of undoubtedly many specific developmental pathways leading to developmental retardation, it does represent an increasingly sophisticated guide for knowing where, when, and why environmental variables affect behavior and outcomes. It represents our progress in assessing environmental influences on developmental retardation and in developing the strategic means of preventing it.

Review of Longitudinal Findings

To support the validity of this progression of developmental retardation, the longitudinal study of infants had to produce a number of findings; for example, (1) groups divergent in SES factors should also differ in trajectories of language production and use at home; (2) these language differences should correlate with concurrently assessed standardized measures of language, IQ, and academic readiness or achievement;

and (3) these early differences (36 months) should predict later achievement differences in first, second, and third grades.

A number of specific findings from the longitudinal study of schooling were also necessary for groups divergent in SES: (1) the groups should be divergent in academic achievement and IQ at first grade, (2) the trajectories of academic development of these groups over elementary and secondary schooling should indicate a wider gap as indicated by differences in trajectories, (3) vocabulary-based differences in reading and language achievement should be noted, (4) differences in the groups' trajectories of engagement with topically relevant subject matter should be noted, and (5) there should be acceleration in the engagement trajectory for a low-SES instructional intervention group, which corresponds to the onset of intervention, followed by a reduction in the achievement gap, including reading and vocabulary achievement.

Early Language Development: Home to School
Early work with preschool language intervention for low-SES children led to a hypothesis concerning

the earliest precursors of language learning in the home (Hart & Risley, 1981, 1989). Consequently, we undertook a longitudinal study (Hart & Risley, 1992) of 45 infants and their families (between 7 to 36 months of age in the home) and their early schooling (between preschool through third grade). The results of this study are shown in Figure 16.2.

Overall, a number of the findings we had expected to find were supported. Differential growth trajectories in spoken vocabulary in children from 7 to 36 months of age were early precursors of diverging growth trajectories in academic skills in the early elementary school grades (Hart & Risley, 1992). Based on our home observation data from 1982 to 1987, we found that parents of low-SES children expressed to their children less-varied vocabularies during the first 36 months of life, and these children in turn had smaller vocabularies than the high-SES children at 36 months. The parents of low-SES children interacted with their children less often, taught less often, asked fewer questions, were less responsive, and were more likely to prohibit explora-

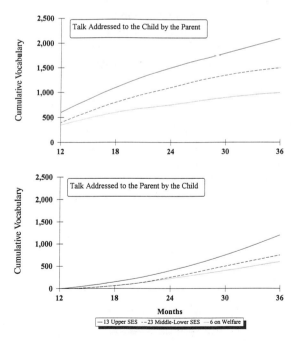

Figure 16.2. Child and parent trajectories of vocabulary use in the context of home interaction.

tion by the child. Hart and Risley's (1992) findings supported the argument that conditional variations of exposure to language in the home (as influenced by SES-related factors) are strongly correlated with children's subsequent IQ and language production.

Data from the subsequent public schooling experience (kindergarten through third grade: 1988–1992) of this cohort indicated that low-SES children, compared to high-SES children, were provided less time on academic subject matter (e.g., reading, math, language arts), on the order of 12 minutes less per day or 48 cumulative hours less. These students performed significantly lower on curriculum-based and standardized test measures of mental age, vocabulary, reading achievement, and other basic academic skills (Walker et al., 1991).

Vocabulary use (VU), mean length of utterance (MLU), and measured IQ at 36 months of age were highly correlated to the Peabody Picture Vocabulary Test (PPVT, a measure of receptive language) some two years later at kindergarten (rs = 0.76, 0.70, and 0.72) and four years later at the end of first grade (rs = 0.74, 0.74, and 0.77). Also, the two home-language observational measures (VU and MLU) and measured IQ at 36 months were moderately correlated to standardized reading, mathematics, and language tests at both kindergarten and first grade. For example, MLU at 36 months accounted for 59% of the variance in the Peabody Vocabulary standard score taken at the end of first grade. Using a model that combined MLU, measured IQ, and family income, it was possible to predict 67% of the variance in the end-of-first-grade Peabody Vocabulary score [R = .82, $F(3,19)$, p = .001]. The correlations in Table 16.1 provide a summary of these relationships.

The most important findings based on these results from observational studies in the home and in the home-school transition strongly suggested that early parenting in low-SES families adversely affected language use and development and that students' subsequent language functioning in school was predictable from natural language data collected in the home between 7 and 36 months of age. Other significant elementary school correlates of home language usage were the students' measured IQ, socioeconomic status, and achievement. Additionally

Table 16.1 Summary of correlations among 36-month predictors of kindergarten and first grade functioning

	36-Month Predictors				Kindergarten					First Grade	
Variables	Vocabulary Use (VU)	Mean Length of (MLU)	IQ	Income	PPVT	Word	Rcomp	Math	Lang	PPVT	T Read
VU	1.00										
MLU	.85**	1.00									
IQ	.64**	.70**	1.00								
Income	.31	.28	.45*	1.00							
PPVT	.71**	.70**	.72**	.39*	1.00						
Word	.62**	.55**	.50**	.04	.49**	1.00					
Rcomp	.43*	.36*	.42*	-.05	.38*	.78**	1.00				
Math	.47**	.38*	.39*	.21	.42*	.65**	.55**	1.00			
Lang	.42*	.23	.33	-.06	.25	.76**	.61**	.65**	1.00		
PPVT	.74**	.74**	.77**	.49**	.90**	.58**	.45*	.56**	.27	1.00	
TRead	.32	.37*	.33	.12	.56**	.54**	.52**	.54**	.42*	.41*	1.00

*r=0.355, p < .05
**r = 0.456, p < .01

Note: Metropolitan Achievement Test (Normal Curve Equivalents): Word = Word recognition, Rcomp = Reading comprehension, Math = Mathematics, Lang = Language; Comprehensive Test of Basic Skills (normal curve equivalents): TRead = Total reading.

evident for those students in elementary school, who were at a disadvantage because of lower language functioning, was the lack of differential academic or language programming at school. In fact, based on the ecobehavioral observational data collected at school, as a group they experienced significantly less daily time devoted to instruction in academic subjects. Thus, in combination, these relationships among home language, ability, early school achievement, and schooling experiences support an environmental process in both the early home and early schooling factors by which students are taught less of the subject matter, thus placing the students at risk for lower performance and early school failure.

Academic Development: Schooling

Early work with a second cohort of students indicated a similar gap between low- and high-SES students attending low- versus high-SES schools in their reading-achievement growth trajectories in first through eighth grades (see Figure 16.3). An achievement gap was present as early as October of first grade, *a developmental difference equal to 0.3 of a grade level at school entry*. At the beginning of sixth grade, we observed a greater gap, 3.8 versus 7.3 grade

levels, now a *developmental gap of 3.5 grade levels*! In eighth grade, we observed a difference of 5.5 versus 11.3, now *a developmental gap of 5.8 grade levels*. We observed similar gaps in developmental trajectories in mathematics and language arts achievement (Greenwood, Delquadri, & Hall, 1989; Greenwood et al., in press).

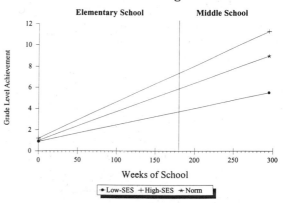

Figure 16.3. Reading achievement growth trajectories for SES groups.

Most important, we found that (1) lower exposure to academic subject matter and (2) lower engagement in academic behaviors played a major role in explaining the gap in academic learning between low- and high-SES children. For example, consider the 180 weeks (Grades 1–5) that define the elementary school experience and the additional 108 weeks (Grades 6–8) that define the middle school influence on students' learning of basic academic skills. As illustrated in Figure 16.4, differences between these students in low- and high-SES schools were directly related to the amount of time academic subject matter was taught and the amount of time in which students were actively engaged (Greenwood, 1991a).

In a 7-hour schoolday at the elementary level (Greenwood, 1991a), low-SES students were taught basic academic subjects for 2.6 hours compared to 2.7 hours for high-SES students (a 6-minute daily difference). Within these different exposure levels, low-SES students were engaged less, 1.3 hours per day compared to 1.7 hours per day for the high-SES group (a 24-minute daily difference). At the middle school level (Greenwood et al., in press), there was no longer a difference between SES groups in the time exposed to academic subjects and the SES gap in engagement had narrowed. Low-SES students were now engaged 1.1 hours per day compared to 1.3 for high-SES students in middle school (a 12-minute daily difference).

When expressed across elementary and middle school (see Figure 16.5), these daily differences in exposure and engagement become diverging trajectories that reflect lasting differences in functional educational histories, based on total accumulations of 1,143 versus 1,507 hours (elementary) and 1,715 versus 2,190 hours (middle) for low- versus high-SES students. At the elementary level alone, we see a cumulative difference of 364 hours by the end of elementary school. At these rates, and assuming no change in their educational program, low-SES students would need to attend school an extra 1.6 years (364 hours/6.5 hours per week = 57 weeks/36 weeks per schoolyear) to attain the same educational experience. The trajectories for these students through middle school (Grades 6–8) show that even though the

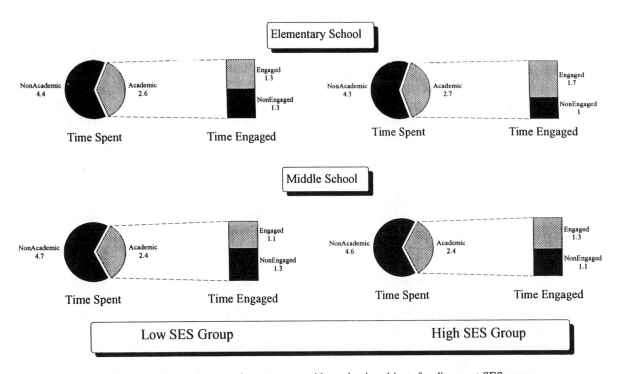

Figure 16.4. Daily hours of exposure to and engagement with academic subjects for divergent SES groups.

Cumulative Hours Engaged With Academic Subjects

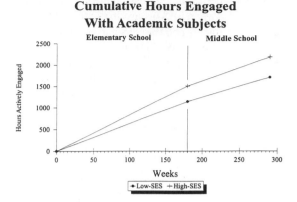

Figure 16.5. Trajectories of cumulative hours engaged with academic subjects for divergent SES groups.

slopes differentiating the SES groups have narrowed at middle school, the cumulative gap is still widening.

Implications of the Problem and Its Cause

Collectively, these results from two separate cohorts of children at different ages investigated across ten years of development support the existence of the progression of retardation. As noted, SES differences corresponded to differences in vocabulary development corresponding to diverging trajectories of engagement and achievement in school. Important linkages between the findings of the two studies include those between language, engagement, and achievement.

These results illustrate how, before entering school, poor children acquire less educational experience that is relevant to academic skill in their homes and subsequently within their schooling. The results also expand the notion of opportunity to respond to include a developmental, life-span dimension that crosses multiple caregiving environments over time. In these terms, the results point to a progressive, cumulative, experiential deficit in language and academic skills caused by variations in exposure and engagement that, in turn, are regulated by the organization of low-SES environments. This deficit is one of engagement in

relevant subject matter, a requisite for skill acquisition, use, and improvement. From these data, clear implications for prevention and remediation have emerged:

1. Environmental change must be systematic, comprehensive, ongoing, and longlived. Temporarily improved environments will have local effects on skill acquisition but will not markedly change developmental trajectories.
2. Prevention that begins early and continues through adulthood has the best prospect of success because of smaller cumulative deficits and lower costs associated with mounting the intervention commensurate to overcome the deficit.
3. The cumulative deficit can be quantified in terms of topically relevant hours of engagement and may be used to guide the necessary intensities of a prevention effort.
4. To achieve the quantity of topically relevant engagement necessary to prevent this form of retardation, an inventory of coordinated, validated multipurpose procedures configured as a systematic prevention intervention package will be needed.
5. Interventionists will need new methods of assessment to monitor both the component and total prevention effort in order to ensure that the children start and remain on the correct trajectory.
6. Intervention that begins late will have markedly less prospects of success because it must deal with a greater cumulative experiential deficit. Remediation will have to be designed to dramatically accelerate exposure and engagement above the normal developmental trajectory, so that children learn more in less time. The shorter the delay in the onset of intervention, the less intensive the effort to accumulate the hours needed to offset a developing experiential deficit.

Is Prevention Possible? What Will It Take?

From the analyses and from the body of intervention research conducted nationally and at the Juniper Gardens Children's Project over the last 26 years (e.g., Bryant & Ramey, 1987; Becker, 1988; Infant Health and Development Program, 1990; Garber, 1988), the prevention of developmental retardation appears scientifically and technically possible. The design needed to accomplish this task will entail a systematic, intergenerational prevention effort within the home, day care, preschool, school, and community environments of young families and children at risk. Planning such a large-scale effort will also require the necessary assessment protocols. The configuration of one such effort, based on procedures previously developed at Juniper Gardens over the past 26 years, is illustrated in Table 16.2.

What Remains to Be Done?

For a life-span prevention effort to work, however, a number of scientific and policy issues remain to be addressed. First, such efforts need to be guided by an integrative theoretical model linked to the functional analysis of behavior and based on data from longitudinal data sets and empirical models of parenting and schooling. Second, methods for constructing and delivering comprehensive, long-term services and education to low-SES families based on the integrative model will be needed. Third, because the poverty rate has increased over the past decade (e.g., Johnson, Sum, & Weill, 1992), the need for such programs and the national benefit to be gained by their success is increasingly less controversial. However, establishing public understanding of an intergenerational solution to the problem and demonstrating the means necessary for implementing comprehensive prevention programs remain major challenges for those engaged in this work, particularly when compared to prevailing views or initiatives that address this problem (e.g., America 2000).

Discussion and Conclusion

As indicated in this and the other chapters in this book, applied behavior analysis has made and continues to make a major contribution to improving educational outcomes through improved caretaking procedures, practices, and programs in the home and school. As important, however, is our improving understanding of the toxic environmental-behavioral processes that lead to developmental retardation in low-SES families and schools, and alternately, those processes that may be used to prevent it.

The important early work in behavior analysis solved problems that were responsive to straightforward adjustments in either contingencies or setting variables in the immediate environment. We learned that these adjustments resulted in important changes, specifically in the acquisition of knowledge and development of technologies where none previously existed (Greenwood et al., 1992). However, in the continuing pursuit of solutions to the larger personal and societal problems arising from poverty, research

Table 16.2 Potential configuration of a systematic, comprehensive prevention program

Age Group	Domain	Setting	Procedures/Programs
Infants/toddlers	Language	Home	Home intervention
		Day care	Infant center
		Day care	Toddler center
Preschoolers	Preacademics	Preschool	Turner House preschool model
		Day care	After-school day-care model
	Survival skills	Preschool	Classroom Survival Skills Model
School-aged children	Academics	School	Classwide responsive teaching
		School	Classwide peer tutoring
		Home	Home tutoring program
		Community center	After-school program. Summer tutoring program
			Parent education program
Adults	Social behavior	Home	Responsive parenting
		Community center	Urban survival skills

is increasingly focusing on the behavioral effects of the more complex problems and issues produced by the interaction of multiple variables from multiple sources and over long periods of life span (i.e., one's history of behavioral development). Applied behavior analysis is only beginning to acquire a life-span, let alone an intergenerational, perspective for its practical application.

To research the lifelong development of academic skills, behavior analysis has responded with conceptual and methodological developments that include: (1) the opportunity to respond (Greenwood, Delquadri, & Hall, 1984), (2) ecobehavioral assessment and analysis (Risley, 1977; Schroeder, 1990), (3) development of procedures for maintaining long-term research within the interactive systems of community settings (Hart & Risley, 1989), and (4) methods of analyzing the effects of environmental contexts on behavioral development (e.g., Hart & Risley, 1992; Patterson, DeBaryshe, & Ramsey, 1989; Sidman, 1986), measurable in terms of the combination of longitudinal and experimental design combined with ecobehavioral assessment (Greenwood et al., 1989).

We are trying to find the scientific solution to developmental retardation by understanding its mechanisms; that is, how multiple variables and transactional processes work with respect to present and past competence. We are trying to advance prevention and treatment by expanding the scope of behavior analysis to account for behavioral development over major periods of the life span.

We have defined the problem of developmental retardation in terms of a cumulative experiential deficit with topically related content (language) and instructionally related content (schooling) in the earliest transactional experiences of children in the home and school. We have identified transactions (accelerating and decelerating) that regulate exposure, what is learned, and the rate that learning of relevant skills takes place. We have hypothesized that the prevention of this cumulative deficit and of developmental retardation is feasible and possible, when started early and when prevention efforts are assessed in terms of cumulative hours of engagement with relevant content. There are procedures and programs that accelerate the desired transactions for poor children, that promote engage-

ment, and that can be used in a developmental, ecologically broad, systematic, and comprehensive prevention effort. However, we still need to extend and fill in the gaps in the current longitudinal database on behavioral development and complete the theoretical basis for the prevention effort that will eventually follow from this work.

If our procedures and practices are to have wide impact on the lives of families and children, we must account for more than just changed behaviors. Additionally, we need the capacity to account for changed lives. The implications of the constructs of exposure and engagement in children's parenting and schooling programs are prime examples because they provide a parsimonious, functional explanation of change over behaviors, programs, settings, and ages. They provide an integrative model linking behavioral ecology, behavior change, and development beyond the traditional view reflected in the experimental analysis of just one or two behaviors. Such a model is important because it links continuing and expanding behavior-change efforts through conceptual and empirical means. It illustrates trends in the evolution of applied behavior analysis toward greater sophistication in the use of more complex methodologies for studying interactive and developmental systems and in addressing issues of general concern in psychology (e.g., ecology, development). This greater sophistication of applied behavior analysis will be necessary if we are to act to prevent predictable negative outcomes and impact lives in socially significant ways.

References

ARREAGA-MAYER, C., & Tapia, Y. (1991). *Evaluating instructional and linguistic features of a bilingual special education classroom: An ecobehavioral approach.* Paper presented at the 20th Annual Conference of the Association for Bilingual Education, January, Washington, DC.

BECKER, W. C. (1988). Special issue devoted to Direct Instruction. *Education and Treatment of Children, 11.*

BRYANT, D. M., & Ramey, C. T. (1987). An analysis of the effectiveness of early intervention programs for high-risk children. In M. Guralnick & C. Bennett (Eds.), *Effectiveness of early intervention* (pp. 33–78). New York: Academic Press.

CARTA, J. J., Atwater, J. B., Schwartz, I. S., & Miller, P. A. (1990). Applications of ecobehavioral analysis to the study of transitions across early education. *Education and Treatment of Children, 13,* 298–315.

COOPER, D. H., & Speece, D. L. (1990). Instructional correlates of students' academic responses: Comparisons between at risk and control students. *Early Education and Development, 1,* 279–300.

GARBER, H. (1988). *The Milwaukee Project: Preventing mental retardation for children at-risk.* Washington, DC: American Association for Mental Retardation.

GREENWOOD, C. R. (1991a). A longitudinal analysis of time, engagement, and achievement in at-risk versus non-risk students. *Exceptional Children, 57,* 521–535.

GREENWOOD, C. R. (1991b). Classwide peer tutoring: Longitudinal effects on the reading, language, and mathematics achievement of at-risk students. *Journal of Reading, Writing, and Learning Disabilities International, 7,* 105–123.

GREENWOOD, C. R., Carta, J. J., & Atwater, J. J. (1991). Ecobehavioral analysis in the classroom: Review and implications. *Journal of Behavioral Education, 1,* 59–77.

GREENWOOD, C. R., Carta, J. J., Hart, B., Kamps, D., Terry, B., Delquadri, J. C., Walker, D., & Risley, T. R. (1992). Out of the laboratory and into the community: Twenty-six years of applied behavior analysis at the Juniper Gardens Children's Project. *American Psychologist, 47,* 1464–1474.

GREENWOOD, C. R., Carta, J. J., Hart, B., Thurston, L., & Hall, R. V. (1989). A behavioral approach to research on psychosocial retardation. *Education and Treatment of Children, 12,* 303–346.

GREENWOOD, C. R., Delquadri, J., & Hall, R. V. (1984). Opportunity to respond and student academic performance. In W. L. Heward, T. E. Heron, J. Trapp-Porter, & D. S. Hill (Eds.), *Focus on behavior analysis in education* (pp. 58–88). Columbus, OH: Charles Merrill.

GREENWOOD, C. R., Delquadri, J., & Hall, R. V. (1989). Longitudinal effects of classwide peer tutoring. *Journal of Educational Psychology, 81,* 371–383.

GREENWOOD, C. R., Delquadri, J. C., Stanley, S. O., Sasso, G., Whorton, D., & Schulte, D. (1981). Allocating opportunity to learn as a basis for academic remediation: A developing model for teaching. *Monograph in Behavior Disorders,* Summer, 22–33.

GREENWOOD, C. R., Terry, B., Utley, C., Montagna, D., & Walker, D. (in press). Achievement, placement, and services: Middle school benefits of classwide peer tutoring used at the elementary school. *School Psychology Review.*

GREER, R. D., McCorkle, N., & Williams, G. (1989). A sustained analysis of the behaviors of schooling. *Behavioral Residential Treatment, 4,* 113–141.

HALL, R. V., Schiefelbusch, R. L., Hoyt, R. K., & Greenwood, C. R. (1989). History, mission, and organization of the Juniper Gardens Children's Project. *Education and Treatment of Children, 12,* 301–329.

HART, B., & Risley, T. R. (1981). Grammatical and conceptual growth in the language of psychosocially disadvantaged children. In M. J. Begab, H. Garber, & H. C. Haywood (Eds.), *Prevention of retarded development in psychosocially disadvantaged children.* Baltimore: University Park Press.

HART, B., & Risley, T. R. (1989). The longitudinal study of interactive systems. *Education and Treatment of Children, 12,* 347–358.

HART, B., & Risley, T. (1992). Variations in American parenting that predict child outcomes at three. *Developmental Psychology, 28,* 1096–1105.

INFANT Health and Development Program. (1990). Enhancing the outcomes of low-birth-weight, premature infants: A multisite, randomized trial. *Journal of the American Medical Association, 263,* 3035–3042.

JOHNSON, C. M., Sum, A. M., & Weill, J. D. (1992). *Vanishing dreams: The economic plight of America's young families.* Washington, DC: Children's Defense Fund.

KAMPS, D., Carta, J., Delquadri, J., Arreaga-Mayer, C., Terry, B., & Greenwood, C. R. (1989). School-based research and intervention. *Education and Treatment of Children, 12,* 359–390.

KAMPS, D., Leonard, B. R., Dugan, E. P., Boland, B., & Greenwood, C. R. (1991a). The use of ecobehavioral assessment to identify naturally occurring effective procedures in classrooms serving students with autism and developmental disabilities. *Journal of Behavioral Education, 4*(1), 367–397.

KAMPS, D., Walker, D., Dugan, E. P., Leonard, B. R., Thibadeau, S. F., Marshall, K., Grossnickle, L., & Boland, B. (1991b). Small group teaching procedures: Programming for increasing opportunities to respond and student performance. *Focus on Autistic Behavior, 6*(4), 1–18.

NARAYAN, J. S., Heward, W. L., & Gardner, R. III (1990). Using response cards to increase student participation in an elementary classroom. *Journal of Applied Behavior Analysis, 23,* 483–490.

PATTERSON, G. R., DeBaryshe, B. D., & Ramsey, E. (1989). A developmental perspective on antisocial behavior. *American Psychologist, 44,* 329–335.

REYNOLDS, A. J. (1991). Early schooling of children at risk. *American Educational Research Journal, 28,* 392–442.

RISLEY, T. R. (1977). The ecology of applied behavior analysis. In A. Rogers-Warren & S. Warren (Eds.), *Ecological perspectives in behavior analysis* (pp. 149–163). Baltimore: University Park Press.

SCHROEDER, S. (Ed.). (1990). *Ecobehavioral analysis and developmental disabilities: The twenty-first century.* New York: Springer-Verlag.

SELINSKE, J., Greer, R. B., & Lodhi, S. (1991). A functional analysis of the comprehensive application of behavior analysis to schooling. *Journal of Applied Behavior Analysis, 24,* 107–117.

SIDMAN, M. (1986). Functional analysis of emergent verbal classes. In T. Thompson & M. D. Zeiler (Eds.), *Analysis and integration of behavioral units* (pp. 213–245). Hillsdale, NJ: Lawrence Erlbaum.

SKINNER, B. F. (1953). *Science and human behavior.* New York: Macmillan.

SKINNER, B. F. (1968). *The technology of teaching.* New York: Meredith.

WALKER, D., Carta, J. J., Greenwood, C. Hart, B., & Taylor, B. (1991). *Identification of risk factors: Links between early language development and risk outcomes for young children.* Paper presented at the meeting of the Society for Research in Child Development, May, Seattle.

CHAPTER 17

Ecobehavioral Assessment of Bilingual Special Education Settings: The Opportunity to Respond

Carmen Arreaga-Mayer
Judith J. Carta
Yolanda Tapia

For the past two decades, the effectiveness of bilingual intervention programs has been the subject of public and academic debate. In the field of bilingual education, the issues of the best type of services (e.g., maintenance versus transition)—coupled with cultural pluralism, heterogeneous populations, exit/entry assessments, and equal protection of the law—often conflict with intervention strategies, confounding the issue of what an ideal bilingual education program should be or should accomplish. No one specific criterion is sufficient to measure and describe the variety of bilingual programs available, nor has any clearly defined variable emerged against which to evaluate the adequacy of bilingual education in general (Amber & Dew, 1983; Fradd & Hallman, 1983; Ortiz & Ramirez, 1988).

The evaluation of special education programs is no less complicated. The issues of referral, nondiscriminatory assessment, categorization and classification procedures, case conferences, mainstreaming, due process, parent involvement, staff training, and coordination of services add to the difficulty of accurately assessing program impact and effectiveness (Arreaga-Mayer, Carta, & Tapia, in press; Baca & Cervantes, 1989; Hakuta, 1985; Maheady et al.,

1983). The enactment of Public Law 94-142, the Education of All Handicapped Act of 1975 (currently the Individuals with Disabilities Educational Act, or IDEA, 1990), with its mandates of individualized educational programming and placement in less-restrictive environments, has created added pressure for educators to develop effective instructional strategies and for administrators and researchers to develop evaluation strategies that facilitate statutory compliance and make sense instructionally.

The merging of the fields of bilingual education and special education into bilingual special education

This research, supported by Grant #H023C00052 from the U.S. Department of Education, Office of Special Education and Rehabilitation Services, was conducted at the Juniper Gardens Children's Project, Life Span Institute, University of Kansas. We express sincere appreciation to Debra Montagna, Claudia Perdomo, Evelia Acosta, and Martha Martinez for their efforts in observer training, observations, and coordination. We also thank Liang-Shye Hou for expert software development and advice. A final note of appreciation is extended to administrators, teachers, and students in the Kansas City, Kansas and Kansas City, Missouri Public School Districts for their cooperation and support in research efforts.

Requests for further information about the ESCRIBE code and data management system should be directed to Dr. Carmen Arreaga-Mayer, 1614 Washington Blvd., Kansas City, KS 66102.

has presented even more demanding complications to program evaluators and educators. Bilingual special-education children not only have limited English language proficiency but also experience specific learning problems and handicapping conditions that interfere with the acquisition of English and the retention of skills or content material (Baca & Cervantes, 1989; Tymitz, 1983). No categorical placement seems to fit the learner with this double set of needs.

Past evaluation studies of bilingual special-education programs have not fully addressed critical issues in methodological design as they apply to the field (Arreaga-Mayer & Greenwood, 1986; Baca & Cervantes, 1989; Bernal, 1983; Cortes, 1986; Maheady, 1985; Tymitz, 1983). What is needed are evaluations that answer more challenging questions, such as What works in the program? Why is it working? Why is it not working? How can those who implement the program make it work better? Answers to these questions require more than the traditional outcomes-only approach to assessment. They require the use of evaluation strategies that are responsive to the complexities of individual children, programs, and contexts.

In the continuing endeavor to prevent and ameliorate academic deficit, particularly by culturally and linguistically diverse populations, researchers at the Juniper Gardens Children's Project have adopted an interactional or ecobehavioral methodology to examine the process variables (i.e., the assessment of teacher behavior, student behavior, and contextual variables) and the hypothesis that the opportunity to respond is an important variable in academic and language achievement. The emphasis has been on identification of instructional variables that reliably influence academic and linguistic performance, and the design of instructional technology based on this knowledge. An ecobehavioral approach to instruction enables analyses of the components of effective instruction.

Ecobehavioral Assessment: A Technology for Measuring Classroom Processes

Ecobehavioral assessment emerged from a combination of three different theoretical fields: (1) *ecological psychology* and its concern with assessment of aspects of the environment within strategies for observational measurements (e.g., Baker & Wright, 1968; Bronfenbrenner, 1979), (2) the repeated measure designs of *applied behavior analysis* (e.g., Baer, Wolf, & Risley, 1987; Bijou, Peterson, & Ault, 1968), and (3) the *process/product research* of education (e.g., Brophy & Good, 1986; Dunkin & Biddle, 1974). Ecobehavioral assessment is a means of assessing program variables by systematic observation while measuring the moment-to-moment effects of an array of situational variables on student behavior. Carta and Greenwood (1985) stated that "in ecobehavioral assessment, the momentary interactions between program variables (ecological stimuli) and student behaviors are the units of analysis for predicting or otherwise investigating program outcomes such as developmental gain or long-term achievement (p. 92)." An advantage of ecobehavioral assessment of classroom practices is the direct examination, either individually or collectively (i.e., in terms of the effect of one on another), of quantified ecological and behavioral variables.

During the last decade, ecobehavioral assessments have been developed in response to the growing demand in education for improved methods of evaluating and developing effective instructional practices that focus on the series of ecological events (e.g., instructional activity, materials, grouping, teacher behaviors) temporarily related to students' academic performance. Researchers have advanced the use of ecobehavioral analysis in evaluating the effectiveness of instruction and interventions in a variety of educational settings: in regular education (Greenwood, Delquadri, & Hall, 1984; Greenwood et al., 1986b), in special education (Greenwood et al., 1990; Thurlow et al., 1984; Ysseldyke et al., 1984), and in early childhood education (Carta, Greenwood, & Robinson, 1987).

Work in ecobehavioral methodology at the Juniper Gardens Children's Project has resulted in the development of several comprehensive observation systems (Carta, Greenwood, & Atwater, 1985; Greenwood et al., 1990; Greenwood et al., 1985, 1986a; Stanley & Greenwood, 1983). This technology has taken on greater applied significance in the evaluation of instructional interventions by demonstrating that an ecobehavioral approach can identify the specific elements of programmatic success in a variety of service delivery settings for monolingual students. Although the ecobehavioral approach equips researchers and educators with a more precise and systematic means of ensuring program effectiveness, fidelity, and replication, it has yet to be applied to bilingual special-education programs (Arreaga-Mayer, Carta, & Tapia, in press). The purpose of this chapter is to illustrate the development and application of an ecobehavioral assessment approach for serving exceptional limited English proficient (LEP) students.

ESCRIBE: The Ecobehavioral System for the Contextual Recording of Interactional Bilingual Environments

To design an instrument for (1) defining the contextual features of the environment; (2) examining the interactions between the environment, teacher, student, languages, and behaviors; and (3) capturing the student behaviors most likely related to academic and linguistic gains, we needed to address a variety of issues. First, we reviewed previous approaches to the identification of effective bilingual special-education programs and of ecological factors previously linked to instructional effectiveness for this population (Arreaga-Mayer, Carta, & Tapia, in press). This activity confirmed the absence of ecobehavioral approaches for evaluating exceptional LEP students and the emphasis in the field for outcome measures (product). Reviews of the literature and initial revisions of ecobehavioral observation systems previously developed at the Juniper Gardens Children's Project (Carta, Greenwood, & Atwater, 1985; Carta et al., 1988) identified ecological factors that had previously been linked to instructional effectiveness in bilingual classrooms.

Second, we conducted informal observations in a variety of service delivery settings for exceptional and academically at-risk LEP students in order to identify the range of contextual features characteristic of these classroom environments. We then developed a list of codes and behavioral definitions based on these observations. Next, an experimental observational code

(paper-pencil version) was pilot-tested on a variety of instructional models and settings. We reviewed the codes and definitions and collected some initial data on interobserver reliability.

Third, we asked a group of identified research experts and teachers in the fields of bilingual and bilingual special education to review the experimental observational code in order to obtain feedback on its content validity. Following their review, we conducted a second pilot study. The ESCRIBE code that emerged from this process assesses four major categories of variables: stationary elements, instructional environment features, teacher languages and behaviors, and student languages and behaviors (see Table 17.1).

Major Categories of Variables

Stationary variables, subcategories, and codes. Stationary variables describe the service delivery setting and instructional model where instruction takes place. These variables are critical to the analysis of instructional environments. The stationary category is composed of four subcategories and 18 codes.

Settings are defined by the physical setting, space, or room in which the target student is located (e.g., regular education classroom, self-contained special education classroom, and instructional lab). *Instructional models* include seven specific bilingual education program designs used with culturally and

Table 17.1 Summary of ESCRIBE categories and subcategories

Echobehavioral Variables			
Stationary Variables	*Instructional Environment Variables*	*Teacher Variables*	*Student Variables*
Setting	Student activity	Teacher definition	Language initiating/ responding
Instruction model	Materials	Teacher focus	Oral responses
Number of adults	Language of materials	Language of instruction	Language of the student
Number of students	Instructional grouping	Corrections/ affirmations	Student activity-related responses
		Teacher behavior	

linguistically diverse learners, such as full bilingualism, structured immersion, and English as a second language (ESL). *Number of adults* is the actual count of adults present who are interacting with or monitoring the students. *Number of students* is the actual count of students within the setting being observed.

Instructional environment variables, subcategories, and codes.   Instructional environment variables describe the structure of the classroom ecology. These are background features considered pertinent in influencing student language and behavior. The instructional environment category is composed of four subcategories and 35 codes.

Student activities are the subject matter or learning tasks given to the target student (e.g., language, reading, and science). *Materials* are the actual curriculum item or media material the target student is using to make academic or language responses during instruction, such as computers, workbooks, and manipulables. *Language of materials* defines the language of the materials the target student is using (e.g., English, non-English, or mixed languages). *Instructional grouping* is the method of instruction as defined by a combination of teacher interaction, activity, materials, and the number of students involved in the same lesson as the target student, such as whole-class instruction and one-to-one instruction.

Teacher variables, subcategories, and codes.   The teacher category consists of five subcategories and 32 codes that provide information about the adult or peer with whom the target student interacts. The teacher variables constitute the code's second ecological variable category. We decided to consider it as a separate category based on the capability of analyzing the individual codes as dependent or independent of the "instructional environment variables," with respect to their influence on student language and behavior.

Teacher definition refers to the person who is providing the most immediate cues and sustained academic instruction to the target student (e.g., language education teacher, peer, and paraprofessional). *Teacher focus* indicates the direction of the teacher's behavior (e.g., target student only, target student and others, and other than target student). *Language of*

instruction refers to the oral or written language used by the teacher or person responsible for instruction, such as English, mixed languages, and no-language. *Teacher correction/affirmation* classifies the teacher's verbal or written academic behavior as either corrective, affirmative, or neither in relation to the target student's language or academic performance. *Teacher behavior* is the category that describes the behavior of the "teacher" chosen in the teacher definition category, such as question academic, nonverbal prompt, attention, and disapproval.

Student variables, subcategories, and codes.   Student behavior is categorized into four separate subcategories: language initiating or responding behaviors, oral responses, language of the student, and activity-related responses. Two main considerations guided this decision. First, we wanted the behavior and language codes to be specific responses that potentially were influenced by the moment-by-moment changes in instructional environment and teacher code categories. Second, we wanted to be able to look at academic and language profiles individually. We were interested in the interrelationships of these four subcategories. For example, we were interested in determining if some children verbalized more frequently when they were engaged in certain types of behaviors. Similarly, we wanted to know whether changes brought about in "language usage" produce corresponding changes in the *language initiating/responding* characteristics of that discourse. Examples of the *oral responses codes* include talk academic and talk management. *Language of the student* is characterized as English, non-English, mixed language, no-language, or can't tell. Examples of the *student activity-related responses* subcategory include writing, reading, talk, noncompliance, and student attention.

Observation and Recording Procedures

The ESCRIBE code targets an individual student as the focus of observation and analysis. This intensive data collection on an individual student enables the recorder to generate sufficiently dense frequencies of events to provide adequate analyses of ecological or teacher variables that influence specific student language or behavior. All ecobehavioral variables (i.e., instructional environment variables, teacher variables, and student variables) are recorded on a 15-second momentary time sampling system in order to produce reliable records (Powell, Martindale, & Kulp, 1975). To observe a target student, observers use a laptop computer that provides them with auditory cues every 15 seconds. They then record a specific category of variables. More specifically, the program cycles through one 15-second interval to collect the instructional environment codes, followed by six sequences of two 15-second intervals to collect the teacher and student codes alternatively. Using this ecobehavioral observation system, a single observer can track a single student during an entire school day or for shorter periods that are of interest.

Analysis of Ecobehavioral Processes

Ecobehavioral analysis can be used to describe observations of specific variables in which the frequency of each coded event can be totaled and expressed in terms of the grand total of all the coded events, as a percentage score, or as an unconditional proportion. These molar descriptions are proportions or session estimates of the relative rates of occurrence of each coded classroom event. This type of analysis will allow independent summary statements about the classroom ecology, such as the percentage of the day spent doing specific activities or using a specific language. Similar descriptions can be made about the proportion of the day that the teacher or the student engage in various behaviors or languages.

In addition, classroom events that occur contiguously (co-occurring in the same time interval or those that follow each other in subsequent intervals) can be combined to form conditional proportion scores (conditional probabilities). Summaries of these jointly occurring events can then be combined to form molecular descriptions; that is, the conditional relationship between ecology and behavioral events. These molecular descriptions are conditional probability statements regarding the likelihood of two or more events (ecological and behavioral) occurring simultaneously in close sequential time intervals. These data provide information about the effects of specific instructional environment variables on teacher and student variables. Thus, the probabilities of various combinations of variables

on the code of theoretical interest can be computed. These computations yield the following types of statements:

1. Given a specific type of activity or material (such as language arts or non-English computer program), in what type of behavior or language was the student most likely engaged?
2. Given a specific classroom structure or grouping (such as one-on-one arrangement), in what type of behavior or language was the teacher most likely engaged?
3. Given a specific service delivery setting (such as regular classroom) or instructional model (such as full bilingualism), in what type of oral response behaviors or languages was the student most likely engaged?

In ecobehavioral analysis, the classroom processes defined using molar and molecular descriptions achieve added significance when they are related to measures of language and academic performance to obtain process/product analyses of achievement gains. Correlating the percentage occurrence scores of individual variables with outcome measures, such as tested levels of criterion-referenced or standardized achievement, provide this type of analysis. These analyses will allow for responses to the following questions:

1. Do students with high rates of oral responding also exhibit high rates of change on achievement or language dominance tests?
2. Do students with high rates of English language initiation exhibit higher gains on English language dominance or English language literacy tests?

This type of analysis enables the determination of those program aspects (i.e., instructional environment components, teacher behaviors/languages, or student behaviors/languages) that are most related to academic and linguistic gains.

Pilot Study

During the 1991–1992 school year, we conducted a pilot study with the ESCRIBE code in four classrooms in which instruction was provided for LEP students who were also identified as receiving special education services or were at risk for developmental disabilities. This study provided a rich quantitative description of potentially influential programmatic and linguistic variables and their subsequent behavioral effects.

Instructional Models

Instructional model refers to the specific educational program designs used with culturally and linguistically diverse learners (CLDL). The terms and descriptions selected for the ESCRIBE system were those most widely accepted by teachers, authors, and researchers. The descriptions of the different models are also limited to those terms that best represent major differences in overall program design. For the purpose of this study, the instructional models described in the following section were utilized.

Native language instruction/immersion model. Students receive all instruction in their native language. English is not taught as part of the curriculum. The instruction should focus on the developmental language skills of thinking, listening, speaking, reading, and writing in the native language.

Full bilingualism model. Students receive content area instruction in English and their native language. The most important concern is that they receive a solid academic curriculum with support for reaching full English language proficiency without negating their first language in the process.

Transitional bilingualism with English as a second language model. Students receive instruction in their native language in all subject areas and instruction in ESL, but only for a limited time. The native language is used only until the children adjust to school and are able to participate in academic subjects in English. The highest priority is the teaching of English, with the goal of mainstreaming LEP students as soon as possible.

Structured immersion model. Students receive instruction totally in the ESL format, with native language tutoring support as needed during the first year or two. The teachers are bilingual and accept students' responses in their native language, but they respond only in English. The materials are highly structured to introduce students step-by-step to the second language.

English as a second language only model. Although not a form of bilingual instruction, ESL was selected as an instructional model for this code since in many instances it is the *only* program available to provide assistance to LEP students. ESL instruction includes English taught from a second-language point of view in grammar or language arts classes and content-area instruction in English, provided at the students' level of English proficiency. The students may go to the ESL resource room or may be divided within the regular or special education classroom into smaller groups to receive this instruction.

ESL also includes programs identified as Cognitive Academic Language Proficiency (CALP) models. These models are content ESL methods for teaching English, through less focus on language itself and more emphasis on hands-on motivating tasks in math, science, and social studies that encourage natural acquisition. As LEP students increase their mastery of English, they are gradually moved into academic classes with native English speakers.

English immersion model. Students receive all instruction in English with no native language support or structured ESL instruction. Regular classroom or a special services classroom where instruction is provided *only* in English are examples of English immersion programs.

Subjects and Settings

This study was conducted in the metropolitan Kansas City area. Our subjects were 36 randomly selected students, enrolled in four elementary-level schools serving culturally and linguistically diverse students and qualifying as LEP by district identification standards (i.e., scores of 1, 2, or 3 in the Language Assessment Scales-Oral, De Avila and Duncan, 1985).

Schools 1 and 3 were traditional English immersion schools with pull-out services for special education, bilingual special education, and ESL services. There were 7 students in school 1 (4 males, 3 females, ages ranging from 7.0 to 9.5 years) and 8 students in School 3 (5 males, 3 females, ages ranging from 7.0 to 8.7 years).

School 2 was a math, science, and language magnet school with special pull-out services provided through instructional labs, special education, bilingual special education, and ESL programs. There were 11 students in School 2 (5 males, 6 females, ages ranging from 7.3 to 10.7 years).

School 4 was a Spanish-language magnet school providing full bilingual instruction (i.e., Spanish-English) and pull-out special education, bilingual special education, language labs, and ESL services. There were 10 students in School 4 (6 males, 4 females, ages ranging from 7.0 to 10.5 years).

Observer Training and Interobserver Agreement

We hired four bilingual (Spanish-English) observers from the community and from the university. Training for these observers took place over a three-week period, for approximately 12 hours per week. They were introduced to the ESCRIBE codes and definitions and to basic laptop computer skills and practiced using the code with videotapes of classroom instruction. The observers then practiced observing in classrooms until they reached a criterion of three consecutive percentage-agreement reliability checks of 80% or higher. The observers completed code-by-code percentage of observation agreement separately for occurrences of behaviors or codes within each subcategory. During the study, interobserver agreement checks were collected for 53 observations, approximately 25% of all observations distributed across subjects and settings. The mean percentage agreement was 99.4% overall, ranging from 92% to 100% across all subcategories.

Data Collection and Analyses

Observations were conducted for the entire school day on 111 variables across 36 students within four elementary-level school settings and 26 different classrooms over a seven-month period. Thirty-four students were observed for 6 days, one student for 5 days, and one student for 3 days. This averaged 2 to 3 days per month of observations for each student. A total of 213 full-day observations were collected throughout the study. The length of individual observations ranged from 180 to 360 minutes, with a mean of 210 minutes. The only activities not observed were lunch, restroom breaks, recess, and errands. On completion of classroom observations, files were transferred from the laptop computers to an IBM-AT computer for storage and data management.

Daily data files were maintained for each subject and each class. These files served as the basis for all analyses. The daily data sets were combined by class, settings, or schools and averaged across each of the sets to address the specific research questions. Molar and molecular statistical analyses were computed using software programs specifically written for use with the ESCRIBE code (Arreaga-Mayer & Hou, 1992a, 1992b). To compute averages for single students across observations, single files were merged and the overall percentage of occurrence was computed. Means across classrooms were computed by averaging the class mean percentage occurrence for specific categories or subcategories.

Results and Implications of Molar Descriptions

The first analyses were based on the combined data set, including all 213 days of observations across the four schools and 26 classrooms. These data allowed global descriptions of ecobehavioral events on a typical classroom day for this population based on our sample of 36 students. Molar descriptions can be used to address a variety of instructional and research questions involving: time devoted to instructional activities, typical teacher behavior, language of instruction, student language-related behaviors, or student activity-related behaviors. The following molar analyses illustrate the type of information that can be obtained with ESCRIBE.

Typical classroom day. The first analyses addressed the question of time devoted to instructional activities. The data in Figure 17.1 show that the most frequently occurring activity was math at 20%. The next most frequently occurring activities were reading at 18%, language arts at 16%, social studies and science at 7%, spelling and transition at 5%, and all other activities occurring less than 5% of the time. These data portray an emphasis on academic skills with these students.

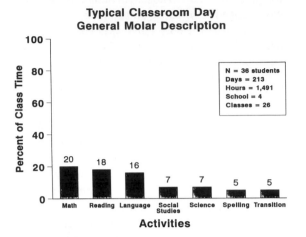

Figure 17.1. Average occurrence of instructional activities.

Second, the data in Figure 17.2 addressed the question of student language–related behaviors. The data revealed that the most frequently coded behaviors were the students' use of No Language and No Talk, both at 92%. The students used the English language 8% of the time and non-English (i.e., Spanish) only 1% of the time. The students were engaged in Academic Talk only 5% of the time, the highest frequency of Oral Responses coded, followed by 2% of the time engaged in Other Talk (i.e., social). The students spent 76% of the day neither initiating nor responding to language (verbal or written); 21% Responding to Language initiated by another adult, peer, or instructional material; and only 4% Initiating Language (verbal or written).

These data are extremely informative about the quality of linguistic opportunities that exceptional or developmentally at-risk LEP students receive during a typical academic day. If LEP students are to increase their use and fluency of the English language or to maintain their native language, the frequency and quality of their language behaviors need to change to include activities that require a larger percentage of oral responses and instructional formats that foster higher levels of initiating and responding language behaviors.

Figure 17.3 addresses the occurrence of student activity-related behaviors. The data indicate that the most frequently coded behavior was Attending (i.e., looking at a teacher who was instructing or discussing, or at a peer involved in an interaction with the target, or at some instructional material), occurring in 38% of all intervals. The total "active engagement" of students in Academic Behaviors (44%) was slightly less than one-half of the school day, whereas the active engagement of students in Oral Language Responses occurred only 7% of the total school day.

Schools comparisons.   The previous data presented an overall picture of the typical day for exceptional and

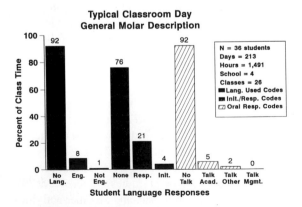

Figure 17.2. Average occurrence of student language-related behaviors.

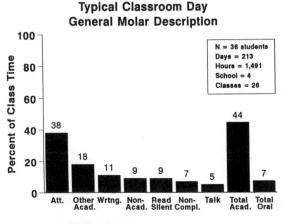

Figure 17.3. Average occurrence of student activity-related behaviors.

academically at-risk LEP students. The analyses that follow sampled another molar comparison capability of the ESCRIBE code: schools comparisons. These analyses can refine global data by providing an in-depth look into variables and by examining effects within and across specific schools, instructional models, or service delivery settings.

Figure 17.4 describes school comparison analyses by settings. It is a comparison of the students' participation in three different service delivery settings— regular classroom, ESL resource room, and special education classrooms—within the same school. This comparison provides a more specific analysis of "active academic responding" behavior by settings. As a whole, students in School 3, a traditional English immersion school, scored higher than the three other schools in every setting. Regular classroom active engagement was the lowest score at 51%, topped by ESL participation at 59%, and finally by special education services at 72%. The lowest engagement in School 1 (also a traditional English immersion school) was during special education services at 27%; in School 2 (the math, science, and language magnet school) during regular education at 41%, and in School 4 (the full bilingualism school) during ESL instruction at 31%. Overall, students were most actively and academically engaged while in the special education setting (mean = 54.0%), followed by ESL engagement (mean = 43.0%), and least engaged in the

regular education setting (mean = 41.5%). Molecular analysis of student activity-related responses by setting can further clarify which behaviors promote higher levels of academic responding, during the special education instruction? Similarly, conditional probability analyses of teacher behaviors and student responses could also provide further explanation.

Table 17.2 delineates molar analyses based on the ESL instructional model for each of the four schools. Exceptional and academically at-risk LEP students receiving ESL instruction spent the largest percentage of their instructional time Attending, with a mean of 46% (ranging from 32% to 58%). Attending does not require active academic or language engagement from the student. The highest percentage of Attending behavior occurred in School 4, the full bilingualism Spanish magnet school, and the lowest percentage in School 3, a traditional English immersion school. In contrast, active Academic Responding averaged 43% (range 31%–59%), with School 4 students scoring the lowest percentage response at 31% and School 3 students scoring the highest percentage at 59%. Oral

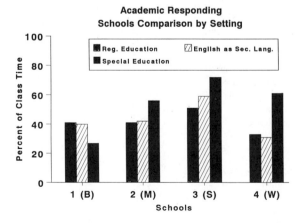

Figure 17.4. Average occurrence of academic responding by setting.

Table 17.2 ESL comparisons - Percentage Occurrences

Student Activity	Schools			
	1	2	3	4
Writing	13	11	15	11
Reading aloud	1	1	1	2
Reading silently	2	4	8	4
Talk	8	10	8	7
Other academic	16	16	27	7
Exercise	0	0	0	0
Nonacademic response	5	5	5	4
Noncompliance response	9	4	5	6
Attending	46	49	32	58
None	0	0	0	0
Can't tell	0	0	0	0
Oral Responses				
Talk academic	7	10	8	8
Talk other	3	1	2	1
Talk management	0	0	0	0
No talk	90	89	90	90
Academic Responding				
Composite	40	42	59	31
Oral Repsonding				
Composite	10	11	10	9

Responding composite scores, the percentage of time that students engaged in verbal behaviors, resulted in an average of 10% occurrence with a range of 9% to 11%. In summary, the learning profile for students participating in ESL programs at these four schools confirmed that LEP students spent an average of 89.7% of their instructional time not engaged in oral language behaviors (oral responses category) and only 43% of their instructional time engaged in active academic responding behaviors (i.e., writing, talking, reading, or manipulating academic materials).

As the bilingual literature and the special education research has demonstrated, exceptional LEP students learn best by active participation, hands-on activities, and continuous opportunities to use oral language skills (Baca & Cervantes, 1989; Garcia, 1992). The data analyses from this pilot study illustrated the opposite instructional and oral language opportunities occurring in these four classrooms. Schools, service delivery settings, and instructional model comparisons will help refine our research hypotheses concerning the problem of low student engagement and the configuration of the school or classroom environment in terms of ecological and teacher behavior as they affect student academic and language responses. Analyses like those illustrated in Tables 17.2 and Figure 17.4 can provide answers to questions such as:

1. Are all service delivery models alike in relationship to ecological, teacher, and student variables?
2. Can we modify these programs, based on ecobehavioral assessment, to provide the skills necessary to effect language and academic gains for exceptional LEP students?

Comparisons within classrooms.   The next analyses addressed the question of student variation within a classroom in response to the instructional programs. The data for three target students in Classroom 9 (School 4: Full Bilingualism Instructional Model) are presented in Table 17.3 with regard to Teacher Behavior and Language of Instruction. All students were identified at risk for exceptionality and participated in full bilingual instruction, language labs, and ESL programs. Each student was observed for six days. Although many similarities were noted, interesting

differences existed among these students served in the same learning environments.

The most frequently occurring teacher behavior for Sancho and Angel was Talk Academic (22%, 30%). Herman's highest frequency of Teacher Behavior was in the No Response subcategory (i.e., no teacher attention or interaction) at 23%, yet Talk Academic also occurred at a fairly high level (21%). All three students received similar frequency occurrence of Teacher Attention behavior.

The most frequently occurring Language of Instruction for Sancho and Angel was English (47%, 46%), whereas Herman received only 37%. Herman received the highest frequency of occurrence in No Language (i.e., no verbal or written language) at 46%, yet Sancho and Angel also received fairly high levels of No Language teacher behavior (40%, 32%). The use of non-English (i.e., Spanish) for instruction, however, varied widely across the subjects at 17%, 12%, and 21%, respectively. These results demonstrated that the Teacher Behaviors and Languages Used for Instruction can show consistency in their structure and

Table 17.3 Comparison of students in Classroom 9 across teacher behavior and language of instruction: Percentage occurrences

		Students	
Category	Herman	Sancho	Angel
Teacher Behavior			
Question academic	8	8	11
Command academic	9	11	10
Talk academic	21	22	30
Talk nonacademic	9	9	10
Nonverbal prompt	7	5	3
Teacher attention	17	19	18
Praise/approval	1	2	1
Disapproval	3	4	2
Read aloud	2	3	2
Sing	0	1	1
No response	23	16	12
Language of Instruction			
English	37	47	46
Non-English	17	12	21
Mixed	0	0	0
No language	46	40	32
Can't tell	0	1	1

can also depict student differences in the magnitude of specific variables.

Descriptions of individual student's daily variations. The two panels in Figure 17.5 illustrate the relative magnitude of one student's percentage scores for two subcategories of Student Activity Responses (upper panel) and Total Academic and Oral Responding (lower panel), while receiving services in a special education resource classroom. These data depict daily variations, and the relative range in magnitudes within subcategory codes.

The upper panel illustrates the daily differences in the student responses of Talk and Reading Aloud

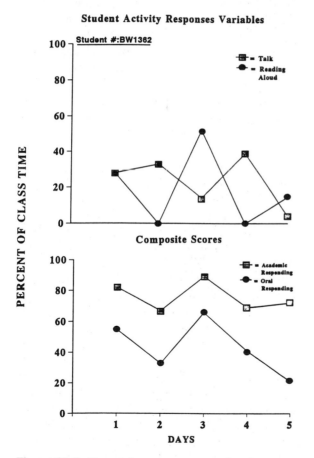

Figure 17.5. Range of occurrence across days for one student in a special education resource classroom.

during special education resource room services. Talk was the most frequently occurring activity response and ranged from 14% to 39% (an average of 24%) over the five days sampled. Reading Aloud occurred less frequently than Talk and ranged from 0% to 52% (an average of 19%). The behaviors exhibited great variability with alternating days of higher frequency, with the exception of day 1 where both behaviors occurred at the same frequency (28%).

The lower panel depicts the overall variations of the composite scores for Academic and Oral Responding (active engagement scores). Academic Responding averaged 76% over the five days sampled (ranging from 67% to 89%), whereas Oral Responding averaged 43% (ranging from 23% to 33%). The student's overall active engagement while participating in special education services was higher for Academic and Oral Responding than his overall typical day with Academic Responding at 45% (ranging from 31% to 57%) and Oral Responding at 12% (ranging from 8% to 17%).

Summary of molar analyses. These analyses are useful in providing general descriptions about the structure of time spent within different ecological variables (e.g., different instructional models, activities, materials, language usages, grouping configurations, service delivery settings) and within various teacher and student behaviors. Molar analyses, as illustrated by the previously discussed data, can be useful in making comparisons across settings, students, and days for individual students or groups of students. Collectively, these particular data confirm an important point; bilingual intervention is not a unitary variable that is either present or not present; rather, it is a multitude of variables of different strengths.

Results and Implications of Molecular Descriptions

We conducted molecular analyses to determine the influences of ecological or teacher behavior variables on students' behavior or language usage from a temporal correlational and causal perspective. Table 17.4 presents one such analysis based upon the consolidation of six full days of observation for one student. This student's teachers were concerned about the fre-

Table 17.4 Conditional probability analysis: Oral Responses ⟷ Setting + Talk

	Regular Classroom Talk	Special Education Talk	Resource Room–ESL Talk	Library Talk	Therapy–Bilingual Special Education Talk
Talk Academic	0.514	0.943	0.870	0.636	1.000
Talk Management	0.143			0.091	
Talk Other	0.329	0.029	0.130	0.273	
No Talk	0.014	0.029			

Note: Number of Strings with Conditional Probability Equal to or Greater Than 0.05 = 5

quency and quality of the student's oral language usage during the school day.

The molecular descriptions based on the conditional probability analysis of the student's oral responses by service delivery setting revealed important temporal correlations. The target student spent the highest percentage of time engaged in Talk Academic while participating in special education. During bilingual special education, the student spent 100% of his "talk behavior" engaged in Talk Academic and 94% when in regular/English-only special education. The student spent 87% of his "talk behavior" in Talk Academic during ESL services, 63% during library, and 51% while in the regular classroom. In contrast, the student spent the highest percentage of time engaged in Talk Other (i.e., social) while in the Regular Classroom and the lowest while receiving special education services. These differences suggest the need to examine additional ecological factors across these settings to further isolate the elements or techniques accelerating oral language usage in the special education settings.

A second sample of molecular analysis addressed the causal relationship between active engagement in academic/language use behaviors (Academic Responding/Oral Responding) and instructional grouping (Whole Class versus Small Group). As presented in Figure 17.6, the highest frequency of Active Academic Responding occurred during the Small-Group Instructional format; however, the frequency of Oral Responding did not demonstrate similar causal effects. Small-Group Instruction provided a significant ecological change resulting in a higher active engagement level of the student's activity-related behaviors but in itself was not a causal factor for increased language usage (i.e., Oral Responding Behaviors).

A descriptive and quantitative analysis of the Academic and Oral Responses during the two instructional-grouping arrangements demonstrated that the small-group arrangement provided the student with a higher percentage opportunity for Active Academic Responding in Writing (18%), Reading Silently (14%), Talk (9%), and Other Academic activities (6%). In addition, while participating in small group, the passive Attending behavior decreased to 34% as compared to 83% in the whole-class grouping. Overall, small-group instruction allowed this student to increase academic engaged time from 15% (whole class) to 47% (small group) and oral responding from 7% (whole class) to 10% (small group).

Summary of molecular analyses. In summation, these analyses demonstrated the use of an ecobehavioral assessment approach to determine the impact of ecological and teacher variables on student behaviors and language usage. Molecular analyses provide critical direction in developing interventions and evaluating effects across a broad array of variables. These scores paired with student outcome measures can provide a detailed picture of classroom processes that are most highly related to academic and linguistic programmatic success.

Conclusions

In summary, bilingual special education/mainstream students spent 67% of their instruction time engaged in Whole-Class Instruction formats, 92% of their classroom day not using any language (verbal or written), 8% using English, and 1% using a non-English

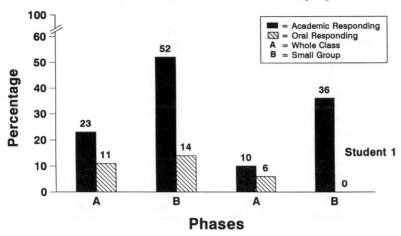

Figure 17.6. Causal relationship between active engagement and instructional grouping.

language (i.e., Spanish). Oral Responding during a typical classroom day totaled only 7%. The highest-coded student activity was passive attention to teacher or materials at 38% and the most-used language for instruction was English at 58%. Although students spent the highest percentage of the day in academic activities (math, 20%; reading, 18%; and language, 16%), their active academic engagement time totaled only 44%.

The preliminary findings from the above mentioned pilot study support use of the ESCRIBE code as a reliable and valid ecobehavioral assessment instrument. In addition, the data suggest that ecobehavioral assessment is a viable approach for describing and evaluating programs for culturally and linguistically diverse learners who are experiencing academic difficulties.

Summary

Currently, research using the ESCRIBE code within the context of an ecobehavioral approach parallels our previous efforts to identify the most-effective ecological procedures with regular, mild handicapped, autistic, and preschool populations (Carta,

Greenwood, & Robinson, 1987; Greenwood et al., 1986; Kamps, Leonard, & Greenwood, 1991). With a new target population—exceptional LEP students—we are using an ESCRIBE database to identify problem areas and accelerator variables within classrooms exhibiting high rates of academic responding. Ecological arrangements (e.g., Activity = Language, Materials = Other media in English language, Instructional grouping = Small group, Teacher behavior = Question academic) can then be used to engineer measurably superior interventions for implementation across students and classrooms.

In summary, the ESCRIBE code provides a methodological improvement for use in the next generation of bilingual and bilingual special-education efficacy studies. It offers an approach for generating the data necessary to support instructional or accountability research in bilingual special-education programs. The ecobehavioral approach will expand the focus of assessment to account for both the independent and the dependent variables that explain student outcomes. This type of evaluation would enable us to design, deliver, and support the most-effective educational programs for this unique and diverse population.

References

AMBER, A., & Dew, N. (1983). *Special education for exceptional bilingual students: A handbook for educators.* Dallas: Evaluation, Dissemination, and Assessment Center.

ARREAGA-MAYER, C., Carta, J. J., & Tapia, Y. (in press). Ecobehavioral assessment: A new methodology for evaluating instruction for exceptional culturally and linguistically diverse students. *Division of Diverse Exceptional Learner (DDEL): Monograph* 1. Reston, VA: Council for Exceptional Children.

ARREAGA-MAYER, C., & Greenwood, C. R. (1986). Environmental variables affecting the school achievement of culturally and linguistically different learners: An instructional perspective. *Journal of the National Association for Bilingual Education, 10*(2), 113–136.

ARREAGA-MAYER, C., & Hou, L. S. (1992a). *Data analysis program for the ecobehavioral system for the contextual recording of interactional bilingual environments (ESCRIBE): Training manual.* Kansas City: Juniper Gardens Children's Project, University of Kansas.

ARREAGA-MAYER, C., & Hou, L. S. (1992b). *Data analysis software packages for the ESCRIBE code: SCORES, TABS, RELIABILITY, KAPPA RELIABILITY and MATRIX.* Kansas City: Juniper Gardens Children's Project, University of Kansas.

BACA, L. M., & Cervantes, H. T. (1989). *The bilingual special education interface.* Columbus, OH: Merrill.

BAER, D. M., Wolf, M. M., & Risley, T. R. (1987). Some still current dimensions of applied behavior analysis. *Journal of Applied Behavior Analysis, 20,* 313–327.

BAKER, R. G., & Wright, P. E. (1968). *Ecological psychology: Concepts and methods for studying the environment of human behavior.* Stanford, CA: Stanford University Press.

BERNAL, E. M. (1983). Trends in bilingual special education. *Learning Disability Quarterly, 6*(4), 424–431.

BIJOU, S. W., Peterson, R. F., & Ault, M. H. (1968). A method to integrate descriptive and experimental field studies at the level of data and empirical concept. *Journal of Applied Behavior Analysis, 1,* 175–191.

BRONFENBRENNER, U. (1979). Contexts of child rearing: Problems and prospects. *American Psychologist, 34,* 844–850.

BROPHY, J., & Good, T. L. (1986). Teacher behavior and student achievement. In M. L. Wittrock (Ed.), *Handbook of research on teaching* (pp. 328–375). 3rd ed. New York: Macmillan.

CARTA, J. J., & Greenwood, C. R. (1985). Ecobehavioral assessment: A methodology for expanding the evaluation of early intervention programs. *Topics in Early Childhood Education, 5,* 88–104.

CARTA, J. J., Greenwood, C. R., & Atwater, J. (1985). *Ecobehavioral system for complex assessment of the preschool environment: ESCAPE.* Kansas City: Juniper Gardens Children's Project, Bureau of Child Research, University of Kansas.

CARTA, J. J., Greenwood, C. R., & Robinson, S. L. (1987). Application of an ecobehavioral approach to the evaluation of early intervention programs (pp. 123–155). In R. Prinz (Ed.), *Advances in behavioral assessment of children and families.* Vol. 3. Greenwich, CT: JAI.

CARTA, J. J., Greenwood, C. R., Schulte, D., Arreaga-Mayer, M., & Terry, B. (1988). *Code for instructional structure and student academic response (CISSAR)—Mainstream special education version (MS2CISSAR): A training manual.* Kansas City: Juniper Gardens Children's Project, Bureau of Child Research, University of Kansas.

CORTES, L. A. (1986). Students' reaction to bilingual special education. Paper presented at the Annual International Convention, Council for Exceptional Children, April, Atlanta. (ED 139 174)

DE AVILA, E. A., & Duncan, S. E. (1985). *Language Assessment Scales-O.* Monterey, CA: CTB/McGraw-Hill.

DUNKIN, M. J., & Biddle, B. J. (1974). *The study of teaching.* New York: Holt, Rinehart & Winston.

FRADD, S., & Hallman, C. L. (1983). Implications of psychological and educational research for assessment and instruction of culturally linguistically different students. *Learning Disability Quarterly, 6*(4), 468–478.

GARCIA, E. E. (1992). Linguistically and culturally diverse children: Effective instructional practices and related policy issues. In H. C. Waxman, J. Walker de Felix, J. E. Anderson, & H. P. Baptiste, Jr. (Eds.), *Students at risk in at-risk schools* (pp. 65–86). Newbury Park, CA: Corwin Press.

GREENWOOD, C. R., Carta, J. J., Kamps, D., & Arreaga-Mayer, C. (1990). Ecobehavioral analysis of classroom instruction. In S. R. Schroeder (Ed.), *Ecobehavioral analysis and developmental disabilities* (pp. 33–63). New York: Springer-Verlag.

GREENWOOD, C. R., Delquadri, J., & Hall, R. V. (1984). Opportunity to respond and student academic performance. In W. Heward, T. Heron, D. Hill, & J. Trapp-Porter (Eds.), *Behavior analysis in education* (pp. 58–88). Columbus, OH: Merrill.

GREENWOOD, C. R., Delquadri, J., Stanley, S. O., Terry, B., & Hall, R. V. (1985). Assessment of ecobehavioral interaction in school settings. *Behavioral Assessment, 7,* 331–347.

GREENWOOD, C. R., Delquadri, J., Stanley, S. O., Terry, B., & Hall, R. V. (1986a). Observational assessment of ecobehavioral interaction during academic instruction. In S. E. Newstead, S. H. Irvine, & P. D. Dan (Eds.), *Human assessment: Cognition and motivation* (pp. 319–340). Dordrecht, Netherlands: Nijhoff Press.

GREENWOOD, C. R., Schulte, D., Kohler, F., Dinwiddie, G., & Carta, J. J. (1986b). Assessment and analysis of ecobehavioral interaction in school settings (pp. 68–98). In R. J. Prinz (Ed.), *Advances in behavioral assessment of children and families.* Vol. 2. Greenwich, CT: JAI.

HAKUTA, K. (1985). *Mirrors of language: A debate on bilingualism.* New York: Basic Books.

KAMPS, D. M., Leonard, B. R., & Greenwood, C. R. (1991). Ecobehavioral assessment of students with autism and developmental disabilities (pp. 201–237). *Advances in behavioral assessment of children and families.* Vol. 5. London: Jessica Kingsley.

MAHEADY, L. (1985). The assessment of the bilingual exceptional child: Trends and models. In L. Baca, J. Starks, & E. Hartley (Eds.), *Third annual symposium: Exceptional hispanic children and youth.* Monograph Series (1), 41–63. Boulder: Bueno Center for Multicultural Education.

MAHEADY, L. A., Towne, R., Algozzine, B., Mercer, J., & Ysseldyke, J. (1983). Minority overrepresentation: A case for alternative practices prior to referral. *Learning Disability Quarterly, 6*(4), 448–457.

ORTIZ, A. A., & Ramirez, B. A. (1988). *Schools and the culturally diverse exceptional student: Promising practices and future directions.* Reston, VA: Council for Exceptional Children (ERIC).

POWELL, J., Martindale, A., & Kulp, S. (1975). An evaluation of time-sample measures of behavior. *Journal of Applied Behavior Analysis, 8,* 463–470.

STANLEY, S. O., & Greenwood, C. R. (1983). *Code for instructional structure and student academic response (CISSAR): Observer's manual.* Kansas City: Juniper Gardens Children's Project, University of Kansas.

THURLOW, M. L., Ysseldyke, J. E., Graden, J., & Algozzine, B. (1984). Opportunity to learn for LD students receiving different levels of special education services. *Learning Disabilities Quarterly, 7,* 55–67.

TYMITZ, B. L. (1983). Bilingual special education: A challenge to evaluation practices. In D. R. Omark & J. G. Erickson (Eds.), *The bilingual exceptional child* (pp. 359–377). San Diego: College Hill Press.

YSSELDYKE, J. E., Thurlow, M. L., Mecklenburg, C., Graden, J., & Algozzine, B. (1984). Changes in academic engaged time as a function of assessment and special education intervention. *Special services in the schools.* Vols. 1 & 2. Binghamton, NY: Haworth Press.

CHAPTER 18

Toward Instructional Process Measurability: An Interbehavioral Field Systems Perspective

Andrew Hawkins
Tom Sharpe
Roger Ray

We are seeing a change in focus from the study of one organism over time to the study of the social interaction between organisms.

Dillon, Madden, and Kumar (1983, p. 564)

It has been an ongoing challenge for educational researchers to systematically capture the many observable variables relevant to instruction as they occur in concert in natural settings. At a conceptual level, many similarities exist between an interbehavioral field systems perspective and the nature of the instructional milieu. The purpose of this chapter is to take advantage of these similarities by describing the value of the field systems orientation as it relates to the measurement of instructional settings, and by detailing the feasibility of a measurement technology based on an interbehavioral framework. Specifically, we address this purpose by (1) conceptualizing a field systems perspective as it relates to the assessment of instructional processes, (2) describing an interbehavioral measurement system that uses current computer-based technology, (3) presenting an example of instructional assessment using a field systems perspective in which longitudinal data point to the efficacy of such an approach in the education and assessment of teachers, and (4) providing future

potential applications of this approach specifically to teacher education and generally to behavior analysis. We hope this type of information will provide behavior analysts with the ability and incentive to focus on the more complex and observable process interactions that are naturally exhibited between teachers and students in context. Our goal is to contribute to the further development of data-driven, behavior-analytic assessment of instructional settings.

Conceptual Foundations

It is easy to agree with Jackson's (1968) perspective that in the context of typical classroom settings, events come and go with astonishing rapidity. Individual teachers engage in hundreds of behavioral interactions within each class period. Accurate observation and analysis is difficult at best and is at least partly responsible for a "science versus art" debate with regard to effective instruction. Many educators contend that a true science of teaching is beyond our grasp, for it "implies that good teaching will someday be attainable by closely following rigorous laws that yield high predictability and control" (Gage, 1978, p. 17). Some argue that effective teaching is spontaneous and intuitive. Clinical assessments within a class setting regarding how multiple variables affect the solution to the myriad of daily instructional problems are said to rely primarily on feeling and artistry (cf., Dawe, 1984; Eisner, 1983; Gage, 1984; Rubin, 1985). In essence, many mainstream contemporary educational researchers agree that scientific attempts to analyze teaching as a preplanned or predictive process are much too difficult and time-consuming. Further, they may even distract from a study of important esthetic, intuitive, and political factors.

A history of debate across paradigmatic communities further complicates the challenge of improving instruction through science and technology (cf., Finn, 1988; Firestone, 1987; Garrison, 1986; Howe, 1988; Huberman, 1987; Shavelson & Berliner, 1988). It is not our intent to malign particular research perspectives or engage in more polemic. Rather, we intend to point toward a particular methodology and its underlying conceptual framework. We believe this to be compatible with, and of great utility for, a feasible scientific approach to measuring instructional effectiveness.

Interbehavioral Field Systems

Behavior-analytic research in natural classroom settings has largely stemmed from a linear approach to experimentation and evaluation (Witt, 1990). Although productive, a linear perspective allows primarily for possible solutions to an immediate concern by examining a limited number of variables. Results are temporally and contextually constricted, often overlooking multiple concurrent and sequential interdependencies. Basic laboratory science functions largely according to linear chains in which functional relationships are established between certain variables. Single factors are usually identified as independent variables, which exert functional control over single dependent variables. However, the subject's behavior in a natural setting is guided by patterns of multiple concurrent and se-

quential stimuli. Drawing from Gottman and Roy's (1990) sequential analysis illustrations, a comparison of conditional and unconditional probabilities of multiple behavioral events as they flow through time may be a valuable analytic tactic. Knowledge of the temporal characteristics of prior events as they have naturally occurred may assist in the kind of prediction desired in science. It seems, therefore, that the nature of classroom instruction may be more fruitfully assessed as an interbehavioral field comprised of distinguishable but inseparable historical, setting, contextual, and behavioral elements that act to simultaneously and conjointly define the whole.

Before proceeding, we want to familiarize you with fundamental field systems terminology. The language used in this chapter is drawn largely from Roger Ray's methodological work (e.g., Ray, 1992; Ray & Delprato, 1989) and from interpretations of J. R. Kantor's many conceptual contributions (1941, 1946, 1953, 1959, 1969; Kantor & Smith, 1975). First, the term *interbehavior* is used to emphasize not only an isolated response to stimulus function, but the multiplistic connections among organisms, organismic action, setting factors, and other relevant enabling and impeding conditions in a particular setting. Clearly, context is of primary importance within an interbehavioral analysis. For example, low student achievement may be interpreted and reacted to differently across accelerated and special education settings by both the teacher and student peers.

The term *field* stems from Kantor's (1959) holistic approach to behavioral psychology and Morris and Midgley's (1990) assertion that the behavioral sciences must become increasingly ecological and contextualistic. A field involves a thorough account of observable events that conceivably operate within a setting. Given the static connotation of the term *field*, the additional term *system* is added to emphasize the dynamic reciprocal interaction of the many elements contained within a field. A systemic dimension accentuates the presence of at least two or more elements that share varying degrees of enabling or constraining influence on one another, and consequently force the field into a constant state of flux. An interbehavioral field system, therefore, may be defined as a unique, constantly changing, spatial and temporal confluence of multiple behavioral and setting elements.

Redefining the Instructional Setting

The application of linear assumptions to the study of whole classrooms has been conceptually unsatisfactory and epistemologically forced. Multiplistic occurrences of a host of interrelated events are characteristic of instructional settings (Scarr, 1985). Altman (1988) and Altman and Rogoff (1987) argued that instructional elements mutually define one another. They understood the instructional whole as a host of inseparable aspects that serve to mutually explain one another in context. These aspects include the historical characteristics of teachers and students, the setting, the lesson content and activities, and the students' and teachers' current behavior. All of these contribute to the "meaning and nature of . . . the [instructional] event" (Altman & Rogoff, 1987, p. 24). It may readily be discerned, therefore, that an interbehavioral field systems perspective and the emergent view of instruction in a natural context are conceptually compatible.

The question, therefore, becomes "*How*, then, can such a rich setting be studied, and *what* questions ought its study be able to answer?" (Salomon, 1991, p. 14). Attempts to redefine a compatible research and evaluation process according to a field systems approach are scarce. Ray and Delprato (1989) offer one of the few generic behavioral systems methodologies available in the literature. A few recently available tactical guides are also more relevant to instructional settings (Frick, 1990; Greenwood et al., 1991; Greenwood, Carta, & Atwater, 1991; Sharpe & Hawkins, 1992a, 1992b). We now turn our attention to a methodological process that draws from these seminal efforts.

An Assessment Protocol

A technology that enables concurrent evaluation of people, settings, and activities within particular instructional episodes shows great promise for educational improvement at a local level. Toward this end, we now describe one instructional measurement system (Sharpe, Bahls, & Wood, 1991) that has been used with undergraduate teacher education students who teach in physical education and special education movement skill settings.[1]

Technological Foundations

The past 20 years may be characterized as a period of rapid technological evolution with readily apparent effects in scientific, technical, and industrial fields. Technology's effect on education in general and teacher education in particular, however, is less discernible (Hawkins & Wiegand, 1987). It is possible that the greatest potential for the application of technology to education may lie in the area of instructional measurement. The assessment of teacher and student process variables as they occur within the context of particular learning environments may be amenable to fresh technological approaches. The recurrent challenge is to find instruments that enable behavioral, ecological, and historical evaluation of particular classroom settings. We believe that this challenge, if met, may lead to direct improvement of educational programs at their most basic level—moment-to-moment teaching/learning activities.

Technological enhancement may make significant contributions to at least two areas in instructional measurement: more exhaustive recording and measurement capabilities in live instructional settings, and instructional evaluation based upon more sensitive data collection. Greater understanding of the variables extant in instructional settings, when coupled with an analysis of the functional relationships among those variables, may enable more effective pedagogical assessment.

Category Systems

When category systems are used to describe and analyze instruction, it must be remembered that such categories are somewhat arbitrary delineations of certain stimulus and response classes. In other words, the

---

[1] Currently, this evaluation instrument is used by the West Virginia University and University of Nebraska-Lincoln undergraduate teacher certification programs in physical education, and it is in the first cycle of implementation and possible adoption throughout the Lincoln Public School System. Experienced practitioners, university faculty, and select graduate students are working cooperatively on evaluation system training, preservice teacher instruction, and on-site assessment (cf., Sharpe et al., 1991).

sum total of behavioral and contextual elements is subdivided into functionally defined groups that are thought to have a relationship to teaching effectiveness according to the informed opinion and literature of teacher educators. It still remains to be seen whether the categories in our example, or in any category system for that matter, are profitable in understanding the relationships in a learning environment. Categories often evolve into multiple subcategories, while others are synthesized to better describe and analyze the relationships in instructional settings. The number of categories that constitute a thorough description of an instructional system must also be balanced against a logistical requirement. In essence, the number of categories must be carefully weighed against the information gained and the ability of observers to collect it. System parsimony enhances the accuracy and reliability of the data collected.

Nevertheless, category systems provide vehicles for a more systematic and objective perspective on our phenomenon of interest: effective instruction. Therefore, our purpose has been to discover technologies that facilitate the use of category systems in instructional assessment.

The Measurement System

The Behavioral Evaluation Strategy and Taxonomy (BEST) and its companion, the Temporal Analysis System (TAS), were developed in concert by the faculty at the Teachers College at the University of Nebraska-Lincoln and the West Virginia University Sport Pedagogy faculty (Sharpe, Bahls, & Wood, 1991; Sharpe, Hawkins, & Wood, in press). Its purpose is to provide a rich empirical source of information from which instructional assessment may be made. BEST was designed to be used by teacher educators in evaluating preservice and inservice teachers in different subject matters. The system incorporates an extensive category system, including teacher and student behaviors, ecological elements, and historical factors. In addition, it can incorporate new or unique situational elements as the user observes them.

Instructional stimuli, student responses, setting events, and historical context categories were derived from a content analysis of qualitative field notes generated in observations of a variety of subject mat-

ter activities by preservice and inservice teachers. Terminology has been taken, when appropriate, from a synthesis of many of the category systems in the teaching evaluation literature, such as the observation tools contained in Darst, Zakrajsek, and Mancini's (1989) compilation and in the work of the Juniper Gardens Children's Project (Dickie, 1989).

The system is designed for use with an electronic recording regimen (e.g., S&K Computer Products Event Recorder, Ltd.). Though traditional paper-and-pencil recording techniques could be used, the user would be constrained in the level of complexity that is amenable to observation. Therefore, we will only explain the electronic strategy in detail.

We prefer using fairly sophisticated technology for data collection because we want to provide immediate, real-time information for each behavioral and contextual category (e.g., frequency, average duration, and percentage of total recording time) and a detailed analysis of patterns in time (e.g., the frequency, relative probability, and parametric significance with which defined categories tend to follow one another in time). Only an electronic recording regimen is able to provide a thorough description of complex instructional settings.

Six to eight hours of instruction and practice on the system generally produces an acceptable level ($r > .85$) of interrater reliability (Kazdin, 1982). System accuracy is assessed through observation comparisons with several short segments of a criterion tape. System reliability is assessed by comparing one accurate observation to another observation conducted on the same criterion tape sample one month later. Interobserver agreement is assessed by comparing two simultaneous independent observations of the same criterion tape sample.

Since the data collected must be viewed in the context of certain ecological factors such as unit planning, placement in the unit, class size, activity, and so on, the teacher educator must have a degree of learned interpretation. This is particularly salient with regard to student categories, which are only definable in terms of a particular lesson's goals. Therefore, an ideal generic data profile that may be transferred across lesson contexts does not exist. Rather, a systematic technology is presented in light of its ability to collect a substantial amount of descriptive data to be used to (1) systematically describe an instructional setting, (2) provide context-specific feedback, and (3) provide a longitudinal account of progress through a series of observations and analyses.

Category system descriptions. The BEST system consists of a 4-category, 14-subcategory, and 107-event classroom observation system (Table 18.1). The system enables the recording of simultaneously occurring teacher and student behaviors. Although the category system appears large, only 20 to 30 of the possible 107

events are typically observed within a particular instructional context. For example, only one event within each of the six ecological subcategories will be operative, and the historical subcategories are recorded before the observation begins. The system is organized around four major categories: ecological, teacher behavior, student behavior, and historical. The focus of analysis is on multiple dimensions of discrete events within each of the three major nonhistorical categories and on the proximal relationships in time, or sequential patterns, among these events (Sharpe, 1990; Sharpe & Hawkins, 1992c).

Table 18.1 BEST categories, descriptions, codes, and examples

Categories	Number of Codes	Description	Examples of Codes
Ecological			
Setting	8	Service delivery setting	Regular class, resource room, partitioned gymnasium
Content	10	Subject matter content	Science, math, English, physical education
Content stage	3	Temporal status of lesson	Introduction, lesson body, review
Materials	6	Physical resources	Task cards, pupil folders, workbooks
Pupil grouping	3	Physical arrangements	Large group, small group, individual
Method of instruction	6	Stimuli method to occasion responding	Command style, task teaching, questioning, peer teaching, self-instruction, cooperative
Teacher			
Behavior	22	Teacher's behavior relative to student	Observation, instruction, interpersonal, managerial
Focus	3	How behavior is directed	Individual, general class, nonstudent
Position	5	Relative proximity to target student	Proximate, distant, central, peripheral, out of room
Student			
Academic	5	Active response	Task appropriate, task engaged, motor, cognitive, verbal
On task	5	Organizational responses	Transition, absorption, waiting, support, peer instruction
Off task	3	Academically competing responses	Active disruption, self-stimulation, passive
Historical			
Teacher definition	11	Organismic history of setting impact	Educational certification, years and type of experience
Student definition	17	Organismic history of setting impact	Age, cultural background, SES achievement and disciplinary history

For illustrative purposes, we've chosen one category system used in physical education and special education movement skill settings. For the purpose of multiple evaluations across a similar practicum, a more simplistic code drawn from the BEST instrument was used. Table 18.2 displays this category system, which was implemented across several teacher certification practica and inservice settings. Comparison of Tables 18.1 and 18.2 should illustrate how instructional measurement tools for particular contexts may evolve from a more global category system.

Recording procedures.   A data entry program integral to a NEC-PC 8300 laptop computer (S&K Computer Products, Ltd.) is used to record classroom events and prompt historical notations. Historical notations and ecological subcategories are entered at the beginning of an observation evaluation and any time thereafter if they change. Real-time recording procedures are used to record teacher and student behavioral events and those ecological characteristics that change during an observation. Real-time recording involves ascribing a subcategory to an alphanumeric key on the NEC-PC. Keys are either pressed to signal the onset and termination of a particular subcategory or pressed and held for the dura-

Table 18.2 Physical education/Movement skill assessment code

Teacher Behavior	Student Behavior	Context
General observation	Motor appropriate	Lesson preview
Specific observation	Motor inappropriate	Lesson body
Encouragement	Supportive	Lesson review
Positive feedback	Instruction of peers	
Negative feedback	Cognitive	Teacher locus: Proximate
Management	Self-management	Distant
Verbal instruction	Waiting	Teacher focus: Individual
Modeling	Off task	Large group
Physical guidance		
Interpersonal		
Off task		

tion of a particular category. A notation program also allows for the recording of atypical characteristics of particular events. Following collection, data are downloaded into a personal computer for analysis, using software developed by S & K Computer Products and the authors.[2]

Instructional Measurement Procedures
Using BEST as an instructional measurement instrument in our teacher education programs includes three steps: (1) data collection and summation of discrete behavioral and contextual elements (i.e., those elements that change in the course of an observation); (2) analysis of the data set for patterns in time; and (3) data-based goal setting for future instructional opportunities. Selected examples from one instructional episode, shown in Table 18.3, illustrate the type of information gleaned.

Discrete element analysis.   Our first step is to examine the summative characteristics of each subcategory used in the observation (refer to Table 18.2). Several measurement dimensions (e.g., frequency, duration, and the temporal percentage of the total observation) are necessary for each subcategory to understand the dynamics of a complex instructional setting more thoroughly. For example, frequency may be more important in assessing high-velocity, low-duration behaviors such as teacher "interpersonal interaction." On the other hand, duration may be a more indicative dimension of some low-frequency behaviors such as teacher "nontask interpersonal," or low-frequency contextual events such as "lesson preview." The number per minute and percentage duration dimensions indicate how an event functioned in relation to the overall class time. An insightful inquiry based on a field systems perspective requires a multidimensional examination.

Analysis of patterns in time.   The analysis of patterns in time describes some of the relationships among contextual and behavioral events as they occur tem-

[2]A complete data collection and analysis protocol and accompanying category system definitions are available from Tom Sharpe at the University of Nebraska.

Table 18.3 Three-step instructional assessment examples

| | Frequency | Discrete Element Data Summation | | |
		Mean Duration (sec.)	Percentage Duration	Number Per Minute
Teacher Behavior				
Specific observation	19	35	24.8	0.59
Interpersonal	5	11	2.1	0.11
Verbal instruction	15	101	16.1	0.33
Management	59	8	48.2	1.31
Teacher Context				
Individual focus	5	28	4.8	0.11
Group focus	57	15	32.1	1.28
Proximate	7	19	4.1	0.17
Distant	11	189	68.2	0.23
Student Behavior				
Motor appropriate	5	185	33.1	0.11
Motor inappropriate	8	135	35.2	0.20
Waiting	4	121	16.0	0.08
Supportive	15	35	16.1	0.33

Analysis of Patterns in Time

Teacher Observation ⟶ Management   @11 (.58)[a]
                                        Verbal Instruction   4 (.21)
                                        Interpersonal   1 (.05)

4(0.80)[b]   Teacher Proximate   ⟵   Motor appropriate
4(0.80)[b]   Student Support
5(1.00)[b]   Individual Focus

6(0.75)[b]   Teacher Distant   ⟵   Motor inappropriate
8(1.00)[b]   General Focus

Notes:
@ 11 = number of times the pattern occurred; (.58) = conditional probability of management following teacher observation
[a] = significant at $p = .05$
[b] = significant at $p = .01$

Examples of Goal Setting

Provide secondary managerial systems to allow for a primary focus on instruction.
Use observation to focus on instructional concerns.
Provide an active supervision pattern to ensure proximity and individual focus when conveying instruction.
Use peers as secondary instructional support sources.

porally. As Table 18.3 displays, frequency, conditional probability (the probability with which a particular subcategory either precedes or succeeds another), and statistical significance (based on conditional and unconditional probabilities, Gottman & Roy, 1990) are represented for preceding and succeeding events around a central subcategory of interest. Pattern-in-time searches may be programmed using preceding events, succeeding events, origination events, and length-of-chain parameters. Then, they may be searched individually or as a logically specified group. For example, all event chains of three that begin with a particular teacher behavior subcategory may be examined (e.g., all behavior chains that begin with verbal instruction and include other key instructional behaviors, such as verbal instruction $\longrightarrow$ specific observation $\longrightarrow$ positive feedback). All conceivable chains of two may be explored and represented by a matrix. All subcategories that either precede or succeed a particular subcategory may also be displayed (e.g., all behaviors that precede and succeed teacher modeling). Lag-time specifications may be specified in a pattern-in-time search (a time parameter between the onset of a central event and the onset of others); this is particularly useful if multiple ongoing events obscure a temporal chain of interest.

The major constraint of previous behavior-analytic efforts is that particular variables of interest have been viewed in a linear fashion, removing them from their context and from their temporal association with one another. Other events have been deemed extraneous to such an evaluation. An interbehavioral analysis stands in contrast to this kind of assessment, and the analysis of patterns in time may be the crux of our approach. In complex settings such as exist in classroom instruction, it is quite clear that many events have the propensity to affect many others in a multidirectional fashion. Therefore, evaluation that primarily focuses on which teacher, student, and contextual events tend to be present, absent, or surround others temporally should lend greater insight into how to enhance instructional settings and processes.

Goal setting. An integral component in our use of the BEST system is data-based goal setting. Approaches based on the contiguous temporal relationships among behavioral and contextual elements, and that make a direct connection with student responses, hold much promise for educational evaluation. An inter-behavioral evaluation strategy seeks to capture such teacher $\longleftrightarrow$ student relations within the larger umbrellas of contextual events and historical antecedents. Therefore, following assessment, goals are provided that relate directly to the discrete element summation and to the analysis of patterns in time. Of course, future observations may assess the degree to which goals are attained.

As Table 18.3 illustrates, high-frequency and high-percentage teacher managerial behavior ($f = 59$, 48.2%) and a low-percentage duration of verbal instruction (16.1%) indicate a need to reorient toward a primarily instructional role. This need is again evident in the analysis of patterns in time. There is a temporal connection between teacher observation and the ensuing management emphasis. Furthermore, the importance of teacher proximity and peer support are also seen in this kind of analysis. There are significant temporal relationships among (1) motor-appropriate student behavior and teacher proximity, (2) motor-appropriate behavior and student support, and conversely, (3) motor inappropriate behavior and teacher distance. The need for more individual focus is also evident, both from the discrete element summation (individual equals low frequency and percentage, and general equals high frequency and percentage) and from the analysis of patterns in time. The strong temporal relationship between individual focus and motor appropriate on the one hand, and general focus and motor inappropriate on the other underscores the need for more individual focus.

A caution. A major criticism of a behavior-analytic approach to assessment lies in its perception as a largely technocratic undertaking, driven more by advanced technologies employed by unreflective technicians than by thoughtful professionals (Schempp, 1987). However, it should not be assumed that particular quantitative levels or specific temporal relationships may be ascribed and extended to effective instruction. Rather, a technical tool merely enables a more representative and thorough picture of complex instructional episodes from a dynamic field systems perspective. A field systems procedure, and others that are akin, still requires the interpretive expertise of an experienced, trained educational evaluator. An interbehavioral system simply provides descriptive and analytic techniques for extracting behavioral and contextual information from instructional settings. The purpose is always to understand more fully the dynamics of complex educational environments.

An Example of Interbehavioral Assessment

To illustrate the value of a field systems approach to instructional measurement, we present two analyses of instructional performance change for selected events within Table 18.2.

Study I

Study I was a longitudinal analysis of different dimensions of selected teacher and student behaviors of physical education and special education majors in the University of Nebraska-Lincoln (UN-L) teacher certification program ($N = 15$). Aggregate data were used for each graph and instructional context and subject matter activities were matched cross-sectionally and longitudinally.

Preservice teachers in the undergraduate certification program were familiarized with the conceptual nature of an interbehavioral field systems approach to instructional measurement in the didactic portions of their introductory and intermediate methods classes. They were then repeatedly assessed according to the Table 18.2 protocol throughout each practicum, student teaching, and in their initial inservice experiences. One aggregate early, mid, and end-of-experience data point for each practicum (i.e., methods practica, student teaching, and inservice) is represented for illustrative purposes in Figures 18.1, 18.2, and 18.3.

Teacher and student behaviors and analytic units were chosen based on initial instruction in the didactic portions of the coursework. For example, before each practicum, the following concepts were repeatedly addressed: (1) increasing class time devoted to instruction and student motor-appropriate time (Figure 18.1); (2) decreasing time devoted to teacher and student management and student waiting (Figure 18.1); (3) increasing the frequency of specific observation, encouragement,

feedback, instruction, and interpersonal interaction (Figure 18.2); and (4) emitting particular instructional behaviors in sequence (Figure 18.3).

As is readily discerned from Figures 18.1 through 18.3, aggregate trends were demonstrated across all variables in the recommended directions. Though only three aggregate points are represented within each practicum, each graph indicates the efficacy of the assessment protocol with regard to improvement both within and across phases for each vari-

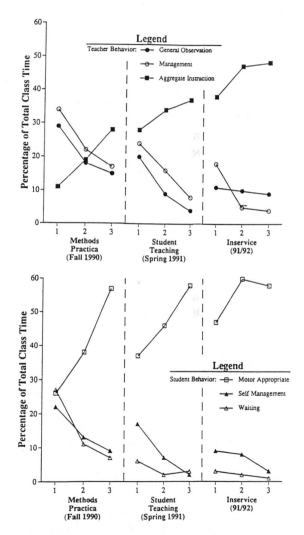

Figure 18.1. Percentage of total class time for selected teacher and student behaviors from the Table 18.2 assessment taxonomy.

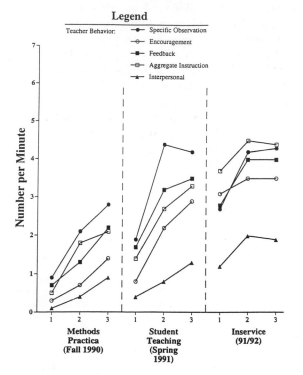

Figure 18.2. Average emission number per minute for selected teacher behaviors from the Table 18.2 assessment taxonomy.

able targeted for change. Of additional interest is the field system orientation's ability to train, alter, and maintain more complex analytic units (e.g., sequences of teacher behaviors).

Study II

Study II involved an aggregate comparison of employed teachers who had been repeatedly exposed to the evaluation process in their undergraduate program (as in Study I, $N = 15$) and a similar inservice teacher group that had not been similarly exposed ($N = 15$).[3] Over the course of one academic year, a series of ten profiles using the BEST instrument were undertaken

[3]Data collection and analysis was made possible by the Oliver E. Bird Fellowship for the *UN-L Training and Generalization Project: A Behavioral Evaluation Strategy and Taxonomy for In-Service Teacher Evaluation*, and UN-L Research Council Grant LWT/10-215-91601 *Real-Time Data Analysis Software Applications*.

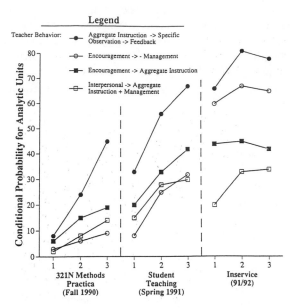

Figure 18.3. Conditional probability for trained teacher behavior analytic units from the Table 18.2 assessment taxonomy.

at regular intervals for each subject in representing the overall performance for the two groups.

Figures 18.4 and 18.5 represent the amount of class time devoted to the teacher behaviors of verbal instruction, management, and interpersonal interactions. A comparison of experimental (Figure 18.4) and control (Figure 18.5) graphs demonstrates that the evaluation process seemed to (1) increase class time devoted to instruction, (2) decrease time devoted to managerial concerns, and (3) prompt greater periods of class time devoted to interpersonal interactions over the course of the academic year.

These findings demonstrate the usefulness of the BEST instrument as a measurement system for teacher education. More important, however, is the use of field systems analyses to understand and develop the temporal relationships among more complex clusters of teacher and student behaviors. Figure 18.6 shows percentages of class time devoted to student success (i.e., accomplishment of a stated subject matter–related task—motor-appropriate behavior), whereas Figure 18.7 portrays the percentage of student-engaged behavior (i.e., attempting a subject mat-

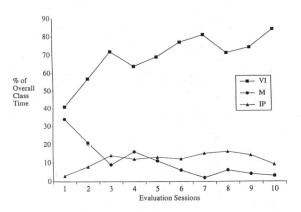

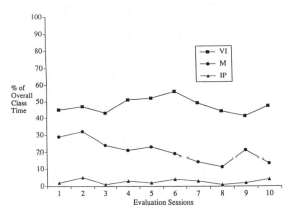

Figure 18.4. Comparison of percentage of total class time devoted to selected teacher behaviors for the evaluation aggregate.

Figure 18.5. Comparison of percentage of class time devoted to selected teacher behaviors for the control aggregate.

ter–related task, but doing so unsuccessfully—motor-inappropriate behavior) for the exposed group across sessions. The findings also represent the probabilities with which selected teacher behaviors evidence themselves in a manner temporally contiguous with the student variables.

The evaluation process fostered interactions that enabled larger percentages of student success with diminished portions of student engagement over the course of the year. Further, teacher proximate (i.e., the teacher in close proximity to a particular student) and individual teacher focus (i.e., the teacher attends to a particular student as opposed to student groups) appear to function as temporal facilitators of student success, as indicated by the heightened conditional probability levels that correlate positively over time with levels of student success. A similar pattern was also seen between teacher distant and general focus probabilities and student engaged (unsuccessful at-

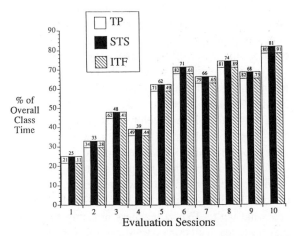

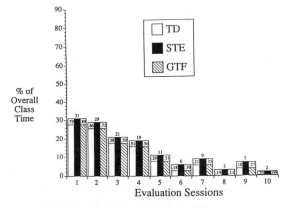

Figure 18.6. Conditional probability of select teacher behaviors occurring in termporal contiguity as a function of the percentage of classtime in which motor-appropriate behavior is evidenced.

Figure 18.7. Conditional probability of select teacher behaviors occurring in temporal contiguity as a function of the percentage of classtime in which motor-inappropriate behavior is evidenced.

tempts), though the levels of student engaged declined across sessions.

When combining student success with student-engaged class percentages across graphs (i.e., the total time students spend in subject matter attempts regardless of success), the evaluation procedure may also be focused on classroom practices, which enable greater portions of time to be devoted to subject matter practice. This was particularly salient in light of the diminished portions of total class time devoted to managerial concerns across the academic year for the experimental aggregate (refer to Figure 18.4).

From these data, it seems that behavior analysis is increasingly capable of examining some of the more-complex response classes of human subjects in educational settings using an interbehavioral technology. This has largely been due to a field systems perspective that has emerged contemporaneously with growing computer technologies. The combination has made possible the technological application of a theoretical framework, which has enabled a more complex data collection, analysis, and evaluation process.

Implications and Applications

It is increasingly clear from this study and the others referenced that technology is enabling behavior analysts to understand, and even control, more complex response ←——→ stimulus configurations. This provides an impetus for evaluating and altering complex behavioral and contextual interactions in classroom settings. If this is the case, then two questions arise: Should we do what is technologically feasible? and Which configurations should be taught now that we know we are capable? Though it is easy to become mired in the particulars of which educational ends justify which technological means, the larger question of the general effects of technology must be considered first.

The question of the effects of technology have not so much to do with the technological revolution itself, but with the philosophical frame of reference of the 20th century. Technological power is oftentimes perceived as dogma, with the technological revolution another form of idolatry (Ellul, 1964). This can be the

case whether the technology involves nuclear weapons, media discourse, or even educational evaluation. In this intellectual climate, science ceases to be the basic process for the discovery of truth and degenerates into the means for the development of technological worship. The limits of technology are determined by the individual or group that controls it. Caution should therefore be exercised to avoid viewing technological approaches to educational evaluation as unduly concentrating on means without seeing the ends (Hawkins & Wiegand, 1987).

Therefore, what purpose may we legitimately expect to have served by enhancing our technological understanding of excellence in teaching? Is it to remain merely a tool for assessment, or may we anticipate applying it to the enhancement of other dimensions of the teaching process, including perhaps the teaching of the prospective teacher (i.e., applying technology to teacher education as well as to evaluation)? Several issues seem to be raised by such a vision, not the least of which is the possibility of computer-driven simulations of the process. Perhaps the most realistic form that such simulation might take is that of an interactive video.

Consider, for example, the possibility that evaluation research such as that reported earlier might lead us directly to the ability to discriminate and articulate those teacher activities most influential in guiding desired student learning of a given topic or skill in a given situation. Anticipating that expert teachers are more expert at teaching some things than others, any given simulation effort will surely have its application and validity restricted by the specific expertise and setting that is under study, thus requiring a variety of different simulation efforts.

If our interest is in developing such a technology, data must come from a variety of experts doing a variety of things before we attempt to articulate any single approach or strategy appropriate to any given circumstance. In addition, variations between individual students help define what is likely to work and what isn't. Expert teachers not only fail when they try to teach all things, they also fail sometimes in teaching their strongest areas to some select students. But what is the feasibility for bringing simulation technology into such a complex process?

Given the fact that data-based assessment programs such as those reported earlier will likely generate a variety of concrete examples of good and not-so-good teaching over a variety of student learning and setting variations, what if the critical features of these various episodes were reconstructed on video-disc as isolated "scenes" for eventual computer-selected simulation application? Such a corpus of video scenes might well illustrate most, if not all, of the positive and negative event features that new teachers are likely to experience, including the individuals and ecological settings with which they will eventually deal.

Imagine the possibility of playing these various scenes in a wide variety of sequences by making computer-based choices of the types of teacher interactions chosen for illustration. Also imagine that each sequence leads to its own learning outcomes, and that the video database includes illustrative examples of all such outcomes. Such a video simulation system has several possibilities for application and may assume many different structural and functional forms.

First, real databases could be used to "seed" the simulation's onset, thereby allowing the simulator to determine sequential transitions from scene to scene. This would be accomplished by following in the same stochastic sequence determined by the type of data being simulated (e.g., poor teaching interaction databases, better teaching databases, and expert teaching databases).

Such a simulator is interactive not with the viewer but with the supplied stochastic database. As such, it mimics typically observed settings, student types, teaching interaction strategies, sequential dependencies among events, durational and other temporal parameters, and so on. It also demonstrates the observed learning outcomes attendant to each type of stochastic database. Good teaching may thus be directly compared to poorer teaching as the user selects the desired playback "script's" level of expertise. And because playback scenes are stochastically driven in sequence, they approximate the actual dynamics and unpredictability of real teaching situations.

Yet another variation on this computer-operated video simulator could allow for the viewer to interact with the sequence playback by using keyboard inputs.

In this scenario, viewers could watch poor teaching sequences until they felt they recognized the types of problems being demonstrated. Then they could intervene to shift the driving stochastic programs to more-effective strategies by interceding with better-interaction selections. As a result, they could "teach" the teacher being observed on the video to use different teaching techniques, thereby learning what really is, and is not, a "better" technique by observing student performance outcomes reported via the simulator's play sequence.

The critical factor in all good simulators is whether an expert observer (such as those doing the coding in the evaluation studies) can detect whether a true human expert is in control, or whether a novice or learner is in control. As such, all interactions with the interactive-video simulator should be automatically "coded" by the simulator and used to contrast with the expert teacher's choices of interaction with the training simulator. When they are statistically indistinguishable, the student has personally learned to "simulate" the expert. When such a performance level has been reached, the student should be placed into real-life situations to train generalization.

Because teaching is interactive on several levels, examples of physical interactions and of interactions that are more qualitative and interpretational in character should be included. This level is conveyed by much subtler, but still potentially objective, events that are more difficult to capture in coded descriptions. These events include verbal intonations and inflections, the frequencies of speaking and pausing, choices of words for their connotative (rather than their denotative) meanings, nonverbal communicative gestures and body language, and even social (versus physical) distances that exist between teacher and student. These are the elements that challenge us most in describing how a true expert teacher works. They are the traditional domain of the "artistic" teachers. Nevertheless, art may also be understood and used as a simulation of reality.

The challenge lies not only in recognizing the task that lies before us in trying to describe and evaluate good teaching, but also in recognizing the tools that are already available for accomplishing that task. Scientific description is of little use if we cannot use it to reconstruct the original sequences and dynamics of events being described. Computer and interactive video simulation is, after all, merely a reconstructive process that makes the original events appear to be real-time depictions to those observing and describing the simulation. Eventually, simulation becomes our own quality check on the reality of scientific progress: if we understand and describe the attendant variables well enough to make our simulations appear real, we probably have the technology necessary to use it to train new observers and participants in the process.

Conclusion

In spite of the productive nature of the behavior-analytic tradition, there is much that is yet unknown about the determinants of more complex forms of human behavior. For example, Bronfenbrenner (1979) has noted that education currently lacks a database on the structure, distribution, and impact of ecological context variables in applied settings. It is likely that the more complex forms of behavior, and the ecology in which they reside, need to be developed in teacher education programs. It is becoming apparent that a spatiotemporal perspective is necessary to provide more accurate educational evaluation and a better understanding of the complete meaning and nature of instructional events. Thus, the need is apparent for more sophisticated evaluation technologies to better assess classroom instruction and to discover how to more effectively enhance the behaviors of prospective teachers and their students. This brings us to our own nascent attempts to employ technologically driven evaluation systems in educational settings, though we recognize the philosophical cautions.

In line with Greenwood, Delquadri, Stanley, Terry, and Hall (1985), we recommend four areas for application of these emergent assessment strategies: (1) the development of a comparative database derived from different instructional settings as temporal conglomerates of contextual and behavioral variables; (2) the implementation of subsequent causal analyses of relationships that frequently appear in such databases; (3) the monitoring of the fidelity of interventions in specific contexts based on causal conclusions; and (4) the assessment of long-term changes in contextual and

behavioral dependencies that have resulted from these interventions.

Greenwood, Carta, Arreaga-Mayer, and Rager (1991) summarized the implications of instructional evaluation efforts comparable to the one described:

> The utility of a search and validate approach to the evaluation of effective instructional practices has only just begun to be undertaken. Because of its . . . analysis of classroom behavior, and temporally related situational features of classroom instruction, it is an approach consistent with current school improvement goals. It is also an approach that focuses on the contributions classroom teachers can bring to the development of effective instructional technology. Clearly, demonstrations of the approach are warranted. [pp. 188–189]

As the technological revolution approaches educational evaluation, careful consideration of the empirical and ethical limits of technology must be undertaken through the scholarly dissemination of its functional possibilities. The end of more thorough and accurate educational evaluation strategies will necessarily combine calculated experimentation with emergent technology.

References

ALTMAN, I. (1988). Process, transactional, contextual, and outcome research: An alternative to the traditional distinction between basic and applied research. *Social Behavior, 3,* 259–280.

ALTMAN, I., & Rogoff, B. (1987). World views in psychology: Trait, interactional, organismic, and transactional perspectives. In D. Stokolis & I. Altman (Eds.), *Handbook of environmental psychology* (pp. 1–40). New York: Wiley.

BRONFENBRENNER, U. (1979). Contexts of child rearing: Problems and prospects. *American Psychologist, 34,* 84–89.

DARST, P. W., Zakrajsek, D. B., & Mancini, V. H. (1989). *Analyzing physical education and sport instruction.* 2nd ed. Champaign, IL: Human Kinetics.

DAWE, H. A. (1984). Teaching: Social science or performing art? *Harvard Educational Review, 54,* 111–114.

DICKIE, R. F. (Ed.). (1989). The Juniper Gardens Children's Project. *Education and Treatment of Children* [Special monograph issue], *12*(4).

DILLON, W. R., Madden, T. J., & Kumar, A. (1983). Analyzing sequential categorical data on dyadic interaction: A latent structure approach. *Psychological Bulletin, 94,* 564–583.

EISNER, E. W. (1983). The art and craft of teaching. *Educational Leadership, 40,* 4–13.

ELLUL, J. [1954] (1964). *The technological society.* Trans. J. Wilkinson. New York: Knopf.

FINN, C. E. (1988). What ails education research. *Educational Researcher, 17,* 5–8.

FIRESTONE, W. A. (1987). Meaning in method: The rhetoric of quantitative and qualitative research. *Educational Researcher, 16,* 16–21.

FRICK, T. W. (1990). Analysis of patterns in time: A method of recording and quantifying temporal relations in education. *American Educational Research Journal, 27*(1), 180–204.

GAGE, N. L. (1978). *The scientific basis of the art of teaching.* New York: Teachers College Press.

GAGE, N. L. (1984). What do we know about teaching effectiveness? *Phi Delta Kappan, 66,* 87–90.

GARRISON, J. W. (1986). Some principles of postpositivistic philosophy of science. *Educational Researcher, 15,* 12–18.

GOTTMAN, J. M., & Roy, A. K. (1990). *Sequential analysis: A guide for behavioral researchers.* New York: Cambridge University Press.

GREENWOOD, C. R., Carta, J. J., & Atwater, J. (1991). Ecobehavioral analysis in the classroom: Review and implications. *Journal of Behavioral Education, 1,* 59–77.

GREENWOOD, C. R., Carta, J. J., Arreaga-Mayer, C., & Rager, A. (1991). The behavior analyst consulting model: Identifying and validating naturally effective instructional methods. *Journal of Behavioral Education, 1,* 165–191.

GREENWOOD, C. R., Delquadri, J. C., Stanley, S. O., Terry, B., & Hall, R. V. (1985). Assessment of eco-behavioral interaction in school settings. *Behavioral Assessment, 7,* 331–347.

HAWKINS, A. H., & Wiegand, R. L. (1987). Where technology and accountability converge: The confessions of an educational technologist. In G. T. Barrette, R. S. Feingold, C. R. Rees, & M. Pieron (Eds.), *Myths, models, and methods in sport pedagogy* (pp. 67–75). Champaign, IL: Human Kinetics.

HOWE, K. R. (1988). Against the quantitative-qualitative incompatibility thesis or dogmas die hard. *Educational Researcher, 17,* 10–16.

HUBERMAN, M. (1987). How well does educational research really travel? *Educational Researcher, 16,* 5–13.

JACKSON, P. W. (1968). *Life in classrooms.* New York: Holt, Rinehart & Winston.

KANTOR, J. R. (1941). Current trends in psychological theory. *Psychological Bulletin, 38,* 29–65.

KANTOR, J. R. (1946). The aim and progress of psychology. *American Scientist, 34,* 251–263.

KANTOR, J. R. (1953). *The logic of modern science.* Chicago: Principia Press.

KANTOR, J. R. (1959). *Interbehavioral psychology.* Granville, OH: Principia Press.

KANTOR, J. R. (1969). *The scientific evolution of psychology.* Vol. 2. Chicago: Principia Press.

KANTOR, J. R., & Smith, N. W. (1975). *The science of psychology: An interbehavioral survey.* Chicago: Principia Press.

KAZDIN, A. E. (1982). *Single case research designs.* New York: Oxford University Press.

MORRIS, E. K., & Midgley, B. D. (1990). Some historical and conceptual foundations of ecobehavioral analysis. In S. R. Schroeder (Ed.), *Ecobehavioral analysis and developmental disabilities: The twenty-first century* (pp. 1–32). New York: Springer-Verlag.

RAY, R. D. (1992). Interbehavioral methodology: Lessons from simulation. *Journal of Teaching in Physical Education* [special monograph issue].

RAY, R. D., & Delprato, D. J. (1989). Behavioral systems analysis: Methodological strategies and tactics *Behavioral Science, 34,* 81–127.

RUBIN, L. J. (1985). *Artistry in teaching.* New York: Random House.

SALOMON, G. (1991). Transcending the qualitative-quantitative debate: The analytic and systemic approaches to educational research. *Educational Researcher, 20,* 10–18.

SCARR, S. (1985). Constructing psychology: Making facts and fables for our times. *American Psychologist, 40,* 499–512.

SCHEMPP, P. K. (1987). Research on teaching in physical education: Beyond the limits of natural science. *Journal of Teaching in Physical Education, 6*(2), 111–121.

SHARPE, T. L. (1990). Field systems data: An exploration of alternative visual representations. *Interbehaviorist, 18*(2), 4–8.

SHARPE, T. L., & Hawkins, A. (1992a). Field systems analysis: A tactical guide for exploring temporal relationships in classroom settings. *Teaching and Teacher Education: An International Journal of Research and Studies, 8,* 171–186.

SHARPE, T. L., & Hawkins, A. (Eds.) (1992b). Field systems analysis: An alternative strategy for the study of teaching expertise. *Journal of Teaching in Physical Education, 12*,1.

SHARPE, T. L., & Hawkins, A. (1992c). Field systems analysis: Prioritizing patterns in time and context among observable variables. *Quest, 44,* 15–34.

SHARPE, T. L., Bahls, V., & Wood, D. (1991). University of Nebraska teacher and student behavioral evaluation strategy and taxonomy (BEST). 3rd ed. Lincoln: University of Nebraska-Lincoln.

SHARPE, T. L., Hawkins, A., & Wood, D. (in press). *Temporal analysis system software guide and users' manual.* Ontario, Canada: S&K Computer Products, Ltd.

SHARPE, T. L., Bahls, V., Seagren, S. & Wolfe, P. (1991) A collaborative approach to practica based teacher preparation: The Nebraska - Lincoln Model. In G. M. Graham & M. A. Jones (Eds.), *Collaboration between researchers and practitioners in physical education: An international dialogue* (pp. 89–96). Champaign, IL: Human Kinetics.

SHAVELSON, R. J., & Berliner, D. C. (1988). Erosion of the education research infrastructure: A reply to Finn. *Educational Researcher, 17,* 9–14.

WITT, J. C. (1990). Complaining, preCopernican thought and the univariate linear mind: Questions for school-based behavioral consultation research. *School Psychology Review, 19,* 367–377.

CHAPTER 19

Developing Competent Learners by Arranging Effective Learning Environments

Vicci Tucci
Daniel E. Hursh

The quality of the human species' day-to-day functioning was enhanced as interactions between and among humans led to more reliable acquisition of reinforcers and escape or avoidance of aversive events. Those behaviors that helped us acquire food, shelter, warmth, and opportunities to reproduce, and allowed us to escape or avoid discomfort, pain, injury, or loss of life were strengthened. Those behaviors that interfered with these contingencies were weakened (Alessi, 1992; Skinner, 1953). For instance, agricultural practices led to settlements. Trading systems allowed us to barter for food, supplies, and other materials. We became more efficient in acquiring everyday survival skills. Industrial practices led to less dependence on human effort and more reliance on mechanical advantage. This in turn increased our efficiency and effectiveness. We began to arrange our daily environ-ments so they served us better. The value of learning became more obvious as we developed educational and social contingencies (Skinner, 1968) that reduced the impact of the harsher elements in our lives.

As our sophistication at dealing with our environment increased, the requirements for operating effectively in those environments increased as well. Beginning roughly with the Industrial Revolution, those requirements have been increasing dramatically. Our response has been to teach basic skills and academic subject matter that prepare learners to behave effectively in these environments.

Observing how we came to function effectively may have led us to improve our educational efforts. Continued improvements in educational practices may have allowed us to behave effectively within existing environments and modify aspects of those environments that needed to be changed. This, in turn, created more complicated environments that required increasingly more sophisticated repertoires; that is ". . . an accumulation of skills, knowledge, and social and ethical practices . . ." (Skinner, 1968, p. 110) for effective functioning. Our educational practices have not kept pace with the rapidly accelerating requirements created by increasingly more complex everyday environments (Tucci, 1986). This relationship between the effects of education and the requirements of our environments across our cultural evolution is displayed in an idealized form in Figure 19.1.

Competent Learners

If our analysis is correct, the effects of our educational efforts are falling at an ever-increasing rate behind the requirements of our constantly changing environments (e.g., the growing sophistication of technology). A probable solution to enhance our educational practices is to develop repertoires in our learners that help them keep pace with these changing requirements. Then, learners would be able to behave effectively in novel circumstances; that is, they would be fully prepared to learn what is necessary to meet the demands of their circumstance. This can be accomplished when our students are equipped to learn under novel conditions. A student who is a sophisticated observer, listener, talker, reader, writer, problem solver, and participator is a competent learner (Tucci, 1986). These sophisticated repertoires allow students to learn under the everyday social and physical contingencies of our culture without relying on more contrived educational contingencies (i.e., the curricular materials and instructional efforts of teachers in classrooms, Skinner, 1968). They augment and expand learning so that students who possess them

become competent learners, whereas students who have only weak or rudimentary versions of these repertoires learn more gradually and require contrived educational contingencies.[1] Figure 19.2 graphically displays the enormous learning advantage competent learners can have over students who possess less sophisticated repertoires.

Producing competent learners allows individuals to function effectively and efficiently in their everyday environments (i.e., without contrived educational contingencies). They can *observe* their circumstances, *listen* to input from others, *talk* to others as needed, *read* and find out what to do, *write* and keep track of what has happened or prompt what to do next, *problem-solve* as necessary, and *participate* until they accomplish what they set out to do. When faced with the need to nourish, communicate, maintain health, transport, entertain, earn a living, socialize, purchase, or maintain a setting, they are equipped with a collection of verbal and nonverbal operants (i.e., repertoires) to respond effectively.

The value of having a population of competent learners can be illustrated by comparing the costs of competent learners with students with less sophisticated repertoires. Figure 19.3 displays the relationship between the costs of these two populations in an idealized graphic manner. The costs of students with

---

[1]The notion that someone possesses a repertoire may seem at odds with the conceptualization of behavior as something someone emits. For the most part, human behavior is operant, and operant behavior is defined by its function. It can be divided into functional response classes wherein the responses are similar to each other by their functional, rather than their formal, properties (Skinner, 1953). Thus, when Skinner (1957) described verbal operants he said, "We observe that a speaker possesses a *verbal repertoire* in the sense that responses of various forms appear in his behavior from time to time in relation to identifiable conditions. A repertoire, as a collection of verbal operants, describes the *potential* behavior of a speaker" (p. 21). It is in this sense that someone is said to *have* a repertoire. "We are concerned here not only with the fact that certain specific forms of verbal behavior are observed but that they are observed under specific circumstances. These controlling circumstances add a dynamic character to 'repertoire' . . ." (Skinner, 1957, p. 22). This dynamic character is captured by Skinner's construct of *repertoire* and provides the power of behavior analysis in its application to human efforts, such as education. For these reasons, repertoire in this article means something someone *possesses* in some strength and something that can be established, strengthened, or weakened.

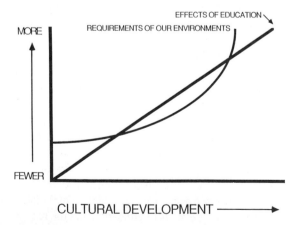

Figure 19.1. An idealized graphic representation of the relationship between the effects of education and the requirements of our environments across the development of our culture.

LEARNING

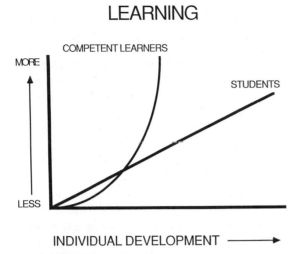

Figure 19.2. An idealized graphic representation of the amount of learning across the development of individuals who are learners or students.

COSTS

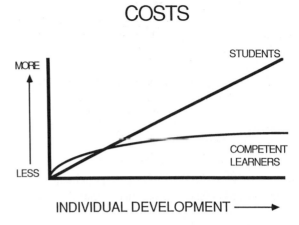

Figure 19.3. An idealized graphic representation of the costs to our culture across the development of individuals who are learners or students.

less sophisticated repertoires are constant because they learn only what is effectively taught during instruction and they have to be carefully instructed on each new task. The costs of may initially be high because sophisticated educational programming may be necessary to develop and strengthen their repertoires. The tremendous benefit of competent learners to themselves and the culture is that as the behavioral repertoires of competent learners are strengthened, these individuals become independent, and the costs to themselves and the culture diminish substantially.

Repertoire Development

Accepting the thrust of our analyses raises the question, "How can we arrange learning conditions that develop and strengthen competent learner repertoires for all students so that we can produce a population of learners who are prepared to match, if not exceed, the ever-changing requirements of our environments?" The answer lies in the integration of behavior analysis, instructional design, and environmental design practices. Teachers whose students become competent learners are constantly arranging and rearranging the

components of their learning environment to strengthen learner repertoires. They are sensitive to the impact of the contingencies they have arranged on these repertoires. They note functional relationships among the various components of the learning environment. They observe how the interactions among their repertoires, their students' repertoires, the curricular materials and instructional formats, and the arrangement of the environment's physical aspects are responsible for the outcomes achieved.

Behavior analysis has provided the basis for arranging effective learning environments (Skinner, 1968). The substance of behavior analysis is the identification, establishment, maintenance, or reduction of functional relationships between behavioral and environmental events. These functional relationships are described as contingencies that consist of the behavior of interest and the environmental events related to it (Morris, 1982) (see Figure 19.4). *Antecedents* are environmental events that occur immediately before the behavior and set the occasion for the behavior. *Consequences* are events that occur immediately after the behavior and increase, maintain, or decrease the probability of a response class of behavior occurring again. The history an individual brings to the current situation is also part of the environment involved in functional relationships. This

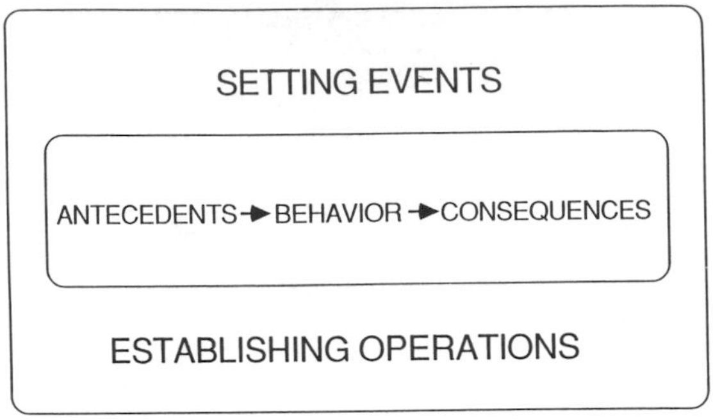

Figure 19.4. A schematic representation of the relationship between behavior and environmental events that can affect behavior.

history includes the biological aspects of the individual and all the environmental events that the individual has experienced. Of particular importance, and in close temporal proximity, are those conditions J. R. Kantor called *setting events* (those conditions that affect the functions of the antecedents or consequences) and those processes Jack Michael has called *establishing operations* (particular sequences of events that make a given set of antecedents or consequences functional with respect to the behavior of interest) (Morris, 1982). A teacher rearranging the desks in the classroom so the students face each other may be a *setting event* that allows the proximity of another student to serve as a discriminative stimulus for conversation between students. Making access to preferred activities only occasionally available to students may serve as an *establishing operation that maintains the effectiveness of these activities as potential reinforcers (via a mild deprivation process). The temporal relationships among antecedents, behavior, consequences, setting events, and establishing operations describe the contingencies that account for functional relationships, which are the basis for repertoire development (Skinner, 1957).*

Sets of related functional relationships can be referred to as repertoires (Skinner, 1957). A *repertoire* is a dynamic entity consisting of a variety of response forms emitted under identifiable conditions. An observer repertoire is strong when the learner accurately describes (tacts) features of his or her en-

vironment. For example, when the teacher asks the learner to describe how two other learners are the same and how they are different, the strong observer does so accurately and reliably. The learner knows what to do, can do it well, and does it under appropriate circumstances. Thus, a repertoire includes knowledge, skilled responding, and social and ethical practices (Skinner, 1968).

Repertoire development is crucial in education because our students must be prepared to succeed in a world where their daily environments are changing as the result of the acceleration of technological and social developments. These developments often occur in the absence of sophisticated instructional programs that allow students to learn how to benefit from the developments. Typical instructional conditions in our students' everyday environments consist of being told how to do something, shown how to do it, given written instructions, told to keep trying until it works out, or some combination of these conditions (Tucci, 1986; Tucci & Hursh, 1991). These instructional conditions require students to have strong competent learner repertoires before they can master what is to be learned. What follows is a description of how behavior analysis, instructional design, and environmental design practices can be combined so teachers can effectively arrange learning environments that develop their students' repertoires to the point that they become competent learners; that is, learners who are equipped to act effectively and efficiently in their everyday environments.

Learning Environments

A learning environment is composed of (1) teachers and the repertoires they bring to the environment, (2) learners and the repertoires they bring to the environment, (3) curricular materials and instructional formats available to the environment; and (4) the physical structures and furnishings in the environment. Instructional conditions created by various arrangements of the parts of the learning environment either establish, strengthen, maintain, or weaken the learners' repertoires. These instructional conditions have different effects with respect to the learners' repertoires because the relative strength of the repertoires determines the manner in which a given instructional condition will function. For example, a teacher-directed instructional condition with a rich schedule of reinforcement may function well to establish and strengthen weak repertoires. Strengthening and maintaining repertoires requires gradual, persistent movement from more teacher-directed instructional conditions with rich schedules of reinforcement to learner schedules of reinforcement with less teacher mediation. These arrangements are typical of semi-directed (teacher available as needed), peer-directed (joint efforts between two or more students), and non-directed (students working individually and independently) instructional conditions (Skinner, 1968; Tucci, 1986; Tucci & Hursh, 1991).

The Competent Learner Model

The Competent Learner Model (Tucci, 1986) brings teachers to mastery of the teaching repertoires necessary to assess the strength of their learners' repertoires under various instructional conditions. Also, it arranges and rearranges the parts of the learning environment to bring about the instructional conditions required to develop and maintain their learner repertoires. The teachers analyze their existing learning environments in terms of the congruence between the strength of their learners' repertoires and the instructional conditions in place throughout various daily activities. Sometimes this straightforward analysis of what is happening leads to changes that enhance learning. For example, if the social studies curriculum includes projects to be completed somewhat independently by teams of learners, and the participator repertoires of a number of the learners are weak, the teacher can see the mismatch between the activity's requirements and the current strength of the learners' repertoires. Before these teams can successfully complete the project, the teacher will have to arrange for more teacher-directed activities while gradually scheduling fewer reinforcers. In effect, increased teacher direction will shift from a high level to a low one as the amount of peer direction increases.

The Competent Learner Model provides lessons that include didactic instruction regarding behavior analysis, instructional design, environmental design practices, and coaching on how to apply these practices during and between didactic sessions. In this manner, teachers master these essential practices. A hallmark of the model is its collegial approach. The instructors (who also coach the teachers) establish their value as facilitators, not as experts. They practice what they preach regarding conditioning and reinforcement to strengthen teachers' repertoires.

The model's goal is to work *with* teachers until they can independently formulate and effectively and efficiently implement instructional programming that strengthens and maintains their students' repertoires. That is, instructional programming moves the learners from dependence on the more contrived educational contingencies of the classroom to effective and efficient functioning under the social and physical contingencies of their everyday environments.

In many ways, the instructors/coaches are in the same position with respect to their teacher colleagues as the teachers are with respect to their learners. That is, they have to formulate and implement instructional programming that brings their teacher colleagues to mastery of behavior analysis, instructional design, and environmental design practices. Such instructional programming has been and continues to be developed by Vicci Tucci, the model's creator.

Tucci developed the model during 20 years of observing learners, teachers, and herself. She focused on developing competent learner repertoires rather than on teaching specific knowledge or training specific skills. The work of Skinner (1953, 1957, 1968), Catania (1984), Sidman (1989), and others formed the basis for the behavior analysis practices that were so valuable. The work of Engelmann and Carnine (1982) and others formed the basis for the instructional design practices.

The core of all of these practices, as they are integrated in the Competent Learner Model, is represented by a series of questions adapted from Skinner's (1968) work. The first question is "What repertoires are to be developed?" This is answered by an assessment of the strength of the learners' repertoires (e.g., how reliable are they as observers, listeners, talkers, and so on). A Competent Learner Repertoire Assessment instrument that teachers use to answer this first question has been developed and continues to be refined (Tucci, 1993). The second question is "Are there any response forms available with which the teacher can begin the process of establishing, strengthening, and maintaining the repertoires?" This question is answered by further teacher observations under a variety of instructional and noninstructional conditions with the goal of identifying existing approximations to the desired response. The third question is "What stimuli have value for the learners?" Observing the stimuli that are regularly produced by the learners' stronger behaviors provides an answer to this question. The fourth question is "What contingencies are required to develop or strengthen the repertoires?" This question is answered by determining the types of instructional programming required to develop or strengthen the repertoires. Strong learners can function well with automatic contingencies, whereas weak learners require arranged educational contingencies. The fifth question is "How can reinforcement be most efficiently scheduled to maintain strong repertoires?" This question is answered by identifying the existing schedule of reinforcement for the repertoire and planning gradual and persistent movement to more and more intermittent and unpredictable schedules of reinforcement. This is accomplished by arranging and rearranging the parts (e.g., physical structure and teacher delivery of lessons) of the learning environment.

The Direct Instruction Curricula and instructional design strategies developed by Engelmann and Carnine (1982) and others became the basis for the instructional design practices employed by the model. They provide logically flawless presentations of what is to be learned in formats that illustrate the range and limits of the concepts, principles, or problem-solving routines being taught, and they require learners to master what is taught. In accomplishing this outcome, these instructional design strategies provide the rich schedules of reinforcement under teacher-directed conditions that support the establishing and initial strengthening of the competent learner repertoires. Further strengthening and maintenance of the repertoires is provided when the teachers move to

semidirected, peer-directed, and nondirected instructional conditions by adjusting the schedules of reinforcement and diminishing the educational contingencies in favor of more automatic social and physical contingencies.

Designing New Schools

The Competent Learner Model has been successful in settings for students with learning difficulties and is being extended to other learners from preschool through high school. When the model was fully implemented, learners met their individual education program objectives, and out-of-district placements of these at-risk learners were near zero. Efforts are underway to obtain support for empirical investigations that can validate this anecdotal evidence (Tucci, 1993). In this process of expanding the model's application, a number of issues became clear, leading us to describe the design of new schools that will produce competent learners consistently.

One of the most obvious notions is that the Competent Learner Repertoires are the core of all learning (see Figure 19.5). They enable learners to acquire knowledge, skilled responding, and social and ethical practices that facilitate their ability to master subject matter that will augment their performance of day-to-day actions. The repertoires allow students to become learners under the typical instructional conditions found in everyday environments (i.e., telling, showing, written instruction, trial-and-error, and combinations of these conditions).

In addition, the school will become a place where educators, members of the community, and parents gather and work together toward shared goals. This will be accomplished by designing learning environments that are created and sustained through the collaboration of private and public community organizations. The school will become a place where educators and other community service providers deliver a continuum of educational, social, recreational, and health care services to enrich and nurture the lives of each child. These schools will require numerous structural and functional components. *Instant communication* will be a necessity and will be

Competent Learner Repertoires©
"Core of All Learning"

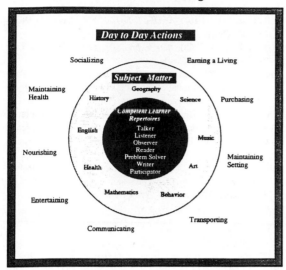

©1991 Tucci Educational Services

Figure 19.5. A schematic representation of the relationship among competent learner repertoires, subject matter, and day-to-day actions.

accomplished by linking all services with a computer network and utilizing high-tech "smart cards" for learners. These cards will allow on-line monitoring of learners' progress and provide the information to help learners who enter a particular setting. These cards function much the way as magnetic strip credit cards only with much greater capacity for storing, recalling, and updating information.

Teachers will work in *instructional teams* that assume responsibility for coordinating, delivering, and monitoring the instruction of mixed-age children (e.g., kindergarteners through third-graders or high school juniors and seniors). Students can move among the teachers who will operate different aspects of the environment based on their instructional strengths. Learning environments will be *arranged for success* in the manner introduced in this chapter. *Real-life scenarios* will be integral components of all curricula to ensure the transfer of what is learned. As students come to master the components of problem-solving routines, the routines will be applied to situations found in their daily environments.

Functional projects will be assigned to give learners the experience of applying what they have learned to learning activities that allow them to function differently and more effectively and efficiently in the world.

The school will have a *student center* setting that will serve as a learning environment, giving students the opportunity to acquire, extend, and practice competencies in a supportive social context. The staff will help them complete their assignments, talk with them about personal matters, and advocate for their well-being by making others aware of their needs. A *school-based government* will demonstrate to learners the value of a democratic process. A *school-based economy* will teach students the value of using their time productively and motivate them to engage in actions that generate desirable outcomes. The school will be constructed or renovated to include *flexible structures and furnishings* that will allow the learning environments to be arranged and rearranged to serve the needs of the learners based on the conditions that will help establish, strengthen, and maintain competent learner repertoires.

Administrators, teachers, and community service providers will become resource managers in a *responsive management* system that uses student performance as the bottom line. This bottom line may be well worth the expense if governments can spend less on correcting the failures of our education system and our society and begin operating better because community members are wiser and more responsible. Businesses may operate more efficiently with more knowledgeable skilled workers. Life on the planet may be better for everyone if a world of competent learners takes responsibility for the effects of their actions. In summary, arranging effective learning environments through the integration of behavior analysis, instructional design, and environmental design practices may enhance our educational practices by focusing on developing competent learners. In doing so, we'll create the opportunity for a most humane and creative future for members of our cultures.

Author Notes

The authors consider the authorship of this article to be equal with readers invited to contact Vicci Tucci,

Tucci Educational Services, 18 Aqua View Drive, La Selva Beach, CA 95076 for more information regarding the Competent Learner Model or reprints of the article.

References

ALESSI, G. (1992). Models of proximate and ultimate causation in psychology. *American Psychologist, 47,* 1359–1370.

CATANIA, A. C. (1984). *Learning.* Englewood Cliffs, NJ: Prentice-Hall.

ENGELMANN, S., & Carnine, D. (1982). *Theory of instruction: Principles and application.* New York: Irvington Press.

MORRIS, E. K. (1982). Some relationships between interbehavioral psychology and radical behaviorism. *Behaviorism, 10,* 187–216.

SIDMAN, M. (1989). *Coercion and its fallout.* Boston: Authors Cooperative.

SKINNER, B. F. (1953). *Science and human behavior.* New York: Free Press.

SKINNER, B. F. (1957). *Verbal behavior.* New York: Appleton-Century-Crofts.

SKINNER, B. F. (1968). *The technology of teaching.* New York: Appleton-Century-Crofts.

TUCCI, V. (1986). An analysis of a competent learner. Paper presented at the annual convention of the Northern California Association for Behavior Analysis, February, San Mateo, CA.

TUCCI, V. (1993). Evaluation of instrument to monitor learners and at-risk learners. Small Business Innovative Research Grant Proposal submitted to the National Institutes of Health, April.

TUCCI, V., & Hursh, D. (1991). Competent learner model: Instructional programming for teachers and learners. *Education and Treatment of Children, 14,* 349–360.

CHAPTER 20

START Tutoring: Designing, Training, Implementing, Adapting, and Evaluating Tutoring Programs for School and Home Settings

April D. Miller
Patricia M. Barbetta
Timothy E. Heron

Well-informed teachers know more today than ever before about how to create effective and positive learning environments. Among other key instructional variables, these teachers recognize that instruction improves when testing and teaching are integrated. They know to measure student learning directly and frequently and to use the data collected from these assessments to make ongoing diagnostic decisions. These teachers further recognize that their classroom instruction is improved when they (1) establish specific instructional objectives; (2) present clear, concise instructions or demonstrations; and (3) provide their students with multiple opportunities to practice learning tasks with feedback. Knowledgeable teachers also provide considerable reinforcement and encouragement for their students' efforts and outcomes.

Still, increased demands on teachers' time and increased diversity in many classrooms have made it much more difficult for even responsive teachers to provide quality instruction. There simply does not seem to be enough hours in the day (or pairs of hands) to do all that needs to be done and to teach all that needs to be taught. The paperwork and meeting requirements seem endless. Higher student-teacher ratios, greater percentages of at-risk students, and increased efforts to integrate students with disabilities into mainstream environments have added to classroom diversity. While this increased diversity has enriched the character of many of our classrooms, it has often added to the difficulty of providing appropriate instruction.

Since students progress optimally when they work at their own pace and level, our best teachers attempt to meet the challenges of today's diverse classrooms by providing more individualized instruction. Some teachers provide students with their own work packets while they deliver one-to-one or small-group instruction. In this classroom structure, however, the students assigned to work independently often engage in unproductive, off-tasks behaviors. Other teachers recruit parent or community volunteers to help individualize instruction. Although this is effective, it has become less viable as more parents and community members work outside the home. Some districts try new administrative arrangements (e.g., team teaching, split classrooms, classroom aides) to help teachers provide more individualized instruction. In a time of economic cutbacks, however, many districts do not have adequate funds to meet the students' needs.

Ironically, many teachers overlook one of the most potentially powerful instructional sources: the students themselves. Using students as tutors offers benefits to students, tutors, and classroom teachers.

The Benefits of Using Students as Tutors

Benefits to Students

In addition to availability, there are a number of benefits to using students as tutors. First, they can be highly effective. Student-tutoring programs have been shown to increase student on-task behavior (Heward et al., 1986) and to produce improvement in a variety of subject areas such as sight words (Barbetta et al., 1991), mathematics (Franca et al., 1990; Thurston & Dasta, 1990; Vacc & Cannon, 1991), social skills (Ehly & Larson, 1976), and higher-level cognitive subjects like oral reading, writing, and reading comprehension (Delquadri et al., 1983; Sindelar, 1982). Several student-tutoring programs have been found to be more effective than some conventional teacher-mediated instruction (e.g., Greenwood et al., 1984). These gains are optimized when the tutoring sessions are highly structured, provide multiple opportunities for students to respond, and provide frequent positive and corrective feedback (e.g., Barbetta et al., 1991; Delquadri et al., 1983; Heron et al., 1983). In addition, student-tutoring programs can be individualized and can provide intensive one-to-one instruction without a large percentage of the class having to work independently (Cooke, Heron, & Heward, 1983).

Tutoring can also help increase social interactions (Custer & Osguthorpe, 1983; Franca et al., 1990; Maheady & Sainato, 1985) and reduce disruptive behaviors (Folio & Norman, 1981). Furthermore, tutoring can be used to increase the chances for success of mainstreamed students with disabilities by setting the occasion for these students to interact with their nondisabled peers (Brown, 1986; Madden & Slavin, 1983). This increased interaction may positively affect social acceptance and increase other social interactions between students with and without disabilities (Guralnick & Groom, 1988; Haring et al., 1987).

Benefits to Tutors

There are also benefits to the students who serve as tutors, such as academic gains (Chiang, Thorpe, &

Darch, 1980; Parson & Heward, 1979) and improved on-task behaviors in other classroom settings (Polirstok & Greer, 1986). Studies by Greer and Polirstok (1982) and Polirstok and Greer (1986) found that when tutors were trained and awarded tokens to use social reinforcement during tutoring, their appropriate academic and social performance and on-task behavior increased in nontutoring settings. Jenkins and Jenkins (1981) observed that tutors showed improved self-concept and attitudes toward school and enhanced racial relations. Tutoring programs have also been shown to reduce truancy and tardiness in tutors (Lazerson et al., 1988). Finally, students involved in changing the behavior of their peers take ownership of learning, become more responsible for completing assignments, and control their behavior more appropriately (Harris & Aldridge, 1983; Miller, 1984).

Benefits to Teachers

A major benefit of student-tutoring programs for teachers is that they can provide individualized instruction without imposing a constant demand on the teachers' time (Drass & Jones, 1971; Ehly & Larson, 1980; Mc-Kellar, 1986; Reisberg & Wolf, 1986). Classwide peer tutoring, for example, is a method for providing individualized instruction simultaneously for any size group. Although the start-up cost in terms of teacher-time can be high, most established tutoring programs can be operated with reduced teacher effort, allowing the teacher to take on more of an administrative and consultant role. Tutoring programs can be an excellent tool to help the general-education teacher include mainstream students with disabilities in large-group academic instruction (Cooke et al., 1982). Tutoring programs have also been shown to decrease disruptive behavior (Folio & Norman, 1981; McKenzie & Budd, 1981).

Tutoring often occurs informally in the classroom, with one student who is proficient in the skill being tutored acting as "teacher" for another student who is having difficulty. The focus of this chapter, however, is on highly structured student-tutoring programs that use the START tutoring steps to design, implement, adapt, and evaluate tutoring programs. We have also included a brief discussion of home-based tutoring, in which parents assume the role of tutor.

The START Tutoring Program

Once a teacher decides to integrate tutoring into her instructional program, the START tutoring steps begin. START stands for Select a tutoring format, Train the tutors, Arrange the environment, Run the program, and Test for effectiveness (see Figure 20.1).

Step 1: Select a Tutoring Format

Tutoring occurs in at least five formats, each of which shares several common design, training, implementation, and evaluation considerations (Miller & Heron, 1991). The most widely used formats are classwide, cross-age, small group, one-to-one, and home-based tutoring. This section presents a discus-

sion of the organization, procedures, and advantages and disadvantages of each format.

Classwide peer tutoring. Classwide peer tutoring (CWPT) involves the entire class simultaneously participating in tutoring dyads. During each session, students can assume reciprocal roles of tutor and tutee (Cooke et al. 1983; Greenwood et al., 1984), or they can participate only as the tutor or tutee (Heward et al., 1986). The pairing of reciprocal tutors can occur on a random basis (Kohler & Greenwood, 1990), in rank order to assure similar skill levels, or with special considerations for students with behavior or achievement problems (Cooke et al., 1983). The pairings can be individualized by pretesting the students and assigning partners and materials to students with similar needs or abilities.

Typically, CWPT sessions last 30 minutes, with 20 to 25 minutes used for instruction and the remaining time spent in testing, generalization activities, and transition to and from tutoring. During instruction, the tutee may be required to respond to tutor questions orally or in writing. As the tutee responds, the tutor provides feedback (i.e., praises correct responses and behaviors, corrects errors). Testing consists of a brief assessment of the skills practiced that tutoring session. Generalization activities involve application of the facts (items) being taught (e.g., use of sight words being tutored in sentences; time trial of tutored math facts).

There are several advantages to using this tutoring format. First, CWPT can be used to teach skills across a wide range of subject areas, ability and age levels, and scheduling considerations. Research has found CWPT to be effective in increasing student achievement in math (Greenfield & McNeil, 1987), reading (Greenwood, 1991; Kamps et al., 1989), social studies (Maheady, Harper, & Sacca, 1988), spelling (Kohler & Greenwood, 1990; Mallette et al., 1991), and vocabulary (Heron et al., 1983). Although CWPT lends itself most readily to factual information, it can be used to teach higher-level skills, such as oral reading, writing, reading comprehension, and hypothesis testing (Sindelar, 1982; Stanley & Greenwood, cited in Delquadri et al., 1986). CWPT has also been shown to be effective in increasing measures of curriculum-

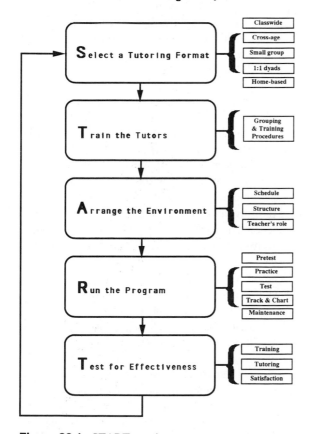

START Tutoring Steps

Figure 20.1. START tutoring steps.

based achievement (Maheady & Harper, 1987) and grades (Maheady, Sacca, & Harper, 1988). Finally, students, teachers, and parents like this format (Greenwood et al., 1984).

The disadvantages include the amount of teacher time needed to plan and prepare the program, train students as tutors, and coordinate the large amount of materials and information produced. Most of these disadvantages can be overcome by developing a functional system for training tutors (to be discussed later), keeping records, and monitoring the program. As much as possible, teachers should ask students to help conduct and monitor the CWPT program.

Cross-age tutoring.   Cross-age (CA) tutoring occurs when an older student is matched with a younger student to deliver instruction. An age difference of two or more years usually delineates the roles. There do not need to be large differences in skill levels between the tutor and tutee, because both members of the dyad benefit from the experience (Brown, Rollins, & McCandless, 1988; Polirstok & Greer, 1986). Although students selected to serve as tutors might miss classroom instructional time, they usually are not adversely affected by the lost time (Chiang, Thorpe, & Darch, 1980).

The tutee's teacher usually determines the skill to be taught and the materials to be used in the tutoring sessions; however, junior and senior high school tutors have also identified skill areas, planned, and developed materials for use in tutoring (Barbetta et al., 1991; Maher, 1984; Russell & Ford, 1983). Teachers may decide to use CA tutoring, if they believe that their students are too young to tutor or that older students would serve as useful role models for their younger counterparts (Johnson & Bailey, 1974).

The tutors come from different sources. In most cases, they come from older classes within the same school, but they can also come from outside. For example, Barbetta and their colleagues (1991) trained high school students during their study hall periods to serve as tutors for students in the nearby elementary school. Cross-age tutoring arrangements have also used nondisabled students to tutor students with disabilities (Haisley, Tell, & Andrews, 1981). More recently, the effectiveness of having special education

students tutor other special education students has been demonstrated (e.g., Cook et al., 1985; Greenwood, Carta, & Hall, 1988; Osguthorpe & Scruggs, 1986).

There are several advantages to using CA tutoring. As with CWPT, this tutoring format has been used to teach a wide variety of subjects to students with varying abilities. Tutees have included students from general education classrooms, students with reading or word recognition difficulties (Barbetta et al., 1991; Polirstok & Greer, 1986; Sindelar, 1982) or learning disabilities (Lazerson et al., 1988), moderately handicapped students (Vacc & Cannon, 1991), mainstreamed exceptional students (Folio & Norman, 1981), students with mental retardation (Maher, 1984), and incarcerated youth with learning disabilities (Kane & Alley, 1980). Another advantage is that the tutors often require fewer training sessions because they bring skills and experience to the tutoring program. One disadvantage is the lack of flexibility due to the need to coordinate schedules. The necessity of a set tutoring schedule and dependence on external help makes CA tutoring a less flexible resource than other tutoring formats.

Small-group tutoring.   Two procedural variations are possible within small-group tutoring. The sessions can be conducted with select students who need additional practice with skills (perhaps instead of independent seat work), or the whole class can participate in the tutoring on a rotating basis. While the teacher works with one group, a second group participates in peer tutoring, and the remainder of the class engages in independent seat work or other cooperative groups. Groups rotate daily (or weekly) so each group engages in each activity.

The advantages include the flexibility of scheduling who participates and when the tutoring occurs. A major disadvantage is that the teacher will typically not be available to monitor the tutoring sessions because he or she will be instructing other students.

One-to-one tutoring.   This method differs procedurally from other tutoring programs in the identification of participating tutors and tutees. Only select tutees, typically students needing remedial support, participate in the one-to-one tutoring format. They are paired with select tutors (perhaps highly skilled peers, peers also in need of remedial work, or CA tutors). Each member of the dyad may receive and provide tutoring in the same content area, or tutors can provide instruction in a content area in which they are highly skilled.

The major advantages of one-to-one tutoring are the specificity of the tutoring, flexibility in scheduling, and the range of subject areas tutored. One disadvantage might be the time needed to train tutors individually and monitor the tutoring sessions, particularly if tutors are less skilled students.

Home-based tutoring. Home-based tutoring programs use the parent (or sibling) as the tutor. Many parents want to help their children's academic skill development (Goldstein et al., 1980), and overwhelming research shows that they can successfully instruct their child at home, when the school provides guidance, sufficient training, and feedback (Heron & Harris, 1993). Not all parents, however, can or should tutor their child at home. Some parents may be too anxious or have limited time or skills.

When home-based tutoring is appropriate, it offers several advantages. First, involving parents formally in the educational process enhances learning (Barbetta & Heron, 1991; Bechner, 1984; Cooper & Edge, 1981; Heron & Harris, 1993; Thurston & Dasta, 1990). Teachers and administrators state there is only so much that can be done at school to increase a child's academic functioning (Heron & Harris, 1993). The extra practice provided by home-based tutoring can help slower learners "catch up" with their classmates and the average and above-average learners progress at a more rapid pace. Second, many parents believe that the 180-day schoolyear does not meet the definition of appropriate education specified in Public Law 94-142 (Stotland & Mancuso, 1981). They are concerned about their child's loss of hard-won academic gains over the summer months. Home-based tutoring can be used during the summer with minimal support from professionals.

Step 2: Train the Tutors

Tutor-training procedures vary along a continuum from unstructured to highly structured (Krouse, Gerber, & Kauffman, 1981) and are generally based on a task analysis of the tutoring role, with the steps systematically trained in order of importance. The more structured and direct the tutor training, however, the more likely tutors will perform the program components (Greenwood, Carta, & Hall, 1988; Parson & Heward, 1979). Studies measuring tutor behaviors (i.e., behaviors instructed during training) have shown that tutors are able to correctly implement instructional procedures (Barbetta et al, 1991; Cooke, Heron, & Heward, 1983; Greenwood et al., 1984), use behavioral terminology (Campbell, Scaturro, & Lickson, 1983), and praise correct responses on an intermittent schedule (Heward et al., 1986). Heward and colleagues (1986), for example, demonstrated that, after a single 30-minute training program consisting of modeling, role playing, feedback, and practice, first-grade students were able to praise their partners on an approximate FR3 schedule of reinforcement (i.e., reinforcement was provided after every three correct responses). The extent and type of training implemented depends on the tutor's skills and the goals and complexity of the tutoring task. The following paragraphs contain general information on grouping, training procedures, and components of tutor training.

Tutor-training grouping. Training can take place in a large group, a small group, or on an individual basis. Large-group training makes it more difficult to individualize instruction. Training in a small group is ideal for providing tutors with more practice and feedback. Although it demands an enormous amount of time, training tutors on an individual basis allows for individualization of specific skills or information that the tutor may lack.

Tutor-training sessions do not need to be extended until students reach 100% mastery. Once they have acquired an adequate knowledge of the tasks involved, their skills can be further shaped and refined during the actual tutoring sessions by the teacher or more skilled peers. Supervision of the tutor-tutee dyads might include quality checks on the accuracy of procedures, academic responses and prompts, record keeping, and positive social interactions. After a time, retraining or refresher sessions may be needed to reinforce the performance of certain tutoring behaviors (Parson & Heward, 1979).

Tutor-training procedures. Role playing, tokens, or instructional packages can be used to teach individuals to follow prescribed tutoring protocols (Thurston & Dasta, 1990; Pigott, Fantuzzo, & Clement, 1986; Polirstok & Greer, 1986; Maheady & Harper, 1987; Heron et al., 1983; Heward et al., 1986). The model, lead, and test instructional sequence championed by Carnine and Silbert (1979) is also considerably effective for training tutors. This training model has been used in several tutoring programs (e.g., Cooke, Heron, & Heward, 1983; Maheady & Sainato, 1985). The structure of model-lead-test actively engages tutors in the training, provides practice in developing new skills, allows students to receive feedback on performance, and provides the teacher with a method for evaluating the training. Scripted lessons can be used to keep training consistent across groups and to cue the trainer's behavior (e. g., Barbetta et al., 1991; Heron et al., 1983). Videotapes of tutoring sessions and previously trained tutors can be useful in training tutors. Teachers may also want to provide a tutoring steps checklist to use for the first few tutoring sessions.

Tutor training typically includes instruction in (1) transitions (to and from tutoring), (2) practice procedures, (3) rules for tutor and tutee behavior, (4) reinforcement strategies for correct responses, (5) error correction procedures, (6) methods of gaining the teacher's attention, (7) testing procedures, and (8) record keeping for tutee performance. Tutors have also been trained in pretesting (Barbetta et al., 1991) and handling behavior problems (Kamps et al., 1989).

The length of training varies considerably (from one 30-minute session to twenty 45-minute sessions), depending largely on tutor and tutee abilities and the goals of tutoring. Barbetta and her colleagues (1991), for example, trained high school students to tutor elementary school students in one 45-minute training session. In contrast, Vacc and Cannon's CA tutor-training program (1991) required 30 hours of training. The training involved learning sign language, behavior management techniques, and problem-solving skills that were above and beyond those usually taught. Another study (Haisley, Tell, & Andrew, 1981) required eighth- and ninth-grade students to undergo intensive training, including six weeks of informal observations and training in a resource center, and twenty 45-minute sessions on direct instruction, task analysis, communication, behavior management, instructional design, and classroom survival skills.

Tutor-training sessions for one-to-one tutoring also differ, depending on the abilities of the tutors and tutees and the tutoring procedures. Training ranges from no formal training (Campbell, Scaturro, & Lickson, 1983) to two 30-minute sessions per week for eight weeks (Osguthorpe, Eiserman, & Shisler, 1985). In some programs, tutors received weekly training or instruction (Eiserman, 1988; Osguthorpe, Eiserman, & Shisler, 1985), played a board game to facilitate discussion and education (Campbell, Scaturro, & Lickson, 1983), or held booster sessions as needed (Shafer, Egel, & Neef, 1984).

Training parent-tutors can take place in the home, at school, or in a clinical setting (Barbetta & Heron, 1991). It is important for parents to understand that tutoring can occur in short time intervals, be a positive experience for them and their children, and still effect academic changes. To achieve these goals, parents should be trained to implement tutoring procedures based on behavioral principles (Elksnin & Elksnin, 1991).

More recently, tutor-training programs have moved toward training students with disabilities as tutors; this may require more intensive training. Maher (1984), for example, trained adolescents with disabilities to be CA tutors for younger students with disabilities. In addition to instruction in the tutoring procedures, training included information on the tutees' disabling conditions, academic areas that could be tutored, and instruction of prerequisite academic skills. The tutor-training activities consisted of didactic presentations by the trainer, individualized meetings with the tutor and the trainer, group discussions, role playing, and simulations.

Step 3: Arrange the Environment

As with effective teacher-mediated instruction, effective student-mediated instruction requires attention to scheduling and program structure. In this section, we discuss each of the tutoring formats with regard to these issues and present a cursory overview of the teacher's role.

Tutoring schedule. Each tutoring format can be scheduled to occur as little as once a week or as often as each school day. For example, to add variety to daily spelling lessons, a teacher may choose to schedule CWPT tutoring just one day per weekly spelling unit. On the other hand, a teacher may decide to include 5 to 10 minutes of CWPT tutoring of spelling words at the end of each daily spelling lesson. Students who need extra help in spelling might be selected to participate in a CA tutoring program or be provided with additional support in small-group or one-to-one tutoring. Teachers should consider following CWPT programs with more relaxed, slower-pace activities such as supplemental worksheets or independent work at learning centers. Parents implementing home-based instruction are encouraged to keep the instructional sessions short (10 to 20 minutes per week) but to schedule them at least three days a week (Barbetta & Heron, 1991).

Tutoring structure. Proper structuring of tutoring programs significantly influences their level of effectiveness and enjoyment. Clear and consistent expectations for tutor and tutee behaviors during the tutoring sessions and during transitions to and from tutoring are critical. Expectations (e.g., using appropriate voice level, following directions, accepting peer feedback, having materials ready) should be identified (with the tutors and tutees) during tutor training and early tutoring sessions and reviewed frequently. For students who have difficulty remembering or following expectations, teachers should post expectation charts and require that they be reviewed before each tutoring session.

Expectations should include rules for appropriate transitioning to and from tutoring sessions. In addition, to improve transitions some CWPT tutoring programs (e.g., Delquadri et al., 1983), predetermine the "movers" (those who move to their partners) and the "stayers" (those who wait for their partners) as well as who will function as the tutor first. The teacher might also consider setting a transition-time goal when using CWPT (e.g., 20 seconds to be prepared for tutoring). Students can then be challenged to meet or beat their goal and receive teacher praise and/or bonus points when successful.

Keeping tutoring materials (e.g., tutoring folders, point sheets, pretesting materials) in a designated area will also improve transition time. Materials for CWPT can be kept in "mail slots" in the classroom. For CA tutoring, mail slots in the hallway or library provide tutors access to tutoring materials without having to interrupt tutees' classrooms. A get-ready-for-tutoring checklist might be helpful for parents who are having a difficult time with their child being prepared for home-based tutoring.

Teacher's role. The teacher's role during tutoring depends largely on the tutoring format and the ages and abilities of the tutors and tutees. When using CWPT, teacher's function as the program developer and tutor monitor. They typically identify the content to be tutored, assist students in preparing the tutoring material, and develop a system for monitoring tutee performance. In addition, they move from dyad to dyad, assisting tutors when they are confronted with a difficult tutoring decision (e.g., prompting an unknown word, forgetting a tutoring step). Along with providing assistance, teachers should reinforce appropriate tutor and tutee behaviors by giving them verbal praise or points or stars on a point sheet or "star card" (to be discussed in more detail later).

With CA tutoring programs, teachers typically identify the materials to be used for tutoring and occasionally provide support for tutor and tutee performance. Whenever possible, however, they should use paraprofessionals, support faculty (e.g., librarian assistant, school secretaries), or parent volunteers to play a major role in program organization and implementation. To show appreciation to CA tutors, teachers and tutees might organize a picnic or party as a culminating activity.

With home-based tutoring, teachers might provide parents with specific information regarding words, facts, or concepts to be tutored by sending home tutoring assignment sheets or by recording messages on the school's answering machine for parents to access (Hassett et al., 1984). To monitor and reinforce parent and child home-based tutoring efforts, teachers could ask parents to send tutoring-session reports to school for review. In addition, the teacher (or parent volunteers, perhaps parents who are tutoring themselves) might occasionally phone parents to reinforce home-based tutoring efforts or solve problems.

Step 4: Run the Program

The START tutoring program described in this section contains the elements critical to effective instruction. These elements include clearly specified instructional objectives, multiple opportunities for tutee response, use of positive feedback for correct responses, programming for generalized outcomes, frequent testing, and program monitoring. The START program has been field-tested with positive results as a classwide (Cooke, Heron, & Heward, 1983), a cross-age (Barbetta et al., 1991), and a home-based tutoring program (Barbetta & Heron, 1991). The START program consists of five components: pretesting, practice, testing, performance tracking and charting, and maintenance testing.

Pretesting.   Before instruction begins, pretesting is administered to determine unknown words, facts, or terms to be practiced during tutoring sessions. The classroom teacher or students, whenever possible, can administer the testing. The pretester takes the following steps:

1. Present one word (fact or term) at a time on a list or sheet to the tutee, giving the tutee two to three seconds to respond to each item (depending on the difficulty level of the material being pretested). The first ten items missed or answered too slowly are used to develop the first set of practice cards. Do not provide any assistance in forming the correct response.
2. Print the unknown items on 3-by-5-inch index cards.
3. As the tutee masters ten practice cards, repeat pretesting to obtain another list of unknown items.

Pretesting adaptations.   Depending on the curricular area to be tutored or ability of the tutee, teachers may want to identify a fewer or greater number of unknown items during each pretesting session. Data on tutee performance, as well as on the level of frustration observed during tutoring sessions, should guide this decision. For example, if the teacher determines that each practice set is to contain ten unknown items and then observes that it is frustrating for the tutee to practice ten at a time, he or she might reduce the set size to seven. Whenever possible, teachers should enlist the help of tutors or paraprofessionals to pretest tutees. They can simply provide them with a pool of items and train them in these procedures. If terms and their definitions are to be practiced (or math facts), the correct response can be printed on the back of the card. Students can also make their own tutoring practice cards. If index cards are too expensive to use, photocopied sheets can be used.

Practice.   The practice component of START tutoring involves the use of a tutoring folder (see Figure 20.2). The folder is constructed of a file folder, library pockets, and a tracking graph. The tutor folder can vary, depending on the academic subject being practiced and the age and interests of the tutees. It is a good idea to have tutees and their tutors design and make their tutoring folders as a time-saving and rapport-building activity. To use the START tutor folder, the tutor takes the following steps:

1. Take the practice cards from the "Go" (working) pocket and show them to the tutee one card at a time. Then prompt a response (e.g., when tutoring sight words, present the practice card and say, "What word?"). The tutee then attempts to say (or write) the correct response. If the tutee responds correctly, say "Good," and present the next card quickly. If the tutee makes an incorrect response, say, "Try again." If, after this prompt, the tutee is still unable to produce the correct response, model the correct answer. The tutee says (or writes) the response following the model.
2. Present as many practice rounds as possible (a round being a practice trial on each card in the set) within the allotted practice time; shuffle cards between rounds.
3. With classwide peer tutoring, small-group, and one-to-one tutoring, after 5 to 10 minutes, the tutors and tutees switch roles.   Role reversals are not

implemented for CA or home-based tutoring. A kitchen timer can be used to help keep track of time.

4. Reinforce appropriate tutee behavior by drawing a star or placing a sticker on the "star card" (see Figure 20.2, right panel). When it is full, the star card is either displayed or traded for a reward, such as a special game time or treat.

Practice adaptations. When running a sight-word tutoring program in which the tutors are still at the acquisition phase, it may be difficult for them to provide a completely accurate model during corrective feedback. Heward, Heron, and Cooke (1982) described a procedure called the "tutor huddle," in which tutors are introduced to and practice new cards they will be responsible for presenting to their tutees. Tutor huddle is implemented by dividing the tutors into small groups to review the words they are scheduled to present that day. Members take turns reading the words as other members of the huddle confirm or correct their responses. The teacher monitors each tutor huddle, providing positive and corrective feedback for performance and behavior.

The START tutoring program can also be used to practice the skills needed to compute word problems (Barbetta & Heron, 1991). The tutor first presents a set of practice cards—in the manner indicated earlier—that contain key phrases that cue the tutee about the correct operation to use when solving a word problem (e.g., sum, together, is both, how much more, is left, difference). Once these cards are mastered, the subsequent sets of practice cards have a word problem on each card. The tutor presents the word-problem practice card and the tutee responds to four separate questions: What do we know? What do we want to find out? Are there any key phrases? and What operation should we use? The tutor gives affirmative and corrective feedback. The tutee solves the word problem and writes his or her answer only during the last presentation of each card during practice.

Enrichment or extension activities can be added to each of the START tutoring formats. For example, if the tutoring objective is to learn math facts, each tutoring session might end with a one-minute time trial. Supplemental activities for tutees learning sight-word vocabulary might include writing the sight words in sentences, story writing, word games, and oral reading exercises. To reinforce the material covered in their tutoring lessons, parents could take advantage of everyday learning opportunities (e.g., grocery shopping, sign reading while riding in the car).

Other practice adaptations involve varying the number of cards to be practiced (depending on the tutee's ability) or the subject being tutored. To program for generality, the type of responses required during tutoring (e.g., from saying to writing) or the response level (e.g., from recognition, to recall, to adaptation exercises) might be altered. Figure 20.3 shows eight card variations (front and back) that can be used with START tutoring programs. These variations represent different curricular areas, grade levels, and

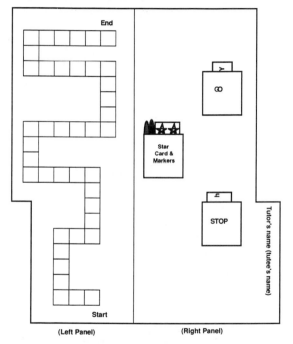

Figure 20.2. Folder mock-up showing left and right panels. Left panel shows cumulative tracking chart. Right panel shows go, stop, and star card pockets. SOURCE: *Adapted from "TUGMATE: A Cross-Age Tutoring Program to Teach Sight Vocabulary," by P. M. Barbetta, A. D. Miller, M. T. Peters, T. E. Heron, and L. L. Cochran, February 1991,* Education and Treatment of Children, 14(1), pp. 19–37. *Copyright © 1991 by Education and Treatment of Children (ETC). Adapted by permission.*

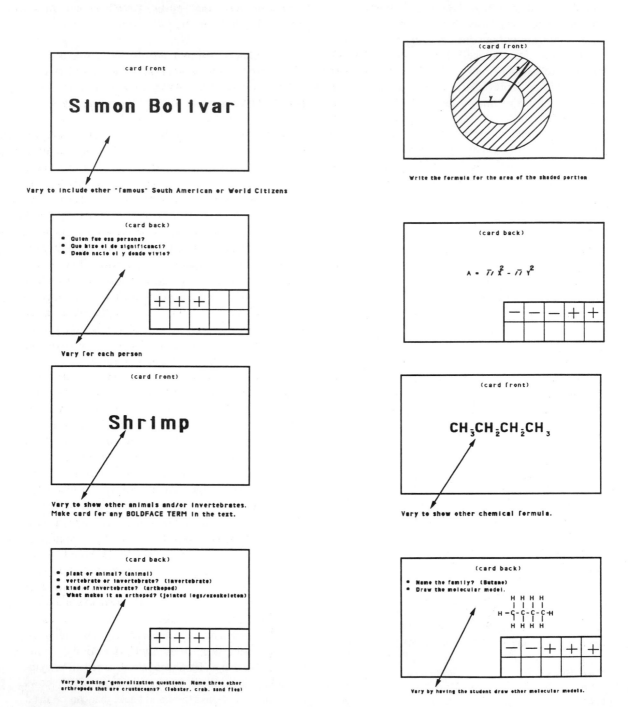

Figure 20.3. Card variations showing how flashcards can be modified across presentation and response modes. Plus and minus signs show correct or incorrect responses, respectively, during testing.

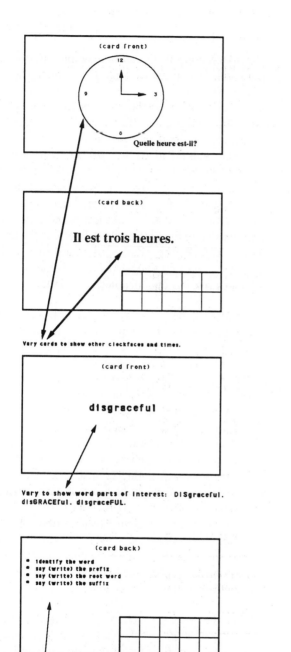

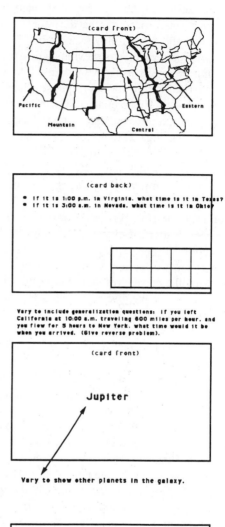

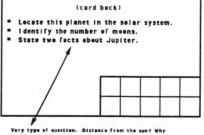

Figure 20.3 continued.

response modes. Each card represents one of a set of ten such cards that would be placed in the Go pocket.

Error correction variations can be divided into three classifications: procedures that the tutor follows, procedures that the tutee follows, and time factors associated with correction. As previously described, some tutoring programs use a "try-again," followed by the tutor modeling the correct response when the tutee errs again (e.g., Heron et al., 1983). With other tutoring programs, a tutor indicates when a response is incorrect by saying "Wrong" or "No" and then providing a prompt, cue, or the correct response before another trial is attempted (Koury & Browder, 1986; Maheady & Harper, 1987; Young, Hecimovic, & Salzberg, 1983).

A second variation of error correction examines the tutee's response pattern. Several studies suggest that error correction during recognition and recall task instruction is most effective when it ends with the student making the correct response rather than with the tutor's corrective feedback (Barbetta, Heron, & Heward, 1993; Barbetta & Heward, in press).

With regard to the timing of corrective feedback, Koury and Browder (1986) found that a constant time-delay procedure used by moderately handicapped tutors during word instruction resulted in a rapid acquisition of words by all tutees and a decrease in the time required for mastery. Briefly, a time-delay procedure transfers stimulus control from a prompt (the tutor saying the presented word) to the natural stimulus (the written word). The presentation of the prompt is delayed until after the natural stimulus has been presented. Koury and Browder (1986) began with tutors saying the word immediately as the word card was presented (zero time delay), and increasing the amount of time between the card being shown and the tutor saying the word (3- to 5-second time delay).

Testing.   After each practice session the tutees are tested. To implement testing in the START tutoring programs, the tutor takes the following steps:

1. Turn the tutoring folder to the reverse side to expose an O (for correct) and an X (for incorrect).
2. Show each card once, holding it up for two to three seconds. If the tutee says (or writes) the response

correctly, place the card on the O. If the tutee does not respond correctly or makes no response, place the card on the X. Do not give corrective feedback during testing.
3. After presenting all the cards, mark the back of each card with an O or X, depending on which pile the card was sorted into.
4. Move any card with three consecutive Os to the Stop (learned) pocket. Return cards without three consecutive Os to the Go pocket.
5. Once all cards are in the Stop pocket, remove them from the folder and place a new set of ten cards into the Go pocket. The program uses a nonreplacement system; that is, no new cards are added until the tutee has mastered all ten flashcards and they have been moved to the Stop pocket. In effect, the Stop pocket reduces the number of times an already learned card is presented and increases the number of response trials on unlearned cards in the set.

Testing adaptations.   There are several ways to adapt the testing procedure, including changing the criteria for mastery or the symbols used for signifying correct and incorrect responses during testing (Os and Xs). Some tutees may require only a two-day mastery criterion. Frequent assessments for maintenance of performance (i.e., maintenance tests given one to two weeks after mastery) would help the teacher determine the sufficient mastery criteria. When used with younger children, the testing symbols could be changed to a happy face and neutral face; when used during Spanish tutoring lessons the words *Si* and *No* might be used. A card-replacement system could also be used. Instead of using the nonreplacement exiting system (as described in Step 5 of Testing), a card-replacement system can be used. When a card is mastered (moved to the Stop pocket), a new card would be inserted into the Go pocket (instead of waiting until all ten cards are mastered).

Performance tracking and charting.   A tracking graph (see Figure 20.2, left panel) is a way for the tutor and tutee to keep a record of the total number of words (or facts) mastered. Also, the graph is used to provide visual feedback and reinforcement for learning the new words or facts. To use the tracking graph, the tutor takes the following steps:

1. Have the tutee color in the number of blocks corresponding to the number of cards that moved to the Stop pocket that day. (By alternating colors daily, the tutor and tutee can monitor each day's progress.)
2. Once the tracking graph is completed, place a new graph in the folder. Give the completed graph to the tutee to post in the classroom or to take home.

Tracking and charting adaptations. As an alternative to (or in addition to) reinforcing individual tutee performances with the tracking group, a teacher might consider providing group-oriented contingencies (Litow & Pumroy, 1975). For example, a reinforcer could be delivered to all tutees when each meets a preestablished criterion. Another method of reinforcer delivery would be to provide a reinforcer contingent on the mean score (or rate of behavior) of each individual within a tutoring group. Third, reinforcement can be delivered based on the performance of one student selected with a purpose or at random (Speltz, Shimamura, & McReynolds, 1982). Fourth, delivery can be team based (Kazdin, 1984), with two or more teams competing for recognition (Delquadri et al., 1983). The performance of team members is recorded on posted team charts, and the team that scores the most tutoring points receives recognition or reinforcement. A version of the Good Behavior Game (Barrish, Saunders, & Wolf, 1969) is another example of a group-oriented contingency. With this delivery method, students can be divided into two or more competing teams, and contingencies exist for each team. The team with the most points receives a reinforcer, and any teams that meet the criterion are rewarded.

Maintenance testing. To administer maintenance testing, the tutor takes the following steps:

1. Each time a set of cards moves from the Stop pocket, collect it, date it seven days ahead, and place it in a designated location (e.g., envelope).
2. Administer a maintenance test on the date indicated, using testing procedures identical to the one used during the daily tutoring sessions. If the tutee responds correctly, take the card out of the system. If the tutee makes an error, add that card to the next set of cards to be inserted in the Go pocket (e.g., nine new cards plus one maintenance card).

Maintenance testing adaptations. The time designated for maintenance testing or the number of sets probed at the same time can be varied. For tutees participating in school-based tutoring, the teacher may decide to send those cards missed on maintenance tests home for practice and review.

Step 5: Test for Effectiveness

When testing the effectiveness of START tutoring programs, three broad categories should be assessed: the effects of tutor training, the effects of tutoring, and the satisfaction of the tutors, tutees, and teachers.

Effects of tutor training. The overall effectiveness of any tutoring program depends in part on whether the tutors are able to carry out the instructional procedures as they were trained. There are several strategies that can be used to determine this. First, teachers should periodically observe tutor behavior using a checklist of tutoring protocol. Tutor awards could be presented to students who are consistently following tutoring protocol, or special awards could be given to tutors who excel in specific tutoring behaviors (e.g., most positive, most prepared). If necessary, a tutoring booster session (a review of tutoring protocol) could be held.

Teachers should consider using students as tutor monitors on a rotating basis. Once a week (or every two weeks), a student could be assigned the responsibility of observing tutoring dyads and evaluating tutoring performance (on a checklist similar to what the teacher would use). If the students are younger, perhaps the tutor monitor could wear a sash or badge signifying his or her title. In addition to serving as a review of tutoring protocol, being tutor monitor would likely be seen as a reward. When using CA tutoring programs, a paraprofessional, parent assistant, or tutor whose tutee is absent could occasionally serve as a tutor monitor. To evaluate the tutoring performance of parents (or siblings) at home, the teacher could send home an occasional tutoring protocol checklist for parents to fill out and return. The teacher would then follow up by praising the parents or siblings for following tutoring protocol.

Effects of tutoring. When students (or parents) are used as tutors, the teachers are still accountable for their students being taught accurately and with efficacy. Therefore, they must carefully and consistently monitor the effectiveness of the tutoring programs on the acquisition, maintenance, and generalization of the skills being tutored. The daily testing component of START tutoring provides teachers with ongoing information regarding the short-term effects of the tutoring program. The tracking charts are an efficient way to gather and display performance data. Teachers may also consider using simple line graphs, cumulative graphs, or standard celeration charts to record student progress. Additional evaluation techniques might include standardized testing (Greenwood et al., 1984), observations, and analyses of permanent student products (Greenfield & McNeil, 1987; Pigott, Fantuzzo, & Clement, 1986). If a tutoring program is not effective, a teacher has several program modification options: (1) tutoring of prerequisite skills, (2) holding more frequent tutoring sessions, (3) decreasing the number of words (concepts, facts) presented per session, (4) using a different tutoring format, and (5) supplementing a school-based tutoring program with a home-based tutoring program.

In addition to teaching new skills, maintaining and generalizing student performance are the desired goals of the tutoring programs. Rather than expect behaviors and skills to generalize across behaviors, settings, or students, teachers must plan for generalization (Stokes & Baer, 1977). Maintenance tests in the START tutoring program are built into the weekly tutoring routine, with previously mastered word (fact) sets being placed in the folder for review. Teachers should also consider assessing for maintenance after longer intervals (e.g., one month). Generalization of performance during tutoring could be enhanced by varying the tutoring partners. Teachers should also consider varying the materials used in tutoring. For example, sight words could be practiced in isolation and in context; math facts could be presented in a vertical and horizontal format; spelling words could be spelled orally and written out.

Satisfaction of tutors, tutees, and teachers.   The satisfaction of the participants is an important factor in the success of the tutoring program and the likelihood of its continued use. Social validity can be measured by using questionnaires and surveys (Maheady, Sacca, & Har-per, 1988), by conducting interviews (Barbetta & Heron, 1991; Maheady, Sacca, & Harper, 1988), and by using rating scales (Brown, Rollins, & McCandless, 1988). Teachers should periodically ask their tutors' and tutees' opinions about tutoring programs and write suggestions for change. To help ensure the continuation of tutoring programs begun by researchers or consultants, steps must be taken to reinforce the persons primarily responsible for the continuation (e.g., teachers, parents, administrators). To accomplish this objective, maintenance contingencies must be built into the program from its onset (D. P. Wacker, personal communication, September 26, 1991). For example, teachers may need to be reinforced for continuing to implement a peer-tutoring program, just as the students involved often need to be reinforced to maintain tutoring behaviors. Intermittent reinforcement and indiscriminate contingencies (perhaps from consultants, administrators, parents, or fellow teachers) can be programmed to maintain the behavior of the behavior change agents and the learners. Charts and graphs of student progress may also be used as a reinforcer for maintaining tutoring programs.

Conclusion

Tutoring in the Classroom

The use of students as tutors is not a new instructional technology. Informal and spontaneous tutoring has occurred in the classroom since the days of the one-room schoolhouse. Recently, however, research efforts have focused on the development of formal, highly structured, peer-tutoring programs that have demonstrated convincingly that peers can successfully effect changes in academic and social skills. The START tutoring program (as well as the many programs referenced in this chapter) has been successfully used in various formats, with tutors and tutees of different ages and abilities, and across a variety of curricular areas. Furthermore, most students seem to enjoy the roles of tutor and tutee.

Home-Based Tutoring

Classroom teachers can be instrumental in influencing parents to implement home tutoring programs. The parents' confidence levels will likely increase when they are given specific instructions for tutoring procedures, praising, error correction, and record keeping. Home-based tutoring programs should be kept simple, short, positive, and fun. Teachers need to reinforce parents as well, perhaps by making occasional phone calls or sending home short notes. Excellent times for sharing ideas for home-based tutoring programs are at open houses or before summer vacations.

Sharing with Colleagues

Teachers using student or parent tutoring should be encouraged to invite other teachers to observe, learn, and participate in their tutoring programs. To cut down on the cost of teacher time, a team of teachers could plan, prepare, and implement a tutoring program. Once tutoring is set up, management takes less time and effort as most teacher time is expended up front. Team teaching may also allow for mainstreaming and social skills development across classes.

Implications for Teacher Educators

Given the positive results of well-designed student and home-based tutoring programs, it is important for teacher trainers in special and general education programs to share these instructional approaches with their students. Preservice and inservice teacher-education programs should provide instruction in the research supporting the use of tutoring as well as specific strategies for successful and continued use.

Tutoring strategies could be introduced during class lectures by using videotape presentations, role playing, or by taking classroom visits to sites using student-tutoring procedures. Parents providing home-based tutoring could be asked to share their tutoring experiences. Teacher educators should consider incorporating peer-tutoring methods in college-level courses by using tutoring to teach the college-level curriculum, or requiring students to implement tutoring programs in school or service settings.

Implications for the Researcher

Despite the accumulating body of research and many years of experience using tutoring programs, several questions concerning the implementation of students (and parents) as tutors have not yet been answered. Much of the tutoring research consists of investigations of intervention packages, providing little information regarding which specific program components (e.g., prompting, practice, error correction) might have contributed to their effectiveness. Given that tutoring programs have focused more on academic than on social outcomes, more information on the effectiveness of peer tutoring to increase social skills, interactions, and peer relations would be desirable. Also research is needed to identify the most effective and efficient methods of tutor training.

Perhaps, most important, research is needed on how to reinforce teachers to employ (or continue to use) school and home-based tutoring programs as an integral part of instruction. Many highly effective tutoring programs exist. Yet when confronted with the challenge of meeting the diverse needs of their students, many teachers still do not use students and parents as tutors. These potentially powerful teaching resources and procedures—resources and procedures that we can ill afford to waste—often go untapped.

References

BARBETTA, P. M., & Heron, T. E. (1991). Project Shine: Summer home instruction and evaluation. *Intervention in School and Clinic, 26,* 276–281.

BARBETTA, P. M., & Heward, W. L. (1993). Effects of active student response during error correction on the acquisition and maintenance of geography facts by elementary students with learning disabilities. *Journal of Behavioral Education, 3,* 217–233.

BARBETTA, P. M., Heron, T. E., & Heward, W. L. (1993). Effects of active student response during error correction on the acquisition, maintenance, and generalization of sight words by students with developmental disabilities. *Journal of Applied Behavior Analysis, 26,* 111–119.

BARBETTA, P. M., Miller, A. D., Peters, M. T., Heron, T. E., & Cochran, L. L. (1991). Tugmate: A cross-age tutoring program to teach sight vocabulary. *Education and Treatment of Children, 14,* 19–37.

BARRISH, H. H., Saunders, M., & Wolf, M. M. (1969). Good behavior game: Effects of individual contingencies for group consequences on disruptive behavior in a classroom. *Journal of Applied Behavior Analysis, 2,* 119–124.

BECHNER, R. M. (1984). *Parent involvement: A review of the research and principles of successful practice.* Washington, DC: National Institute of Education.

BROWN, J. C., Rollins, H. A., & McCandless, B. R. (1988). Effects of a contingency management remedial reading program administered by cross-age tutors. *Journal of Human Behavior and Learning, 5,* 53–62.

BROWN, W. (1986). Handicapped students as peer tutors. *Academic Therapy, 22*(1), 75–79.

CAMPBELL, A., Scaturro, J., & Lickson, J. (1983). Peer tutors help autistic students enter the mainstream. *Teaching Exceptional Children, 15*(2), 64–71.

CARNINE, D., & Silbert, J. (1979). *Direct instruction reading.* Columbus, OH: Merrill.

CHIANG, B., Thorpe, H. W., & Darch, C. B. (1980). Effects of cross-age tutoring on word recognition performance of learning disabled students. *Learning Disability Quarterly, 3,* 11–19.

COOK, S. A., Scruggs, T. E., Mastropieri, M. A., & Casto, G. C. (1985–1986). *Journal of Special Education, 19*(4), 483–492.

COOKE, N. L., Heron, T. E., & Heward, W. L. (1983). *Peer tutoring: Implementing classwide programs in the primary grades.* Columbus, OH: Special Press.

COOKE, N. L., Heron, T. E., Heward, W. L, & Test, D. W. (1982). Integrating a Downs Syndrome child in a classwide peer tutoring system: A case report. *Mental Retardation, 20,* 22–25.

COOPER, J. O., & Edge, D. (1981). *Parenting strategies and educational methods.* Louisville: Eston Corp.

CUSTER, J. D., & Osguthorpe, R. T. (1983). Improving social acceptance by training handicapped students to tutor their non-handicapped peers. *Exceptional Children, 50*(2), 173–174.

DELQUADRI, J. C., Greenwood, C. R., Stretton, K., & Hall, R. V. (1983). The peer tutoring spelling game: A classroom procedure for increasing opportunity to respond and spelling performance. *Education and Treatment of Children, 6,* 225–239.

DELQUADRI, J., Greenwood, C. R., Whorton, D., Carta, J. J., & Hall, R. V. (1986). Classwide peer tutoring. *Exceptional Children, 52,* 535–542.

DRASS, S. D., & Jones, R. L. (1971). Learning disabled children as behavior modifiers. *Journal of Learning Disabilities, 4,* 16–23.

EHLY, S. W., & Larson, S. C. (1976). Peer tutoring to individualize instruction. *Elementary School Journal, 76,* 475–480.

EHLY, S. W., & Larson, S. C. (1980). *Peer tutoring for individualized instruction.* Boston: Allyn & Bacon.

EISERMAN, W. D. (1988). Three types of peer tutoring: Effects on the attitudes of students with learning disabilities and their regular class peers. *Journal of Learning Disabilities, 21,* 249–252.

ELKSNIN, L. K., & Elksnin, N. (1991). Helping parents solve problems at home and school through parent training. *Intervention in School and Clinic, 26,* 230–233.

FOLIO, M. R., & Norman, A. (1981). Toward more success in mainstreaming: A peer teacher approach to physical education. *Teaching Exceptional Children, 13*(3), 110–114.

FRANCA, V. M., Kerr, M. M., Reitz, A. L., & Lambert, D. (1990). Peer tutoring among behaviorally disordered students: Academic and social benefits to tutor and tutee. *Education and Treatment of Children, 13,* 109–128.

GOLDSTEIN, S. R., Strickland, B., Turnbull, A. P., & Curry, L. (1980). An observational analysis of the IEP conference. *Exceptional Children, 46,* 278–286.

GREENFIELD, S. D., & McNeil, M. E. (1987). The effects of an intensive tutor training component in a peer tutoring program. *The Pointer, 31,* 31–36.

GREENWOOD, C. R. (1991). Longitudinal analysis of time, engagement, and achievement in at-risk versus non-risk students. *Exceptional Children, 57,* 521–535.

GREENWOOD, C. R., Carta, J. J., & Hall, R. V. (1988). The use of peer tutoring strategies in classroom management and educational instruction. *School Psychology Review, 17*(2), 258–275.

GREENWOOD, C. R., Dinwiddie, G., Terry, B., Wade, L., Stanley, S. O., Thibadeau, S., & Delquadri, J. C. (1984). Teacher versus peer mediated instruction: An ecobehavioral analysis of achievement outcomes. *Journal of Applied Behavior Analysis, 17,* 521–538.

GREER, R. D., & Polirstok, S. R. (1982). Collateral gains and short-term maintenance in reading and on-task responses by inner-city adolescents as a function of their use of social reinforcement while tutoring. *Journal of Applied Behavior Analysis, 15,* 123–139.

GURALNICK, M. J., & Groom, J. M. (1988). Peer interactions in mainstreamed and specialized classrooms: A comparative analysis. *Exceptional Children, 54,* 415–425.

HAISLEY, F. B., Tell, C. A., & Andrews, J. (1981). Peers as tutors in the mainstream: Trained "teachers" of handicapped adolescents. *Journal of Learning Disabilities, 14,* 224–226.

HARING, T. G., Breen, C., Pitts-Conway, V., Lee, M., & Gaylord-Ross, R. (1987). Adolescent peer tutoring and special friend experiences. *Journal of the Association for Persons with Severe Handicaps, 12,* 280–286.

HARRIS, J., & Aldridge, J. (1983). 3 for me is better than 2 for you. *Academic Therapy, 18,* 361–364.

HASSETT, M. E., Engler, C., Cooke, N. L., Test, D. W., Weiss, A. B., Heward, W. L., & Heron, T. E. (1984). A telephone-managed, home-based summer writing program for LD adolescents. In W. L. Heward, T. E. Heron, D. S. Hill, & J. Trapp-Porter (Eds.), *Focus on behavior analysis in education* (pp. 89–103). Columbus, OH: Merrill.

HERON, T. E., & Harris, K. C. (1993). *The educational consultant: Helping professional, parents, and mainstreamed students.* 3rd ed. Austin: PRO-ED.

HERON, T. E., Heward, W. L., Cooke, N. L., & Hill, D. S. (1983). Evaluation of a classwide peer tutoring system: First graders teach each other sight words. *Education and Treatment of Children, 6,* 137–152.

HEWARD, W. L., Heron, T. E., & Cooke, N. L. (1982). Tutor Huddle: Key element in a classwide peer tutoring system. *Elementary School Journal, 83,* 115–123.

HEWARD, W. L., Heron, T. E., Ellis, D. E., & Cooke, N. L. (1986). Teaching first grade peer tutors to use praise on an intermittent schedule. *Education and Treatment of Children, 9,* 5–15.

JENKINS, J. R., & Jenkins, L. M. (1981). *Cross-age and peer tutoring: Help for children with learning problems.* Reston, VA: Council for Exceptional Children.

JOHNSON, M., & Bailey, J. S. (1974). Cross-age tutoring: Fifth graders as arithmetic tutors for kindergarten children. *Journal of Applied Behavior Analysis, 7,* 223–232.

KAMPS, D., Locke, P., Delquadri, J., & Hall, R. V. (1989). Increasing academic skills of students with autism using fifth grade peers as tutors. *Education and Treatment of Children, 12,* 38–51.

KANE, B. J., & Alley, G. R. (1980). A peer-tutored, instructional management program in computational mathematics for incarcerated, learning disabled juvenile delinquents. *Journal of Learning Disabilities, 13,* 148–151.

KAZDIN, A. E. (1984). *Behavior modification in applied settings.* Homewood, IL: Dorsey Press.

KOHLER, F. W., & Greenwood, C. R. (1990). Effects of collateral peer supportive behaviors within the classwide peer tutoring program. *Journal of Applied Behavior Analysis, 23,* 307–322.

KOURY, M., & Browder, D. M. (1986). The use of delay to teach sight words by peer tutors classified as moderately mentally retarded. *Education and Training of the Mentally Retarded, 21,* 252–258.

KROUSE, J., Gerber, M. M., & Kauffman, J. M. (1981). Peer tutoring: Procedures, promises, and unresolved issues. *Exceptional Education Quarterly, 1*(4), 107–115.

LAZERSON, D. B., Foster, H. L., Brown, S. I., & Hummel, J. W. (1988). The effectiveness of cross-age tutoring with truant junior high students with learning disabilities. *Journal of Learning Disabilities, 21,* 253–255.

LITOW, L., & Pumroy, D. K. (1975). A brief review of classroom group-oriented contingencies. *Journal of Applied Behavior Analysis, 3,* 341–347.

MCKELLAR, N. A. (1986). Behaviors used in peer tutoring. *Journal of Experimental Education, 54,* 163–167.

MCKENZIE, M. L., & Budd, K. S. (1981). A peer tutoring package to increase mathematics performance: Examination of generalized changes in classroom behavior. *Education and Treatment of Children, 4,* 1–15.

MADDEN, N. A., & Slavin, R. E. (1983). Mainstreaming students with mild academic handicaps: Academic and social outcomes. *Review of Educational Research, 53,* 519–569.

MAHEADY, L., & Harper, G. R. (1987). A class-wide peer tutoring program to improve the spelling test performance of low-income third- and fourth-grade students. *Education and Treatment of Children, 10,* 120–133.

MAHEADY, L., & Sainato, D. M. (1985). The effects of peer tutoring upon the social status and social interaction patterns of high and low status elementary school students. *Education and Treatment of Children, 8,* 51–65.

MAHEADY, L., Harper, G. R., & Sacca, K. (1988). A classwide peer tutoring system in a secondary resource room program for the mildly handicapped. *Journal of Research and Development in Education, 21*(3), 76–83.

MAHEADY, L., Sacca, M. K., & Harper, G. F. (1988). Classwide peer tutoring with mildly handicapped high school students. *Exceptional Children, 55,* 52–59.

MAHER, C. A. (1984). Handicapped adolescents as cross-age tutors: Program description and evaluation. *Exceptional Children, 51,* 51–63.

MALLETTE, B., Harper, G. F., Maheady, L., & Dempsey, M. (1991). Retention of spelling words acquired using a peer-mediated instructional procedure. *Education and Training in Mental Retardation, 26,* 156–164.

MILLER, A. D., & Heron, T. E. (1991). Peer and cross-age tutoring: Training issues, reinforcement and correction procedures, and outcomes. Paper presented at the 17th annual convention of the Association for Behavior Analysis, May, Atlanta.

MILLER, M. (1984). The three faces of mainstreaming. *Academic Therapy, 19,* 561–565.

OSGUTHORPE, R. T., & Scruggs, T. E. (1986). Special education students as tutors: A review and analysis. *Remedial and Special Education, 7*(4), 15–26.

OSGUTHORPE, R. T., Eiserman, W. D., & Shisler, L. (1985). Increasing social acceptance: Mentally retarded students tutoring regular class peers. *Education and Training of the Mentally Retarded, 20,* 235–240.

PARSON, L. R., & Heward, W. L. (1979). Training peers to tutor: Evaluation of a tutor training package for primary learning disabled students. *Journal of Applied Behavior Analysis, 12,* 309–310.

PIGOTT, H. E., Fantuzzo, J. W., & Clement, P. W. (1986). The effects of reciprocal peer tutoring and group contingencies on the academic performance of elementary school children. *Journal of Applied Behavior Analysis, 19,* 93–98.

POLIRSTOK, S. R., & Greer, R. D. (1986). A replication of collateral effects and a component analysis of a successful tutoring package for inner-city adolescents. *Education and Treatment of Children, 9,* 101–121.

REISBERG, L., & Wolf, R. (1986). Developing a consulting program in special education: Implementation and interventions. *Focus on Exceptional Children, 19*(3), 1–14.

RUSSELL, T., & Ford, D. F. (1983). Effectiveness of peer tutors vs. resource teachers. *Psychology in the Schools, 20,* 436–441.

SHAFER, M. S., Egel, A. L., & Neef, N. A. (1984). Training mildly handicapped peers to facilitate changes in the social interaction skills of autistic children. *Journal of Applied Behavior Analysis, 17,* 461–476.

SINDELAR, P. T. (1982). The effects of cross-age tutoring on the comprehension skills of remedial reading students. *Journal of Special Education, 16*(2), 199–206.

SPELTZ, M. L., Shimamura, J. W., & McReynolds, W. T. (1982). Procedural variations in group contingencies: Effects on children's academic and social behaviors. *Journal of Applied Behavior Analysis, 15,* 533–544.

STOKES, T. F., & Baer, D. M. (1977). An implicit technology of generalization. *Journal of Applied Behavior Analysis, 10,* 349–367.

STOTLAND, J. F., & Mancuso, E. (1981). *Mainstreaming of children in schools: Research and programmatic issues.* New York: Academic Press.

THURSTON, L. P., & Dasta, K. (1990). An analysis of in-home parent tutoring procedures: Effects on children's academic behavior at home and in school and on parents' tutoring behaviors. *Remedial and Special Education, 11*(4), 41–52.

VACC, N. N., & Cannon, S. J. (1991). Cross-age tutoring in mathematics: Sixth graders helping students who are moderately handicapped. *Education and Training of the Mentally Retarded, 26,* 89–97.

YOUNG, C. C., Hecimovic, A., & Salzberg, C. L. (1983). Tutor-tutee behavior of disadvantaged kindergarten children during peer teaching. *Education and Treatment of Children, 6,* 123–135.

CHAPTER 21

Three "Low-Tech" Strategies for Increasing the Frequency of Active Student Response During Group Instruction

William L. Heward

There are many conceptual models for education, and they differ significantly in their frames of reference, the variables considered relevant, and the degree to which those variables can be objectively measured and experimentally manipulated. Two touchstones for evaluating the goodness of any educational model are the extent and quality of empirical evidence attesting to the model's effectiveness and its relevance to the realities of classroom practice. When judged by these criteria, the collection of instructional models properly identified as "behavioral" and/or "direct instruction" fares pretty well. Within the so-called behavioral approach to education, there are different sets of terminology and conflicting opinions as to which instructional variables are most important. Proponents of all behavioral/direct instruction models would agree, however, that effective teaching is characterized by: clear specification of learning objectives, assessment of the student's entry skills relative to those objectives, structured classroom activities in which students are actively engaged with well-designed curricular materials, systematic use of both positive and corrective feedback for student performance, and a formative and summative evaluation of learning (e.g., Ber-

liner, 1980, 1984; Brophy & Good, 1986; Bushell & Dorsey, 1985; Christensen, Ysseldyke, & Thurlow, 1989; Gersten, Carnine, & White, 1984; Rosenshine & Stevens, 1986).

These teaching activities can be organized under four basic functions: assessment, planning, instruction, and evaluation (e.g., Stephens, 1977). Although assessment, planning, and evaluation are important components of teaching, students come into actual contact with the teaching program only during instruction.

Preparation of this chapter and many of our studies were supported in part by Leadership Training Grants from the U.S. Department of Education to The Ohio State University. The Psychology Department at Keio University, Tokyo and, in particular, Professors Masaya Sato and Takyuki Sakagami, provided support and assistance that were greatly appreciated during the preparation of this chapter. This research is the product of the hard work and good ideas of many classroom teachers and university students, but each of the following individuals contributed significantly to the ASR research program while graduate students at OSU: Patricia M. Barbetta, Rodney A. Cavanaugh, Nancy L. Cooke, Frances H. Courson, Ralph Gardner III, Teresa A. Grossi, Jonathan W. Kimball, Janani S. Narayan, and David W. Test. If the research we summarize contributes to the practice of education, it is because of the combined energy, creativity, scientific curiosity, and good sense of this group of people.

The Learning Trial as the Basic Unit of Instruction

In teaching models based on behavior analysis, the three-term contingency represents the point of contact between the learner and the teacher. In the context of education, the three-term contingency can be called a learning trial. A learning trial consists of three major elements: antecedent (i.e., curricular) stimuli, the student's response to those stimuli, and consequent stimuli (i.e., instructional feedback) following the response. The learning trial is a basic unit of analysis for examining teaching and learning from both the teacher's perspective (that is, an opportunity to teach) and the student's perspective (or an opportunity to learn) (Heward, 1987). For example, the number of learning trials (called *learn units*) delivered per lesson is the primary measure of a teacher's effectiveness in the Comprehensive Application of Behavior Analysis (CABAS) model developed by Doug Greer and his colleagues (see Chapter 13 in this text). "A learn unit is the smallest divisible unit of teaching and incorporates interlocking three-term contingencies for both the teacher and the student. . . .

when used in concert with rigorous assessment of learning objectives they are direct measures of schooling effectiveness" (Greer & Linhardt, 1992, pp. 4-5).

Although teaching (perhaps too often) and meaningful learning (occasionally) can occur via a single learning trial, direct systematic instruction usually requires a sequence of learning trials. Figure 21.1 illustrates two ways in which a series of learning trials can take place within the unavoidable dimension of time. When a student is first learning a new skill or content knowledge, feedback ideally follows each response (as shown in the top part of Figure 21.1). Feedback during this stage should focus on the accuracy and topography of the student's response. By providing feedback following each response, the teacher reduces the likelihood of the student practicing errors (Van Houten, 1984). As the student begins to demonstrate some accuracy with the new behavior, a series of responses can and should be emitted before feedback is obtained (as shown in the bottom half of Figure 21.1). During the practice stage of learning, instruction should be designed to help the student develop fluency with the target skill, and

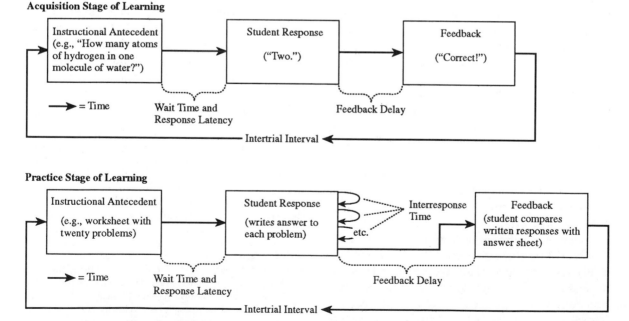

Figure 21.1. Schematic representations of a series of learning trials during the acquisition and practice stages of learning.

feedback should emphasize the rate or speed with which the student performs (see Chapter 14 in this text; Van Houten, 1984). Instruction during the practice stage can still be analyzed as a series of complete learning trials; however, one feedback episode serves multiple student responses.

Each time period between the three components of the learning trial—wait time and response latency, feedback delay, and intertrial interval—influences the number of learning trials that can be delivered (teacher's perspective) and experienced (student's perspective) during a given time. Wait time, feedback delay, and intertrial interval are teacher-controlled variables; the teacher can experimentally manipulate each one and observe its effects on the number of learning trials and student performance (e.g., Koegel, Dunlap, & Dyer, 1980). Each of these time elements (including response latency) can also be measured as a dependent variable to determine if and how they are affected by various instructional arrangements.

Behaviorists, of course, have not been alone in recognizing the importance of events taking place just before and just after a student responds during instruction. For example, the three stages of the "teaching cycle" described by Zahorik (1985)—soliciting, responding, and reacting—correspond to the three elements of the three-term contingency. The distinguishing contribution of behavior analysis has been its search for and identification of functional relations between the elements of the learning trial and the subsequent development of effective teaching practices based on those relations.

Some educators argue that the learning trial is too simplistic a concept to represent the complex interactions between student and teacher, that the three-term contingency does not accommodate certain "higher-order" types of teaching and learning. They may be correct. But there is evidence to suggest that a great deal of important teaching and learning is functionally described by the learning trial. In their review of the literature on effective teaching, Rosenshine and Berliner (1978) concluded that instruction in classrooms in which students made significant achievement gains was characterized by "a pattern of 'controlled practice' consisting of factual questions, student academic responses, and adult academic feedback" (p. 10). Rosenshine

and Berliner, who are not behavior analysts, had described the three-term contingency perfectly. They concluded that teachers do not have to ask so-called higher-order questions to be effective: "The frequency of factual, single-answer questions is positively related to achievement gain in most of these studies" (p. 10). In fact, a high frequency of open-ended questions correlated negatively with achievement in the Project Follow Through classroom observations (Stallings & Kaskowitz, 1974).

Most behavioral research in education has focused on the first and third elements of the learning trial. Applied behavior analysis made its initial and most widely recognized contributions to education by demonstrating the powerful effects of consequences—most notably, contingent reinforcement—on student performance. Behavior analysts have also focused their science on the role of antecedent stimuli in the form of curricular materials. Although still far from finished, this research has produced many components of an effective technology of teaching, some of which are described in this text.

Even though John Dewey more than 75 years ago (1916) emphasized that "students learn by doing," until recently educational researchers have overlooked the middle component of the three-term contingency—the student's response—as an independent variable. Since the late 1970s, however, the relation between active student engagement and academic achievement has been the focus of a large and growing body of research.

Vance Hall and his colleagues at the Juniper Gardens Children's Project first directed the attention of the behavior analysis community to the importance of active student participation during instruction, a variable they termed *opportunity to respond* (Delquadri, Greenwood, & Hall, 1979; Hall, Delquadri, & Harris, 1977; Hall et al., 1982). They didn't set out to research opportunity to respond (OTR). Like other behaviorists working in education in the 1960s and 1970s, they focused on how reinforcement and other consequences could be manipulated to improve student performance. Their early papers tell an interesting story of the serendipitous manner in which they discovered the relationship between opportunity to respond and the school success of children who are at risk for academic failure and developmental delay.

Over the past 15 years, the Juniper Gardens research group has published numerous studies documenting the positive correlation between opportunity to respond and academic achievement and has been a leader in the behavior analysis community in the development and field testing of instructional strategies that provide high levels of OTR in the classroom. For reviews of this work, see Greenwood (1991; Chapter 16 in this text) and Greenwood, Delquadri, and Hall (1984).

Behavior analysts were not the only researchers to discover the relation between active student engagement and academic achievement. Educational researchers who use the methodology of groups comparison and statistical inference reached the same conclusion as the behavior analysts at about the same time. Rosenshine & Berliner (1978) described the finding in these words:

> The primary finding is this, student time spent engaged in relevant content appears to be an essential variable for which there is no substitute. . . . Teachers who make a difference in students' achievement are those who put students into contact with curriculum materials and find ways to keep them in contact. [p. 12]

Within mainstream educational research, the concept of academic learning time, or ALT, evolved as the primary measure of student engagement and "contact" with the curriculum. For reviews of literature on academic learning time, see Fisher and Berliner (1985), Fisher and colleagues (1980), and Rosenshine (1979).

Active Student Response

In this section, ASR is first defined and then compared to other measures of instructional time and student engagement. Then, three benefits of increasing the frequency of active student response during instruction are discussed.

A Definition of Active Student Response

Active student response (ASR) can be defined as an observable response made to an instructional antecedent. To say it less technically, ASR occurs when a student emits a detectable response to ongoing instruction. The kinds of responses that qualify are as varied as the kinds of lessons that are taught. Depending on the instructional objective, examples include words read, problems answered, boards cut, test tubes measured, praise and supportive comments spoken, notes or scales played, stitches sewn, sentences written, workbook questions answered, and fastballs pitched. The basic measure of how much ASR a student receives is a frequency count of the number of academic responses emitted within a given period of instruction.

A comment on the adjective *active* is warranted. To a behaviorist, calling a response *active* is like saying that water is *wet*. Behavior, by definition, is action—movement, regardless of scale, of some part of the body through space and time (Johnson & Pennypacker, 1980; Skinner, 1938). In spite of its theoretical redundancy, the concept of active student response holds practical importance for the classroom.

First, research shows that learning is enhanced by students' engagement with relevant instructional materials (Rosenshine & Berliner, 1978; Stallings, 1980). By requiring students to actively respond during instruction, the teacher can ensure that relevant responses are occurring. An active response in this sense means a response that produces movement or change in the environment that can be detected by someone who can provide feedback to the student, be it teacher, peer, or the student herself. Relatedly, research also shows that active student participation (e.g., reading words, answering questions, marking answers) correlates more strongly with achievement than does passive responding (e.g., paying attention, listening to the teacher, watching other students respond) (e.g., Greenwood, Delquadri, & Hall, 1984; Narayan et al., 1990).

Another reason for focusing the teacher's attention on active responses is that while some students can and do learn without emitting responses that an observer can detect, the existence and extent of that learning cannot be determined without having the student respond "publicly" at some point. Both Katie and Brandon may quietly and intently watch their teacher demonstrate how to bisect an angle, but the only way to evaluate what each student has learned is to observe his or her performance of the skill. In education, this evaluation is typically done in the form of a test, which is often given after instruction is finished and the teacher and children have moved on to another part of the curriculum. When it is then discovered that Katie can bisect angles but Brandon cannot, the teacher has little recourse but to ascribe the differential outcomes to variables attributable to the students, such as low intelligence, lack of motivation, perceptual difficulties, poor breakfasts, and so on. The list of student attributes and nonclassroom variables educators use to explain away ineffective instruction is both extensive and creative (Heward & Orlansky, 1992; Lovitt, 1977).

Comparing ASR with Other Measures

Administrators and researchers use numerous variables to objectively measure "how much" education is provided. Figure 21.2 compares ASR with several of the most widely used measures of instructional delivery and student participation in that instruction. The oldest and most common measure is *available time*, which consists of the total number of school days and classroom hours making up the school calendar. Although it holds enormous importance for administrators (staffing), teachers (union bargaining and compensation), parents (child care), and students (summer vacation), available time greatly overestimates the amount of instruction actually provided. In her review of the use of time in the classroom, Stallings (1980) concluded that the length of the school day or class period was not related to academic achievement: "Clearly, student learning depends on how the available time is used, not just the amount of time available" (p. 11).

Allocated time refers to the amount of time scheduled for instruction. At the school-building level, the time allocated for academic instruction can

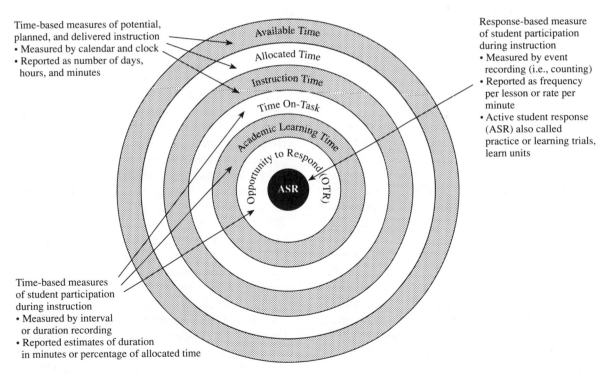

Figure 21.2. Relationships between active student response (ASR) and other commonly used measures of student participation in education.

be determined by examining the class schedule. At the classroom level, allocated time can be determined by totaling the number of minutes reserved for academic instruction in the teacher's plan book. Because of nonacademic activities and management functions, allocated time in the classroom will always be less than the amount of allocated time reported by the principal's office. Although teachers allocate a high proportion of the available time for academic instruction, studies of correlations between amount of allocated time and achievement have produced nonsignificant results (Guthrie, Martuza, & Seifert, 1976; Smith, 1976; Welch & Bridgman, 1968). While perhaps surprising at first, this finding can be understood by reviewing the discrepancies between allocated time and engaged time found in classroom observational studies. For example, Hall and colleagues (1982) reported that while six elementary teachers allocated 75% of the available time each school day for academic instruction, their students spent the largest portion of that time, up to 45% of the instructional day, passively attending to the teacher, and only 25% in academic responding. The message is loud and clear: administrators and teachers can plan any number of hours and minutes for instruction, but the critical factor is how that allocated time is used. Or, as Stallings (1980) put it, "How long does it take to get the show on the road?" (p. 12).

The next circle in Figure 21.2, *instruction time*, refers to the number of minutes that instruction is actually delivered. For many reasons, some of which are out of the teacher's control, the actual time spent in instructional activities is usually less than the time originally allocated. Instruction time provides a closer indicator of what actually happens in the classroom than allocated time, because its measurement requires both students and teachers to be placed within a matrix of various instructional activities (e.g., silent reading, seatwork). Although not a direct measure of student behavior during these activities, instruction time shows the amount of time that students were at least present in various activities. Stallings (1980), who referred to this variable as "time allocated to specific activities," reported that the amount of instruction time spent in specific reading activities significantly affected reading gains made by students in

87 secondary remedial classrooms. Interestingly, the kinds of instructional activities most correlated with achievement gains were what Stallings called "interactive on-task instruction" and were characterized by having students reading aloud and teachers providing support and corrective feedback.

Like available and allocated time, instruction time is not a direct and ongoing measure of what students actually do during instruction. The remaining circles in Figure 21.2 represent various measures of actual student participation during instruction.

On-task behavior is a direct measure of student behavior during instruction. To be judged as on task, a student must be attending to the ongoing instructional activity. While on-task behavior is not undesirable, research has shown that increasing a student's on-task behavior does not necessarily result in a corresponding increase in the amount of academic responses the student emits (e.g., Ferritor et al., 1972; Harris, 1986; McLaughlin & Malaby, 1972; Marholin & Steinman, 1977). Stallings (1980) found that students in classrooms where no achievement gains were made spent 50% of available time in noninteractive on-task activities such as silent reading and seatwork while the teacher graded papers or made lesson plans.

The concept of *academic learning time* was developed at the Far West Regional Laboratory in the Beginning Teacher Evaluation Study (Fisher et al., 1980) as a measure of student engagement during classroom instruction. ALT is a measure of the time a student spends actively engaged in academically relevant materials that are moderately difficult. It has proved to be the strongest correlate of academic achievement (Fischer et al., 1980; Fischer & Berliner, 1985; Rosenshine & Berliner, 1978). In a review of the teaching effectiveness literature, Rosenshine (1979) concluded that content covered and engaged time (both represented by ALT) had consistently produced better correlations with achievement than any other variable.

While the ALT literature offers a great deal of empirical support for the basic relation between active responding and achievement, molar ALT's, onecategory definition of student engagement used by the concept does not enable an analysis of specific types of academic responses (Greenwood et al., 1984). As a time-based measure, ALT cannot provide an account of the actual number of learning trials in which a student participated during instruction.

As noted earlier, Vance Hall and his colleagues coined the term *opportunity to respond* in 1977, and it has become the most widely used term in the behavioral literature to refer to active student participation during instruction. As operationalized by the Juniper Gardens group, OTR is an ecobehavioral measure of the "interaction between: (a) teacher-formulated instructional antecedent stimuli (the materials presented, prompts, questions asked, signals to respond, etc.), and (b) their success in establishing the academic responding desired or implied by the materials" (Greenwood et al., 1984, p. 64).

The precise measurement of OTR is conducted with variations of a sophisticated observational system called the *Code for Instructional Structure and Student Academic Response* (CISSAR) (Stanley & Greenwood, 1981). An observer using the CISSAR code records, using a 10-second interval, momentary time-sampling procedure, the occurrence of up to 53 different setting or behavioral events across six different categories: classroom activity (reading, math, transition), task (paper-pencil, media), structure (small group, individual), teacher position (in front, out of the room), teacher behavior (teaching, no response), academic response (writing, reading aloud), task management responses (attention, raise hand), and competing or inappropriate responses (disrupt, look around). The data gathered can then be used to analyze the interactional effects of various academic activities, tasks, classroom structures, and teacher behavior with student responding. Because opportunity to respond incorporates seven different categories of appropriate academic responding and considers attention or on-task behavior as competing responses, it provides both a more specific and a more conservative measure of student engagement during instruction than measures of academic learning time. OTR has proved to be an excellent tool for both descriptive and intervention research in which students' active participation during instruction is a featured variable (see Arreaga-Mayer, Carta, & Tapia, Chapter 17 in this text; Greenwood, 1991; Greenwood, Delquadri, & Hall, 1984; Greenwood et al.,

1985; Greenwood et al., Chapter 16 in this text; Stanley & Greenwood, 1983).

Active student response is represented by the smallest circle in the center of Figure 21.2 because it is the most direct measure of a student's academic responding during instruction. ASR offers several advantages as a measure of student participation during instruction. First, it is a direct measure of the primary behavior of interest: the occurrence of a student's specific responses to the curriculum. Second, ASR reveals not only how much instruction has been delivered in terms of learning trials experienced, but also how much learning has taken place. While ALT and OTR have both been shown to predict academic achievement, ASR provides a direct measure of behavior change as it occurs (Alexander, 1983). Third, primary ASR data are reported as frequency counts; a standard and absolute behavioral dimension that is sensitive to changes in the instructional environment and is not limited by artificial ceilings as are time-based measures that are reported in minutes or as a percentage of observed intervals (Johnson & Pennypacker, 1980). Fourth, ASR can be measured during instruction delivered via structured discrete trials, incidental teaching, or free operant responding; in instructional settings as varied as whole-class, small-group, peer tutoring, computer-assisted, or self-study; and across all curriculum contexts. Fifth, and perhaps most important, ASR is a simple measure that practicing teachers can use to directly assess how much active instruction their students are receiving.

Although ALT and OTR include ASR, neither of these time-based measures provide an account of discrete learning trials. Percentage of "engaged" time is not as direct a measure of a student's *behavioral* interaction with ongoing instruction as a frequency count showing the number of learning trials in which the student participated. A time-based measure may show that two math students were actively engaged with a paper-and-pencil task for 80% of the observed intervals, but it would not reveal that one student calculated 20 common denominators and the other student only 10. From an ASR perspective, time is seen as the ongoing dimension in which all instruction and learning must take place instead of the primary independent variable. In other words, the time that a student is engaged is considered less important than the number of academic responses the student makes within that time.

Three Benefits of Increasing ASR During Instruction

1. **ASR generates more learning.** The primary advantage of increasing each student's frequency of ASR is increased academic achievement. If all variables are held constant (e.g., quality of curriculum materials, students' prerequisite skills, and motivational variables), an ASR-rich lesson will produce more learning than a lesson of equal duration in which students make fewer active responses. In addition to its role in teacher-led group instruction, higher learning rates have been reported when students are provided with increased ASR during classwide peer-tutoring programs (Heron et al., 1983; Greenwood, Delquadri, & Hall, 1989) and during teacher-delivered error correction (Barbetta, Heron, & Heward, 1993; Barbetta & Heward, 1993; Drevno et al., in press). To review the large body of literature that supports increasing active student engagement during instruction is beyond the purpose and scope of this chapter. For reviews of this research, see Fisher and Berliner (1985); Greenwood, Delquadri, and Hall (1984); and Greenwood et al., Chapter 16 in this text.

2. **ASR provides important feedback to the teacher.** When students actively and regularly respond during a lesson, the teacher obtains immediate feedback on the effectiveness of instruction. Suppose a teacher is demonstrating how to solve long-division problems. He writes a problem on the chalkboard and carefully demonstrates and explains each step of its solution. Knowing that student participation is desirable and wanting to keep the students' attention, the teacher conducts a dialogue with the class. He then generates active participation by an individual student or two by asking, "Who can tell me _____?" or "What is the product of these two numbers?" Sometimes the teacher answers his own questions. After repeating the demonstration and explanation with a second and

perhaps even a third example problem, the teacher turns to the class and asks, "Do you understand?"

The students who respond say yes, even though some in the class do not understand at all. There are many reasons students learn to tell the teacher they understand when, in fact, they do not. First, the teacher often reinforces answering yes by smiling or praising the student. And when students tell the teacher they understand, it seems to make the teacher happy. Another class of contingencies can be grouped under "not wanting to look bad in front of one's peers." Everyone else in the class usually says they understand. Escape and avoidance contingencies also play a major role in supporting the students' behavior of telling the teacher they understand when they really don't. The student who admits to not understanding may be subjected to a variety of aversive consequences, such as a disappointed look from the teacher, recriminating questions around the general theme of "Why don't you understand?" recommendations to pay better attention next time, and, perhaps worst of all, a reenactment of the entire demonstration. This all-too-common scene is described very well by children's author Alan Gross (1980) in *What If the Teacher Calls on Me*?

> She keeps saying, "Do you understand? Do you understand?"
> So finally, I say, "Yes, I understand." But I don't—not really.
> If you tell her you understand, then usually she lets you sit down.
> Maybe something's wrong with me. Other people seem to understand.

Also contributing to the number of "false" yes responses is the fact that sometimes a student *thinks* he understands, when in reality he does not. Watching someone else perform a task is not the same as performing it; especially if that demonstration is accompanied by a narrative designed to make it sound easy. A skill that appears simple to the novice when executed by a competent performer whose behavior is under stimulus controls that are not apparent often turns out to be complex and impossible to perform independently.

Of course, every now and then a brave soul does admit to not understanding. The teacher might question the student about what aspect of the problem she doesn't understand but the student may not be able to answer, especially if instruction was conducted in the whole-problem manner described above. In the end, the teacher has little recourse but to present the entire demonstration again.

By providing sufficient ASR throughout instruction of a new skill, a teacher need never ask students if they "understand." To continue the long-division example, suppose our hypothetical teacher provides each student in the class with a structured worksheet (see Figure 21.3) and places a transparency of the worksheet on an overhead projector. He tells the students they are going to learn the first step in solving long-division problems, and that they will find this easy to learn because they are already fluent in the math skills needed to solve this type of problem. Instruction begins with the teacher pointing to the model problem at the top of the worksheet, telling the students they will be using the terms shown in the model problem to identify the parts of a division problem, and that they should refer to the model problem as often as needed. Next, the teacher reads

The first step in solving a long-division problem:

Rule 1 - If the first digit of the dividend is either equal to or larger than the divisor, begin solving the problem by dividing into the first digit of the dividend.

Rule 2 - If the first digit of the dividend is smaller than the divisor, begin solving the problem by dividing into the first two digits of the dividend.

Let's do some together:

Now it's your turn:

Figure 21.3. Example of a structured worksheet used by students to actively respond during a teacher-directed lesson on long division.

Rule 1, and then reads it together with the class. He then tells how Rule 1 was applied to the first two example problems, pointing out that the correct number of digits in the dividend have already been circled on the students' worksheet. Using choral responding, the teacher and class then apply Rule 1 to the third and fourth example problems, circling the 8 and the 5 together. This process is then repeated with Rule 2.

Using a combination of choral and written responses, the teacher and students then apply the two rules to a series of problems in the following fashion:

Teacher: Let's use these two rules on a few problems together. (Points to the first problem.) The first problem is eighty-two divided by six. When I say "Class," everyone please answer by responding yes or no. Is the first digit of the dividend either equal to or bigger than the divisor? Class.

Students: Yes.

Teacher: Correct. So we would begin solving this problem by dividing into how many digits of the dividend? Class.

Students: One.

Teacher: Good. On your worksheet, circle the eight in the dividend. (Circles 8 on the overhead projector and points to the next problem.) The next problem is three hundred and fifty-five divided by five. Is the first digit of the dividend either equal to or bigger than the divisor? Class.

Students: No.

Teacher: Correct. Is the first digit of the dividend smaller than the divisor? Class.

Students: Yes.

Teacher: So we begin solving this problem by dividing into how many digits of the dividend? Class.

Students: Two.

Teacher: Excellent. On your worksheet, circle the thirty-five in the dividend.

The teacher and students continue this procedure with the next four problems. He then turns the overhead projector off and instructs the students to apply the two rules to the six problems at the bottom of the worksheet, circling the correct number of digits in the dividend of each problem. The teacher circles the correct answers on the transparency and after a minute or two turns on the overhead projector. The students look at the screen for feedback on their responses and self-correct as necessary.

This whole-class activity would take approximately about 15 minutes, with every student in the classroom actively responding many times. Each student response is part of a complete learning trial including immediate feedback. The teacher has little need to ask the students if they "understand." Observation of the students' responses during instruction provides direct evidence of their level of "knowing." Students may also feel more comfortable asking for help because they can be specific about what is giving them trouble.

Without the kind of feedback provided by frequent active student response, teachers may unknowingly continue ineffective instruction while students fall further behind, or waste precious instructional time "teaching" material the students already know. The direct "real-time" access to student performance provided by frequent ASR enables teachers to modify instruction as it occurs. ASR-rich instruction is one method of putting teachers into the "close, continual contact with relevant outcome data" recommended by Bushell and Baer in Chapter 1 of this text.

3. **ASR is correlated with increased on-task behavior.** Increased levels of on-task behavior and/or reduced off-task and disruptive behavior have been found in numerous studies as correlates or functional outcomes of increased ASR (e.g., Carnine, 1976; Gardner et al., 1993; Lingenfelter, 1990; Miller, Hall, & Heward, 1993; Morgan, 1987; Sainato, Strain, & Lyon, 1987). Although on-task behavior is a weak correlate of learning or active student participation (e.g., McLaughlin & Malaby, 1972; Stallings, 1980) and its production should not be the primary purpose of any intervention designed to improve academic achievement, three positive outcomes might occur when students pay attention during group instruction and do not disrupt others: (1) an on-task student is better able to see and hear instructional stimuli than the off-task student, (2) reductions in a student's disruptive behavior make it more likely his or her peers will be able to see and hear the ongoing lesson, and (3) teachers like it when their students are well behaved and on task. The third factor may prove to be a most-impor-

tant outcome in determining teachers' adoption and continued use of high-ASR teaching strategies.

How Much Active Student Participation Occurs in Classrooms?

Given the consensus in the research literature on the importance of active student participation, observational studies of classroom behavior should report high levels of student engagement. Descriptive studies of students' behavior in classrooms, however, have found that in some classes the largest portion of the available teaching time is used for management and transition tasks. Student "participation" during the time that remains is most often in the form of passive attending to the teacher. For example, Hall, Delquadri, Greenwood, and Thurston (1982) reported that while teachers in six elementary schools allocated 75% of the school day for academic instruction, their students spent less than 1% of the day actively responding in each of the following ways: reading aloud, answering questions, asking questions, and reciting. The largest portion of the school day, up to 45% of the time available for instruction, was spent passively attending to the teacher.

Studies of how much opportunity to respond is provided to students receiving special education services are also disappointing (Thurlow et al., 1984). Stanley and Greenwood (1983) compared the amount of academic responding by students in Title I and general education classrooms and concluded the special education students would have to have their school year extended by six weeks to make up for the 11 additional minutes of academic responding by their nondisabled peers each day in the regular classroom.

ASR is a simple concept and its relation to student learning, while not completely understood, is relatively straightforward. Providing all students with sufficient amounts of ASR to enable them to acquire and become fluent in the knowledge and skills of the curriculum, however, presents the classroom teacher with some challenging engineering problems. How can a teacher deal with every student responding at once? How can feedback be delivered in timely and effective fashion if student responding is increased significantly?

The Visual Response System: High Technology for Increasing ASR During Group Instruction

I first became intrigued by the potentially powerful effects of high-ASR instruction through my experience with a specially designed teaching environment called the Visual Response System (VRS). In 1971 I was introduced to an early prototype of the VRS by its creator, Raymond Wyman (1968, 1969). As a newly hired graduate research assistant in Professor Wyman's Northeast Regional Media Center for the Deaf at the University of Massachusetts, my job was to design and conduct applied research to determine if this technology would improve the education of students with hearing impairments. For someone wanting to learn how the principles of behavior might be used to improve instruction, the VRS offered an excellent opportunity. The VRS classroom that evolved from our early work consists of eight to ten student desks arranged in a U-shaped configuration. The VRS's most striking feature is that each student desk has a built-in overhead projector. During a lesson, each student responds to every instructional item by writing on, placing or moving an object onto, or pointing at, and so on, the stage of their overhead projectors (Heward, 1978a, 1978b).

Early research found the VRS to be an effective environment for teaching written language to students with prelingual hearing impairments, an academic area in which deaf students are notorious underachievers (Eachus, 1971; Heward & Eachus, 1979). I wondered how the VRS would work with students experiencing other kinds of academic difficulties and thought this might provide an interesting direction for my research as a new faculty member at Ohio State University (OSU). Four VRS classrooms were constructed in Columbus-area schools, and for five or six years they were productive research sites. The studies conducted in the VRS covered a wide range of curriculum areas, independent variables, and student participants. The VRS proved to be an effective technology for teaching a wide variety of academic, social, and daily living skills to secondary special education students: computation of math fractions (Shadding, 1982), written composition and punctua-

tion (Buckley, 1980; Cowardin, 1978; Jackson, 1980), photosynthesis concepts (Test & Heward, 1980), completion of employment applications (Heward, McCormick, & Joynes, 1980), self-management skills (Marshall & Heward, 1979), use of city and state highway maps (Cooke, Heron, & Heward, 1980), money management skills (Seavey, 1979), and road signs and traffic laws (Test & Heward, 1983). In a VRS in a public elementary school, fifth-graders improved their reading comprehension (Grossman, 1981) and fourth-grade students learned nutrition concepts (Young, 1980). For his dissertation, Dave Test (1983) set up a temporary VRS in a group home and taught money-handling skills to adults with developmental disabilities.

Despite these encouraging results, there were only about 15 VRS classrooms in operation across the country by 1983, and my fantasy of a VRS in every school came to an end. Although equipment and construction costs and space requirements no doubt limited widespread adoption of the system, the amount of training needed for teachers to competently use the VRS was also a significant factor working against its adoption (Heward, Test, & Cooke, 1981; Test, 1978).

With its overhead projectors and electromechanical counters, the VRS did not pass as high tech in terms of its hardware; but by other dimensions, the VRS was a high-tech approach to better instruction: it was not readily available, it was expensive, the equipment was prone to breakdown and repairs, and special training was required to use it correctly. By contrast, low technology is widely available, relatively inexpensive, resistant to downtime because it uses readily available materials or equipment of proven reliability, and requires little or no special training to use correctly.

The system's contribution was as an environment in which instructional variables can be controlled and their effects on students' learning can be seen. The VRS embodied or enabled the effective use of 11 positive instructional features (Heward, 1978a, 1978b). While most of these features are usually part of well-designed instruction in any setting (e.g., a variety of reinforcers, evaluation of instruction as a direct by-product of the lesson), three key instructional features are not often incorporated into group instruction in the conventional classroom: high rates of active student response, immediate visual access to students' responses as they were being emitted, and student-student interaction. We then began to look for low-technology methods of adapting key instructional features of the VRS to the conventional classroom (Test et al., 1983).

Low-Tech ASR Teaching Strategies

Each of the three strategies for increasing ASR described in this chapter—choral responding, response cards, and guided notes—qualifies as a relatively low-tech approach to improving classroom instruction; each strategy has a research base demonstrating its effectiveness in producing measurably superior gains in academic achievement; and each strategy is generally liked by the students and teachers who have used it.

Choral Responding

Choral responding—each student in the class responding orally in unison—is the easiest-to-implement method for increasing ASR during group instruction. It is not a new idea; teachers used choral responding (CR) frequently in the days of the one-room schoolhouse. While children in preschool and primary classrooms today occasionally respond in unison and many foreign language teachers still use CR on a regular basis, few contemporary teachers systematically use CR as part of their daily instructional routine. This is especially true at the secondary level where many teachers may be reluctant to use CR, feeling the tactic is appropriate only for use with young children.

Overview of choral responding research. Although choral responding has been an integral component of several experimentally evaluated instructional programs—most significantly, the Distar Direct Instruction Model of Project Follow Through (Engelmann & Bruner, 1988)—there is relatively little experimental research on the effectiveness of CR as a teaching procedure in its own right.

Sindelar, Bursuck, and Halle (1986) found CR more effective than ordered questioning (one student

responding at a time) in teaching sight words to 11 elementary students with learning disabilities or mild mental retardation. Carnine (1976) presented Distar reading materials to a four first-grade remedial reading students and found that a fast pace (intertrial interval of one second or less) resulted in more learning trials presented by the teacher, higher ASR, increased accuracy of student responses during instruction, and better on-task behavior. Sainato, Strain, and Lyon (1987) experimentally assessed choral responding with a group of ten preschool children with developmental disabilities. Learning trials with CR were presented to the children at two different rates, three per minute and five per minute. Like Carnine (1976), Sainato and colleagues (1987) reported higher rates of student participation, increased levels of correct responding, and decreased levels of off-task behavior with the faster presentation rate.

Table 21.1 provides a summary of seven experiments involving choral responding conducted at Ohio State University. A direct comparison of the effects of students' actively participating by choral responding versus passively attending to instruction can be seen in Figure 21.4. Sterling and colleagues (1993) used an alternating treatments design to compare the effects of choral responding and on-task (OT) instruction on the acquisition and maintenance of health facts during small-group lessons. Five students with learning handicaps (four students identified as developmentally handicapped and one student identified as learning disabled) participated in daily small-group instruction on weekly sets of 20 unknown health facts (10 facts assigned to the CR condition and 10 to the OT condition). Each session lasted approximately 15 minutes and included both ASR and OT instruction. Instruction began with the teacher shuffling all 20 health fact cards. She then presented a round of practice trials on each health fact. A practice trial consisted of the teacher holding up a health fact card with the correct answer side showing as she read the corresponding health question (e.g., "What does the heart do?" "It pumps blood.") Students participated either in ASR or OT instruction. After the first round of practice trials, the teacher shuffled the cards and presented a second round. Choral response instruction consisted of the teacher cueing the students to

Table 21.1 Summary of classroom research on choral responding at The Ohio State University

Study	Students and Setting	Teacher	Curriculum Area and Dependent Variables	Independent Variable and Experimental Design	Results (ASR data/test scores reported as mean per student, unless noted.)
Morgan (1987)	Special school for students with SBH; small-group instruction with 4 poor readers, data taken on 2 lowest readers (S1 and S2)	Experimenter	Reading (sight words): (1) LTs per min; (2) participation (% of LTs student responded); (3) accuracy of student responses; (4) on-task behavior.	Pacing of CR manipulated by controlling the ITI. Phase 1, Slow Only (ITI = 3"); Phase 2, ATD of Slow and Fast (ITI < 1"), each pace for one-half of 20-min. session; Phase 3, Fast Only.	(1) LTs per min., slow = 5.8, fast = 8.7; (2) participation, S1: slow = 94%, fast = 95%; S2: slow = 52%, fast = 79%; (3) accuracy, S1: slow = 92%, fast = 94%; S2: slow = 76%, fast = 96%; (4) on-task behavior, S1: slow = 92%, fast = 97%; S2: slow = 59%, fast = 82%.
Bosch (1988)	1st-grade students in Chapter I reading program (N = 9; three groups of 3)	Classroom teacher	Reading (sight words): (1) Number of words read correctly approx. 5 hrs. after first session with each set (max. score = 5); (2) number of words read correctly after five sessions with each set (max. score = 5); (3) percentage of words read correctly on end-of-study posttest; (4) percentage of words read correctly on follow-up test 4 weeks after study.	Students provided with high, low, and no ASR to each word. Phase I: high = 15 CR opportunities, low = 3, and no = 0. Phase II: high = 9, low = 3, and no = 0. New set of 15 unknown words each week; 5 words per level of ASR; four sets per phase. Words shuffled and presented 3 times each per session (e.g., 15 ASR × 3 rounds).	(1) Test after one session - Phase I: high = 3.0, low = 1.7, no = 1.4; Phase II: high = 3.2, low = 2.2, no = 1.5; (2) test after five sessions - Phase I: high = 4.3, low = 3.9, no = 3.0; Phase II: high = 4.3, low = 3.8, no = 2.5; (3) posttest - Phase I: high = 80%, low = 63%, no = 50%; Phase II: high = 70%, low = 47%, no = 22%; (4) follow-up test - Phase I: high = 75%, low = 65%, no = 56%; Phase II: high = 68%, low = 48%, no = 45%.
Lingenfelter (1990, Experiment I)	1st-grade general education classroom in suburban elementary school (N = 21, 4 target students observed during CR)	Classroom teacher	Reading (sight words): (1) ASR rate per min.; (2) on-task behavior; (3) number of sight words read correctly on daily tests.	Daily 10-min. sessions in which students participated for half of each session by CR and by raising their hands to be called on to respond individually for the other half of the session in an ATD. Weekly set of 15 unknown words used for each condition.	(1) ASR: HR = 0.7, CR = 11.3; (2) on-task behavior: 3 target students higher on task during CR, 1 student similar levels of on task during both conditions; (3) sight word tests: mixed results, some students had higher scores on HR words, some had higher scores on CR words.

Table 21.1 (continued). Summary of classroom research on choral responding at The Ohio State University

Study	Students and Setting	Teacher	Curriculum Area and Dependent Variables	Independent Variable and Experimental Design	Results (ASR data/test scores reported as mean per student, unless noted.)
Lingenfelter (1990, Experiment II)	Special education classroom in inner-city elementary school, 8 students with DH, 4 students observed during CR	Classroom teacher	Same as Experiment I	Same as Experiment I.	(1) ASR: HR = 0.8, CR = 8.6; (2) on-task behavior: 3 target students higher on task during CR, 1 student higher on task during HR; (3) Sight word tests: 5 of 8 students had higher mean scores on words taught with CR.
Cashman (1990)	Special education classroom in inner-city elementary school; 9 students with DH, CR in two groups of 4	Classroom teacher	Reading (sight words): (1) ASR rate per min.; (2) ASR accuracy; (3) on-task behavior; (4) words read correctly on daily tests.	ATD comparing CR with different intertrial intervals (ITIs: < 1", 3", and 5"). Two different ITIs (e.g., 1" vs. 5") were compared during each of the study's four phases by using a different ITI for each half of the daily 10-min. sessions.	(1) ASR rate: < 1" ITI = 24.0; 3" ITI = 10.4; 5" ITI = 8.0; (2) ASR accuracy: < 1" ITI = 91%; 3" ITI = 89%; 5" ITI = 89%; (3) on-task behavior: < 1" ITI = 81%; 3" ITI = 73%; 5" ITI = 72%; (4) daily test: although differences were slight, 7 of 9 students had higher mean scores on words taught with fastest pace (i.e., < 1" ITI).
Sterling, Barbetta, Heward, & Heron (1993)	Special education classroom in suburban elementary school, 4 students with DH, 1 with SLD	Classroom teacher	Health: (1) number of health facts stated correctly on daily tests given 5 hrs. after instruction (max. score = 10) (2) total number of health facts learned; (3) percentage of facts stated correctly on maintenance test 2 weeks after instruction.	ATD of daily 15-min. sessions in which 10 facts were taught with CR and 10 facts were taught with OT (students were praised for looking at the health fact card and listening to the teacher read the fact). Each of 5 sets of 20 unknown facts was used for 5 consecutive days.	(1) Daily tests: Day 1, CR = 3.3, OT = 1.3; Day 2, CR = 4.4, OT = 2.1; Day 3, CR = 5.4, OT = 2.5; Day 4, CR = 6.2, OT = 3.2; Day 5, CR = 6.8, OT = 3.5; (2) total facts learned: CR = 22.8, OT = 11.8; (3) maintenance tests: CR = 76%, OT = 63%.
Williams (1993)	Special education classroom in inner-city elementary school, 4 students with SBH, 2 students observed during CR	Classroom teacher	Social studies facts: (1) LTs per min.; (2) correct student responses per min.; (3) on-task behavior; (4) percentage correct on next-day quiz scores.	ATD across daily 10-min. sessions in which facts were reviewed by either fast (ITI < 1") or slow-paced (ITI = 5") CR.	(1) LTs per min.: Slow = 2.1, Fast = 3.4; (2) correct responses per min.: S1: slow = 1.5, fast = 2.1; S2: slow = 1.6, fast = 2.2.; (3) on-task behavior: S1: slow = 24%, fast = 36%; S2: slow = 35%, fast = 44%; (4) next-day quiz scores: S1: slow = 35%, fast = 50%; S2: slow = 70%, fast = 85%.

Notes: ASR = active student response, ATD = alternating treatments design, CR = choral responding, DH = developmental handicaps, HR = hand raising, ITI = intertrial interval, LT = learning trial, OT = on-task instruction, SBH = severe behavior handicaps, SLD = specific learning disabilities.

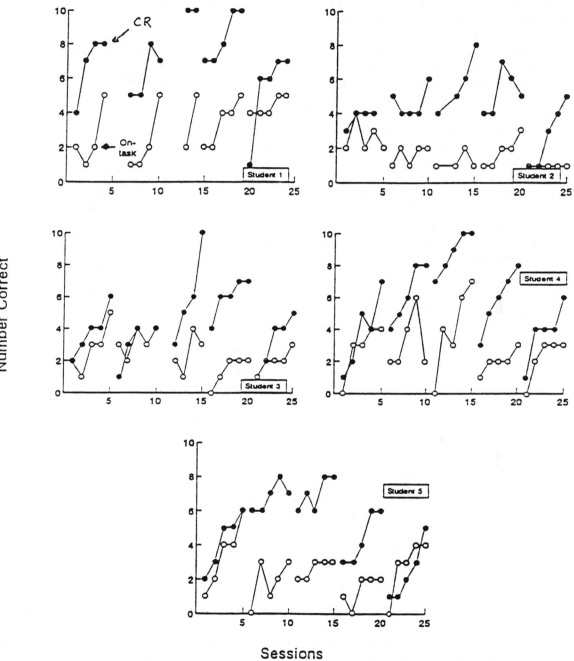

Figure 21.4. Number of health facts stated correctly by special education students on end-of-day tests as a function of choral response (CR) or on-task (OT) instruction. SOURCE: *R. Sterling, P. M. Barbetta, W. L. Heward, & T. E. Heron,* Effects of Active Student Response During Instruction on the Acquisition and Maintenance of Health Concepts by Elementary Students with Learning Disabilities, *1993. Manuscript submitted for publication, The Ohio State University. Used by permission.*

respond in unison with the word "Class," after she modeled the question and its answer. After the group chorally responded, the teacher then cued them to respond two more times by twice saying, "Again, class." She provided verbal praise (e.g., "Good!" "Yes!") after each choral response. During OT instruction, the teacher read each health fact and its answer and then praised the students for listening and attending to the card (e.g., "Good looking!"). On end-of-day tests given to each student approximately five hours after instruction, all five students made more correct responses on health facts taught with CR instruction than they did on health facts taught with OT instruction (see Figure 21.4). CR also produced consistently superior results on maintenance tests administered two weeks after instruction.

Bosch (1988) varied the number of times first-grade remedial-reading students chorally responded to sight words during small-group lessons. Measures of initial acquisition and two follow-up tests found that the students learned and retained more "high-ASR" (9 or 15 CR) sight words than "low-ASR" (3 CR) words, and more "low ASR" words than "no ASR" (0 CR) words.

Three of the OSU studies on choral responding were designed as systematic replications of Carnine's (1976) study and produced similar results (Cashman, 1990; Morgan, 1987; Williams, 1993). When choral response opportunities were presented at a fast pace (intertrial interval $\leq$ one second), small-group instruction was characterized by greater ASR, higher response accuracy, and better on-task behavior than CR at a slow pace (ITI = three or five seconds). Williams (1993) administered next-day quizzes as a measure of learning social facts practiced with fast- and slow-paced CR. Both target students scored better on facts that had been taught by fast-paced CR.

Guidelines and suggestions for using choral responding in the classroom. Choral responding is best suited for curriculum content that meets three criteria: students can answer with short responses (1 to 3 words, numbers, or other vocal elements), there is only one correct answer per question or item, and the questions or items can be presented at a fast, lively pace. Choral responding is most effective and most enjoyable for teacher and students when conducted in a systematic and energetic manner. The following recommendations for conducting CR are based on those presented by Heward, Courson, and Narayan (1989).

1. *Provide clear directions and model one or two trials.* A teacher should begin the CR activity by telling and modeling for the students the kind of questions that will be presented and the type of response they are to make. For example, "Each time I point to a triangle and say 'What kind?' everyone should answer together by saying 'equilateral,' 'isosceles,' or 'scalene.' Watch and listen as I show you how to do it." The teacher then models several trials, playing both roles.

2. *Provide a thinking pause as needed.* A thinking pause—a few seconds between presenting the question or problem and signaling for the students' response—gives students time to think of, compute, or select their answers. The length of the thinking pause should be determined as a function of the complexity of the content and the students' relative skill. Gradually reducing the thinking pause can help promote students' proficiency. A thinking pause of four to six seconds is appropriate for many activities. It may be difficult to maintain the desired rhythm of CR for materials requiring a thinking pause of more than ten seconds.

3. *Use a clear, consistent cue to signal students to respond.* Students should be taught to respond immediately to a standard signal. The signal might be a word such as "Class" or "Now," used by the teacher across all CR activities. Or, the cue might be content or activity specific, such as "How many?" or "Which word?" Visual cues such as a hand or arm movement or touching the next problem or item on the blackboard overhead projector also work very well. Students should be given practice in responding in unison to whatever cue is selected. If a thinking pause of about three seconds or more is used, the teacher should say "Get ready!" immediately before giving the CR cue. This warning signal greatly improves the unison nature of the students' participation.

4. *Provide feedback for the "majority" response.* When it is conducted well, CR consists of a fast-paced series of learning trials, with immediate feedback following each CR. Progressively disclosing the cor-

rect answers on an overhead projector as students choral-respond to a series of projected questions or problems is an excellent tactic for providing immediate feedback. Providing feedback is easy when only correct responses are heard. A quick, positive comment such as "Great!" "Yes!" or "You're right!" is provided and the next item presented. If the clear majority of students answer correctly and just a few incorrect responses are heard, the teacher should repeat or point out the correct answer as in, "Yes, the word *barn* is the predicate in that sentence." When a significant number of incorrect responses are heard, perhaps a fourth to a third or more of the class, the teacher should repeat the correct answer, then immediately repeat the complete learning trial for CR by the whole class. By repeating, several trials later, any item for which any incorrect responses were given, the teacher can check on the effectiveness of the corrective feedback.

5. *From time to time randomly call on individual students.* Two procedures can be used to assess the performance of individual students during a CR activity. The first is simply to try to discriminate the voice of a particular student. With practice this is not as difficult as it may sound, although it cannot be done under some conditions. Eye contact and a smile directed toward a student who has just answered correctly can be an effective reinforcer. When an incorrect answer is voiced by a particular student, the teacher should listen carefully for that student's response when the same item is repeated. The second method is to intersperse responses by individual students within a series of choral responses. The teacher should always ask the question or present the problem before calling an individual student's name, so the entire class will attend to the item. In this way each student in the group will ready a response in preparation for the teacher's cue, be it for a choral or an individual response. The teacher should avoid calling on individual students in order to catch them making a mistake. This is especially important with students for whom failure in front of their peers is an all-too-common experience. Instead, teachers should use the individual response tactic to provide students with learning problems with opportunities to succeed before their classmates.

6. *Maintain a lively pace.* The key to conducting choral responding at a lively pace is to prepare the instructional stimuli prior to the lesson. Advance preparation not only reduces the likelihood of long intertrial intervals while the teacher "makes up" a new question or problem, it also frees the teacher to focus on the students' responses. The overhead projector is an excellent device for presenting instructional stimuli for a CR activity. Transparencies that include numerous opportunities for active student response can be prepared ahead of the lesson (Cooke & Test, 1984). For example, a science teacher might prepare a transparency showing the molecular construction of a dozen or more chemical compounds. By randomly pointing to the different molecular structures and saying, "What compound?" the teacher could conduct CR at a lively pace.

There are numerous ways in which CR might be modified. Hand movements or finger responses might be used to supplement or even replace oral responses (McKenzie & Henry, 1979; Pratton & Hales, 1986). Choral responding might also be conducted as a form of peer tutoring. Students might earn the privilege of being "teacher" for the day, getting to present the instructional stimuli and provide feedback.

Response Cards

Response cards are cards, signs, or items that are held up simultaneously by all students to display their response to a question or problem presented by the teacher. Not only do response cards enable every student in the class to respond to each question or item, but students can learn by watching others. When response cards are used, as opposed to choral responding, the teacher can more easily detect the responses of individual students.

Table 21.2 summarizes the research on response cards (RC) conducted to date at OSU. The first two response card studies (Lenox, 1982; Hoagland, 1983) were designed to determine if VRS-type instruction could be effective in the conventional classroom. Students sat in U-shaped configurations and simultaneously displayed their answers by holding up paper or cardboard "signs" in place of the opaque objects (e.g., coins, shapes) or "response slides" (acetate mounted in cardboard frames for 35-mm slides) used

Table 21.2 Summary of classroom research on response cards (RC) at The Ohio State University

Study	Students and Setting	Teacher	Curriculum Area and Dependent Variables	Independent Variables and Experimental Design	Results (ASR data/test scores reported as mean per student, unless noted.)
Lenox (1982)	Special education classroom in suburban secondary school, 8 students with developmental disabilities	Experimenter	Employment applications: (1) ASR rate; (2) ASR accuracy; (3) 36-item master application; (4) scores on three applications on which no instruction was given	MBD across four sets of master application items with preprinted and write-on RCs (14 total sessions averaging 38 min.)	(1) ASR per min. = .99; (2) ASR accuracy = 96%; (3) 10.8 items correct on pretest, 34.4 correct on 1-week follow-up test; (4) similar gains on generalization applications
Hoagland (1983)	Special education classroom in suburban secondary school, 6 students with SLD	Classroom teacher	Driver's education: (1) ASR rate; (2) ASR accuracy; (3) 20-item test of traffic signs and laws; (4) three students took Ohio DMV test 3 mos. later	Instruction with preprinted (True/False, Yes/No, and traffic signs) and write-on RCs in MBD across three groups of signs and laws (16, 40-min. sessions)	(1) ASR per min. = .80; (2) ASR accuracy = 92%; (3) 11 correct on pretest, 18.3 correct after instruction; (4) two students passed Ohio DMV test on first try; third student passed on third attempt
Wheatley (1986)	Special education classroom in inner-city middle school, 9 students with developmental disabilities	Experimenter	Functional math (money-handling skills): (1) ASR rate; (2) ASR accuracy; (3) 5-item same-day quizzes	ATD of 20-min. sessions using either (1) HR in which one student at a time responded, or (2) preprinted (True/False, numerals) and write-on RCs (29 total sessions)	(1) ASR per min.: RC = .98, HR = .51; (2) ASR accuracy: RC = 82%, HR = 76%; (3) daily quiz score: RC = 4.0, HR = 1.4
Narayan, Heward, Gardner, Courson, & Omness (1990)	4th-grade general education classroom in inner-city elementary school (N = 20)	Experimenter	Social studies (1) ASR per session; (2) ASR accuracy; (3) 10-item same-day quizzes	ABAB design of daily, 20-min. sessions with HR or write-on RC (31 total sessions)	(1) ASR per session: HR = < 2, RC = 30; (2) ASR accuracy: HR = 82%, RC = 83%; (3) 19 of 20 students had higher mean quiz scores on RC lessons
Narayan (1988, Experiment II)	4th-grade general education classroom in inner-city elementary school (N = 18)	Experimenter	Social studies [review of material taught in Exp. I]: (1) ASR per session; (2) 40-item test with 20 items reviewed by each method	ATD: HR was used for half of each 20-min. session and True/False RCs were used during the other half of the session (4 total sessions)	(1) ASR per session: HR = 4, RC = 87; (2) test scores: HR = 63%, RC = 72%; (3) 16 of 18 students had higher test scores on items reviewed with RCs

Table 21.2 (continued). Summary of classroom research on response cards (RC) at The Ohio State University

Study	Students and Setting	Teacher	Curriculum Area and Dependent Variables	Independent Variable and Experimental Design	Results (ASR data/test scores reported as mean per student, unless noted.)
Gardner, Heward, & Grossi (in press)	5th-grade general education classroom in inner-city elementary school (N = 22)	Experimenter	Science (various topics): (1) ASR per session; (2) ASR accuracy; (3) 16-item next-day quizzes; (4) 40-item biweekly review tests	ABAB design of daily, 50-min. lessons with either hand-raising (HR) or write-on RC (26 total sessions)	(1) ASR per session: HR = 1.5, RC = 21.8; (2) ASR accuracy: HR = 92%, RC = 93%; (3) mean quiz score: HR = 56%, RC = 70%; (4) mean review test score: HR = 49%, RC = 70%
Sweeney, Gardner, Hunnicutt, & Mustaine (1992)	3rd-grade general education classroom in inner-city elementary school (N = 26); 5 target students, 2 academically at-risk	Classroom teacher	Social studies: (1) ASR per session; (2) ASR accuracy; (3) student preference for 3 modes of participation; (4) 12-item next-day quizzes	ATD of hand-raising (HR), write-on RCs (WORC), and preprinted True/False RCs (PPRC) followed by ABAB of WORC and PPRC (55 total sessions)	(1) ASR per session: HR = 1.1, WORC = 20.9, PPRC = 26.4; (2) ASR accuracy: HR = 80%, WORC = 89%, PPRC = 93%; (3) 25 of 26 students chose WORC 1st, PPRC 2nd, and HR as 3rd "most-liked" method; (4) quiz scores improved across conditions during ATD and maintained during ABAB
Gardner, Bullara, Heward, Cooper, & Sweeney (1993)	4th-grade general education classroom in inner-city elementary school (N = 25); 3 target students with histories of off-task and disruptive behavior during group instruction	Classroom teacher	Social studies: percentage of observed intervals of (1) off-task behavior and (2) disruptive behavior of 3 target students	ABAB design of daily, 20-min. lessons with either hand-raising (HR) or write-on RC (36 total sessions)	Clear functional relations between RC and reduced off-task and disruptive behavior for all 3 students. (1) Off-task: HR = 50%, 42%, 75%, RC = 8%, 6%, 7%; (2) Disruptive: HR = 20%, 25%, 55%, RC = 4%, 8%, 12%. (Means per student per experimental condition.)
Cavanaugh, Heward, & Donelson (1993)	9th-grade general science class in suburban secondary school (N = 23; 8 in special education or identified as academically at risk)	Classroom teacher	Earth science (various topics): (1) 12-item next-day quizzes; (2) 42-item weekly tests over material presented over past 2 weeks	ATD design in which key points from lecture and/or demonstration were reviewed during the final 10-15 min. of each session by (1) teacher-led verbal review and discussion, or (2) students using write-on RC to respond to teacher-posed questions about key points	(1) Quiz scores: 14 of 15 general education students and all 8 special education students earned higher mean quiz scores following lessons in which RC were used for review; (2) weekly tests: results mixed, but mean scores by all students were higher for test items reviewed with RC than for verbal review items

Notes: ATD = alternating treatments design, HR = hand raising, MBD = multiple-baseline design, RC = response cards, SLD = specific learning disabilities.

by students in the VRS. The positive results of these studies led to a series of five subsequent studies in which RC were compared experimentally to hand raising and one-student-at-a-time recitation, the most commonly used method of student participation during whole-class instruction (Gardner, Heward, & Grossi, in press; Narayan, 1988; Narayan et al., 1990; Sweeney et al., 1992; Wheatley, 1986). Elementary and middle school students in both general and special education classrooms participated in these studies, and the subject matter included functional math, social studies, and science.

The Narayan et al. (1990) experiment is representative of this group of studies. First, when RC were used, each student made approximately 30 responses per 20-minute lesson compared to less than 2 responses per lesson when students raised their hands to be called on to respond individually (HR). The higher ASR rate achieved with RC takes on additional significance when its cumulative effect over the course of a 36-week school year is calculated. Based on the results of this study, if RC were used instead of HR for just 20 minutes per day, each student would make more than 5,000 additional academic responses per school year. Second, the mean daily quiz scores obtained by 19 of the 20 students in the class was higher for RC lessons than for HR lessons. And third, all but one student preferred RCs over raising their hands. After raising their hands several times at the beginning of a HR lesson, five or six students often stopped paying attention and "dropped out" by putting their heads on their desks. This behavior was not observed during RC lessons.

Gardner and colleagues (1993) explored the possibility of a functional relationship between the use of RC and reductions in off-task behavior during classwide instruction. Three students with histories of disruptive and off-task behavior were observed during daily 20-minute social studies lessons in which students participated either by HR or RC. The graphic displays for all three students revealed clear and socially significant functional relations with little or no overlap in data paths between use of RC and reduced levels of both classes of inappropriate behavior. This finding is consistent with the results of several choral responding studies showing higher levels of on-task behavior

during lessons in which students emit higher rates of ASR (Carnine, 1976; Cashman, 1990; Lingenfelter, 1990; Morgan, 1987; Sainato, Strain, & Lyon, 1987).

The results of our most recently completed RC study showed that high school earth science students scored higher on next-day quizzes and weekly tests when they used RC to actively respond during a teacher-led review of key points at the conclusion of each lesson than on quizzes and tests following verbal reviews by the teacher with class discussion (Cavanaugh, Heward, & Donelson, 1993).

Types of response cards.   While response cards can take many forms, there are two basic types: preprinted and write on. When using *preprinted response cards*, each student selects the card with the answer he or she wishes to display from a personal set of cards. Examples of preprinted RC include: yes/true and no/false cards, numbers, colors, traffic signs, molecular structures, and parts of speech. Instead of receiving a set of different cards, each student can be given a single preprinted RC with multiple answers (e.g., a card with clearly demarked sections identified as proteins, fats, carbohydrates, vitamins, and minerals). In its most humble version, we call this type of multiple response card a "pinch card," because the student responds by simply holding up the card with thumb and forefinger and "pinching" or pointing to the part of the card displaying his or her answer. Colored plastic clothespins make an excellent "pinching" tool; students simply clip the clothespin on the selected part of the response card and hold the card overhead. Preprinted RC may also have a built-in device for displaying answers, such as a cardboard clock with movable hour and minute hands.

Preprinted response cards have several advantages: (1) higher ASR rates can be generated, (2) instruction can begin with few errors by starting with only two cards and adding more cards (i.e., choices) as students' repertoires develop, and (3) they are easier for the teacher to see than write-on response cards. Possible disadvantages include: (1) students are limited to the responses printed on the cards, (2) instruction is limited to recognition tasks only, and (3) the cards are not appropriate for lessons with a large number of different answers.

When using *write-on response cards*, students mark or write their answers to each instructional item on blank cards or boards, which are erased between learning trials. A set of 40 durable write-on RC can be obtained by purchasing a 4-foot-by-8-foot sheet of white laminated "bathroom" board, which is carried by most builder-supply stores and lumberyards. The cost is generally less than $20, including the charge for cutting the sheet into individual 9-inch-by-12-inch response cards. Using dry erasable markers makes the writing easily seen and the clean up simple. Students can also use small chalkboards as write-on response cards, but responses may be difficult for the teacher to see in a full-size classroom. Write-on response cards can also be custom-made to provide background or an organizing structure for student responses. For example, music students might mark notes on a response card with permanent treble and bass clef scales, and students in a driver's education class might draw where their car should go on a response card that has permanent traffic patterns and intersections (Hoagland, 1983).

Potential advantages of write-on response cards include: (1) curriculum material with multiple correct answers can be used, (2) students can emit creative responses, (3) a more demanding recall-type response is required rather than the simpler recognition-type response, and (4) spelling can be incorporated into the lesson. Possible disadvantages of write-on response cards include: (1) the ASR rate may be lower due to the time needed for writing and erasing, (2) error rates are likely to be higher, and (3) variations in the size and legibility of students' writing can make their responses difficult for the teacher to see.

Suggestions for using response cards in the classroom. The following suggestions are based on anecdotal observations and the experimental results of the RC studies summarized earlier. General suggestions for using both types of response cards include: (1) model several learning trials and let students practice using them; (2) maintain a lively pace throughout the lesson (i.e., keep intertrial intervals short); (3) provide clear cues when students are to hold up and put down their cards; (4) provide feedback based on the "majority response" (for details, see the section on

choral responding); (5) if an item results in too many errors, present it again several trials later; and (6) remember that students can benefit and learn from watching others, don't let students think it's cheating to look at their classmates' response cards

Suggestions for using preprinted response cards include: (1) design and construct the cards to be as easy to see as possible (e.g., consider size, print type, color codes); (2) make the cards easy for students to manipulate and display (e.g., put the answers on both sides of the cards so students can easily see what they are showing the teacher, attach a group of cards to a ring or chain so students can hold the entire set at once); (3) begin instruction with a small set of cards (perhaps only two), gradually adding additional cards as students' skills improve.

Suggestions for using write-on response cards include: (1) limit language-based responses to one or two words; (2) keep a few extra markers on hand; (3) be sure students do not hesitate to respond because they are concerned about making spelling mistakes— consider (a) using a prepractice routine in which students write new words on their response cards and receive feedback, (b) writing new words or important technical terms on the chalkboard or overhead projector and telling students to refer to them during the lesson, or (c) telling students to try their best but that misspellings won't be counted against them; and (4) after a good lesson, allow students to draw on the cards for a few minutes.

Guided Notes

A great deal of the curriculum content that middle- and secondary-level students are expected to learn is presented via the teacher lecture. As the teacher presents new information, reviews material included in assigned reading, and demonstrates or illustrates a process or relationship, students are expected to participate by listening, watching, asking questions, and recording the most important information for future study.

Research has shown that students who take accurate notes during class and who study them later achieve higher test scores than students who only listen to the lecture and read the text (Baker & Lombardi, 1985; Carrier, 1983). Although various strategies and formats for effective note-taking have been identified (Kierwa, 1987), most students receive no explicit instruction on how to take good notes (Beirne-Smith, 1989; Saski, Swicegood, & Carter, 1984). For students with disabilities who are integrated into regular curriculum content classes, note-taking can be extremely frustrating. Their listening, language, and, in some cases, motor deficits make it difficult for them to identify what is important and to write it down correctly and quickly enough during a lecture. While writing one concept in a notebook, the student with learning problems may miss the next two points. When teachers develop guided notes to accompany their lectures, both students with disabilities and their nondisabled peers benefit.

Guided notes are teacher-prepared handouts that "guide" a student through a lecture with standard cues and prepared space in which to write the key facts, concepts, and/or relationships. Two examples of guided notes are shown in Figure 21.5. The guided notes we have developed at OSU evolved from the transparencies used to prompt written responses from students in the VRS (Heward & Test, 1979). Guided notes share some characteristics with the framed outlines and study guides developed by Tom Lovitt and his colleagues as a method of enhancing the effectiveness of lecture presentations by organizing content and providing students with a means of actively responding to the material (Bergerud, Lovitt, & Horton, 1988; Horton & Lovitt, 1989; Lovitt et al., 1986).

Summary of OSU research on guided notes. Carol Kline's (1986) thesis was the first of an ongoing series of experimental evaluations of guided notes (GN) that we conducted at OSU (see Table 21.3). Carol was unhappy with the results of her efforts to teach American history to secondary students with learning disabilities. Although she used a high-interest, low reading-level text developed for students with poor reading skills and followed up each reading assignment with lectures and class discussions, most of Carol's students failed miserably when tested on the content she had worked so hard to cover. As a means of increasing each student's ASR during class and to try to improve their success with the content, we decided to try guided notes. At the beginning of every

class session throughout the study—during both the baseline/own notes and GN conditions—Carol encouraged her students to take good notes. All ten students earned higher scores on quizzes administered after lectures with guided notes than when they took their own notes during the teacher's presentations. If letter grades had been assigned based on their quiz scores, the average grade in the class would have been an A- when guided notes were used, compared to a D when students took their own notes.

The results of the first GN experiment were encouraging, but students must usually maintain what they learn from a lecture for more than a few minutes after class. In the second GN study, scores on next-day quizzes were the primary dependent variable (Yang, 1988). All 5 mainstreamed students with learning disabilities and 17 of the 18 nondisabled students in the middle-school science class earned higher scores on next-day quizzes following GN lectures. Pados (1989) also used next-day quizzes to evaluate the effects of guided notes in teaching American history in a fifth-grade classroom. Not only did the 2 students with learning disabilities who were mainstreamed into the class and all 11 general education students obtain higher quiz scores with guided notes, but so did 6 of the 7 students in the class who were enrolled in the district's program for gifted and talented children.

Note-taking, whether by guided notes or any other format, should serve at least two functions. In addition to a process function, which provides opportunities to actively respond during the lecture, note-taking serves a product function, providing a written summary of key facts, concepts, and relationships for future review and study (Kierwa, 1987). Since research has shown that successful students take more accurate notes than unsuccessful students (e.g., Norton & Hartley, 1986), it was also important to determine if, and to what extent, guided notes help students produce a more accurate record of the lecture than when taking their own notes. Pados (1989) measured the accuracy of note-taking by calculating the percentage of key lecture concepts or facts accurately recorded in the students' notes. The mainstreamed students with learning disabilities correctly recorded a mean of only 18% of all lecture facts

American History   Name _____
Guided Notes   Session 16

Road to Revolution II

A. *New Problems and New Troubles*
  1. The French and Indian War _____ .
     a. The British thought the colonists _____
        _____ .
     b. Britain thought the colonists _____ .
  2. In 1764, Parliament decided to _____ the colonists to help
     pay the bills for the war.
     a. Colonists had to pay a tax on _____
        and _____ .
     b. _____ collected the taxes.
  3. _____ , the British lawmaking group.
  4. _____ , the people who collected the taxes. They were allowed
     to keep part of the taxes themselves.
B. *The Stamp Act (1765)*
  1. Under this law, colonists had to buy _____
     for all kinds of paper products.
     a.
     b.
     c.
C. *"Taxation without Representation"*
  1. "Taxation without representation" means _____
     _____ by a lawmaking group in which you have no representation.
     a. Colonists could not _____
        _____ .
     b. Colonists also could not _____
        _____ .
  2. James Otis, a young lawyer from Massachusetts, referred to the Stamp Act as _____
     _____ .
D. *Protest and Repeal*
  1. _____ , a group of colonists formed to protest the taxes.
     a. It was founded by _____ .
     b.
     c.
     d.
  2. In 1766, the British Parliament *repealed* the Stamp Act (tax).
     a. "Repeal" means _____ .
  3. The colonists thought _____ .

Figure 21.5. Examples of guided notes used by fifth-grade students learning American history and by university students in special education studying generalized outcomes. SOURCES: *G. E. Pados, 1989,* A Comparison of the Effects of Students' Own Notes and Guided Notes on the Daily Quiz Performance of Fifth-grade Students. *Unpublished masters thesis, The Ohio State University, Columbus. W. L. Heward, 1992, Student Guided Notes for Planning and Implementing Instruction for Generalized Outcomes. Unpublished course materials, The Ohio State University, Columbus. Used by permission..*

ED S & R 764, Unit V: PCS & Train Loosely   Guided Notes - 1

I. Rationale, Definition, and Basic Strategy

A. As with teaching enough examples, the rationale underlying the recomendation to "program common stimuli" is stimulus control. Responses are less likely to be emitted under conditions that differ significantly from those that were present during training. *Remember*: **stimulus control exists when:**

_____

_____

_____

Including stimuli in the teaching setting that are _____

_____

B. **Program common stimuli** means including stimuli in the training environment that

_____

_____

C. In other words, significant stimuli present in the generality setting(s) must be identified and incorporated into the training program. Possible stimuli to make *common* can be identified by:

• Looking

• Asking

• Guessing

D. Even though efforts have been made to include stimuli in the training environment that are common in the nontraining environment(s), some behaviors may show little generality.

A more proactive approach to programming common stimuli is to *contrive a controlling stimulus* that can function as a discriminative stimulus in the generality setting and can be included in the training program. Baer (1981) recommends that the stimulus selected for this important role be both:

• Functional

• Transportable

Examples of contrived common stimuli:

_____

_____

E. Some stimuli make better common stimuli than others. When choosing a stimulus to be made common to both teaching and social generality setting(s), consider using

_____ Why? _____

Figure 21.5. (continued).

Table 21.3 Summary of classroom research on guided notes at The Ohio State University

Study	Students and Setting	Teacher	Curriculum Area and Dependent Variables	Independent Variable and Experimental Design	Results (ASR data/test scores reported as mean per student, unless noted.)
Kline (1986)	Special education classroom in inner-city secondary school, 10 students with SLD	Classroom teacher	U.S. history: scores on 10-item same-day quizzes[a]	ABAB design of daily, 15- to 20-min. lectures in which students (A) took their own notes (Own Notes), or (B) completed GN (24 total sessions)	All 10 students had higher quiz scores when GN were used. Mean score by phase: Own Notes 1 = 6.2; GNs 1 = 9.2, Own Notes 2 = 6.8; GNs 2 = 9.1
Yang (1988)	General education classroom in suburban middle school (N = 23; 5 with SLD)	Classroom teacher	Science (oceanography): scores on 10-item next-day quizzes	ABAB design of daily, 15- to 20-min. lectures in which students (A) took their own notes, or (B) completed GN (35 total sessions)	17 of 18 general education students and all 5 SLD students had higher quiz scores when GN were used. Mean score by phase: Own Notes 1 = 5.4; GNs 1 = 7.1, Own Notes 2 = 5.1; GNs 2 = 7.7
Pados (1989)	5th-grade general education classroom in suburban elementary school (N = 20; 2 with SLD, 7 in program for gifted and talented [G&T] students)	Classroom teacher	U.S. history: (1) Scores on 10-item next-day quizzes; (2) Accuracy of students' notes as a percentage of key concepts/facts from lecture accurately recorded in students' notes	ABAB design of daily, 15- to 20-min. lectures in which students (A) took their own notes, or (B) completed GN. Prior to quiz, SLD students reviewed their completed notes with resource room teacher (35 total sessions)	(1) All 11 general education students, both SLD students, and 6 of the 7 G&T students had higher quiz scores when GN were used. General education, Own Notes = 6.4, GN = 8.0; SLD, Own Notes = 6.4, GN = 9.3; G&T, Own Notes = 8.4, GN = 9.2; (2) Accuracy of notes: General education, Own Notes = 34%, GN = 97%; SLD, Own Notes = 18%, GN = 89%; G&T, Own Notes = 38%, GN = 97%
Virgalitte (1988)	Special classroom in school for incarcerated juvenile offenders, 9 students with SLD	Classroom teacher	Employment applications: 10-item next-day quizzes over parts of employment applications	ABAB design of daily, 15- to 20-min. lectures in which students (A) took their own notes, or (B) completed GN (18 total sessions)	All 9 students had higher quiz scores when GN were used. Mean score by phase: Own Notes 1 = 5.6, GN 1 = 8.2, Own Notes 2 = 5.1, GN 2 = 8.8

Table 21.3 (continued). Summary of classroom research on guided notes at The Ohio State University

Study	Students and Setting	Teacher	Curriculum Area and Dependent Variables	Independent Variable and Experimental Design	Results (ASR data/test scores reported as mean per student, unless noted.)
Courson (1989)	Special class for SLD and academically at-risk students in suburban middle school (N = 9 with SLD, 10 at risk)	Classroom teacher	Social studies (Africa): (1) 10-item next-day quizzes; (2) percent correct on 30-item biweekly review tests; (3) accuracy of students' notes	ABAB design as in previous GNs studies with ATD within GNs phases in which students used either short- or long-form GNs (42 total sessions)	All 19 students had higher mean scores on daily quizzes and bi-weekly tests when GNs were used. (1) Quizzes: Own Notes = 5.1, short-form GNs = 7.9, long-form GNs = 8.3; (2) Tests: Own Notes = 43%, GNs = 80%; (3) Accuracy of notes: Own Notes = 19%, short-form GNs = 97%, long-form GNs = 94%
Hamilton (1991)	Special classroom in school for incarcerated juvenile offenders (N = 9, 6 with SLD)	Experimenter	Social studies (achievements of African Americans): (1) 10-item next-day quizzes; (2) accuracy of students' notes	ABAB design of daily, 15-min. lectures in which students (A) took their own notes, or (B) completed GN (22 total sessions)	(1) All 9 students had higher quiz score when GNs were used. Mean score by phase: Own Notes 1 = 4.2, GNs 1 = 6.7, Own Notes 2 = 4.0, GNs 2 = 8.0; (2) accuracy of notes: Own Notes = 38%, GNs = 85%
White (1991)	Special education classroom in inner-city secondary school, 8 students with SLD	Classroom teacher	U.S. history: (1) percentage of lecture concepts/facts accurately recorded in students' own notes; (2) percent correct on 14-item next-day quizzes	Following an initial baseline in which students took their own notes, GNs were introduced and used for one-half of each day's 20-min. lecture. The ATD showed each student's note-taking skills as a function of using GNs. Students took their own notes for the whole lecture during the final phase.	(1) Accuracy of notes: Baseline (Own Notes only) = 17%; Phase 1 of ATD (no lecture transparencies): GNs = 81%, Own Notes = 57%; Phase 2 of ATD (lecture outlines shown by OHP): GNs = 94%, Own Notes = 79%; Final phase (Own Notes only) = 84%. (2) Quiz scores: Baseline = 28%; Phase 1 of ATD (no lecture transparencies): GNs = 49%, Own Notes = 48%; Phase 2 of ATD (lecture outlines shown by OHP): GNs = 69%, Own Notes = 77%; Final phase (Own Notes only) = 86%

Notes: ATD = alternating treatments design, GN = guided notes, SLD = specific learning disabilities.
[a]During all conditions in each of these studies, students were given from 3 to 5 minutes to study their notes just before taking each quiz or review test.

or concepts when they took their own notes, compared to an overall accuracy of 89% when they used guided notes. Guided notes also resulted in large improvements in the accuracy of the lecture notes taken by both the general education students (own notes = 34%, GN = 97%) and by the students in the gifted program (own notes = 38%, GN = 97%).

For some students, taking accurate lecture notes may not be enough to ensure success on subsequent tests. Additional contingencies may be necessary to increase the probability that the student studies and reviews those notes. Even though all five of the special education students in the Yang (1988) study earned higher next-day quiz scores with guided notes than when they took their own notes, the improved scores for four of the students were still below passing. In the study's final phase, a procedure was implemented in which the special education students took the guided notes they had completed in science class to the resource room later in the day for several minutes of review and study supervised by the resource room teacher. The quiz scores for all five students with learning disabilities were higher during the GN with review phase than during the first GN phase when no review was conducted.

Pados (1989) included supervised review of lecture notes in the resource room as part of the general procedure for the two students with learning disabilities throughout all phases of her study. The resource room teacher only reviewed the information included in the students' notes; the special education teacher supplied no additional information or content. The mean quiz score for the LD students was 93% during the combined GN phases with resource room review, compared to 64% when they took their own notes to the resource room for review. In two systematic replications evaluating guided notes with the resource room review procedure, Lazarus (1991, in press) found that the supervised review procedure produced improved test scores over and above the use of guided notes alone.

Fran Courson's (1989) dissertation evaluated the effectiveness of two different GN formats during a social studies unit in a special classroom of 19 learning disabled or academically at-risk seventh graders. With short-form GN, the students filled in blanks with single words or short phrases, while the long-form GN required them to write sentences or phrases in the open spaces following asterisk (*) cues. Every student earned higher next-day quiz scores with either GN format than they did when taking their own notes, but no difference of significance (educational or statistical) was found between the two GN formats. Figure 21.6 shows the next-day quiz scores earned by one student throughout the study and illustrates the basic pattern of results found across students. Similar results were obtained on two-week review tests: students performed better on items that had been instructed with either GN format (80% versus 43%), but neither format produced significantly better maintenance. Short-form GN produced slightly higher note-taking accuracy (97%) compared to the long-form GN (94%), but note-taking accuracy with either format was much greater than when students took their own notes (19%).

In the most recently completed study in this line of research, White (1991) assessed the extent to which using guided notes might improve the accuracy of students' unassisted note-taking. Following a baseline in which the students took their own notes throughout daily 20-minute lectures on American history, eight secondary students with learning disabilities used GN for half of each day's lecture and took their own notes during the other half of the lecture. Each of the eight students improved the accuracy of his or her note-taking during the study, from a group mean of 17% during baseline to 84% during the study's final phase when GN were no longer used. Figure 21.7 shows the accuracy of note-taking accomplished by the students across each phase of the study. All eight students also improved their performance on next-day quizzes from the initial baseline/own notes phase (group mean = 28%) to the final phase in which they were again taking their own notes for the entirety of each lecture (group mean = 86%). Sixteen high school teachers independently conducted a blind rating of the students' own notes in terms of their accuracy, usefulness for study, and how they compared to notes taken by other high school students. The teachers' mean ratings of the notes taken by six of the students during the baseline ranged from "useless" to "poor" on all three attributes,

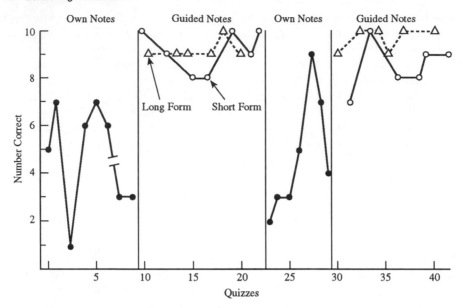

Figure 21.6. Number of correct answers on social studies quizzes given one day after teacher lectures.   SOURCE: *F. H. Courson, 1989,* Differential Effects of Short- and Long-Form Guided Notes on Test Scores and Accuracy of Note Taking by Learning Disabled and At-Risk Seventh Grade Students During Social Studies Instruction. *Unpublished doctoral dissertation, The Ohio State University, Columbus. Used by permission.*

with the remaining two students' baseline notes receiving ratings of "average." The teachers rated the notes taken by all eight students during the final phase of the study as "average" or "very good."

A great amount of research remains to be done. We don't know the range of curricular areas, student characteristics, and formats for which GN can be effective. In addition, White's (1991) study suggested a whole new program of thematic research exploring how GN might be used, not only to help students succeed in their current content academic subjects, but to produce generalized improvements in their note-taking skills.

In addition to the data showing superior test performance as a function of guided notes, the combined empirical results and anecdotal information from the GN research suggests the following advantages: (1) students must actively respond to and interact with the lesson's content (i.e., ASR is increased); (2) since the location and number of key concepts, facts, and relationships are cued or highlighted, students are better able to determine if they are "getting it" and therefore seem more likely to ask the teacher to repeat or clarify a point of information; (3) students produce a standard set of accurate notes for subsequent study and review; (4) teachers must carefully plan the lesson or lecture in order to use GN; and (5) teachers are more likely to stay "on task" with the sequence and contents of the lesson.

To the teacher who may be concerned that providing students with GN is spoonfeeding them or making it too easy to learn, I ask you to consider this: students who are using GN are actively responding and interacting with the curriculum content. That's not making it "too easy"; that's helping them learn. By contrast, we may be making it "too easy" for our students when we allow them to sit quietly and passively attend to ongoing instruction.

Suggestions for using guided notes in the classroom. When developing guided notes, be sure to (1) include background information so students' note-taking responses focus on the important facts, concepts, and relationships they need to learn; (2)

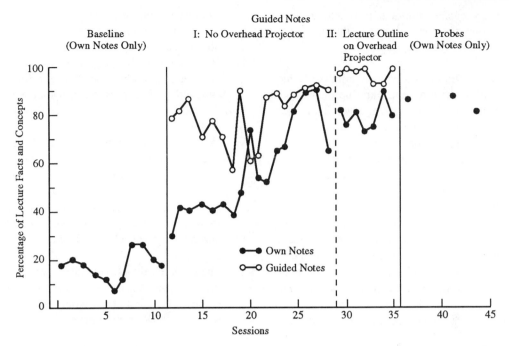

Figure 21.7. Mean percentage of facts and concepts accurately recorded by eight students with learning disabilities using their own notes and guided notes. SOURCE: *D. M. White, 1991,* Use of Guided Notes to Promote Generalized Note Taking Behavior of High School Students with Learning Disabilities. *Unpublished masters thesis, The Ohio State University, Columbus. Used by permission.*

provide consistent cues (e.g., asterisks, lines, bullets) so students will know where, when, and how many concepts they should record; (3) don't use a simple fill-in-the-blank format in which students need only listen or look up now and then to copy down a word; (4) don't require students to write too much, the most common error when creating early versions of GN; (5) make sure the GN include all critical facts, concepts, and relationships the students are expected to learn; (6) use a word processor so changes and updates are easy to make; (7) consider gradually fading the use of GN as a means of teaching students how to take notes in classes for which GN are not used; and (8) consider adding follow-up activities and contingencies for students' completion and study of notes; daily quizzes not only offer such a contingency but provide additional ASR as well.

Using High-ASR Teaching Strategies Across the Curriculum and Throughout the School Day

Choral responding, response cards, and guided notes are three relatively easy-to-implement, low-cost, and widely effective strategies for increasing ASR. Teachers can adapt and combine the three methods in numerous ways to best meet their instructional objectives and fit their students' current levels of performance. These low-tech strategies can also be used in conjunction with other proven methods for providing students with high rates of meaningful ASR, such as classwide peer tutoring (see Miller, Barbetta, & Heron, Chapter 20 in this text) or time trials (Miller & Heward, 1992), as well as with emerging technologies such as videodisc curriculum materials (e.g., Hofmeister, Engelmann, & Carnine, in press).

Elementary teachers might increase active student response across the curriculum and throughout the school day in the following ways:

1. Choral responding is used in a gamelike fashion as a two- to three-minute warm-up or review at the beginning of reading, language, math, social studies, and science lessons.

2. Students use write-on response cards to display their answers as their teacher demonstrates how to solve a new kind of arithmetic problem. During a language lesson, students select a preprinted response card showing the part of speech (e.g., noun, verb, preposition) as their teacher points to various words in a projected sentence. When the students can consistently recognize parts of speech, their teacher switches to write-on response cards, which elevates instruction to a higher level of knowledge by requiring the students to recall each part of speech.

3. Reading and math lessons usually conclude with two or three 1-minute time trials as a fluency-building or maintenance activity for skills already acquired but not yet mastered by the students. Students self-score each time trial, marking the results of their best effort on a personal chart or graph.

4. At the intermediate level, students complete guided notes while the teacher lectures or demonstrates new subject matter during social studies and science lessons. Students in the primary grades complete simpler versions of guided notes and structured worksheets as they follow the teacher's explanation and demonstration of a new concept or procedure (e.g., matching number sets).

5. Most lessons in social studies and science end with short 5-minute quizzes over the day's content. Students score their own quizzes, self-correct any errors, and record their scores on a chart or graph showing their cumulative progress.

6. In addition to teacher-directed lessons, a daily 20 to 25-minute classwide peer-tutoring session in reading and math (or whatever curriculum area needs the most work) might be conducted.

7. Choral responding is used during various transitions and downtime to provide students with additional ASR (Johnson, 1990).

8. Paraprofessionals and senior citizen volunteers provide systematic opportunities for ASR by conducting choral response, response card, and time trial activities (Courson & Heward, 1988, 1989).

9. Arrangements are made for significant others (e.g., bus drivers, playground supervisors) to promote maintenance and generalization of learned knowledge and skills by providing students with additional opportunities to respond, such as asking children to count to 20 by 2s as described by Bushell and Baer (see Chapter 1 in this text).

10. Finally, all self-directed practice, cooperative learning activities, classroom learning centers, and homework assignments would all be designed with high ASR as a top priority.

At the secondary level, a science teacher could use choral responding, response cards, and guided notes on a regular basis by structuring a 50-minute class period like this: (1) the lesson begins with 3 to 5 minutes of choral responding in which students warm up for the day's lesson by reviewing concepts they have been learning; (2) students then complete guided notes during a 15-minute lecture or demonstration by the teacher; (3) for the next 20 minutes, small groups of students perform hands-on laboratory experiments, perhaps filling in a structured worksheet with key procedural steps, results, and observations; and (4) on some days response cards are used during the last 5 minutes of the period to review the day's lesson (Cavanaugh, Heward, & Donelson, 1993), whereas on other days the period ends with two 1-minute time trials as a maintenance and fluency-building activity for concepts learned in previous lessons. The actual time spent with each activity would, of course, vary from day to day, and 5 minutes are left unscheduled to allow for transition time.

Using the rates of active student engagement obtained in previous research as a basis, a daily schedule of instruction even approaching the two examples outlined here would likely provide each student with several hundred more learning trials each week and many thousands of additional responses over an entire school year.

A high number of student responses do not guarantee effective instruction. Even though they could easily be counted and might look like ASR, not every "academic" response a student makes during a lesson qualifies as ASR. Four suggestions will help the teacher recognize and provide "good ASR" in the classroom. First, *don't be fooled by on-task behavior*. On-task behavior is not a bad thing, but research has shown that increasing on-task behavior does not necessarily result in an increase in active student response. Second, *be sure students practice the target skill*. A distinguishing characteristic of direct instruction is that students practice the actual skill targeted for learning (or components of the target skill) not skills that bear only an assumed or passing relation to the terminal skill. When attempting to add variety to a lesson, or when providing practice on prerequisite skills leading up to the terminal skill, do not inadvertently reduce or eliminate ASR on the terminal skill. Third, *check instructional materials for faulty stimulus control*. Well-designed instructional materials require students to practice the target skill the teacher intends to teach and do not promote either correct or incorrect responses for the "wrong reason" (Vargas, 1984). Finally, provide feedback for student responses. Don't forget the last element of the learning trial. Students learn best when they receive instructional feedback on their responses.

ASR Is Not a Silver Bullet

Although I believe it to be a critical component of effective teaching, increasing the frequency with which students actively respond during instruction is but one part of the teaching-learning equation. ASR focuses on the middle component of the three-term learning trial. Just as systematic feedback must be provided if learning is to be maximized, high rates of ASR emitted in the absence of carefully selected and properly designed instructional materials can be meaningless. Siegfried Engelmann (1992a) uses driving a car as an analogy for effective teaching. The

skills used in driving a car (e.g., accelerating, cornering, passing, braking) are analogous to the methods and tactics a teacher uses during instruction (e.g., pacing of the presentation, praising correct responses, correcting errors). The car itself can be seen as the curriculum. No matter how impressive the driver's skills, he or she won't get very far in a broken-down automobile. And to win a race, any race, a highly reliable car that has proved its ability to go fast is a must. Extending Engelmann's analogy to ASR: a teacher could be the Mario Andretti of education as far as providing students with opportunities to respond is concerned, but if those responses are emitted in the context of a poorly designed curriculum, the students won't get very far in their learning. Using Engelmann's analogy, learning strategies and tactics for increasing ASR are one part of driver's training for teachers. Learning to discriminate well-designed curriculum materials from ineffective materials must also be part of that training (cf., Engelmann, 1992b; Vargas, 1984).

Just as high rates of ASR will not turn a bad curriculum into a good one, providing students with many opportunities to respond will not make up for other mistakes that ignore or shortchange basic elements of good educational practice. Two examples from the ASR research at OSU will illustrate this important point. In our effort to eliminate a possible ceiling effect (noted in an earlier study) that might have obscured the full effects of response cards, we changed the primary dependent variable from a 10-item same-day quiz used in the earlier study to a 16-item next-day quiz (Gardner et al., in press). Although students performed better on quizzes covering RC-taught content than on quizzes covering lessons in which they had participated by raising their hands, their mean quiz score with RC was just 70%. In order to expose students to enough curriculum content to create 16 quiz questions, a large amount of new content had to be presented each day. So even though students emitted a much higher number of ASR per lesson when response cards were used, there was usually time for only one or two learning trials per fact or concept.

In one of our guided notes studies, it became apparent that four of the five students with learning disabilities who were mainstreamed into the class did not possess the basic tools and prerequisite skills to help them benefit from the regular science program (Yang, 1988). Even though these students' scores on next-day quizzes improved by more than 50% when they used GN, they were still performing below passing. Two more of the students with learning disabilities earned passing scores in the study's final phase when they reviewed their guided notes with the resource room teacher. Even though student achievement improved considerably when the high-ASR strategy was implemented in these two studies, the heavy instructional load (Gardner et al., in press) and inappropriate student placement (Yang, 1988) were likely factors in the less-than-desired performance by some students in each class.

Much More Research Is Needed

The basic relation between increased ASR and academic achievement has shown considerable generality. But research to date has produced only a crude relationship—all things being equal, when students actively respond during the lesson, they will learn more than when they passively attend to the ongoing instruction. Many important details about the relation between ASR and learning, however, remain unknown. In addition to research examining the effects of increased ASR on achievement across different curriculum areas and students' age and ability levels, research is needed on the following questions:

1. *How much ASR produces the most effective learning outcomes*? In 1978, Rosenshine & Berliner wrote:

> Right now, we *do not know* how much academic engaged time is reasonable or humane. Nor do we know whether engaged time in different materials or different academic activities yields different results. Research on these questions is urgently needed. [p. 14]

That research is still needed today. In addressing this question, ASR would be manipulated as the independent variable and various measures of student learning would constitute the dependent variable.

Parametric analyses of the effects of varying frequencies of ASR are one approach toward generating the needed data. For example, Bosch (1988) varied the number of times first grade remedial-reading students chorally responded to sight words during small-group lessons. Measures of initial acquisition and two follow-up tests found that the students learned and retained more "high-ASR" sight words than "low-ASR" words, and more "low-ASR" words than "no-ASR" words. Such studies represent only the barest beginning toward answering "How much ASR is needed?" Many studies of this type are needed before we can begin to answer important questions such as: How much ASR is needed for students to initially acquire and then reach fluency in the critical knowledge and skills that comprise the curriculum? Is there an optimum frequency of ASR during instruction? Does the optimum frequency of ASR vary across learning tasks, age, skill levels, or other variables suspected or unknown?

2. *What instructional methods most reliably produce various levels of ASR*? As research begins to teach us about optimal rates of ASR, studies can then be designed to systematically determine what teaching methods will produce those rates. In these experiments, different combinations and arrangements of instructional variables (e.g., selection of materials, presentation pace, student response materials, response mode, feedback, and error correction procedures) would constitute the independent variable and measures of ASR would be the primary dependent variable. Measures of student learning should also be collected as secondary supportive data in such studies. Studies addressing this broad question would manipulate features of any element or combination of elements within the learning trial. For example, Carnine (1976), Morgan (1987), and Williams (1993) investigated the effects of teacher pacing of instruction on student performance during instruction (ASR, accuracy, on-task behavior) by manipulating the duration of the intertrial interval.

3. *How can teachers provide feedback for increased rates of academic responding*? A probable reason for the low ASR levels observed in many classrooms is the high response cost for teachers who provide students with more opportunities to respond

(Hall et al., 1982). Teachers already work long hours grading, evaluating, and otherwise providing feedback to their students. If we are going to ask teachers to increase ASR significantly, we must work with them to discover efficient strategies for delivering instructional feedback for all of the new responses. Efficient and effective methods for providing feedback can be found in the work on self-correcting learning materials (Mercer, Mercer, & Bott, 1987), peer tutoring (Miller, Barbetta, and Heron, Chapter 20 in this text), and self-scoring (e.g., Hundert & Buchner, 1978). Research is also needed on other ways that teachers provide students with effective feedback that is efficient in terms of teacher time.

Lovitt (1982) suggested that intermittent checking be investigated as a method for providing feedback when students create increased amounts of academic products. Providing feedback to students on their writing is one of the most difficult, time-consuming tasks for teachers and may be one reason that students receive too little ASR for writing. Heward, Heron, Gardner, and Prayzer (1991) described a "selective grading" procedure in which students write every day, but the teacher randomly selects, reads, and marks individualized feedback on the compositions of perhaps 20% of the class. Specific portions of the selected students' papers are used as instructional examples the next day with the whole class, and individual students and the class receive academic and social rewards via interdependent group-oriented contingencies. The results of two exploratory studies reported by Heward and colleagues (1991), one in a fourth-grade classroom and the other in a middle-school English class, suggested that selective grading is a promising technique for meeting the challenge of providing feedback for daily compositions.

4. *What are the effects of increasing ASR during other kinds of instruction?* Most of the research investigating the relation between active student engagement and learning has been conducted within the context of classroom-based instruction. It would be interesting to study the effects of increasing ASR within other instructional contexts. Homework is one area that is ripe for such investigations; vocational and work-related skills, daily living skills, and sports and leisure skills may also be positively influenced by more ASR.

5. *What are the long-term, cumulative effects of high-ASR instruction?* Suppose an elementary teacher were to systematically provide, across the curriculum, throughout the school day, and over the course of the school year, a schedule of high-ASR activities similar to the one outlined earlier. How much total ASR would each student receive? More important, how much learning might occur if choral responding, response cards, guided notes, peer tutoring, time trials, and so on, were used on a systematic basis, day in and day out? The investigation of the effects of systematic peer tutoring on academic achievement conducted by Charlie Greenwood and his colleagues at the Juniper Gardens Children's Project is an excellent example of the kind of large-scale longitudinal research that is needed in this area (Greenwood, 1991; Greenwood, Delquadri, & Hall, 1989).

6. *What training and administrative contingencies are most effective in influencing inservice educators to implement high-ASR teaching methods?* The classroom teacher is the most important player. Research on what must be done to facilitate teachers' adoption and continued implementation of instructional methods that provide each student with many opportunities to respond should be a top priority. We should start by looking at the instructional methods themselves. Many strategies might be effective if systematically applied, but the strategies with the highest probability of use will probably exhibit the user-friendly characteristics of low technology (i.e., low cost, readily available, reliable, and easy to implement). Next, we must work side-by-side with classroom teachers to design, evaluate, redesign, and disseminate effective strategies.

Conclusion

The results of research on increasing students' frequency of active engagement during instruction (whether this variable is called ASR, OTR, or learn units) are encouraging for both researchers and practitioners. An executive summary of this body of research might read as follows: When compared to teaching methods in which students passively attend and actively participate by infrequent responses, teaching strategies that increase the frequency with which each student makes academic responses during instruction have (1) consistently produced better performance on same-day, next-day, and follow-up tests of the content taught; (2) resulted in higher levels of on-task behavior (or conversely, reduced levels of off-task, disruptive, and "looking bored" behavior); and (3) been preferred by the vast majority of students over traditional methods of classroom participation.

Not only are the outcomes of increasing ASR significant, but the means for providing each student in the classroom with more learning trials are currently available. Active student responding is neither a hard-to-pin-down hypothetical construct nor a variable, such as socioeconomic status, on which the teacher can hope to have little or no effect. ASR is, as Bloom (1980) put it, an alterable variable; that is, one that both makes a difference and can be affected by teaching practices.

There is no research that documents the learning outcomes that might accrue if ASR-intensive instruction were implemented in elementary and secondary general education classrooms across the curriculum and across the school day. Nevertheless, given the improvements in students' academic performance when this instruction is just part of their school day, increasing every student's ASR seems a good way to go.

There is no doubt that planning and conducting ASR-intensive instruction would entail a great deal of hard work. But teachers already work hard. The disappointing level of academic achievement displayed by many students in public education is not caused because their teachers don't work hard enough. But it may be caused, in part, because teachers work too hard in the wrong way—performing for students when the students should be responding, and grading papers when self- and peer-scoring are both more cost-effective and provide additional ASR.

In comparing the development of education and medicine, Carnine (1992) noted that while both fields began in a state in which decision making was determined by dogma and expert opinion, "the acquisition of a scientific perspective has enabled medicine to rise

to a new stage characterized by higher effectiveness and decisions based on what has proven effective. An over reliance on dogma has contributed to a circular movement of recycled fads that has stunted growth in the effectiveness of education" (p. 27). Change in education most often occurs through revolution. This stands in stark contrast to the evolutionary process of selection by consequences, which characterizes the steady development of fields guided by scientific practices (Heward & Cooper, 1992).

Increasing active student response in the classroom will not in itself turn education into a discipline guided by scientific decision making, but it is one way that classroom teachers can put themselves in touch with the immediate consequences of their efforts. When instruction is designed around high-ASR activities, not only is it hard for students to passively attend, it is equally difficult for teachers to avoid direct and daily feedback on the effectiveness of their teaching. This is one means of achieving the "close, continual contact with relevant outcome data" recommended by Bushell and Baer in Chapter 1 of this text. In this way, strategies that increase active student responding may play a functional role in the selection of measurably superior instructional practices.

References

ALEXANDER, K. (1983). Beyond the prediction of student achievement: Direct and repeated measurement of behavior change. *Journal of Teaching in Physical Education, 3* (Summer Monograph I), 42–47.

BAKER, L., & Lombardi, B. R. (1985). Students' lecture notes and their relation to test performance. *Teaching of Psychology, 12*, 28–32.

BARBETTA, P. M., & Heward, W. L. (1993). Effects of active student response during error correction on the acquisition and maintenance of geography facts by elementary students with learning disabilities. *Journal of Behavioral Education, 3*, 217–233.

BARBETTA, P. M., Heron, T. E., & Heward, W. L. (1993). Effects of active student response during error correction on the acquisition, maintenance, and generalization of sight words by students with developmental handicaps. *Journal of Applied Behavior Analysis, 26*, 111–119.

BEIRNE-SMITH, M. (1989). A systematic approach for teaching notetaking skills to students with mild learning handicaps. *Academic Therapy, 24*, 425–437.

BERGERUD, D., Lovitt, T. C., & Horton, S. (1988). The effectiveness of textbook adaptations in life science for high school students with learning disabilities. *Journal of Learning Disabilities, 21*(2), 70–76.

BERLINER, D. C. (1980). Using research on teaching for improvement of classroom practice. *Theory into Practice, 19*, 302–308.

BERLINER, D. C. (1984). The half-full glass: A review of research on teaching. In P. L. Hosford (Ed.), *Using what we know about* (pp. 51–77). Alexandria, VA: Association for Supervision and Instruction.

BLOOM, B. S. (1980). The new direction in educational research: Alterable variables. *Phi Delta Kappan, 61*, 382–385.

BOSCH, C. (1988). Effects of high, low, and zero opportunities to respond during instruction on the acquisition and maintenance of sight words by first graders in a remedial reading program. Unpublished masters thesis, The Ohio State University, Columbus.

BROPHY, J., & Good, T. (1986). Teacher behavior and student achievement. In M. C. Wittrock (Ed.), *Handbook on research on teaching.* 3rd ed. (pp. 328–375). New York: Macmillan.

BUCKLEY, C. (1980). Effects of verbal prompts and feedback on generalization of punctuation skills. Masters thesis, The Ohio State University, Columbus.

BUSHELL, Jr., D., & Dorsey, D. (1985). Behavioral models of teaching. In T. Husen & T. N. Postlewaite (Eds.), *International encyclopedia of education* (pp. 437–442). New York: Pergamon Press.

CARNINE, D. W. (1976). Effects of two teacher presentation rates on off-task behavior, answering correctly, and participation. *Journal of Applied Behavior Analysis, 9*, 199–206.

CARNINE, D. W. (1992). The missing link in improving schools: Reforming educational leaders. *Direct Instruction News, 11*(3), 25–35.

CARRIER, C. A. (1983). Notetaking research: Implications for the classroom. *Journal of Instructional Development, 6*, 19–29.

CASHMAN, C. T. (1990). The effects of fast- versus slow-paced instruction during choral responding. Senior honors thesis, The Ohio State University, Columbus.

CAVANAUGH, R. A., Heward, W. L., & Donelson, F. (1993). Comparative effects of teacher-presented verbal review and active student response during lesson closure on the academic performance of high school students in an earth science course. The Ohio State University, Columbus. Manuscript submitted for publication review.

CHRISTENSEN, S. L., Ysseldyke, J. E., & Thurlow, M. L. (1989). Critical instructional factors for students with mild handicaps: An integrative review. *Remedial and Special Education, 10*(5), 21–31.

COOKE, N. L., & Test, D. W. (1984). Instructional transparencies for the directive teacher. *The Directive Teacher, 6*(1), 22–23.

COOKE, N. L., Heron, T. E., & Heward, W. L. (1980). Teaching map skills to special education students. *Journal of Geography, 79*, 253–258.

COURSON, F. H. (1989). Differential effects of short- and long-form guided notes on test scores and accuracy of note taking by learning disabled and at-risk seventh grade students during social studies instruction. Ph.D. dissertation, The Ohio State University, Columbus.

COURSON, F. H., & Heward, W. L. (1988). Increasing active student response through the effective use of paraprofessionals. *The Pointer, 33*(1), 27–31.

COURSON, F. H., & Heward, W. L. (1989). Using senior citizen volunteers in the special education classroom. *Academic Therapy, 24*, 525–532.

COWARDIN, J. H. (1978). Modifying the syntactical maturity of compositional writing by academically handicapped secondary students. Ph.D. dissertation, The Ohio State University, Columbus.

DELQUADRI, J., Greenwood, C. R., & Hall, R. V. (1979). Opportunity to respond: An update. Paper presented at the Annual Meeting of the Association for Behavior Analysis, May, Milwaukee.

DELQUADRI, J., Greenwood, C. R., Whorton, D., Carta, J. J., & Hall, R. V. (1986). Classwide peer tutoring. *Exceptional Children, 52*, 535–542.

DEWEY, J. (1916). *Democracy and education.* New York: Macmillan.

DREVNO, G. E., Kimball, J. A., Possi, M. K., Heward, W. L., Gardner III, R., & Barbetta, P. M. (in press). Effects of active student response during error correction on the acquisition, maintenance, and generalization of science definitions by elementary students. *Journal of Applied Behavior Analysis.*

EACHUS, H. T. (1971). Modification of sentence writing by deaf children. *American Annals of the Deaf, 116*, 29–43.

ENGELMANN, S. (1992a). *Comments made during Teleconference on Applied Behavior Analysis.* Columbus, OH: The Ohio State University.

ENGELMANN, S. (1992b). *War against the schools' academic child abuse.* Portland, OR: Halcyon House.

ENGELMANN, S., & Bruner, E. C. (1988). *Reading mastery: Fast cycle (DISTAR).* Chicago: Science Research Associates.

ENGELMANN, S., Becker, W. C., Carnine, D. W., & Gersten, R. (1988). The Direct Instruction Follow Through Model: Design and outcomes. *Education & Treatment of Children, 11*, 303–317.

FERRITOR, D. E., Buckholdt, O. N., Hamblin, R. L., & Smith, L. (1972). The noneffects of contingent reinforcement for attending behavior on work accomplished. *Journal of Applied Behavior Analysis, 5*, 7–17.

FISCHER, C. S., Berliner, D. C., Filby, N. N., Marliave, R., Cahen, L. S., & Dishaw, M. M. (1980). Teaching behaviors, academic learning time, and student achievement. In C. Denham & A. Lieberman (Eds.), *Time to Learn* (pp. 7–22). Washington, DC: National Institute of Education.

FISCHER, C. W., & Berliner, D. C. (Eds.). (1985). *Perspectives on instructional time.* New York: Longman.

GARDNER, III, R., Heward, W. L., & Grossi, T. A. (in press). Effects of response cards on student participation and academic achievement: A systematic replication with inner-city students during whole-class science instruction. *Journal of Applied Behavior Analysis.*

GARDNER, III, R., Bullara, D. T., Heward, W. L., Cooper, J. O., & Sweeney, W. J. (1993). Effects of response cards on elementary students' participation and disruptive behavior during whole-class instruction. The Ohio State University, Columbus.

GERSTEN, R., Carnine, D., & White, W. A. T. (1984). Direct instruction. In W. L. Heward, T. E. Heron, D. S. Hill, & J.

Trapp-Porter (Eds.), *Focus on behavior analysis in education* (pp. 36–57). Columbus, OH: Merrill.

GREENWOOD, C. R. (1991). A longitudinal analysis of time, engagement, and achievement in at-risk and non-risk students. *Exceptional Children, 57*, 521–535.

GREENWOOD, C. R., Delquadri, J., & Hall, R. V. (1984). Opportunity to respond and student academic achievement. In W. L. Heward, T. E. Heron, D. S. Hill, & J. Trap-Porter (Eds.), *Focus on behavior analysis in education* (pp. 58–88). Columbus, OH: Merrill.

GREENWOOD, C. R., Delquadri, J., & Hall, R. V. (1989). Longitudinal effects of classwide peer tutoring. *Journal of Educational Psychology, 81*, 371–383.

GREENWOOD, C. R., Delquadri, J., Stanley, S. O., Terry, B., & Hall, R. V. (1985). Assessment of eco-behavioral interaction in school settings. *Behavioral Assessment, 7*, 331–347.

GREER, D. R., & Linhardt, R. F. (1992). A parametric study of the Comprehensive Application of Behavior Analysis to Schooling. Teachers College, Columbia University. Manuscript submitted for publication.

GROSS, A. (1980). *What if the teacher calls on me?* Chicago: Children's Press.

GROSSMAN, M. A. (1981). Teaching reading comprehension skills to fifth graders in the Visual Response System. Masters thesis, The Ohio State University, Columbus.

GUTHRIE, J. T., Martuzo, V., & Seifert, M. (1976). *Impacts of instructional time in reading.* Newark, DE: International Reading Association.

HALL, R. V., Delquadri, J., & Harris, J. (1977). The opportunity to respond: A new focus for applied behavior analysis. Paper presented at the Annual Meeting of the Association for Behavior Analysis, May, Chicago.

HALL, R. V., Delquadri, J., Greenwood, C. R., & Thurston, L. (1982). The importance of opportunity to respond in children's academic success. In E. B. Edgar, N. G. Haring, J. R. Jenkins, & C. G. Pious (Eds.), *Mentally handicapped children: Education and training* (pp. 107–140). Baltimore: University Park Press.

HAMILTON, S. L. (1991). Effects of guided notes on academic performance of incarcerated juvenile delinquents with learning disabilities. Masters thesis, The Ohio State University, Columbus.

HARRIS, K. R. (1986). Self-monitoring of attentional behavior versus self-monitoring of productivity: Effects on on-task behavior and academic response rate among learning disabled children. *Journal of Applied Behavior Analysis, 19*, 417–424.

HERON, T. E., Heward, W. L., Cooke, N. L., & Hill, D. S. (1983). Evaluation of a classwide peer tutoring system: First graders teach each other sight words. *Education & Treatment of Children, 6*, 137–152.

HEWARD, W. L. (1978a). Visual Response System. *Exceptional Children, 44*, 466–468.

HEWARD, W. L. (1978b). Visual Response System: A mediated resource room for children with learning problems. *Journal of Special Education Technology, 2*, 40–46.

HEWARD, W. L. (1987). Some thoughts on the development and delivery of systematic instruction. *Jornal de Psicologia, 6*(1), 20–24.

HEWARD, W. L. (1992). Student guided notes for Planning and Implementing Instruction for Generalized Outcomes. Unpublished course materials, The Ohio State University, Columbus.

HEWARD, W. L., & Cooper, J. O. (1992). Radical behaviorism: A productive and needed philosophy for education. *Journal of Behavioral Education, 2*, 345–365.

HEWARD, W. L., & Eachus, H. T. (1979). Acquisition of adjectives and adverbs to sentences written by hearing impaired and aphasic children. *Journal of Applied Behavior Analysis, 12*, 391–400.

HEWARD, W. L., & Orlansky, M. D. (1992). *Exceptional children: An introductory survey of special education.* 4th ed. New York: Macmillan/Merrill.

HEWARD, W. L., & Test, D. W. (1979). *Visual Response System demonstration project: Final report.* ERIC Reports, ED 198 684.

HEWARD, W. L., Test, D. W., & Cooke, N. L. (1981). Training teachers to use technology: Experience with the Visual Response System. *Teacher Education and Special Education, 4*, 15–26.

HEWARD, W. L., Courson, F. H., & Narayan, J. S. (1989). Using choral responding to increase active student response during group instruction. *Teaching Exceptional Children, 21*(3), 72–75. *ADI News, 1990, 9*(2), 30–33.

HEWARD, W. L., McCormick, S., & Joynes, Y. (1980). Completing job applications: Evaluation of an instructional program for mildly retarded juvenile delinquents. *Behavioral Disorders, 5*, 223–234.

HEWARD, W. L., Heron, T. E., Gardner III, R., & Prayzer, R. (1991). Two strategies for improving students' writing skills. In G. Stoner, M. R. Shinn, & H. M. Walker (Eds.), *A school psychologist's interventions for regular education* (pp. 379–398). Washington, DC: National Association of School Psychologists.

HOAGLAND, C. A. (1983). Teaching learning disabled students traffic signs and laws. Masters thesis, The Ohio State University, Columbus.

HOFMEISTER, A., Engelmann, S., & Carnine, D. (in press). Technology and teacher enhancement: A videodisc alternative. *Technology in Education.* Alexandria, VA: Association of Supervision and Curriculum Development.

HORTON, S. V., & Lovitt, T. C. (1989). Using study guides with three classifications of secondary students. *Journal of Special Education, 22*, 447–462.

HUNDERT, J., & Bucher, B. (1978). Pupils' self-scored arithmetic performance: A practical procedure for maintaining accuracy. *Journal of Applied Behavior Analysis, 11*, 304.

JACKSON, M. A. (1980). Teaching punctuation skills in the Visual Response System. Masters thesis, The Ohio State University, Columbus.

JOHNSON, L. K. (1990). Password: Organizing exits from the resource room. *Teaching Exceptional Children, 23*(2), 82–83.

JOHNSON, J. M., & Pennypacker, H. S. (1980). *Strategies and tactics of human behavioral research.* Hillsdale, NJ: Lawrence Erlbaum.

KIERWA, K. A. (1987). Notetaking and review: The research and its implications. *Instructional Science, 16,* 233–249.

KLINE, C. S. (1986). Effects of guided notes on academic achievement of learning disabled high school students. Masters thesis, The Ohio State University, Columbus.

KOEGEL, R. L., Dunlap, G., & Dyer, K. (1980). Intertrial interval duration and learning in autistic children. *Journal of Applied Behavior Analysis, 13,* 91–99.

LAZARUS, B. D. (in press). Guided notes, review, and achievement of students with mild handicaps. *Education and Treatment of Children.*

LAZARUS, B. D. (1991). Guided notes, review, and achievement of secondary students with learning disabilities in mainstream content courses. *Education and Treatment of Children, 14,* 112–127.

LENOX, S. L. R. (1982). The effects of a modified Visual Response System instructional program on teaching job application skills to mildly retarded secondary students in a conventional classroom. Masters thesis, The Ohio State University, Columbus.

LINGENFELTER, T. M. (1990). Comparing the effects of individual and choral responding during large-group instruction in a primary classroom. Senior honors thesis, The Ohio State University, Columbus.

LOVITT, T. C. (1977). *In spite of my resistance . . . I've learned from children.* Columbus, OH: Merrill.

LOVITT, T. C. (1982). Response to Hall et al. In E. B. Edgar, N. G. Haring, J. R. Jenkins, & C. G. Pious (Eds.), *Mentally handicapped children: Education and training* (pp. 141–149). Baltimore: University Park Press.

LOVITT, T. C., Rudsit, J., Jenkins, J., Pious, C., & Benedetti, D. (1986). Adapting science materials for regular and learning disabled seventh graders. *Remedial and Special Education, 7*(1), 31–39.

MCKENZIE, G. R., & Henry, M. (1979). Effects of testlike events on on-task behavior, test anxiety, and achievement in a classroom rule-learning task. *Journal of Educational Psychology, 71,* 370–374.

MCLAUGHLIN, T. F., & Malaby, J. (1972). Intrinsic reinforcers in a classroom token economy. *Journal of Applied Behavior Analysis, 5,* 263–270.

MARHOLIN II, D., & Steinman, W. (1977). Stimulus control in the classroom as a function of the behavior reinforced. *Journal of Applied Behavior Analysis, 10,* 465–478.

MARSHALL, A. E., & Heward, W. L. (1979). Teaching self-management to incarcerated youth. *Behavioral Disorders, 4,* 215–226.

MERCER, C. D., Mercer, A. R., & Bott, L. (1987). *Self-correcting learning materials.* Columbus, OH: Merrill.

MILLER, A. D., & Heward, W. L. (1992). Do your students really know their math facts? Using daily time trials to build fluency. *Intervention in School and Clinic, 28,* 98–104.

MILLER, A. D., Hall, S. W., & Heward, W. L. (1993). Effects of sequential 1-minute time trials with and without intertrial feedback on general and special education students' fluency with math facts. Ohio State University, Columbus. Manuscript submitted for publication.

MORGAN, D. (1987). Effects of fast and slow teacher presentation rates on the academic performance of special education students during small-group reading instruction. Masters thesis, The Ohio State University, Columbus.

NARAYAN, J. S. (1988). Comparison of hand raising and response card methods of group instruction on fourth-grade students' opportunity to respond and academic achievement. Masters thesis, The Ohio State University, Columbus.

NARAYAN, J. S., Heward, W. L., Gardner, III, R. Courson, F. H., & Omness, C. (1990). Using response cards to increase student participation in an elementary classroom. *Journal of Applied Behavior Analysis, 23,* 483–490.

NORTON, L. S., & Hartley, J. (1986). What factors contribute to good examination marks? The role of notetaking in subsequent examination performance. *Higher Education, 15,* 355–371.

PADOS, G. E. (1989). A comparison of the effects of students' own notes and guided notes on the daily quiz performance of fifth-grade students. Masters thesis, The Ohio State University, Columbus.

PRATTON, J., & Hales, L. W. (1986). The effects of active participation on student learning. *Journal of Educational Research, 79*(4), 210–215.

ROSENSHINE, B. (1979). Content, time, and direct instruction. In P. L. Peterson & H. J. Walberg (Eds.), *Research on teaching: Concepts, findings, and implications* (pp. 28–56). Berkeley, CA: McCutchan.

ROSENSHINE, B., & Berliner, D. C. (1978). Academic engaged time. *British Journal of Teacher Education, 4,* 3–16.

ROSENSHINE, B., & Stevens, R. (1986). Teaching functions. In M. C. Wittrock (Ed.), *Handbook on research on teaching,* (pp. 376–391). 3rd ed. New York: Macmillan.

SAINATO, D. M., Strain, P. S., & Lyon, S. L. (1987). Increasing academic responding of handicapped preschool children during group instruction. *Journal of the Division of Early Childhood Special Education, 12,* 23–30.

SASKI, J., Swicegood, P., & Carter, J. (1984). Notetaking formats for learning disabled adolescents. *Learning Disability Quarterly, 6,* 265–273.

SEAVEY, D. V. (1979). An instructional package designed to teach money management skills to students with special needs. Masters thesis, The Ohio State University, Columbus.

SHADDING, A. L. (1982). Evaluation of a Visual Response System instructional program to teach computation of math fractions to secondary students enrolled in a remedial mathematics program. Masters thesis, The Ohio State University, Columbus.

SINDELAR, P. T., Bursuck, W. D., & Halle, J. W. (1986). The effects of two variations of teacher questioning on student performance. *Education and Treatment of Children, 9,* 56–66.

SKINNER, B. F. (1938). *The behavior of organisms: An experimental analysis.* New York: Appleton-Century.

SMITH, N. M. (1976). Time allotments and achievement in social studies. Unpublished manuscript. Baltimore: John F. Kennedy Institute for Habilitation, Johns Hopkins University.

STALLINGS, J. (1980). Allocated academic time revisited, or beyond time on task. *Educational Researcher, 9* (September), 11–16.

STALLINGS, J., & Kaskowitz, D. (1974). *Follow Through classroom observation evaluation, 1972–73.* Stanford, CA: SRI Project URU-7370, Stanford Research Institute.

STANLEY, S. O., & Greenwood, C. R. (1981). *CISSAR: Code for instructional structure and student academic response: Observer's manual.* Kansas City: Juniper Gardens Children's Project, Bureau of Child Research, University of Kansas.

STANLEY, S. O., & Greenwood, C. R. (1983). Assessing opportunity to respond in classroom environments through direct observation: How much opportunity to respond does the minority disadvantaged student receive in school? *Exceptional Children, 49,* 370–373.

STEPHENS, T. M. (1977). Teaching skills to students with learning and behavior disorders. Columbus, OH: Merrill.

STERLING, R., Barbetta, P. M., Heward, W. L., & Heron, T. E. (1993). Effects of active student response during instruction on the acquisition and maintenance of health concepts by elementary students with learning disabilities. Ohio State University. Manuscript submitted for publication.

SWEENEY, W. J., Gardner, R., Hunnicutt, K. L., & Mustaine, J. (1992). Increasing active student response through the use of write-on and pre-printed response cards with academically at-risk learners in an urban elementary third grade social studies class. Ohio State University, Columbus. Unpublished manuscript.

TEST, D. W. (1978). The development, implementation, and evaluation of a training program designed to provide in-service teachers those skills necessary to teach effectively in the Visual Response System. Masters thesis, The Ohio State University, Columbus.

TEST, D. W. (1983). Teaching coin summation to mentally retarded individuals. Ph.D. dissertation, The Ohio State University, Columbus.

TEST, D. W., & Heward, W. L. (1980). Photosynthesis: Teaching a complex science concept to juvenile delinquents. *Science Education, 64,* 129–139.

TEST, D. W., & Heward, W. L. (1983). Teaching road signs and traffic laws to learning disabled students. *Learning Disability Quarterly, 6*(1), 80–83.

TEST, D. W., Cooke, N. L., Heron, T. E., & Heward, W. L. (1983). Adapting Visual Response System technology to the regular classroom. *Journal of Special Education Technology, 6*(2), 15–26.

THURLOW, M. L., Ysseldyke, J. E., Graden, J., & Algozzine, B. (1984). Opportunity to learn for LD students receiving three different levels of special education services. *Learning Disability Quarterly, 7*(1), 55–67.

VAN HOUTEN, R. (1980). *Learning through feedback.* New York: Human Sciences Press.

VAN HOUTEN, R. (1984). Setting up performance feedback systems in the classroom. In W. L. Heward, T. E. Heron, D. S. Hill, & J. Trapp-Porter (Eds.), *Focus on behavior analysis in education* (pp. 114–125). Columbus, OH: Merrill.

VARGAS, J. S. (1984). What are your exercises teaching? An analysis of stimulus control in instructional materials. In W. L. Heward, T. E. Heron, D. S. Hill, & J. Trap-Porter (Eds.), *Focus on behavior analysis in education* (pp. 126–141). Columbus, OH: Merrill.

VIRGALITTE, J. K. (1988). Effects of using guided notes on teaching employment applications to juvenile delinquents with mild handicaps. Masters thesis, The Ohio State University, Columbus.

WELCH, W. W., & Bridgman, R. G. (1968). Achievement gains as a function of teaching duration. *School Science and Mathematics, 68,* 449–454.

WHEATLEY, R. K. (1986). The effects of hand raising and response card conditions on nine intermediate developmentally handicapped students during and after money instruction. Masters thesis, The Ohio State University, Columbus.

WHITE, D. M. (1991). Use of guided notes to promote generalized note taking behavior of high school students with learning disabilities. Masters thesis, The Ohio State University, Columbus.

WILLIAMS, V. I. (1993). Effects of two teacher presentation rates on student participation and academic achievement during small group instruction by students with severe behavior disorders. Masters thesis, The Ohio State University.

WYMAN, R. (1968). A visual response system for small group interaction. *Audio-visual Instruction, 13,* 714–717.

WYMAN, R. (1969). A progress report on the Visual Response System. *American Annals of the Deaf, 114,* 838–840.

YANG, F. M. (1988). Effects of guided lecture notes on sixth graders' scores on daily science quizzes. Masters thesis, The Ohio State University, Columbus.

YOUNG, B. K. (1980). Teaching nutrition concepts to fourth grade students in the Visual Response System. Masters thesis, The Ohio State University, Columbus.

ZAHORIK, J. A. (1985). Reactions and feedback in the classroom. In T. Husen & T. N. Postlewaite (Eds.), *International Encyclopedia of Education* (pp. 4192–4200). New York: Pergamon Press.

CHAPTER 22

Applied Behavior Analysis: An Insider's Appraisal

Thomas C. Lovitt

Bill Heward mentioned that he had received a number of calls and letters about my participation in this conference (Behavior Analysis in Education: Focus on Measurably Superior Instruction). Most of the inquirers were puzzled, but a few were actually irate. Folks were wondering why he had selected me to attend the conference, much less kick it off. Several offered alternatives to Bill in the event that I came to my senses and backed out, or he came to his senses and sent me to a faraway place that dealt with a topic other than Applied Behavior Analysis.

Some of the madding crowd who contacted Bill admitted that they knew I had written a few pieces for the *Journal of Applied Behavior Analysis* and other applied behavior analysis journals in the late 1960s and early 1970s, but they thought I had either passed on to another methodology—perhaps one more qualitative—or simply passed on. Bill, the honorable person he is, held his ground and told the critics to be patient. He explained that he knew I had not been ringing the applied behavior analysis bell loudly or frequently of late, but he saw this as an opportunity for me to come back into the fold, to become a "born-again ABA" (I guess that would be a BAABA).

In an attempt to establish some credibility as an applied behavior analyst, I'll just mention that in the mid-1960s I worked with Ogden Lindsley in the College of Education and Richard Schiefelbusch in the Bureau of Child Research at the University of Kansas. In fact, I was Lindsley's first doctoral student at Kansas. In addition, I crossed paths briefly with the cast of applied behavior analysts who had immigrated to Kansas from Washington: Don Baer, Vance Hall, Betty Hart, Todd Risley, Jim Sherman, Montrose Wolf, and their respective entourages.

A Few Significant Epochs

Before going any further, I would like to comment on a few terms and offer a mild disclaimer. As for the terms, I will refer to a singular applied behavior analyst as an ABA, to two or more applied behavior analysts as ABAs, and to the *Journal of Applied Behavior Analysis* as *JABA*. Now for the disclaimer. Throughout, I will make reference almost exclusively to articles from *JABA* as being representative of the work of ABAs, realizing full well there are other journals that cater to ABAs: *Behavior Modification*,

Behaviorism, Education & Treatment of Children, Journal of Behavioral Education, and *The Behavior Analyst.* Articles on applied behavior analysis are also published in a wide variety of education and psychological journals that are not exclusively devoted to that methodology, although that certainly hasn't always been the case. But I will refer mostly to articles in *JABA* since that is the field's flagship journal and it has been around for almost 25 years now.

Admittedly, I haven't been as active in mainline applied behavior analysis circles the past 10 or 15 years as I once was. My interests and commitments have been more with public schools, principals, pupils, parents, and teachers than with research methodologies of any particular type. Although I acknowledge my roots and cherish my heritage as a behaviorist, because of my work in schools and with the activities and individuals associated with them, my adherence to a particular mode of discovery has been of secondary importance.

When it comes to publishing school research most journal editors and reviewers are rather under-whelmed, in spite of the fact they may be calling for more teachers to use validated techniques. They are generally unwilling to give the school researcher a break; that is, to be more lenient with respect to matters of design and analysis. This is particularly true if the researcher has the assigned teacher carry out the intervention on a topic he or she would ordinarily deal with, at a time when he or she would usually schedule it, and with all of the students in the class. Although we have managed to squeak a few school-based pieces by reviewers of various journals in the past years, one has to be rather thick-skinned to keep up the effort. For example, a few years ago, we ran what we thought was a multiple baseline design across teachers. Not only had they started the project at different times, they were in different schools and cities. A reviewer was unimpressed with our write-up of that study, however. He or she said: "The authors violated the canons of multiple baseline research in that they reported no stable baselines and their analyses rested solely on mean scores. In the future I recommend that the authors either study research design or hire a knowledgeable consultant." Now I

didn't mind that last shot about boning up on research design, but I was a little upset that I had violated a canon.

Over the years we have made a few modest efforts to fit our school studies into other research designs. Moreover, we have run a few *t*-tests, an analysis of variance or two, some correlations, and even a multi-variate analysis. Currently, we are trying our hand at some qualitative research by sending out surveys and interviewing teachers, parents, principals, and pupils. So, methodologically, I have been a wanderer.

The Beginning of *JABA* in 1968

I'll never forget my excitement when the first issue of *JABA* hit the streets in 1968. I read it from cover to cover. There was the lead article by Vance Hall and colleagues (1968), "Effects of Teacher Attention on Study Behavior," and the wonderful piece by Betty Hart and friends (1968), "Effect of Contingent and Non-Contingent Social Reinforcement on the Cooperative Play of a Preschool Child," and of course the article by Donald Baer, Montrose Wolf, and Todd Risley (1968) that told us what applied behavior analysis was and how to do it.

I knew that I had found *the* journal. Prior to *JABA* about the only journal that reported behavioral pieces was the *Journal of Experimental Analysis of Behavior.* Although it was certainly experimental, analytic, and behavioral, to make use of its findings readers were required to generalize from titration schedules with naive pigeons to daily schedules with rowdy sixth-graders. Finally, with *JABA* there was a practical (applied) journal that focused on education. At last, a journal had been conceived that would offer tactics and strategies to teachers that were useful in their situations.

I had assumed further that after the first issue or two, the articles in *JABA* would be written in such a way that teacher trainers and teachers themselves could read them and immediately put the ideas into practice. I thought the *JABA* editors would shape us into a more teacher-friendly format. Perhaps the ar-ticles could have been written up in three sections. The first could be a "Who Can Benefit" part, in which we were told about the type of youth who might profit most from the technique. Section two could be a step-by-step explanation of the "Procedures." The final section could tell the teacher how to "Monitor" the effects of the practice once they put it into operation. There was no such evolution. The articles continued to follow the same stilted form they began with. After several years some authors did begin to use the first person instead of the third and the active voice instead of the passive. That helped. But the formats remained the same, boring: An introduction in which the authors make a case for their research by referencing a call for more research on that topic they had made in an earlier article. A method section in which the subjects (not students, children, teachers, or anything human) are explained, the apparatus and measurement devices are detailed, the procedures for carrying out the experiment are outlined. A results section in which charts, tables, and figures show or illustrate such exciting data as "average percent attending per 5-minute trial." A discussion section in which the authors either set themselves up for their next experiment, if this one turned out as they had hoped, or plead to others to carry on the torch if it didn't or if they are bored with the research.

More disturbing than the "inconsiderate" format of the articles was that the frequency of *JABA* articles dealing with education began to fall off, or so it seemed to me.

A Shift in Emphasis in 1979

Up to about 1979 there had been a reasonable number of education articles in each *JABA* issue to keep an education person interested, but then the tide turned. (Only 15 articles on education, defined ever so broadly, were published in 1979.) Although I had been a loyal subscriber to *JABA* since 1968, I lost enthusiasm in 1979 and let my subscription lapse. To show how *JABA* had swung away from education, the following are some articles published in 1979:

• "FI schedules and Persistence at Gambling in the U.K. Betting Office" (Dickerson)
• "Theoretical, Practical, and Social Issues in Behavioral Treatments of Obesity" (Wooley, Wooley, & Dyrenforth)
• "Program Evaluation Research: An Experimental Cost-Effectiveness Analysis of an Armed Robbery Intervention Program" (Schnelle et al.)

• "Behavioral Treatment of Caffeinism: Reducing Excessive Coffee Drinking" (Foxx & Rubinoff)
• "Suppression of Self-Stimulation: Three Alternative Strategies" (Harris & Wolchik)
• "Satiation Therapy: A Procedure for Reducing Deviant Sexual Arousal" (Marshall)

Granted, those and many of the other noneducation articles that appeared in *JABA* are important topics, but it struck me at the time that ABAs, at least those writing for *JABA,* were more inclined to show that the applied behavior analysis methodology was suitable for any and all concerns than for solving complex educational matters. Of course there wasn't an educational crisis in 1979. Or was there?

In retrospect, it appears that ABAs believed they had taken care of education. They could put it aside and move on to other fields: medicine, business, ecology, and community involvement to name a few. They could in turn handle problems in those areas.

Of course, there were some sterling educational pieces in 1979: two discussion articles on self-management, one by O'Leary and Dubey, and the other by Rosenbaum and Drabman, and the clever writing piece with children with hearing impairments by Heward and Eachus. But since 1979, it was slim pickings for we teachers.

JABA from 1979 to Present

Even though I dropped my subscription in 1979, I would periodically sneak a look at some of the issues. I work in a place where that is easy to do. I would drop into Owen White's or Felix Billingsley's office, colleagues of mine, rummage through their *JABAs* and ask them about new developments. "What are the ABAs up to now?" Both Owen and Felix are avid ABAs. And the past year or so I have been able to visit with Ilene Schwartz and look over her *JABAs.* Ilene is beyond avid, she is a devout ABA. She has all the copies of *JABA* in leather-bound sets. Not only did I want to know what the ABAs were up to and, which new topics they had taken on, but I wanted to know if they were giving education another chance.

Thankfully, they had not totally neglected education. In 1988, *JABA* came out with a volume of selected education articles that had appeared in that journal since 1968 (Sulzer-Azaroff et al., 1988). It is a wonderful collection. There are 73 articles in the book grouped in 10 categories: conceptual, preschool children, language and social behavior, instructional processes and academic performance, classroom management, peers as tutors, behaviorally disordered students, college instruction, teacher and parent training, and health and safety. There is also a complete listing of behavioral education articles from 1968 to 1987 in that volume.

Over the years ABAs have indeed produced some terrific educational articles. I believe I have read most of them. Following are six of my favorites, ones I have recommended in paraphrased form to teachers:

1. Hopkins, Schutte, and Garton, 1971, "The Effects of Access to a Playroom on the Rate and Quality of Printing and Writing of First and Second Grade Students." A simple, straightforward procedure for teaching writing to an entire class, in fact a split class.
2. Ferritor, Buckholdt, Hamblin, and Smith, 1972, "The Noneffects of Contingent Reinforcement for Attending Behavior on Work Accomplished." They demonstrated that time on task is not necessarily related to production.
3. Brigham, Graubard, and Stans, 1972, "Analysis of the Effects of Sequential Reinforcement Contingencies on Aspects of Composition." They relied on quantitative and qualitative measures to show that the writing of 13 remedial students could be improved.
4. Harris and Sherman, 1974, "Homework Assignments, Consequences, and Classroom Performance in Social Studies and Mathematics." This study was carried out with all the pupils in two sixth-grade classes. Their data indicated that when contingencies were arranged for the accurate completion of homework, student performances at school improved.
5. Johnson and Bailey, 1974, "Cross-Age Tutoring: Fifth Graders as Arithmetic Tutors for Kindergarten Children." They showed that a passel of fifth-graders could teach important skills—counting objects, counting by tens, naming decades—to kindergartners. Their research was the forerunner of the excellent current studies on peer-mediated

instruction by Greenwood, Maheady, Jenkins, and others.
6. Smith, Schumaker, Schaeffer, Schaeffer, and Sherman, 1982, "Increasing Participation and Improving the Quality of Discussions in Seventh-Grade Social Studies Classes." In this study, with several classes of seventh graders, the researchers showed that properly arranged contingencies could increase not only the frequency that students participated in discussions, but the quality of their contributions as well.

Renewed Interest in Education

In the Spring of 1992, *JABA* came out with a monograph, "The Education Crisis: Issues, Perspectives, Solutions." I thought Eureka, the ABAs have rediscovered education! I couldn't wait to read the issue, all 17 articles plus the introduction by Scott Geller! I thought those rascals, the ABAs, they have really been thinking about education all along; they have just been pondering the many important issues in private for the past dozen years, and now they are revealing their master plan. I read the issue from cover to cover.

Carnine (1992) wrote about expanding the notion of teachers' rights to tools that work. Lindsley (1992) asked why effective teaching tools weren't more widely adopted. Axelrod (1992) wrote on the dissemination of an effective technology. Others wrote about the presumed benefits of ABA technology to education.

In an effort to get their message out, the *JABA* folks sent copies to as many individuals in education as they could think of: current subscribers, those who had been in the fold and dropped out, those who had never been in the guild, and others. I apparently qualified on several counts because they sent me four copies.

Message of the Education Crisis Issue

The authors responded brilliantly to many of the issues and perspectives of the education crisis and posed several possible solutions to the crisis. But the major theme of the issue, as I understand it, was this: "We, the ABAs, have a finely crafted set of procedures, ones that have been skillfully developed over the past 25 or so years. They have been amply tested in applied settings and are ready to be used more widely. If you school people would just make use of them there would no longer be an education crisis."

Sid Bijou had a similar message in 1970 when his article, "What Psychology Has to Offer Education— Now," was published in *JABA*. He offered six general principles for teachers to follow that are derived from applied behavior analysis: (1) state in objective terms the desired terminal or goal behavior, (2) assess the child's behavioral repertory relevant to the task, (3) arrange in sequence the stimulus material for reinforcement, (4) start the child on that unit in the sequence to which he or she can respond correctly about 90% of the time, (5) manage the contingencies of reinforcement to strengthen successive approximations to the terminal behavior, and (6) keep records of the child's responses as a basis for modifying the materials and teaching procedures.

As for school psychologists, Bijou's suggestions for adopting behavior-analytic principles and techniques were more specific. He saw them performing four functions: (1) working closely with kindergarten and first-grade teachers to identify children who were at risk of failing or not doing well in school, and modifying programs for them so that they would be successful; (2) working with counselors, teachers, and others to set up remedial programs based on behavioral principles; (3) assisting teachers to deal with problems of classroom management and subject-matter programming in their classrooms; and (4) conducting inservice sessions for instructional assistants (aides) so they are better able to help their assigned teachers. Great advice! The only school psychology program I know of that encourages their graduates to behave like that is the one at the University of Oregon with Gary Stoner, Mark Shinn, and Hill Walker (1991). Bless them!

Bijou's message for teachers and school psychologists was one of optimism. It was up-beat. Of course, that was in 1970—we were younger then.

In contrast, the message of the ABAs in the recent education crisis issue didn't come through as a statement of joy and hope, but rather as confused and somewhat whiny: *What do they want? It's all there*

for the taking. Why don't they use the right stuff? The signature lamentation of these Rodney Dangerfields was direct instruction. The common complaint about direct instruction went like this: "Direct instruction won the Follow Through contest in the late 1960s; it beat out all others; therefore, it should be used today much more widely than it is." Engelmann was so disgusted with education because they haven't adopted the proper methods, in particular direct instruction, he sued the state of California. Lindsley, writing in the *JABA* education crisis issue (1992), informed us that he was so fed up with education for not using the "right stuff," particularly precision teaching, he is taking his six-cycle charts into the world of business. Well!

Applied Behavior Analysts' Responses to the Crisis in Education

Other ABAs have responded differently to the plight that their wares have not been as widely used as they should have been. Carnine, writing in the education crisis issue, is of the opinion that an agency should be formed to screen educational practices and recommend only those that measure up to their standards, something like the Food and Drug Administration or the Good Housekeeping seal of approval, I suppose. He apparently believes that direct instruction and other applied behavior analysis techniques would be disseminated more widely if such a screening process were set up.

That's not a bad idea, having some sort of governing body to pass judgment on educational practices. But all the glitzy, trendy, research-based techniques notwithstanding, we all know teachers who can teach complex behaviors with few if any tools. We have all known teachers who can teach most children to read, write, and cipher with only a hornbook and a slate. And on the flip side, we have all known teachers who can foul up any technique, procedure, or strategy, even those that are based on research and are carefully scripted.

In the research project mentioned earlier, the one in which I violated the canons, we identified research-based techniques on four themes: study skills, social skills training, adapting materials, and self-management. Once identified, the practices were described and explained to groups of teachers. Following those sessions, the teachers went to their respective schools and put the ideas into practice. After they had completed a little study with the techniques, we followed up their efforts and analyzed their data. Those data showed that some teachers were extremely successful; that is, the great majority of their youngsters improved, some were sort of successful, and others were not at all successful. Not too surprising, but it does indicate that teachers, pupils, and other circumstances make a difference. Simply because an agency or the literature endorses a product as being sound or effective won't guarantee that it will be successful across-the-board.

Actually, there is such an agency as the one Carnine recommends. The federal government set up the Joint Dissemination Review Panel some years ago. Individuals who had carried out government-funded projects could write up the results of their projects and send the report to this panel. These panel members would look over the report; if they thought it had merit, they would recommend that the producers apply for funds through the National Defusion Network. If things went smoothly with that agency, the developers were encouraged to describe their product at awareness sessions attended by potential consumers. If the consumers were interested in adopting the program, they could apply for funds. If funds were granted, they would set out to replicate the developer's program. That process has changed somewhat in recent years, but the general plan is still in effect. In addition to that federal dissemination agency, some private groups get involved in dissemination and will fund products they believe should be replicated. One of them is the National Center for Learning Disabilities.

Another way to increase the probability that the good behavior-analytic practices are properly disseminated would be to write up the techniques in ways that teachers understand. Jon Bailey (1991) chided ABAs on this score, when he said that they have continued to write up their research in ways that appeal to editors of journals and promotion committees rather than in formats that respond to teachers' needs.

Phil Bornstein and I worked with Ray Beck a few years ago to design a prereferral program known as RIDE (Responding to Individual Differences in Education) (Weast, Beck, Gabriel, Bornstein, Lovitt, & Conrad, 1987). For that program we selected over 200 articles that explained research practices, the majority of which were of the applied behavior analysis type, and paraphrased them so teachers could more easily read them and put them into practice. There is now a microcomputer program that incorporates those tactics. But even though the techniques were backed up by research, were rewritten for teachers, and are easily accessed, there is no guarantee they will be effective across-the-board. Like plumbers, mechanics, and carpenters, some teachers are better able to use tools than others.

Related to dissemination and the problem of fidelity of implementation—that is, recognizing the fact that some teachers are better able to put endorsed and supported techniques into practice than are others—some educators have recommended that producers make certain that potential users *really know* how to use their materials. Baer, Wolf, and Risley (1987) mentioned this as a possibility. With such an approach, potential consumers are required to come to the place where the product was developed, sit through a carefully scripted set of lessons, respond to questions raised by the developers, buy the kit or package, accept a certificate regarding their attendance, sign an oath saying they will use the product as designed, come back to the home office for periodic retraining, and purchase the program updates as they come out. As you know, there are several programs of this type around the country; some pertain to learning strategies, others to social skills training, and several to reading instruction. I don't think much of this approach either, and for the same reasons I noted earlier about the agency concept; there are factors other than the technique itself that must be taken into account.

Alternative Actions

Other options are available for ABAs who are concerned that their techniques are not being put into effect by teachers as frequently as they should be.

Wait Until Consumers Are Ready

One approach we ABAs might consider is to carry out our research as did Barbara McClintock, the geneticist who recently died (Kolata, 1992). According to reports, she worked alone and chose not to publish some of her most revolutionary research on genetics for years, explaining that she thought no one would accept her findings. Furthermore, she rarely appeared at professional meetings to discuss her research. Instead, McClintock patiently waited until she believed the world was ready to hear about her discoveries of molecular tools that dissect genetic material before writing or talking about them. We ABAs could do likewise, wait patiently until the world is ready for our approaches, all the while perfecting our methodology. Only when the educational community was ready for them would we unveil the techniques.

Ask Consumers What They Want

Another approach for ABAs to consider—one that is more functional than whining, waiting, threatening, or suing—would be to take our case to the consumers. For a short time, ABAs could become qualitative salespersons. That's fashionable these days. We could go into classrooms with slides, films, videos, or pamphlets that describe the products and show teachers how these procedures work. Some teachers might sign up for a trial run right on the spot, informing the producer that they had never heard of the product but it looked terrific. It was just what they needed. Others, who knew about the product but hadn't tried it or used it for a while and dumped it, could tell the producers why they had never tried the package or explain why they had put it aside if they had used it at one time. Depending on what those nonusers said, ABA producers could make adjustments in their practices and try again. That could be the marketing twist that Axelrod (1992) spoke of in the education crisis monograph. It does make sense to attend to consumers' wishes.

While we are at it, we ABA producers could ask teachers who had latched on to other ideas or practices, particularly ones that were not supported by data, why they had done so. I believe that is what really piques us, when teachers and schools adopt practices that have little or no empirical support. There

are plenty of those instances. In my neck of the woods Instructional Theory into Practice (ITIP), an instructional approach out of Southern California, has been a big seller. Most of the districts in and around Seattle have bought into it at one time or another. In the district where I live, staff development is in fact synonymous with ITIP training. This significant involvement of the practice flies in the face of Slavin's report in the *Phi Delta Kappan* a few years ago (1989). According to him, there have been no studies to support its positive effects on pupils, teachers, schools, or anything else. The Orton-Gillingham-Slingerland method for teaching reading is also firmly entrenched in my area. And there are scant data to support its selection over direct instruction, reading recovery, whole language, or any other reading program.

Carry Out Dissemination Research

Yet another option for disgruntled ABAs would be to carry out dissemination research. If ABAs had a product they believed teachers should use, they could set it up in a class or two in one school. As the teachers attempted to put the idea into practice, the producer would be there watching and listening. The producer would keep notes and records on what was happening: about their difficulties with getting started, about keeping it going, with acquiring data, with pupils of certain types, about the time required to use it. The producer would also gather quantitative data from the teachers and the youngsters. When the product was up and running in one school, the producer could move on to another school and continue observing, interviewing, writing notes, and keeping data. He or she would continue the process, moving on to other schools. Perhaps, in an effort to test the limits of the procedure, each new school would be somewhat different than the one before. After a while, the producer would visit the initial sites to see if there had been any slippage and would stick around to straighten things out if there had been. Baer, Wolf, and Risley, in their applied behavior analysis–revisited article in 1987, suggested that something like this would be a worthwhile form of research. I certainly agree.

If we are truly interested in disseminating our wares, we might recommend that our universities modify the contingency system under which we operate. Instead of being paid off for the number of articles in refereed journals, researchers would be rewarded for the number of successful disseminations.

And finally, if ABAs become extremely peeved with school people because they won't use our procedures, we could start teaching school ourselves. Along that line, I have a little reminder posted in my office. It says: "Tom, if at any time you get so bummed out with teachers because they won't use the wonderful things you have come up with, all you have to do is go back to Kansas City, or some other place in Missouri, and start teaching school." I have a lifetime teaching certificate in that wonderful state.

What Do We ABAs Have to Disseminate?

Just what *do* we ABAs have to disseminate to schools besides direct instruction and possibly precision teaching? Most assuredly, we have a creditable and vast portfolio of practices to offer. We have indeed come up with some of the right stuff. Broadly speaking, we have informed educators in every way, shape, and form how to arrange contingencies that increase the probability of behaviors occurring or not occurring. More specifically, we have given them dozens of strategies for managing behavior: positive and negative reinforcement, response cost, time out, extinction, punishment, differential reinforcement of low rates of responding, satiation, shaping, fading, and chaining. Related to those principles, ABAs have thoroughly investigated and promoted such practices as self-management, token economies, contingency contracts, and group contingencies of various types. Certainly, if all or parts of those approaches were properly applied in schools, the education crisis would be under heavy siege, but I am not as convinced as are some of my ABA mates that the war would be over.

What Problems Should We Address?

I certainly don't agree with Jere Brophy (1983) when he said that although the efforts of behavior analysts in education were interesting, they reminded him of a child with a hammer who discovered that everything in his environment needed hammering. As I said earlier, ABAs have made significant contributions to education; they go far beyond the hammer level. But if we want to take our influence up a notch or two, we must deal with some of the more pressing issues of education, issues we have neglected for the most part. I'll just note a few: parental involvement, collaboration, dealing with diversity, dropouts, teenage pregnancies and sexually transmitted diseases, violence in schools, IEPs, deferred diplomas, year-around schools, extended school year, national or state tests for teachers and pupils, vouchers, merit pay, and alternative certification. And if we ABAs really want to get involved in educational reform, we must pay attention to not only *how* things are taught but *what* is taught. We should roll up our sleeves and become active in determining curriculum. It's one thing to argue about *how* something should be taught, either directly or indirectly, and quite another to deal with *what* is taught. Therein lies a major challenge.

How Can Applied Behavior Analysts Influence Education?

Following are four ways in which ABAs, or others for that matter, can get more involved with education and schools, and in so doing increase the probability that our practices will be more widely used than they now are.

Working in Schools

First and foremost, if we want to influence teachers, we must spend considerable time in the schools. We must go regularly and often to an elementary or secondary school. Once we find a school, it is necessary to stay there for a number of weeks or even months. And while there, it is essential that we watch, listen, and ask questions. It is imperative, according to Saul Axelrod (1992), to find out what consumers want and in what form they want it. Too many ABAs and other educational researchers have solutions in search of problems. They don't know what the problems and needs of schools and teachers are.

It's not at all difficult to find a school that will welcome us, particularly if we are willing to spend time there and adapt to their culture. There is no shortage of schools. In Washington, which isn't one of our more populous states, there are about 300 high schools, about as many middle schools or junior highs, and over 1,000 elementary schools. In the Seattle area alone, there are about 50 high schools.

If researcher-disseminators spent a couple of days a week in a high school for nine months they would learn a great deal. For one thing, they would learn that the basic curriculum has not changed much in the past 60 years and, for another, that the populations of most urban schools have changed considerably since they went to school. They would also learn that there are several cultures and subcultures in the schools, special and regular education being the most obvious. On the side, they would pick up some terrific stories about teachers, pupils, parents, and administrators and would greatly enhance their credibility as educators or researchers. It is particularly important to work with schools now because most of them are in the throes of restructuring and in the process are considering all sorts of ideas for change from a variety of sources.

Work with Educators of Other Types

If ABAs intend to influence schools significantly, we must realize that there are others out there who are also concerned about education. In the 1992 education crisis monograph, there was not one reference to any of the Secretaries of Education, past or present. There was no mention of a Boyer, a Bennett, or an Alexander. Some might believe that is to their credit, but the authors of those 18 pieces in the crisis issue also neglected to mention such eminent educational figures as Elliot Eisner, Chester Finn, John Goodlad, Sara Lawrence Lightfoot, and Ted Sizer. Moreover, there was not a single reference to articles in the *Phi Delta Kappan,* one of the most widely read journals in education. And there were only three citations of articles in *Educational Leadership*, another noteworthy educational magazine, and all three of those were in Scott Geller's introduction. It's a good idea to be proud of our methodology and to interact with individuals like ourselves, but it's probably not a good

idea to totally neglect the ideas and criticisms of others.

Work in Places Other than Schools and with Individuals Other than Teachers

If we intend to get our message across to educators, we will have to influence a broad field. We will have to work with parent groups. In special education, parent groups have in the past 25 years greatly modified federal, state, and district policies that deal with children with disabilities. ABAs should take a page from their book. In addition, ABAs should seek the attention of legislators and gain access to education committees. We should lobby to be included on the various commissions and task forces that are periodically appointed by presidents, governors, mayors, and others to deal with educational issues. In Washington a blue ribbon commission on education was recently formed. There are over two dozen members on that committee, only three or four of whom are active educators, and of course, none of them are ABAs. And by all means, in our efforts to influence schools and education, we should get the attention of school board members, if not actively campaign to get on boards ourselves.

Work with Colleges of Education

If ABAs intend to influence education, particularly the training of new teachers, we must be aware that that takes place primarily in colleges of education. Although departments of human development, psychology, sociology, and anthropology contribute significantly to developing strategies and tactics for use by school people to educate children, the places in which education is most influenced are the colleges of education. I know that is a terrifying thought to many, that the fate of our schools and children is in the hands of colleges of education—I shudder myself— but that's where teachers, principals, school psychologists, and counselors who work in schools are instructed. More specifically, kindergarten through 12th-grade teachers are prepared in departments of curriculum and instruction.

Therein lies another challenge. According to J. E. Stone (1991), writing in an issue of *News and Views,* colleges of education are staffed largely by developmentalists. He stated that they urge teachers to find activities that are first engaging to students and second of educational relevance, instead of arranging motivating incentives for student performances. (The first two of those goals don't seem all that out of line to me, although they should give some thoughts to reinforcement theory.) Incidentally, Stone was also disappointed that direct instruction wasn't any more popular than it was. Saul Axelrod, writing in the education crisis issue, was generally in accord with Stone, saying that colleges of education were staffed by professors whose methods differed significantly from those of the ABAs. Ah, the Evil Empire.

But since we ABAs are experts at modifying behaviors, we should rise to the occasion and change the minds, spirits, and methodologies of the developmentalists. Such an opportunity!

Wrap Up

Thanks for indulging me. I hope I haven't been too negative about ABAs. As I have been criticizing the methodology and our practices, I have included myself right there with them, for *Ich bin ein ABA*. As a final word or two, I believe that applied behavior analysts *can* have a direct and significant impact on the crisis of education if we make adjustments with the three words of our name. We should take the applied in *applied* more seriously with respect to schools and education. We should work in schools, with ordinary teachers, on regularly arranged tasks, and with usual schedules. Moreover, it is essential to work with all the youth in classes, report data from all of them, and do something different with those who did not react positively to our treatment. With respect to *behavior*, we should use measures that are more natural and more commonly understood, such as playing the piano, building a workbench, writing a story, speaking in German, and designing a building. And related, we should lighten up a bit with our *analysis*. If we use more lifelike measures, relate the performances of our clients to those of "professionals," and determine the extent that they approach those standards, there will be less need for parametric and nonparametric statistics, designs, controls, and sampling.

References

AXELROD, S. (1992). Disseminating an effective educational technology. *Journal of Applied Behavior Analysis,* Monograph Number 7, 24–28.

BAER, D. M., Wolf, M. M., & Risley, T. R. (1968). Some current dimensions of applied behavior analysis. *Journal of Applied Behavior Analysis, 1,* 91–97.

BAER, D. M., Wolf, M. M., & Risley, T. R. (1987). Some still-current dimensions of applied behavior analysis. *Journal of Applied Behavior Analysis, 20,* 313–327.

BAILEY, J. S. (1991). Marketing behavior analysis requires different talk. *Journal of Applied Behavior Analysis, 24,* 445–448.

BIJOU, S. W. (1970). What psychology has to offer education—now. *Journal of Applied Behavior Analysis, 3,* 65–71.

BRIGHAM, T. A., Graubard, P. S., & Stans, A. (1972). Analysis of the effects of sequential reinforcement contingencies on aspects of composition. *Journal of Applied Behavior Analysis, 5,* 421–429.

BROPHY, J. E. (1983). If only it were true: A response to Greer. *Educational Researcher, 12,* 10–12.

CARNINE, D. (1992). Expanding the notion of teachers' rights: Access to tools that work. *Journal of Applied Behavior Analysis,* Monograph Number 7, 7–13.

DICKERSON, M. G. (1979). FI schedules and persistence at gambling in the U.K. betting office. *Journal of Applied Behavior Analysis, 12,* 315–323.

FERRITOR, D. E., Buckholdt, D., Hamblin, R. L., & Smith, L. (1972). The noneffects of contingent reinforcement for attending behavior on work accomplished. *Journal of Applied Behavior Analysis, 5,* 7–17.

FOXX, R. M., & Rubinoff, A. (1979). Behavioral treatment of caffeinism: Reducing excessive coffee drinking. *Journal of Applied Behavior Analysis, 12,* 335–344.

HALL, R. V., Lund, D., & Jackson, D. (1968). Effects of teacher attention on study behavior. *Journal of Applied Behavior Analysis, 1,* 1–12.

HARRIS, S. L., & Wolchik, S. A. (1979). Suppression of self-stimulation: Three alternative strategies. *Journal of Applied Behavior Analysis, 12,* 185–198.

HARRIS, V. M., & Sherman, J. A. (1974). Homework assignments, consequences, and classroom performance in social studies and mathematics. *Journal of Applied Behavior Analysis, 7,* 505–519.

HART, B. M., Reynolds, N. J., Baer, D. M., Brawley, E. R., & Harris, F. R. (1968). Effect of contingent and non-contingent social reinforcement on the cooperative play of a preschool child. *Journal of Applied Behavior Analysis, 1,* 73–76.

HEWARD, W. L., & Eachus, H. T. (1979). Acquisition of adjectives and adverbs in sentences written by hearing impaired and aphasic children. *Journal of Applied Behavior Analysis, 12,* 391–400.

HOPKINS, B. L., Schutte, R. C., & Garton, K. L. (1971). The effects of access to a playroom on the rate and quality of printing and writing of first- and second-grade students. *Journal of Applied Behavior Analysis, 4,* 77–87.

JABA. (1992). The education crisis: Issues, perspectives, solutions. *Journal of Applied Behavior Analysis, 25*(1).

JOHNSON, M., & Bailey, J. S. (1974). Cross-age tutoring: Fifth graders as arithmetic tutors for kindergarten children. *Journal of Applied Behavior Analysis, 7,* 223–232.

KOLATA, G. (1992). Dr. Barbara McClintock, 90, gene research pioneer, dies. *The New York Times,* September 4, pages A1 and C16.

LINDSLEY, O. R. (1992). Why aren't effective teaching tools widely adopted? *Journal of Applied Behavior Analysis,* Monograph Number 7, 14–19.

O'LEARY, S. G., & Dubey, D. R. (1979). Applications of self-control procedures by children: A review. *Journal of Applied Behavior Analysis, 12,* 449–465.

MARSHALL, W. L. (1979). Satiation therapy: A procedure for reducing deviant sexual arousal. *Journal of Applied Behavior Analysis, 12,* 377–389.

ROSENBAUM, M. S., & Drabman, R. S. (1979). Self-control training in the classroom: A review and critique. *Journal of Applied Behavior Analysis, 12,* 467–485.

SCHNELLE, J. F., Kirchner, R. E., Galbaugh, F., Domash, M., Carr, A., & Larson, L. (1979). Program evaluation research: An experimental cost-effectiveness analysis of an armed robbery intervention program. *Journal of Applied Behavior Analysis, 12,* 615–623.

SLAVIN, R. E. (1989). PET and the pendulum: Faddism in education and how to stop it. *Phi Delta Kappan, 70,* 752–758.

SMITH, B. M., Schumaker, J. B., Schaeffer, J. B., Schaeffer, J., & Sherman, J. A. (1982). Increasing participation and improving the quality of discussions in seventh-grade social studies classes. *Journal of Applied Behavior Analysis, 15,* 97–110.

STONE, J. E. (1991). Developmentalism: A standing impediment to the design of the "New American School." *News and Views, 10,* 1–3.

STONER, G., Shinn, M. R., & Walker, H. M. (Eds.). (1991). *Intervention for achievement and behavior problems.* Silver Spring, MD: National Association of School Psychologists.

SULZER-Azaroff, B., Drabman, R. M., Greer, R. D., Hall, R. V., Iwata, B. A., & O'Leary, S. G. (Eds.). (1988). Behavior analysis in education 1968–1987. *Journal of Applied Behavior Analysis,* Reprint Series, Vol. 3, Department of Human Development, University of Kansas, Lawrence.

WEAST, J., Beck, R., Gabriel, S., Bornstein, P., Lovitt, T., & Conrad, D. (1987). Project RIDE (responding to individual differences in education) (multimedia and microcomputer program). Longmont, CO: Sopris West.

WOOLEY, S. C., Wooley, O. W., & Dyrenforth, S. R. (1979). Theoretical, practical, and social issues in behavioral treatments of obesity. *Journal of Applied Behavior Analysis, 12,* 3–25.

PART 5

Transition to Adulthood

Chapter 23
Teaching Generalized Skills to Persons with
Disabilities
    Carolyn Hughes

Chapter 24
Helping High-Risk Black College Students
    Mark A. Jackson, Richard W. Malott

CHAPTER 23

Teaching Generalized Skills to Persons with Disabilities

Carolyn Hughes

Behavior analysts have been successful at teaching secondary students with disabilities a variety of skills that are critical when working and living in the community, including job skills (Davis et al., 1992; Test, Grossi, & Keul, 1988), home management and community living skills (Day & Horner, 1989; Welch, Nietupski, & Hamre-Nietupski, 1985), social interaction skills (Chadsey-Rusch et al., 1984; Storey & Gaylord-Ross, 1987), and recreational and leisure skills (Bambara & Ager, 1992; Wilson, Rusch, & Lee, 1992). Efforts have been less encouraging with respect to teaching individuals the strategies they need to maintain and adapt their performance when conditions are different from those encountered during instruction (Horner, Dunlap, & Koegel, 1988). For example, an employee may lose her new job in a library because she speaks at the same volume she learned when delivering orders at her job at McDonald's. Or a high school student may fail to board the city bus that takes him to work when he sees a new driver at the steering wheel.

Traditional Instructional Models

Although applied behavior analysis offers a technology for influencing distal instructional outcomes, strategies that promote generalized change are rarely incorporated into everyday teaching (Berg, Wacker, & Flynn, 1990; Haring, 1988; Horner, Dunlap, & Koegel, 1988). Behaviorally derived instructional methods were initially introduced to individuals with disabilities beginning in the 1960s in the environments in which these individuals typically spent time (e.g., segregated residential, work training, and educational settings) (Repp, 1983). For example, Hunter and Bellamy (1976) used task analysis and prompting methods to teach people with severe mental retardation employed in a sheltered workshop to assemble complex cable harnesses. Subsequent research conducted in integrated settings (e.g, competitive employment, community residences, general education schools and classrooms) targeted teaching skills that were necessary for everyday life (Rusch, Rose, & Greenwood, 1988). To illustrate, individuals with disabilities have been taught to eat at fast-food restaurants (Nietupski et al., 1985), ride buses (Coon, Vogelsberg, & Williams, 1981), prepare meals (Martin et al., 1982), and work in community employment (Wehman, Hill, & Koehler, 1979). Importantly, although settings have differed across investigations over the past 30 years (i.e., segregated versus integrated), the instructional procedures utilized have been similar in that they have often failed to either address or achieve generalization of skills beyond the instructional situation. Specifically, Nietupski's team (1985) and Coon, Vogelsberg, & Williams (1981) found that teaching skills in a classroom setting in a "train and hope" fashion (Stokes & Baer, 1977) did not generalize to community settings. In contrast, Martin and colleagues (1982) and Wehman, Hill, & Koehler (1979) failed to assess generalization across meal preparation or employment skills, respectively.

Increasing the probability that individuals with disabilities will perform valued skills in noninstructional settings requires more than ensuring that they acquire specific targeted behaviors during instruction. An individual must be able to respond to variations and inconsistencies that are continually encountered over time (Berg, Wacker, & Flynn, 1990; Rusch, Martin, & White, 1985). Frequently, the failure to incorporate these variations into instructional programming restricts generalized responding across diverse conditions.

Recent investigations have taught individuals to assume increased responsibility for their behavior (Hughes, 1991). The primary reason for this shift from externally managed to self-managed strategies likely resulted from the observation that external change agents, such as teachers, could neither be continually present nor control all relevant variables across the myriad environments in which an individual participates. Consequently, individuals performed well under circumstances that closely resembled instructional conditions, but poorly when conditions varied. Rusch and colleagues (1984) demonstrated that dishwashers with mental retardation spent more time working when job trainers were present than when the trainers were absent from the workplace. Heward (1987) suggested that teaching students to act as their own change agents could promote the generalization of behavior change across people, tasks, situations, and time because the only change agent continually available to a person is that person himself or herself.

Two Strategies for Promoting Generalization: Self-Instruction and Multiple-Example Teaching

Generalization and maintenance have been systematically studied since Stokes and Baer's seminal article in 1977. They identified several strategies (e.g., training loosely, using indiscriminable contingencies, and programming common stimuli) that have shown promise in promoting generalized outcomes. As yet, however, no single strategy has been unequivocally effective in promoting both generalization and maintenance of selected newly learned skills. For example, a variation of Stokes and Baer's "training sufficient exemplars" has been referred to as *general case programming* (Horner, Sprague, & Wilcox, 1982). This strategy has promoted generalized responding across such diverse skills as street crossing (Horner, Jones, & Williams, 1985), soap dispensing (Pancsofar & Bates, 1985), and crimping and cutting electronic capacitors (Horner & McDonald, 1982). Maintenance, however, has not been systematically assessed using general case programming. Instead, instruction is applied continuously throughout the intervention.

In contrast, "recruiting natural supports" such as the assistance of co-workers (a form of Stokes and Baer's [1977] "introduce to natural maintaining contingencies") has been associated with the maintenance of job tasks in integrated employment settings. For example, Schutz, Jostes, Rusch, and Lamson (1980) taught co-workers in a university cafeteria to provide performance feedback to employees with disabilities when they were sweeping and mopping the floor. Recruiting natural supports in the form of co-worker feedback was associated with performance maintenance; however, generalized responding to related kitchen tasks was not observed.

To facilitate both generalization and maintenance of targeted skills, a model has been developed to teach students with disabilities a strategy they may use to promote their own behavior change (i.e., to serve as their own change agents). This six-step model for teaching generalization and maintenance combines traditional self-instruction (Meichenbaum & Goodman, 1971) (i.e., a variation of Stokes and Baer's "mediating generalization") with teaching more than one example of a response (i.e., Stokes and Baer's "training sufficient exemplars"). The remainder of this section describes the two generalization strategies.

Self-Instruction

Self-instruction can be an effective instructional strategy for promoting independent performance among persons with disabilities (Graham & Harris, 1989; Guevremont, Osnes, & Stokes, 1988; Roberts, Nelson, & Olson, 1987). Self-instruction involves teaching individuals to verbalize a sequence of statements that directs task performance or to prompt appropriate responses to a situation. Most applications of self-instruction have been based on a teaching sequence developed by Meichenbaum and Goodman (1971) consisting of combinations of components that include a rationale for instruction, modeling, practice, corrective feedback, and reinforcement. Typically, the sequence is presented during several brief instructional periods (e.g., one or two 2-hour sessions or four or five 30-minute sessions).

Meichenbaum and Goodman's (1971) teaching sequence consisted of five steps: (1) the teacher performs the task, instructing aloud while the participant observes; (2) the participant performs the task while the teacher instructs aloud; (3) the participant performs the task while self-instructing aloud; (4) the participant performs the task while whispering; and (5) the participant performs the task while self-instructing "covertly." Contemporary applications of self-instruction typically omit the last two steps of this sequence because of research requirements for measuring self-instructions verbalized by individuals during performance observation (cf. Agran et al., 1992). Self-instructional statements that individuals are taught to verbalize while performing a task are usually the same as those taught in the 1971 instructional sequence and include (1) stating the problem (Statement 1), (2) stating the response (Statement 2), (3) self-evaluating (Statement 3), and (4) self-rein-

forcing (Statement 4). For example, Guevremont, Osnes, & Stokes (1988) increased accuracy on academic tasks by teaching students with disabilities to complete tasks while stating (1) "What do I have to do first?" (Statement 1), (2) "I have to circle the words that have the same letters" (Statement 2), (3) "This is one, so I circle it" (Statement 3), and (4) "Good job" (Statement 4).

Self-instruction and independent performance. A critical feature of the self-instructional sequence is that assistance is gradually withdrawn and responsibility for continued performance is ultimately assumed solely by the participant. Self-instruction may be considered a self-management technique because participants learn to use a procedure for independently "managing" their own behavior. Self-instruction is frequently associated in the literature with independent performance following the removal of instructional assistance (Agran & Martin, 1987; Hughes, 1991).

Self-instruction taught with single examples. Initial applications of self-instruction to increase independent performance of everyday skills taught individuals to self-instruct in response to single examples of a desired response (Agran, Fodor-Davis, & Moore, 1986; Rusch, Martin, & White, 1985). Specifically, participants were taught to complete a sequence of housekeeping tasks in a hospital (Agran, Fodor-Davis, & Moore, 1986), to request materials to complete film orders in a university film center (Rusch et al., 1988), or to increase the time spent working in a university cafeteria (Rusch et al., 1985). These investigations demonstrated that self-instruction could be effective at teaching acquisition and maintenance of relevant employment skills.

Interestingly, generalization was assessed only in the Rusch group (1988) study. Rusch and his colleagues taught a young man with severe mental retardation to self-instruct to request assistance when he needed materials to complete orders in the university film center where he was employed. Following self-instructional teaching, the young man's requests for assistance increased when the materials he needed to complete the orders were missing (single-example teaching). However, he needed instructional feedback during the work performance sessions before his requests generalized from the teaching setting to the work situation. Additionally, his requests for assistance when materials were missing did not generalize to instances when there were not enough materials to complete orders. Rusch and his colleagues concluded that although self-instruction taught with a single response example may be effective at producing acquisition and maintenance, it may not be sufficiently powerful to produce generalized responding in community settings.

Multiple-Example Teaching

Because of the failure of single-example self-instructional teaching to produce generalized responding, investigators have examined the effects of teaching self-instruction in combination with multiple examples that are representative of situations that require individuals to perform independently (cf. Hughes & Rusch, 1989). *Multiple-exemplar training* has been described in the literature as an effective method for producing generalized responding (Stokes & Baer, 1977; Berg, Wacker, & Flynn, 1990). Using this procedure, multiple examples of the full range of stimuli and response requirements encountered in the generalization setting(s) are taught in order to produce a generalized response. An example of this procedure, general case programming, consists of the following steps: (1) define the instructional universe, (2) define the range of relevant stimulus and response variations within the universe, (3) select examples from the instructional universe for use in teaching and probe testing, (4) sequence teaching examples, (5) teach the examples, and (6) test with nontrained probe examples (Horner, Sprague, & Wilcox, 1982). Using general case programming, diverse generalized community skills have been taught, including generalized vending machine use (Sprague & Horner, 1984), generalized street crossing (Horner, Jones, & Williams, 1985), generalized assembly tasks (Horner & McDonald, 1982), and generalized household cleaning (Wacker & Berg, 1984). For example, Horner, Jones, & Williams (1985) taught three individuals

with moderate and severe mental retardation to cross streets independently. Initially, they taught the individuals to cross 8 different types of intersections. Following the initial teaching condition, the researchers conducted ongoing instruction and assessment during which generalization occurred across 20 uninstructed street intersections.

A New Approach: The Generalized Skills Model

Although multiple-exemplar teaching (e.g., general case programming) has been effective in producing generalized responding, instruction is typically applied continuously throughout investigations of this strategy. Because long-term maintenance is usually not assessed in these studies (cf. Horner, Jones, & Williams, 1985), little is known about an individual's performance after assistance is terminated. Conversely, self-instruction is associated with weak generalized effects despite its powerful influence on maintenance.

The Generalized Skills Model: Self-Instruction with Multiple Examples

In an effort to produce a more robust procedure for increasing important everyday skills (i.e., a procedure that would produce *both* generalization and maintenance), an instructional model has been developed that combines self-instruction with teaching multiple examples (see Figure 23.1). This *generalized skill model* has evolved over the past few years through efforts at systematic replication of a strategy that teaches people to act as their own change agents. The model has been effective at producing generalized responding across diverse skills such as problem solving (Hughes & Rusch, 1989; Hughes, 1992), task sequencing (Hughes & Hugo, 1993), and initiating and maintaining conversation (Hughes et al., 1993). The remainder of this chapter describes initial application of the model, outlines the model's components, traces systematic replications of the model, and discusses future areas of research.

F. R. Rusch and I initially applied the model (Hughes & Rusch, 1989) to teach generalized problem

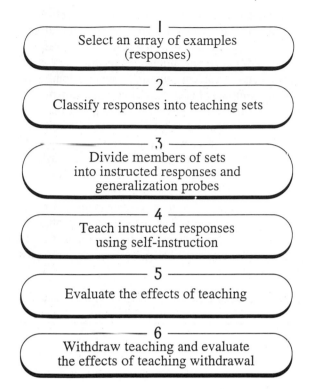

Figure 23.1. The generalized skills model.

solving to two individuals with severe mental retardation who were employed by a janitorial supply company that packaged liquid soap. In this study, we investigated the use of self-instruction to produce a generalized response to an array of problems that were identified by the work supervisor as likely to occur throughout the workday and to be ignored by the employees. For example, we observed that when they were confronted with a work-related problem (e.g., task materials in wrong place), the employees either stopped working (e.g., when materials could not be found) or continued to work but ignored the consequences of the problem (e.g., a bag of soap leaking).

To some extent the evolution of the model was serendipitous. After extensive observations and interviews, we extrapolated from our previous investigations of self-instruction (Rusch et al., 1988) that teaching with single examples of work-related problems would not produce generalization across the diverse situations to which the employees were expected to respond in this environment. The Rusch investigation showed us that teaching with a single response example would produce maintenance of a single task response but not generalized responding across an array of unpredictable situations.

Therefore, we had to produce a model that would result in independent performance across a variety of situations. We experimented with a novel adaptation of self-instruction in order to produce generalized responding. It seemed logical to assume that since single-example instruction equated with single-example responding, systematically introducing many examples of a desired response into self-instructional teaching would equate with generalized responding across many different situations. The remainder of this section describes the steps we took in developing and implementing our model.

Identifying examples.   First, we asked the work supervisor to identify typical work-related "problem situations" that occurred throughout the day and the correct responses to these problems. For example, the supervisor observed that the employees occasionally ran out of materials when working or that their work stations were blocked by obstacles. The employees were expected to respond independently by "solving the problem" posed by these situations by obtaining the required materials or removing the obstacles. The array of problem situations identified by the supervisor and verified by observation were examples of the stimulus conditions to which employees were expected to respond. Based on the supervisor's survey of the work setting, we selected ten examples representative of the array of identified responses to serve as teaching examples (see Table 23.1).

Classifying examples.   We observed that the employees were expected to solve a broad range of problems requiring a variety of functionally dissimilar responses (see Table 23.1). For example, they were expected to remove any liquid soap spilled in their work areas, refill empty tape dispensers, and plug in disconnected appliances. In contrast, previous investigations that used more than one teaching example focused on within-class generalization, such as generalized use of soap dispensers (Pancsofar & Bates, 1985) or crossing similar intersections (Horner, Jones, & Williams, 1985). To increase generalization to a broader class of problems likely to occur throughout the workday, we classified the ten responses under investigation (Table 23.1). Although the responses were theoretically within the "problem solving" response class, three functionally different operations were observed across the responses—plugging in appliances, finding missing items, moving obstacles. For teaching purposes, functionally related responses such as moving obstacles were considered members of the same "teaching set." We reasoned that teaching several members of a set (i.e., a variation of Stokes and Baer's [1977] "training sufficient exemplars") would produce generalized responding across the entire set of responses.

Dividing members of teaching sets into instructed and uninstructed responses. To assess generalized responding across sets of functionally related responses (in addition to evaluating generalization across the broad class "problem solving"), we randomly assigned members of each set either to a group of five responses to be instructed or to five generalization probes (uninstructed responses) (see Table 23.1). For example, because Problem Situation 1 (paper towel in sink) and Problem Situation 2 (trash on table) both required moving an obstacle, these two responses were assigned to different groups. As indicated in Table 23.1, instructed responses for one employee (Myra) served as generalization probes for the other employee (Les). Conversely, instructed responses for Les served as generalization probes for Myra.

Table 23.1 Work-related problem situations and correct responses

Problem Situation	Instruction	Correct Response
1. Paper towel in drain of sink; sink full of water[a]	Instructed by trainer to wring out rag in sink	Remove paper towel; drain sink (Move obstacle)
2. 5 pieces of trash on table[b]	Instructed by trainer to begin work	Throw trash in basket located within 2m of table (Move obstacle)
3. Radio is unplugged	Instructed by trainer to turn on radio	Plug in radio and turn on (Plug-in appliance)
4. Box is on table next to soap-dispensing machine	Instructed by trainer to put tray on table	Put box in proper place or seek assistance (Move obstacle)
5. Bundle on table where work is to be conducted	Instructed by trainer to begin working	Put bundle in proper place (Move obstacle)
6. Tape dispenser is empty	Instructed by trainer to get tape dispenser	Find tape and fill tape dispenser (Find missing item)
7. Cardboard pad is in box with chip boards	Instructed by trainer to get more chip boards	Find pad and put in proper place (Find missing item)
8. Chair is in center of work room	Instructed by trainer to hang rag by sink	Put chair next to table (Move obstacle)
9. Puddle of soap on table where work is to be conducted	Instructed by trainer to begin working	Wipe soap with rag (Move obstacle)
10. Box containing hair nets is in wrong place	Instructed by trainer to get hair net	Find box and put in proper place (Find missing item)

[a]Trained Responses for Myra; Generalization Probes for Les: 1, 3, 5, 7, 9
[b]Trained Responses for Les; Generalization Probes for Myra: 2, 4, 6, 8, 10

Source: From "Teaching Supported Employees with Severe Mental Retardation to Solve Problems" by C. Hughes and F.R. Rusch, 1989, *Journal of Applied Behavior Analysis.* Adapted by permission.

Our decision to teach *five* examples of desired responses was based on literature investigating the use of multiple-exemplar training to produce generalized responding (Hupp & Mervis, 1981; Pancsofar & Bates, 1985; Stokes & Baer, 1977). Research has not yet determined the number or type of teaching examples needed to produce generalized responding. In some instances, teaching as few as two examples that vary across stimulus features (e.g., color, shape, location) has resulted in generalized responding (Pancsofar & Bates, 1985; Stokes, Baer, & Jackson, 1974). Research indicates, however, that if different sequences of movements are required across responses, more than two examples may be required to produce generalized responding (Haring, 1985; Haring & Laitinen, 1992).

In our judgment, at least five teaching examples were needed to encompass the full range of response requirements the employees were expected to perform.

Teaching instructed responses using self-instruction. Our observation of the employees' performance during baseline revealed that Myra made no correct responses to either instructed or uninstructed problem situations, and Les made only four correct responses out of a total of 50 problem presentations (see the upper two panels of Figure 23.2). Consequently, we introduced self-instructional teaching with the group of instructed responses in a sequential fashion across employees.

Based on a review of the empirical literature (Hughes, 1991), we established guidelines for teach-

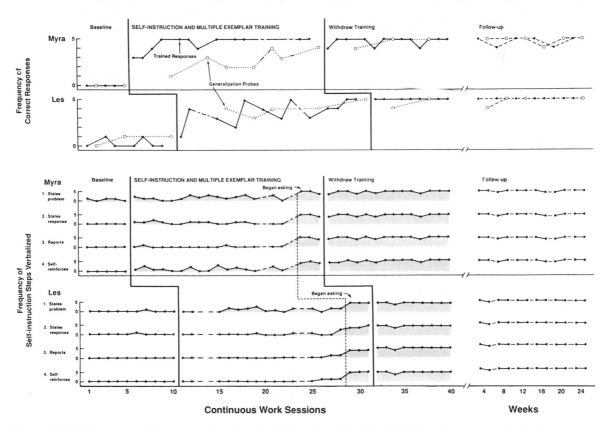

Figure 23.2. Frequency of correct responses to trained and untrained problem situations (generalization probes) and frequency of self-instruction steps verbalized during performance. Broken lines indicate data missing due to employee absence. *SOURCE: From "Teaching Supported Employees with Severe Mental Retardation to Solve Problems," by C. Hughes and F. R. Rusch, 1989,* Journal of Applied Behavior Analysis, *p. 369. Reprinted by permission.*

ing self-instruction: (1) use an instructional sequence that programs for generalization, (2) teach all four self-instruction steps of the Meichenbaum and Goodman (1971) sequence regardless of the level of disability, and (3) adapt a number of teaching sessions according to the subject disability. The variation of the Meichenbaum and Goodman sequence we used is compared to the original sequence in Table 23.2. (Instructional strategies suggested by Stokes and Baer [1977] to program generalization are indicated in parentheses following each teaching step.)

We taught each employee individually to self-instruct during approximately 30 minutes immediately preceding observation of actual work performance using the instructional sequence depicted in Table 23.2. They were taught to self-instruct in response to the five problem situations chosen for teaching, which were presented randomly across all teaching sessions. The self-instructional statements were adapted from

Meichenbaum and Goodman (1971) and consisted of (1) stating the problem (e.g., "Tape empty"), (2) stating the correct response to solve the problem (e.g., "Need more tape"), (3) self-reporting (e.g., "Fixed it"), and (4) self-reinforcing (e.g., "Good").

Evaluating teaching effects.   We took repeated measures of the employees' frequency of correct responding and self-instructing to instructed and uninstructed problem situations throughout the investigation (see Figure 23.2). To ensure the consistency of opportunities to respond throughout the study, we presented five randomly assigned problem situations during each observation session, chosen from an employee's group of instructed or uninstructed problem situations (generalization probes). Generalization probes occurred on an average of once every three sessions during baseline and teaching and once every four sessions during the Withdraw Training condition.

Table 23.2 Comparison between current model and Meichenbaum and Goodman's (1971) training sequence

Current Model	*Meichenbaum and Goodman (1971)*	*Comparison*
1. Trainer provides rationale for self-instruction training and tells subjects to respond as if in response to work demands (Program Common Stimuli).	Trainer does not provide rationale or tell subjects to respond as if in response to work demands.	Different
2. Trainer models multiple examples of tasks while self-instructing aloud (Teach Sufficient Exemplars and Mediate Generalization).	Trainer models multiple examples of tasks while self-instructing aloud (Teach Sufficient Exemplars and Mediate Generalization).	Same
3. Subject performs tasks while trainer instructs.	Subject performs tasks while trainer instructs.	Same
4. Subject performs tasks while self-instructing aloud.	Subject performs tasks while self-instructing aloud.	Same
5. Subject does not perform tasks while whispering.	Subject performs tasks while whispering.	Different
6. Subject does not perform tasks while self-instructing covertly.	Subject performs tasks while self-instructing covertly.	Different
7. Trainer provides corrective feedback and prompting, if needed.	Trainer provides corrective feedback and prompting, if needed.	Same
8. Trainer reminds subject in training to self-instruct when working (Mediate Generalization).	Trainer does not remind subject to self-instruct when working.	Different

Source: "Independent Performance Among Individuals with Mental Retardation: Promoting Generalization through Self-Instruction," by C. Hughes, 1991, in M. Hersen, R. M. Eisler, & P. M. Miller (Eds.), *Progress in Behavior Modification* (Vol. 27, pp. 7–35). Copyright 1991 by Sage Publications. Reprinted by permission.

Our findings indicated that following the introduction of self-instruction with multiple examples, both employees generalized their use of the teaching components (i.e., verbalized self-instruction steps and correct responses to instructed problems) and their responding to uninstructed problem situations during work performance sessions.

Evaluating teaching withdrawal.   As a measure of social validation, we asked the work supervisor to specify an acceptable range of performance for the employees. The supervisor indicated that at least four of the five problem situations presented per session should be responded to correctly across three consecutive sessions to meet her expectation of "job independence." Consequently, we withdrew teaching sequentially across the employees when correct responding stabilized at four or five correct responses to instructed and uninstructed problems per session (i.e., Session 27 for Myra and five sessions later for Les). Both employees maintained criterion performance, without needing external assistance, during the Withdraw Training condition and during six months of follow-up data collected at monthly intervals.

Systematic Replications of the Model

My subsequent research (1992) replicated the effects of the initial application of the model across four residents of a group home who had severe mental retardation. I taught these individuals to self-instruct in response to diverse task-related problems likely to occur in their home. My findings indicated that the residents used the self-instructional strategy to solve both instructed and uninstructed problems and that responding maintained during a six-month follow-up period.

With my colleagues, I conducted further investigations to extend the parameters of the model (Hughes & Hugo, 1993; Hughes et al., 1993). We conducted the studies in integrated high school settings with students with mild to severe mental retardation. Hugo and I taught generalized task sequencing across a functional skill cluster (e.g., making toast) to seven students with moderate or severe mental retardation

in a vocational high school. Initially, we taught self-instruction as a preteaching strategy, with one response example after which multiple examples of responses were introduced. Interestingly, two students who never acquired the preteaching strategy (i.e., never learned to self-instruct) also did not learn to perform either instructed or uninstructed task sequences (see second and third panels, Figure 23.3). All five students who acquired the self-instructional sequence generalized and maintained performance across all instructed and uninstructed task sequences.

My colleagues and I (Hughes et al., 1993) taught four high school students with mild and moderate mental retardation to initiate and maintain conversation across new conversational partners (i.e., partners not associated with instruction). The partners included students with and without disabilities and the conversations were conducted across instructed and uninstructed settings. Figure 23.4 indicates that all four students learned to generalize conversational initiations across multiple partners and settings as a result of learning to self-instruct with multiple partners. Social comparison data revealed that the rate of initiating approximated that of a random sample of high school students without disabilities (see band indicating "Range of Expected Behavior" on each panel in Figure 23.4). Additional findings demonstrated that the rate of initiating correlated with the partners' responses.

Future Areas of Research

Several dimensions of the generalization model warrant further investigation. For example, in our studies (Hughes and Hugo, 1993; Hughes et al., 1993), we used two previously untested features in replicating the model. These features included the use of sign language in teaching students to self-instruct and the use of peers (i.e., students without disabilities) to teach the self-instructional strategy. In both investigations, we taught students with mental retardation and either with or without hearing and speech impairments to self-instruct via verbal instructions accompanied by signed instructions. During independent performance, the students were allowed either to self-instruct ver-

Figure 23.3. Frequency of correct responses to trained and untrained task sequences (generalization probes). Broken lines indicate data missing owing to student absence.

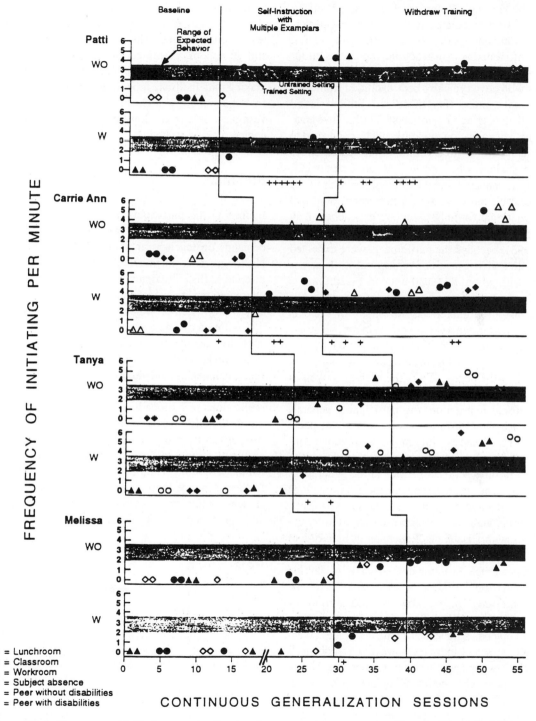

Figure 23.4. Frequency of initiating conversational topics per minute across peers with and without disabilities.

bally or by signing. Both verbal and signed self-instructions were associated with independent performance by students participating in the two studies. The use of signed self-instructions represents an innovative approach to teaching because it focuses on students who have typically been excluded from self-instructional training (i.e., those with limited verbal skills or with hearing impairments). Further investigation of the generalization model should be conducted to determine if similar effects could be replicated across additional students who have limited verbal repertoires.

Using students without disabilities to teach self-instructing also represents a departure from traditional self-instructional formats. Students as teachers may be especially appropriate in our investigation (Hughes et al., 1993), because the participants were expected to generalize their use of conversational skills across students with whom they had not conversed. In this study, the multiple-teaching-examples component of the generalization model was the variety of students who taught participants to converse using self-instruction. The "conversation" that was taught by the students was a "pool" of initiations and responses suggested by the peer teachers themselves as well as by many other students in the high school. Following conversational instruction, the participants generalized their use of self-instruction to converse with peers with whom they had not initiated or maintained conversation. The use of peers as teachers should be replicated in further investigations of the generalization model across more extensive social interactions such as making and maintaining friendships.

Additional areas of research are suggested by the Individuals with Disabilities Education Act (IDEA) of 1990 (P.L. 101-476). This legislation stipulates that services that promote the transition from school to adult life must be based on a student's choice, preferences, and interests. *Individual student choice* is a critical factor associated with the successful transition from school to postschool outcomes for students with disabilities (Wehman, 1990). Research indicates, however, that individuals with disabilities typically have limited opportunities to make or express choices (cf. Houghton, Bronicki, & Guess, 1987; Kishi et al., 1988), although choice making is associated with developing independence and personal autonomy (Guess, Benson, & Siegel-Causey, 1985).

If we expect students with disabilities to make wise choices as they enter adult life, we need to begin to teach them strategies to help them do so while they are still in school. Application of our generalization model as a means of teaching choice and decision making may facilitate more independent and successful outcomes for adults. Further research should investigate the use of the generalization model as a choice-making strategy.

Summary

Increasing the participation and integration of students with disabilities in everyday life places new demands on teachers and related service providers. No longer is it sufficient to simply teach selected discrete skills. Students must learn to respond to unpredictable life events and to changing expectations across varying environments. This chapter has traced the evolution of a new approach to teaching everyday skills to students with disabilities. The generalized skills model addresses the need for individuals to function independently apart from instructional situations. The model has emerged from systematic replications of a procedure for teaching self-instruction with multiple examples of desired responses. To date, it has been effective at producing generalized problem solving, task sequencing, and initiating and maintaining conversation. The model's potential to further influence favorable community outcomes for students with disabilities should be explored through additional empirical applications.

References

AGRAN, M., & Martin, J. E. (1987). Applying a technology of self-control in community environments for individuals who are mentally retarded. In M. Hersen, R. Eisler, & P. Miller (Eds.), *Progress in behavior modification* (Vol. 14, pp. 108–151). Newbury Park, CA: Sage Publications.

AGRAN, M., Fodor-Davis, J., & Moore, S. (1986). The effects of self-instructional training on job-task sequencing: Suggesting a problem-solving strategy. *Education and Training of the Mentally Retarded, 21,* 273–281.

AGRAN, M., Fodor-Davis, J., Moore, S., & Martella, R. (1992). Effects of peer-delivered self-instructional training on a lunch-making work task for students with severe handicaps. *Education and Training in Mental Retardation, 27,* 230–240.

BAMBARA, L. M., & Ager, C. (1992). Using self-scheduling to promote self-directed leisure activity in home and community settings. *Journal of the Association for Persons with Severe Handicaps, 17,* 67–76.

BERG, W. K., Wacker, D. P., & Flynn, T. H. (1990). Teaching generalization and maintenance of work behavior. In F. R. Rusch (Ed.), *Supported employment: Models, methods, and issues* (pp. 145–160). Sycamore, IL: Sycamore Publishing.

CHADSEY-Rusch, J., Karlan, G. R., Riva, M. T., & Rusch, F. R. (1984). Competitive employment: Teaching conversational skills to adults who are mentally retarded. *Mental Retardation, 22,* 218–225.

COON, M. E., Vogelsberg, R. T., & Williams, W. (1981). Effects of classroom public transportation instruction on generalization to the natural environment. *Journal of the Association of the Severely Handicapped, 6,* 46–53.

DAVIS, C. A., Williams, R. E., Brady, M. P., & Burta, M. (1992). The effects of self-operated auditory prompting tapes on the performance fluency of persons with severe mental retardation. *Education and Training in Mental Retardation, 27,* 39–50.

DAY, H. M., & Horner, R. H. (1989). Building response classes: A comparison of two procedures for teaching generalized pouring to learners with severe disabilities. *Journal of Applied Behavior Analysis, 22,* 223–229.

GRAHAM, S., & Harris, K. R. (1989). Improving learning disabled students' skills at composing essays: Self-instructional strategy training. *Exceptional Children, 56,* 201–214.

GUESS, D., Benson, H. A., & Siegel-Causey, E. (1985). Concepts and issues related to choice-making and autonomy among persons with severe disabilities. *Journal of the Association for Persons with Severe Handicaps, 10,* 79–86.

GUEVREMONT, D. C., Osnes, P. G., & Stokes, T. F. (1988). The functional role of preschoolers verbalizations in the generalization of self-instructional training. *Journal of Applied Behavior Analysis, 21,* 45–55.

HARING, N. G. (Ed.). (1988). *Generalization for students with severe handicaps: Strategies and solutions.* Seattle: University of Washington.

HARING, T. G. (1985). Teaching between-class generalization of toy play behavior to handicapped children. *Journal of Applied Behavior Analysis, 18,* 127–139.

HARING, T. G., & Laitinen, R. E. (1992). Extending complex repertoires of critical skills. In R. J. Gaylord-Ross (Ed.), *Issues and research in special education* (Vol. 2, pp. 125–155). New York: Teachers College Press.

HEWARD, W. L. (1987). Self-management. In J. O. Cooper, T. E. Heron, & W. L. Heward (Eds.), *Applied behavior analysis* (pp. 515–549). Columbus, OH: Merrill.

HORNER, R. H., & McDonald, R. S. (1982). A comparison of single instance and general case instruction in teaching a generalized vocational skill. *Journal of the Association for the Severely Handicapped, 7,* 7–20.

HORNER, R. H., Dunlap, G., & Koegel, R. L. (Eds.). (1988). *Generalization and maintenance: Life-style changes in applied settings.* Baltimore: Brookes.

HORNER, R. H., Jones, D., & Williams, J. A. (1985). Teaching generalized street crossing to individuals with moderate and severe mental retardation. *Journal of the Association for Persons with Severe Handicaps, 10,* 71–78.

HORNER, R. H., Sprague, J., & Wilcox, B. (1982). General case programming for community activities. In B. Wilcox & G. T. Bellamy, *Design of high school programs for severely handicapped students* (pp. 61–98). Baltimore: Brookes.

HOUGHTON, J., Bronicki, G. J. B., & Guess, D. (1987). Opportunities to express preferences and make choices among students with severe disabilities in classroom settings. *Journal of the Association for Persons with Severe Handicaps, 12,* 18–27.

HUGHES, C. (1991). Independent performance among individuals with mental retardation: Promoting generalization through self-instruction. In M. Hersen, R. Eisler, & P. Miller (Eds.), *Progress in behavior modification* (Vol. 27, pp. 7–35). Newbury Park, CA: Sage Publications.

HUGHES, C. (1992). Teaching self-instruction utilizing multiple exemplars to produce generalized problem-solving by individuals with severe mental retardation. *American Journal on Mental Retardation, 97*(3), 302–314.

HUGHES, C., & Hugo, K. (1993). Teaching generalized task sequencing to high school students with disabilities. Manuscript submitted for publication.

HUGHES, C. H., & Rusch, F. R. (1989). Teaching supported employees with severe mental retardation to solve problems. *Journal of Applied Behavior Analysis, 22,* 365–372.

HUGHES, C., Killian, D. J., Alcantara, P. R., Niarhos, F., & Harmer, M.L. (1993). Peers as teachers of generalized conversational skills with high school students with disabilities. Manuscript submitted for publication.

HUNTER, J., & Bellamy, T. (1976). Cable harness construction for severely retarded adults: A demonstration of a training technique. *AAESPH Review, 1,* 2–13.

HUPP, S. C., & Mervis, C. B. (1981). Development of generalized concepts by severely handicapped students. *Journal of the Association for the Severely Handicapped, 6,* 14–21.

KISHI, G., Teelucksingh, B., Zollers, N., Park-Lee, S., & Meyer, L. (1988). Daily decision-making in community residences: A social comparison of adults with and without mental retardation. *American Journal on Mental Retardation, 92,* 430–435.

MARTIN, J. E., Mithaug, D. E., Agran, M., & Husch, J. V. (1990). Consumer-centered transition and supported employment. In J. L. Matson (Ed.), *Handbook of behavior modification with the mentally retarded* (pp. 357–389). 2nd ed. New York: Plenum Press.

MARTIN, J. E., Rusch, F. R., James, V. L., Decker, P. J., & Trtol K. A. (1982). The use of picture cues to establish self-control in the preparation of complex meals by mentally retarded adults. *Applied Research in Mental Retardation, 3,* 105–119.

MEICHENBAUM, D., & Goodman, J. (1971). Training impulsive children to talk to themselves: A means of developing self-control. *Journal of Abnormal Psychology, 77,* 116–126.

NIETUPSKI, J., Clancy, P., Wehrmacher, L., & Parmer, C. (1985). Effects of minimal versus lengthy delay between simulated and in vivo instruction on community performance. *Education and Training of the Mentally Retarded, 20,* 190–195.

PANCSOFAR, E., & Bates, P. (1985). The impact of the acquisition of successive exemplars on generalization. *Journal of the Association for Persons with Severe Handicaps, 10,* 3–11.

REPP, A. C. (1983). *Teaching the mentally retarded.* Englewood Cliffs, NJ: Prentice-Hall.

ROBERTS, R., Nelson, R., & Olson, T. (1987). Self-instruction: An analysis of the differential effects of instruction and reinforcement. *Journal of Applied Behavior Analysis, 20,* 235–242.

RUSCH, F. R., Martin, J. E., & White, D. M. (1985). Competitive employment: Teaching mentally retarded employees to maintain their work behavior. *Education and Training of the Mentally Retarded, 20,* 182–189.

RUSCH, F. R., Rose, T., & Greenwood C. R. (1988). *Introduction to behavior analysis in special education.* Englewood Cliffs, NJ: Prentice-Hall.

Rusch, F. R., McKee, M., Chadsey-Rusch, J., & Renzaglia, A. (1988). Teaching a student with severe handicaps to self-instruct: A brief report. *Education and Training in Mental Retardation, 23,* 51–58.

RUSCH, F. R., Menchetti, B. M., Crouch, K., Riva, M., Morgan, T., & Agran, M. (1984). Competitive employment: Assessing employee reactivity to naturalistic observation. *Applied Research in Mental Retardation, 5,* 339–351.

RUSCH, F. R., Morgan, T. K., Martin, J. E., Riva, M., & Agran, M. (1985). Competitive employment: Teaching mentally retarded employees self-instructional strategies. *Applied Research in Mental Retardation, 6,* 389–407.

SCHUTZ, R. P., Jostes, K. F., Rusch, F. R., & Lamson, D. S. (1980). Acquisition, transfer, and social validation of two vocational skills in a competitive employment setting. *Education and Training of the Mentally Retarded, 15,* 306–311.

SPRAGUE, J. R., & Horner, R. H. (1984). The effects of single instance, multiple instance, and general case training on generalized vending machine use by moderately and severely handicapped students. *Journal of Applied Behavior Analysis, 17,* 273–278.

STOKES, T., & Baer, D. (1977). An implicit technology of generalization. *Journal of Applied Behavior Analysis, 10,* 349–367.

STOKES, T., Baer, D., & Jackson, R. (1974). Programming the generalization of a greeting response in four retarded children. *Journal of Applied Behavior Analysis, 7,* 599–610.

STOREY, K., & Gaylord-Ross, R. (1987). Increasing positive social interactions by handicapped individuals during a recreational activity using a multicomponent treatment package. *Research in Developmental Disabilities, 8,* 627–649.

TEST, D. W., Grossi, T., & Keul, P. (1988). A functional analysis of the acquisition of janitorial skills in a competitive work setting. *Journal of the Association for Persons with Severe Handicaps, 13,* 1–7.

WACKER, D., & Berg, W. (1984). Evaluation of response outcome and response topography on generalization of skills. Division of Developmental Disabilities, The University of Iowa, Iowa City.

WEHMAN, P. (1990). School-to-work: Elements of successful programs. *Teaching Exceptional Children, 23,* 40–43.

WEHMAN, P., Hill, J. W., & Koehler, F. (1979). Helping severely handicapped persons enter competitive employment. *AAESPH Review, 4,* 274–290.

WELCH, J., Nietupski, J., & Hamre-Nietupski, S. (1985). Teaching public transportation problem solving skills to young adults with moderate handicaps. *Education and Training of the Mentally Retarded, 20,* 287–295.

WILSON, P. G., Rusch, F. R., & Lee, S. (1992). Strategies to increase exercise-report correspondence by boys with moderate mental retardation: Collateral changes in intention-exercise correspondence. *Journal of Applied Behavior Analysis, 25,* 681–690.

CHAPTER 24

Helping High-Risk Black College Students

Mark A. Jackson
Richard W. Malott

The Problem of Attrition for Minority Students

Student attrition in higher education is a serious problem for colleges and universities. For example, at Western Michigan University, 24% of the enrolled freshmen do not return for their sophomore year (Asher, 1987). National attrition statistics are comparable at 25% (Bureau of the Census, 1980). This problem is even more serious for many black students, especially given the options available to those who either do not or cannot complete the requirements for a college degree.[1] For example, Asher (1987) also reported that 36% of the regularly admitted black freshmen did not return their sophomore year. Attrition is an even greater factor at the high school level. When compared with white high school students, black high school students are decidedly less likely to graduate from high school, let alone enroll in college (McNett, 1983). Forty-three percent of black youth

age 18 and 19 have failed to graduate from high school, compared to only 25% of the white youth (Boyer 1981; College Entrance Examination Board, 1985).

The high school dropout rate for minority[2] students in many large urban cities is often higher; in New York City, recent statistics have reported an attrition rate among black males of almost 75%. In Detroit, where 88% of the public school population is black, the dropout rate is well over 50% (Riley, 1986).

A college degree can result in a significant improvement in income compared with a high school diploma or less. For example, the mean annual earnings for black males in the United States with four years of high school was $13,762, as compared to an average of $18,223 with four years of college (Bureau of the Census, 1980). (Four years in high school or college may not have resulted in a diploma for many individuals.)

---

[1]This chapter addresses the problems of those black university students who are at risk of not graduating or not graduating with adequate preparation. Certainly not all black students are at risk. But the proportion that is at risk is large enough to justify the great concern of the university and the black community.

[2]Although this review focuses primarily on black students, several statistics are not limited to blacks, but deal with all minorities. However, one can generally assume that the largest proportion of minority students is black.

The situation is equally distressing when viewing the employment rates for high school graduates. For example, only 59% of black (and other minority) high school graduates are employed, as compared to 90% of white high school graduates (Bureau of the Census, 1986). Furthermore, the career options are limited for a high school graduate without a college degree. Therefore, the global view may be described as this: blacks are less likely to graduate from high school; those who graduate from high school are less likely to go to college. Those who go to college are less likely to graduate from college. Those who graduate from college are perhaps less likely to have impressive grade point averages (GPAs). Those who graduate from college may also be less likely to have "impressive" majors (Williams, 1984). Therefore, they might be less likely to make substantial contributions to society as well as receive the benefits of society (earn money) in proportion to their human potential. If such a scenario is the case, their projected standard of living is discouraging when compared to their white counterpart.

The income and unemployment data mentioned above emphasize the importance of black students attending college for four years. The difference between the yearly incomes of $13,000 and $18,000 for blacks may more greatly affect the general standard of living than the difference between $18,000 and $26,000 for whites. In other words, the closer to the poverty line, the more crucial an extra thousand dollars is to meeting the necessities of life rather than the niceties.

Racism and job discrimination may contribute to the income discrepancies between equally educated blacks and whites. However, the collection of data on income discrepancies between these groups does not control for comparable major fields of study and GPAs between the two groups, or for comparable rates of graduation after completing four years of high school or college. For example, more white students have good academic accomplishments in high school; and perhaps because of their good academic accomplishments, they more often choose difficult fields of study that pay higher salaries (e.g., engineering, physics, and business). And black students most often choose lower-paying fields of study (e.g., educa-

tion, communications, and social work). Furthermore, a higher percentage of whites may actually graduate after four years of college. (Of course, the discrepancies between academic accomplishments, difficulty of major fields, and graduation rate after four years may result from earlier discrepancies in the opportunity to obtain elementary and secondary education of a comparable quality. The existence of these earlier discrepancies argues for an increased effort at the high school, grade school, and probably preschool level. But it does not argue against assuming the responsibility to help those current college students who are at risk.)

Possibly those black students who are at risk of not graduating have not been helped effectively to achieve a sufficient repertoire to adequately compete with other college students. In other words, they have been allowed to progress through college with inadequate educational repertoires (academic, motivational, time-management, etc.) and are now getting "shortchanged." Then, the issue of discrepant incomes should focus first, on increasing the number of blacks graduating with a college degree and second, on increasing the *value* of the college degree those students obtain.

In this chapter, we focus on efforts at the university to increase the number of blacks earning college degrees and to increase the value of those degrees; however, the roots of the problem go much deeper, and effective behavioral intervention must also occur at those levels. For example, black children are more likely to attend poorer grade schools and high schools with fewer resources. In addition, they are more likely to come from environments that cannot provide the entering repertoire and continuing support needed for academic success at any level.

The University's Perspective

As universities have increased their recruitment efforts to compete for a shrinking college-bound population, many have developed special programs to provide assistance to minority students who have a high risk of not graduating. Many academically at-risk minority students attend universities because of special admission policies that give the students a chance to attend the university though they do not meet the high school grade point average or entrance test requirements. Unfortunately, the level of supportive resources and attention focused on helping the academically at risk among the minority students decreases drastically soon after they enroll. Of the five largest universities in Michigan, for example, only one has a support program for minority students that extends beyond the first year ("Similar Programs," 1986). Because of shifts in both age and ethnic/racial demographics, colleges will soon face more minorities in the general population over the next few decades (McNett, 1983; Hodgekinson, 1987).

Hodgekinson discussed the fact that minority [public school] students in Michigan were 42% of all students in 1982 (15% in 1970). He suggested that this is primarily a function, *not* of increased black immigration or fertility, but of a sharply decreased white fertility rate in Michigan. This trend of increasing minority percentages of the population and decreasing white fertility rates exists nationwide. Hodgekinson further predicts that public postsecondary institutions will face shrinking enrollments as the college-age group declines. It seems plausible that universities might best prepare for this shift in demographics by further developing their technologies and programs to adequately serve the anticipated increase in minority students.

Reasons for Attrition

Many efforts by colleges to decrease student attrition focus on areas that, at best, are indirectly related to academic performance. Some university administrators prefer to discuss retention in a more global sense; for example, Turner (1980) noted that a wide range of factors (most of which involve student satisfaction) must be considered when attempting to identify the variables controlling minority college-student attrition. Universities spend hundreds of thousands of dollars providing educational, social, and recreational activities ranging from personal and career counseling to faculty-student interaction programs. Much of this money is directed toward

programs and activities that help students feel more comfortable while on the college campus—activities and programs such as student groups, dances, and concerts. In other words, these are efforts to keep the students from attending other schools, in contrast to more specific efforts designed to help them stay in school. It might be argued that these efforts help students be happier and more comfortable, with the assumption that comfortable, happy students might be more likely to stay in college; but these efforts are not geared toward improving academic performance. While student comfort and satisfaction should be issues of concern for administrators, this review will limit the discussion to retention activities and programs whose purpose is to directly affect students' academic performance. As a result, we consider programs addressing (1) inadequate academic preparation, (2) insufficient motivation, and (3) poor performance management.

Inadequate Academic Preparation

According to Asher (1987), a larger percentage of high-risk black students do not return after the freshman year as compared with regularly admitted white students (25.6% versus 19.5%).[3] So an important task is the remediation of basic academic skills. Many of these high-risk students have yet to receive the type of academic preparation necessary to effectively compete on the college level. Sometimes, students may even receive good grades in their high school courses and establish respectable GPAs. However, standardized test scores such as the ACT (American College Test)[4] and SAT (Standardized Achievement Test) often suggest that severe deficits exist in the

---

[3]Most "high-risk" students are admitted under the status of academic probation, dictating that if their cumulative grade point average remains below 2.0 after two consecutive semesters, they will be dismissed from the university. Regularly admitted students can be considered to have an additional semester inasmuch as they do not enter the university on academic probation.

[4]The ACT and SAT are designed to aid universities in evaluating the qualifications of applicants for admission. The tests in the ACT are achievement oriented, emphasizing the application of skills learned in the areas of English, mathematics, social studies, and natural science. A score is reported for each subtest, and the average of the four subtest scores is reported as a composite score.

college-bound minority population as compared to nonminority students (given similar GPAs, black students are still more likely to have lower ACT scores than white students). The College Entrance Examination Board (CEEB, 1985) reported that the average ACT composite score for high school students tested in the United States was 18 (range = 1–36). The average score for white students was 19, while the average score for black students was 13. This deficit is clearly shown by the disproportionate percentage of black high school students failing to score in the middle and upper ranges (American College Testing Service, 1985), while their self-reported GPAs are not that dissimilar. The top graph in Figure 24.1 shows that 70% of the black students in Michigan taking the ACT in 1985 scored in the lower range (1–15), as compared to only 24% of the white students. Furthermore, only 11% of the black students scored in the upper (21–36) range as compared to 46% of white students. This upper range includes the students who have the greatest chance of academic success at the university level. The percentage of blacks lacking entry-level skills may be even greater than these data suggest because these data include few of the large number of black students who do not graduate from high school. These data show that many black college students will need remedial help. (Incidentally, it is comforting to argue that tests like the ACT and SAT are biased in favor of white middle-income students and biased against black low-income students. The implications of that argument are that, if the tests were truly unbiased, they would show no differences between the two groups. However, the purpose of those tests is to predict success in college. And they do. If the tests were designed so that both groups of students achieved the same results, they would fail to predict college success, because the two groups do have different levels of success in college.)

The bottom graph in Figure 24.1 shows the absolute number of students in each category. Generally, universities actively seek students who fall in the 26 to 36 range, but almost no black students meet this criterion. Universities are willing to accept students who fall in the 21 to 25 range, but few black students even fall in this range. Nearly 1,000 black students fall in the undesirable range (16–20), and the great

majority (nearly 4,000) fall in the definitely unqualified range (1–15). This suggests that interuniversity competition over 500 qualified black students will contribute little to proportional representation of the black community on university campuses. The solution does not lie in enhanced recruitment.

Typically, many high-risk black students gain admission to college, do poorly in their courses, and subsequently withdraw voluntarily or are academically dismissed (Lanward & Hepworth, 1984). At Western Michigan University, for example, the Martin Luther King Program for high-risk minority freshmen experienced a 44.2% first-year attrition rate in the 1985–1986 academic year (in spite of the possibility of extended probation).

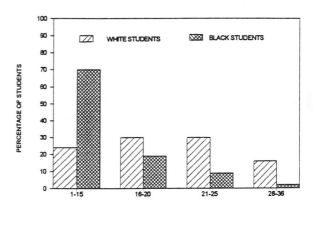

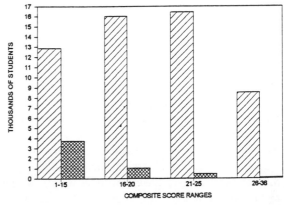

Figure 24.1. ACT composite scores for Michigan high school students in 1985.

Poor Motivation

Most colleges and universities attempt to address the issue of high-risk minority students by offering admission under academic probation. Through the probationary period, the university stipulates that the student has one or two semesters to establish a GPA meeting the minimum requirements or be dismissed from the university. Most educators would probably agree that such probationary programs are designed to affect motivational deficits as a possible source of low grades. Apparently, this type of ultimatum is designed, at least in part, to provide the incentive to produce the study behavior necessary to result in satisfactory academic accomplishments. Advocates of this policy seem to believe that at least one reason high-risk students do not do well is because they do not possess the motivation to do well. Yet, if students' test scores show they have academic deficits, and not necessarily just motivational deficits, a probationary contingency alone probably will not help them overcome their academic deficits.

Because these students often have high rates of absenteeism, low assignment completion, and low quality of assignments completed, administrators sometimes conclude that "these students really don't want to be in college." Further inquiry, however, might reveal many low-performing students who want to do well in their classes and eventually graduate from college, but they still have much difficulty and little success with attendance, quality of assignments, and completion of assignments. The reasons they are doing poorly are usually as much a mystery to them as to their instructors.

Motivation in this context refers to the extent to which a student values the outcome produced by a certain activity. We often assume that if people do not do what is needed to achieve a particular outcome, then they must not value that outcome. Often, this assumption is false. For example, people who try desperately to lose weight or stop smoking may value the outcomes of losing weight and quitting smoking. However, because of poor self-management skills, they may be unable to maintain those activities related to losing weight and smoking cessation. Similarly, high-risk students may want to do well in their classes; but due to poorly developed time management and self-management skills, they too may be unable to maintain their efforts toward improvement.

Poor Performance Management

Procrastination is the postponement of an activity. Further analysis of procrastination often reveals that the person engages in more reinforcing activities than the postponed activity. For example, the (often small) immediate rewards for studying must compete with more interesting and enjoyable (and less effortful) activities. The problem of "not getting important things done" therefore becomes an issue of ineffective time management and/or self-management. Unfortunately, it is difficult for students to get and use these self-management skills. In addition, due to limited probationary periods, academically at-risk students may have only two or three semesters to acquire this crucial repertoire and improve their performance and grades.

During the probationary period, students are not likely to contact a training program intensive enough to allow them to learn the skills they need in the time available. They may therefore give up and drop out of college, quoting popular sayings like "college just isn't for everybody." Or they may be academically dismissed by an administration that was "generous enough to offer them an opportunity to succeed in higher education—an opportunity the students did not seem to feel was sufficiently valuable to take advantage of," as allegedly shown by their frequent absences and low-quality work.

We in the education and helping professions act as if people are only worthy of our help when they continue to actively and *enthusiastically* participate in whatever we want them to do. If they do not, we may quickly turn to the safety of the notion that "you can't help people who won't help themselves." This provides a convenient excuse for those unwilling to be held accountable for the failures of those they are responsible for helping. Perhaps a more accurate message would be "those who most need our help often make it very inconvenient for us to help them; and so we are no longer inclined to offer our assistance."

In summary, this section has addressed university perspectives on three types of retention activities that directly affect high-risk college student performance. *Inadequate academic preparation* can only be dealt with directly with supportive or remedial skill-building activities. *Insufficient motivation* suggests many factors that may or may not be academically related. However, motivational retention efforts must be more specific to the academic tasks. They should not be a delayed, global motivational "threat" of a poor course grade or dismissal from the university after two semesters' poor performance. Finally, the problem of *poor performance management* can often be related to ineffective time-management and/or self-management skills. This calls for the teaching of specific organizational techniques designed to get students to do what they have to do when they must do it. It may also call for support systems to help them use those techniques.

Current Strategies Designed to Affect Attrition

As we have said, several distinct reasons may exist for high-risk student attrition. University officials have developed several different types of programs to improve the retention of the high-risk student. The following sections will review efforts that addressed the problem of attrition from the perspectives of (1) a more common traditional perspective, (2) the performance-management orientation, and (3) learning-to-learn strategies.

Traditional Support Programs

To counteract the lack of academic preparation, most colleges and universities offer remedial or skill-building courses in reading, writing, and arithmetic. But many black students graduate from high school with such severe deficits in these areas that they are often poorly prepared to perform adequately, sometimes even in the lower remedial courses (as will be discussed later). If universities are going to offer average black students a real opportunity to obtain a four-year college education, the universities must provide (and even require) the skill remediation to raise these students to the level of a regularly admitted college student.

On the other hand, Francisco (1983) alleged that colleges and universities were not nearly as serious as they claimed to be with respect to the issue of minority student attrition (or attrition in general). He questioned the effectiveness of long-standing support programs for black students: Although progress had been made in the numbers of minority students attending postsecondary institutions over the last 15 years, "the number of Black students receiving a 4-year degree or completing an undergraduate or graduate course of study has not increased proportionately" (p. 115). More specifically, Francisco pointed to the lack of published research in the area of special support programs. He found that although many colleges and universities currently boast of their support services to minority students, few had provided objective data on the most significant outcome: the number of students graduating from the institutions. Limited financial resources and limited or nonexistent program evaluations characterize university retention programs. He concluded that these shortcomings should stand as evidence of the relative unimportance or low priority of black student retention to the institutions.

Most university programs (not just retention programs), however, function with limited resources and scant program evaluation. Perhaps it is not cost efficient to run these (or perhaps, any) programs "as well as they should be run"; that is, by providing everything necessary for effective functioning. So evaluations of program effectiveness are scarce at the university level across-the-board. The benefits of program evaluation are long term, at best. So when faced with a limited budget, programs invest in areas with a more immediate demand (e.g., providing classes for the students who need to take them).

Offering special admission and some type of support program for high-risk black students appears to be a noble gesture; but if it were not a cost-effective gesture, colleges and universities would probably not continue it. In other words, colleges may benefit from the additional dollars brought in by the additional students, but are the students benefiting from the special admission? Support efforts that involve poor monitoring or evaluation mechanisms may not be benefiting these students and, quite possibly, may hinder them by setting them up to fail. In addition, Williams

(1984) agreed that "if . . . administrators are given the responsibilities and resources to reduce the attrition rate of minority students over a set epoch, . . . decision makers should replace such administrators if the job is not accomplished" (p. 1). But such decisions can only properly result from thorough, ongoing program evaluation.

In this light, it is imperative that those directing retention programs ensure that the variables measured are those that are most important to the students' academic status at the university (i.e., assignment completion, class attendance), as opposed to those unobservable and only indirectly related variables (e.g., student comfort or satisfaction). Although comfort and satisfaction are also of interest, they are generally difficult to measure reliably and do not determine how well a student does in course work.

In a review of black student retention, the Office of Civil Rights for the Department of Education admitted that "although there is a preponderance of literature addressing the issue of disproportionality, there is significantly less uniformity with respect to descriptions of underlying causes of the problem" (Research and Evaluation Associates, 1983, p. 3). Besides the level of academic preparation (called the "most central determinant" affecting retention of black students), other key factors identified in this review included financial aid, the need to get a job, poor health, personal problems, motivation, personal values, self-concept, and degree aspirations.

Understanding attrition is further complicated by the different methods of evaluation used by traditional studies. Although most of the traditional studies in the following section report positive and even statistically significant results, many unfortunately involved the use of unobservable or subjective measures to assess the effectiveness of their particular programs. The use of such measures increases the difficulty of forming accurate predictive relationships between existing conditions and subsequent outcomes.

What follows is the rationale for several traditional support programs: Walton (1979) proposed that the presence of a "strong support person" contributing to the development of the students' "academic readiness" could possibly increase the retention of minority students. Walton stated ". . . the person who func-

tions as a role model for the minority student is perhaps the single most important key to retention" (p. 124). High (1986) suggested that attrition of minority students admitted to college through special admissions programs might be decreased by offering a set of five workshops over the freshman year. Beck (1980) further proposed that the deficiencies most detrimental to the success of high-risk students were "poor self-concept and inadequate clarification of life goals" (p. 4). Dolyard and Martin (1973) made the assumption that "most students seeking admission to college have the basic ability to succeed academically, but have not learned to make adequate use of these abilities" (p. 57). Whyte (1978) explored the effects of three modes of counseling on the academic achievement and "internal/external locus of control" of high-risk college freshmen. Lanward and Hepworth (1984) solicited volunteers from high-risk freshmen to enroll in a two-credit support course.

These traditional programs have face validity, at least from a common-sense cognitive perspective. But generating program rationales with face validity is much easier than empirically showing their effectiveness. Some evaluation reports of these programs presented no actual data, some no statistical significance, and all seemed seriously flawed in one or more ways. Lack of random assignment of students to experimental and control programs was the most common flaw.[5] None showed convincing evidence of their effectiveness.

A common problem with retention programs is the premise that those who really want help will seek it out. Most of the retention efforts provided by colleges (except required prerequisite remedial courses) are voluntary. Therefore, a common shortcoming is that these programs do not require participation. If these services are not required, and the assumption is true that some type of self-management or motivational problem exists with high-risk black students, then it seems likely that many would find it just as effortful and less rewarding to participate in supportive activities as to participate in their regular course work.

---

[5]A more detailed critique of these and other empirical evaluations may be obtained from the authors.

Contributing to biased evaluations, a voluntary support/retention program can, by virtue of its self-selected clientele, only report on the performance of the participants. There is usually a sizable population of students who do not participate in the retention program, and their performance often goes unreported. If such programs do not keep track of the total number of students qualifying for supportive assistance (as compared with only those who take advantage of it), data obtained on those who participate could be misleading. Probably those students who volunteer differ from those who do not with respect to factors that are important to retention. Furthermore, the services of such retention programs then fail to reach a segment of the population they are designed to serve.

Performance-Management Programs

One area absent from most retention/support programs is the management of academic performance. Many high-risk students possess the academic skills necessary to succeed in college; however, they suffer academically because they do not devote the amount of time needed to study. Failure to devote sufficient study time could be due to procrastination or to not having enough time. For example, a student may work full-time, have conflicting home obligations, or be taking an unusually large course load. However, informal observation of low-performing students suggests that inadequate study time is seldom the problem. The problem is usually poor time management.

Hudesman, Avramides, & Loveday (1983) explored the effects of academic contracting and semi-structured counseling sessions on the GPAs of community college students in academic difficulty. The authors reported a statistically significant higher increase in the mean GPA for the 47 students in the experimental group (1.316 to 1.688) as compared to the 23 students in the control group (1.113 to 1.259). Ottens (1982) designed the Guaranteed Scheduling Technique to manage students' procrastination. Unfortunately, Ottens provided no results other than the report that students responded favorably to the system. Prather (1983) set up a "behaviorally-oriented study skills program" with 24 low-performing cadets (GPAs

below 2.0) at the US Air Force Academy. Prather reported a significantly higher increase in the mean GPA of the program participants as compared to control students (0.54 vs. 0.02). Pennypacker and Pennypacker (1978) set up a universitywide personalized system of instruction to decrease the dropout rate of underachieving college students. The dropout rate for students participating in the center's courses (many of whom were minority students and athletes) decreased from 40% to less than 6% in the first two years of the program. Unfortunately, these studies had methodological flaws similar to those reviewed earlier (e.g., insufficient detail for replication and lack of randomly assigned control groups).

We conducted a series of studies at the Center for Self-Management of Academic Performance in the Psychology Department at Western Michigan University. In the first study, Yancey (1983) evaluated the effectiveness of an academic-management course offered to undergraduate college students on academic probation. He hypothesized that academic performance declined when behavioral consequences for studying are too delayed, too small and cumulative, or too improbable to adequately and reliably support academic behavior. When in an environment with many other more reinforcing contingencies to compete with academics, students will often delay working on their academic tasks until shortly before the deadlines (e.g., cramming the night before a test). But high-risk students are among those who can least afford such a luxury. However, if these students reserved an appropriate amount of time for completion of their academic tasks, they might be likely to spend more time working on these assignments and by that raise their grades.

Therefore Yancey developed a system that would reliably and strategically deliver reinforcers for high levels of academic performance. Participants earned points in the academic-management course by completing various self-monitoring worksheets on a daily and weekly basis. The students met with a graduate assistant every other week to specify the academic tasks they needed to complete for the upcoming weeks. In addition, they were required to study at least five hours per week in the study center to complete their assignments. Yancey reported that the students participating in the self-management course outperformed the control group on all relevant measures, including a higher GPA (2.14 vs. 1.70), although the differences obtained were not significant at the 0.05 level. Unfortunately, no data were provided on the possible variations in the other courses taken by the students and their relative difficulty across and within the groups.

A follow-up study, conducted in the Center for Self Management by Jager (1984), required probationary students to graph their daily accomplishments and spend at least ten hours per week studying in a study center. When compared to the control group, students who participated in the academic management course obtained a significantly greater increase in their semester and cumulative GPAs. The academic-management group showed a significantly greater increase in their semester GPAs (0.66) than the control group (0.26; p < .05). However, Wittkopp's replication study (1984) failed to show a statistically significant difference.

As another follow-up, Lowe (1987) evaluated a sequence of similar programs with 40 high-risk black college freshmen on academic probation from the Martin Luther King Program (MLK). She also studied 88 upperclassmen on academic probation from the College of Arts and Sciences at Western Michigan University. Again, this study failed to show statistically significant effects on GPAs. Lowe noted considerable difficulty in sustaining the MLK students' participation in the course activities. She concluded that because of their sporadic attendance, these students did not have sufficient contact with the procedures to decide whether these procedures would have any effect on their academic performance.

Jackson (1990) also worked with high-risk, black MLK students at Western Michigan University to follow up Jager (1984), Wittkopp (1984), and Lowe (1987). Unfortunately, he also failed to show a statistically significant superiority of the study-management group.

Kelly and Stokes (1982) evaluated the effects of a student-teacher contracting procedure on the academic productivity of junior high and high school dropouts. Students received $2.35 for each hour they attended school and were productively engaged. A reversal experimental design showed that the students' productivity more than doubled during contracting conditions (range = 56–103 items answered correctly) as compared with their productivity during baseline (range = 0–36 correct items).

The poor results of these performance management studies with high-risk college students may suggest two possible new approaches: First, no one has reported the use of financial incentives contingent on effective hourly participation. Kelly and Stokes's (1982) success with junior high and high school students suggests that this approach may succeed at the university level.

Second, a more comprehensive support program may be needed. For example, a centralized effort must overcome the difficulties in obtaining timely and reliable data on the students' performances from the instructors. Furthermore, high-risk students would probably benefit from a program involving both study management and an academic-skill-strengthening component, with performance in each area centrally monitored. Typically, academic skills programs are neither regularly used nor contingently related to any type of effective behavioral consequence, because these measures are not monitored by any university office. Therefore, we cannot assume that our high-risk students participate in or benefit from the academic skills assistance offered.

For example, the Special Services Program for low-income and first-generation college students at Western Michigan University reported the following: Out of 247 high-risk students who qualified for free individual tutoring, study skills, and supplemental instruction, only 118 responded by participating in at least one program activity. In addition, out of the 32 high-risk black students who qualified for this program, only 7 attended the initial interview session; and only 9 met with tutors for their remedial writing courses (T. Staufer, personal communication, April 1987). When universities attempt to increase their minority enrollments, they attract students who may not have seriously considered college previously. Furthermore, these students may reject the notion that they need educational and motivational support. This, of course, is the population most in need of structure and guidance.

Learning-to-Learn Strategies

An important concern with high-risk students has been study skills and strategies. A student who did not know "how to study" would have problems in academics. In discussing the *learning-to-learn* approach to improved thinking, Heiman (1984) said that the key to improving the thinking and learning of unsuccessful students should involve the examination of successful students' learning strategies. Brethower (1982) said ". . . most of what students do when they set out to study is counterproductive. Much time goes into 'getting ready to study,' a set of activities very difficult to discriminate from 'procrastinating'" (p. 4). It seems plausible that students will use whatever study strategies they do not mind doing. High-risk students probably have poor study strategies. And they continue to use them either because they believe they can get satisfactory (although, marginal) results or because learning and carrying out new strategies would involve more effort than most high-risk students will normally invest. It is possible that it would be especially hard to convince high-risk college students that their current methods of study are inadequate for college, if those same methods produced good grades in high school. However, we might expect that a couple of semesters of poor college performance would lead them to the conclusion that a change in study methods would be worth considering. But, in any event, our experience is that convincing a student of the need for change is a disappointingly small step toward the student's making a substantive change in study behavior.

Heiman (1984) suggested that successful students commonly use the following learning techniques: (1) They ask questions of new materials, engaging in a covert dialogue with the author or lecturer, forming hypotheses, reading or listening for confirmation; (2) they identify the component parts of complex principles and ideas, breaking down major tasks into smaller units; (3) they devise informal feedback mechanisms to assess their own progress in learning; and (4) they focus on instructional objectives, identifying and directing their study to meet course objectives.

Heiman then translated these techniques into a set of exercises that failing students could apply directly to their academic work. They included general learn-

ing-skills exercises applicable to any curriculum, as well as subject-specific learning skills. Heiman reviewed the results of the uses of the learning-to-learn system at Boston College and Roxbury Community College. Both studies produced statistically superior results in favor of learning-to-learn, although the randomization of experimental and control subjects was not clear. Most high-risk students probably do not have effective learning strategies. So their academic performance might improve significantly if these deficiencies could be identified early and addressed reliably.

An Alternative to the Traditional Ineffective Retention Program: The Three-Contingency Model of Performance Management

We conclude with an analysis of the problems and solutions in terms of the three-contingency model of performance management (R. W. Malott, 1992b, in press) and the performance-management model of cultural change (M. E. Malott, in press).

We believe that both the main source of the problem and the source of the solutions to the problem of high-risk black students are to be found in the behavioral contingencies surrounding the students' academic work. Figure 24.2 shows this in a set of contingency diagrams (Malott, 1992b). A convenient unit of behavior for our analysis is *doing one study session* or, more succinctly, *studying*. Studying is imbedded in several behavioral contingencies in the student's natural environment. One contingency is the *slightly higher* mastery of the academic subject that will result from a single study session. But unfortunately, this contingency is usually ineffective in controlling study behavior, because the increment in level of mastery is too small to adequately reinforce the response unit of studying for one session. (This is so although the accumulated increments over four years of studying could become large enough to be a powerful reinforcer.)

Furthermore, this ineffective natural contingency battles two natural punishment contingencies (Figure 24.2): One is the punishing effects of the increment of

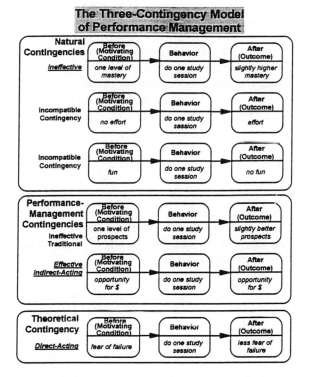

Figure 24.2. The three-contingency model of performance management applied to the study behavior of those black college students who are at high risk of academic failure.

psychological effort the student must exert while studying (e.g., reading, writing, thinking, and using the dictionary). The other is a penalty contingency involving the loss of reinforcers (chatting with friends and watching TV). However, even without these incompatible contingencies, the natural contingency involving a slight increment in academic mastery may still not be powerful enough to reinforce the necessary study behavior.

Because the increment in mastery is too small to reinforce studying, high-risk students need supplemental performance-management contingencies, if they are to do the required studying. A traditional, ineffective intervention essentially involves various modes of explaining to the students what wonderful reinforcers will be available because of four years of hard studying and explaining what horrible aversive conditions will occur, if the students do not study hard

for the next four years. Unfortunately, this intervention is no more valuable for high-risk students than the ineffective natural contingency. One session's studying still produces too small an improvement in the students' prospects to reinforce that studying (Figure 24.2). (Contrary to popular belief, the four-year delay in this outcome of studying may not be the culprit; the culprit may be the small though cumulative significance of the outcomes of each single instance of studying [Malott & Garcia, 1991] The student can procrastinate one more hour, or day, or week with no significant adverse effect; but a year's worth of such procrastinating can accumulate to one more statistic on student attrition.)

This traditional approach is based on the common error of failing to distinguish between commitment and adherence (Malott, 1992c). It is easy to get high-risk students to commit to a rigorous study schedule, and most interventions stop there. It is much harder to get those students to adhere to that schedule. This is where behaviorally based performance-management interventions are needed.

A plausible solution might be a variation on the Kelly and Stokes (1982) pay-for-performance contingency. A crucial and usually neglected feature of this contingency is that it involves deadlines (limited holds or limited opportunities to earn the reinforcers). Large tasks are divided into small, often hourly units. If the task is not completed on time, the student loses the opportunity to earn the pay for that hour's work. There is little room for procrastination. This is probably an effective, indirect-acting, rule-governed analog to an avoidance contingency; *doing one study session* avoids the loss of the opportunity to earn that session's pay (Figure 24.2).

The response unit might be sufficiently small that avoidance of loss of the pay would directly reinforce studying. But most often delivery of that pay would be too delayed (e.g., the end of the day) for this to be a direct-acting contingency of avoidance-based reinforcement. In other words, if the student did not know the rule describing the contingency, the contingency probably would not control studying.

How does knowing the rule influence control by this indirect-acting contingency? We must infer a theoretical contingency (Figure 24.2): Stating the deadline rule acts as an establishing operation to establish the stimuli arising from not studying as an aversive condition (e.g., *fear of failure*). This then allows for a direct-acting escape contingency where *doing one study session* decreases that aversive condition (e.g., produces *less fear of failure*).

Elements to Consider for the Academic Monetary-Incentive Program

Educators will likely meet resistance when discussing monetary incentives for academic performance. Opponents strongly believe students should not be paid to study. Rather, the students should recognize the obvious benefits of education and academic excellence and derive the motivation to do the necessary tasks. They may argue that high-achieving students self-motivate in this way (we doubt this), but this is not an option for low-achieving students.

With respect to the issue of paying students to study, we suggest that a monetary-incentive program would be essentially the same as an academic scholarship program. In fact, scholarships are widely praised as rewards or motivations for high levels of academic performance. Unfortunately, unless students *begin with* and consistently hold this high level of performance, they may quickly fall out of the range (generally 3.5 to 4.0 GPA) where scholarships are awarded.

We recommend the following features for an academic monetary-incentive program, especially for students who do not have a history of high academic achievement:

1. Assign a monetary point value to each important academic task (assignment completion, lecture notes and reading notes, attendance, quality, timeliness). A common mistake is to compensate students only for attendance, thereby increasing attendance but not affecting assignment completion.
2. Specify the value of the assignments (as a syllabus shows the point-value of assignments). Provide weekly feedback on the assignment completion (and earnings). Post graphs of performance.
3. Specify and follow all deadlines, assignment sizes, format requirements, and resources to be used. Assignments that fail to meet the predetermined standards should be penalized with deductions in points.

4. Deliver monetary incentives in a payroll format (weekly or biweekly). It is often necessary to have student employees to distribute the funds this frequently. This type of arrangement suits the needs of the program well.
5. Hire graduate or undergraduate assistants or enroll student helpers for practicum credit. They will serve as liaisons, monitor student client accomplishments, and keep the records of the program. Specify their duties and assign point-values that can be used toward a grade (or toward pay) as with the student clients in the program. Also graph and post the student staff performance.
6. Provide remediation for inadequate assignments, but reduce by about 10% the total points to be earned; this encourages an earnest effort on the student's initial trial.
7. If possible, select structured academic environments for the development of this program, like a summer program for transition from high school to college. It will be easier to sustain the cooperation of instructors in providing the necessary information about student academic performance. Otherwise, the staff may have to rely on the student clients to provide information on their own performance (self-reports).

The Performance-Management Model of Cultural Change

Unfortunately, we must have a major cultural change, if we are to reliably carry out that small pay-for-performance contingency for all the high-risk black students who need it, for all the courses where they will need it, for all the years they will need it. As difficult as it is to get high-risk students to do what needs to be done, it is equally difficult to get the people in the chain of support to do what needs to be done. We should apply the three-contingency model of performance management to the behavior of those people as well; however, for now we will only look at a potentially effective performance-management contingency for some key members of that chain of support (Figure 24.3).

Someone must supervise the student's pay-for-performance contingency. That might be a professor or a teaching assistant. But this supervisor will need an

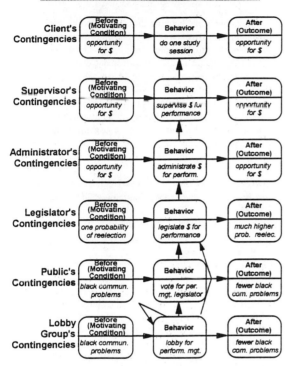

The Performance-Management Model of Cultural Change

Figure 24.3. The performance-management model of cultural change suggesting the support systems needed to improve the performance of those black college students who are at high risk of academic failure.

effective performance-management contingency to support the considerable amount of necessary behavior. Pay-for-performance might be optimal (Figure 24.3). This pay could be for setting up the performance-management contingency with high-risk black students (process) and for their achieving good academic performance (outcome). Our experience has been, that without some sort of added performance-management contingencies by whatever name, the faculty will not do what needs to be done—no matter how well intentioned and sympathetic they are—to make a difference. Adherence must follow commitment.

Similarly, university administrators must provide the funding and monitoring needed for this system. An effective performance-management contingency could involve making their personal bonuses and significant departmental, college, and university allocations contingent on their productive support of this program (Figure 24.3). Our experience in this area has been that administrative support of affirmative action programs comes and goes as financial contingencies imposed by state legislature come and go. Again, *adherence* to effective affirmative action is difficult to achieve even though a dedicated administration is strongly *committed* to it.

What contingencies seem to control the behavior of even the most idealistic legislators? Those contingencies involving the *probability of reelection* (Figure 24.3). And who controls these contingencies? The public and special-interest or lobby groups (major businesses and both religious and secular private and governmental public-interest groups). Most of these special-interest or lobby groups not only control the legislators' contingencies directly but also indirectly by influencing the voting of the public (Figure 24.3).

It is difficult to increase the probability of going to the voting center and voting (in some countries it is against the law not to vote). However, it is probably less difficult to influence the nature of the actual vote. Most attempts to influence the nature of the vote involve providing the voters with rules describing the consequences of one or another candidate being elected. These rules may then function as establishing and incentive operations (Malott, Whaley, & Malott, 1993).

Finally, the penultimate cultural-change buck stops with the leaders of the special-interest or lobby groups. Either they are sufficiently impressed with behavioral approaches to performance management and their community problems are sufficiently aversive that they will escape that aversiveness by *lobbying for performance management* or there is little hope that effective action will be taken to provide adequate college education for the black community.

In conclusion, first, as behavior analysts we must develop and demonstrate an effective, robust technology for working with high-risk black college students. Second, we must lobby the special-interest or lobby groups for that technology and those students.

References

AMERICAN College Testing Service. (1985). *American College Test.* McInshire, IL: American College Testing Service.

ASHER, J. (1987). First-year attrition rates for beginning freshmen. Office of Institutional Research, Western Michigan University, Kalamazoo.

BECK, M. (1980). Decreasing the risk of high-risk students. *Community and Junior College Journal, 31,* 4–6.

BOLYARD, C., & Martin, J. (1973). High-risk freshmen. *Measurement and Evaluation in Guidance, 6*(1), 57–58.

BOYER, E. L. (1981). High school/college partnerships that work. *Current Issues in Higher Education, 1,* 1–4.

BRETHOWER, D. M. (1982). Thinking about learning—teaching students to be scholars. *Journal of Learning Skills, 21,* 3–10.

BUREAU of the Census. (1980). *Earnings by occupation and education.* Subject Report No. PC80-2-8B. Washington, DC: Government Printing Office.

BUREAU of the Census. (1986). *Statistical abstract of the United States: 1986.* 106th ed. Washington, DC: Government Printing Office.

COLLEGE Entrance Examination Board. (1985). *Education and excellence: The educational status of black Americans.* New York: CEEB.

FRANCISCO, R. P. (1983). Special programs for black students in higher education: The need for reorganization during a conservative era. *Journal of Non-White Concerns, 11*(3), 114–121.

HEIMAN, M. (1984). Learning to learn: A behavioral approach to improving thinking. Presented at the Conference on Thinking at the Harvard Graduate School of Education, August, New Haven.

HIGH, J. (1986). A description of model minority student orientation and academic strategy sessions. Presented at the Second Annual Minority Retention Conference, November, Atlanta.

HODGEKINSON, H. (1987). *Michigan: The state and its educational system.* Washington, DC: Institute for Educational Leadership.

HUDESMAN, J., Avramides, B., & Loveday, C. (1983). The effects of academic contracting and semi-structured counseling sessions on GPA for students in academic difficulty. *Journal of College Student Personnel, 24*(3), 287–279.

JACKSON, M. A. (1990). A study-management course for high-risk, black college freshmen. Ph.D. dissertation, Western Michigan University, Kalamazoo.

JAGER, V. (1984). Using performance management to improve the academic success of high-risk college students. Master's thesis, Western Michigan University, Kalamazoo.

KELLY, M., & Stokes, T. (1982). Contingency contracting with disadvantaged youths: Improving classroom performance. *Journal of Applied Behavior Analysis, 82*(15), 447–454.

LANWARD, S., & Hepworth, D. (1984). Support-systems for high-risk college students: Findings and issues. *College and University, 59* (2), 119–128.

LOWE, R. (1987). The effects of a performance management course to improve the academic performance of probationary students and academically high risk minority students. Master's project, Western Michigan University, Kalamazoo.

MCNETT, I. (1983). *Demographic imperatives: Implications for educational policy.* Report to the Forum on "The Demographics of Changing Ethnic Populations and Their Implications for Elementary-Secondary and Postsecondary Educational Policy," Los Angeles.

MALOTT, M. E. (in press). Enforcement of seat belt laws: A behavioral systems analysis. In M. Sato, N. Sugiyama, & M. Boyle (Eds.) *Theoretical and applied issues in behavior analysis.* Tokyo: Niheisha.

MALOTT, R. W. (in press). The three-contingency model of performance management applied to organizational behavior management. In M. Sato, N. Sugiyama, & M. Boyle (Eds.) *Theoretical and applied issues in behavior analysis.* Tokyo: Niheisha.

MALOTT, R. W. (1992a). Notes from a radical behaviorist: Saving the world with contingency diagraming. *ABA Newsletter, 15* (1), 45.

MALOTT, R. W. (1992b). Notes from a radical behaviorist: The three-contingency model of performance management. *ABA Newsletter, 15*(2), 6.

MALOTT, R. W. (1992c). Notes from a radical behaviorist: Commitment vs. adherence and cognitivism vs. behaviorism. *ABA Newsletter, 15*(3), 19.

MALOTT, R. W., & Garcia, M. E. (1991). The role of private events in rule-governed behavior. In L. J. Hayes & P. Chase (Eds.), *Dialogues on verbal behavior* (pp. 237–254). Reno, NV: Context Press.

MALOTT, R. W., Whaley, D. L., & Malott, M. E. (1993). *Elementary principles of behavior* (2nd ed.). *Englewood Cliffs, NJ: Prentice-Hall.*

OTTENS, A. J. (1982). A guaranteed scheduling technique to manage students' procrastination. *College Student Journal, 16* (4), 371–376.

PENNYPACKER, H. S., & Pennypacker, J. B. (1978). A university-wide system of instruction: The personalized learning center. *Handbook of Behavior Analysis.* New York: Irvington Publishers.

PRATHER, D. (1983). A behaviorally oriented study-skills program. *Journal of Experimental Education, 51,* 131–133.

RESEARCH and Evaluation Associates, Inc. (1983). Black student retention—Review of the literature. A report developed for the Office of Civil Rights, U.S. Department of Education.

RILEY, N. (1986). Footnotes of a culture at risk. *The Crisis, 93*(3), 23–28.

SIMILAR programs offered at state schools. (1986). *Kalamazoo Gazette,* December 14, p. 1.

TURNER, R. (1980). Factors influencing the retention of minority students in the 1980's: Opinions and impressions. *Journal of Non-White Concerns,* July, 204–214.

WALTON, J. M. (1979). Retention, role-modeling, and academic readiness: A perspective on this ethnic minority student in higher education. *Personnel and Guidance Journal, 10,* 124–127.

WHYTE, C. B. (1978). Effective counseling methods for high-risk college freshmen. *Measurement and Evaluation in Guidance, 10,* 198–201.

WILLIAMS, C. (1984). Retention of black college students: Where should we go during the 80's? A paper presented at a forum at Massachusetts Institute of Technology, Cambridge.

WITTKOPP, C. (1984). The effects of the center for self-management of academic performance on high-risk students. Master's thesis, Western Michigan University, Kalamazoo.

YANCEY, B. D. (1983). The effects of behavior-management on probationary students' academic behavior. Master's thesis, Western Michigan University, Kalamazoo.

PART 6

Behavior Analysis in Education and Public Policy

Chapter 25
Behavior Analysis in Education, and Public
Policy: A Necessary Intersection
    Susan A. Fowler

CHAPTER 25

Behavior Analysis in Education and Public Policy: A Necessary Intersection

Susan A. Fowler

Perceptions control much of human behavior, and the perceptions people have about our profession—behavior analysis—and its intersection with education will affect our future role in education. The perceptions and misperceptions that others have about our language, values, interventions, outcomes, and intent shape the reception and adoption of our techniques in education and society in general. As Dorothy said, in the *Wizard of Oz*, "Toto, I have a feeling we're not in Kansas anymore."

In 1988 I repeated this phrase to myself the first few weeks that I joined the ranks of civil servants in my short-lived career at the US Department of Education in Washington, D.C. I continued to repeat it, as I was occasionally invited by my colleagues to comment on the ethics of behavioral interventions that were proposed in research applications addressing school-based interventions. Most of these interventions used some mild form of response deceleration techniques, like brief time-out and response cost, to reduce undesirable behaviors such as tantrums or peer aggression. Typically, they used these interventions in conjunction with techniques that increased desirable behaviors, such as task persistence or positive peer interaction.

In general, some staff were reacting to a perception that adults used external strategies to control and suppress child behavior and that behavior changes always depended on these externally administered controls. They wanted evidence that the students would eventually exercise choice and self-control to manage their own behavior. Sometimes we call this *maintenance of treatment gains* or *generalization*. They called it self-determination and autonomy.

It struck me that their negative responses to behavioral interventions in these grant applications were often a result of the author's failure to make the case that (1) the eventual changes would, or at least might, maintain without extensive external controls, given appropriate strategies for the withdrawal of external controls and the identification of natural communities of reinforcement that would support the behavior change; (2) the intervention would provide the child with alternative behaviors that would compete with the undesirable behaviors; and (3) the child could choose which behavior to use given that reinforcers for the new behavior outweighed those for the old behavior and that the response cost of emitting the new behavior was less than that for the old behavior.

The moral of this story follows. In the rejected proposals, the strategies for maintenance of behavior change and shift from external controls were rarely made explicit and interventions were judged to be coercive and controlling. Outcome words like *choice, self-determination*, and *self-management* were not emphasized.

How can we remedy the fact that the methods and outcomes of behavior analysis are often shortchanged or misinterpreted?

Considering Our Terminology: Does It Help or Hinder?

Each discipline has its own language and jargon—as Humpty Dumpty said in a rather scornful tone in Lewis Carroll's (1992) *Through the Looking Glass*, "When I use a word, it means just what I choose it to mean—neither more nor less." (p. 124). It's difficult to communicate with others who attribute meanings or definitions to terms in behavior analysis that do not reflect our definition. As Tom Lovitt noted in Chapter 22 of this text, language changes over time and the use and meanings of our vernacular change as well. That's why dictionaries are frequently updated. The term *negative reinforcement* is a clear example. How many practitioner-educators understand what we choose it to mean? Most educational practitioners tend to infer that it means to punish—that is, negative connotes bad. Can we afford to be purists and still keep it in our vocabulary? That's a different question from asking if we can still use the concept. (See Skiba & Deno, 1991, for a detailed discussion of this issue.)

I doubt that most behavior analysts operating in the world of education would deny that our words cause us difficulty today. In the recent special issue of the *Journal of Applied Behavior Analysis* (JABA) on the crisis in education, Axelrod (1992) noted:

the language and practices of applied behavior analysis run counter to the language and practices of American culture. The language of our culture is one of freedom, independence, and psychoanalysis. . . . Thus when we use terms like consequences, control, reinforcement, and punishment, we are seen as coercive and controlling. This image is further strengthened when behavior analysts use procedures termed time-out, over-correction and contingent shock. [p. 31] . . . The perception is not attenuated by the fact that behavior analytic principles were initially discovered in the laboratory, using pigeons and rats as subjects. [p. 32]

To bring the point home to education more sharply he then cited Bailey (1991) who stated that, "teachers . . . won't buy into a seemingly mechanistic and deterministic technology of behavior change. This is foreign to them and inconsistent with the rest of their training" (p. 446).

Given the culture of education today, how can we find a goodness of fit between our paradigm and language and that of the education majority? I suggest that we consider, as Sam Odom and Tom Haring pointed out in Chapter 8, the cultural context in which we live. Let's look at the language of the culture. Current key words include *cognition, critical thinking, self-reflection, motivation, mastery, empowerment*, and *child-centered philosophy*. Consistent with our national history, these terms promote individualism and achievement and focus on internal, sometimes difficult to define, constructs. They often deal with affective domains and emotions. Many of these terms suggest a process or an outcome, which I believe can be operationalized; they also reflect a philosophy, which we must address. One element of that philosophy is choice. Another element is self, whether self-concept, self-esteem, or self-control.

Building a Clear Vision of Our Goals for Education

We believe that we are effective when we use behavioral strategies to solve problems in the school and to create new opportunities for children to participate—otherwise we wouldn't continue to *choose* our methodology. What we share with many others in education is a desire for children to learn, to be excited about learning, and to use what they've learned to learn more. Ultimately, we also want them to graduate and to contribute productively to society.

I suggest that we focus on this goal—that we want children to learn, to be happy about learning, to feel good about learning. Furthermore, we want their learning to be generative, and we want their teachers and parents to support the process of learning and to appreciate their children's efforts and outcomes. Finally, as Bushell and Baer have stated in Chapter 1, we want principals and administrators to support and reward teachers; we want the public to support and reward effective schools. Perhaps if we focus on these outcomes, we can talk about behavior analysis as a means to that end—perhaps one of several *choices* or means, perhaps one of the most *cost-effective choices*. We can then promote the common vision of education and behavior analysis as a *choice* for enhancing educational outcomes. We can affirm with other educators that we agree that children should acquire critical thinking skills, be self-reflective, be empowered and enabled, be motivated, and experience mastery.

This common vision of outcomes unites us with other constituencies, whereas our choice of methods often separates us from them. As Bailey (1991) stated, "We need to promote the view that behavior technology gives children dignity and cultivates their freedom" (p. 447).

Encouraging Appropriate Choices by Publishing Professional Standards

The setting of professional standards is a rite of passage. Standards define practice; they set a criterion by which performance can be judged and compared. They attempt to clarify what is acceptable practice from unacceptable practice. Nearly all accepted professions have published standards—many have licensure or credentialling. Now we might argue (and probably have) whether behavior analysis is a set of practices—a technology—that cuts across professions or if its practice is a profession. If we want our technology to be embedded throughout education, I recommend that we push for standards of practice versus standards of the profession. In my area of early childhood, a very powerful set of standards has been developed by the National Association for the Educa-

tion of Young Children (NAEYC) to describe a set of practices, termed *developmentally appropriate*, for young children between infancy and age 8 (Bredekamp, 1987). NAEYC has also developed accreditation criteria and procedures for early childhood programs, which provide a vehicle for determining the way in which the standards of developmentally appropriate practice are implemented at the program level. They have influenced thousands of practitioners and programs since 1987 and many of their standards are now institutionalized in state and federal regulations and govern the funding and licensing of programs.

We need a manual of standards for behavior analysis in education that identifies the basic principles and asserts their value to education and the range and limits of their use in education, using the current rhetoric of education. The standards will provide guidance and a choice of appropriate versus inappropriate implementation for practitioners.

Just as the first edition of standards published by NAEYC was far from perfect, so ours may be flawed in places. Public discussion and debate will lead to revision, just as it is doing with NAEYC today. They are revising their standards, partly in response to the behavioral early childhood and special education community's concern over examples in their standards that misinterpret and bash behaviorism.

I would suggest a format of appropriate practice paired with descriptions of inappropriate practice. We are often maligned for poor implementation of our technology. How often do we hear about the teacher who misused time-out or who used a combination of positive procedures to prompt adaptive class behavior, before even considering time-out?

I recognize that behavior analysis is an individualized, contextual set of practices, but the practices are based on well-defined principles. We should articulate examples of their use and misuse in education and not wait for others to do it for us.

Promoting Consumer Input

Fantuzzo and Atkins (1992) summarized the current impact of behavior analysis in the special *JABA* issue

on the education crisis: "The fact is that many behavior change interventions have been developed to
improve the education process, but few have been
chosen" (p. 37). Our most critical stakeholders are
teachers and parents. Yet much of our history of
interventions may be characterized as unidirectional;
that is, to paraphrase Fantuzzo and Atkins, the classroom too often has been treated as an "applied lab" for
demonstrating our intervention. Once it's been
demonstrated, we leave. The implicit message has
been "I made it happen. Now you make it work"
(1992. pp. 38–39).

  We know we have to go beyond demonstrating
change to demonstrating maintenance and generalization—after all, Stokes and Baer's seminal paper was
published in 1977—but we often fail to make the
paradigmatic shift from psychology experiment to
educational intervention. We can never be satisfied
with short-term behavior change in a single individual. Much of the education world has shifted
from a unidirectional model of intervention to a
reciprocal model or multidimensional model involving systems change. We often neglect to extend our
effects to the level of systems change. Can we change
classrooms so that they support individual changes?
Systems change requires moving, at a minimum, to
classroom-based technology. The research that perhaps best exemplifies this is classwide peer tutoring
(CWPT), as described by Greenwood, Delquadri, and
Hall (1989).

  To promote systems change, we need to establish
partnerships with schools and teachers and move to a
consultation-based model instead of an expert model.
To do so, again as noted by Fantuzzo and Atkins
(1992) and elegantly analyzed by Peck, Killan, and
Baumgart (1989), we must "involve teachers in the
decision process at all levels by (a) selecting the goals
for intervention, (b) considering how learning principles can be used to develop a workable classroom
intervention, and (c) determining how the evaluation
will be conducted and which criteria will be used to
judge success" (Fantuzzo & Atkins, 1992, p. 40).

  By having teachers set the agenda, we are making
our efforts more relevant to educators; teachers will
quickly identify (in case they don't already know)
which (and how many simultaneous) methods are

workable. The peer-tutoring work by researchers
such as Greenwood, Delquadri, & Hall (1989); Miller,
Barbetta, and Heron (Chapter 20, in this text);
Maheady, Sacca, and Harper (1988); and their respective colleagues are fine examples of this approach.
Standards might help define personal and consultant
support for more intensive interventions.

Expanding Our Choices of Marketing and Dissemination Strategies

This subject was well articulated by Carl Binder in
Chapter 3, "Measurably Superior Instructional
Methods: Do We Need Sales and Marketing?" Many
of our procedures have been implemented in special
education classrooms or with the most difficult
clients. As Sam Deitz noted in Chapter 4, this can be
a two-edged sword. On the one hand, it shows that we
are effective with some tough cases; on the other hand,
it suggests that we are a remedy for only tough cases
and special education. We're not seen as pertaining
to the mainstream. I often hear from some of my
colleagues in the College of Education at the University of Illinois, "Behavior analysis or modification is
okay for people with disabilities, but keep it away
from our kids."

  Second, we've concentrated on reducing disruptive behavior and leaving pedagogy, curricular content, and format to teachers, assuming that they are
experts in that area. When the disruptive behavior is
reduced, teachers see no further need for behavior-
analytic procedures. We have failed to establish a
relationship between the teaching of academics and
behavior analysis.

  How do we correct this image problem? As many
others have suggested, we can't limit our work to our
professional conferences and journals. We have to
submit and publish more articles in regular education
journals. And we need to teach undergraduate classes
in education. Interestingly, in my department of special education, the one undergraduate class addressing
special education which is required of all education
majors, is packed with principles and application of
behavior analysis. For the past three years, the students have voted this class and its instructors as the

most outstanding class of all their undergraduate courses. Their comments usually include "I really learned strategies to improve my teaching." Publishing standards that can be widely described and disseminated may also help this marketing problem.

Building Coalitions with Other Constituency Groups

We can choose to stand alone or to build partnerships with other professional associations and organizations invested in education. To do so, we need to return to a shared vision of education and focus on the common goals.

As Carnine (1992), in *JABA*'s special issue on education, emphatically urged: "Target those responsible for providing tools to teachers. Some specific target organizations and groups include (a) state textbook adoption committees, (b) national curriculum organizations, (c) superintendents, (d) educational publishers, (e) teacher and administrator certification programs, and (f) educational researchers" (p. 16). I know from my experience in other organizations that it is the united voice of multiple professional organizations that has effected changes in public policy and produced legislation that supports what we consider to be best practice.

Our consumers belong to other organizations, such as the National Education Association, the American Educational Research Association, and the Council for Exceptional Children, to name a few. Most don't belong to the Association for Behavior Analysis (ABA); which, although growing, has only 2,000 members. If ABA is our professional organization, and we want behavior analysis to be recognized, then ABA needs to become visible and valuable to other organizations. How does that happen? Well, ABA is a membership organization, so it has to happen through us—each member has to be a link to other groups.

We need to encourage ABA (and Division 25 of the American Psychology Association) to maintain mailing lists of other relevant groups, so we can disseminate our policies and positions and establish a presence at relevant conferences.   In addition, in order to influence research priorities, regulations, and legislation, we need a strong link to legislative and executive branch activities.

Promoting Public Advocacy

If we want to ensure that behavior analysis remains a practice that can be applied in education, then we need to protect and promote its role in federal and state legislation and regulations and monitoring court cases. "The importance of having behavioral procedures adopted by policy makers cannot be overstated" (Stolz, 1981). Billions of dollars for human services are tied through federal and state regulations to specific models of service delivery. For instance, states are proposing and developing regulations regarding what constitutes positive behavioral interventions and appropriate behavioral assessments. The regulations are an attempt to minimize inappropriate practice. Regulations also serve a gatekeeping function—identifying who is deemed qualified or not to engage in certain practices— and sometimes dictate what practices are reimbursable through third-party insurance payments. Behavior analysts need to be involved in the formulation of such regulatory statements if we want our interests protected. In fact, we have seen the extraordinary effectiveness of parents and special education advocacy groups in the area of developmental disabilities that have lobbied successfully for governmental standards regarding various behaviorally based treatments. Why have these successes not permeated all of education?

As Stolz noted in 1981 in her article on dissemination, public policy is rarely based on outstanding evaluation data, rather it is responsive to a pressing social problem. So perceived solutions often emerge from sociopolitical movements, and not from research. Which brings us back to the place of our language in today's education world: Are we perceived as part of the current social movement in education? Will we be included if we are perceived to be too far to the left or right? As educators, what can we do to use the right words or "almost the right words" to maintain the integrity of our procedures and to ensure their generalized use and maintenance in society? I think we have to look carefully at our language. We need to develop a vision of how and in what ways we can meet the pressing needs of children, families, and teachers. We need standards to articulate those methods. And we need active participation and dialogue with our consumers, other constituency groups, and government agencies.

In 1963 Hubert Humphrey spoke about behavioral research:

> We need people to build bridges from research to community programs. The bridges must lead from scientific symposia to the halls of Congress, to federal office buildings, state legislatures, city halls, school boards, chambers of commerce, trade unions, service clubs, PTA's, churches and temples, neighborhoods and street corners, and every other arena of opinion and action. [p. 291]

Humphrey was right then and his words ring true today. I know from my brief stint in civil service how powerful and effective some professional organizations are. They effectively use negotiations and compromise to build consensus so they have a language accepted by a diverse constituency, a vision that is clearly articulated, and standards to measure the achievement of that vision. Then they're effective at marketing that vision and those standards, forging consumer support, building coalitions, and advocating at the community, state, and federal level for the adoption of their vision.

Creating that intersection between our language and vision of behavior analysis in education and public policy regarding education will be our challenge for now and well into the year 2000. We must be aggressive in finding common ground or we risk losing the opportunity for our effective technology to be an accepted set of practices in education.

References

AXELROD, S. (1992). Disseminating an effective educational technology. *Journal of Applied Behavior Analysis, 25*, 31–36.

BAILEY, J. (1991). Marketing behavior analysis requires different talk. *Journal of Applied Behavior Analysis, 24*, 445–448.

BREDEKAMP, S. (1987). *Developmentally appropriate practice in early childhood programs serving children birth through age 8.* Washington, DC: National Association for the Education of Young Children.

CARNINE, D. (1992). Expanding the notion of teacher's rights: Access to tools that work. *Journal of Applied Behavior Analysis, 25*, 13–19.

CARROLL, L. (1992). *Through the looking glass and what Alice found there.* New York: Dell.

FANTUZZO, J., & Atkins, M. (1992). Applied behavior analysis for educators: Teacher centered and classroom based. *Journal of Applied Behavior Analysis, 25*, 37–42.

GREENWOOD, C. R., Delquadri, J., & Hall, R. V. (1989). Longitudinal effects of classwide peer tutoring. *Journal of Educational Psychology, 81*, 371–383.

HUMPHREY, H. H. (1963). The behavioral sciences and survival. *American Psychologist, 18*, 290–294. cited in S. B. Stolz, (1981), Adoption of innovations from applied behavior research: "Does anybody care?" *Journal of Applied Behavior Analysis, 14*, 491–505.

MAHEADY, L. J., Sacca, M., & Harper, G. (1988). Classwide peer tutoring with mildly handicapped secondary students. *Exceptional Children, 55*(1), 52–59.

PECK, C. A., Killen, C. C., & Baumgart, D. (1989). Increasing implementation of special education instruction in mainstream preschools: Direct and generalized effects of nondirective consultation. *Journal of Applied Behavior Analysis, 22*, 197–210.

SKIBA, R. J., & Deno, S. L. (1991). Terminology and behavior reduction: The case against punishment. *Exceptional Children, 57*, 298–313.

STOKES, T. F., & Baer, D. M. (1977). An implicit technology of generalization. *Journal of Applied Behavior Analysis, 10*, 349–367.

STOLZ, S. B. (1981). Adoption of innovations from applied behavior research: "Does anybody care?" *Journal of Applied Behavior Analysis, 14*, 491–505.

NAME INDEX

Aase, J. M., 133
Abel, E. L., 132
Abramowitz, A. J., 143, 200
Adams, M. J., 116, 125, 150, 151, 152, 156, 157
Adler, J., 62
Ager, C., 335
Agran, M., 337
Ainsworth, M., 133
Albers, A., 163, 164, 165, 166
Aldridge, J., 266
Alessi, G., 181, 257
Alexander, K., 289
Alexander, R., 60
Algozzine, B., 44
Allen, K. E., 76
Allen, L. J., 143
Alley, G. R., 268
Allington, R. L., 156
Allis, S., 62
Alpert, C., 104, 106
Altman, I., 243
Amber, A., 225
Anderson, B. E., 118, 119, 120, 122
Anderson, L. M., 40
Andrews, J., 268, 270
Andronis, P. T., 14, 180, 182
Angelo, D. H., 105
Arbogast, A., B., 174
Archer, A., 174
Aristotle, 88
Arreaga-Mayer, C., 35, 215, 225, 226, 227, 231, 254, 289
Arrington, R. L., 38
Arthur, L., 61
Ascione, F. R., 143
Asher, J., 349, 351
Atkins, M., 35, 40, 369, 370
Atwater, J., 215, 226, 227, 243
Auerbach, I. T., 117
Ault, M. H., 226
Ault, M. J., 137, 143
Avramides, B., 356
Axelrod, S., 35, 38, 39, 40, 43, 44, 200, 324, 327, 328, 329, 368
Ayllon, T., 161
Azrin, N., 24

Babbitt, R. L., 162, 163, 166
Babcock, N. L., 109
Baca, L.M., 225, 226, 234
Baer, D. M., 5, 7, 8, 76, 77, 79, 80, 82, 91, 103, 107, 137, 138, 139, 226, 278, 292, 312, 316, 321, 322, 326, 327, 336, 337, 338, 340, 341, 342, 369, 370

Bagnato, S. J., 78
Bahls, V., 243, 244
Bailey, D. B., 78, 96
Bailey, J. S., 268, 324, 326, 368, 369
Baker, L., 303
Baker, R. G., 226
Bambara, L. M., 102, 105, 335
Bandura, A., 89
Barbetta, P. M., 187, 190, 266, 268, 269, 270, 271, 272, 273, 276, 278, 290, 296, 297, 311, 315, 370
Barford, D., 132
Barkely, R. A., 137, 141, 142
Barnet, S., 154
Barnhart, C., 119
Baroody, A. J., 205, 206
Barr, H. M., 133
Barrett, B., 58, 180, 183
Barrish, H. H., 277
Barton, E. J., 143
Bast, R. J., 132, 133
Bates, D. F., 192
Bates, P., 336, 340, 341
Bates, S., 192
Batstone, D., 315
Baumann, J. F., 154
Baumgart, D., 370
Bechner, R. M., 269
Beck, M., 355
Beck, R., 326
Becker, M., 133
Becker, W. C., 116, 126, 162, 163, 220
Beckett, J. A., 96
Beckwith, L., 133
Beirne-Smith, M., 304
Bejar, R., 133
Belfiore, P., 143
Bellamy, T., 335
Bennett, W. J., 58, 59
Benoit, D., 136
Benson, H. A., 346
Bereiter, C., 118, 119, 120
Beretz, M. M., 157
Berg, W. K., 335, 336, 338
Bergerud, D., 304
Bergson, H., 89
Berkeley, G., 89
Berlin, J. A., 17
Berliner, D. C., 8, 242, 283, 285, 286, 288, 290, 314
Berman, T. E., 136
Bernal, E. M., 226
Biddle, B. J., 226
Bigge, M. L., 59, 64, 65

Biglan, A., 81, 87, 92, 94, 96
Bijou, S. W., 91, 137, 138, 139, 226, 325
Billingsley, F. F., 137, 323
Binder, C. V., 16, 17, 21, 22, 25, 28, 29, 40, 44, 59, 174, 175, 177, 180, 183, 184, 190, 191, 192, 193, 370
Birnbaum, J., 63
Birnbrauer, J. S., 24
Bishop, K., 143
Bishop, N., 78
Blankenship, A. B., 22, 23
Bloom, B. S., 316
Bloomfield, L., 119
Bloomster, M., 124
Blurton-Jones, N. G., 89
Bolyard, C., 355
Bonfante, J., 62
Booth, C., 62
Bornstein, P., 326
Bosch, C., 295, 298, 314
Bott, L., 315
Bower, B., 150, 151, 157
Boyer, E. L., 349
Brazelton, T. B., 93
Bredekamp, S., 61, 68, 77, 80, 93, 369
Breen, G., 22, 23
Brethower, D. M., 358
Bricker, D. M., 78, 89, 95
Bridgman, R. G., 288
Briggs, E. D., 134
Brigham, T. A., 324
Brock, D., 62
Bronfenbrenner, U., 89, 226, 254
Bronicki, G. J. B., 346
Bronowski, J., 177
Brookfield-Norman, J., 76
Brophy, J. E, 162, 226, 283, 328
Browder, D. M., 276
Brown, J. C., 268, 278
Brown, J. S., 90, 92
Brown, L. T., 179
Brown, W., 266
Bruder, M. B., 95
Bruner, E., 25, 116, 119, 174, 202, 294
Bruner, J., 93
Bryant, D. M., 220
Bryant, N. D., 199
Buckholdt, D., 324
Buckley, C., 293
Budd, K. S., 266
Budzynski, T. H., 135
Bullara, D. T., 301

Burd, L., 132, 133
Burgess, D. M., 134, 142
Burke, P., 109
Burns, C., 26
Bursuck, W. D., 294
Bushell, Jr., D., 4, 6, 7, 283, 292, 312, 316, 369
Butterfield, E. C., 89
Byrne, B., 156

Calfee, R., 157
Campbell, A., 269, 270
Campion, N., 51
Cannon, G. S., 109
Cannon, S. J., 266, 268, 270
Carney, L. J., 133
Carnine, D., 16, 36, 37, 38, 40, 44, 89, 116, 121, 157, 158, 174, 188, 189, 190, 205, 262, 270, 283, 292, 294, 298, 302, 311, 314, 316, 324, 325, 371
Carrier, C. A. 303
Carroll, L., 368
Carta, J. J., 61, 78, 79, 215, 225, 226, 227, 237, 243, 254, 268, 269, 289
Carter, J., 304
Cashman, C. T., 296, 298, 302
Caswell, S. B., 101, 103
Catania, A. C., 261
Cavallaro, C. C., 105
Cavanaugh, R. A., 301, 302, 312
Cervantes, H. T., 225, 226, 234
Chadsey-Rusch, J., 335
Chall, J. S., 124, 125, 150
Chambliss, M. J., 157
Chandler, L., 95
Chaney, J. H., 150, 152
Charlop, M. H., 105, 143
Chase, P. M., 169
Chasnoff, I. J., 132, 133
Chermak, G. D., 133
Chess, S., 138, 139
Chiang, B., 266, 268
Christensen, S. L., 283
Chubb, J. E., 15
Ciscar, C. L., 143
Clark, D. C., 179
Clark, L. H., 59, 63, 66
Clarren, S. K., 133
Clement, P. W., 270, 278
Cobb, P., 154
Cochran, L. L., 272
Cole, K., 101, 103, 105, 106
Collins, A., 90, 92
Connell, P. J., 106
Cook, S. A., 268
Cooke, N. L., 266, 267, 269, 270, 272, 273, 293, 299
Coon, M. E., 335, 336
Cooper, D. H., 215

Cooper, J. O., 269, 301, 316
Cortes, L. A., 226
Courson, F. H., 189, 298, 300, 308, 309, 310, 312
Cowardin, J. H., 293
Cripe, J. J., 78, 89, 95
Cross, C. T., 62, 63, 65, 70
Crowell, F., 109
Cuban, L., 43,
Culbertson, S. A., 177
Cullinan, B., 152
Cunningham, P., 153, 157
Custer, J. D., 266

Dale, P., 101, 103, 105, 106
Darch, C. B., 266, 268
Darling-Hammond, L., 58
Darst, P. W., 244
Dasta, K., 266, 269, 270
DaVerne, K. C., 78
Davies, B., 103, 104, 143
Davis, C. A., 335
Davis, K. L. S., 174
Dawe, H. A., 242
Day, H. M., 335
DeAvila, E. A., 230
DeBaryshe, B. D., 222
Deitz, S. M., 34, 36, 38, 162, 370
Deloughry, T., 62
Delprato, D. J., 242, 243
Delquadri, J. C., 45, 161, 162, 165, 213, 214, 215, 218, 222, 226, 254, 266, 267, 271, 277, 285, 286, 289, 290, 292, 315, 370
Democritus, 88, 89
Dempsey, M., 267
DeNapoli, J., 189
Deno, S., 157, 368
D'Entremont, D. M., 133
Descartes, R., 88, 89
DeStefano, D. M., 95
DeVries, R., 89, 93
Dew, N., 225
Dewey, J., 57, 59, 60, 65, 66, 89, 285
Diamond, D., 166
Dickerson, M. G., 323
Dickie, R. F., 244
Dickinson, A., 60, 66
Dickinson, E., 154
Dillon, W. R., 241
Dimino, J., 44
Dixon, R., 205
Dixon, S. D., 133, 134
Dodd, C. J., 134
Dolch, E, 124
Doleys, D. M., 200
Donahoe, J. W., 40, 185
Donelson, F., 301, 302, 312
Dorsey, D., 283
Drabman, R. S., 323
Drass, S. D., 266
Drevno, G. E., 290

Dubey, D. R., 323
Duguid, P., 90, 92
Duncan, S. E., 230
Dunkin, M. J., 226
Dunlap, G., 142, 208, 285, 335
Dunlap, L. K., 208
Dunst, C. J., 96
Durand, D. J., 133
Durkin, D., 116, 117, 118, 119, 120, 125, 156
Dyer, K., 285
Dyrenforth, S. R., 323

Eachus, H. T., 293, 323
Edge, D., 269
Edmonds, R., 161
Egel, A. L., 270
Ehly, S. W., 266
Eiserman, W. D., 270
Eisler, R. M., 342
Eisner, E. W., 242, 329
Elkind, D., 68, 77
Elksnin, L. K., 270
Elksnin, N., 270
Elliot, D. J., 133
Ellson, D., 57, 58, 61, 68
Ellul, J., 252
Elmore, R. F., 47, 55
Emrick, J., 109
Englemann, S., 16, 25, 34, 38, 44, 89, 116, 118, 119, 120, 121, 174, 182, 184, 188, 202, 262, 294, 311, 312, 325
Erikson, E., 57
Eshelman, J., 61
Euripides, 154
Evans, J., 109, 188

Fantuzzo, J., 35, 40, 270, 278, 369, 370
Farran, D. C., 75
Fawcett, S., 107
Ferrell, D. R., 79
Ferritor, D. E., 288, 324
Ferster, C. B., 177, 182
Fey, M. E., 102, 103
File, N., 109
Finn, C. E., 15, 242, 329
Finney, R., 35
Firestone, W. A., 242
Fischer, C. W., 286, 288, 290
Flanagan, D., 149
Fleury, P., 133
Flynn, T. H., 335, 336, 338
Fodor-Davis, J., 337
Fogel, A., 92
Folio, M. R., 266, 268
Ford, D. F., 268
Foster, H., 191
Fowler, S. A., 7
Fowler, W. A., 118, 119, 120
Fox, A. A., 133

Fox, J. J., 91
Foxx, R., 24, 323
Fradd, S., 225
Franca, V. M, 266
Francisco, R. P., 354
Freebody, P. 156
Freidling, C., 143
Frick, T. W., 243
Friedman, K., 103, 106
Friedman, P., 103, 106
Friesen, D. T., 117
Fuchs, L., 157
Fulrother, R., 133

Gage, N. L., 242
Gagne, R. M., 178, 179, 191
Galileo, G., 89
Garber, H., 220
Garcia, E. E., 234
Garcia, G. E., 156
Garcia, M. E., 359
Gardner, R. III, 214, 292, 300, 301, 302, 313, 314, 315
Garrison, J. W., 242
Gartner, A., 44
Garton, K. L., 324
Gast, D. L., 79
Gates, A. I., 120, 156
Gaylord-Ross, R., 335
Gazdag, G., 105
Geller, S., 324, 329
Gerber, M. M., 269
Gersten, R., 44, 119, 122, 125, 205, 283
Gesell, A., 89
Gewirtz, J. L., 91
Gilbert, M. B., 16
Gilbert, T. A., 16
Gilbert, T. F., 188
Girolametto, L., 102, 103, 105
Glaser, R., 188
Glasgow, R. E., 81, 92
Gleason, M., 174
Glenn, S. S., 81, 92, 96
Gobbi, L., 105
Goecke, T., 133
Goetz, E. M., 76, 117
Goldiamond, I., 180, 182
Goldstein, H., 79, 103, 104, 105, 110, 142, 143
Goldstein, S. R., 269
Good, T. L., 155, 226, 283
Goodlad, J. L., 8, 329
Goodman, J., 337, 342
Goodman, K., 150, 153, 154, 157
Gottman, J. M., 242, 247
Gould, S. J., 14
Graham, S., 337
Graubard, P. S., 324
Gray, S., 115, 121, 125
Green, T. H., 89

Greenfield, S. D., 267, 278
Greenwood, C. R., 35, 45, 161, 162, 165, 213, 214, 215, 218, 219, 221, 222, 226, 227, 237, 243, 254, 266, 267, 268, 269, 278, 285, 286, 288, 289, 290, 292, 315, 324, 335, 370
Greer, R. D., 35, 162, 163, 164, 165, 166, 167, 169, 170, 214, 266, 268, 269, 284
Griesbach, L. S., 131, 132, 133, 136
Griffin, G., 58
Griffith, D. R., 132, 134, 135, 137
Griffith, P. L., 156
Groom, J. M., 266
Gross, A., 290
Grossen, B., 174
Grossi, T. A., 301, 302, 335
Grossman, M. A., 293
Grouws, D. A., 155
Guess, D., 138, 139, 140, 346
Guevremont, D. C., 337
Guralnick, M. J., 78, 266
Gurney, D., 143
Guthrie, J. T., 288

Haddox, P., 25, 182, 202
Haisley, F. B., 268, 270
Hakuta, K., 225
Hales, L. W., 299
Hall, R. V., 43, 44, 45, 55, 161, 162, 165, 213, 214, 215, 218, 222, 226, 254, 268, 269, 285, 286, 288, 289, 290, 292, 315, 321, 322, 370
Hall, S. W., 292
Halle, J. W., 103, 105, 109, 294
Hallman, C. L., 225
Hamblin, R. L., 324
Hamilton, S. L., 308
Hamlet, C. C., 200
Hamre-Nietupski, S., 335
Hanner, S., 174, 182
Hanson, M. J., 95
Hardman, M., 95
Haring, N. G., 142, 191, 335
Haring, T. G., 87, 89, 90, 105, 266, 341, 368
Harper, G., 44, 267, 268, 270, 276, 278, 370
Harris, A. M., 117
Harris, J., 266, 285
Harris, K. C., 269
Harris, K. R., 288, 337
Harris, M., 12, 13, 81, 92, 96
Harris, S. L., 323
Harris, V. M., 324
Hart, B., 76, 89, 95, 101, 103, 105, 215, 216, 217, 222, 321, 322
Hartley, J., 304
Haskins, R., 115

Hassett, M.E., 271
Haughton, E. C., 16, 17, 180, 183, 186, 191, 192, 193
Hawking, S. W., 158
Hawkins, A., 243, 244, 245, 252
Hawkins, R. P., 80, 169
Hayes, L. J., 87, 90, 92
Hayes, S. C., 87, 90, 92, 94
Hecimovic, A., 276
Heckler, J. B., 16
Hegel, G. W. F., 64, 88, 89
Heiman, M., 358
Heiman, S. E., 21
Henry, M., 299
Hepworth, D., 352, 355
Heron, T. E., 187, 190, 266, 267, 269, 270, 271, 272, 273, 276, 278, 290, 293, 296, 297, 311, 315, 370
Hersen, M., 342
Hertz, V., 143
Heward, W. L., 163, 185, 189, 190, 214, 266, 267, 269, 270, 272, 273, 276, 284, 287, 290, 292, 293, 296, 297, 298, 300, 301, 302, 304, 305, 311, 312, 315, 316, 321, 323, 336
High, J., 355
Hill, J. W., 335, 336
Hineline, P. N., 38
Hingson, R., 131
Hoagland, C. A., 299, 300, 303
Hobbes, T., 89
Hodgekinson, H., 351
Hodgkinson, H. L., 44, 149, 150, 151, 158
Hofmeister, A., 311
Holmes, S. A., 29
Homme, L. E., 188
Hopkins, B. L., 7, 324
Horner, R. H., 89, 142, 143, 335, 336, 338, 340
Horton, S., 304
Hou, L. S., 231
Houghton, J., 346
Howard, J., 133
Howard, V. F., 134, 136
Howe, K. R., 242
Hoymer, H. E., 133
Huberman, M., 242
Hubler, E., 154
Hudesman, J., 356
Hughes, C., 336, 337, 338, 340, 341, 342, 343, 346
Hugo, K., 343, 338
Hume, D., 89
Hummel, J. H., 36
Humphrey, H., 372
Hundert, J., 315
Hunnicutt, K. L., 301
Hunt, J. M., 75

Hunt, M. P., 59, 64, 65
Hunt, P., 105
Hunter, J., 335
Hunter, M., 59
Hupp, S. C., 341
Hursh, D., 260, 261

Idol, L., 109
Ingham, M., 162, 163, 164, 165, 166
Inman, D., 109
Iwata, B. A., 143

Jackson, M. A., 293, 357
Jackson, P. J., 174, 176, 179
Jackson, P. W., 241
Jackson, R., 341
Jager, V., 357
James, W., 65, 88, 89, 90
Janney, R., 109
Jastak, J. F., 119
Jastak, S., 119
Jenkins, J. R., 266
Jenkins, L. M., 266
Jenson, W. R., 51
Jimenez, R. T., 156
Johnson, C. M., 221
Johnson, D. M., 179
Johnson, G., 174
Johnson, J. E., 61
Johnson, K. M., 61
Johnson, K. R., 16, 17, 22, 23, 25,
    28, 29, 69, 169, 173, 174, 175,
    176, 177, 180, 181, 182, 183,
    185, 187, 188, 189, 191, 192
Johnson, L., 175
Johnson, L. K., 312
Johnson, M., 133, 268, 324
Johnston, J. M., 13, 286, 289
Johnston, M. B., 208
Jones, D., 336, 338, 340
Jones, K. L., 132, 133
Jones, R. L., 266
Jostes, K. F., 336
Joyce, J., 154
Joynes, Y., 293
Juel, C., 156

Kaczmarek, L., 110, 111
Kafka, F., 154
Kaiser, A. P., 76, 95, 103, 104, 106
Kameenui, E. J., 116, 149, 150, 154,
    156, 157, 158, 205
Kamps, D., 215, 237, 267, 270
Kane, B. J., 268
Kantor, J., 91, 242, 260
Karlan, G. R., 142
Karnes, M. B., 75, 78
Karweit, N., 115
Kaskowitz, D., 285
Kauffman, J. M., 269
Kaye, K., 131

Kazdin, A. E., 244, 277
Keetz, A., 95, 103
Keller, F. S., 16, 34, 37, 188, 189
Kelly, M., 357, 359
Kelly, T. M., 166
Kennedy, C. H., 87, 89, 90
Kennedy, J. F., 70, 181
Kennedy, T., 175
Kerr, M. M., 45, 46
Keul, P., 335
Kevo, H., 174
Kiewra, K. A., 304
Killan, C. C., 370
Kinder, B. D., 44, 188, 189, 190
King, E. M., 117
Kishi, G., 346
Klaus, R., 115, 121
Klein, N., 109
Kline, C. S., 304, 307
Kling, J. W., 178
Knudson, G. P., 118, 120
Koegel, R. L., 142, 285, 335
Koehler, F., 335, 336
Koenig, C. H., 192
Kohlberg, L., 57, 89, 93
Kohler, F. W., 43, 44, 55, 267
Kolata, G., 327
Kouri, T. A., 101, 103
Koury, M., 276
Kramer, R., 57
Kramlinger, T., 23
Krantz, P. J., 143
Kraut, R. E., 68
Kropenske, V., 133
Krouse, J., 269
Kuerschner, S., 200
Kulp, S., 229
Kumar, A., 241
Kurtz, P. F., 143
Kusserow, R. P., 132

Lachman, J. L., 89
Lachman, R., 89
LaDue, R. A., 133
Laitinen, R. E., 341
Lamb, M. A., 47
Lamm, N., 163, 164, 166
Lamson, D. S., 336
Lanward, S., 352, 355
Larson, S. C., 266
Layng, T. V., 16, 17, 22, 23, 25, 28,
    29, 69, 173, 174, 175, 176, 177,
    179, 180, 182, 183, 185, 189,
    191, 192
Lazarus, B. D., 309
Lazerson, D. B., 266, 268
LeBlanc, J. M., 102
Lederman, D., 62
Lee, B. L., 132
Lee, S., 335
Leeper, H. A., 133
LeLaurin, K., 76

Lenox, S. L. R., 299, 300
Leonard, B. R., 237
Leonard, L. B., 103
Lerner, R. M., 92
Lewis, H., 109
Lewis, M., 103, 105
Liberman, A., 150, 153, 154, 157
Liberman, I., 150, 153, 154, 157
Lickson, J., 269, 270
Lieberman, A., 109
Lightfoot, S. L., 329
Lignugaris-Kraft, B., 35
Lilly, M. S., 44
Lindsley, O. R., 16, 17, 35, 37, 178,
    190, 192, 209, 321, 324, 325
Lingenfelter, T. M., 292, 295, 296,
    302
Linhardt, R. F., 284
Lipsky, D. K., 44
Liston, D., 47
Litlow, L., 277
Lochhead, C., 28
Locke, J., 88, 89
Locurto, C., 115
Lodhi, S., 163, 164, 166, 214
Lombardi, B. R., 303
Loveday, C., 356
Lovitt, T. C., 287, 304, 315, 368
Lowe, R., 357
Lubinski, C., 134
Lubinski, D., 92
Lucretius, 89
Luke, B., 132, 133
Lynch, E. W., 95, 96
Lyon, S. L., 292, 294, 302

Mace, C., 200
Mace, F. C., 138, 143
MacDonald, J. D., 105
MacGintie, W. H., 120
MacGregor, S. N., 133
MacKay, H. A., 143
Madden, N. A., 127, 266
Madden, T. J., 241
Madsen, C. H., 162
Mager, R. F., 3, 9
Maggs, A., 205
Maheady, L., 44, 225, 226, 266, 267,
    268, 270, 276, 278, 324, 370
Maher, C. A., 268, 270
Mahoney, G., 77, 103, 105
Mahoney, M., 25
Majewski, F., 133
Malaby, J., 288, 292
Malagodi, E. F., 81
Mallette, B., 44, 267
Malott, M. E., 358, 361
Malott, R. W., 22, 26, 141, 358, 359,
    361
Mancini, V. H., 244
Mancuso, E., 269
Marchand-Martella, N. E., 35

Marholin, II, D., 288
Markle, S. M., 179, 188, 189, 191
Marr, M. J., 87, 90
Marshall, A. E., 293
Marshall, A. M., 103, 109
Marshall, W. L., 323
Martin, J., 355
Martin, J. E., 335, 336, 337
Martindale, A., 229
Martsolf, J. T., 132, 133
Martuzo, V., 288
Maslow, A. H., 57
Mason, J. M., 116, 117
Mather, N., 150
Matthews, J., 28
Mayer, G. R., 137, 138, 180
McCandless, B. R., 268, 278
McClannahan, L.E., 143
McClean, M. E., 78
McClintock, B., 327
McConnell, S. R., 76, 79
McCorkle, N., 162, 163, 165, 166,
167, 169, 214
McCormick, L. 140
McCormick, S., 293
McDonald, R. S., 89, 143, 336, 338
McDonnell, A., 95
McEvoy, M. A., 76, 78
McGee, G. G., 105, 143
McKeller, N. A., 266
McKenzie, G. R., 299
McKenzie, M. L., 266
McKinny, P., 189
McLaughlin, M., 109
McLaughlin, T. F., 134, 144, 288,
292
McLean, M. E., 95, 96, 105
McNeil, M. E., 267, 278
McNett, I., 349, 351
McQuarter, R. J., 103
McReynolds W. T., 277
Meichenbaum, D., 337, 342
Mercer, A. R., 315
Mercer, C. D., 315
Merkel, G., 154
Mervis, C. B., 341
Meyer, L. 109
Michael, J., 91, 260
Midgley, B. D., 242
Miller, A. D., 187, 190, 267, 273,
292, 311, 315, 370
Miller, G. A., 132, 134, 204
Miller, L., 101, 109
Miller, M., 266
Miller, P., 185
Miller, P. D., 157
Miller, P. N., 342
Miller, R. B., 21
Mills, P., 106
Milstein, J. P., 143
Moe, T. M., 15
Moellenberg, W. P., 40

Moore, S., 337
Morgan, D., 292, 295, 298, 302, 314
Morphett, M., 116
Morris, E. K., 87, 90, 91, 94, 242,
259, 260
Morrison, C., 117
Mulligan, M., 95
Mullis, I., 185
Mustaine, J., 301

Narayan, J. S., 189, 214, 286, 298,
300, 302
Neef, N. A., 105, 270
Neisworth, J. T., 78, 94
Nelson, R., 337
Nietupski, J., 101, 106, 335, 336
Nino-Murcia, G., 136
Norman, A., 266, 268
Norton, L. S., 304

Ockwood, L., 101, 106
Odom, S. L., 75, 76, 78, 79, 80, 94,
95, 96, 109, 143, 368
O'Leary, S. G., 143, 200, 323
Oliver, C., 105
Olney, C. W., 25
Olson, M. W., 156
Olson, T., 337
Omness, C., 300
O'Neill, R. E., 135
Orlansky, M. D., 287
Ortiz, A. A., 225
Osguthorpe, R. T., 266, 268, 270
Osnes, P., 78, 337
Osterloh, J. D., 132
Ostrosky, M., 94
O'Sullivan. P. J., 156
Overholser, J. C., 132, 133

Pados, G. E., 304, 305, 307, 309
Palmer, D. C., 40, 185
Pancsofar, E., 336, 340, 341
Parson, L. R., 266, 269
Parsonson, B. S., 5
Patriarca, L., 47
Patterson, G. R., 222
Pearson, P. D., 156
Peck, C. A., 370
Peltzman, S., 12
Pennypacker, H. S., 8, 13, 15, 16,
17, 28, 90, 173, 192, 286, 289,
356
Pennypacker, J. B., 356
Pepper, S., 81, 87, 88, 89, 90, 91
Perfetti, C., 153
Peters, M. T., 273
Peterson, R. F., 226
Peterson, S., 109
Pfiffner, L. J., 200
Phillips, B., 133
Phillipson, R., 133
Piaget, J., 57, 59, 89

Pigott, H. E., 270, 278
Plato, 88
Polirstok, S. R., 266, 268, 270
Polloway, E. A., 131, 132, 133, 136
Popham, W. J., 59
Porter, A. C., 157
Posner, R. A., 12
Powell, A., 77, 103, 105
Powell, J., 229
Prather, D., 356
Pratton, J., 299
Prawat, R. S., 157
Prayzer, R., 315
Proper, E. C., 60
Pryor, K., 26
Pryzwansky, W. B., 109
Pumroy, D. K., 277

Quayle, D., 175

Rackham, N., 27
Rager, A., 254
Ramey, C. T., 220
Ramirez, B. A., 225
Ramsey, B., 115, 121
Ramsey, E., 222
Randels, S. P., 133
Ravitch, D., 60, 63, 64
Ray, R. D., 242, 243
Reavis, H. K., 51
Reese, E. P., 174
Reese, H.W., 87, 90
Regis, E., 158
Reis, K., 109
Reisberg, L., 266
Reitz, A. L., 45, 46
Repp, A. C., 335
Resnick, D. P., 115
Resnick, L., 115, 184, 185
Reynolds, A. J., 215
Reynolds, M. C., 63
Rhode, G., 51
Riggs, L. A., 178
Riley, N., 349
Risley, T. R., 76, 79, 103, 105, 215,
216, 217, 222, 226, 321, 322,
326, 327
Robbins, J. K., 174, 179
Roberts, M. D., 161
Roberts, R., 337
Robinson, C., 77
Robinson, S. L., 226, 237
Roehers, T., 136
Rogers, S., 109
Rogers-Warren, A., 76, 103, 105
Rogoff, B., 243
Rolider, A., 199, 200, 201, 202, 203,
204
Rollins, H. A., 268, 278
Romer, L. T., 137
Rose, J., 60
Rose, T., 335

Rosen, L. A. 200
Rosenbaum, M. S., 323
Rosegrant, T., 93
Rosenshine, B., 283, 285, 286, 288, 314
Ross, D., 205
Rossett, H. L., 133
Rousseau, J. J., 64, 65
Rowan, B., 55
Roy, A. K., 242, 247
Rubin, L. J., 242
Rubinoff, A., 323
Ruggles, T. R., 102
Rusch, F. R., 335, 336, 337, 338, 339, 340, 341
Ruskin, R. S., 185, 187, 188, 189, 194
Russell, T., 268

Sacca, M. K., 268, 278, 370
Sailor, W., 138
Sainato, D. M., 79, 266, 270, 292, 294, 302
Salomon, G., 243
Salzberg, C. L., 276
Saski, J., 304
Saunders, M., 277
Savard, C., 118, 121
Scarr, S., 243
Scaturro, J., 269, 270
Schaeffer, J., 324
Schaeffer, J. B., 324
Scheirer, M. A., 68
Schelling, F. W. J., 89
Schempp, P. K., 248
Scheutz, G., 101, 106
Schiefelbusch, R. L., 140, 321
Schmidt, B., 15, 28
Schneider, J. W., 133
Schnelle, J. F., 323, 331
Schon, D. A., 45, 47
Schreibman, L., 208
Schroeder, S., 222
Schumaker, J. B., 324
Schutte, R. C., 324
Schutz, R. P., 336
Schwartz, I., 77, 80, 82, 107, 323
Schwartz, R. G., 103, 105
Scruggs, T. E., 268
Seavey, D. V., 293
Seifert, M., 288
Selinske, J., 214, 163, 164, 166
Semb, G. B., 187, 188, 189
Shadding, A. L., 293
Shafer, M. S., 270
Shakespeare, W., 154
Sharpe, T. L., 243, 244, 245, 246
Shavelson, R. J., 242
Sheehan, R., 109
Sherburne, S., 79
Sherman, J. A., 324

Sherman, J. G., 185, 187, 188, 189, 194, 321
Shimamura, J. W., 277
Shinn, M. R., 325
Shisler, L., 270
Shores, R. E., 79
Sidman, M., 5, 40, 91, 92, 93, 140, 141, 222, 261
Siegel-Causey, E., 139, 140, 346
Silberman, C. E., 4
Silbert, J., 116, 174, 270
Simeonsson, R. J., 93, 94
Simmons, D, C., 157
Sims, E. V. J., 125
Sindelar, P. T., 266, 267, 268, 294
Singer, G., 81, 92
Sizer, T., 329
Skellenger, A., 94
Skiba, R. J., 368
Skinner, B. F., 5, 11, 12, 16, 17, 27, 45, 67, 89, 90, 91, 140, 161, 173, 177, 179, 187, 189, 193, 214, 257, 258, 259, 260, 261, 262, 286
Slavin, R. E., 51, 125, 266, 327
Smith, B. M., 324
Smith, D. W., 132, 133
Smith, F., 153
Smith, L., 324
Smith, N. M., 288
Smith, N. W., 242
Smylie, M. A., 155
Snyder, G., 174, 175, 176, 177, 183
Speece, D. L., 215
Speltz, M. L., 277
Spradlin, J. E., 103, 109
Sprague, J., 336, 338
Sprinthall, N. A., 57
Sprinthall, R. C., 57
Stahl, S. A., 157, 185
Stallings, J., 161, 285, 286, 287, 288, 292
Stanley, S. O., 226, 254, 267, 289, 292
Stanovich, K. E., 153, 155, 156, 157
Stans, A., 324
Starr, I. S., 59, 63, 66
Staufer, T., 357
Steinman, W., 289
Stephens, J. M., 161
Stephens, T. M., 283
Stepich, D., 185
Sterling, R., 294, 296, 297
Sternberg, R. J., 92
Stevens, R., 283
Stevenson, H. W., 59, 62
Stigler, J. W., 59, 62
Stokes, T. F., 7, 78, 278, 336, 337, 338, 340, 341, 342, 357, 359, 370
Stolovitch, H., 193

Stolz, S. B., 371
Stone, J. E., 26, 57, 59, 60, 186, 329
Stone, J. G., 116
Stoner, G., 325
Storey, K., 335
Stotland, J. F., 269
St. Pierre, R. G., 60
Strain, P. S., 43, 44, 55, 76, 79, 87, 187, 292, 294, 302
Stratton, R. P., 179
Streck, J., 174, 176, 181, 183, 188
Streissguth, A. P., 132, 133, 134, 142
Strickland, D., 152
Striefel, S., 142
Stromer, R., 142,143
Stoyva, J. M., 135
Sulentic, C., 125
Sullivan, M. W., 103
Sulzer-Azaroff, B., 34, 38, 40, 137, 138, 169, 180, 323
Sum, A. M., 17, 221
Sweeney, W. J., 301, 302
Swicegood, P., 304
Sykes, G., 47

Tannock, R., 102, 103
Tapia, Y., 215, 225, 227, 289
Taylor, B., 215
Tell, C. A., 268, 270
Terry, B., 35, 254
Test, D. W., 293, 294, 299, 304, 335
Tharp, R., 26
Thiagarajan, S., 193
Thomas, A., 138, 139
Thomas, D. R., 162
Thomas, V., 205
Thompson, T., 92
Thorndike, E. L., 89
Thorpe, H. W., 266, 268
Thurlow, M. L., 44, 226, 283, 292
Thurston, L. P., 266, 269, 270, 292
Tiedt, I. M., 51
Tiedt, P. L., 51
Tiemann, P. W., 178, 179
Timm, M. A., 76, 79
Tomlinson, T. M., 62, 63, 65, 70
Torrey, J. W., 116, 117
Trivette, C. M., 96
Tucci, V., 258, 260, 261, 262
Turner, R., 351
Twardosz, S., 78
Tymitz, B. L., 226

Ultee, C. A., 133

Vacc, N., 266, 268, 270
Vacha, E. F., 134
Valdiviesco, C., 109
van Baar, A. L., 133
Van Dyke, D. C., 133

Van Eyk, D., 193
Van Houten, J., 205, 206
Van Houten, R., 188, 199, 200, 201,
    202, 203, 204, 205, 206, 284,
    285
Vargas, E., 63, 68
Vargas, J. S., 313
Vellutino, F., 153
Vincent, L., 96, 105, 195
Virgalitte, J. K., 307
Vogelsburg, R. T., 335, 336
Vygotsky, L. S., 151, 154

Wacker, D. P., 278, 335, 336, 338
Wahler, R. G., 91
Walberg, H. J., 57, 58, 61, 63, 65, 68
Walker, D., 215, 216, 217
Walker, H. M., 325
Walton, J. M., 355
Wang, M. C., 63
Ward, S. L., 133
Warren, K. R., 132, 133
Warren, R. P., 154
Warren, S. F., 76, 95, 102, 103, 105
Warr-Leeper, G. A., 133
Washburne, C., 116
Watkins, C. L., 15, 16, 17, 21, 22,
    25, 28, 29, 57, 59, 175, 190
Watson, J. B., 89
Weast, J., 326
Wehman, P., 335, 336
Weill, J. D., 221
Weisberg, P., 115, 117, 118, 119,
    121, 122, 124, 125, 126

Weiss, R. S., 104, 105, 109
Weissman-Frisch, N., 109
Weistuch, L., 103, 105
Welch, J., 335
Welch, W. W., 288
Weller, C., 103
Welsh, P., 62
West, J. F., 109
Weston, D. R., 134
Wetherby, B., 142
Whaley, D. L., 361
Wheatley, R. K., 300, 302
White, D. M., 308, 309, 310, 311,
    336
White, G. W., 109
White, O. R., 191, 323
White, W. A., 205
White, W. A. T., 283
Whitman, T., 208
Whyte, C. B., 355
Wiegand, R., 243, 252
Wilcox, B., 336, 338
Wilcox, M. J., 101, 103, 105
Will, M. C., 44
Williams, B. F., 134, 136
Williams, C., 350, 354
Williams, G., 162, 163, 165, 166,
    167, 214
Williams, J. A., 336, 338, 340
Williams, V. I., 296, 298, 314
Williams, W., 335, 336
Wilson, P. G., 335
Winett, R. A., 36, 80, 161
Winkler, R. C., 36, 80, 161

Winograd, T., 89
Wise, A., 58
Wishon, P., 63
Witt, J. C., 242
Wittkopp, C., 357
Wlodkowski, R. J., 60, 61, 64
Wolchik, S. A., 323
Wolery, M., 76, 79
Wolf, M. M., 79, 80, 226, 277, 321,
    322, 326, 327
Wolf, R., 266
Wolpow, R. I., 161
Wood, D., 243, 244
Wood, T., 154
Woodhead, C., 60
Wooley, O. W., 323
Wooley, S. C., 323
Wright, P. E., 226
Wyman, C., 293

Yackel, E., 154
Yancey, B. D., 356
Yang, F. M., 304, 307, 309, 314
Yatvin, J., 150
Yoder, P. J., 95, 103, 104, 105, 106,
    143
Young, B. K., 293
Young, C. C., 276
Ysseldyke, J. E., 44, 156, 226, 283

Zahorik, J. A., 285
Zakrajsek, D. B., 244
Zeichner, K. M., 47
Zemke, R., 23

SUBJECT INDEX

ABA, 67, 371
Academic development:
  and achievement, 218–220
Academic engagement, definition
  of, 213–214
Academic learning time (ALT),
  288–289
Academic performance:
  and opportunities to respond, 213–222
Accepting correction, 210
Active student respond (ASR):
  advantages of, 286–287, 289, 290–292, 316
  definition of, 286
  descriptive studies of, 292
  feedback provided to teacher by, 290–292
  four characteristics of "good ASR," 313
  increasing across the curriculum and throughout school day, 311–312
  measurement of, 289
  needed research on, 314–315
  and other measures of student participation, 287–290
  strategies for increasing, 283–316
Acquisition stage of learning, 284–285
ACT, 351–352
Adaptive behavior, teaching 209–210
Adduced contingencies, 17
AFCD, 121
African-American college students, 349–361
Aid to Families with Dependent Children (AFCD) program, 121
Allocated time for instruction, 287–288
ALT, 288–289
American 2000 program, 59, 68
American College Test (ACT), 351–352
American Educational Research Association (AERA), 371
American Psychology Association (APA), 371
  Task Force on Psychology in Education, 34
Antecedents, definition of, 259
Applied behavior analysis:
  and early intervention, 76–77
  principles and strategies in education, 325–330
  impact on education, 321–330

Applied behavior analysis: (continued)
  and teacher education, 43–56
ASR. *See* Active student response
Association for Behavior Analysis (ABA), 67, 371
Attrition of African-American college students, 349–361
Automatic reinforcement, 179

Bank Street model of education, 60
Behavioral Evaluation Strategy and Taxonomy (BEST), 244–249
  category systems of, 245–246
  as instructional measurement instrument, 246–249
  recording procedures for, 246
Behavioral interventions:
  with children prenatally exposed to alcohol and drugs, 134–142
  differential reinforcement, 137–138
  errorless learning, 137
  functional analysis of behaviors, 135
  rule-governed behavior as, 141–142
  systematic desensitization, 135–137
  task analysis, 137
  task variation as, 138
  verbal behavior, 138–140
Behavior analysis:
  appeal to pragmatists, 58
  in education, 367–372
  its future in education, 16–18
  marketing strategies for, 370–372
  promoting public advocacy of, 371–372
  in public policy, 367–372
  terminology of, 368
Behavior analysts, and school reform, 43–44
Behaviorism:
  advantages of contextualistic perspective of, 91–93
  as a contextualistic system, 90–91
  as a mechanistic system, 89–90
BEST, 244–249
Bilingual education, models of, 230
Black students who are academically at-risk, 349–361
  learning-to-learn strategies, 358
  monetary incentive program for, 360
  performance-management program for, 356–361
  problems of attrition, 349–350
  reasons for attrition of, 351–354

Black students who are academically at-risk (continued)
  traditional support programs for, 354–356
  universities perspective on, 350–351
Bureau of Child Research at the University of Kansas, 321

CABAS, 162–170
California Achievement Test, 183
Center for Self-Management of Academic Performance at Western Michigan University, 356–357
Center for the Study of Reading at the University of Illinois, 151
Child abuse and neglect, 150
Child-centered view of education, 77, 78
Children prenatally exposed to alcohol and drugs, 131–143
  behavioral interventions with, 134–142
  characteristics of, 132–134
  early intervention with, 135–142
Children with learning problems, 199–210
  methods to motivate, 200, 202
  problems with labeling and memory, 202–205
  teaching by rules, 205–208
Choral responding, 294–299
  curriculum content appropriate for, 298
  definition of, 294
  guidelines for using, 298–299
  in Morningside Model of Generative Instruction, 189
  research on, 294–298
CISSAR, 289
Classwide peer tutoring (CWPT), 267–268, 370 (*See also* Peer tutoring)
Cocaine, children prenatally exposed to, 132
Code for Instructional Structure and Student Academic Responding (CISSAR), 289
Communication functions, 108–109
Communication skills interventions, 101–111
  challenges to across-the-day implementation, 106–111
  and communicative functions, 108–109

3

Communication skills interventions (continued)
    hybrid approaches, 103–106
    inservice training for, 109
    interactive model, 102–103
    social validation of, 107–108
    teachers' generalization and maintenance of, 110–111
Competent learner model, 261–262
Competent learners:
    assessment of, 262
    definition of, 258–259
    development of, 257–264
    repertoires of, 262–263
Comprehensive application of behavior analysis to schooling (CABAS), 162–170
Comprehensive Education Reform Act (Tennessee, 1984), 59
Comprehensive Employment and Training Act (CETA), 175
Conditional discriminative stimuli, 91–92
Consequences, definition of, 259–260
Contextualism (contextual behaviorism):
    advantages of, 91–93
    applications in early childhood education, 93–97
    basic elements of, 88–89
    implications for early childhood education, 87–97
    judging usefulness of, 89, 92
Contingencies of reinforcement, institutional, 12–15
Contingency adduction, 182–183
Contingency contracting:
    for academic productivity, 357
    for student teaching practicum, 48–49
Council for Exceptional Children (CEC), 371
Cross-age tutoring, 268 (See also Peer tutoring)
    in Morningside Model of Generative Instruction, 187
Cultural diversity, 36
Cultural evolution, 11
    role of verbal behavior in, 11
Cultural materialism, 96
Cultural practices, formula for probability of retention, 14
Curriculum leaps, 183

DAP. See Developmentally appropriate practice
Default contingencies, 61
Demographic characteristics of school-age children, 149–150

Developmentalism:
    conflict with behavioral approaches, 65–67
    emphases of the theory of, 57
    as impediment to school reform, 59–63
    popular acceptance of, 63–65
    recommendations for combating, 67–70
Developmentally appropriate practice (DAP), 76–77, 78, 369
Developmental retardation, 215–216
    and low academic achievement, 215
    longitudinal findings on, 216
Differential reinforcement, 179
    and children prenatally exposed to alcohol and drugs, 137–138
Differential reinforcement of alternative behaviors (DRA), 180
Differential reinforcement of low rates of behavior (DRL), 180
Differential reinforcement of other behavior (DRO), 180
Direct Instruction, 38, 126–127, 162, 163
    curricula, 262
    in Morningside Model of Generative Instruction, 188–190
    with preschoolers, 115–127
Direct Instruction System for Teaching Arithmetic and Reading (DISTAR), 29, 116–122, 124
Disadvantaged children, teaching reading to, 115–127 (See also Head Start)
Discovered knowledge, 13–14
Discrimination training, 179

Early Childhood Day Care Center (ECDCC), 120–121
Early Childhood Day Care Project, 121
Early childhood education, 75–83 (See also Early intervention)
    implications of contextualism for, 87–97
    prediction and control of behavior in, 94
    selection of learning objectives for, 94–95
Early intervention, 75–83
    community involvement in, 82–83
    definition of, 75
    goals of, 77–79
    program outcomes in, 79–82
    in reading, 115–127
    social context, 81–83
    social validity in, 81–83
    with alcohol- and drug-exposed children, 131–143

Ecobehavioral assessment:
    analysis of instructional processes, 229
    molar analyses as result of, 231–235
    molecular analyses as result of, 235–23
Ecological System for the Contextual Recording of Interactional Bilingual Environments (ENSCRIBE):
    categories and variables measured by, 227–228
    molar outcomes/implications from, 231–235
    molecular outcomes/implications from, 235–256
    observations and recording procedures, 228–229
    pilot study with, 229–236
Education, systems change in, 370
Educational reform:
    developmentalism as an impediment to, 57–70
    facilitation by disseminating applied behavior analysis, 325–330
    and mathematics instruction, 154–156
    perspectives of a college of education dean, 33–41
    and pragmatic nondevelopmentalists, 58–59
    problems behavior analysts should address, 328
    and reading instruction, 151–154
    recommendations for improving instruction in reading and mathematics, 157
Education Improvement Act (Tennessee, 1992), 59
Embedding instructional items in curriculum materials, 208–209
    color mediation procedure, 208
Endurance, building students', 192–193
Error correction, 210
Errorless learning strategies, 137
Establishing operations, 260
Evaluation, of early intervention programs, 82–83

FAS, 131–132
Feedback, during learning, 284–285
Fetal alcohol syndrome (FAS), 131–132
Flashcard instruction, 199–200
Fluency, definition of 17
Fluency aims, 184, 190–191
Fluency building, 177–184, 188–192
    with peer coaches, 190

Fluency building (continued)
  sprinting as a tactic for, 189
  of tool skills, 188, 190
Formism, 88–89
Fred S. Keller Preschool, 167
Functional analysis of behavior,
  with children prenatally exposed
  to alcohol and drugs, 135
Functional relationships, 259–260

Gates Primary Reading Test, 118
General case programming, 336, 338
Generalization and maintenance of
  behavior change:
  with children prenatally exposed
  to alcohol and drugs, 142
  by persons with disabilities, 335–
  346, 367
  strategies for promoting, 335–343
  teachers' use of communication
  interventions, 110–111
Generalized-skills model, 338–346
  components of, 338–343
  definition of, 338
  example of, 339
Generative instruction, 173–194
Guided notes, 303–311
  advantages of, 310
  definition of, 304
  effects on students' own note-
  taking, 309–310
  examples of, 305–306
  research on, 304–310
  short form vs. long form, 309–310
  suggestions for using, 310–311

Head Start, 15, 76
High-risk black college students,
  349–361

IDEA, 76, 346
Impact of behavior analysis in
  education, 33–41
Indiscriminable contingencies of
  reinforcement, 336
Individuals with Disabilities Act of
  1990 (P.L. 101-476):
  and preschool children, 76
  and students transitioning from
  school to adult life, 346
Inservice training, for communica
  tion interventions, 109
Instructional settings, arrangement
  of 243
Instruction time, 288
Interbehavior, definition of, 242
Interbehavioral assessment, example
  of, 249–252
Interbehavioral field systems:
  definition of, 242–243
  perspectives of, 241–254
Invented wisdom, 13–14

JABA. *See Journal of Applied*
  Behavior Analysis
Jargon, 25–27
Job Training and Partnership Act
  (1985), 175
Joint Dissemination Review Panel,
  326
Journal of Applied Behavior
  Analysis, 33, 39, 40, 80, 321–
  325, 368, 370, 371
Journal of Behavioral Education,
  322
Journal of Experimental Analysis of
  Behavior, 322
Journal of Teacher Education, 36
Juniper Gardens Children's Project,
  161, 165, 226, 244, 285–286
  results from, 213–222

Kentucky Educational Reform Act
  (1990), 59

Language, development of, 216–218
Language experience approach.
  See Reading instruction
Learning disabilities, students at
  Morningside Academy with, 175
Learning environments:
  components of, 260–261
  effective, 257–264
Learning problems, teaching
  children with, 199–210
Learning trial, 284–185 (*See also*
  Learning unit)
Learn units (*See also* Learning trial):
  advantages of, 166
  cost-benefit analysis of, 167
  definition of, 163
  frequency in public high school
  classrooms, 165
  as series of interlocking operants,
  163–164
  three-term contingency as basis
  of, 163–164
  type of, 168–169
  validity of, 169
Limited English proficient (LEP)
  students, 227–238

Malcolm X College, 28, 173–177
Margaret Chapman School, 167–168
Martin Luther King program for
  college students, 357
Mathematics instruction:
  NCTM Standards, 154–156
  recommendations for, 157
Mean length of utterance (MLU),
  217–218
Measurement of effective instruction,
  3–9
  by 3C/ROD, 7–9, 316
  by curriculum steps completed, 6–7

Measurement of effective instruction
  (continued)
  rate and accuracy of learn units as,
  161–170
  relevance of audience to, 7–9
  role of frequency data in, 177–
  178
  role of professional judgment in,
  4–5
  using criterion-referenced objec
  tives completed as, 166
Mechanism, 88–89
Mediational techniques:
  and children with learning
  problems, 202–204
  color mediation approach, 203–204
Memory aids:
  broken-word procedure as, 205
  and children with learning
  problems, 204–205
Milieu language teaching, 95, 103–
  104
Minority students, problems of attrition of, 349–350
Morningside Academy, 29, 173–194
Morningside Model of Generative
  Instruction, 173–194
  curriculum for, 174
  daily instructional procedures,
  186–194
  endurance building, 193
  generative instruction, definition
  of, 181
  guarantees, 174–175
  history of, 173–177
  as product of selectionism, 185–
  186
  programming for intellectual
  skills, 178–183
  seven tenants of, 183–185
  students with learning dis
  abilities, 175
Motivation, 200, 202
Multicultural education, in teacher
  education, 51
Multiple-example teaching, 336–
  346
  definition of, 338
  general case programming using,
  336–338

NAEYC. *See* National Association
  for Education of Young
  Children
NASP, 69
National Association for Education
  of Young Children (NAEYC),
  60, 61, 68, 77, 127, 369
National Association of Manufacturers,
  63
National Association of School
  Psychologists (NASP), 69

National Center for Learning
  Disabilities, 326
National Council for Accreditation
  of Teacher Education
  (NCATE), 58
National Council for Teachers of+
  Mathematics (NCTM), 151, 154
National Diffusion Network, 326
National Education Association
  (NEA), 60, 371
Natural contingencies of reinforce
  ment, 38, 336
Naturalistic communication interven
  tion, 101–111
Naturalistic language training, 95
NEA, 60, 371
New American School Development
  Corporation (NASDC), 58–59
NCATE, 58
NCTM, 151, 154
Note-taking, 304 (*See also* Guided
  notes)

On-task behavior:
  of children with learning
    problems, 209–210
  and increased active student
    response, 292
  and student involvement in instruc
    tion, 288
Opportunity to respond, 285–286
  in bilingual special education
    programs, 231–236
  compared with active student
    response (ASR), 289
  definition of, 214
  as measured by ENSCRIBE,
    227–236
Organizations:
  Type F(unctional), 13–14
  Type S(tatic), 13–14

Peabody Picture Vocabulary Test
  (PPVT), 217–218
Peer tutoring, 51, 265–279
  benefits of, 266
  classwide, 267–268
  cross-age, 268
  daily testing component, 276
  for fluency building, 190
  folders and flashcards, 272–275
  home-based, 269
  maintenance testing component,
    267
  needed research on, 279
  one-to-one, 268–269
  practice component, 272–276
  pretesting students, 272
  small-group, 268
  and teacher education program,
    50–51, 53
  teacher's role during, 271–272

Peer tutoring (continued)
  tracking and charting students'
    performance, 276–277
  tutor training, 269–270
Personalized Systems of Instruction
  (PSI), 34–35, 37, 162, 188
Positive reinforcement, and
  children prenatally exposed to
  alcohol and drugs, 140–141
Poverty, 149–150
Practice stage of learning, 284–285
Precision Teaching, 178, 183, 190
Programmed instruction, 188–189
Programming common stimuli, 336
Program outcomes:
  in early intervention, 79–80, 81–
    83
  evaluation of, 80
Progressive education ,57,64
Project Follow Through, 15, 16
Promoting use of behavior analysis
  in education, 21–30, 325–330
  collaborating with nonbehavioral
    education, 67–68, 329
  marketing communication, 25
  market research, 22–24
  product development, 24–25
  public vs. private sector, 28–30
  sales, 27–28
  working in colleges of education,
    329–330
PSI. *See* Personalized System of
  Instruction
Public Law 94–142 (Individuals
  with Disabilities Education
  Act), 87, 225
Public Law 99–457 (Education of
  the Handicapped Act Amend
  ments of 1990), 78, 87
Public policy, and behavior
  analysis, 367–362

RARE, 43–56
Rate, developing, 209
Reading instruction:
  comprehension as function of,
    120
  DISTAR program, 116, 119, 120
  Gates Primary Reading Test, 118
  and preschool children, 115–127
  recommendations for, 157
  self-taught readers, 116–118
  teaching early reading, 116–121
  using Direct Instruction model, 119
  whole language/language ex
    perience approach, 151–154
Reflective and Responsive Educator
  Program (RARE), 43–56
  capstone experience, 51–52
  instructional procedures of, 47–
    48, 50–52
  philosophy of, 45

RARE (continued)
  principles of, 45
  program model and components
    of, 46–48
  program outcomes, 52–55
Repertoires of learners, develop
  ment of, 259–260
Response cards, 299–303
  advantages of, 299, 302–303
  definition of, 299
  preprinted, 302
  research on, 299–302
  suggestions for using, 303
  write-on, 303
Rule-governed behavior:
  with children prenatally exposed
    to alcohol and drugs, 141–142
  and study behavior of college stu
    dents, 359–360
Rules, teaching by, 205–208

SAT, 351–352
Schedules, and children prenatally
  exposed to alcohol and drugs,
  138
School reform, 43–44 (*See also*
  Educational reform)
Seattle Children's School, 173
Selectionism, 90
  basic tenant of, 11–12
  effects on the Morningside Model
    of Generative Instruction, 185–
    186
  in field guided by scientific prac
    tices vs. education, 316
  role of cost and benefits in, 15–16
  role of frequency in, 17
  variation and selection in educa
    tion, 15–16
Self-determination, 367–368
Self-instruction, 336–346
  definition of, 337
  independent performance, 337
  guidelines for teaching, 342–343
  with single examples, 337
Self-management, 368
Setting events, 260
Social content, in early intervention,
  81–83
Social validity:
  in early intervention, 77, 80–83
  of communication interventions,
    107–108
Socio-economic status, and
  academic achievement, 213–
  222
Standard celeration chart, 178, 191–
  192
Standardized Achievement Test
  (SAT), 351–352
Structured worksheets, to increase
  active student response, 291–292

Student-centered education, 37–38
Students as tutors. *See* Cross-age tutoring; Peer tutoring
Students' responsibility to study and work hard, 69–70
Substance abuse, with children prenatally exposed to alcohol and drugs, 131–134
Systematic desensitization, with children prenatally exposed to alcohol and drugs, 135–137

TAS, 244
Task analysis, 137
Teacher-centered education, 37
Technical language of behavior analysis, 25–27
Temporal Analysis System (TAS), 244

Tennessee State Department of Education, 68
Three-contingency model of performance management, 358–361
Three-term contingency:
  as basis for analyzing and measuring instruction, 284–285
  as basis for learn units, 163–164
  as self-correcting mechanism for effective instruction, 185
  viewed from mechanistic and contextualistic perspectives, 89–92, 97
Tool skills, 188, 190–191
Train and hope, 336
Training sufficient exemplars, 336–337
Transition from school to work, strategies for, 335–337

U.S. Department of Education, 175
U.S. Department of Energy, 175
U.S. Department of Labor, 175

Verbal behavior:
  and children prenatally exposed to alcohol and drugs, 138–140
  in cultural evolution, 12
Visual Response System (VRS), 293–294
Vocabulary use, 217–218

Whole language approach. *See* Reading instruction
World hypotheses, 88–89